RSHA

RSHA

REICH SECURITY MAIN OFFICE—
ORGANISATION, ACTIVITIES, PERSONNEL

STEPHEN TYAS

FONTHILL

Acknowledgements

The author gratefully acknowledges Max Williams for providing many of the photographs from his collection that are used here.

Fonthill Media Language Policy

Fonthill Media publishes in the international English language market. One language edition is published worldwide. As there are minor differences in spelling and presentation, especially with regard to American English and British English, a policy is necessary to define which form of English to use. The Fonthill Policy is to use the form of English native to the author. Stephen Tyas was born and educated in Conisbrough, Yorkshire; therefore British English has been adopted in this publication.

Fonthill Media Limited
Fonthill Media LLC
www.fonthillmedia.com
office@fonthillmedia.com

First published in the United Kingdom
and the United States of America 2022

British Library Cataloguing in Publication Data:
A catalogue record for this book is available from the British Library

ISBN 978-1-78155-867-6

Typeset in Minion Pro 10pt on 13pt
Printed and bound in England

Contents

Acknowledgements		4
List of Ranks		7
List of Abbreviations		9
Introduction		11

1	Liquidation Reports Nos 1 and 2: *Ämter* I and II of the RSHA	17
2	Situation Report No. 3—*Amt* III of the RSHA	51
3	Situation Report No. 4: *Amt* IV of the RSHA	103
4	Organisation of the German Police (up to 1938)	217
5	Liquidation Report No. 6: *Amt* VI of the RSHA—*Gruppe* VI A	238
6	Liquidation Report No. 7: *Amt* VI of the RSHA—*Gruppe* VI B	253
7	Situation Report No. 8: *Amt* VI of the RSHA—*Gruppe* VI C	299
8	Situation Report No. 9: *Amt* VI of the RSHA—*Gruppe* VI D	352
9	Situation Report No. 10: *Amt* VI of the RSHA—*Gruppe* VI E	391
10	Situation Report No. 11: *Amt* VI of the RSHA—*Gruppe* VI F	426
11	Liquidation Report No. 12: *Amt* VI of the RSHA—*Gruppe* VI G	450
12	RSHA *Gruppe* VI S	459
13	Situation Report No. 21: *Amt* VI of the RSHA—*Gruppe* VI Wi (Wirtschaft)	536
14	RSHA VI Z	544
15	Liquidation Report No. 23: *Amt* VII of the RSHA	565
16	RSHA *Amt* N	580
17	Training Schools of the *Sicherheitspolizei* and the *Sicherheitsdienst*	590
18	Liquidation Report No. 26: RSHA *Militärisches Amt*	600
19	Situation Report No. 27: RSHA *Mil Amt* A	609

20   Situation Report No. 28: RSHA *Mil Amt* B   616

21   Situation Report No. 29: RSHA *Mil Amt* C   626

22   Liquidation Report No. 30: RSHA *Mil Amt* D   637

23   Liquidation Report No. 31: RSHA *Mil Amt* E   644

24   Liquidation Report No. 32: RSHA *Mil Amt* F   655

25   Liquidation Report No. 34: RSHA *Mil Amt* i   662

Suggested Reading about RSHA   665

List of Ranks

SS-Ranks

SS-*Mann*	enlisted man/private
SS-*Sturmmann*	Private first class
SS-*Rottenführer*	Corporal
SS-*Unterscharführer*	Corporal
SS-*Scharführer*	Sergeant
SS-*Oberscharführer*	Sergeant
SS-*Hauptscharführer*	Sergeant
SS-*Sturmscharführer*	Sergeant Major
SS-*Untersturmführer*	2nd Lieutenant
SS-*Obersturmführer*	1st Lieutenant
SS-*Hauptsturmführer*	Captain
SS-*Sturmbannführer*	Major
SS-*Obersturmbannführer*	Lieutenant Colonel
SS-*Standartenführer*	Colonel
SS-*Oberführer*	Brigadier
SS-*Brigadeführer*	Major General
SS-*Gruppenführer*	Lieutenant General
SS-*Obergruppenführer*	General

Police Ranks

(These ranks have no corresponding modern terms, and given in order of seniority)

Büro Angestellter (clerk)
Kriminal Angestellter

Kriminal Assistent
Kriminal Oberassistent
Kriminal Sekretär
Kriminal Obersekretär
Kriminal Inspektor
Kriminalkommissar
Kriminalrat
Kriminal Direktor
Polizei Assistent
Polizei Sekretär
Polizei Obersekretär
Polizei Inspektor
Polizei Oberinspektor
Polizeirat
Reichskriminaldirektor

Civil Service

(These ranks indicate a professional university educated official)

Regierungs Assessor
Regierungs Inspektor
Regierungs Oberinspektor
Regierungsrat
Oberregierungsrat
Regierungs- und Kriminalrat
Oberregierungs- und Kriminalrat

plus associated Administrative (*Verwaltung*) ranks such *Ministerialrat*, Ministerial Registrator, *Regierungsamtmann, Amtsmann*, and *Amtsrat*.

List of Abbreviations

BdS	*Befehlshaber der Sicherheitspolizei und des* SD
Büro Ange	*Büro Angestellter*
CdS	*Chef der Sicherheitsheitspolizei und des* SD
CIWR	Counter-Intelligence War Room
Gst.	*Geschäftsstelle*
IdS	*Inspekteur der Sicherheitspolizei und des* SD
KA	*Kriminal Assistant*
KD	*Kriminal Direktor*
KdS	*Kommandeur der Sicherheitspolizei und des* SD
KI	*Kriminal Inspektor*
KIA	Killed in action
KK	*Kriminalkommissar*
KOA	*Kriminal Oberassistent*
KOS	*Kriminal Obersekretär*
KR	*Kriminalrat*
Krim Ange	*Kriminal Angestellter*
KS	*Kriminal Sekretär*
MI 5	Security Service (British)
MI 6	Secret Intelligence Service (British)
MIA	Missing in action
ORR	*Oberregierungsrat*
ORuKR	*Oberregierungs- und Kriminalrat*
OSS	Office of Strategic Services (US)
PI	*Polizei Inspektor*
POI	*Polizei Oberinspektor*
Pol Rat	*Polizeirat*
POS	*Polizei Obersekretär*
PS	*Polizei Sekretär*

RD	*Regierungsdirektor*
RFSS	*Reichsführer*-SS (Himmler)
RMdI	*Reichsministerium des Innern*
ROI	*Regierungs Oberinspektor*
RS	*Regierungs Sekretär*
RuKR	*Regierungs- und Kriminalrat*
RR	*Regierungsrat*
SSHA	SS-*Hauptamt*
SS-*Brif*	SS-*Brigadeführer*
SS-*Gruf*	SS-*Gruppenführer*
SS-*Hschaf*	SS-*Hauptscharführer*
SS-*Hstuf*	SS-*Hauptsturmführer*
SS-*Obf*	SS-*Oberführer*
SS-*Ogruf*	SS-*Obergruppenführer*
SS-*Oschaf*	SS-*Oberscharführer*
SS-*Ostubaf*	SS-*Obersturmbannführer*
SS-*Ostuf*	SS-*Obersturmführer*
SS-*Rotf*	SS-*Rottenführer*
SS-*Schaf*	SS-*Scharführer*
SS-*Staf*	SS-*Standartenführer*
SS-*Stubaf*	SS-*Sturmbannführer*
SS-*Stuschaf*	SS-*Sturmscharführer*
W/T	Wireless Transceiver (radio receiver/transmitter)

Introduction

There were many reasons behind the research for this book. My original idea was an 'RSHA Handbook', but it has turned out much longer. The main reason being to provide a clear and accurate view of how the German security services, the *Gestapo*, and the SD, operated not only in Germany but in German-occupied territories in Europe and beyond the borders of the Reich. Too many publications attribute all-seeing and all-knowing abilities to these agencies, which was simply not the case. It is all too easy to use modern-day tools such as overhead cameras in public places and people using mobile phones to film incidents when these technical advancements had not been invented at the time. In their place, the *Gestapo* placed greater emphasis on watch and wait, the use of informers, acting upon denunciations, and waiting for enemies of the state to make mistakes that came to their notice before taking action. The SD, especially when it became RSHA III, produced secret reports for the top-level Nazi government ministers which showed how public opinions reflected what the government was doing, or not doing. From time to time, these SD reports proved poor reading for ministries not doing their job and complaints to *Reichsführer*-SS Heinrich Himmler for his subordinates highlighting someone else's deficiencies. Whereas the public giving their opinions to the SD were regarded as confidential, the Gestapo had no such qualms about arresting and sending to concentration camps anyone flouting Nazi laws.

Before the outbreak of the Second World War in September 1939, the term 'Gestapo' had become notorious across Europe, perceived as a brutal and evil secret police. *Reichsführer*-SS Himmler who was in charge of all SS organisations and SS-*General* Reinhard Heydrich, delegated by Himmler to direct the security police and the security service, decided an alternative term would be needed to deceive civilian populations in occupied countries. When the German security services went into territories behind their advancing armies, units known as *Einsatzgruppen* with their subordinate *Kommandos*, under the direction of Himmler and Heydrich, all wore standard wartime field grey uniforms. To avoid using the word Gestapo, all the men had a diamond-shaped badge on the left uniform sleeve stating 'SD'. This overall SD term covered officers, NCOs, and enlisted men from the *Gestapo*, the Criminal Police, the SD itself, and *Waffen*-SS men attached to these *Einsatzgruppen*. A deception to lull suspicious civilian populations.

Towards the end of the Second World War in Europe, the intelligence services of Britain and the USA still had no clear view of how the Berlin headquarters of the German security police and security services, the Reich Security Main Office (RSHA—*Reichssicherheitshauptamt*), operated. How it directed its operations, intelligence gathering, and counter-intelligence forces against the Allies especially after RSHA had absorbed the *Abwehr*, the military intelligence service of the German armed forces, in the wake of the attempted assassination of Hitler on 20 July 1944.

As early as 5 December 1944, Dick White, director-general of Britain's security service, MI5, wrote about the role of a counter-intelligence war room (CIWR) to be used against Germany. CIWR would be composed of MI5 officers and intelligence officers from Britain's secret intelligence service (MI6) and the American intelligence service (OSS). Their job would 'be concerned with enquiries into the clandestine organisations of the Nazi regime which have to be totally destroyed ... the War Room will concern itself with the *Abwehr, Sicherheitspolizei* and *Geheimstaatspolizei*'.[1]

What happened over the course of 1945 was that captured German officials of these organisations were extensively interrogated in Germany and in Britain and their interrogation reports passed to CIWR. These were pieced together with captured German documents and what appears to have been some of the top secret German Enigma radio messages decoded at Bletchley Park. On the basis of these sources CIWR then issued over 100 liquidation and situation reports about the German intelligence agencies. Most concerned German mobile forces used at the military fronts for reconnaissance and agent placement behind the lines. These reports were written by CIWR intelligence officers for other intelligence officers in the field to help in their further interrogation of suspects, the whereabouts of wanted war criminals, and newly identified officials who needed to be captured, interrogated, and interned as they were all 'automatic arrest' categories. CIWR had no interest in the top-level members of the Nazi government (Goebbels, Göring, Bormann, etc.) who were the responsibility of other agencies. CIWR was solely interested in intelligence officers (*Abwehr, Gestapo*, and SD) who directed offensive intelligence gathering about the Allied armed forces and those directing German counter-intelligence measures against the Allies.

Twenty-five CIWR reports have been used here to show how German prisoners viewed the RSHA in Berlin and explained their own former agencies and their former colleagues. The views of these German prisoners provided Allied intelligence agencies with a wealth of details about the various departments of the RSHA, its organisation, personnel assignments, and how the individual sections operated. With the collapse of Germany and surrender, with the capture of so many German intelligence officials, the Allies were not so much interested in the early history of the RSHA other than in a general sense, but more interested in the last eighteen months to two years and whether a Nazi underground subversive organisation had been created to undermine the Allied occupation of Germany. As a result, for example, few captured *Gestapo* or SD officers mentioned the role of Adolf Eichmann, the deportation of Jews from many occupied countries to Auschwitz, and other extermination camps or the mass shootings of Jews in the Soviet Union. This may mean they were not asked about such activities during interrogation or avoided answering on the grounds of self-incrimination. With few exceptions, the fate of the Jews was not reported, though many felt able to state that they had fought against communism and other political threats to the state. The CIWR reports do not report any racial ideology that may have been identified among the German prisoners and its very absence may indicate the little interest about it among the Allied intelligence agencies. At the time, an OSS officer based in London, William J. Casey (later head of the CIA), said information about concentration camps and the persecution of Jews was 'shunted aside because of the official policy in Washington and London to concentrate exclusively on the defeat of the enemy'.[2]

Other aspects of RSHA history that were ignored includes the evacuation and dispersal of RSHA III, IV, VI, and VII offices and their officials from Berlin. The building at Prinz-Albrecht-Strasse 8 in Berlin housed Amt IV offices, the other Ämter were scattered across Berlin. RSHA III were round the corner at Wilhelmstrasse 103 while RSHA VI main offices was Berkaerstrasse 32 in Schmargendorf; RSHA VII mainly at Emser Strasse 12 in Wilmersdorf. The most significant factor in the dispersal of offices from Berlin was increasing Allied air-bombardment of Berlin city centre. RSHA III lost many able senior SS officers in air-raids, the large daylight raid of 29 April 1944 being the most serious. Apart from losing personnel, the consequent damage to telephone and teleprinter networks caused further disruption. In the summer of 1944, many RSHA offices had been evacuated to two purpose-built barrack-type areas in woodland east of Berlin and just short of Küstrin/Oder. They were known as 'Dachs I' and 'Dachs II'. This was an ill-fated location because by January 1945 it stood in the path of advancing Soviet armies, so staff and equipment were uprooted and returned to Berlin. In February 1945, RSHA VI began evacuating its staff to Bavaria and locations in Bohemia and Moravia (the Protectorate). RSHA III and IV began in March 1945 with most Amt IV offices relocating to the Hof area in northern Bavaria. Through early and mid-April 1945, a northern staff (Nordstab) of RSHA official was organised to travel via Schwerin and further northwards to Flensburg in Schleswig-Holstein. A southern staff (Südstab) evacuated in stages from Hof south towards Munich and Austria. The last convoy of officials from Berlin included SS-*Sturmbannführer* Horst Kopkow and it called at the Berlin-Lankwitz home of RSHA Amtschef IV, Müller, on 22 April 1945 for final instructions before heading west and north towards Schwerin, narrowly avoiding Soviet forces creating an armoured circle around Berlin.

The twenty-five reports marked 'Secret' represent every RSHA Amt, training schools, and offices created following the absorption of the *Abwehr* into the RSHA. These are shown by the chapter headings used here for each of them. The CIWR devoted some time to developing the report on RSHA IV—the *Gestapo*—but more time was devoted to the individual offices of RSHA VI, the SD foreign intelligence agency. These offices were responsible for different geographical areas of the world and therefore of most interest to British and American intelligence agencies. The reports on RSHA VI offices were collated from a mix of interrogation reports and therefore the sources of information used by RSHA VI across the world as shown in the reports can only be those acceptable for publication. Those names unacceptable, those now claimed by Allied agencies, are undoubtedly excluded. It is notable that the forgery of British and US bank notes by RSHA VI F (*Unternehmen* Bernhard) although mentioned, there is very little detail reported. The immense RSHA VI intelligence gathering and agent placement operations in the Soviet Union, *Unternehmen* Zeppelin, is only partially explored and explained. These two episodes provide an indication that there was a degree of exclusion in the reports, possibly for Allied exploitation.

The same format runs throughout the reports, the style of writing used varies according to their author. Punctuation varies considerably and has not been changed. Typographic errors and a small number of other spelling errors have been corrected. Many names and locations were capitalised, and these have been made lower case. There was a lack of umlauts in words such as 'Fuhrer' and 'Fuehrer' and these also have been corrected. The reports by American intelligence agencies use American spellings (e.g., organization, labor) and these have been retained. Where German terms have been used, these too have been retained. Throughout the original reports, there was a failure to add 'SS-' to the ranks of SS officers and this has been corrected in line with modern usage; similarly, there was little use of 'RSHA' to denote a particular office and again this has been corrected. These corrections and amendments are designed to assist the reader in clarifying what is discussed in the reports. The layout of the appendices and annexes are slightly different due to the differences between a manual typewriter tabulation keys and those in Word, which meant changing the fonts to keep everything on a line. All the CIWR reports ended with lists of SS officers and officials who served in the respective Amt. These names contained numerous errors both of name and rank and these have been corrected. Other than these changes mentioned, the texts of the reports are those in the originals.

The CIWR had fulfilled its tasks by the end of 1945 when it was dissolved, leaving a small caretaker section to finish the small number of reports still being written. Allied occupation of Germany was now well established in its various zones and extradition of war criminals between the zones was well underway. There was no SS organised stay-behind agent network, and though small squads of Werwolf continued into 1946 and 1947, they were dispersed and arrested by Allied intelligence and the new German police force.

In May 1945, the RSHA building stood derelict, a bombed-out skeleton, like the rest of the government quarter along nearby Wilhelmstrasse. Being unsafe, the remaining walls were brought down during the early days of Allied occupation of the city. In 1972, when the author tramped over the ruins, it must have looked very much as it did in late 1945: the Berlin Wall ran the length of Prinz-Albrecht-Strasse with the East Berlin sector on the eastern side, and the American Zone on the western side. Today, in modern Berlin, Prinz-Albrecht-Strasse is now Niederkirchner Strasse, renamed by the East Berlin authorities to commemmorate Käthe Niederkirchner, a young German communist who parachuted into Poland in 1943 on behalf of Soviet Intelligence and was captured. Niederkirchner was imprisoned here in the cells of *Gestapo* headquarters before being sent to Ravenbrück concentration camp for women where she was shot without trial on 28 September 1944 following orders from SS-*Sturmbannführer* Horst Kopkow. The ruins of *Gestapo* headquarters are now a modern exhibition centre, *Topographie des Terrors* (Topography of Terror), which depicts the horrors, persecutions, atrocities, and racial exterminations carried out by the Nazi regime.

The RSHA disappeared into history at the end of the war, but some of its officials were soon employed by all the Allied intelligence agencies and the new West German intelligence service, the Organisation Gehlen. It would be another fifty years before some of these RSHA officials were unmasked as mass killers.

Post-war interrogation reports of captured *Gestapo* and SD officials at British and American interrogation centres were exchanged between the two agencies. For this reason, the same interrogations can be found in the National Archives of the United Kingdom (Kew) and the United States (College Park). However, the security organs in the UK continue to retain a major part of these interrogations as long-dead Nazi criminals may come back to haunt them. Researchers can find more British interrogations of Nazi criminals and security suspects among the archives of US National Archives than can be found in UK National Archives at Kew.

Notes

1 The National Archives, Kew (UK), KV 4/100; MI 5 file dealing with 'Functions and Organisation of Counter-Intelligence War Room 1944–1945. Letters, reports and minuting involving the Security Service, SIS, OSS and SHAEF and the allotment of roles in the proposed German War Room.'

2 Casey, William J., *The Secret War Against Hitler* (Washington, DC, 1986), p. 218; also Breitman, Richard, *Research in OSS records: One Historian's Concerns*, in: George C. Chalou, *The Secrets War: The Office of Strategic Services in World War II* (Washington, DC, 1992) for a comparison between the requirements of intelligence and knowledge of the Holocaust.

1

Liquidation Reports Nos 1 and 2: *Ämter* I and II of the RSHA

INDEX

Part I:	*Amt* I from 1939 to 1940
Part II:	The Development and Functions of *Amt* I from 1941–1945
Part III:	The Development and Functions of *Amt* II from 1941–1945
Part IV:	Miscellaneous
Appendix I:	Organisational Chart of *Amt* I in 1939–1940
Appendix II:	Organisational Chart of *Amt* I in 1941
Appendix III:	Organisational Chart of *Amt* II in 1941
Appendix IV:	Comparative Table of the Development of *Amt* I into *Ämter* I and II
Appendix V:	Organisational Chart of *Amt* I in 1944–1945
Appendix VI:	Organisational Chart of *Amt* II in 1943
Appendix VII:	Organisational Chart of *Amt* II in 1945
Appendix VIII:	The Mobile Organisation of *Amt* II in 1945
Appendix IX:	Personnel Index of *Amt* I
Appendix X:	Personnel Index of *Amt* II

Preamble

It is not possible to trace the history and development of RSHA *Amt* I and *Amt* II separately as they have in fact a common root, nor is it possible to give a completely clear picture of the changes which have occurred within the two *Ämter* themselves as these changes are many and complicated. This paper, however, sets out the salient features of this development and while this account is largely of historical and academic interest, the history of *Amt* I is of importance in that it shows perhaps better than any other *Amt* the large part which the personal ambitions and jealousies among the *Amtschefs* played in the final determination of the organisation of the RSHA.

It should be noted that there is no connection whatever between the RSHA *Amt* II of 1939–1940 and the *Amt* II of 1941 onwards: the original *Amt* II became the subsequent *Amt* VII under SS-*Staf* Six, this development being fully dealt with in the Liquidation Report on *Amt* VII. Until the end of 1940, therefore, the function of the final *Amt* I and *Amt* II were very largely covered by the original *Amt* I.

Part I

Amt I from 1939 to the end of 1940

1. The scope of the Original Amt I:

There is little need to discuss the origins of *Amt* I; it is sufficient to say that as the organisational department of the new RSHA it developed very largely from the corresponding section of the SD-*Hauptamt*, being intended to cover the administration of the other services merging with the SD in the new organisation. Examination of the organisational chart of the new *Amt* I which is shown at Appendix I shows, however, that the powers accorded to the *Amt* were indeed extensive. The Amt not only dealt with the normal administrative duties covering the organisation of the RSHA and personnel questions of the Sipo, *Gestapo*, and SD, but extended its sphere of interest to cover questions of law, passports, visas, and the supervision of the technical side of RSHA communications. These functions which by their nature exercised a degree of supervision over the other *Ämter* gave *Amt* I a position of considerable power during the early months of RSHA history.

2. The struggle for Power:

The study of the history of RSHA makes it clear that the various reorganisations which took place from time to time were not so much the result of a desire for greater efficiency but were rather a reflection of the struggle for authority between the *Amtschefs* themselves. An *Amtschef* can of course be no more powerful than his *Amt* is important and not the least concerned with the question of the authority of the *Amtschefs* was the CdS himself, Heydrich, who was ever anxious that no single *Amtschef* should become so powerful as to jeopardise the position of Heydrich himself.

3. Best and the other *Amtschefs*:

In the original allocation of power therefore on the formation of the RSHA, SS-*Brif.*

Dr Best was probably in the strongest position as not only was he *Amtschef* I with the wide field that that *Amt* accorded him but was *Gruppenleiter* IV E in charge of counter-espionage with Schellenberg as his deputy. It is worth noting that the weakest *Amtschef* on the formation of the RSHA was Jost as *Amtschef* VI, not only because of his personal characteristics but because the *Amt* itself as a new department in SD activity was not a strong one and not likely to appeal to Müller of *Amt* IV, Ohlendorf of *Amt* III, still less to the ambitious Dr Six. The early history of *Amt* I therefore is the story of the rivalry of the *Amtschefs* and the fear of Heydrich that Best was in too powerful a position.

4. The Best-Heydrich Quarrel and the reorganisation of Amt I:

The bad relations which existed between Best and Heydrich for the reasons stated above came to a head before the end of 1940, as a result of which Best relinquished his appointment as *Amtschef* to take up an appointment as *Kriegsverwaltungschef* in Paris. Heydrich now had the opportunity of reorganising *Amt* I with the object of dividing its extensive powers between two *Ämter* thus weakening the position of the new *Amtschefs*. By the end of 1940, the reorganisation had taken place with the result that the original *Amt* II under Dr Six now became the new *Amt* VII, while *Amt* I split into the new *Ämter* I and II with SS-*Brif.* Streckenbach as *Amtschef* I and SS-*Staf* Nockemann as *Amtschef* II.

5. Results of the reorganisation:

Heydrich's policy of divide and rule brought varying fortune to the remaining *Amtschefs*. Dr Six now found himself in charge of a new *Amt* VII of grossly decreased importance and his star was on the wane, *Amt* III remained unaffected, but Müller of *Amt* IV came out rather well in the reorganisation not only because Best had been removed from *Amt* I and from his position as *Gruppenleiter* IV E but also he had shared to a certain extent in the spoils afforded by the dissolution of *Amt* I. The Central Visa Office and the control of foreign workers travel which had been part of the functions of the former *Gruppe* I A (b) were incorporated into *Referat* IV C1.

6. The new *Amt* I:

The organisational chart of the new *Amt* I is shown at Appendix II. It will be seen that this new *Amt* is concerned solely with questions of personnel, training, physical training, and discipline and in taking over the relevant departments of the old *Amt* I, has given them further sub-divisions. In only two aspects did the new *Amt* maintain a position of any importance: firstly in the question of appointments and in the posting of personnel to operation units in occupied territory with the formation of the new *Einsatzkommandos*. Secondly, *Gruppe* I D of the new *Amt* gave the *Amt* considerable authority in questions of discipline.

7. The new *Amt* II:
The new *Amt* II was given much wider scope. Apart from the normal functions of organisation it was concerned with the important subject of confiscation of property as well as the control of passports and the supervision of RSHA communications. Notice should also be taken of the new departments II C 9, II C 10, and II D 6 giving the *Amt* supervision of all funds. This function was later to become one of the most important activities of *Amt* II, both in the payment of personnel of the Sipo and SD and in the distribution of special funds for intelligence purposes.

Part II

The Development and Functions of *Amt* I from 1941–1945

A. The Organisational Development

1. The General Trend:
The subsequent history of *Amt* I is easy to follow as the general tendency was always towards a simplification of its duties and a restriction of its scope. The *Amt* maintained a position of comparative importance while Streckenbach remained the *Amtschef*, a tendency which was strengthened during the period after Heydrich's death in 1942 and before the appointment of Kaltenbrunner as his successor. Even before Streckenbach relinquished his appointment as *Amtschef* in January 1943, however, the scope of the *Amt* was already in the decline. Its importance still centred round its authority over appointments and promotions, and power in matters of discipline.

2. The disappearance of *Gruppe* I C in 1942:
Before the end of 1942, *Gruppe* I C which dealt with physical training and military training was transferred to the SS-*Hauptamt*. At that time the SS-*Hauptamt* consisted of eight *Hauptämter* of which one under SS-*Ogruf* Berger dealt with recruitment and training. *Gruppe* I C therefore now became a department of Berger's SS-*Hauptamt* under SS-*Staf* Daniels dealing with 'Sport'. *Gruppe* I C reappeared again before the end of 1944 but with entirely different functions. This is dealt with in paragraph 4 below.

3. The disappearance of *Gruppe* I D:
A similar fate befell *Gruppe* I D some time at the end of 1942. The *Gruppe* which dealt with matters of discipline was removed from the control of *Amt* I and placed under the direct control of the CdS. The reason for the change was the resentment felt by the

other *Ämter* at the authority which *Gruppe* I D vested in the hands of the *Amtschef* I, in that the *Gruppe* had disciplinary authority over all members of the RSHA and its subordinated agencies. The SS-court which *Gruppe* I D controlled acted without legal restriction and was severe in its judgments, small offences being punished by prison sentence or transfer to rehabilitation units of the *Waffen-*SS. The *Gruppe* I D therefore became directly subordinated to the CdS though the final review of all sentences passed by the court rested in Himmler himself. The *Gruppe* passed under the control of SS-*Stubaf* Dillersberger, with the title of *Untersuchungsführer* Chef Sipo.

4. The creation of the new *Gruppe* I C in 1944:
The *Amt* subsequently underwent one major change by the creation in November 1944 of a new *Gruppe* I C having as its sphere of interest what was called '*Weltanschauliche Führung*'. The *Gruppenleiter* was SS-*Ostubaf* Gschwend. The creation of this new *Gruppe* represented a 'penetration' of *Amt* I by the SS-*Hauptamt*, the underlying idea being that the SS-*Hauptamt* should be responsible for the education of members of the RSHA and its subordinate formations on the general official attitude of the Party. The *Gruppe* was to exercise its functions through representatives with each IdS and BdS. In point of fact the *Gruppe* was organised at too late a date to have any effect and while the *Gruppe* existed on paper it did not at any time function on any recognised organisational lines. The breakdown of *Gruppe* I C therefore is not known for the very good reason that it did not exist. Gschwend had as his deputy SS-*Ustuf* Moebus.

5. The creation of *Gruppe* I *Mil-Pers.*:
The absorption of the *Abwehr* in the summer of 1944 caused a further change in the organisation of *Amt* I through the appointment of *Oberstleutnant* Hübner as *Gruppenleiter* of a new *Gruppe* I *Mil-Pers*. The function of the new *Gruppe* is self-explanatory, Hübner being given the task of supervising military personnel. Ehrlinger made every effort to have effective control over his new *Gruppe* in the selection and appointment of *Abwehr* personnel but was unsuccessful owing to Schellenberg's personal interest in the building up of the new *Mil Amt*.

6. The *Amtschefs*:
When Best relinquished his appointment in the summer of 1940 he was replaced by SS-*Brif* Streckenbach who was instrumental in maintaining *Amt* I in a comparatively strong position, mainly through *Gruppe* I D, during his tenure of office until January 1943. Streckenbach was a strong personality but his successor SS-*Brif* Erwin Schulz was weak in comparison and the decline in authority of *Amt* I dates from his appointment. Schulz, as a result of friction between himself and Müller, *Amtschef* IV, was dismissed from this office and transferred to BdS Salzburg in March 1944 where he remained until his arrest in May 1945. Schulz was succeeded by SS-*Staf* Erich Ehrlinger who remained in command until the end.

7. The dis-organisation of *Amt* I:

The *Amt* suffered severely on two occasions as a result of air attacks on Berlin. In November 1943, the *Amt* building was severely damaged and some 35 deaths in personnel caused. A second loss was suffered in April 1944 from similar causes and as a result of the inevitable confusion caused by loss of personnel, offices and to a certain extent, records, the *Amt* in its later stages underwent considerable changes but was disorganised rather than reorganised. Nominally the structure of the *Amt* on paper remained unchanged, though it is to be noted that in February 1944 *Referat* I A6 was incorporated in I A1 but the air-raids and the general war situation which caused a continual flow of physically fit personnel to fighting units had their inevitable effect. The final organisation divided *Gruppe* I A into two *Abteilungen*, I A1 under Wanninger and I A2 under Schraepel. The organisational chart of *Amt* I such as it existed in the later stages is shown at Appendix V.

B. The functions of *Amt* I

1. Appointments of Personnel:

The only function of any importance which *Amt* I retained until the end was that of appointments and promotions. The appointments to other *Ämter* had to be made through *Amt* I which also acted as a pool for officers who had been dismissed from other *Ämter* prior to postings to other units under the RSHA or to the *Waffen*-SS.

Employment in the RSHA normally involved deferment from service in a fighting unit or transfer to the RSHA from a fighting unit. Such transfers were not easy, especially in the case of younger men and in the latter stages of the war when the needs of fighting units grew considerably. *Amt* I was responsible for the arranging of such transfers and normally adopted the practice of drafting the person concerned to the *Waffen*-SS and then posting him to the Headquarters Company of the *Waffen*-SS in the RSHA.

2. The *Einsatzkommandos*:

Amt I was likewise responsible for appointments to the *Einsatzkommandos*, composed of Sipo and SD personnel, which operated with the armies in occupied territory. In such appointments *Amt* I wielded considerable authority: the *Einsatzkommandos* served two useful purposes from the point of view of the personnel section, as they were a convenient method of getting rid of 'undesirable' personnel and at the same time offered rich prizes in the field of promotion. Both these advantages were fully exploited.[1]

3. Promotions:

It was in the question of promotions that *Amt* I appeared important in the eyes of the RSHA. Promotion depended on the vacancies allowed by the War Establishment

(*Planstellenwesen*) and the War Establishment came under the control of SS-*Ostubaf* Braune, Ehrlinger's deputy. The question was one of constant controversy, and frequent changes were made both in the War Establishments themselves and in the relationship between appointment and rank, always a source of discontent. In these squabbles and discussions, Braune was an important figure whose opinion on promotions and appointments carried much weight.

Part III

The Development and Functions of *Amt* II from 1941–1945

A. The Organisational Development

1. General:
Like *Amt* I, *Amt* II saw its scope progressively restricted between the years of 1941 to 1945. The *Amt* tended to become more and more a purely organisational section and lost its control over passports and communications, the former eventually passing to *Amt* IV and latter being incorporated in the new RSHA *Amt* N. The organisational chart of *Amt* II such as it stood in the latter half of 1943 is shown at Appendix VI. Comparison with the organisation shown at Appendix III shows that in fact the two former *Gruppen* A and B have disappeared: what in effect has happened is that the old *Gruppe* C has become the new *Gruppen* A and B, while the former *Gruppe* D has become the new *Gruppe* C.

2. The disappearance of *Gruppe* II A in 1941:
Gruppe II A did not remain long in the form it possessed in 1941. *Referat* II A3 became the new *Referat* II B4, but the rather wide scope of II A4 and II A5 seems to have disappeared at an early date. II A5 reappears as a mere sub-section of *Referat* II B1 while II A4 disappeared entirely. The remaining functions of the original *Gruppe* II A were incorporated into *Gruppe* II C when that *Gruppe* replaced II A.

3. The transfer of *Gruppe* II B to *Amt* IV:
It has been noted that on the reorganisation of *Amt* I at the end of 1940 the Central Visa Office (*Sichtvermerkstelle*) had passed to IV C1 though the Passport *Referat* had remained in the new *Amt* II as *Gruppe* II B. *Gruppe* II B did not remain long in *Amt* II, however, and joined RSHA *Amt* IV to join up with the *Sichtvermarkstelle*, probably very early in 1943. In subsequent changes in *Amt* IV, the department became IV B4 after the major reorganisation in the summer of 1944, having previously been a separate *Gruppe*, *Gruppe* IV F.

4. The formation of *Amt* N in September 1944:

By the middle of 1944, it had become obvious that *Amt* II was not suited to the supervision of RSHA communications, a field of activity which required technical knowledge beyond the functions of an administrative unit. A new *Amt* therefore was created, *Amt* N, under SS-*Staf* Sansoni in September 1944. The functions of the new *Amt* were the training of telephone and W/T personnel, the procurement and distribution of signal equipment. The formation of *Amt* N meant that II C1 and II C2 disappeared from *Amt* II.

5. The final reorganisation under Spacil:

The final organisation of *Amt* II became complicated beyond clarification in the last months when SS-*Staf* Josef Spacil reorganised the *Amt* to conform with the war situation. As a result of Allied bombing, it became necessary to divide the *Amt* into an executive and an operational staff, the former group remaining in Berlin, and the latter evacuating to Bad Sulza. Further, plans for the evacuation of the RSHA [from Berlin] were by now underway and *Amt* II had to create a very mobile and pliable organisation to cope with the altered situation. The general effect was that the numbered Referate largely lost their significance while Spacil formed special 'groups' operating directly under his command. This fluid organisation is shown at Appendix VIII while the organisation is shown at Appendix VII. The formation of *Gruppe* FZ, created in February 1945, should be noted.

6. The *Amtschefs*:

The original *Amtschef* SS-*Staf* Nockemann was transferred to the Eastern Front in early 1943 where he was later killed in action [in fact, Nockemann was killed in action on 19 December 1941 on the Eastern Front]. His successor was SS-*Staf* Prietzel who proved himself inefficient and was sent to Norway at the end of 1943. By the end of the year the organisational side of the RSHA began to cause Kaltenbrunner some concern and Kaltenbrunner appointed SS-*Oberführer* Spacil who had been his administrative assistant when Kaltenbrunner had been *Leiter* of the SS-*Oberabschnitt* Donau. Spacil was a man of some efficiency but found the task of reorganising *Amt* II on satisfactory lines too difficult a task in face of the many complications caused by the deteriorating war situation. Spacil remained in charge until the final collapse. There is some doubt as to the actual date of Spacil's appointment. There is documentary evidence showing him as *Amtschef* as early as October 1943, but he himself maintains that he was not appointed until July 1944, a contention which is supported from other sources including Kaltenbrunner.

B. The Functions of *Amt* II

1. Administration of Funds:

By far the most important function of *Amt* II, indeed its only function of any real importance in the last two years of its existence, lay in its control of allocation of funds. It was responsible for the payment of salaries to the Sipo and SD personnel of the RSHA, though in this it acted merely as a book-keeping department as the actual funds were held by the treasury of the NSDAP and the SD and by the Ministry of the Interior for the Sipo.

2. SD Finances:

The payment of SD funds was made through SS-*Staf* Hoppe, *Referent* for II A4 and *Referent* for the SD *Verwaltung* section of Spacil's 'mobile' organisation. Hoppe was responsible for drawing up the monthly estimate which was countersigned by Ohlendorf, RSHA *Amtschef* III, before being presented to the Party Treasurer Schwarz. The monthly budget was probably in the region of 1,000,000 Reichsmarks. On receipt of the funds from the Party Treasury, Hoppe was responsible for distribution of part of the money to Ohlendorf of *Amt* III for secret purposes, the remainder being sent direct to the IdS for further allocation to the SD-*Abschnitte*. Auditing of the SD account was done by SS-*Wirtschafts Verwaltungshauptamt*.

3. Financial arrangements of other *Ämter*:

The remaining *Ämter* of the RSHA, I, II, IV, VII, *Amt* N, and *Amt* San (*Amt* V administration was controlled by the *Orpo* and not by *Amt* II) were dealt with directly by *Amt* II in question of pay. Normally *Amt* II had a paymaster representative in the Stapo Kassen at lower levels responsible for the distribution of funds received from *Amt* II through the KdS or BdS. It is to be noted that VI S operational units were catered for by the Wehrmacht in matters of pay, rations and equipment.

4. Foreign Currency:

Questions of Foreign Exchange assets were dealt with by the *Devisen Referat*, RSHA II A1b under SS-*Hstuf* Pfeiler, the money being received from the SS-*Wirtschafts Verwaltungshauptamt* for further distribution to the *Ämter*. *Amt* VI of course by the nature of its work received most of the foreign currency, usually in the region of 75%. The remaining *Ämter* received only small and occasional allocation for specific purposes, the residue being used by *Amt* II itself for purchase of equipment etc.

5. Other *Referat*:

There is little need to explain the functions of the remaining *Referat* of RSHA *Amt* II as these functions are self-evident from the title of the *Referat*. Mention should be made of the *Referat für* N-Zwecke whose function it was to obtain valuable articles such as jewelry, gold, etc. for the payment of foreign agents. *Gruppe* FZ was responsible for equipping with weapons the special mobile formations organised in the later stages of the war.

6. *Amt* II and the Redoubt Plan:

As the administrative section of the RSHA, *Amt* II had a prominent part to play in the projected plan for the Alpine Redoubt. The *Amt* was responsible for the establishment of food dumps for resistance groups and for the transfer of RSHA funds to places of safe keeping. The plan for the provision of food dumps failed to materialise, but the transfer of funds was carried out. The *Devisen Referat* was evacuated with the Operational Group of the *Amt* to Bad Sulza [145 miles south of Berlin] in October 1944 but the funds remained in Berlin until continued air-attacks made it imperative to have them transferred to Bad Sulza in February 1945. To conform with the Alpine Redoubt plan, the funds were to be hidden in caches throughout the Redoubt area but owing to the speed of the Allied advance it was found they could only be hurriedly buried in the early part of May 1945. It is believed that most of the funds have now been recovered.

The Berlin account of *Amt* II was withdrawn from the Reichsbank in the second half of April 1945, part being given to Ohlendorf for the purposes of the Nordstab, the remainder being taken to Salzburg for division among the various agencies centred there.

Part IV

Miscellaneous

1. Arrests:

Arrested personnel of *Amt* I and *Amt* II are shown at Appendices IX and X. *Amt* II is very largely covered by the arrest of RSHA *Amtschef* Spacil though the arrest of SS-*Hstuf* Pfeiler and SS-*Ustuf* Mandel who were in charge of the hiding of part of the *Amt* funds in the Redoubt should if effected complete picture of the disposition of these funds. In *Amt* I the chief target is the *Amtschef* Ehrlinger who is known to have gone north with the Nordstab and was last reported in the Flensburg area in early May 1945. SS-*Stubaf* Wanninger is the most important arrest so far.

2. Main Sources:

On *Amt* I:	SS-*Stubaf* Wanninger, *Gruppenleiter* I A
	Captured documents.
On *Amt* II:	SS-*Obf* Spacil, *Amtschef* II
	Reg.Ob.Insp. Tempelhagen, *Geschäftsstelle* II
	Captured documents.

Issued by section W.R.C.3.a, 21 October 1945.

Appendix I

Organisational Chart of RSHA *Amt* I in 1939–1940

Amtschef I			SS-*Brif* Dr Best
Hauptbüro des RSHA and *Gesellschäft Amt* I			SS-*Stubaf* Trinkl
Hauskommandant			SS-*Hstuf* Bünsch

Gruppe	*Referat*	*Sachgebiet*	*Referent*
Gruppenleiter: SS-*Staf* Zindel			
I A (a)		Recht	
	I A1	*Gesetzgebung* I	SS-*Hstuf* Neifeind
	I A2	*Gesetzgebung* II	SS-*Stubaf* Meyer
	I A3	*Verwaltungsrecht*	SS-*Hstuf* Ehlers
	I A4	*Reichsverteidigung*	SS-*Stubaf* Thorn
	I A5	*Justitiar*	SS-*Stubaf* Mylius
Gruppenleiter: *Min Rat* Krause			
I A (b)		*Passwesen und Auslanderpolizei*	
	I A6	*Passwesen*	*Reg Rat* Kröning
	I A7	*Auslanderpolizei*	Dr Wetz
Gruppenleiter: vacant			
I B		*Organisation*	
	I B1	*Organisation der Sipo*	SS-*Stubaf* Bilfinger
	I B2	*Organisation der* SD	SS-*Ostuf* Paeffgen
	I B3	*Organisation der Grepo*	SS-*Staf* Trummler
	I B4	*Angelegenheiten des Abwehrbeauftragten*	SS-*Stubaf* Renken
		des Reichministerium des Innern	
Gruppenleiter: SS-*Staf* Tesmer			
I C (a)		*Personalien der Sipo*	
	I C1	*Personalien der Stapo*	SS-*Stubaf* Hafke
	I C2	*Personalien der Kripo*	SS-*Stubaf* Kaphengst
Gruppenleiter: SS-*Staf* Willich			
I C (b)		*Personalien des* SD	
	I C3	*Personalangelegenheiten*	vacant
	I C4	*Stellenbesetzungen des* SD	SS-*Stubaf* Braune

Gruppenleiter: unoccupied

I D	*Dienststrafsachen*	
I D1	*Dienststrafensachen der Sipo*	SS-*Stubaf* Mylius
I D2	*Dienststrafsachen*	SS-*Stubaf* Hänsch

Gruppenleiter: Dr Siegert

I E (a)	*Haushalt und Wirtschaft der Sipo*	
I E1	*Haushalt*	SS-*Stubaf* Bergmann
I E2	*Wirtschaft*	SS-*Stubaf* Kreklow

Gruppenleiter: Ober.Reg.Rat Berk

I E (b)	*Haushalt und Wirtschaft des* SD	
I E3	*Haushalt*	SS-*Hstuf* Radtke
I E4	*Wirtschaft*	SS-*Stubaf* Brocke

Gruppenleiter: SS-*Staf* Willich

I F	*Erziehung*	
I F1	*Weltanschauliche Erziehung*	vacant
I F2	*Fachliche Schulung*	vacant
I F3	*Dienstliche Leibesübungen*	vacant
I F4	*Kampfsport*	vacant

Gruppenleiter: SS-*Stubaf* Rauff

I G	*Technische Angelegenheiten*	
I G1	*Funk*	vacant
I G2	*Fernschreiben und Fernsprechwesen*	SS-*Stubaf* Walter
I G3	*Kraftfahrwesen*	SS-*Hstuf* Pradel
I G4	*Waffenwesen*	SS-*Stubaf* Leopold
I G5	*Flugwesen*	SS-*Stubaf* Leopold

Appendix II

Organisational Chart of RSHA *Amt* I in 1941

Amtschef I	SS-*Brif* Streckenbach
Geschäftstellenleiter Amt I	*Reg.Oberinspektor* Selberg
Deputy	*Pol.Sek.* Herr

Gruppe	*Referat*	*Sachgebiet*	*Referent*
Gruppenleiter: SS-*Staf* Brunner			
I A		Personnel	
	I A1	Personnel matters of *Sipo*	SS-*Stubaf* Mohr and SD
	I A2	Personnel matters of *Stapo*	SS-*Stubaf* Tent
	I A3	Personnel matters of *Kripo*	SS-*Stubaf* Schräpel
	I A4	Personnel matters of SD	SS-*Stubaf* Braune
	I A5	Party and SS Personnel matters	vacant
	I A6	Welfare	SS-*Ostubaf* Trinkl
Gruppenleiter: SS-*Staf* Erwin Schulz			
I B		Education	
	I B1	Ideological Education	SS-*Stubaf* Dr Engel
	I B2	Successors	SS-*Stubaf* Hotzel
	I B3	Planning of Instruction in Schools	SS-*Stubaf* Sandberger
	I B4	Other Plans of Instruction	SS-*Stubaf* Rennau
Gruppenleiter: SS-*Stubaf* von Daniels			
I C		Training	
	I C1	General Matters concerning physical training	vacant
	I C2	Physical Education and Military Training	vacant
Gruppenleiter: SS-*Brif* Streckenbach			
I D		*Dienststrafensachen*	
	I D1	Official Penal Matters	SS-*Stubaf* Friedrich Schulz
	I D2	SS Disciplinary Matters	SS-*Stubaf* Hänsch

Appendix III

Organisational Chart of RSHA *Amt* II in 1941

	Amtschef II	SS-*Staf* Nockemann	

Gruppe	*Referat*	*Sachgebiet*	*Referent*
Gruppenleiter: vacant			
II A		Organisation and Law	
	II A1	Organisation of *Sipo* and SD	SS-*Hstuf* Dr Schweder
	II A2	Legislation	SS-*Stubaf* Neifeind
	II A3	Justiciary Matters:	SS-*Stubaf* Suhr
		Claims for Indemnification	

II A4	Matters concerning Defence of the Reich	SS-*Stubaf* Renken
II A5	Miscellaneous:	SS-*Stubaf* Richter
	- Determination of hostility to *Volk* and State;	
	- Confiscation of property of foes of *Volk* and State in Berlin;	
	- Retraction of German citizenship.	

Gruppenleiter: *Min Rat* Krause

II B		Basic Questions of Passports and Foreign Police	
II B1	Passports	Dr Hoffmann & Dr Baumann
II B2	Passports II	*Reg.Rat* Weistz
II B3	Identification and ID cards	*Reg.Rat* Kelbling
II B4	Basic Questions of Foreign Police and Border Security	*Ober.Reg.Rat* Kröning

Gruppenleiter: SS-*Staf* Dr Siegert

II C (a) Domestic Arrangements of *Sipo*

II C1	Domestics Arrangements and Pay	SS-*Staf* Dr Siegert
II C2	Board and Material Expenses	SS-*Stubaf* Kreklow
II C3	Lodgings and Prisoners	SS-*Stubaf* Dr Bergmann
II C4	Business office: Accounts of *Chef Sipo u.d.* SD; Clothing accounts of *Grepo*	SS-*Stubaf* August Meier

II C (b) Domestic Arrangments of the SD

II C7	Domestic Arrangements and Pay	SS-*Hstuf* Radtke
II C8	Procurement, insurance, real estate, construction, vehicles	SS-*Stubaf* Fritz Schmidt
II C9	Audit and Examination	SS-*Ostubaf* Brocke
II C10	Finance and Accounts	SS-*Ostubaf* Brocke

Gruppenleiter: SS-*Ostubaf* Rauff

II D		Technical Matters	
II D1	Wireless, Photography, Films	SS-*Stubaf* Gottstein
II D2	Teleprinter and Telephones	SS-*Stubaf* Walter
II D3	Motor Vehicles of the *Sipo*	SS-*Hstuf* Pradel
II D3 (b)	Motor Vehicles of the SD	SS-*Hstuf* Gast
II D4	Weapons	SS-*Stubaf* Lutter
II D5	Aviation	SS-*Stubaf* Leopold
II D6	Management of the Technical Funds of the *Sipo* and SD	vacant

Appendix IV

Comparative Table of the Development
of RSHA *Amt* I into *Ämter* I and II

Amt I, 1940	*Sachgebiet*	Allocation in *Amt* I and *Amt* II, 1941
I A (a)		
1	*Gesetzgebung* I	II A2
2	*Gesetzgebung* II	II A2
3	*Verwaltungsrecht*	-
4	*Reichsverteidigung*	II A4
5	Justitiar	II A3
I A (b)		
6	*Passwesen*	II B1 }
		II B2 }
7	*Ausländerpolizei*	II B4
I B		
1	Organisation *der Sipo*	II A1
2	Organisation *des* SD	II A1
3	Organisation *der Grenzpolizei*	-
4	*Angelegenheiten des Abwehrbeauftragten des* RMdI	-
I C (a)		I A1
1	*Personalien der Staatspolizei*	I A2
2	*Personalien der Kriminalpolizei*	I A3
I C (b)		
3	*Personalangelegenheiten*	I A4
4	*Stellenbesetzungen des* SD	-
I D		
1	*Dienststrafsachen der Sipo*	I D1
2	*Dienststrafsachen*	I D2
I E (a)		II C (a)
1	*Haushalt*	II C1 }
		II C2 }

2	*Wirtschaft*	II C3 }
		II C4 }
I E (b)		
3	*Haushalt*	II C7
4	*Wirtschaft*	II C8
I F		
1	*Weltanschauliche Erziehung*	I B1
2	*Fachliche Schulung*	I B2-4
3	*Dienstliche Liebesübungen*	I C1
4	*Kampfsport*	I C2
I G		
1	*Funk*	II D1
2	*Fernschreiber und Fernsprechwesen*	II D2
3	*Kraftfahrwesen*	II D3a & II D3b
	(1) *der Geheimen Staatspolizei*	
	(2) *des SD*	
4	*Waffenwesen*	II D4
5	*Flugwesen*	II D5

New Departments in the new RSHA *Amt* I:

I A4	Party and SS Personnel matters
I A6	Welfare

New Departments in the new RSHA *Amt* II:

II A5	*Sippenhaft*, German citizenship
II B3	Identity Cards
II C9	Auditing and examination of SD accounts
II C10	Finances and accounts of SD
II D6	Management of Technical Funds of SD

Appendix V

Organisation of RSHA *Amt* I, 1944–1945

RSHA *Amt* I:	Personal, *Ausbildung und Organisation der Sipo u.d.* SD
Amtschef I:	SS-*Obf* Ehrlinger
Geschäftstelle:	SS-*Hstuf* Ergenzinger

Gruppe	Referat	Sachgebiet	Referent
Gruppenleiter: SS-*Stubaf* Wanninger			
I A		Personal	
	I A1	*Allgemeine Personalangelegen-*	SS-*Stubaf* Wanninger
		heiten, Sipo und SD	
	I A2	Personal (*Gestapo*)	SS-*Stubaf* Hülf
	I A3	Personal (*Kripo*)	SS-*Staf* Schräpel
	I A4	Personal (SD)	SS-*Ostubaf* Braune
	I A5	Personal (*Partei und* SS)	SS-*Ostubaf* Braune

Gruppenleiter: SS-*Stubaf* Dr Zirpins			
I B		*Nachwuchs, Erziehung*	
	I B1	*Politische-weltanschauliche*	SS-*Stubaf* Dr Engel
	I B2	*Nachwuchs*	SS-*Ostubaf* Dr Rennau
	I B3	*Ausbildung, Fortbildung*	SS-*Stubaf* Dr Zirpins
	I B4	*Leibeserziehung, Wehrausbildung*	SS-*Ostuf* Folkerts
	I B5	*Laufbahnrichtlinien, Prüfungsamt,*	SS-*Stubaf* Gindel
		Fondsverwaltung	

Gruppenleiter: SS-*Ostubaf* Gschwend			
I C		*Weltanschauliche Führung*	

Gruppenleiter: *Oberstleutnant* Hübner			
I *Mil-Pers.*		*Militärisches Personal*	

Note: The above organisation was subsequently modified by the division of *Gruppe* I A into two *Abteilungen*, I A (I) under Wanninger and I A (II) under Schräpel. Details of this organisation are still lacking.

Appendix VI

Organisation of RSHA *Amt* II in September 1943

Amt II:	*Haushalt und Wirtschaft*
Amtschef II:	SS-*Staf* Prietzel
Geschäftstelle:	SS-*Stubaf* Graetz
Deputy:	SS-*Hstuf* ROI Tempelhagen
Hauptbüro:	SS-*Stubaf* Amtsrat Pommerening
Deputy:	SS-*Hstuf* Weber
Hauskommandant:	SS-*Hstuf* Holtmann

Gruppe	Referat	Sachgebiet	Referent

Gruppenleiter: SS-*Ostubaf* Kreklow

II A		Haushalt, Besoldung, Rechnungswesen	
	II A1	Haushalt der Sipo	SS-*Hstuf* ROI Müller
	II A2	Besoldung der Sipo	*Amtsrat* Terborg
	II A3	Gebürnis und Rechnungstelle des RSHA	SS-*Stubaf* RR Meier
	II A4	Haushalt, Besoldung und Rechnungswesen des SD	SS-*Staf* Helldobler

Kasse des RSHA (*Sipo*)

Leiter: *Amtsrat* Lüder
Staff: SS-*Hstuf* POI Hercht
         POI Wetzel
         POI Schmidt

Rechnungsamt des RSHA (*Sipo*)

Leiter: *Amtsrat* Heinmöller
Staff: POI Hoffmann
         POI Koppehl
         POI Liepelt
         PI Papenfuss
         PI Kalix
         PI Loewke
         PI Franke

Gruppenleiter: SS-*Ostubaf* Dr Bergmann

II B		Wirtschaftsangelegenheiten, usw.	
	II B1	Unterkunft, Rohstoffe	SS-*Ostubaf* Dr Bergmann
	II B2	Bekleidung, Geschäftsbedürfnsse	*Amtsrat* Rievers
	II B3	Gefangenenwesen	SS-*Ostubaf* Dr Bergmann
	II B4	Justitiarangelegenheiten usw.	SS-*Ostubaf* Dr Kaufmann

Gruppenleiter: SS-*Ostubaf* Hafke

II C		Technische Angelegenheiten	
	II C1	Funk, Foto und Filmwesen, kriminaltechn. Geräte	SS-*Stubaf* Mehlstaübl
	II C2	Fernschreib- und Fernsprechwesen	SS-*Stubaf* AR Walter
	II C3	Kraftfahrwesen	SS-*Stubaf* Pradel
	II C4	Waffenwesen	SS-*Stubaf* AR Lutter
	II C5	Nachschub	vacant (acting, PI Rath)

Appendix VII

Organisation of RSHA *Amt* II in 1945

Amt II:	*Haushalt und Wirtschaft*
Amtschef II:	SS-*Obf* Spacil
Geschäftsstelle:	SS-*Stubaf* Grätz
Hauptbüro:	SS-*Stubaf* Pommerening
Hauskommandant:	SS-*Hstuf* Holtmann

Gruppe	Referat	Sachgebiet	Referent

Gruppenleiter: SS-*Ostubaf* Kreklow

II A		*Haushalt und Rechnungswesen*	
	II A1	*Haushalt und Devisen*	SS-*Hstuf* Müller
	II A2	*Fürsorge*	SS-*Stubaf* Dietrich
	II A3	*Besoldung, Wirtschaftsstelle der Sipo*	SS-*Stubaf* Meier
	II A4	*Wirtschaftsstelle des* SD	SS-*Staf* Helldobler

Gruppenleiter: SS-*Ostubaf* Dr Bergmann

II B		*Beschaffungen und Gefangenenwesen*	
	II B1	*Beschaffungen*	SS-*Ostubaf* Dr Bergmann
	II B2	*Ausrüstung*	SS-*Stubaf* Rievers
	II B3	*Gefangenenwesen*	SS-*Ostubaf* Dr Bergmann
	II B4	*Bekleidung*	SS-*Hstuf* Uterhardt

Gruppenleiter: SS-*Ostubaf* Hafke

II C		*Kraftfahrwesen und Transport*	
	II C3	*Kraftfahrwesen*	SS-*Hstuf* Just
	II C4	*Transportwesen*	SS-*Hstuf* Just

Gruppenleiter: SS-*Stubaf* Müller

FZ		*Feldzeugmeisterei*	
	II FZ 1	*Waffen und Munition*	
	II FZ 2	*Geräte*	
	II FZ 3	*Zeugamt*	

Appendix VIII

The Mobile Organisation of RSHA *Amt* II in 1945

Amtschef II:	SS-*Obf* Spacil
Adjutant:	SS-*Ostuf* Schiebel
Asst *Amtschef*:	SS-*Ostubaf* Dr Karl
Adjutant:	SS-*Ustuf* Panhans

Gruppe A—*Gruppenleiter*: SS-*Ostubaf* Kreklow

Budget and Salaries	SS-*Hstuf* Müller
Foreign Exchange	SS-*Hstuf* Pfeiler
Dependents' and Family Benefits	SS-*Stubaf* Dierich
Assistance to Victims of Bombing	SS-*Hstuf* Cohrs
Disbursing and Accounting	SS-*Stubaf* Meier
Examining and Auditing	*Amtsrat* Heinmöller

Gruppe B—*Gruppenleiter*: under Spacil's direct supervision

Clothing and Equipment	SS-*Hstuf* Uterhardt
Rations	SS-*Stubaf* Rievers
Offices and Billets	SS-*Ostubaf* Dr Bergmann
Plans and Construction of Dispersal Sites	SS-*Ostubaf* Dr Bergmann
Contracts	SS-*Ostubaf* Dr Bergmann
PX Rations, Tobacco, Agents, Bribes	SS-*Ostubaf* Dr Bergmann

Gruppe C—*Gruppenleiter*: SS-*Ostubaf* Hafke

Vehicles, Fuel, Spare Parts	SS-*Hstuf* Just
Radio Receivers for Offices and Billets	SS-*Hstuf* Müller
Maintenance Units	SS-*Ustuf* Kränzle
Construction of Repair Shops	SS-*Ustuf* Krautsdorfer

Gruppe FZ—*Gruppenleiter*: SS-*Stubaf* Müller

Procurement of weapons and equipment from OKH, OKW and SS-*Hauptamt*	SS-*Stubaf* Müller
Supply Officer	SS-*Stubaf* Luther

Gruppe, Miscellaneous—*Gruppenleiter*: under Spacil's direct supervision

Legal Dept	SS-*Stubaf* Dietrich
Mail and Message Centre	SS-*Stubaf* Pommerening
Hauskommandant	SS-*Hstuf* Holtmann
Air Raid Protection Service	SS-*Hstuf* Ballauf
Liaison with Customs Service	SS-*Hstuf* Scharr
Auditing Italy, Operation Bernhard	SS-*Ustuf* Günther
Evacuation Service	SS-*Hstuf* Fichtner

Appendix IX

Alphabetical Index of RSHA *Amt* I personnel

Note: 1) Arrested personnel are underlined;

2) This list contains the names of *Amt* I officers from 1941-1945. It does not include officers of *Gruppe* I C and *Gruppe* I D which left the *Amt* in 1942, except the *Gruppenleiter*.

Name	Rank	*Referat*	Remarks
Abel, Helmut	SS-*Hstuf*	I A2	
Achterberg, Helmut	SS-*Stubaf*	I D	
Albinus, Werner	SS-*Ustuf*	I A3	
Anderson, Franz	SS-*Ostuf*	I A2	
Bahr, Herbert	SS-*Ostuf*	I A5	
Baschin, Albert	SS-*Ustuf*	I A3	
Bauer,	*Krim.Ob.Sek.*	I A1	
Beckhoff, Friedrich-Wilh.	SS-*Hstuf*	I A4	
Best, Dr Karl Werner	SS-*Brif.*	*Amtschef* I	1940, left the *Amt*
Beyer, Paul	SS-*Ustuf*	I Gst.	Nov. 1943, *Leiter* Kanzlei
Bolduan, Karl	SS-*Ustuf*	I A1	Nov. 1943
Bonatz, Wilhelm	SS-*Stubaf* RuKR	I A3	Nov. 1943
Braune, Fritz	SS-Ostubaf	I A4, I A5	Referent
Brettschneider, Johannes	*Reg.Ob.Insp*	I A 3	Nov. 1943
zum Broock, Heinrich	SS-*Hstuf*	I	
Brunner, Karl	SS-*Staf*	I A	1941, *Gruppenleiter*
von Buelow, Harry	SS-*Ostubaf*	I Org	1944, with SSHA
Bunde, Willy	*Reg.Sek*	I A2	
Burchards, Günther	SS-*Hstuf*	I A4	
Burgdorf, Wilhelm	SS-*Stubaf*	I A5	
Buss, Daniel	SS-*Ostuf*	I B2	Nov. 1943

Christof, Robert	SS-*Hstuf*	I A3	
von Daniels, Herbert	SS-*Staf*	I C	to 1942, *Gruppenleiter*; transfer to SSHA
Dannecke,	SS-*Hstuf*	I Org	
Daun, Walter	SS-*Ustuf*	I A1	
Dierich, Heinrich	SS-*Stubaf*	I A6	Nov. 1943
Dietterich, Gustav	SS-*Ustuf*	I A5	Nov. 1943
Dillersberger, Dr Walther	SS-*Stubaf*	I D	1940–42, *Gruppenleiter*; then CdS *Untersuchungsführer*
Dommick, Kurt	SS-*Hstuf*	I A1	
Ehrle, Helmut	SS-*Ustuf*	I A1	Nov. 1943
Ehrlinger, Erich	SS-*Obf.*	*Amtschef* I	1944–1945
Eichler, Ernst	*Reg.Rat*	I A3	Nov. 1943
Eimers, Reinhard	SS-*Hstuf*	I	
Engel, Dr Siegfried	SS-*Stubaf*	I B1	*Referent*
Ergenzinger, Fritz	SS-*Hstuf*	I Gst.	Adjutant to Ehrlinger
Feder, Herbert	SS-*Hstuf*	I A4	
vom Felde, Gustav	SS-*Ostubaf*	I A	*Gruppenleiter*; killed in air-raid, Oct. 1943
Fleischhammer, Dr Georg	*Krim.Rat*	I B	Nov. 1943
Folkerts, Gerhard	SS-*Ostuf*	I B4	Referent
Folz, Ewald	SS-*Ostuf*	I	
Friedrich, Johannes	SS-*Ustuf*	I A5	Nov. 1943
Frohberg, Walter	*Pol.Sek*	I A6	
Gagstädter, Johannes	*Pol.Insp.*	I A5	Nov. 1943
Gindel, Willy	SS-*Stubaf*	I B5	*Referent*
Glaser, Karl	SS-*Ustuf*	I A4	Nov. 1943
Gottschalk, Friedrich	SS-*Stubaf*	I A1	1944, *Referent*
Graaf, Kurt	SS-*Stubaf*	I A5	Nov. 1943
Graetz, Paul	SS-*Stubaf*	I Gst.	1945, *Leiter*
Greiffenberger Wilhelm	SS-*Stubaf*	I A4	
Gschwend, Wilhelm	SS-*Ostubaf*	I C	Nov. 1944, *Gruppenleiter*
Gütschow, Walter	SS-*Ostuf*	I A1	Feb. 1944
Gutt, Fritz	SS-*Ostuf*	I A1	
Haensch, Dr Walter	SS-*Ostubaf*	I D	transfer to CdS *Untersuchungsführer*
Hammer, Erich	SS-*Hstuf*	I B4	
Hanne, Günther	SS-*Hstuf*	I B	
Härtl, Albert	SS-*Ustuf*	I A5	
Hebekerl, Wilhelm	*Pol.Sek.*	I A6	
Heise, Ernst	*Pol.Insp.*	I A1	

Heinze, Friedrich	SS-*Ostuf*	I A	
Herr, Walter	SS-*Ostuf*	I Gst.	
Herrmann, Heinrich	SS-*Ostuf*	I A2	
Heuser, Ernst	SS-*Hstuf*	I A2	died in air raid, 29 April 1944
Höpker, Fritz	SS-*Hstuf*	I A1	Nov. 1943
Hoffmann, Albert	*Reg.Ob.Insp.*	I A2	died in air raid, 29 April 1944
Hoffmann, Ernst	SS-*Hstuf* KK	I A3	Nov. 1943
Hosch, Alfons	SS-Hstuf	I A6	Nov. 1943
Hotzel, Rudolf	SS-Ostubaf	I B	1943–1944, *Gruppenleiter* and *Referent*, I B1
Hubner,	*Oberst*	I *Mil Pers*	1944–1945, *Gruppenleiter*
Hülf, Wilhelm	SS-*Ostubaf*	I A2	*Referent*
Jakob, Gustav	SS-*Stubaf Pol.Rat*	I A2	Nov. 1943
Janek, Franz	SS-*Hstuf*	I A5	Nov. 1943
Janne, Friedrich	SS-*Stubaf*	I A2	June 1944, transfer to Stapo Munich
Junghans, Martin	SS-*Stubaf*	I A5	Nov. 1943
Kampitz, Julius	SS-*Ostuf*	I A5	Nov. 1943
Klaus, Walter	SS-*Ostuf*	I A1	
Klemm, Max	*Krim.Ob.Sek*	I A3	Nov. 1943
Klimesch, Paul	*Pol.Ob.Sek*	I A2	Nov. 1943
Kloth, Wilhelm	SS-*Ostuf*	I A1	Feb. 1944
Knigge, Hans	SS-*Stubaf*	I	Apr. 1945, Amt I Training
Knobel, Paul	*Pol.Ob.Sek*	I A2	Nov. 1943
Krack, Carl-Ludwig	SS-*Stubaf*	I A2	*Referent*; died in air raid Oct. 1943
Kretz, Lothar	*Pol.Ob.Sek*	I A2	KIA, Oct. 1943.
Kutter, Alfred	SS-*Stubaf*	I A5	Nov. 1943
Langer, Ernst	*Amtsrat*	I A1	Feb. 1944
Lehmann, Dr Robert	SS-*Hstuf*	I B	Nov. 1943
Leiterer, Dr Albert	SS-*Ostubaf*	I A2	Nov. 1943
Loba, Kurt	SS-*Ostuf*	I B4	Nov. 1943
Losse, Josef	SS-*Stubaf Pol.Rat*	I A2	
Maisel, Wilhelm	SS-*Ostuf*	I A4	Nov. 1943
Maly, Dr Hans	SS-*Hstuf Krim.Rat*	I A3	Nov. 1943
Merbach, Fritz	*Pol.Insp.*	I A6	April 1945, Welfare
Meyer, Dr Heinrich	SS-*Stubaf*	I A	

Meyrer, Georg	SS-*Ostuf* POS	I Gst.	
Moebus, Hans	SS-*Ostuf*	I C	Deputy to Gschwend
Möckel, Albrecht	*Pol.Insp.*	I A6	Nov. 1943
Möhlmeyer, Georg	SS-*Ostuf*	I A5	Nov. 1943
Mohr, Robert	SS-*Stubaf* RR	I A1	1941, *Referent*
Molder, Werner	SS-*Ostuf* PI	I	Adjutant to Ehrlinger
Mulack, Hans	*Krim.Ob.Sek*	I A3	Nov. 1943
Müller, Hans-Joachim	SS-*Ostuf*	I A1	
Munder, Reinhold	SS-*Ustuf*	I A2	Nov. 1943
Mylius, Paul	SS-*Stubaf* RR	I A5	MIA, Oder Front, 1945
Neifeind, Dr Kurt	SS-*Hstuf*	I A	KIA, Hungary, Dec. 1944
Neumann, Johannes	SS-*Hstuf*	I	
Nowack, Paul	Amtsrat	I A2	Nov. 1943
Oestreich, Max	*Reg.Sek*	I A2	Nov. 1943
Paetzold, Artur	SS-*Ostuf*	I	Adjutant for Kaltenbrunner
Peters, Kurt	*Krim.Sek*	I B3	Nov. 1943
Pfoser, Alfons	SS-*Ustuf*	I B2	Nov. 1943
Platta, Reinhold	*Reg.Ob.Insp.*	I A3	Nov. 1943
Ponath, Walter	SS-*Ostuf* PI	I A1	Feb 1944
Rachfahl, Bruno	*Pol.Ob.Insp.*	I A3	Nov. 1943
Regitschnig, Willibald	SS-*Hstuf*	I	June 1944
Rennau, Dr Heinrich	SS-*Ostubaf*	I B2	*Referent*
Resch, Fritz	*Reg.Ob.Insp.*	I A3	Nov. 1943
Ringel, Werner	SS-*Ustuf*	I Org.	
Roock, Kurt	*Reg.Sek*	I A2	Nov. 1943
Ruddersdorf, Georg	*Min.Reg.*	I A2, I A3	Nov. 1943
Rutsch, Karl	*Pol.Ob.Insp.*	I A2	Nov. 1943
Sachse, Karl	SS-*Hstuf* POI	I A2	Nov. 1943
<u>Sandberger</u>, Dr Martin	SS-*Staf*	I B3	1941, *Referent*; later *Gruppenleiter* VI A
Scheefeld, Felix	SS-*Hstuf* PI	I A6	Nov. 1943
Schleicher, Friedrich-Wilh.	*Krim.Sek*	I A3	Nov. 1943
Schrader, Otto	SS-*Hstuf* PI	I B1	Nov. 1943
Schraepel, Georg	SS-*Staf*	I A3	1944, *Leiter* Abt I A
Schreck, Willi	SS-*Hstuf*	I A4	Nov. 1943
Schrefeld, Herbert	SS-*Ostuf* PI	I A1	Nov. 1943
<u>Schulz</u>, Erwin	SS-*Brif*	*Amtschef* I	Jan. 1943–1944
Schwinge, Herbert	SS-*Stubaf*	I A5	1943–1944, *Referent*
Seekel, Dr Friedrich	SS-*Stubaf*	I Org	later I B3

Selberg, Fritz	SS-*Hstuf* ROI	I Gst.	1941–1945, *Leiter*; 1945, I Org.
Senftleben, Arthur	SS-*Stubaf Amtsrat*	I A2	Nov. 1943
Spidla, Friedrich	SS-*Ostuf* PI	I A3	died in air raid, 29 April 1944
Splitter, Willi	SS-*Ostuf* ROI	I A1	to 1945
Steffen, Erich	*Pol.Sek*	I	Nov. 1943
Steiner, Franz-Xaver	SS-*Ustuf*	I A	1945
Stieg, Willi	*Min.Reg.*	I A6	Nov. 1943
Streckenbach. Bruno	SS-*Brif.*	*Amtschef* I	1941–Jan 1943
Teege, Wilhelm	SS-*Hstuf Pol.Rat*	I A6	Nov. 1943
Tent, Karl	SS-*Stubaf* RR	I A2	1941, *Referent*
Thielecke, Hans	SS-*Ostuf*	I A4	1943–1944
Thomas, Alfred	SS-*Stubaf*	I B2	Deputy *Referent*; KIA in Brussels, 20 Jan. 1943
Thorn, Willi	SS-*Stubaf*	I A4	1940–1942
Trautmann, Dr Franz	SS-*Ostubaf*	I A2	1941–1943, *Referent*; killed in air raid 14 Dec. 1943
Trinkl, Edmund	SS-*Ostubaf*	I A6	Nov. 1944, to RuSHA
Viehöfer, Walter	SS-*Hstuf* POI	I Org	to 1945
Vollmer, Walter	SS-*Ostubaf* ORR	I A2	to 1945
Vopel, Fritz	SS-*Stubaf Pol.Rat*	I A2	to 1945
<u>Wanninger</u>, Heinz	SS-*Stubaf*	I A1	later *Referent*, I Org; and *Gruppenleiter* I A
Wehmann,	*Reg.Ob.Insp.*	I A1	in charge of detachments for work in foreign countries, April 1945
Will, Heinz	SS-*Ustuf*	I A4	Nov. 1943
Zastrow, Otto	SS-*Hstuf*	I A2	died in air raid, 29 April 1944
Zapp, Paul	SS-*Stubaf*	I B1	1941
Ziethmann, Emil	SS-*Hstuf Pol.Rat*	I A2	died in air raid, 29 April 1944
Zirpins, Dr Walter	SS-*Stubaf* RuKR	I B	*Gruppenleiter*

Appendix X

Personnel Index of RSHA II

Note: This list contains names of officers in RSHA *Amt* II during the period 1941–1945. These officers in *Gruppen*, transferred to other *Ämter* are included, the transfer being indicated under 'Remarks'. Personnel known to be arrested are underlined.

Name	Rank	Referat to-from 1944	1944 re-org.	Remarks
Albrecht, Werner	SS-*Ostuf* PI	II C4	FZ I	
Alexnat, Erich	SS-*Ostuf*		II	*Persönlicher Referent* to Spacil
Anderson, Paul	SS-*Ostuf* ROI	II HB		died in air-raid, 29 April 1944
Apfelbeck, Albert	SS-*Hstuf*		II	*Leiter* Rosenheim Depot
Baensch, Julius	SS-*Hstuf*	II HK		1944, to BdS Oslo
Ballnus, Albert	SS-*Hstuf* POI	II HK	II HK	
Bank, Otto	SS-*Hstuf*	II C9	II A4	
Barkmann, Herbert	SS-*Ostuf*	II D2	II C2	
Barz, Heinrich	SS-*Ostuf* PI	II C4	II A3	
Bassenge, Theo	SS-*Ostuf*	II C4	II FZ	
Baumann, Christian	SS-*Stubaf* RR	II B1		1943, to RSHA IV A6
Beck Dr Friedrich	SS-*Ostuf*	II D11	II C1	
Behringer, August	SS-*Hstuf*	II C3	II B1	
Bergmann, Dr Rudolf	SS-*Ostubaf*		II B	1945, *Gruppenleiter*
Besigk, Kurt	SS-*Ostuf* PI	II C2	II A3	
Bleck, Paul	PI	II D6	II C2	
Bohn, Hellmut	SS-*Hstuf* PI	II C5	II B1	
Bölter, Gustav	POS	II A5		Nov. 1943, *Referent*
Boning,	POI		II A1	
Borchardt, Helmut	SS-*Htsuf* POI	II C4	II FZ	
Borth, Kurt	SS-*Hstuf* PI		II A1	

Bossdorf, Gerhard	SS-*Ostuf* PI		II B5	
Brocke, Carl	SS-*Staf*	II C(b)	II A4	
Brumme, Emil	SS-*Ostuf*		II HB	
Buche, Gerhard	SS-*Ustuf*		II C4	
Burdach, Paul	*Min.Reg.*		II HB	
Bürger, Paul	*Krim.Insp.*	II D2	II C2	
Cohrs, Rudolf	SS-*Hstuf*	II C2	II B2	
Czekowski, Arthur	SS-*Ostuf*	II D3b		Nov. 1943
Deharde, Heinrich	SS-*Hstuf*	II HB	II HB	KIA, April 1945
Dierich, Heinrich	SS-*Stubaf*		II A2	
Dietrich,	SS-*Stubaf*	II B	II HB	Legal Matters
Dilger, Wilhelm	SS-*Stubaf*	II C8	II A4	*Referatsleiter*
Dobbrick, Ernst	SS-*Ustuf*	II B		Nov. 1943
Dohrmann, Fritz	SS-*Ustuf*	II D13	II C	
Dörnbrack, Paul	SS-*Ustuf*	II D3a	II FZ	
Doll, Werner	SS-*Ostuf* PI		II A3	
Ehlert, Bruno	*Pol.Rat*	II C2	II B2	
Einfeld, Heinz	SS-*Ostuf*	II HB		Nov. 1943
Engel, Ludwig	*Pol.Sek.*	II HB		Nov. 1943
Ernst, Johann	SS-*Ostuf* tOS	II D3a	II FZ	
Ertel, Gerhard	*Pol.Sek.*	II C4	II A3	
Eschmann, Hugo	KOS		II HK	
Fichtner, Herbert	SS-*Ustuf*		II	
Fischer, Gerold	SS-*Ustuf*	II HK	II A4	
Franke, Paul	*Pol.Insp.*	II C4	II A3	
Franken, Adolf	ROI	II A3	II B4	
Fraude, Johannes	*Pol.Sek.*	II C4	II A3	
Freuwört, August	*Pol.Insp.*	II C4	II A3	
Frohlich, Fritz	SS-*Hstuf* PI	II D1	II C3	
Gassmann, Eduard	SS-*Ustuf*	II D13	II C3	
Gast, Wilhelm	SS-*Hstuf*	II D3b	II C4	
Geissen, Alfred	SS-*Ostuf* PI	II C4	II A3	
Genböck, Josef	SS-*Ustuf*	II HB		1944, to RSHA VI
Gericke, Erhard	SS-*Ostuf* PI	II C4	II A3	
Gnilka, Herbert	SS-*Ostuf* PI	II C4	II A3	
Goetz, Arthur	*Pol.Ob.Sek.*	II C4	II A3	
Gottstein, Reiner	SS-*Stubaf*	II D1		Feb. 1945, KIA Hungary
Graetz, Paul	SS-*Stubaf*		II Gst.	*Leiter*
Grau, Gustav	SS-*Hstuf*	II C2	II A2	
Graul, Franz	*Reg.Amtmann*	II C2	II B2	

Gruhlke, Paul	SS-*Ustuf*	II D3a	II C3	
Günther, Rudolf	SS-*Ustuf*		II	*Unternehmen* Bernhard accounts
Haase, Karl	SS-*Ustuf* tOS	II D2	II C2	
Hafke, Kurt	SS-*Ostubaf*	IIC	II C	*Gruppenleiter*
Hamann, Wilhelm	SS-*Ostuf* tOS	II D3a	II C3	
Hanke, Hans	KOS		II C3	
Hartmann, Hans	SS-*Hstuf* POI		II C2	
Haupt, Gerhardt	SS-*Ostuf*	II D2		Sept. 1944, to RSHA N
Hausler, Hermann	*Pol.Sek*	II D6		Sept. 1944, to RSHA N
Heidenreich, Gerhard	SS-*Ustuf*		II HB	
Hein, Georg	SS-*Ostuf* PI	II C4	II A3	
Heine, Georg	*Pol.Sek.*	II B		Nov. 1943
Heinmoller, Heinrich	*Amtsrat*		II A	*Rechnung-sprüfungsstelle*
Heinrich, Gerhard	SS-*Ostuf*	II D3b	II C3	
Helldobler, Franz-X.	SS-*Staf*		II A4	*Referent*
Hercht, Walter	SS-*Hstuf* POI		II A	*Kasse des* RSHA
Herrmann, Willy	SS-*Stubaf*	II C7-C9	II A4	
Hoffmann, Alfred	SS-*Ustuf*		II HK	
Hoffmeister, Günther	SS-*Ustuf*	II D11	II D2	Sept. 1944, to RSHA N
Höhne, Walfried	SS-*Ustuf*	II D2	II C2	Sept. 1944, to RSHA N
Holtmann, Hans	SS-*Hstuf*		II HK	*Hauskomman-dant* II
Holz, Gerhard	SS-*Ostuf*	II C10	II A4	
Hoppe, Hans	SS-*Hstuf*	II C4	II A4	*Verwaltungs-führer* SD
Höpping, Fritz	SS-*Ustuf*	II D12	II A4	
Horn, Dr Rudolf	*Krim.Rat*	II C3		arrived in 1943
Horst, Alfons	SS-*Stubaf*	II C10	II A4	
Hucko, Wilhelm	SS-*Hstuf* KR		II C3	Sept. 1944, to RSHA N
Hünicke, Willy	SS-*Ustuf* tS	II D3a	II C3	
Jacoby, Heinz	*Pol.Sek.*	II C4	II A3	
Just, Willy	SS-*Hstuf* tI	II D3a	II C3	
Kalix, Oswald	SS-*Ustuf* PI		II C4	*Rechnungsamt d.* RSHA

Karl, Dr	SS-*Ostubaf*		II	Deputy *Amtschef*
Kaufmann, Dr Heinz	SS-*Ostubaf*	II A3	II B4	Referent
Keese, Heinrich	*Min.Reg.*	II A		Nov. 1943, *Gruppenleiter*
Kelbling, Rolf	SS-*Stubaf* RR	II B3		1943, *Referent*, then transferred to RSHA IV
Kemper, Gustav	SS-*Ustuf* tOS	II D3a	II C3	
Kempf, Adolf	*Amtsrat*	II D6	II C1	Sept. 1944, to RSHA N
Kettlitz, Gustav	SS-*Hstuf* PR	II C2	II B2	
Kiesewalter, Erwin	SS-*Hstuf* POI	II D3a	II C3	
Kirsten, Karl-Heinz	*Pol.Sek.*	II HB		Nov. 1943
Kleemann, Otto	*Reg.Amtmann*	II C1	II A2	
Klencke, Rudolf	SS-*Ostuf*	II HB		Nov. 1943
Klenert, Max	SS-*Hstuf* tOI	II D2	II C2	Sept. 1944, to RSHA N
Kletzsch, Georg	*Pol.Insp.*	II A3		Nov. 1943
Kloth, Wilhelm	SS-*Ostuf* PI	II C1	II B4	
Knaack, Paul	*Pol.Ob.Sek*	II C4	II A3	
Knoll, Hermann	SS-*Hstuf* POI	II C3	II B1	
Knoop, Eduard	SS-*Ustuf* PI	II A3		
Knuth, Erich	*Pol.Ob.Insp.*	II C1	II A2	
Koppehl, Friedrich	*Pol.Ob.Insp.*	II		1944, *Rechnungsamt* d. RSHA N
Krafft, Erwin	SS-*Ustuf* tOS	II D3a	II C3	Sept. 1944, to RSHA N
Krambs, Paul	SS-*Hstuf*		II A4	
Kränzle, Karl	SS-*Ustuf*		II C5	
Kratz,	SS-*Ustuf*		II A4	
Krause, Johannes	*Min.Rat.*	II B		1941, *Gruppenleiter*; 1943, to RSHA IV B4
Krautsdorfer,	SS-*Ustuf*		II C3	
Kreklow, Dr Arnold	SS-*Ostubaf*		II A	1944, *Gruppenleiter*
Kroning, Rudolf	SS-*Ostubaf*	II B4		1943, to RSHA IV
Kull, Leonhard	SS-*Ustuf*	II D13	II A4	
Kunert, Felix	SS-*Ostuf* PI	II C4	II A3	

Kunze, Fritz	SS-Ostuf	II C10	II A4	
Kurth, Walter	SS-Ustuf tOS	II D2	II C1	Sept. 1944, to RSHA N
Ladewig, Johannes	Amtsrat	II B4		late 1943, to RSHA IV
Lampart, Kurt	SS-Ustuf tOS	II D2	II C2	1943, to BdS Italien
Latossek, Adolf	SS-Ostuf PI	II A3, C4		
Lauterbach, Kurt	Reg.Sek.	II B1		late 1943, to RSHA IV
Lehmann, Willi	Min.Reg.	II B4		late 1943, to RSHA IV
Leopold, Georg	SS-Stubaf		II D5	later, Liaison Officer to Luftwaffe
Leppin, Hubert	Reg.Sek.	II C4	II A3	
Liedtke, Harry	SS-Ostuf	II C4	II A3	
Liepelt, Hans	Pol.Ob.Insp.	II		Rechnungsamt d.RSHA
Link, Eugen	SS-Stubaf	II C9	II A4	
Lisiecki, Hans	SS-Ustuf PS	II Gst.		Nov. 1943
Loewke, Otto	SS-Ostuf PI	II		Rechnungsamt d.RSHS
Loock, Johannes	Reg.Amtmann	II C2	II A2	
Loreck, Karl	SS-Hstuf POI	II C4	II A3	
Lüders, Heinrich	Amtsrat	II		Kasse u. Abrechnung
Lüders, Willi	SS-Ostuf PI	II C4	II A3	
Lutter, Erich	SS-Stubaf PR	II D4	II FZ 3	
Magiera, Karl	SS-Ostuf		II A4	
Manikowski, Edmund	SS-Ostuf		II HK	
Marks, Wilhelm	SS-Hstuf	II D11	II C1	Sept. 1944, to RSHA N
Martin, Gerhard	SS-Ustuf tI	II D3a	II C3	
Mauruszat, Otto	SS-Hstuf	II C3	II B1	
Mehlstäubl, Ferdin.	SS-Stubaf	II D1	II C1	
Meier, Anton	SS-Stubaf	II C4	II A3	Referent
Merbach, Otto	SS-Ostuf	II D3b	II C4	
Meyer, Heinrich	SS-Ostif tOS	II D2	II C1	Sept. 1944, to RSHA N
Mittelsdorf, Herbert	SS-Ostuf	II HB		Nov. 1943
Modrow, Herbert	SS-Ustuf PS	II		Kleiderkammer

Morisse, Karl	SS-*Ustuf*	II		
Moser, Rudi	*Reg.Sek*	II A		Nov. 1943
Müller, Ernst	SS-*Hstuf* PR	II C1	II A1	*Referent*
Müller, Fritz	SS-*Ostuf*	II C10	II C3	
Müller, Heinrich	SS-*Ostuf*	II D3b	II A4	
Narr, Peter	SS-*Hstuf*	II C1	II A1	
Neifeind, Dr Kurt	SS-*Stubaf*	II A2		*Referent*; later KIA in Hungary, Dec. 1944
Niederhausen, Fritz	SS-*Ostuf* tOI	II D3a	II C3	
Niemsch, Paul	*Pol.Insp.*		II C3	
Nockemann, Dr Hans	SS-*Staf*	*Amtschef* II		KIA, Russia, Dec. 1941
Nordeck, Kurt	SS-*Ostuf* PI	II B		Nov. 1943
Obst, Erich	SS-*Ostuf*	II D2	II C2	Sept. 1944, to RSHA N
Panhans,	SS-*Ostuf*		II	Adjutant to *Amtschef*
Papenfuss, Willi	*Pol.Insp.*		II	*Rechnungsamt* d. RSHA
Paul, Herbert	SS-*Ostuf* PI		II	Kdt, Lager Bad Sulza
Paust, Karl-Heinrich	SS-*Ostuf*	II B		Nov. 1943
Penn, Hans	SS-*Hstuf*	II B		Nov. 1943
Pfeiler, Paul	SS-*Hstuf* POI	II C2	II A1	
Platta, Reinhold	POI		II B2	
Pohl, Hans	*Pol.Insp.*	II C4	II A3	
Pohlmann, Günther	SS-*Ostuf*	II D11	II A4	
Pommerening, Helmut	SS-*Stubaf*		II HB	*Leiter*, Hauptbüro
Potter, Adolf	SS-*Hstuf* tOS	II D2	II C2	Sept. 1944, to RSHA N
Pradel, Friedrich	SS-*Stubaf*	II D3	II C3	
Prauser, Oswald	*Pol.Sek.*	II Gst		Nov. 1943
Prietzel, Kurt	SS-Staf	*Amtschef* II		*Amtschef* 1942–1943; 1944–1945, at BdS Oslo
Prömper, Wilhelm	SS-*Hstuf* POI	II C2	II B2	
Pusch, Heinz	SS-*Ustuf* tOS	II D2	II C2	Sept. 1944, to RSHA N

Quade, Bruno	SS-*Ustuf* PS		II C4	
Quarg, Herbert	SS-*Hstuf* ROI	II C1	II B1	
Quiel, Hans	*Pol.Insp.*	II C4	II A3	
Radtke, Oskar	SS-*Hstuf*	II C7	II A4	
Rapsch, Heinz	SS-*Ustuf*	II D12	II B	
Rath, Hans	SS-*Ostuf* PI	II C5		1943
Rauff, Walther	SS-*Ostubaf*	II D		1941–1942, *Gruppenleiter*
Rehbein, Gerhard	SS-*Ustuf*	II C10	II HK	
Remer, Willy	SS-*Ostuf* POI	II C4	II A3	
Renken, Walter	SS-*Stubaf* RR	II A4		1941–1943, *Referent*; then posted to RSHA IV
Restemeier, Erich	SS-*Ostuf* PI	II A4		1943, posted to RSHA III
Richter, Erich	*Reg.Ob.Insp.*	II B1		1943, posted to RSHA IV
Richter, Paul	SS-*Ustuf*	II HB		Nov. 1943
Riek, Franz	*Pol.Insp.*	II D6	II C1	Sept. 1944, to RSHA N
Riesel, Fritz	*Min.Reg.*		II C	
Rievers, Wilhelm	SS-*Stubaf*	II C2	II B2	
Rohloff, Willi	SS-*Ostuf* PI	II C4	II A3	
Röhrich, Hans	SS-*Ostuf* PI	II B2	II A5	
Ruddat, Hermann	*Pol.Insp.*	II B2		1943, posted to RSHA IV
Schadewald, Otto	*Pol.Ob.Insp.*	II C4	II A3	
Scharr, Walter	SS-*Hstuf*		II	Liaison, *Zollgrenzschütz*
Schau, Max	*Amtsrat*	II B4		1943, posted to RSHA IV
Schiebel, Kurt	SS-*Ostuf*		II	Adjutant to Spacil
Schlemme, Ferdin.	SS-*Ustuf*	II HB		Nov. 1943
Schmidt, Alfred	SS-*Ustuf*		II A2	
Schmidt, Erhart	SS-*Ustuf* tOS	II D3a		
Schmidt, Walter	SS-*Ostuf*	II HB		Nov. 1943
Schmiel, Wilhelm	SS-*Ostuf* PI	II C2	II A1	
Schnappauf, Karl-Hz.	SS-*Ustuf*	II HB		Nov. 1943
Schnerr, Karl	SS-*Hstuf*	II C10	II A4	
Schramm, Walter	SS-*Ostuf* PI	II C4	II A3	

Schreibvogel, Karl	SS-*Hstuf* POI	II D6	II A1	
Schroter, Friedrich	*Pol.Ob.Insp.*	II C4	II A3	
Schrul, Günther	SS-*Ustuf*	II D3b	II C3	
Schubert,	SS-*Ostuf*		II	*Leiter*, Bad Sulza Camp
Schuhmann, Friedrich	SS-*Ostuf*		II A2	
Schuler, Heinz	SS-*Hstuf*	II A		Admin.Officer for RSHA *Mil. Amt*, *Referent* VI A2
Schultz, Helmuth	SS-*Ustuf*		II HB	
Schumann, Friedrich	SS-*Hstuf*	II D13	II A2	
Schünke, Otto	SS-*Hstuf* POI	II C4	II A3	
Schuster, Alfred	SS-*Ustuf* PS	II C4		*Leiter*, Schliersee Depot
Schuster, Gottfried	*Amtsrat*	II B3		1944, to RSHA IV G
Schwarz, Heinz	*Reg.Sek.*	II C1	II A1	
Schwarzbold, Georg	*Reg.Sek.*	II C4	II A3	
Schweder, Dr Alfred	SS-*Hstuf*	II A1		1941–1942, *Referent*; then to BdS Krakau
Selberg, Fritz	SS-*Hstuf* ROI	II A1		1945, with RSHA I Org
Siegert, Dr Rudolf	SS-*Obf.*	II C		1941, *Gruppenleiter*, then *Amtschef* 1941–1942
Spacil, Josef	SS-*Obf.*		*Amtschef* II	1 March 1944– Apr. 1945
Spannaus, Günther	SS-*Hstuf*	II C9	II A4	
Spengler, Werner	*Pol.Insp.*	II C4	II A3	
Stein, Hans	SS-*Ustuf*	II D12	II A3	
Sternberg, Paul	SS-*Ustuf* tOS	II D3a	II B1	
Stöckl, Andreas	*Reg.Amtmann*	II C3	II B3	
Störmer, Willi	*Reg.Sek.*	II B1		
Sukkel, Anton	SS-*Ustuf*	II D3a	II B1	
Tempelhagen, Walter	SS-*Hstuf* POI		II B	
Terborg, Paul	SS-*Hstuf*	II A2		Nov. 1943, *Referent*
Teuber, Paul	*Amtsrat*	II C3	II B3	

Vornefeld, Theodor	SS-*Ostuf* PI	II C4	II A3	
Wächter, Heinz	SS-*Ustuf* tOS	II C2		Sept. 1944, to RSHA N
Walter, Kurt	SS-*Stubaf* PR	II D2	II A1	1945, to RSHA N
Wasse, Rudolf	*Pol.Insp.*	II C4	II A3	
Weber, Horst	SS-*Hstuf*		II HB	
Weistz,	*Reg.Rat*	II B2		1943, to RSHA IV B4
Wentritt, Harry	SS-*Ustuf*		II B1	
Wettich, Arthur	SS-*Ostubaf*	II C10	II A4	1944, to BdS Prag
Wetzel, Friedrich	*Pol.Ob.Insp.*		II B	*Kasse des* RSHA
Wiechert, Richard	SS-*Ustuf*		II C3	
Wiedemann, Adalbert	SS-*Ustuf*		II B	1944, to BdS Den Haag
Wienecke, Hans	SS-*Ustuf*		II	
Wilke, Wilhelm	SS-*Stubaf* RR	II B2		1943, to RSHA IV
Winter, Kurt	SS-*Ustuf*	II HB	II C3	
Woelke, Julius	*Reg.Sek.*		II B	
Wolff, Guido	SS-*Ostuf*	II D6	II C3	Dec. 1944, to RSHA N
Wollatz, Werner	SS-*Ustuf*	II D3b		KIA Ukraine 29 Jul. 1943
Wuchter,	SS-*Ustuf*		II C2	
Ziessow, Walter	SS-*Ustuf* tOS		II C2	Sept. 1944, to RSHA N

Notes

* The National Archives, Kew, UK: KV 3/178 and KV 3/185, Liquidation Reports No. 1 and No. 2, Ämter I and II of the RSHA.

1 It was not only RSHA *Amtschef* IV Müller, who had no trust in Schulz, nor did the *Chef* RSHA, Kaltenbrunner, see the National Archives, Kew, KV 3/117, Interrogation Report 030/125 dated 10 December 1945, by SS-*Hstuf* Rudolf Müller. It is reported that service in *Einsatzgruppen* killing squads in Russia was open to 'undesirable personnel' and that such service fast-tracked other SS-officers. While there is available evidence for the former, there is very little to justify the latter.

2

Situation Report No. 3— *Amt* III of the RSHA

INDEX

Part I: The Development of the SD 1933–1939
Part II: The Functions of *Amt* III
Part III: The Creation of *Amt* III in 1939 and its Development
Part IV: *Amt* III and its position in Nazi Germany
Part V: *Amt* III and Post-occupational Plans

Appendix I: Organisation of *Amt* III, 1939–1940
Appendix II: Organisation of *Amt* III, 1940–1943
Appendix III: Organisation of *Amt* III, 1943–1944
Appendix IV: Organisation of *Amt* III, 1944–1945
Appendix V: Alphabetical Index of *Amt* III personnel, 1939–1945

Preamble

In contrast to other *Ämter*, the arrest and interrogation of leading RSHA *Amt* III personnel since the surrender has not tended in a general sense to confirm what was the widely accepted view of the functions of *Amt* III; its position in the RSHA; and its relations with the other *Ämter*, especially with *Amt* IV. Unfortunately, the reports on such personalities as Ohlendorf, the *Amtschef*, have been unsatisfactory as, while throwing previous conclusions into doubt, they do not supply alternative overall pictures, which can be considered acceptable. Ohlendorf himself has been evasive generally, misleading on specific points, while the interrogation of prominent personalities in the British Zone has clarified some points, but added to the confusion on others. This is especially true of the part which *Amt* III was meant to play in resistance, both in occupied territory and after defeat. So far it has been largely a case of *quot homines, tot sententiae* (there are as many opinions as there are men) and it is significant that probably the best assessments of the *Amt* have come from personalities not forming part of it. The present paper is therefore a Situation Report in that, while it modifies opinions previously held, it does not claim to give the final answer.

Part I

The Development of the SD from 1933–1939

1. General

The position held by *Amt* III before and after the creation of the RSHA in 1939 can only be appreciated when seen against the proper background of the German police and security service as a whole. In common with most of the other *Ämter*, the SD *Inlandnachrichtendienst* did not follow any clearly defined line of policy from its inception until its dissolution, and the outwardly homogenous exterior which the RSHA provides on paper hides a long history of inter-departmental jealousies and personal rivalries. No *Amt* was ever any more important, or more efficient than the leading Party personalities, above all Himmler, allowed it to become, and the motives were dictated by considerations of personal prestige and power, and especially by personal relationships with the Führer himself. This latter consideration is of special importance in the case of *Amt* III, whose ultimate function was to mirror public criticism of the regime itself.

The SD remained throughout its history a Party organisation; unlike the *Sicherheitspolizei*, it did not at any time became an instrument of the State. This fundamental difference between the SD on the one hand, and the *Gestapo* and *Kripo* [the *Sicherheitspolizei*] on the other, together with the equally important distinction that unlike the police services, the SD had no executive powers or rights, explains its creation, its subsequent development, and its decreasing importance in the eyes of the RFSS and the CdS, who looked to the executive branches as instruments of power, and ever sought to merge the two lines into a single body, an effort which did not meet with complete success.

2. The early Party Intelligence Services

It has to be remembered that the NSDAP began as a political party, and was in its early years strongly localised in south-eastern Germany. Its early fight was against the other political parties in Germany, as well as against the State itself, and in particular against the police and security services of the State. Its ultimate objective was not to combat the police services by destroying them, but by assuming control over them and subsequently using them for its own purposes. Until the realisation of that aim from the *Machtübernahme* in 1933 onwards, the Party developed its own political intelligence service along somewhat haphazard lines, the restricted purpose of which was the surveillance of the political groups against which it was fighting; this information service was not in any way centralised in one organisation within the Party itself, but rather the component parts of the Party, the SS, the SA, and the Propaganda Service under Goebbels, worked for their own specific needs.

3. Heydrich and the PI-Dienst

By 1931, the Party had itself grown to such proportions, its influence within the country had become so great, and its ultimate assumption of power seemed so probable that the importance of centralising its intelligence work into a separate organisation became apparent. In that year Himmler, then *Reichsführer*-SS, gave the task of developing such a service to *Oberleutnant zur See* Reinhard Heydrich. By the following year Heydrich had organised his 'Press Informatiion Dienst', the PI-Dienst itself being an integral part of the SS. There was, however, no desire on the part of the other branches of the Party to surrender their own services to the new organisation, and the relative strength of the leading Party members was such that not even Himmler could impose his will on the others. The PI-Dienst therefore existed side by side with the former intelligence services, all of them continuing to work on the somewhat narrow Party requirements of the time. By late 1934 the PI-Dienst had become the *Sicherheitsdienst*.

4. Effect of the *Machtübernahme*

The situation changed entirely with the Nazi assumption of power in 1933; the Party fully realised that its regime could best be sustained by force in the shape of police forces directly under its control. Now with the instruments of government in its hands, it could proceed to the penetration of the existing police services from the top and not from the bottom. The steps in the gradual but inevitable control by the Party of all political and civil police forces in Germany have been described in detail in the Situation Report on Amt IV, and need not be repeated in detail here. The most important development was Himmler's appointment as deputy chief of Goering's *Gestapo* in the spring of 1934. From that date, the SD was destined to take a new orientation. Meantime it had been strengthened within the Party itself, as Himmler was now strong enough to decree that all existing Party intelligence services were to be dissolved and incorporated into the *Sicherheitsdienst*.

5. The SD-*Hauptamt* in 1934

By 1934, the SD had taken more definite form by the creation of the SD-*Hauptamt* with Heydrich as its head. Organisationally the *Amt* was on the following lines:

Amtschef—Heydrich

Organisation and Personnel – Dr Best

Abt. I	Central *Abteilung*	SS-*Ostuf* Oberg
Abt. II	Staff Office	SS-*Ostuf* Löffler
Abt. III	Political Section	SS-*Hstuf* Hohn
Abt. IV	Economic Section	SS-*Stubaf* Pleischinger
Abt. VI	Security Section	SS-*Stubaf* Jost

By this time, the SD had moved its headquarters to Berlin itself, while an outside organisation had been built up consisting of twelve *Oberabschnitte*, each with three or four *Unterabschnitte*, the area given to an *Oberabschnitt* being roughly the area of a *Wehrkreis*.

The importance of the SD at this time was lessened in the eyes of its chief, Heydrich. Its functions were themselves of a rather negative character; at that early stage, although the Party has assumed control of the State, it had not yet succeeded in identifying itself completely with the State. The early functions of the SD were confined to pointing out the shortcomings of the State as reflected by the faults in public life. It in fact sounded public opinion for the benefit of the Party in its opposition to other State departments. But Heydrich devoted little time to its work; both he and Himmler were more concerned in developing the new *Gestapoamt*, as that *Amt* was an instrument of repression which served better and more immediate purpose.

6. The *Gestapo* and the SD in the early stages

Thus early the difference between the two services was apparent; the main concern of Himmler, aided and abetted by Heydrich, was the creation of a centralised German police service under the control of the Party, and as the Party had no organisation of wide enough scope to replace the existing services, the tendency was to absorb these existing services and achieve penetration at the highest levels. The fusion was ultimately represented in the persons of Himmler and Heydrich themselves, Himmler in his capacity as *Chef der Deutschen Polizei*, and Heydrich as *Chef der Sipo*, both appointments being achieved by 1936. In the same year all political police forces in Germany came under the control of the *Gestapo*. The effect of these changes was that Himmler now had his executive instrument in the *Gestapo*, and the strengthening of his stranglehold on the German people was developed through that *Amt*. The Party was now supreme, but its supremacy was not achieved through its own internal organisation. The SD could now only develop as an Intelligence Service, though covering the same spheres of interest as the *Gestapo* itself.

The development of the two services side by side was not harmonious; the division of work between them, although moderately clear on paper, was not so in practice. There arose inevitably conflicts and quarrels, and it was not until early in 1938 that a '*Grundsatzvereinbarung*' was reached, determining the spheres of responsibility between the Sipo and the SD, which still continued to exist as two entirely separate departments with only a nominal collaboration between the two in the person of Heydrich in his joint appointment as *Chef der Sipo* and *Chef des* SD-*Hauptamtes*. The situation in one respect suited Heydrich, as with his own position secure, he could play off one organisation against the other, ensuring that neither could become so strong as to jeopardise his own position.

7. The development of the SD in 1937–1938
Meanwhile the SD itself, as the direct instrument of the Party, had been able to play a prominent part in the events in the East and in south-eastern Europe leading up to the *Anschluss* and the Czech crisis. By 1937 the SD-*Hauptamt* itself had undergone a re-organisation, consisting now of three *Ämter*, the former *Abteilungen* I and II being merged into a new *Amt* I, *Abteilungen* III, IV and V into a new *Amt* II, while Jost's small *Abteilung* VI had developed into the security section, *Amt* III. *Amt* I as the administrative section is of little importance, while *Amt* III, the forerunner of *Amt* VI of the RSHA, is dealt with in the Liquidation Reports on that *Amt*. It was *Amt* II which contained the roots of the subsequent *Amt* III of the RSHA.

8. *Amt* II of the SD-*Hauptamt*
Amt II developed considerably during 1937 and 1938 with a corresponding extension of the outside organisation in the SD-*Abschnitte*. The *Amt* itself was divided into two *Hauptabteilungen* II/1 and II/2, in turn composed of *Abteilungen* and *Referate*, designated by a rather curious numbering system. The following departments have been identified, and for the sake of convenience, the corresponding sections of the subsequent *Amt* III are shown:

Section	*Sachgebiet*	Allocation in RSHA
II/111	Freemasonry	II B1
II/112	Jews	II B2
	Marxism	II B4
	Political Churches	II B3
II/12	Liberalism	II B5
II/21	Cultural Spheres	III A
II/211	Sciences	III A1
II/212	*Volkstum*	III A3
II/213	Race and National Health	III B3
II/214	Art	III A4

II/221	Law	III B1
II/222	Administration	III B2
II/223	Education	III A2
II/224	Press and Literature	III A 5
II/225	General National Life	III B4
II/23	Economic Life	III C
II/231	Food	III C1
II/232	Commerce	III C2
	Transport	III C3
II/233	Currency and Banks	III C4
II/234	Industry	III C5
II/235	Finance	III C6
II/236	Labour and Social Questions	III C7

It is to be noted that this breakdown shows the organisation of *Amt* II in the SD-*Hauptamt* such as it existed immediately prior to the creation of the RSHA, and some sections may not have existed as early as 1937. Further, the references to II B1–B5 in column 3 above refer of course to the original *Amt* II of the RSHA, that is, the forerunner of *Amt* VII. Lastly, the remaining references in column 3 are to the original *Amt* III, details of which are given in Part II, Paragraph A (1), and Appendix I.

By the end of 1938 the *Oberabschnitte* had been dissolved, the new field organisation being based on a series of SD-*Leitabschnitte* and SD-*Abschnitte*, similar in organisational structure but differing in importance according to the area which they controlled.

9. Conflict between the *Gestapo* and the SD

The growing strength of the SD, which by now in 1938 was extending its functions to cover counter-intelligence and the Ausland, did nothing to bridge the increasing breach between it and the *Gestapo*. Heydrich, anxious for a high degree of homogeneity, had in 1934 appointed Dr Best, the former Administrative Officer of the SD, as the Administrative Officer of the *Gestapo* with the triple assignment of organising the new *Gestapo* throughout Germany, bringing the *Kripo* under the control of Heydrich, and completing the task by incorporating the SD into a unified service. The creation of the *Sicherheitspolizei* in 1936 had brought the *Gestapo* and the *Kripo* under joint control, but the task of incorporating the SD into the *Sicherheitspolizei* proved too difficult. The objections came from both sides; the Ministry of the Interior opposed the inclusion into the State Police Service of personnel of no training whatever, and when Heydrich sought to overcome the difficulty by making members of the *Sipo* honorary members of the SD, the latter, the '*Alte Kämpfer*' of the Party, jealous of their status, were equally strong in their objections to the inclusion in their ranks of such outsiders. It is to be remembered that the *Gestapo* was not staffed entirely by Party personnel. The mere problem of manpower had meant that Dr Best had been forced to include in its ranks former members of the *Kripo*, who numbered some 30% of the total strength, while the SS and SA accounted for only some 40%. In view of the opposition from both sides, Heydrich was forced to abandon his original project and the two services remained distinct from each other.[1]

The conflict in functions remained equally unsolved: it is true that the *Gestapo* was the executive branch while the SD acted as the information service supplying the *Gestapo* with its ammunition. But this apparently ideal system must be treated with great reserve, as both Services tended to assume the functions of the other. The *Gestapoamt* as early as 1937 was busy setting up its own intelligence service which developed by 1942 into the *Gegnernachrichten- dienst*—an information network of considerable size. The *Gestapo* in that direction therefore was quickly becoming independent of the SD. As mentioned in Paragraph 7, the SD on its side had its own departments dealing with '*Innere Gegner*', while its counter-intelligence functions were developing under *Amt* III of the SD-*Hauptamt*. Lastly, however feeble the efforts may have been, it was the SD which took the first steps at organising an '*Auslandsnachrichtendienst*'. The *Gestapo* under Müller had already its eye on counter-intelligence as its own sphere, while the appointment of the *Polizei Attaches* by 1938 marked its first official steps over the borders of the Reich. Unofficially the *Stapostellen* themselves were beginning to extend their activities to the Ausland. And against this background of conflict between the *Sipo* and the SD, was the added complication of the common enemy, the *Abwehr*, jealous of its rights as the sole agency in the field of counter-espionage and intelligence abroad. The conflict over functions was of course mainly a result of the conflict in personalities, personal prestige, and personal power.

10. The creation of the RSHA in 1939 and its effects

The setting up of the RSHA in September 1939 represented the culmination of the joint efforts of Himmler and and Heydrich to create a unified German Police Service, covering both the overt and secret spheres. By the formation of a central authority controlling both the *Sipo* and the SD, the differences which existed previously regarding spheres of interest were, on paper at least, eliminated. The *Gestapo*, or *Amt* IV as it was now to be named, became the sole executive arm of the RSHA, apart of course from the *Kripo* in its normal civil police functions, while the former functions of the SD were divided among three new *Ämter*, II, III and VI, the first competent for research on specific sects and movements, the last charged with the task of setting up an extended *Auslandsnachrichtendienst*, while *Amt* III for its part was responsible for all aspects of German life. The new *Amt* II was later to become *Amt* VII and disappear into insignificance.

It is at this stage in its development that the position of the SD with its *Inlandnachrichtendienst* gives rise to some doubt; the SD had developed in 1933 from the information service of the Party working against the political opponents of the Party in the early days of its struggle. With the gradual elimination of political opponents from the *Machtübernahme* onwards, the SD had functioned as an information service reflecting public opinion, giving the Party valuable help in its struggle with the State; criticism of the State was welcome as the Party was seeking to penetrate and control all walks of public life. By 1939 the situation had changed, as the Party had succeeded almost entirely in identifying itself with the State, and now criticism of the State was criticism of the Party.

It has been said of RSHA *Amt* III that it kept its finger on the public pulse so that the Party should be aware of public opinion which a totalitarian regime deprives of self-expression. There can be no doubt that such a function in a country like the Reich was a necessity if the government wished to keep in touch with the people and modify its policy in accordance with public opinion. The crux of the analysis of *Amt* III lies in deciding whether its creation in 1939 was in fact a conscious effort on the part of the regime to sound public opinion for its own audience, and whether that policy was pursued throughout the history of *Amt* III—a question which forms the subject matter of Part IV (below).

Part II

The Functions of RSHA *Amt* III

A. General.

The function of *Amt* III was to organise within Germany an intelligence network capable of assessing public reaction to governmental measures; the reports thus obtained embodied criticism and suggested remedies, the reports themselves being submitted to the department concerned. The *Inlandnachrichtendienst* existed therefore as a corrective to the repressive methods of a totalitarian regime. The *Amt* had no executive authority, and unlike the *Gestapoamt*, it did not submit reports on individuals, though in some instances it might pass information locally to the *Stapostelle* if action on the part of the *Gestapo* seemed necessary.

This broad function gave the *Amt* a supervisory capacity over all walks of German life, and ideally the *Amt* sought to present a cross-section of public opinion on general matters, though in addition it might be required to submit a specialised report on a specific subject. The range of *Amt* III was therefore considerable; there were few aspects of national life it did not cover and few classes or strata of the people in which it did not have agents.

B. Functions of *Gruppe* III A.

1. General.

The *Gruppe* as a whole dealt with the general question of law, legislation, and its administration. The *Gruppenleiter* until January 1944 was SS-*Staf* Gengenbach who was killed in the same automobile accident as SS-*Ostubaf* Gräfe, *Gruppenleiter* VI C. Gengenbach was a man of considerable ability, and during his tenure of office had considerable influence on questions of the administration of German law. This *Gruppe* of course met with favour in high places, as the antipathy of Hitler and Himmler to lawyers and jurisprudence was considerable—the Führer himself delivered in 1942 a tirade against lawyers and their alleged obstruction to the carrying out of Nazi justice. The conflict was inevitable. *Gruppe* III A in accordance with *Amt* III general policy had its agents placed in the highest legal circles, and the reports it submitted reflected the attitude of the professional lawyer to abuse by the Nazi Party of German justice. The difficulties facing *Amt* III in the proper despatch of its functions were strongest in *Gruppe* III A, as objective reports could hardly fail to be critical of the existing regime. The test of the effect of the *Gruppe* came when Himmler himself took over the Ministry of the Interior and was thereby in a position to act on the recommendations submitted by *Amt* III; it is significant that Himmler took no action at all.

2. *Referat* III A1.

This *Referat* dealt with personal matters affecting the staff of *Amt* III, including the payment of salaries. It does not appear to have exercised any particular function in the general sphere of *Gruppe* III A work.

3. *Referat* III A2 and III A3.

Referat III A2 dealt with criminal jurisdiction and civil law and was responsible for the submission of reports giving public reaction to legal measures as they were introduced. At the same time it kept a watch on important personalities of the judiciary and professors of the Faculty of Law. In addition to covering the home sphere, this *Referat* also studied, through its representatives in occupied territory, the reaction of occupied countries to German legislation, and likewise maintained a watch on leading legal personalities in these countries.

    Referat III A3 performed a similar functions in the sphere of administration, both at home and in occupied territory.

4. *Referat* III A4.

The designation of this *Referat*—'*Allgemeine Volksleben*'—was in fact a cover for a much more specialised function. The *Referat* dealt with the Party itself, and submitted reports on the effects of the Party on the people, and in particular on public reaction to the Party leaders themselves. In view of the delicacy of such a field, great care was taken to maintain a high degree of secrecy in the workings of the *Referat*, as is evidenced by the misleading title given to it. The reports were kept a close secret and were not revealed to those most likely to be susceptible to their contents—the *Gauleiter* and the high ranking Party chiefs themselves. It is not surprising of course that the reports were of a highly damaging type, but in view of their subject matter and the attitude of such personalities as Himmler himself, they were not passed on to the appropriate authorities for any action to be taken on them. It was *Referat* III A4 for instance which submitted a report on the activities of Goering and the now famous special report of *Amt* III on the inefficiency of the Luftwaffe.

After the July [1944] Plot, *Referat* III A4 also dealt with the *Wehrmacht*, a field of activity until then forbidden to the SD. It has been reported, but not completely confirmed, that the *Wehrmacht* became a special *Referat* III A5 under Dr Seydel, while *Referat* III A5 (below) became a new *Referat* III A6. This change did not occur until December 1944.

5. *Referat* III A5.
This *Referat* was a small one dealing with police administration, and in particular with the position of the SD in relationship to the police and the Party. This had until 1943 been dealt with by *Referat* II A1 of *Amt* II.

C. *Gruppe* III B.

1. General.
Gruppe III B was formed only in early 1940, but as a result of the development of the war, grew into a *Gruppe* of considerable size and influence. Dealing as it did with racial questions, there was no inevitable cleavage between the *Gruppe* and the Party itself, as in the case of *Gruppe* III A. *Gruppe* III A dealt with the reaction of Germans to German rule, while *Gruppe* III B dealt in effect with the reaction of Germans to other nationalities, and the attitude of a people trained for twenty years to consider itself the Master Race and was not likely to diverge to any extent from that of the government which had directed its training. Far from acting as a brake on official policy on questions of minorities, *Gruppe* III B largely contributed to directing it.

2. *Gruppe* III B and Foreign Minorities.
The *Gruppe* enjoyed almost unlimited power in questions of determining claims to German nationality and in the policy adopted towards those minorities within the Reich deemed not to be of pure German stock. The *Gruppe* had authority to enforce the transfer back to Germany of families originally of German descent and which had settled in the neighbouring countries, at the same time being competent for the resettlement of minorities previously resident in Germany. In these matters the *Gruppe* did not of course enjoy executive rights, but official German policy was based on its recommendations.

3. *Gruppe* III B and German Minorities.

A further interest of the *Gruppe* in minority questions was the safeguarding of the rights of German minorities abroad. Full scope for the carrying out of a policy of preferential treatment was afforded during the period when large areas of Europe were under German occupation. The general principle was the simple one that a German national, no matter where he might find himself, was entitled to advantages over other nationals.

4. *Gruppe* III B and Foreign Workers.

Distinct from the question of foreign and German minorities was the position of those foreign workers imported into Germany to meet the growing demand for manpower. The supervision of these workers and all questions relating to their treatment and privileges accorded them came within the competence of *Gruppe* III B, a subject on which there was close liaison with the *Gestapo*. The general tenor of III B recommendations was that however vital the supply of such labour might be, no privileges should be granted that tended to remove the emphasis from German superiority. In this *Gruppe* III B came into conflict with the *Deutsche Arbeitsfront*, which, taking a more realistic attitude, sought to improve the morale of foreign workers by various concessions, all of which were rejected by *Amt* III. It was *Gruppe* III B which was responsible for the promulgations of the law enforcing compulsory abortion in the case of pregnancy of female foreign workers.

5. Employment of Foreign Workers as Agents.

In September 1944, *Amt* III issued a circular to all SD-*Abschnitte* instructing them to begin the organisation of a *Nachrichtdienst* destined to cover the foreign workers. It was pointed out that previous reports on foreign workers had come from German sources and were unsatisfactory, and that in order to remedy this state of affairs, authority was now given for the recruitment of agents among the foreign workers themselves. An interesting feature was the creation of a new type of *Amt* III agent (see Part III, Paragraph D), named a '*Leitagent*' who was to be responsible for the running of the network among the workers themselves. The *Leitagenten* were to be trained by the *Amt* itself and posted to the SD-*Abschnitte* in sufficient strength to have one *Leitagent* for each SD-*Aussenstelle*. The *Leitagenten* were recruited mainly in the East, as III B2 had adopted the practice of employing paid foreign agents at a comparatively early date, the agents now being lent to III B1.

6. *Gruppe* III B and the Vlassov Movement.

In the latter half of 1944 a special section was set up in *Gruppe* III B under SS-*Ostubaf* Buchardt of *Referat* III B2 to deal with the Vlassov enterprise. Vlassov was a Russian general who had been contacted as early as 1942 as a possibly rallying point for anti-Russian elements in German occupied territory in the East. The plan was dropped, however, and it was not until the deteriorating situation on the Eastern Front in 1944 that it was revived, this time through the SS-*Standarte* Kurt Eggers, the propaganda unit of the *Waffen*-SS. The question was raised with Himmler and *Amt* III, and in September 1944 the first steps were taken to form a Vlassov Movement, the aims from the German side being threefold: the formation of fighting units recruited among Russian prisoners of war, the dropping of agents beind the lines to carry out anti-communist propaganda, and an intensification of similar propaganda among Russian workers in Germany. In November 1944 the Vlassov manifesto was issued after the first meeting of the 'Committee of Liberation of the People of Russia'.

The enterprise was a joint affair among the *Ämter* of the RSHA, as in addition to the purely military aspects and the propaganda interest of the SS-*Standarte* Kurt Eggers, *Amt* III was involved in the question of Russian Workers, *Amt* IV in the security supervision of the movement as a whole, and *Gruppe* VI C from the point of view of possible exploitation for espionage and sabotage purposes. The enterprise was undertaken at too late a date to have much chance of success.

7. RSHA *Gruppe* III B and *Amt* VI.
The interest of *Gruppe* III B in occupied territory led to frequent conflict with *Amt* VI; in principle it had been decided at an early date that occupied territory coming under German civil administration would come within the province of *Amt* III. In practice, however, there was frequent friction between the two *Ämter*, in particular in connection with Slovakia which until 1944 was dealt with by *Amt* III. It was finally decided by Kaltenbrunner that *Amt* VI should be allowed to operate in the country.

8. *Gruppe* III B and Public Health.
A less important function of *Gruppe* III B was its responsibility for submitting reports on the general health of the German people. It was under the direction of *Gruppe* III B that the mass X-ray survey of the German population was undertaken, the results of the survey being submitted to the Ministry of Health.

D. *Gruppe* III C.

1. General.
Under its broad function of dealing with 'Culture and Science', *Gruppe* III C was in fact the largest *Gruppe* of the *Amt*, its interests covering the widest sphere, and the subjects of most immediate importance in maintaining the morale of the country as a whole. The value of *Amt* III to the Party largely depended on whether, firstly, *Gruppe* III C was able to report efficiently and objectively, and, more important still, whether the reports of the *Gruppe* met with any response—an aspect which is dealt with more fully in Part IV (below).

2. *Referat* III C1.

This *Referat*, dealing with Science, fulfilled largely the same functions in this sphere as *Referat* III A2 in the field of Law—its task was to assess the effects of science and learning on educational measures imposed by the competent Ministry. There was however not the same element of conflict that has been noted in III A2; the reason lay in the fact that it was not too difficult to introduce into scientific and university circles the true type of Nazi fanatic, irrespective of his true educational attainments. At an early date therefore any 'dangerous' elements had already been removed from German scientific circles. It had not been so easy on the other hand to replace the existing legal personnel. The *Referat* therefore reflected official Nazi policy and was instrumental in maintaining it in spite of any adverse reports on official policy received from the 'Old Guard' in German science. Of special importance was the fact that all appointments to university posts had to be approved by *Referat* III C1, a system which of course guaranteed that only suitable Nazi types received the appointments.

3. *Referat* III C2.

This section dealt with Education and Religious Life. When the new *Gruppe* IV B was created in *Amt* IV in 1942 the personnel of *Referat* III C2 dealing with the Church were transferred for all working purposes to the *Gestapo*, as the attitude to the Church at that time was one of police supervision rather than of intelligence. The official attitude to the Church, supported by *Referat* III C2, was one of antagonism, and the subject came more within the competence of *Amt* IV than *Amt* III. *Amt* III did however submit reports on the general attitude of the public to religious movements, laying particular stress on any trends with suggested a replacement of the established churches with neo-pagan festivals, a development which was encouraged.

In the field of education there was less harmony between official policy and the general tenor of *Gruppe* III C reports. Inevitably there were criticisms of the lowering of educational standards as a result of the war, and especially owing to the strength and policy of the Hitler Youth Movement—a factor which led to a great increase in juvenile delinquency. In 1942 a special survey of the situation was ordered under the title of '*Jugendverwahrlösung und stinkende Moral im dritten Kriegsjahr*', with results that reflected so little credit to official policy that no *Gruppe* III C consolidated report was issued. The attitude of *Amt* III to the education of youth led to constant friction with the Hitler Youth Movement.

4. *Referat* III C3.

The section dealing with Popular Culture and Art was mainly concerned with reports on the perpetuation of old Germanic customs and costumes. It reflected the official support given to this subject, as since the earliest days the Nazi Party had fostered all national rites and customs and resisted any foreign influences. *Referat* III C3 was comparatively unimportant.

5. *Referat* III C4.

The importance of *Referat* III C4 dealing with Press and propaganda is of course evident. The section came under SS-*Ostubaf* Kielpinski, who had been successful in organising an intelligence service capable of presenting to the Propaganda Ministry public reaction to official speeches or newspaper articles only a matter of hours after the speech had been delivered. The *Referat* covered in addition public reaction to Allied propaganda.

6. *Referat* III C5

Referat III C5 was set up as late as the summer of 1944 as a result of Kaltenbrunner's recommendation that *Amt* III should adopt a more positive and less negative role. The *Referat* dealt with questions of research into armament development under SS-*Staf* Dr Wilhelm Spengler, the *Gruppenleiter* [RSHA III C], and acted in an advisory capacity in such matters. There was close liaison with the *Reichspostministerium* under Ohnesorge, whose department had been engaged on inventions and development of existing equipment.

E. *Gruppe* III D.

1. General.

An important factor in the work of *Gruppe* III D was the strong personal interest of the *Amtschef*, Ohlendorf, in its activities. Ohlendorf himself was a graduate in economic law, and did not lose his interest in economic matters during his period of service as RSHA *Amtschef* III. From 1939 Ohlendorf was Chief of the *Geschäftsführung* of *Reichsgruppe* Handel [Trade], and in 1943 was appointed Under Secretary [of State] in the Ministry of Economics, an appointment of particular importance and interest, as it represented the only occasion on which a member of the SD held an important joint appointment under the SD and the State. *Gruppe* III D therefore very largely as an instrument of the Ministry of Economics, and as a result of Ohlendorf's personal interest, the ramifications of the SD economic intelligence network were widespread. The *Gruppe* was particularly active in occupied territories.

2. The *Referate*.

There is little need to treat the *Referate* of *Gruppe* III D separately, as only the subject matter differs, not the working methods or aims. The *Referate* with their *Sachgebiete* are shown in Appendix IV. The reports submitted by the *Referate* gave a detailed survey of all aspects of German economy, but more important was probably the information obtained through the *Abteilungen* III in occupied territory on the economic situation in the countries under German control, the information thus obtained being used in the further exploitation of that country by the Germans. It is to be noted that in occupied territory, *Abteilung* III D was responsible for the recruitment of foreign labour for work in Germany.[2]

F. *Abteilung* III G.

This *Abteilung*, the *Geschäftsnachrichtendienst*, was *Amt* III's contribution to the general security measures taken after the July [1944] Plot. The *Gruppe*, which functioned originally as III N, had the task of reporting on the morale and political opinions of leading circles in society. The *Abteilung* had previously existed on a minor scale, but after the July Plot was increased in stature and placed as an independent *Abteilung* directly under the supervision of the *Amtschef*. Its reports were not submitted directly to higher authorities as in the case of the *Gruppen*, but was passed to the *Gruppe* most directly concerned, depending on the status of the person on whom the report was made.

Part III

The Creation of *Amt* III in 1939 and its Development

A. Organisation and Development of the *Amt*.

1. General.
The organisational structure of *Amt* III remained fairly static throughout its history, for although several changes occurred from time to time, the functions of the *Amt* remained virtually unaltered. The chief developments in the actual organisational and structure are briefly noted in the following paracgraphs.

2. Organisational structure in 1939
The organisational structure of *Amt* III in early 1940 is shown at Appendix I. The original structure of the *Amt* had only three *Gruppen*, as the *Gruppe* III B which is shown at Appendix I was only set up in the early days of 1940. Previously *Gruppe* III B was the 1940 *Gruppe* III C, while *Gruppe* III C in 1939 was the 1940 *Gruppe* D. This will be seen from the comparative table in Paragraph 8 of Part 1 (above). In the early stages therefore *Amt* III merely continued the functions of *Abteilung* II/2 of the SD-*Hauptamt*, the only extension being in the creation of the new *Gruppe* III B early in 1940. The new *Gruppe*, a small one of only three *Referate*, was destined to develop into one of the largest in the *Amt*, the reason of course being the problems arising out of the extension of *Amt* III to cover occupied territory, and later out of the large influx of foreign workers into Germany itself.

3. Developments in 1941–1943.
The *Amt* underwent several changes in 1941; comparison of Appendices I and II show that the differences are, however, mainly changes in the designation of the *Gruppen*. III A and III C changed titles, III B and III D remaining unchanged. In addition to the major changes, there were minor adjustments in the *Referate*, none of which are important enough to call for special attention, except that the creation of *Referat* III B5 indicated the extension of *Amt* III activity to occupied territory.

4. Changes in 1943–1944.
The changes in 1943 were minor in character. *Gruppe* III A set up a new *Referat* III A5 dealing with Law and the Police, while in *Gruppe* III D there appeared the two special sections, III D West and III D East, dealing with occupied territory in those areas, these new sections however disappearing again in the course of 1944.

In the summer of 1944 a new *Referat* in *Gruppe* III C was set up with the designation *Referat* III C5, dealing with weapon research and development, a department in which Kaltenbrunner himself displayed considerable interest. It will be noted too that before the end, *Referat* III B5, dealing with occupied territory, had been incorporated into *Referat* III B1, for the obvious reason of course that by the end of 1944 the territory occupied by the Germans had shrunk considerably.

5. The creation of *Abteilung* III G in 1944.
The only major development of interest in the latter history of *Amt* III was the creation of *Gruppe* III G shortly after the July Plot. The functions of this *Gruppe* are dealt with in Part II (above), but it should be noted that the *Gruppe* originally existed as *Gruppe* III N, which designation it retained for a short time only.

6. Evacuation and Dissolution of *Amt* III.
In view of its functions as an intelligence service with its central office in Berlin advising the government as a result of the information received from the SD-*Abschnitte*, *Amt* III could not follow the same pattern of evacuation adopted by the other *Ämter*. The component parts of *Amt* IV could function by themselves without reference to Berlin, while the *Gruppen* of *Amt* VI could go different ways without materially affecting each other. An SD-*Abschnitt*, on the other hand, served only as an information service to the central office. *Amt* III therefore resembled a closely-knit organisation in which the head was useless without the body, while the limbs served no useful function if the head were removed. The tendency in *Amt* III was accordingly to retain the organisation intact as long as possible, though reducing the staff both at the RSHA and at regional levels to meet the insistent demands for manpower for the [armed] forces.

The *Amt* therefore remained in Berlin virtually until the end, proceeding north with the Nordstab of the RSHA late in April [1945]. There was only a small element of *Amt* III in the *Südstab* under Spengler and Kielspinski. *Gruppe* Spengler went south to join the *Südstab* in the so-called Alpine Redoubt, abandoning however its true *Amt* III functions. Its assignment, a futile one, was to form a static intelligence headquarters, while the individual officers were to act as liaison officers between the Werwolf groups and Spengler's headquarters. The *Gruppe* consisted of about a dozen *Amt* III officers with a small clerical staff. With the general collapse in the Redoubt area, the *Gruppe* Spengler dissolved together with the other RSHA elements in the south. The SD-*Abschnitte* in the final stages are largely covered by Part V (below).

B. Regional organisation within Germany.

The original regional organisation of the SD in Germany had been on the lines of the SS structure of SD-*Oberabschnitte* and dependent SD-*Unterabschnitte*. With the gradual disassociation from the SS, and the corresponding identification with the *Sicherheitspolizei*, this organisational structure was modified to conform more to the regional organisation of the *Gestapo* and *Kripo*, the outside offices being renamed SD-*Leitabschnitte* and SD-*Abschnitte*, and as the SD was in fact a Party organisation it tended to follow the Party territorial divisions of *Gaus* and *Kreise*, a SD-*Leitabschnitt* being roughly competent for a *Gau*, and an *Abschnitt* for a *Kreis*. The SD-*Abschnitte* in turn had dependent branch offices known as SD-*Hauptaussenstellen* and SD-*Aussenstellen*.

The SD-*Abschnitte* came of course within the same chain of command of IdS and BdS, as described in the Situation Report on *Amt* IV (q.v.). Again, as in the case of the *Stapostellen*, the SD-*Abschnitte* were not subordinate to the SD-*Leitabschnitt*, the differences merely indicating the importance of the area covered; but the *Aussenstellen* were controlled by the *Abschnitte*. In common with *Amt* IV, many SD-*Stellen* in Germany were downgraded during the war in order to meet the problem of manpower, some SD-*Abschnitte* becoming SD-*Hauptaussenstellen*.

Organisationally, the SD-*Abschnitte* were formed on the pattern of the *Amt* itself, although local conditions might give rise to modifications.

C. *Amt* III outside Germany.

1. *Amt* III in occupied territory.
Little need to be said regarding the organisation of *Amt* III outside Germany. In occupied territory the *Amt* normally had representation on the staff of the BdS or in the *Einsatzkommandos*, the structure of the *Abteilung* III following closely on that of the *Amt* itself. As in the case of *Amt* IV, local conditions sometimes required some degree of modification.

2. *Amt* III and neutral territory.

There is no reason to believe that *Amt* III extended its representation into neutral territory, though there are instances of *Amt* III *Abschnitte* submitting reports from agents who had occasion to travel to neutral territory. It is not likely that the SD-*Abschnitte* in question actually despatched agents on missions to neutral territory, but rather advantage was taken of the journey of an agent already registered to brief him on certain topics in keeping with the country he intended to visit. It was customary too for the SD-*Abschnitt* on such occasions to inform *Amt* VI of the impending journey and request any brief which the *Gruppe* might have to submit. Thus the SD-*Abschnitt* Karlsruhe informed *Referat* VI B3 that an agent was due to visit Switzerland in the near future, and requested that the *Referat* should supply a brief on which the agent could prepare a report on his return. In such cases the background of the agent was given, together with an assessment of his reliability. It is to be remembered that until 1942 most of the SD-*Leitabschnitt* had an *Amt* VI representative on the staff and this type of collaboration is likely to have been developed at an early date.

3. Relations between *Amt* III and *Amt* VI.

The relations between *Amt* III and *Amt* VI in occupied territory have already been mentioned in Part II, Paragraph C (7) (above).

D. The Working Methods of *Amt* III.

1. General principles.

It has been mentioned in Part II (above) that the general function of *Amt* III was to present to the government an objective summary of public opinion in the country, at the same time embodying in its reports recommendations for improvement in the existing regime. Such a commitment required certain conditions, and it is worth while repeating these conditions as seen by the *Amtschef* Ohlendorf.

(a) The *Amt* would require complete independence in its work in order to be free from all external influences.
(b) The reports would require to be entirely anonymous in order that no action could be taken against those persons criticising existing conditions.
(c) The *Amt* would require to be free from bureaucratic control.
(d) The *Amt* should work independently of the police services and should avoid duplication of their work.

There is little ground to dispute the accuracy of these conditions and the nature of the methods employed by *Amt* III in its work reflects the attempts made to maintain them.

2. Types of agents employed by *Amt* III.

It is difficult to draw a clear line of distinction between *Amt* III officials and the various types of agents employed. It was a matter of policy in the *Amt* to introduce into personnel highly placed experts in the various branches of public life in which the *Amt* was interested, and further, to release such personnel after a period of service in order that they should not lose touch with their own circles through too much routine work in the *Amt* itself.

The agents employed were too of a high grade type, the emphasis being laid on enthusiasm for the work and ability to carry it out, qualifications which were considered more important than membership if the SS or the Party. As far as possible agents were not paid for their work, the willingness to work without payment being a reflection on their interest and enthusiasm. The only exception to this rule was in the case of the *Leitagenten* mentioned in Part II, Paragraph C (5) above, and in Paragraph 6 below.

It is to be noted too that *Ehrenamtliche Mitarbeiter* (see below) could be employed in the offices of the *Amt* itself, though they did not require to be members of the SD, SS, or any other Party formation.

3. The *Ehrenamtlicher Mitarbeiter*.

The *Ehrenamtlicher Mitarbeiter* was the highest type of *Amt* III agent, though his importance depended on his position in public life and on the type of work he had undertaken to perform. This type of agent does not land himself to clear definition, as he could be only casually employed or be given a specific assignment only from time to time in accordance with the current requirements of the *Amt*. An '*Ehrenamtlicher Mitarbeiter*' could be given the task of controlling an *Aussenstelle*, even though unpaid for his work, and in fact more than half of the *Aussenstellen* of *Amt* III were run on this voluntary basis.

4. The *Hauptamtlicher Mitarbeiter*.

The *Hauptamtlicher Mitarbeiter* was properly speaking the full time salaried SD officer, holding SS rank in keeping with the function discharged. The term '*Hauptamtlich*' was general, however, and could be applied in the case of the '*Leitagent*' as they too were in receipt of pay, though not of course SD officers.

5. The *V-Mann*.

In contrast to the *Ehrenamtlicher Mitarbeiter*, the *V-Mann* was a permanent link in the SD chain and did not work on a casual basis. *V-Männer* were normally run from the SD-*Abschnitte* and *Aussenstellen*, and came under the jurisdiction of the local *Hauptamtlicher Mitarbeiter* or of the *Aussenstellen*. The *V-Mann* in turn operated a network of '*Zubringer*' who submitted reports as required. In this chain the *Zubringer* was allowed to know only the identity of the *V-Mann*, while the *Hauptamtlicher Mitarbeiter* acted as the cut-out between the *V-Mann* and the *Leiter* of the *Dienststelle*.

6. The *Leitagent*.

Leitagenten were used in the first instance only in Eastern Europe and marked a departure from normal *Amt* III policy in that they were paid for the work they undertook. *Leitagenten* were recruited, however, only among foreign workers, and were given the task of organising their own network among the foreign workers themselves. In September 1944 this system was extended to cover the whole of Germany (see Part II, Paragraph C (5) above). Where the foreign worker thus employed did not control a network he was referred to as an '*Einzelagent*'.

7. *Amt* III Reports.

As *Amt* III did not report on individuals but on subjects the results of its work were reflected in the reports issued by the *Amt* itself, these reports representing a symposium of the reports received from the smallest links in the chain; the *Zubringer* canalised through and collated at the various levels of *Aussenstelle*, *Abschnitt*, *Referat*, and *Gruppe*. In this way the *Amt* itself acted as the central evaluating office for the whole *Reich*.

The *V-Männer* normally reported verbally to the *Aussenstelle*, which acted mainly as a collecting centre for the reports of the *V-Männer*; these reports were then passed without elaboration to the *Abschnitt*. The *Abschnitt* was responsible for consolidation of these reports, which it in turn submitted to the *Sachbearbeiter* in the *Amt*, giving the background of the sources, but not the identities. The reports were meant to incorporate both the general conclusion of the *Abschnitt* and liberal quotations from the sources themselves in order that the *Amt* could have a clearer picture of the background of the agents themselves.

The *Amt* was then responsible for the issue of a final consolidated report. In the early stages of the war routine reports were issued daily, later twice weekly, to the Party and government authorities on general topics. These reports became less frequent and had more restricted distribution as the war progressed, for reasons which are dealt with in Part IV below.

In addition to the routine reports, the *Amt* was also responsible for the issue of special reports covering specific subjects which were distributed only to the departments concerned.

Part IV

Amt III and its Position in Nazi Germany

General.

1. General Difficulties.

It is now apparent that the role of *Amt* III in Germany was misinterpreted on the Allied side, as in some directions the importance of the *Amt* has been overrated, in other directions its influence unsuspected. To give a true assessment of its position and value in Nazi Germany is not an easy matter, nor even possible, as the testimony of Ohlendorf in particular must be taken with the greatest reserve. The general tendency on the part of leading *Amt* III characters under interrogation has been to 'whitewash' the *Amt* and to idealise its aims and objectives.

2. Effects of the centralisation of *Amt* III.

It is not possible to judge the *Amt* as a whole by a study of its SD-*Abschnitte*, as one can, for instance, assess *Amt* IV by analysing the activities of the *Stapostellen*. However excellent the information obtained by an SD-*Abschnitt* may have been, that information had no positive value until it had been again processed at the *Amt* and passed to the authority concerned. The value of the information obtained by the enormous *Amt* III network stretching all over Germany and occupied territory depended entirely on whether the *Amt* passed it on, and thereafter, on whether it reached the department for which it was intended. A *Stapostelle*, on the other hand, could take local action on its own initiative, a feature of *Amt* IV being the decentralisation of authority. *Amt* VI for its part passed on information as it was received after only normal evaluation and the information could consist of individual items. The characteristic feature of *Amt* III was that it collated, evaluated and distributed information received from all over the country—the *Abschnitt* did not see in concrete form any results of its own work, nor did the *Amt* pass on a report as it was received from a single *Abschnitt*. The essential feature of *Amt* III is its high degree of centralisation; it follows from this that to assess *Amt* III means an analysis of the attitude of its leading characters to its functions and purposes on the one hand, and a similar analysis of the attitude of those Ministries and Departments for whose benefit the work of the *Amt* was intended.

3. Gaps in present information.

An immediate gap lies therefore in the fact that interrogation has been confined to one side only—the leading *Amt* III characters, and, as has been stated, their statements cannot be accepted without qualification. To a certain extent Ohlendorf's contentions have been supported by Kaltenbrunner, but neither of these two characters have impressed by their candour or frankness, and while it may be true that Himmler disapproved of the work of the *Amt* in certain directions and nullified its effectiveness, that is only half the story; it is apparent that *Amt* III in other directions worked in full sympathy with official policy and served an eminently useful role in the designs and development of the Nazi Party.

4. *Amt* III and other Departments.

It can however be stated with certainty that the apparent homogeneity of the German Intelligence Services [GIS] which the study of a mere organisational chart of the RSHA suggest, the alleged sinister part played by the *Inlandsnachrichtendienst* in collaboration with *Amt* IV, and the carefully conceived role of *Amt* III as an instrument of the Party, were in fact grossly exaggerated. The outstanding feature of the GIS which interrogation of its leading personalities has revealed has been the consant internal conflict between those leading figures and the departments the GIS had been set up to serve. This has long been suspected in the case of *Amt* VI, its place in the RSHA, and its relations with the Foreign Office. It is now clear that *Amt* III was no exception to the general rule, both in respect of its relations with the other *Ämter*, and government departments. It is profitable therefore to examine what these relationships were in the light of the eevidence now available.

A. *Amt* III and its relations with other Departments.

1. *Amt* III and the *Gestapo*.

Reference has already been made in Part I above, to the differences that arose between the SD and the *Gestapo* in the years preceding the creation of the RSHA. The setting up of that organisation removed to some extent the causes of friction as far as spheres of interest were concerned, but did little to remove the basic reasons for the rivalry and dispute between the two services—the fact that the *Sipo* remained State Police while the SD continued to be a Party organisation paid out of Party funds. The quarrel became acute when attempts were made to fuse the two services by introducing *Sipo* personnel into the SD and SS, as such officers were granted SS rank acceptable to their Civil Service rank, and *Oberregierungsrat* becoming SS-*Ostubaf*, thus becoming senior to many old SD officers who enjoyed only minor SS ranks.

Cooperation on a working basis between the two *Ämter* must be seen against that background of jealousy and rivalry. In the early stages before the war the SD had played the role of reporting on individuals, reports on which the *Gestapo* took appropriate action. This outward appearance of collaboration became of decreasing importance as time went on owing to two main factors; firstly the *Gestapo* was developing by 1937 its own *Nachrichtendienst*, while *Amt* III was gradually becoming less subjective and more objective in its work. The Heydrich decree of August 1941 (see Liquidation Report on *Amt* IV, Part III) laid down the manner in which the two *Ämter* were to cooperate, but in practice the degree of cooperation was in direct relation to the degree of decentralisation; thus in occupied territory the distinction between *Amt* III and *Amt* IV was less clearly marked than in Germany, while in Germany itself the extent of collaboration decreased from the SD-*Aussenstellen* upwards. We find thus that in Holland for example the *Abteilung* III personnel even carried out arrests and generally worked in closer contact with *Abteilung* IV than did the SD-*Aussenstelle* with a *Stapostelle* in Germany. The policy of *Amt* III was to dissociate itself from any form of police work and to avoid reporting on personalities except in those cases where action was obviously necessary, a security duty which applied in any case equally well to any other service in Germany.

2. *Amt* III and Himmler.

Of prime importance in the development of *Amt* III was the attitude of Himmler himself; it is now clear that that attitude was far from favourable, at least in those aspects of the work of the *Amt* which lent themselves to criticism of the regime. The personal relationship between Himmler and Ohlendorf was not cordial, the latter being commonly referred to by Himmler as a 'gloomy theorist'. Himmler's chief complaint was against what he considered the negative aspect of *Amt* III work, and more than once he attempted to change its working methods. In particular, Himmler ordered the SD in the spring of 1943 to use its intelligence network to combat defeatism, a function more in keeping with *Amt* IV. The *Amt*, therefore, in so far as it was meant to act as a corrective to the excesses of the Nazi regime, lacked support where support was most needed, in the person of the RFSS.

3. *Amt* III and the Party.

It is a curious paradox that the SD began as the instrument of the Party for combatting political opponents, a function later to become the province of *Amt* IV, not a Party organisation, while however the development of the SD as a *Nachrichtendienst* did not meet with the approval of the Party, which tended to look upon its own intelligence service as detrimental to Party interests. The objection lay in the fact that the scope of the SD became virtually unlimited, while at the same time the SD had the authority to submit reports to other government departments. The quarrel on the authority of *Amt* III centred round Bormann, who objected strongly to the independence of the SD; the real objection was not of course to the independent status of *Amt* III, but to the uncontrolled critical content of some of its reports. The Party had in fact taught bloody instructions, which being taught were now returning to plague the inventor. A totalitarian regime does not suffer criticism gladly.

4. *Amt* III and Goebbels.

The attitude of Goebbels to *Amt* III and its work was based on fundamentally the same reasons; his main concern was to prevent any *Amt* III reports having a bearing on the morale of the people from reaching departments which he considered were not concerned with such matters. Again, the underlying reason was that the morale of the people depended very largely on the efficiency of Goebbels' propaganda, and such reports tended to reflect adversely on him. This objection in principle because of a personal enmity with the *Amt* III report on the public reaction to the speech of Goebbels after the Stalingrad disaster was pointedly unfavourable. The value of *Referat* III C4 to Goebbels should have been incalculable, and was no doubt great, but in fact he carried out his functions in accordance with his own policy and preconceived ideas, and was not responsive to criticism of that policy. In the summer of 1943 Himmler, at the instigation of Goebbels, forbade reports of the effect of propaganda on public opinion.

5. *Amt* III and the *Gauleiter*.

The *Gauleiter* for their part attacked the independence of the SD-*Abschnitte* in their areas and frequently pressed that the *Stellen* should come under their administrative control. Again the objection was based on their fear of the subject matter of the reports which might reflect unfavourably on themselves. The *Gauleiter* attempted unsuccessfully to force the SD-*Abschnitte* to disclose the identity of their *V-Männer* for reasons that can well be imagined.

6. Summing Up.

The above review of RSHA *Amt* III relations with other departments and personalities is sufficient to show the position of the *Amt* in Germany was no sinecure. While *Amt* III enjoyed a certain amount of independence, there were many influences at work which affected its working methods and its effectiveness, but how great the effect of these influences is still a matter of interest. The following paragraphs represent an attempted assessment of the position of *Amt* III in Germany.

B. *Amt* III Reports and their Influence.

1. The *Lageberichte*.

At the outbreak of war *Amt* III was committed to the daily issue of a report summarising the reaction of the country to the war and the measures introduced as a result. This report under the title '*Meldungen aus dem Reich*', was circulated to all high Nazi officials and to government ministries. At this early stage the reports achieved a high level of objectivity and gave a faithful reflection of the general situation at the time. It is most probable that for a period after its creation *Amt* III functioned as it was meant to—in giving the State the means whereby it could study public opinion and thereafter frame its own policy accordingly.

But while objectivity in the reports was an essential, it was equally necessary that the reports should embody criticism on certain points, as was recommendations for improvement. It was at this point that the real test of their future usefulness arose; whether the criticisms would reach the proper quarters so that appropriate action could be taken. It was here too that the first weakness became apparent; that it was only at the highest levels of the RSHA that any decisions could be taken on these two essential points. The influences against objective criticism operated at the very levels where such criticism was most required.

2. Influences within the *Amt* itself.
Amt III reports normally consisted of two parts; the '*Stimmungsbericht*' dealing with the general situation, and a second part embodying recommendations and suggestions for improvement. It was in the second part that the influence of Nazi training itself made itself felt, as the *Referenten* at that time under the strict rule of Heydrich coloured their recommendations to suit official policy. At each stage of evaluation therefore the original *Abschnitt* report tended to be toned down until in its final form it had been modified to fall in line with general *Amt* III policy. Objectivity did not long remain a characteristic of *Amt* III reports.

3. Effects of the SD-*Abschnitte*.
The general effect of such a procedure on the originators of the subject matter of *Amt* III reports, the SD-*Abschnitte*, was that they in turn began to treat objectivity with less respect, either toning down their own reports to suit general policy, or exaggerating the situation in the hope that the final draft in the *Amt* might more closely represent the truth. In both cases the SD-*Abschnitte* tended less and less to give a true picture of the situation.

4. Objections to the Reports.
The other influences affecting the value of *Amt* III work came in the efforts to restrict the wide circulation of its reports, for reasons which have been dealt with in Paragraph B. The most effective stop in the process was Himmler himself, through whom all *Amt* III reports which criticised some high personality had to pass. Such reports did not pass that point unless Himmler himself saw personal advantage in allowing them to do so. Strong objections to wide circulation also came from the *Propagandaministerium*, and as a result of Goebbels' influence, the circulation became restricted to Himmler, Bormann, Goering, Lammers, and Goebbels. By July 1943 the '*Meldungen aus dem Reich*' were stopped altogether, and with this suppression, the only existing link between the Party and public opinion ceased. The *Amt* III reports were now restricted to special subjects, and no longer gave a general review.

5. The negative aspects of *Amt* III.
It can be said, therefore, that *Amt* III failed in the function in which it was most necessary that it should succeed; for a variety of reasons it gradually ceased to report

objectively, and did not provide the State and Party with the means whereby the excesses of totalitarianism could be corrected, the State itself being an unwilling customer for the advice which *Amt* III could have provided. The fundamental reasons for the failure lay in the faults inherent in the Nazi regime itself. Such a regime based as it was on the necessity for suppressing all opposition, could not maintain an intelligence service whose function was virtually to criticise the regime, for such criticism meant opposition which should be suppressed and not fostered.

6. The positive aspects of *Amt* III.

It is this aspect of *Amt* III work and failure which Ohlendorf in particular has been at pains to stress, as neither the attempt nor the failure reflect unfavourably. This failure, however, represents only one side of *Amt* III work; in many aspects *Amt* III noted as an instrument of official policy, especially in the field of *Gruppe* III B and *Gruppe* III D. The recommendations and reports submitted by *Gruppe* III B did not in any material way conflict with accepted views, while the information obtained through *Gruppe* III D must have been invaluable to the Ministry of Economics, especially in so far as it covered occupied territory. How great this influence of the *Amt* was in these two spheres in particular is uncertain, but it must have been considerable.

Part V

Amt III and Post-Occupational Plans

1. General.

The role which *Amt* III was to play in resistance and post-occupational movements remains obscure and undetermined, as the evidence so far available is conflicting on major policy and minor points. It may well be the case however that this obscurity is dependent on the fact that no clear policy ever existed in the Amt itself, due to a lack of direction from higher authority. It is however certain that no well laid plans could have been possible in view of the now well established fact that the official attitude did not countenance the possibility of defeat, and to plan for such eventuality was a confession of defeatism.

Nevertheless, it had long been feared on the Allied side prior to the German collapse that *Amt* III with its well conceived and well concealed organisation offered the best medium for any attempt on the part of the GIS to continue its activities after the cessation of hostilities and during the period of Allied occupation, so that a somewhat close examination of existing evidence on any attempt to that direction is more than justified.

2. Limitations of *Amt* III.

There were in the first place definite limitations to the part which *Amt* III could play in a post-occupational role; the *Amt* controlled what was purely an information network, held together largely by personal contact, especially at the lower levels. It was therefore admirably suited to continuing to operate as an intelligence network under occupation, provided arrangements had been made to canalise the information from occupied to non-occupied territory. There were, however, the severe limitations that *Amt* III had no W/T facilities for its agents, as the use of W/T had never been envisaged. To have undertaken W/T training for the purposes under review would of course have been a confession of defeatism, and the matter could not in any case have been raised officially. Nor could the SD network easily adapt itself to resistance or sabotage, as in the case of the *Gestapo*; its scope was accordingly limited, but even in its limitations it still remained a potentially valuable asset with proper preparation. In the event the role it was to play was dictated by circumstances.

3. Occupied Territory.

The question first arose in occupied territory when the Allied advances made it obvious that a general withdrawal was inevitable. No attempt was made in any theatre by *Amt* III to provide for a continuation of its work after withdrawal; the W/T question in any case was an insuperable barrier, but even apart from such consideration, the territory after withdrawal became the province of *Amt* VI, so that *Amt* III had no real interest in attempting to make plans. Generally speaking, its personnel were allotted to the other *Abteilungen*, as in Holland, where, for example, the III B officer engaged in running line-crossing operations in conjunction both with *Abteilung* VI and the *Abwehr* FATs.

4. German Territory.

A different situation arose in Germany itself towards the end of 1944, when it seemed that parts of German territory were about to pass into Allied control, especially in the Alsace-Lorraine sector.[3] It was not so obvious that such occupied territory should become the interest of *Amt* VI, and again, well established SD-*Abschnitte* with their networks of longstanding were facing the prospect of being overrun. The problem which now presented itself therefore was what action should be taken by such SD-*Abschnitte*, and what use if any was to be made of *Amt* III agents in Germany who found themselves in areas under Allied control. It was now, at the end of 1944, that the question of the part to be played by *Amt* III in such matters was forced upon the *Amt* itself, not of course by the higher authorities, who saw a situation that might be exploited, but by the officers who themselves found the problem inescapable.

It can be stated with certainty that for the reasons mentioned in Paragraph 1 above, no coordinated policy was ever decided upon, but such measures as were taken were due to force of circumstances; the following paragraphs give a brief chronological review of *Amt* III activity from the end of 1944 onwards, with the reservation that they are based on evidence that is often conflicting and sometimes intentionally misleading.

5. Events in Alsace-Lorraine.

The events in Alsace-Lorraine from September 1944 onwards represented not so much independent action on the part of *Amt* III, but rather an attempt to make available to *Amt* VI the facilities which the SD-*Abschnitte* in the area offered. In the autumn of 1944, Sandberger of *Gruppe* VI A discussed with Höppner of *Gruppe* III A the question of cooperation between the two *Ämter* in the West in occupied German territory, the results of which discussions were seen in the creation of *Kommando* Zuvogel in Alsace-Lorraine. The general instruction given to SD-*Abschnitte* in the West was that they were to prepare an intelligence network in their areas capable of providing information on the relations between the German population and the occupying forces, working in liaison with the armies.

The chief difficulty in such an enterprise lay in communications; it was soon obvious that *Amt* III had no agents trained in W/T, and requests for W/T transmitters on behalf of the *Amt* went, generally speaking, unheeded. Only in the case of Alsace-Lorraine did any concrete results emerge, and only because of the facilities afforded by *Gruppe* VI F.

The organisation of the scheme came under SS-*Ostubaf* Ott, *Leiter* of the SD-*Abschnitt* Saarbrücken. It was decided to use a special W/T set working in liaison with low-flying aircraft, a development which *Gruppe* VI F were anxious to study in practice.[4] The failure of the German counter-offensive in the Ardennes spelt the doom of the enterprise; in the first instance it had been intended to use only Germans as agents, but by February 1945 it was found necessary to use French nationals. In March 1945 efforts were made to set up a W/T school for the instruction of the agents, but events moved too fast, and the *Kommando* dissolved with the general surrender, having achieved nothing in the way of results.

6. Subsequent Trends.

The subsequent development of *Amt* III activity in post-occupational roles followed two distinct lines; firstly there was the effort on the part of the SD personnel themselves to attempt to maintain the SD network intact throughout Germany so that it could operate during the occupation by the Allies and report to a central government. It will be noted that in this scheme the essential condition was that some form of central German government would be allowed to remain, and in the event it was hoped that the Dönitz government would fulfil this function.

Distinct from this development was the plan which was drawn up in the course of April 1945 in Munich, which aimed at the utilisation, not of SD personnel, but of former SD agents in foreign worker circles, an enterprise which was not in fact a pure *Amt* III undertaking, but represented a fusion between *Amt* III and *Amt* VI in the last days before the collapse.

7. Attempt of *Amt* III to go underground.

The first discussions regarding the possibility of *Amt* III going underground arose at the end of 1944, when the *Gruppenleiters* themselves approached Ohlendorf on the subject. Again it is important to note that the enterprise, such as it was, did not come as a result of official direction from the highest authorities, as in official circles the possibility of defeat was still not countenanced.

Ohlendorf himself opposed this scheme in view of the official attitude to post-occupational planning, but later agreed to preparations being made. The subject was therefore not seriously discussed until March 1945, with SS-*Stubaf* Jaskulsky, *Leiter* of III S, being given the task of dealing with the technical and administrative problems involved. It was decided that in those areas of Germany where the SD-*Abschnitte* were likely to be overrun the *Leiter* of the SD-*Abschnitt* would select the most reliable of his *V-Männer* for post-occupational activity, without however the *V-Männer* beforehand of this intention. A minimum of three officials of the SD-*Abschnitte* themselves were to go underground with the purpose of forming subsequently a *Nachrichtenkopf* for re-establishing contact with the selected *V-Männer* at an opportune moment. What was therefore envisaged was a continuation of the SD organisation in Germany on a much reduced scale.

Some ten SD-*Abschnitt* Leiters were selected for the enterprise, covering mainly the area of Northern Germany, but when these officials were informed of the plan they protested at the lack of detailed information on what exactly their functions were to be, and quite apart from any other consideration, the scheme was stillborn because of the attitude of the SD personnel themselves. When it became obvious to Ohlendorf that the scheme was not developing as had been envisaged, it was decided to cancel the enterprise, and during the last days in Schwerin instructions were issued to that effect.

The attempts made by *Amt* III to go underground did not therefore get beyond the elementary planning stage, and the reasons for this failure can be attributed to the fact that preparations were begun at far too late a date, and this in turn was a result of the official attitude to the possibility of defeat in the highest circles. An additional factor was the technical difficulties involved, as the information network would have to depend on a courier system, as *Amt* III had no W/T equipment of its own.

It is to be noted that Ohlendorf, as well as other leading *Amt* III characters involved, had claimed that the fundamental idea behind these attempts was to place the organisation at the disposal of the occupying forces. In the light of available evidence, such claims are unacceptable.

8. The III B Underground Movement.

In early April 1945 a conference was held in Berlin between *Oberfeldrichter* Schoen of *Gruppe* VI A and representatives of *Amt* III. At this meeting it was decided that the two *Ämter* should work jointly in the exploitation of foreign workers within the Reich which meant in fact that the *Nachrichtendienst* which *Gruppe* III B had organised in foreign labour circles since September 1944 would be used conjointly with *Amt* VI for post-occupational purposes. It was agreed that SS-*Stubaf* Perey of *Gruppe* III B should go south to join the small *Südstab* of *Amt* III under Spengler with authority to give effect to these decisions.

Perey therefore arrived in Munich in the second week of April 1945 armed with his authority to organise a 'great European underground movement' on the lines of the French Maquis, the enterprise going under the name of '*Unternehmen Regenbogen*'. The scheme on paper was more ambitious than circumstances justified. It was decided to divide the country into four sections; north-east, north-west, south-east and south-west, each sector exploiting the foreign workers in its area. The workers were formed into groups according to nationalities, e.g., a French group, a Dutch group, a Belgian group, a Flemish group, etc.. They were instructed to spread pro-German propaganda based more or less on anti-communism, and were to remain until contacted, in the meantime doing what they could to gather arms and recruit more agents for the planned intelligence network.

The enterprise was again a complete failure, and information concerning the personalities and organisation was in Allied hands soon after the plans themselves had been drawn up.

Main sources:

SS-*Gruf* Otto Ohlendorf	*Amtschef* III
SS-*Staf* Dr Hans Ehlich	*Gruppenleiter* III B
SS-*Stubaf* Eberhard Löw z. Steinfurth	*Gruppe* III B
SS-*Stubaf* Dr Wilhelm Höttl	*Gruppe* VI B
SS-*Ogruf* Dr Ernst Kaltenbrunner	CdS (*Chef* RSHA)

Report issued by W.R.C.3a on 14 December 1945.

Appendix I

Organisation of RSHA *Amt* III in 1940

Note: This chart represents the organisation of RSHA *Amt* III in the early days of 1940. When the *Amt* was first created, *Gruppe* III B below did not exist. The three *Gruppen* of the *Amt* were A, B and C, corresponding to *Gruppen* A, C and D in this Appendix.

RSHA *Amt* III—*Deutsche Lebensgebiete*
Amtschef—SS-*Standartenführer* Otto Ohlendorf

Gruppe	Referat	Sachgebiet	Referent
Gruppenleiter A—*Kulturelle Gebiet*—SS-*Stubaf* Spengler			
A		*Geschäftsstelle*	SS-*Hstuf* Jarosch
	S	*Sonderfragen und Sachinspektion*	SS-*Hstuf* Beyer
	L	*Lektorat*	-
	ZB	*Zentralstelle Bundische Jugend*	SS-*Ostuf* Hermann
	1	*Wissenschaft*	SS-*Ostuf* Turowski
	2	*Erziehung*	SS-*Ostuf* Seibert
	3	*Volkskultur*	-
	4	*Kunst*	SS-*Stubaf* Spengler
	5	*Presse, Schriftum, Rundfunk*	SS-*Hstuf* Kielpinski
	6	*Religioses Leben*	SS-*Stubaf* Elling
Gruppenleiter B—*Volkstum*—SS-*Stubaf* Ehlich			
B	S	*Sonderfragen und Sachinspektion*	-
	L	*Lektorat*	-
	1	*Volkstumarbeit*	SS-*Hstuf* Hummitzsch
	2	*Umwanderung*	SS-*Stubaf* Ehlich
	3	*Rasse und Volksgesundheit*	SS-*Hstuf* Schneider
Gruppenleiter C—*Gemeinschaftsleben*—SS-*Stubaf* Gengenbach			
C	S	*Sonderfragen und Sachinspektion*	SS-*Oschaf* Wegener
	L	*Lektorat*	SS-*Ustuf* Reinhart
	1	*Recht*	SS-*Hstuf* Deppner
	2	*Verwaltung*	SS-*Hstuf* Heinze
	3	*Verfassung*	SS-*Hstuf* Heinze
	4	*Allgemeine Volksleben und Nationalsozialismus*	SS-*Uschaf* Seynstahl

Gruppenleiter D—*Wirtschaft*—SS-*Hstuf* Seibert

D	S	*Sonderfragen und Sachinspektion*	SS-*Ostuf* May
	L	*Lektorat* III C	-
	1	*Ernährungswirtschaft*	SS-*Ostuf* Haase
	2	*Handel und Handwerk*	SS-*Hstuf* Seibert
	3	*Verkehrswesen*	SS-*Hstuf* Seibert
	4	*Währung, Banken, Börsen,*	SS-*Ostuf* Reden
		und Versicherungswirtschaft	
	5	*Industrie und Energiewirtschaft*	SS-*Ostuf* Zehlein
	6	*Finanzwirtschaft*	SS-*Hstuf* Kröger
	7	*Arbeits- und Sozialwesen*	SS-*Stubaf* Leetsch
	8	*Wehrwissenschaft*	SS-*Hstuf* Seibert

Appendix II

Organisation of RSHA *Amt* III, 1941–1943

RSHA *Amt* III—*Deutsche Lebensgebiete*
Amtschef—SS-*Standartenführer* Otto Ohlendorf

Gruppe	*Referat*	*Sachgebiet*	*Referent*

Gruppenleiter A—*Fragen der Rechtsordnung und des Reichsaufbaus*—SS-*Stubaf* Gengenbach

A		*Geschäftsstelle*	SS-*Ostuf* Klauss
	1	*Allgemeine Fragen der*	SS-*Hstuf* Beyer
		Lebensgebietsarbeit	
	2	*Rechtsleben*	SS-*Hstuf* Malz
	3	*Verfassung und Verwaltung*	-
	4	*Allgemeines Volksleben*	-

Gruppenleiter B—*Volkstum*—SS-*Ostubaf* Ehlich

B	1	*Volkstumarbeit*	SS-*Hstuf* Hummitzsch
	2	*Minderheiten*	-
	3	*Rasse und Volksgesundheit*	SS-*Hstuf* Schneider
	4	*Einwanderung und Umsiedlung*	SS-*Stubaf* Müller
	5	*Besetzte Gebiete*	SS-*Stubaf* Löwzu Steinfurth

Gruppenleiter C – *Kultur* – SS-*Stubaf* Spengler

C	1	*Wissenschaft*	SS-*Hstuf* Turowski
	2	*Erziehung und religioses Leben*	SS-*Hstuf* Seibert

	3	*Volkskultur und Kunst*	SS-*Hstuf* Rössner
	4	*Presse, Schriftum, Rundfunk*	SS-*Hstuf* Kielpinski

Gruppenleiter D – *Wirtschaft* – SS-*Stubaf* Seibert

D	1	*Ernährungswirtschaft*	SS-*Stubaf* Seibert
	2	*Handel, Handwerk und Verkehr*	-
	3	*Finanzwirtschaft, Währung, Banken, Börsen, Versicherungen*	SS-*Hstuf* Kröger
	4	*Industrie und Energiewirtschaft*	-
	5	*Arbeits- und Sozialwesen*	SS-*Stubaf* Leetsch

Appendix III

Organisation of RSHA *Amt* III, 1943

RSHA *Amt* III—*Deutsche Lebensgebiete*
Amtschef—SS-*Brigadenführer* Otto Ohlendorf

Gruppe	*Referat*	*Sachgebiet*	*Referent*

Gruppenleiter A—*Fragen der Rechtsordnung und des Reichsaufbaus*—SS-*Ostubaf* Gengenbach

A	1	*Allgemeine Fragen der Lebensgebietsarbeit*	SS-*Stubaf* Sepp
	2	*Rechtsleben*	SS-*Stubaf* Malz
	3	*Verfassung und Verwaltung*	SS-*Stubaf* Reinholz
	4	*Allgemeines Volksleben*	SS-Ustuf Hongen
	5	*Allgemeine Polizeirechtsfragen, Polizeiwirkungsrecht, Polizeiverfassungsrecht, Spezialgesetzte polizeilicher Natur und Gesetzgebungstechnik*	SS-*Ostubaf* Neifeind

Gruppenleiter B—*Volkstum*—SS-*Staf* Ehlich

B	1	*Volkstumsarbeit*	SS-*Stubaf* Strickner
	2	*Minderheiten*	SS-*Hstuf* Hirnich
	3	*Rasse- und Volksgesundheit*	-
	4	*Staatsangehörigkeit u. Einbürgerung*	SS-*Stubaf* Ramin
	5	*Besetzte Gebiete*	SS-*Ostubaf* Löw zu Steinfurth

Gruppenleiter C—*Kultur*—SS-*Ostubaf* Spengler

C	A	*Sonderfragen*	SS-*Stubaf* Hirche
	1	*Wissenschaft*	SS-*Stubaf* Turowski
	2	*Erziehung und religioses Leben*	SS-Stubaf Böhmer
	3	*Volkskultur und Kunst*	SS-*Stubaf* Rössner
	4	*Presse, Schriftum, Rundfunk,*	SS-*Stubaf* Kielpinski
		Einsatzauswärtungsstelle	

Gruppenleiter D—*Wirtschaft*—SS-*Ostubaf* Seibert

D	a	*Lektorat, einschliesslich*	
		Wirtschaftspresse, Zeitschriften	
		und Schriftum	
	b	*Kolonialwirtschaft*	
	S	*Sonderfragen und Sachinspektion*	SS-*Stubaf* Maly
	West	*Besetzte Westgebiete*	SS-*Stubaf* Zehlein
	Ost	*Besetzte Ostgebiete*	SS-*Stubaf* Hanisch
	1	*Ernährungswirtschaft*	SS-*Stubaf* Tegtmeyer
	2	*Handel, Handwerk und Verkehr*	SS-*Stubaf* Buchheim
	3	*Finanzwirtschaft, Währung,*	SS-*Hstuf* von Reden
		Banken und Börsen, Versicherungen	
	4	*Industrie und Energiewirtschaft*	SS-*Ostuf* Tiedt
	5	*Arbeits- und Sozialwesen*	SS-*Ostubaf* Leetsch

Appendix IV

Organisation of RSHA *Amt* III, 1944–1945

RSHA *Amt* III—*Deutsche Lebensgebiete*
Amtschef—SS-*Gruppenführer* Otto Ohlendorf
Abteilung III B—*Geschäftsstelle und Sachinspektion*
Abteilungsleiter—SS-*Stubaf* Jaskulski

Gruppe	*Referat*	*Sachgebiet*	*Referent*

Gruppenleiter A—*Fragen der Rechtsordnung und des Reichsaufbaus*—SS-*Ostubaf* Höppner

A	1	*Allgemeine Fragen des*	-
		Lebensgebietsarbeit	
	2	*Rechtsleben*	*Recht.anw.* Seidel
	3	*Verfassung und Verwaltung*	ORR Mäding
	4	*Allgemeines Volksleben*	SS-*Ustuf* Höngen

	5	*Allgemeine Polizeirechtsfragen*	SS-*Ostubaf* Rothmann
	S	*Geschäftsstelle und Sachinspektion*	SS-*Stubaf* Jaskulski

Gruppenleiter B—Volkstum und Volksgesundheit—SS-Staf Ehlich

B	S	*Sachinspektion*	SS-*Stubaf* Perey
	1	*Deutsches und Germanesdes Volkstum*	SS-*Ostubaf* Löw zu Steinfurth
	1a	*Deutsches Volkstum Südosten*	SS-*Ostuf* Hohlfeld
	1b	*Deutsches Volkstum Osten*	SS-*Hstuf* Hoeven
	1c	*Deutsches Volkstum Norden*	SS-*Ostubaf* Löw zu Steinfurth
	1d	*Deutsches Volkstum Westen* (Holland and Belgium)	SS-*Stubaf* Süss
	1e	*Deutsches Volkstum Westen* (France)	SS-*Stubaf* Perey
	2	*Fremdes Volkstum*	SS-*Stubaf* Buchardt
	2a	*Allgemeine Fragen (Auslanderarbeiter)*	SS-*Ustuf* Morawski
	2b	Estonians, Lithuanians, Latvians	SS-*Stubaf* Kortkampf
	2c	Czechs, Slovaks, Slovenes	SS-*Stubaf* Hirnich
	2d	Poles	SS-*Stubaf* Strickner
	2e	Russians	SS-*Ostuf* Pech
	2f	Ukraine	SS-*Stubaf* Schenk
	3	*Rassenpolitik u. Volksgesundheit*	SS-*Staf* Ehlich
	3a	*Bevölkerungs- u. Rassenbiologie*	*Fräulein* Wittmaack
	3b	*Gesundheitsführung*	Dr Gröger
	3c	*Gesundheitsfursorge*	Pietsch
	4	*Staatsangehörigkeit u. Einburgerung*	*Min.Rat* Duckhardt
	4a	*Allgemeine Fragen*	*Min.Rat* Duckhardt
	4b	*Einburgerung A–K*	*Amtsrat* Stumm
	4c	*Einburgerung L–Z*	*Amtsrat* Koplin

Gruppenleiter C—Kultur und Wissenschaft—SS-Staf Spengler

C	S	*Sachinspektion*	-
	1	*Wissenschaft*	SS-*Ostubaf* Rössner
	2	*Erziehung u. religioses Leben*	SS-*Stubaf* Böhmer
	3	Volkskultur und Kunst	SS-*Ostubaf* Rössner
	4	*Presse und Propaganda*	SS-*Ostubaf* Kielpinski
	5	*Waffenforschung und Waffenentwicklung*	SS-*Staf* Spengler

Gruppenleiter D—Wirtschaft—SS-Staf Seibert

D	1	*Ernährungswirtschaft*	SS-*Stubaf* Tegtmeyer
	2	*Handel, Handwerk u. Verkehr*	Dr Oesterreich

3	Banken, Versicherung, und Finanzwirtschaft	SS-*Stubaf* Reden
4	Industrie und Energie	SS-*Hstuf* Tiedt
5	Sozialwirtschaft	SS-*Ostubaf* Leetsch
S	Sachinspektion	SS-*Hstuf* Hempel
a	Lektorat	*Frau* Wehring

Gruppenleiter G—*Gesellschaftsnachrichtendienst*—SS-*Stubaf* Wenger

G	1	Nachrichtenversammlung	SS-*Hstuf* Cern
	2	Nachrichtenauswertung	SS-*Ostuf* Krüger
	3	Sachinspektion	-

Appendix V

Alphabetical Index of RSHA III personnel, 1939–1945

Note: Personnel known to be under postwar arrested are underlined.

Name and Rank	*Referat*	Remarks
Amelung, SS-*Stubaf* Waldemar	III B	1941–1945
Andersch, SS-*Ustuf* Heinz	III	June 1944
Barlen, Dr	III C4i	
Bau, SS-*Uschaf* Arthur	III D3	May 1943
Beck, SS-*Ustuf* Alfred	III A4	arrested by USFET
Berg, SS-*Stubaf* Alfred	III B5a	from Feb. 1941
Bergemann, SS-*Ostuf* Günther	III	
Bethcke, SS-*Hstuf* Theodor	III A4	
Beyer, SS-*Hstuf* Dr Hans-Joachim	III B1	*Referent*, 1940
Beyer, SS-*Stubaf* Herbert	III D5	evacuated to Bavaria, April 1945
Binding, SS-*Obf* Dr Kurt	III	
Bock, SS-*Ustuf* Hans	III	1944
Bockardt, SS-*Hstuf* Karl	III C2	1941–1944
Böhme, *Polizeiinsektor* Paul	III A3	1943
Böhmer, SS-*Stubaf* Dr Rudolf	III C2	evacuated to Bavaria, April 1945
Böhrsch, SS-*Hstuf* Dr Herbert	III B1	1940–1943
Boker, SS-*Oschaf* Adolf	III A1d	1943
Brandenburg, SS-*Stubaf* Walter	III	Liaison Officer to

		Ostministerium
Brandt, SS-*Rotf*		III B5a
Breier, SS-*Hschaf* Josef	III D1	1943
Buchardt, SS-*Ostubaf* Dr Friedrich	III B2	Worked in *Sonderkommando Ost* with Vlassov; at Innsbruck, April 1945
Buchheim, SS-*Stubaf* Erich	III D2	died in air raid, 29 April 1944
Carlsohn, SS-*Ustuf* Erich	III C4	1943
Chikowski, SS-*Ostuf* Artur	III D3b	1943
Damm, SS-*Ustuf* Heinz	III G	still in Berlin, 10 April 1945
Debald, SS-*Sturmmann* Matthias	III C3g	1943
Deisel, SS-*Hstuf* Theo	III C3	evacuated to Bavaria, April 1945
Deppner, SS-*Hstuf* Dr Erich	III C1	1940, then posted to BdS Den Haag
Dreher, SS-*Ustuf* Max	III D5	1943
Dressler, Kinnar von	III C3f	*Intendent*, 1943
Driesch, SS-*Ustuf* Heinrich	III D4	1943
Duckhardt, *Ministerialrat* Dr	III B4	Nov. 1943
Ehlich, SS-*Staf* Dr Hans	III B	*Gruppenleiter* B; arrested British Zone
Eichholz, SS-*Hstuf* Albert	III B1	1944–1945; then BdS Ungarn
Eickhoff, SS-*Hschaf* Heinz	III D5	1943
Eitner, SS-*Stubaf* Hermann	III D2	1943
Elling, SS-*Ostubaf* Georg	III A6	1940, III A3; 1941–1943, A6; May 1943 to Vatican; arrested in Italy
Endelmann, SS-*Schaf* Günther	III C4	1941–1943; then to KdS Lublin
Erreger, SS-*Sturmmann* Franz	III *Registratur*	1943
Farr, *Regierungsrat* Werner	III A3	1943
Felke [*sic*], SS-*Hstuf*	III D	
Ficke, SS-*Hstuf* Bernhard	III C5	evacuated to Bavaria, April 1945
Fischer, SS-*Hstuf* Dr Helmut	III C1	arrested by USFET
Frankenberg, SS-*Ostuf* Prof Richard	III B1	to 1943; then to BdS Oslo
Frenz, SS-*Sturmmann* Wilhelm	III C4	1943
Friedemann, SS-*Bewerber* Arno	III *Registratur*	1940, 1943
Gengenbach, SS-*Staf* Dr Karl	III A	*Gruppenleiter* III A; killed in vehicle accident near Munich, 25 Jan. 1944
Gern, SS-*Hstuf* Peter	III G	still in Berlin, Feb. 1945
Ghedina, SS-*Hstuf* Dr Gustav	III A	Sept. 1943, to BdS Italien
Gregor, SS-*Ostuf* Alfred	III C1	

Greil, SS-*Stuschaf Pol.Sek* Emil	III Gst.	1943
Groeger, Dr	III B3	
Grost, SS-*Oschaf* Dr Julius	III D3	died in an air-raid, 29 April 1944
Hachmann, SS-*Ustuf* Klaus	III D1	Nov. 1943, to BdS Athens
Hanusch, SS-*Hstuf* Rudolf	III D2	died in an air-raid, 29 April 1944
Haupt, SS-*Hstuf* Gerhardt	III D	1943–1945
Heffrich, SS-*Mann* Josef	III *Registratur*	1943
Heim, *Frau*	III A5	
Heinritz, SS-*Hstuf* Dr Martin	III D2	died in an air-raid, 29 April 1944
Heinze, SS-*Hstuf* Wolfram	III C5	March 1945, with SS-*Jagdverband*
Hempel, SS-*Hstuf* Wilhelm	III D2	
Hercht, SS-*Hstuf* POI Walter	III A3	
Herrmann, SS-*Hstuf* Emil	III A ZB	*Referent*, 1940
Herrschaft, SS-*Sturmmann* Hans	III B1	Nov. 1943
Heyer, SS-*Bewerber* Harold	III B4	1943
Heyner, SS-*Hschaf* Kurt	III B3	1940–1944
Hirche, SS-*Hstuf* Dr Emil	III Ca	Nov. 1943
Hirnich, SS-*Stubaf* Dr Erwin	III B2c	Jan. 1944, evacuated to Bavaria, 1945
Hoengen, SS-*Stubaf* Alfred	III A4	1943–1945; arrested British Zone
Höppner, SS-*Ostubaf* Dr Karl-Heinz	III A	*Gruppenleiter* A, 1944–1945; arrested in British Zone
Hoeven, SS-*Hstuf* Harry	III B1c	1940–1944
Höhnig, SS-*Hschaf* Max	III D	
Hohlfeld, SS-*Ostuf* Horst	III B1	1941–1945
Holz, SS-*Rotf* Konrad	III C2	1943
Hummitzsch, SS-*Ostubaf* Heinz	III B1	*Referent* 1940–1943; then BdS Brussels
Ilges, SS-*Stubaf* Wolfgang	III A3	1941–1943
Imhäuser, SS-*Mann* Walter	III D5	1943
Isigkeit, SS-*Uschaf* Horst	III C4	1943
Jäger, SS-*Hstuf* Leonhard	III D4	April 1945, to Flensburg with *Nordstab*
Jahnel, SS-*Sturmmann* Sepp	III *Registratur*	1943
Jarosch, SS-*Hstuf* Erwin	III Gst	1940; later went to RSHA IV
Jaskulsky, SS-*Stubaf* Dr Hans	III S	1940–1945; Flensburg in April 1945

Jedamzik, SS-*Stubaf* Eduard	III A	1944–1945; evacuated to Bavaria, 1945
Keller, SS-*Ustuf* Hans-Albrecht	III C	Nov. 1943
von Kielpinski, SS-*Ostubaf* Walter	III C4	1940–1945; evacuated to Bavaria, 1945
Klafft, SS-*Oschaf* Herbert	III D2	1944; then to BdS Italien
Klam, SS-*Hschaf* Paul	III B2	1943
Klauss, SS-*Ostuf* Herbert	III *Verw.*	1941–1943 *Verwaltungschef*
Kleist, SS-*Oschaf* Heinz	III *Registratur*	1940–1943
Klimek, SS-*Bewerber* Ewald	III B1	1941, 1943
Klughardt, SS-*Hschaf* Adolf	III B	1943
Knorr, SS-*Ostuf* Kurt	III A3	1943
Koellerer, SS-*Hstuf* Adolf	III D1	1940–1943, then to SD-*Ast* Augsburg
Kohnert, SS-*Ostuf* Fritz	III A4	1942–1944, then to BdS Denmark
Koplin, *Amtsrat*	III B4	
Kortkampf, SS-*Stubaf* Gerhard	III B2	1944–1945
Kriebitz, SS-*Ostuf* Kurt	III A	1944
Kröger, *Ministerialrat*	III B	
Kröger, SS-*Hstuf* Heinz	III D3	III D6, 1940; *Referent* III D3, 1941
Kumbier, SS-*Hstuf* Joachim	III D2	from 1940
Lehmann, SS-*Ostuf* Willy	III C	1940
Leetsch, SS-*Ostubaf* Dr Hans	III D1	1940–1945; at Flensburg, July 1945
Leloneck, SS-*Oschaf* Helmuth	III C4	1943–1945
Leposchutz, SS-*Rotf* Dr H	III A3	1943–1945
Leutkart, SS-*Stubaf* Thomas	III C	*Hilfsreferent*, 1943–1944
Liepart, SS-*Mann* Karl	III C4	1943
Löw zu Steinfurth, SS-*Ostubaf* Eberhard	III B5	*Referent*, 1940–1945; arrested British Zone
Lucke, SS-*Ostuf* Dr Hans	III C3	1943
Mäding, SS-*Stubaf* Dr Erhard	III A3	*Referent*, 1943–1945; arrested British Zone
Makowski, SS-*Stubaf* Hans	III C	1944–1945
Malz, SS-*Stubaf* Dr Heinrich	III A2	*Referent*, 1941–1945; *Adjutantur* Dr Kaltenbrunner, 1945; arrested British Zone
Markwardt, SS-*Hschaf* Willi	III D1	1940–1943, III D2; from 1943, III D1
Maulaz, SS-*Stubaf* Dr Kurt	III	1942–1943, then to BdS Paris

Maurer, SS-*Hstuf* Rolf	III D2	KIA in Russia, 8 Feb. 1943
May, SS-*Stubaf* Rudolf	III D5	*Leiter* III S, 1940–1945
Mayr, SS-*Hstuf* Heinz	III A	1941–1945; evacuated to Bavaria, 1945
Mehrbeck, Dr	III C4	*Lektorat*
Meier, SS-*Rotf* Josef	III A3	1943
Metze, SS-*Uschaf* Horst	III Db	1943
Molsen, SS-*Stubaf* Dr Heinrich	III	1944
Morawski, SS-*Ustuf* Walter	III B2	1943–1945
Müller, SS-*Ustuf*	III S	
Müller, SS-*Stubaf* Bruno	III B4	*Hilfsreferent*, 1940–1941
Müller, SS-*Oschaf* Karl	III A1d	
Müller, SS-*Hstuf* Reinhard	III C4	1940–1945; at Flensburg with *Nordstab*
Müller, SS-*Hschaf* Willi	III C2	
Müller, SS-*Hstuf* Wolfgang	III G	1944–1945
Nagel, SS-*Hstuf* Heinz	III C3	1943–1944
Neifeind, SS-*Ostubaf* Dr Kurt	III A5	1943–1944, then to BdS Paris
Nentwig, SS-*Ostuf* Hans	III D5	1943–1945
Neunkirchen, SS-*Hstuf* Paul	III C4a	from 1943
Nimz, SS-*Ostuf* Heinz	III C1	1940–1945
Nitsche, SS-*Ostuf* Ernst	III *Registratur*	1940–1945
Novack, SS-*Mann* Stephan	III *Registratur*	1943
Oehme, SS-*Hstuf* Walter	III C4	1943
Ohlendorf, SS-*Gruf* Otto	*Amtschef* III	1939–1945; arrested British Zone
Oesterreich, Dr	III D	
Pacher, SS-*Stubaf* Franz	III B2c	1945, arrested in Austria
Pape, SS-*Hstuf* Hans-Georg	III S	to 1945
Pech, SS-*Ostuf* Maximilian	III B2c	1944–1945
Pensel, SS-*Schaf* Friedrich	III A4	1943
Perey, SS-*Stubaf* Josef	III B1	1944–1945
Perl, SS-*Schaf*	III A4	1943
Peterlein, SS-*Uschaf* Helmut	III C1	1943
Pettschauer, SS-*Rotf* Heinz	III B5	1943
Pietsch, SS-*Rotf* Ernst	III B3	1943
Pongratz, SS-*Ustuf* Dr Alfred	III C1	1943
von Ramin, SS-*Stubaf* Hans-Henn	III B4	1941–1943, then to SD Litzmannstadt
Reinhardt, SS-*Ostuf* Dr Heinz	III A3	1941–1944, then to RSHA VI
Reinholz, SS-*Hstuf* Wolfgang	III A3	1941–1942
Renard, SS-*Hstuf* Dr Gerhard	III D	1944–1945

Ressing, SS-*Hschaf* Otto	III B1	1943
von Reden, SS-*Stubaf* Erich	III D2	111 D4, 1940; III D2, 1942; III D3, 1943–1945
Rodenberg, SS-*Stubaf* Dr Carl-H.	III B3	1941–1943, then to RSHA V
Rössner, SS-*Ostubaf* Dr Hans	III C3	1941–1945; arrested British Zone
Rothenburg, SS-*Stubaf* Dr	III B3	
Rother, SS-*Hschaf* Willi	III B5	1943
Rothmann, SS-*Ostubaf* Heinrich	III A2	1942–1945; evacuated to Bavaria, 1945
Schäper, SS-*Ostuf* Heinz	III S3	1942–1945
Schenk, SS-*Stubaf* Walter	III B2	1944–1945
Scherbaum, SS-*Uschaf* Kurt	III D	1943
Schienberg, SS-*Hschaf* Walter	III *Registratur*	1940
Schlamp, SS-*Hstuf* Fritz	III	from Sept. 1944
Schmauder, SS-*Bewerber* Philip	III A1d	1943
Schneider, SS-*Hstuf* Robert	III B3	*Referent*, 1941; KIA in Russia, 1942
Schonherr, SS-*Ostuf* Hans	III D5	1943
Schramm, SS-*Sturmmann* Albert	III C1	1943
Schröder, SS-*Stubaf* Kurt	III D5	to Nov. 1944, then to BdS Ungarn
Schubert, SS-*Hstuf* Heinz	III B	*Abt.Leiter* III B, Nov. 1943–Dec. 1944, then to SD Augsburg
Schulte, SS-*Ostuf* Gerd	III A ZB	1940
Schumann, SS-*Mann* Friedrich	III *Registratur*	1943
Schunke, SS-*Mann* Erich	III D5	1943
Seibert, SS-*Staf* Willy	III D2	*Referent*, 1940–1943, *Gruppenleiter* D, 1943–1945
Seidel, *Rechtsanwalt*	III A	
Seidel, SS-*Hstuf* Erich	III B2	1941–1945; at Flensburg, May 1945
Selke, SS-*Hstuf* Dr Lothar	III	from Sept. 1944
Seller, SS-*Hstuf* Herbert	III C4	1939–1945
Sepp, SS-*Stubaf* Dr Fritz	III A1	1941–1944, then SD-LA Königsberg
Seydel, SS-*Stubaf* Dr Helmut	III A2	arrested in British Zone
Seynstahl, SS-*Ostuf* Hans	III C4	1940–1941
Sigismund, SS-*Hstuf* Olaf	III C	1941–1944, then SD-A Weimar
Spengler, SS-*Staf* Dr Wilhelm	III C	1941–1945, *Gruppenleiter* from 1943
Sprenkmann, SS-*Hstuf* Fritz	III D5	1943–1945
Stadtler, Professor	III D	

Stanke, SS-*Hstuf* Eberhard	III C1	1944–1945
Steinbuch, SS-*Rotf* Gerhard	III C1	1943
Steinle, SS-*Oschaf* Hermann	III C3	1940–1944
Stiller, SS-*Hstuf* Kurt	III B	1944
Stolz, SS-*Hstuf* Karl	III D4	1943
Storz, SS-*Hstuf* Dr Alfred	III B4	1941–1944, then BdS Italien
Strickner, SS-*Stubaf* Dr Herbert	III B2	1942–1944, III B1; 1944–1945, III B2d
Strohm, SS-*Hstuf* Dr Eberhard	III G	1943–1945
Stumm, *Amtsrat*	III B4c	
Süss, SS-*Stubaf* Herbert	III B1	1941–1943, III B5; 1944–1945, III B1
Sweerts-Sporck, SS-*Sturmann*	III D4	
Tegtmeyer, SS-*Stubaf* Heinrich	III D1	1942–1945; at Flensburg, May 1945
Theiss, SS-*Ostuf* Adolf	III C2	1943
Tiedt, SS-*Hstuf* Dr Friedrich	III D2	1940–1943, III D2; 1943–1945, III D4
Toporissek, SS-*Oschaf* Heinrich	III A1	1943
Tourneau, SS-*Stubaf* Walther	III	
Trenz, SS-*Hstuf* Josef	III D4	1941–1945
Turowski, SS-*Stubaf* Dr Ernst	III C1	1941–Dec. 1943, then to BdS Italien
Ufken, SS-*Ustuf* Erich	III A1	1941–1944, then to BdS Trieste
Unterkreuten, SS-*Oschaf*	III	evacuated to Bavaria, April 1945
Volke, SS-*Ostuf* Heinz	III C	1943
Walter, SS-*Hstuf* Leo	III D3	1943
Wegener, SS-*Stubaf* Dr Ulrich	III G	1940–1943, III A; 1943–1945, III G
Weinsack, SS-*Schaf* Rudolf	III B5	
Weiss, SS-*Uschaf* Willi	III A2	1942–1945
Wolff, SS-*Hstuf* Erich	III Ca	1945
Zehlein, SS-*Stubaf* Dr Hans	III D4	1940–1943
Zielinski, SS-*Uschaf* Walter	III D4	
Zimmermann, SS-*Hstuf* Walter	III A1d	1942–1945

While Kaltenbrunner and Ohlendorf were being interviewed in London during the summer of 1945 about RSHA III, and CIWR compiling their Situation Report (above), taking into account interrogations in Germany and Austria of Ehlich, Löw zu Steinfurth and Höttl, one longstanding RSHA III *Gruppenleiter* was still under interrogation: SS-*Standartenführer* Willy Seibert. He had been *Gruppenleiter* III D, now detained at the British interrogation centre at Bad Nenndorf (CSDIC/

WEA) and being questioned. Seibert's final interrogation report, FR 37, was issued on 25 January 1946, a month after the CIWR situation report. Seibert had joined the SD-*Hauptamt* in Berlin in 1936 and worked in what became *Amt* III D from that time until the end of the war. His account of how RSHA III D worked complements the brief explanation by CIWR.

Appendix to FR 37—SS-*Staf* Willy Seibert

Penetration of economic life by RSHA *Gruppe* III D.

I. Introduction.
1. Economic matters, which in the early days (1934) of the SD-*Hauptamt* played only a minor part, came under *Zentralamt* II/2 and were dealt with by *Sachgebiet* II/23. With the reorganisation of the SD-*Hauptamt*, *Zentralamt* II became RSHA *Amt* III and *Sachgebiet* II/23 received the designation *Gruppe* III D. In the following report the department dealing with economic matters is referred to throughout as *Gruppe* III D.

II. Development of *Gruppe* III D.
2. 1936–1938
When Seibert joined *Amt* III in 1936 the penetration of economic life by *Gruppe* III D was quite insignificant. At the time *Gruppe* III D had to face a number of difficulties. For its information it depended entirely on V-men, recruited by the SD-*Abschnitte* from among officials in government departments dealing with economic matters and from among the employees of private business and industrial undertakings. Information was therefore limited, and as the HQ staff of III D consisted of only seven or eight persons in 1936, the build-up of the organisation proceeded slowly and with difficulty. Further, the activities were viewed with suspicion by Reich authorities and private enterprise alike. Both saw in it a kind of super-detective agency for ferreting out opponents of the Party. That this misconception arose was understandable, as RSHA *Amt* III formed part of an organisation which included the *Gestapo* and *Kripo*.

Gradually *Gruppe* III managed to dispel this mistrust. Its reports to the competent Reich authorities clearly showed that the aim of the *Gruppe* was to establish the effects of Government measures in the economic sphere. The authorities learned from these reports the usefulness of the *Gruppe*'s work and used them as a means of supplementing their own information.

3. 1938–Sept. 1939 and Agreement with Ministry of Labour

Early in 1938 a great impetus was given to the work of III D. In one of its reports the *Gruppe* informed the Ministry of Labour that there were too many workers in the area of a particular regional Labour Office (*Landesarbeitsamt*). The Ministry interpreted this report as a criticism of its work and declared that it would not countenance further interference by *Gruppe* III D. In order to clear up the affair a conference was arranged between RSHA *Amt* III and high officials of the Ministry of Labour. During the discussion a complete change in the attitude of the Ministry's officials took place. Not only did they acknowledge that reports of this nature were useful and even necessary for the efficient working of the Ministry, but they also considerably facilitated the work of *Gruppe* III D by drawing up an agreement with the *Gruppe*. As far as Seibert can remember the points were as follows:

a) As the intelligence service of the Party and State, the task of SD (III) is to obtain information of the effects of measures taken by Government departments and report on these.

b) RSHA will report to the *Reichsarbeitsministerium*. Arrangements will be made for a mutual exchange of information.

c) Regional offices of the Ministry of Labour (*Landesarbeitsämter*) will cooperate with SD-(*Leit*)*Abschnitte*. Arrangements will be made for an exchange of information.

d) Offices of the Ministry of Labour (*Arbeitsämter*) will cooperate with SD-*Aussenstellen* and arrangements will be made for an exchange of information.

e) All personnel under me are free to work for the SD. This will count as Party service.

(signed) Seldte (*Reichsminister*)

This agreement radically changed the position of III D. Soon other Government departments dealing with economic matters concluded similar agreements. From an under-cover service, whose existence had formerly been kept secret even from Dr Schacht for fear that he would refuse to support such a department (or even oppose it), *Gruppe* III D could now openly pursue its enquiries, and the reports which it issued were regarded by most departments as an essential aid for their own work.

The War Period

4. Rapid improvements in the status of *Gruppe* III D.

At the outbreak of war, Goering, as *Vorsitzender des Ministerrates für Reichsverteidigung*, ordered *Amt* III to submit a daily report (later this report was issued twice a week) to all Ministries, showing the results of and reactions to all

Government measures in the economic sphere. Private enterprises now began to realise that III D channels presented the quickest way by which difficulties, whether in the field of raw materials, labour etc., could be brought to the notice of the authorities, and came with their problems to the III D *Referenten* at their SD-*Abschnitt*. Thus III D no longer depended for its information on the services of V-men, it now obtained a large amount of voluntary information from many quarters in commerce and industry.

Cooperation with State Ministries

5. RUK (Ministry of Armaments)
In September 1943, RSHA *Amt* III supplied a report to RUK entitled 'The Production of Unessential Goods'. This report was viewed with such approval by Minister Albert Speer that he commissioned *Amt* III to produce regular reports of this nature. In order to facilitate the work of *Amt* III, in October 1943 Speer concluded an agreement similar to that existing between *Amt* III and the Ministry of Labour, with the following additional clause:

> 'Security regulations as laid down for factories do not apply to members of SD-*Stellen* (III D *Referenten*) who are provided with a special pass. They are to be treated as employees of my Ministry.'

III D *Referenten* were thus able to investigate problems personally within a factory and III D now had an official status in its dealings with industry.

Penetration into state economic departments expanded rapidly. Members of III D were accepted on the Planning Staff (*Arbeitsstab*) of many departments and proved very valuable, as they were able to take an objective view of difficulties and in many cases were able to estimate beforehand what effects certain measures would have.

The *Referatsleiter* of III D4 and *Seibert* attended conferences of the RUK in uniform, and kept III D currently informed of the policy of the Minister; at the same time they were able to offer the Ministry expert advice on the probable effects of intended measures. Seibert and the *Referatsleiter* of III D4 also accompanied Ministry officials on visits to factories. III D was thus able to make useful contacts with heads of firms and leading personalities in industry and commerce.

6. *Wirtschaftsministerium* [Ministry of Economics]
Cooperation with the *Wirtschaftsministerium* had existed over a number of years. It received a great impetus, however, when the head of RSHA *Amt* III, Ohlendorf, and *Staatssekretär* Dr Hayler entered the Ministry at end 1943. Officials made considerably more use of *Amt* III reports and readily provided information required by the *Amt*. Cooperation with the Commissioners of the Ministry, e.g.

the Commissioner for Rubber, Leather etc. was good, and III D was well informed of their policy and of the measures they intended to introduce.

7. Ministry of Transport
As an agreement between the Ministry of Transport and III D had been concluded, excellent facilities for penetration were afforded. Close cooperation was maintained with all the subordinate offices. During the war, transport was of prime importance for the supply of fuel, raw materials etc. to industry and for transport movements. As a result of wholesale bomb damage, transport problems became acute in the last years of the war. In this sphere the work of III D became correspondingly important. By the end of the war a *Referent* of III D2 had his office in the Ministry, so that he could discuss the III D short reports (*Kurzmeldungen*) on the spot with the competent officials. Seibert visited *Staatssekretär* Ganzenmüller every few weeks to discuss matters affecting policy. The *Reichsbahn Direktorate* in particular placed great value on III D reports, and, wherever possible, took action on them.

8. Ministry of Food and Agriculture
Good cooperation with the Ministry of Food and Agriculture had existed even before the written agreement was concluded. For a number of years members of III D1 (Agriculture) had attended all important conferences of the Ministry and knew all the leading personalities of the Ministry well. The *Referatsleiter* of III D1 visited the Ministry weekly and Seibert every four to six weeks. The Ministry asked for daily reports as far as possible. In addition to these, reports on special subjects were issued from time to time as requested by the Ministry.

9. Ministry of Labour
The agreement between the Ministry of Labour and III D is mentioned in para 3. RSHA *Amt* III was particularly well informed on questions of employment of labour and much useful material was supplied to the branch offices of the Ministry. The *Leiter* of III D5 (labour problems, housing and welfare) acted as Liaison Officer to Sauckel, the Commissioner for Employment of Labour. In an official capacity, and wearing uniform, he took part in all the important conferences which Sauckel summoned, thus ensuring a speedy and accurate evaluation of III D reports.

10. Autonomous Administrative Bodies
Penetration into independent administrative bodies (technical groups, Reich groups, Chambers, Committees, Rings, Fighter Staff and Armaments Staff) was good. During the war all these bodies were responsible for the execution of state tasks and cooperation existed under the same conditions as at the Ministries. Leading members of all these bodies soon learned that III D presented an opportunity of bringing their specific problems quickly to the notice of the highest

authorities. Particularly close was the cooperation with *Reichsgruppe* Handel [Trade] and its sub-offices (Ohlendorf had held an important post in this *Gruppe* before he entered the Ministry of Economics).

A *Referent* of III D4 (Industry) was permanently attached to the Armaments Staff and attended the daily conference there. This *Referent* learned at these conferences of intended changes in production etc. and was able to inform the III D *Referenten* of the SD-*Abschnitte* accordingly.

Penetration of Private Concerns

11. Seibert points out that a distinction must be made between RSHA *Amt* III's penetration into such matters as production, raw material, employment of labour on the one hand, and the inner workings and ramifications of big business on the other.

12. As regards questions of labour and materials penetration was very good. As these were of such importance to the war effort, III D concentrated on them and neglected the other side. Reports on these problems did not as a rule deal with the situation at individual factories, but were collations on such subjects as the following:

a)   Effects of closing down factories.
b)   Effects of changing factories over to the production of a different type of article.
c)   Supplies of raw materials.
d)   Supplies of fuel.
e)   Unessential production.
f)   Faulty use of manpower.
g)   Over-organisation.

Reports of this nature were issued almost daily.

13. Junkers Works, Dessau

In April 1945, OKL [Luftwaffe High Command] ordered the Junkers Works at Dessau to produce a six-engined bomber. The first fifteen aircraft were to be completed by July 1945, and serial production was to be assured from August 1945. On 5 April 1945 Seibert received a report from SD-*Abschnitt* Dessau stating that, at a time when the situation obviously called for fighter aircraft, the High Command was placing orders for the construction of a new type of bomber aircraft, a fact that was having a disquieting effect in the factory and among experts in the aircraft industry, this order was being interpreted as a sign that the people at the top were losing their nerve.

14. Messerschmitt Works, Augsburg

SD-*Abschnitt* Augsburg was very well informed about the Messerschmitt Works. It had current and detailed information about the production of the jet-fighter Me 262. Soon after serial production of the Me 262 had begun, OKL suddenly laid down that it was to be modified to enable it to be used as a bomber. This naturally involved important structural alterations. III D received a report from the SD-*Abschnitt* that this order was not being carried out to the letter, that a percentage of aircraft was being turned out as bombers, but that fighters were still being produced.

15. Schweinfurt Ball-bearing Works

SD-*Abschnitt* Nuremberg was very well informed about the ball-bearing works in the Schweinfurt area. After the severe Allied bombing of the works, *Generaldirektor* Kessler was entrusted with the task of rebuilding the works in another area. The III D *Referent* in Nuremberg was requested by Kessler to give special attention to the difficulties encountered in such a transfer of industry and to keep Kessler and RSHA *Amt* III informed daily. These reports were provided and proved very useful.

16. Henschel Factory, Kassel

In Kassel the III D *Referent* worked in close collaboration with the heads of the Henschel factory. One of the most important engineers at the factory, Stieler von Heydekamp, was also head of the committee for tank construction (*Ausschuss Panzerbau*), and through him the III D *Referent* obtained a good insight into tank construction in general.

17. Conclusion

In conclusion Seibert states that by good cooperation with the leading people in factories etc., the SD-*Abschnitte* were very well informed about routine matters and any special difficulties which arose. Any firms of which the III D *Referenten* did not know the leading personalities could easily be entered with the special pass issued to III D *Referenten*. Seibert emphasises that during the last year of the war there was no case of a head of a firm refusing to give information. Indeed, after the conclusion of the formal agreement, III D *Referenten* were kept fully occupied and could scarcely cope with all the visitors and reports received from industry.

Methods

18. Direction

Information was obtained by the *Referenten* of the SD-*Abschnitte* and passed on to RSHA *Amt* III D. From these reports *Amt* III was able to see where penetration was good or lacking, and was able to direct the SD-*Abschnitte* accordingly.

19. Work Groups

At most SD-*Abschnitte* the III D *Referent* organised small work groups (*Arbeitskreise*). These consisted of unpaid officials and in an industrial area of the heads of factories, and in an agricultural area of the chief farmers, whose confidence the III D *Referent* had been able to gain. The group met as a rule once a week or once a fortnight. Visits to the SD-*Abschnitt* from III D were arranged; thus the *Abteilungsleiter* of III D or Seibert was able to attend meetings of these work groups.

Shortly before the end of the war Seibert attended a meeting of a work group in Hamburg. There were ten or twelve persons present, all either leading engineers or heads of factories. The subject debated was 'The Withholding of Manpower in Shipyards and in Factories'. Each person present stated his views and experiences. A secretary kept minutes of the meeting so that the III D *Referent* could prepare a report. In addition to this main topic of discussion, individual reports from the SD-*Aussenstellen* to the SD-*Abschnitt* were presented and discussed. At this meeting Seibert noted that the III D *Referent* in Hamburg had an exceptionally good insight into the shipyards and factories in that city. Seibert suggests that this III D *Referent*, SS-*Hstuf* Werner, could give additional information on penetration of III D into industry.

Channels of Reports

20. RSHA *Amt* III and III D had no direct means of receiving reports from or making enquiries directly to industry. It was laid down that the SD-*Abschnitte* were to be the link between III D and industry. This rule was adhered to for the best part, but in the following exceptional cases the link was a direct one:

a) The head of a factory summoned to attend a conference of the Armaments Staff of the *Reichswirtschaftsministerium* in Berlin, who knew a III D official personally, occasionally visited III D and reported on conditions at his factory.
b) The head of a factory, who in his area had a problem which affected another area would sometimes arrange through the SD-*Abschnitt* to have an interview with III D in Berlin.
c) The head of a factory, who at the same time was a member of a Ring, Chamber or Committee of Industry, sometimes brought his problem directly to III D.

Seibert emphasised that these cases were irregular. The directive remained that all reports and enquiries between industry and III D should go via the SD-*Abschnitte*.

Reports of RSHA *Amt* III

A. *Meldungen aus dem Reich*

21. At the beginning of the war, Goering ordered that *Amt* III send in regular reports to the chief Party, State and *Wehrmacht* offices on the effects of measures which had been introduced. This was done daily at first. After a few months these reports were submitted only twice weekly. They consisted of information received from III A, B, C and D and were known as '*Meldungen aus dem Reich*'.

22. The '*Meldung*' was divided into five parts and followed a uniform pattern, *viz.*:

a)   General picture of morale—produced by III A
b)   Legal questions—produced by III A
c)   Public Health—produced by III B
d)   Cultural questions, and education—produced by III C
e)   Economics and Industry—produced by III D

23. Distribution

The distribution of these reports was laid down originally by Goering, it included:

> Commissioner for the Four-Year-Plan (Goering)
> *Parteikanzlei* (Party Chancellery) (Bormann)
> *Reichskanzlei* (Reich Chancellery) (Lammers)
> OKW (*Amt allgemeiner Wehrmachtsangelegenheiten*)
> Propaganda Ministry (Goebbels)
> *Fachminister* (Specialist Minister) and *Staatssekretäre* (Secretaries of States) from whose spheres reports had been obtained.

Later the distribution was increased by Ohlendorf to include any other authorities who were concerned or interested. Normally, however, the distribution was laid down separately for each report. Seibert gives the following as a typical distribution list of a normal '*Meldung*':

> Commissioner for Four-Year-Plan   } Concerned with
> Party Chancellery   } or interested in
> Reich Chancellery   } Parts a–c
> Ministry of Propaganda   }
> Ministry of the Interior   … in Part c
> Ministry of Justice   … in Part b
> Health Minister   … in Part c
> Reich Medical Chamber   … in Part c
> Ministry of Economics   … in Parts a and c

Ministry of Transport	... in Parts a and c
Ministry of Armaments	... in Part c
Reich Dept for Coal	... in Part c
Reich Dept for Crude Oil	... in Part c
Ministry of Education	... in Part d

Occasionally an office received only the part which concerned it.

Special Reports

24. By request special reports were produced by one *Gruppe* and published by the *Amt*. On rare occasions composite special reports, prepared by several *Gruppen*, were also published. Other special reports were produced giving more complete details of problems dealt with in the '*Meldungen aus dem Reich*'.

25. Distribution

Reports requested by one office were normally only sent to that office. Other special reports were distributed to all departments and bodies who might be interested.

   As an example of the distribution of a special report on 'The Fixing of a New Scale of Wages in the Metal Industry is Disadvantageous to Skilled Workers', Seibert has suggested the following:

> Commissioner for the Four-Year-Plan (Goering)
> Party Chancellery (Bormann)
> Minister of Labour (Seldte)
> Commissioner for the Employment of Manpower (Sauckel)
> Leader of the German Labour Front (Ley)
> German Labour Front Special Office for Metal Industry
> Minister of Economics (Funk)
> Minister for Armaments (Speer)

Short Reports

26. Short reports were issued by *Gruppen* and/or *Abteilungen* daily. They consisted of memoranda on subjects, the investigation of which had been requested.

27. Distribution

The distribution list of such reports was normally drawn up by the *Leiter* of the *Abteilung*, but in the case of a more important memo the *Gruppenleiter* sometimes fixed the distribution himself.

Abteilung III D1 sent memoranda almost daily to the offices of the Ministry of Food. A report entitled 'Lack of Storing Space for Grain' had the following distribution:

> Personal *Referenten* of *Reichsminister* Backe
> Secretary of State Ricke (Ministry of Food)
> Reich Department for Grain
> Competent officials of the Ministry of Food

A report entitled 'Lack of Leather is holding up Shoe Repairs' went to:

> Ministry of Economics, Handicrafts Dept
> Ministry of Economics, *Referat* Leather
> *Reichsstelle* for Leather
> *Reichsstelle* for Rubber
> Head of *Reich* Shoemakers' Guild Association
> *Parteikanzlei*, Economics Gruppe.

This report was issued by CSDIC/WEA (Bad Nenndorf) on 25 January 1946.

Notes

* The National Archives, Kew, KV 3/187: Situation Report No. 3—RSHA III.
* The National Archives, Kew, KV 3/187: Willy Seibert Final Iterrogation (FR 37).
1 The report did not fully explain that members of the *Kriminalpolizei* (*Kripo*) and the *Geheime Staatspolizei* (*Gestapo*) were part of the German civil service whose salaries were paid by the State; the SD, being a Nazi Party organization its members were paid salaries from Party funds.
2 RSHA Abt. III D may have issued guidelines but the local recruitment of foreign labour, especially in the East, was the work of the German civil administration.
3 Alsace Lorraine (sometimes called Elsaß and Lothringen) were annexed by Germany in 1940. These regions of northeast France bordering Germany were based at Metz.
4 This arrangement of early mobile telephones involved a person on the ground talking to a person in an aircraft circling over head, up to 10,000 feet. The Germans copied this from captured telephones taken from US agents arrested in France. The OSS called it the Joan-Eleanor system, J-E for short.

3

Situation Report No. 4: *Amt* IV of the RSHA

INDEX

Part I: Organisational Development of *Amt* IV
Part II: The Function of *Amt* IV
Part III: The *Gegnernachrichtendienst* and *Dienststelle* IV N
Part IV: The *Gestapo* outside Germany
Part V: Miscellaneous

Appendix I: Organisation of *Amt* IV, 1939–1940
Appendix II: Organisation of *Amt* IV, 1941–1943
Appendix III: Organisation of *Amt* IV, 1943–1944
Appendix IV: Organisation of *Amt* IV, 1944–1945
Appendix V: Chart of the organisational development of *Amt* IV, 1939–1945
Appendix VI: Alphabetical Index of *Amt* IV personnel, 1939–1945

Part I

Organisational Development of *Amt* IV

A. The Development of the *Gestapo* before the War.

(Note: Part A of Part I of this Publication should be read in conjunction with Part I of the Situation Report on *Amt* III, dealing with the development of the *Sicherheitsdienst* before the war.)

1. General.

No attempt will be made to deal in detail with the many-sided activities of *Amt IV* in this publication, which is largely restricted to the C.I. [counter-intelligence] aspects of the *Gestapoamt*, and to giving some picture of the important part which the *Amt* as a whole played in the events leading up to the creation of the RSHA, and in the subsequent power politics which marked the development of relations between the various *Ämter* of the RSHA.

Broadly speaking, in the outwardly co-ordinated police system which the RSHA represented, the *Gestapo* played the part of the executive department, and as such was regarded as an instrument of power on which the continued existence of the Party depended. It found its support therefore in the highest strata of the Nazi Party, and was in consequence the strongest and most influential of the *Ämter*. Curiously enough, however, it was not a Party organisation, and to appreciate this peculiar situation it is necessary to trace the history of the Gestapo from its creation in 1933.

2. The Nazi Party and the Police Services in 1933.

When the Nazi Party assumed power in January 1933 its primary objective was to obtain control over a unified *Reich* police service, which at that time did not exist. Germany itself was divided into *Länder*, each of which had its own police service, while the Party itself had its *Sicherheitsdienst* [SD] under Heydrich, which represented a security service of the SS itself, and as such had territorial jurisdiction. It was therefore a Party security service, and not a secret state police, and the first efforts of the Party were directed towards extending its jurisdiction over the various police services by the appointment of high-ranking SD personnel to positions of authority in these services. In this way, shortly after the *Machtübernahme*, Himmler had become chief of the political police in Bavaria, with Heydrich as his second-in-command, the latter at the same time fulfilling the function of chief of the SD *des* RFSS.

3. Goering and the *Gestapo* in Prussia.

Meantime Goering as Prime Minister of Prussia had founded the *Politische Polizei* in that state, known as the *Staatspolizei* or Stapo. By April 1935 this organisation had had become the *Geheimestaatspolizei* with Goering as its chief and *Oberregierungsrat* Diels virtually directing its activities. It was this organisation of Goering's which was to become the subsequent RSHA *Amt IV*, retaining its title of *Gestapo*, and it is to be noted that the authority for its creation was under Prussian law, which technically remained the only authority until the dissolution of the RSHA. The subsequent chain of events were confined to the absorption of the *Gestapo* into a unified police system, and placing it eventually under the control of the Party, though not dissolving it and replacing it by a Party organisation.

4. Efforts to gain control of the *Gestapo*.

The years 1933 to 1936 represented the continual efforts of Himmler to acquire control over Goering's organisation, which he finally achieved by a succession of measures. By 1934 Himmler had become the *Politische Polizeikommandeur der Länder*, in which capacity he controlled the various provincial police forces, without however these forces losing their own identity and independence. The police forces in Germany still remained under the control of the state organisation under the Ministry of the Interior.

5. Himmler as Deputy Chief of the *Gestapo* in 1934.

In the spring of 1934 the ascendancy of Himmler was shown by his appointment as Deputy Chief of the Prussian Gestapo in place of Diels, While therefore being subordinate to Goering the strong position which he held as *Reichsführer*-SS and *Politische Polizeikommandeur* made him of course stronger than Goering himself, and marked the first step towards the absorption of the *Gestapo* into the Party itself. In June 1936 Himmler was appointed *Chef der Deutschen Polizei* in the Reich Ministry of the Interior, being directly responsible in this capacity to the Minister of the Interior himself. In his capacity however as *Reichsführer*-SS he was at the same time directly responsible to Hitler, and in this way was able to circumvent the Minister of the Interior—a state of affairs which was recognised by a law in May 1937 giving Himmler equal status with the Minister of the Interior in the issue of decrees concerning the German Police Services. Again it is important to note that any decree issued by Himmler under this authority were ministerial and not Party decrees.

6. Creation of the *Sicherheitspolizei* in 1936.

Armed with this power however, Himmler was not long in creating the centralized police service under virtual Party control, which had been his main branches, the *Ordnungspolizei* and the *Sicherheitspolizei*, the latter of which represented a fusion of the *Gestapo* and the *Kripo*. The important development was that Heydrich was appointed chief of the new *Sicherheitspolizei*, which meant in fact that the Party now also controlled the *Gestapo*. The other important feature was that the *Sicherheitspolizei* was granted control over the whole of Germany in its functions, while in September 1936 the *Gestapoamt* was made responsible for the duties of the political police forces which were to assume the general name of *Geheimestaatspolizei*.

7. The '*Gesetz für die Geheimestaatspolizei*' in 1936.

Thus by 1936 the Party has assumed complete control of all secret police in Germany through the appointment of Heydrich as Chief of the *Sipo*, but again it is to be noted that the personnel of the *Gestapo* still remained in the main state servants, and only at the higher levels was there any marked degree of infiltration by the Party. The power of the *Gestapo* was also confirmed in February 1936 by the Prussian law entitled '*Gesetz für die Geheimestaatspolizei*', which gave the *Gestapo* authority to arrest and imprison without reference to the courts of law. It will be noted that the fact that this decree was issued as a Prussian law indicated that the existence of the *Gestapo* under its original decree was still recognised.

8. The Ascendancy of the SD in 1938.

In February 1938 a further decree issued by the Reich Ministry of the Interior gave the SD responsibility for the control of all persons, activities and events which might interfere with the dominance of the Nazi Party. This decree meant that the *Sipo* came under the control of the SD—a state of affairs which had of course virtually existed through the position of Heydrich as Chief of the *Sipo*. During this period Heydrich still remained Chief of the SD-*Hauptamt*, which contained the germs of the later *Ämter* III and VI of the RSHA. But his chief concern was in developing the *Gestapoamt*, as that *Amt* was an executive branch, the functions of which gave its Chief the power to supervise any persons or groups opposed to him.

9. The Creation of the RSHA in 1939.

There now existed two organisations—the *Gestapoamt* under the control of the *Sicherheitspolizei*, and the SD-*Hauptamt* under the control of the *Sicherheitsdienst*. There now remained only one step towards further centralisation, which came with the creation of the RSHA in 1939, effecting the fusion of the *Gestapo*, *Kripo*, and SD, and making them subordinate to the CdS. The *Ämter* of the RSHA are too well known to require repetition. For the purpose of this publication, the *Gestapo* now became *Amt* IV under SS-*Gruf* Müller, and its subsequent development is dealt with in Part B. Heydrich of course became the new CdS, and in this capacity now controlled on behalf of the Party all police forces, secret or otherwise, in Germany. But the strongest and most powerful weapon in his hands was *Amt* IV.

    The above summary of the development of the *Gestapo* has been given on broad lines only; no account has been taken of the development of the relations on a working basis between the *Gestapo* and the SD, a subject which is dealt with in the Situation Report on *Amt* III. It is in fact impossible to treat these two services separately in the period preceding the creation of the RSHA, and this account of the development of the *Gestapo* should be read in conjunction with Part I of the Situation Report on *Amt* III.

B. The Development of *Amt* IV between 1939 and 1944.

1. The Organisation of *Amt* IV, 1939–1940.

The organisation chart of *Amt* IV such as it was constituted on the creation of the RSHA in 1939 is shown at Appendix I. The most important *Gruppe* at this early stage was *Gruppe* IV A as it dealt with the opposition groups within Germany, the emphasis at the time being strongly on the communist circles, against which all *Stapostellen* were very active. Later more attention was paid to religious sects, as was evidenced by the creation of a new *Gruppe* IV B in 1941. This early organisation was of course a tentative effort, as the *Gestapo* has assumed a wider field than it had before, while its scope was greatly increased by the succession of military victories in 1940, and the subsequent posting of *Gestapo* personnel to the various *Sipo* and SD *Einsatzkommandos* operating with the armies in the field. By the end of 1940 the BdS had been set up in occupied territory, and on the staff of the BdS the *Gestapo* was usually the most strongly represented of all the *Ämter*. The changes, therefore, in the general situation and the extended field of *Amt* IV activities soon brought about a re-organisation of the *Gruppe* at RSHA level, the re-organisation taking place by the early part of the year.

2. Re-organisation in early 1941.
The re-organisation of *Amt* IV coincided with the general re-organisation of the RSHA, which saw the splitting up of the original *Amt* I and the creation of *Amt* VII. In this general post, *Amt* IV had taken over the *Zentralsichtvermerkstelle* from *Amt* I, which was incorporated into *Referat* IV C1, the department acting as the Central Card Index and Record Office for the *Amt*.

More notable however was the creation of the new *Gruppe* IV B dealing wirh religious sects, previously a mere *Referat* in *Gruppe* IV A, a change which indicated the growing importance attached by *Amt* IV to the danger to the State of religious activity. It is noteworthy too that this new department, under SS-*Stubaf* Hartl, worked in close co-operation with *Referat* III C2 of *Amt* III, the latter department having direct representation in the *Gestapo* offices.

The new *Gruppe* IV B also extended the scope of *Amt* IV to cover Freemasonry in *Referat* IV B3, while the notorious Eichmann was now in charge of the Jewish *Referat* IV B4, which subject had previously been merely a sub-section of *Referat* IV D3. The original *Gruppe* IV B now completely disappeared, its functions being absorbed into the remaining *Gruppe* (see Appendix V).

Notable too was the creation of small independent sections not controlled by the *Gruppen* but coming under the direct supervision of the *Amtschef* [Müller]. The most important of these was the *Dienststelle* IV N under Halmanseger, which had previously been *Referat* IV C4, the change indicating the increased importance attached to *Amt* IV's Information network, a subject which is dealt with in detail in Part III.

Similarly, the former *Referat* IV D5 had now become the special section IV (P) dealing with liaison with foreign police services. A further indication of the growing influence of *Amt* IV was the creation of the *Geschäftsstelle* acting as the administrative office for the *Gruppe* and at the same time absorbing the former *Referat* IV C3.

The effects of the military campaigns are also shown by the creation of the new *Referat* IV D4 dealing with the occupied territories in Western and North-Western Europe. *Gruppe* IV E on the other hand remained practically unchanged under Schellenberg, the future *Amtschef* VI, although by 1941 it had absorbed the old IV B3 dealing with commerce and industry.

3. Re-organisation in autumn 1943.

Amt IV continued under the organisational structure adopted in 1941 with few changes until the autumn of 1943; then the change was a simple one and merely represented the absorption of *Gruppe* II B of *Amt* II dealing with passports, and the subsequent creation of a new *Gruppe* in *Amt* IV, IV F under *Min Rat* Krause. With the creation of this new *Gruppe*, the *Zentralsichtvermerkstelle* which had been part of *Referat* IV C1, passed over to the new *Gruppe* to become *Referat* IV F5. This *Gruppe* presumably also absorbed into *Referat* IV F4 the old IV (P) dealing with foreign police.

The only other change of note during the three years was the creation of an additional *Referat* in *Gruppe* IV D, *Referat* IV D5, which dealt with occupied territory in the East.

C. *Amt* IV after the absorption of the *Abwehr* in 1944.

1. General Trends.

The re-organisation of the *Gruppe* in the summer of 1944 coinciding with the absorption of the *Abwehr* into *Amt* IV marked the creation of a completely new structure, the changes being easy to visualise on general lines, but complicated in details. The re-organisation was the culmination of the long struggle between the SD and the *Abwehr*, and when the *Abwehr* was finally to be dissolved in the summer of 1944, there arose a further struggle between Schellenberg and Müller for the major share in the spoils. The victory went in substance to Schellenberg with the creation of the *Mil.Amt* under *Amt* VI, while in the sphere of counter-espionage which Müller had wished to appropriate in its entirety to *Amt* IV, the creation of the new *Gruppe* VI Z gave control of counter-espionage to neutral territories to *Amt* VI. Müller had to be content with those elements of *Abwehr* III F dealing with counter-espionage within Germany itself, while at the same time [*Abwehr*] *Abteilungen* III C and III N were also taken over by *Amt* IV.

2. The new *Gruppen* A and B.

The *Amt* was now divided into two *Gruppen*, A and B, the general division being that the former elements of *Amt* IV came under *Gruppe* IV A, while *Gruppe* IV B represented the counter-espionage section of the *Amt*, being roughly a fusion of the former *Gruppe* IV D and IV E, and those elements of the *Abwehr* which had been taken over. This broad distinction however had many exceptions. IV E2 for example became IV A3b, while *Gruppe* IV B also included elements of the former *Gruppe* IV F. The redistribution of functions are shown at Appendix V, but again it is not possible to be precise.

3. The Creation of *Gruppen* IV C and IV ZABP.
Shortly after the reorganisation, a further modification took place by the creation of the new *Gruppe* IV C, replacing the newly created IV A3c, and absorbing the *Zollgrenzschutz* of the *Finanzministerium*. This change is dealt with in detail in Part II C.

A further special section was created in IV ZABP, which represented the absorption of the former censorship department of *Abwehr* III. The changes involved in the major reorganisation are dealt with in more details in Part II under the functional aspects of *Amt* IV.

D. The organisational structure of the *Gestapo* in Germany.

1. General Structure.
The *Gestapo* in Germany exercised its authority through a series of subordinate offices throughout the country, but the organisation, which seems simple on the surface, has certain complications due to the nature of the origins of the *Gestapo* itself, and to the fact that the *Gestapo* remained a State organisation under Party control. It was mentioned in Part I, A, Para. 6, that in September 1936 the *Gestapa* was made responsible for the supervision of all political police forces in Germany, which forces were thenceforth to assume the title of *Geheimestaatspolizei*. Again therefore the new *Gestapo* framework covering Germany was built on an existing organisation, the essential features of which were not dissolved. The former *Staatspolizei* taken over by the *Gestapo* in 1936 had a regional organisation in Germany consisting of *Staatspolizeileitstellen, Staatspolizeistellen* and *Staatspolizeiaussenstellen*, contracted respectively to *Stapolst, Stapost*, and *Stapo-Aust*. The new *Gestapoamt* did not replace these designations, but introduced a new method exercising control over them.

2. The *Stellen* in Germany.
It is important to note that the *Stapostellen* were not subordinated to the *Leitstellen*, the difference in designation indicating the area controlled, a *Leitstelle* usually being established in a *Wehrkreis*, the *Stapostellen* in a *Regierungsbezirk*. Orders from *Amt* IV were passed directly to the two types of *Stellen* and not to the *Stapostelle* through the *Leitstelle*. This feature led to much confusion, as a *Stapostelle* might well come within the area of a *Stapoleitstelle*, resulting in considerable duplication and overlapping. The *Stapoleitstelle* could however act as a co-ordinating for the *Stapostellen* in its area, but not as a directing agency.

Both the *Stapoleitstellen* and the *Stapostellen* might control an indefinite number of branch offices according to the importance of the area which they controlled. These branches went under the name either of *Aussenstelle* or *Aussendienststelle*; the *Aussendienststelle* being of a higher grade than the *Aussenstelle*, as it in turn could have subordinate formations, while the *Aussenstelle* could not. During the course of the war, many *Stapostellen* were downgraded to *Aussendienststellen* as a result of manpower problems incurred by the creation of the *Einsatzkommandos* and BdS in occupied territory.

3. The IdS and BdS.

With the creation of of the *Sicherheitspolizei* in 1936, efforts were made towards the centralisation at regional levels of co-ordinated control under the Party, corresponding to the position at Headquarters of Heydrich himself. This was achieved to a certain extent by the creation of the *Inspekteure der Sipo und des* SD, or IdS, who exercised a supervisory function over the *Stapostellen* and SD-*Abschnitte* in areas under his control, which normally corresponded to a *Wehrkreis*. In occupied territory a similar function was carried out by the *Befehlshaber der Sipo und des* SD (BdS) with the important addition that the BdS had complete command over the forces under his control in matters of training and discipline, etc. In the latter stages of the war it was customary for an IdS in an area near the operational fronts to be upgraded to BdS for more efficient co-ordination in defence.

The general tendency was for the IdS and BdS to centralise in his department the direction and supervision of the *Gestapo* and SD-*Stellen* under his command, a tendency which became more marked as the war progressed. In consequence, the *Stapoleitstellen* and the SD-*Leitabschnitte* lost most of their independence and represented at regional level a degree of centralisation of power which had first recurred at the highest level with the creation of the *Sicherheitspolizei* in 1936. The chain of command from *Amt* IV to the *Stapostellen* was therefore through the IdS and BdS.

4. Internal organisation of the *Stapostelle*.

Little needs to said about the internal organisation of *Stapostellen* in Germany, as with certain modifications they were organised more or less on the lines of the *Amt* itself, there being at this level a re-organisation in the summer of 1944 corresponding to the major change in the *Amt* itself. Prior to the changes in 1944, the *Stapostelle* normally had three sections, of which the first was administrative and the third a liaison section with the *Abwehr* on counter-espionage matters. *Abteilung* II was sub-divided into lettered sections with further numbered *Referate*, e.g. II A4, a section which would correspond in the *Amt* to *Referat* IV A4, etc. The only difference therefore was that while the *Amt* used Roman IV, the *Stellen* used Roman II.

With the major re-organisation in 1944, sections II and III were abolished at *Stapostellen* level, being replaced by a new section IV. As counter-espionage for the new *Gruppe* IV B was conducted through the old *Abwehrstellen*, there was no need for any lettered sections at regional level as the sections corresponded only with *Gruppe* A in the *Amt*. Otherwise the *Stapostelle* used the same designation as the *Amt*; for example, *Abt* IV 3d in a *Stapostelle* would correspond to *Hilfsreferat* IV A3d in the *Amt*.

There is little point in analysing any further the organisation of the *Stapostellen* as each *Stelle* modified its organisation according to local conditions, either omitting a section for which there was no use, or adding a section of its own to deal with some local problem. On the other hand it is to be noted that in occupied territory, the BdS represented an RSHA in miniature, and in such cases the breakdown of *Abteilung* IV of the BdS usually closely followed the breakdown of *Amt* IV at RSHA level. Even in this case, however, minor variations are frequently met with.

Part II

The functions of the *Gestapo*

General.

The functions of the *Gestapo* are dealt with in this Part according to the final organisational structure of the *Amt*. These functions for the most part call for little comment, as basically they remained the same throughout the war, though some aspects of the work increased in importance with the changes in the war situation, as in the case of, for example, of the supervision of foreign workers, when such large numbers were sent to the *Reich* during and after 1942. There is therefore little development in *Amt* IV work that calls for study, except in minor points which are noted in their proper context. Geographically speaking, too, there is little difference to be found in *Gestapo* work except for such emphasis as local conditions may have imposed, so that the work of an *Abteilung* IV of an *Einsatzkommando* in Tunis differs in no material fashion from the work of a *Stapostelle* in East Prussia. To describe the functions of the *Referate* of the *Amt* therefore is to describe the work of the *Gestapo* wherever it had representation, the only difference being that the outside organisations acted in an executive capacity, while the *Amt* acted as an evaluatory and supervisory body.

There are important qualifications to be made to the above. Broadly speaking, the *Amt* itself had its own executive side carrying out arrests etc. while at the same time it maintained an intelligence network in order to acquire the information on which action could be taken. While therefore the functions of the *Gestapo* remained more or less constant, there was an ever present tendency for the information network to go beyond its recognised scope, that of obtaining information on subversive elements dangerous to the state. This extension did not confine itself to subject matter, but was in evidence also in the tendency to go beyond the *Reich* and occupied territory as a sphere of interest. This more important aspect of the work of *Amt* IV is dealt with in Parts III and IV (below). The tendency reflected the ambition of the *Amtschef* Müller, who was ever anxious to bring within the competence of the *Gestapo* functions carried out by other departments, and was most anxious to extend his interest to the Ausland, an ambition which led to conflict between Schellenberg and himself. As a result of Müller's anxiety to appropriate all sorts of functions to *Amt* IV, we find that the activities of *Amt* IV cover an extraordinarily wide field, an important consequence of which is that in specialised departments dealing with remoter subjects such as passports, visas, customs, etc, the personnel include a high number of what are, properly speaking, civil servants, in some cases not even members of the SS.

The *Gestapo* was of course the main security organisation of the German state, whose function was to combat and suppress any element which might endanger the state and the Party. The military successes in the early part of the war saw the *Gestapo* extend these functions to occupied territory where there was a considerable extension in the scope of the original *Gruppe* IV E which was most actively engaged in combatting resistance movements.

When the major reorganisation came in 1944, resulting in the absorption of *Abwehr* III F, the *Amt* took over counter-espionage activity in the *Reich* itself, and it is under this reorganisation that the functions of the *Amt* will be considered. It is misleading, however, to be categorical about the difference in function between the two resultant *Gruppen* A and B. Broadly speaking, *Gruppe* A was functional and *Gruppe* B territorial, though under this division it is difficult to explain away *Referat* IV B4. It would be wrong too to state that the old *Abwehr* III F became the new *Gruppe* IV B. It would seem that the former *Gruppe* IV D which dealt with occupied territory found that its work consisted mainly in combatting resistance movements, which gave the *Gruppe* an increasingly important counter-espionage function. At that stage of the war its *raison d'être*—occupied territory—had largely ceased to exist. The tendency in the re-organisation was therefore for the territorial *Gruppe* IV D to join the new IV B, while the old IV E gave its functional aspects (economic and industrial counter-espionage) to IV A, and its regional section to IV B. The new *Gruppe* IV E represented therefore much more a fusion between IV D and IV E than an absorption of *Abwehr* III F. At the level of the *Amt*, several III F officers such as Rohleder joined the *Gruppe*. On lower levels the change made little difference, III F continuing to function as before except that it came under the control of the local *Stapostelle* in whose organisation it sometimes even retained its own identity by being named *Abteilung* IV/III. Again, as in all cases of change and re-organisation during the latter half of 1944 and onwards, these changes must be seen against a background of continual [Allied] air bombardment which rendered an effective and smooth change over virtually impossible.

A further effect of the re-organisation was that the work of the *Amt* was no longer based on the method of attack used by the enemy, but on his political attitude. Thus, the case of a communist agent arrested in France would be dealt with by the competent section in IV A and not by the territorial section such as it existed previously in IV D.

A. The functions of *Gruppe* IV A.

1. *Referat* IV A1.
This *Referat* with its two *Hilfsreferate* IV A1a and IV A1b represented the former IV A1 and IV A3, both of which remained unchanged from 1939 until the re-organisation in 1944. The *Referat* was the real basis of *Amt* IV work and the primary reason for its existence, dealing as it did with opposition groups within Germany of both extremes of political outlook. Of its two sub-sections IV A1a dealing with communism was naturally the more important.

Hilfsreferat IV A1a: This section dealing with 'Left' movements was *Referat* IV A1 from 1939 until the summer of 1944. It represented the oldest section of the *Gestapo*, as from the inception in 1933, communism had been the most active opponent of the Nazi Party. While engaged in combatting communism in all parts of Germany and German occupied territory, the *Referat* tended to become more and more a *Länderreferat*, as it was in fact directed against Russia. Its sphere covered dealing with German PWs returning from the USSR, as it became evident that Russia was using that method as a way of introducing agents into Germany, while it was also concerned with those elements in Russia itself which had set up anti-Nazi organisations, such as the Seydlitz Group, the German League of Officers, etc. The *Referat* liaised closely with *Referate* IV A2a and IV A2b.

Hilfsreferat IV A1b: IV A1b dealt with combatting 'Rightist' movements, and was principally concerned in this function with the supervision of the old aristocracy and former monarchial circles. The *Referat* assumed special importance after the July [1944] Plot, and was principally concerned with the investigations arising out of that plot.

2. Referat IV A2.
This *Referat* was not one of the most important in the *Amt*. It dealt with sabotage, and from 1942 onwards, with the playing back of parachute agents. While its functions covered all German controlled territory, its activities by force of events were mainly directed against Russia, as sabotage against Germany came mainly from that quarter prior to the war and immediately after the declaration of war on Russia in 1941. It was not until the resistance movements became fully developed

in Western Europe in 1943–44 that the emphasis was somewhat removed from the East. Similarly, the number of W/T agents dropped in Germany was considerably greater in the East than in the West. It was because of this special interest in Russia that there was close liaison between IV A2 and IV A1.

Hilfsreferat IV A2a: This department became the specialist department dealing with sabotage in the *Gestapo*, its functions extending to cover all aspects of enemy sabotage, as well as sabotage by individuals and small subversive groups in Germany. Prior to the outbreak of war, this activity had been dealt with by *Abteilung* II A1 of the old *Gestapoamt* and, as mentioned above, was confined very largely to Eastern Europe. After the outbreak of war, there was a period of a comparatively lull in sabotage activities, which was seen broken by considerably increased activity in Eastern Europe after June 1941. In the latter stages, with the growth of Russian counter-attacks and with the considerable development of resistance movements sponsored and armed by the Allies in the West, acts of sabotage became so frequent that IV A2a was forced to decentralise its interest and authority, action in all cases being taken by the *Stapostelle* or BdS concerned, while only the more important cases were handled by IV A2.

The *Referat* was responsible for the maintenance of a central sabotage museum and records department based on a careful analysis of all acts of sabotage carried out during the course of the war, which on the basis of these records and exhibits noted as a training establishment for the *Gestapo* on counter-sabotage methods. It issued in addition, manuals on sabotage to all *Stapostellen*, to which amendments were issued to keep the *Stellen* abreast of latest developments. This publication was supplemented by a fortnightly review of sabotage cases issued by the BdS in occupied territory, though in eastern occupied territory the task of combatting sabotage became so great that special *Bandenkampfverbände* were organised.

Early in 1944 the department was also given the task of investigating all cases of assassination or attempted assassination, until then the province of *Hilfsreferat* IV A4a, with which department it now collaborated in its investigations. It was IV A2a, for instance, which had to examine the circumstances of the explosion in the July Plot [1944].

A further function of the *Referat* was the study of forged documents of a political nature, a record of all cases of such captured material being kept, so that new cases were referred back to IV A2a for that department to determine from its records which Intelligence Service had been the issuing authority. The department was not, however, responsible for the production of forged documents, that being the province of VI F3. The section existed prior to the reorganisation in 1944 as *Hilfsreferat* IV A2c, but was part of IV A2a after the summer of 1944.

Hilfsreferat IV A2b: IV A2b, dealing with counter-intelligence and action against agents dropped by parachute into Germany, only developed from 1942. Until then the cases of parachute agents in Germany had been very few in number, and again, as in the case of IV A2a, subsequent development was mainly in the

Russian sphere. The main interest of the department lay in '*Funkspiel*' in playing back captured W/T operators, but it is not easy to decide where the interests clashed with those of *Gruppe* IV E, the counter-espionage section of the *Gestapo*. In occupied territory the combatting of parachuted agents was dealt with by *Abteilung* IV E of the BdS. By the time, however, that such activity developed in the West, IV A2b had become recognised as the specialist section on such matters, and all cases of '*Funkspiel*' initiated by the *Gestapo* had to be referred to that section before action could be taken.

The department had its birth more or less in the uncovering of the '*Rote Kapelle*' organisation, a widespread Russian network in Germany with ramifications into high circles in the *Luftwaffeministerium*. The first detections were carried out in Belgium through the D/F'ing on the part of the *Orpo*, the case then being handled by *Abteilung* IV of the BdS. Through leads obtained by the arrests in Belgium, the *Gestapo* was able to unravel the network in France and Berlin. The '*Gegenspiel*' in the *Rote Kapelle* case kept going for some three years, and was a highly successful phase of *Amt* IV work. Based on this initial success, the *Referat* developed its *Funkspiel* work mainly in the East, though there were a few cases of attempts to turn round agents in western Germany.[1]

It should be noted that *Hilfsreferat* IV A2b was the section responsible for the installation of W/T agents in the West to act as stay-behind agents in face of the Allied advance. This aspect of IV A2b work is dealt with in Part V, paragraph A.

2. *Referat* IV A3.
This section as a whole represented those sections of the former *Gruppe* IV E which did not have a purely territorial aspect and were therefore not absorbed into the new *Gruppe* IV B. It dealt with industrial security and with counter-espionage cases which did not fall within the territorial limits set out in the new IV B. The *Referent* immediately on the re-organisation was SS-*Staf* Huppenkothen, replaced by SS-*Stubaf* Quetting, the expert in industrial counter-espionage work, when Huppenkothen replaced Panzinger as *Gruppenleiter* IV A.

Hilfsreferat IV A3a: IV A3a had a general counter-espionage assignment covering those aspects of the subject not covered by *Gruppe* IV B and *Referat* IV A3b. It was responsible for the periodic issue of a counter-espionage news-sheet to all *Stapostellen*. Its range of subjects covered such topics as treason against the State, deserters, passive resisters, and the use of carrier pigeons.

Hilfsreferat IV A3b: The *Hilfsreferent* IV A3b, SS-*Stubaf* Quetting, who at the same time held the position of *Referent* IV A3, was a specialist in the subject of industrial counter-espionage and security, the *Sachgebiet* of the section, which had previously been *Referat* IV E1 in *Gruppe* IV E. The department was responsible for the safeguarding of industry in general, for which purpose it maintained a network of V-*Leute* in the larger companies, and also kept a watch on corruption in industrial management and finance. With the absorption of the *Abwehr*, the *Referat* took over that section of *Abwehr* III having similar functions, *Abteilung* III Wi.

Hilfsreferat IV A3c: Originally this sub-section dealt with Border Control, but on the creation of the new *Gruppe* IV G in October 1944, disappeared and was absorbed in the new *Gruppe* (see paragraph C). Subsequently the *Hilfsreferate* of *Referat* IV A3 were renumbered and a new IV A3c was formed taking over some of the functions of IV A3b, but details are not known. In any case, the change did not get beyond the paper stage.

4. *Referat* IV A4.

Referat IV A4 under SS-*Ostubaf* Eichmann dealt with 'philosophical opponents', this term covering religious sects, Jews and Freemasons.

Hilfsreferat IV A4a: Religious sects had originally been the province of *Abteilung* II B2 of the old *Gestapa*, and in the original organisation of *Amt* IV was dealt with by *Referat* IV A4 under SS-*Ostuf* Roth. In the early days of the war, with things going well for Germany, action against religious sects was vigorously undertaken, as is evidenced by the creation in early 1941 of the new *Gruppe* IV B under SS-*Stubaf* Hartl (see Appendix II). The close collaboration which existed between *Gruppe* IV B and *Gruppe* III C of *Amt* III is worthy of note. After the flight of Hess to Britain in May 1941, a minor panic ensued regarding sects, and as a result all Christian Science activities were banned in Germany, while at the same time *Gruppe* IV B set up a small section to study the whole question of occultism. Hartl left the *Gruppe* by the end of 1941, later joining *Amt* VI, while Roth took command again.

With the change in the general war situation by the end of 1942, the emphasis on combatting religious sects was considerably lessened as it became prudent not to antagonise unduly the neutral countries. The *Gruppe* therefore decreased in importance and became *Referat* IV A4a in the summer of 1944.

Hilfsreferat IV A4b: SS-*Ostubaf* Eichmann, the *Referent* IV A4, was the *Amt* IV specialist on Jewish affairs from the earliest days. His department dealt with all aspects of the Jewish problem—imprisonment, confiscation of property, exchanges, etc, and virtually acted as an independent office. IV A4b also dealt with the subject of Freemasonry.[2]

5. *Referat* IV A5.

Referat IV A5 dealing with 'Special Cases' had no *Referent*, though SS-*Staf* Rang acted in the absence of a regular appointment. The *Referat* had two sub-divisions as follows:

Hilfsreferat IV A5a: This section represented the '*Schutzdienst*' of the *Gestapo*, supplementing the bodyguards for prominent personalities provided through the '*Reichssicherheitsdienst des* RFSS' by arranging security precautions at public meetings etc, addressed by leading Nazi personalities. It also dealt with any attempted assassinations, working in liaison with IV A2a and with the *Forschungsamt*, which department provided material through its monitoring of telephone conversations.

Hilfsreferat IV A5b: This section was a fusion of the former IV C3 and IV C4 dealing with internal Party matters and with the Press. Its more important function was the supervision of leading Nazi personalities, collecting information on their private affairs and dealings, reporting to the '*Parteileitung*' before any action could be taken. (The *Referat* was absorbed a previous section designated as IV S which investigated the character and criminal record of all Party officials). As can be imagined the section became involved in many difficulties as a result of jealousies and rivalries existing within the Party. Many cases of fraud and embezzlement had to be hushed up because of the high ranking personalities involved.

6. *Referat* IV A6.
This *Referat* represented the former *Referate* IV C1 and IV C2, the *Referent* being SS-*Ostubaf* Berndorff.

Hilfsreferat IV A6a (*Schutzhaft*): This section was an important department of *Amt* IV, dealing with all aspects of imprisonment arising out of action by other *Gestapo* departments. It did not itself order arrests, but all *Gestapostellen* in Germany were obliged to pass proposals for detention through IV A6a, which maintained complete dossiers on all persons in concentration camps or under detention elsewhere. This section was therefore an administrative and records section only, having a card index of some 500,000 arrested personnel, excluding Jews, who were dealt with entirely by IV A4b.

Hilfsreferat IV A6b (Central Card Index): The Central Card Index of the *Gestapo* reflected the wide scope of their activities, it numbered some five million cards, including Jews, internees, and those people who had been the subject of *Gestapo* vetting at some time or another. IV A6b was therefore the Central Registry of the *Gestapo*, and represented the former *Referat* IV C1. In addition to maintaining the central card index it maintained personal files, and until the reorganisation in summer 1944 also included the Central Visa Office.[3]

Hilfsreferat IV A6c: This sub-section was created as a direct result of the July Plot [1944] following on a decree issued by Hitler that relatives of the officers implicated in the plot were subject to arrest irrespective of whether they had taken any part in it or not. The treatment was extended to cover the families of those officers known to have deserted to the Russians, and finally to cover the families of deserters of all types on any front.

B. The functions of *Gruppe* IV B.

1. *Referate* IV B1, IV B2 and IV B3.
General: As *Referate* IV B1, IV B2 and IV B3 differed only in territory controlled and not in functions performed, they can be conveniently be considered together, the territories for which they were responsible being shown in Appendix IV. As

previously mentioned the new *Gruppe* IV B represented the absorption by the *Gestapo* of the counter-espionage functions of *Abwehr* III in Germany and German occupied territory. The functions of the *Gruppe* went beyond mere counter-espionage and the *Gruppe* was responsible for the general supervision of *Gestapo* work in the territory it controlled, as well as with the supervision of foreign nationals in Germany of the various countries for which the *Gruppe* was competent. The *Gruppe* was concerned mainly with political aspects in occupied territory.

Relations with *Abwehr* III F: The absorption of the *Abwehr* III F counter-espionage functions did not materially affect the work of *Amt* IV; at lower echelons the only effect was that the *Abwehr* III F *Stellen* continued to work as before, but were nominally subordinated to the local *Stapostelle*. At higher levels, several leading III F personalities joined *Amt* IV. Otherwise the *Gestapo* did not have either the staff nor the experience to take over the functions of III F, of which department it related most of its existing personnel. In operational areas the former *Abwehr* III F had been reorganised into the mobile *Abwehr* III FAKs and FATs directly under the command of the *Oberbefehlshaber* of the respective armies. The liaison between the *Gestapo* and the III FAKs was largely a nominal one, and was strongest probably in Holland, mainly as a result of the close cooperation which had existed in that country between *Abteilung* IV E of the BdS and *Abteilung* III of *Abwehr Ast* Hague.

Counter-Espionage work in Occupied Territory: In occupied territory, especially in France, Belgium and Holland, the *Gestapo*, working through the *Abteilung* IV E of the respective BdS, met with a considerable amount of success in combatting resistance movements. The outstanding success was in Belgium and Holland where *Abteilung* IV E of the BdS The Hague was instrumental in arresting numerous parachute agents depatched from the UK and in liaison with *Abwehr Abteilung* III F engaged in a prolonged '*Funkspiel*'. The part played by *Abteilung* IV E was a comparatively minor one. The original investigations were carried out by *Abteilung* III of *Abwehr Ast* The Hague, who at the opportune moment informed IV E that arrests could be carried out. Once the arrests were effected, IV E referred back to the RSHA any proposed '*Funkspiel*' cases, and on permission being granted (the competent *Referat* was of course IV A2b, previously mentioned) the actual working of the captured set was carried out by IV E. The '*Spielmaterial*' however was supplied by *Abteilung* III F of the *Abwehr Ast*. The resultant arrests in resistance movements in Belgium and Holland were considerable. In Paris, too, the *Abteilung* IV E under SS-*Stubaf* Kieffer was very active in similar directions. It has been claimed on behalf of the Paris *Dienststelle* that through penetration of parachute agents dropped during the period preceding the invasion, the *Stelle* was able to decipher the code messages sent to resistance groups through the BBC, and as a result correctly forecast the actual date of the landing; while this claim remains unverified, it is probably correct, though it must be noted that the essential information, that is, the place chosen for the landing, was not obtained.[4]

The strength of *Amt* IV in combatting resistance movements lay, of course, in their power to arrest without reference to courts of law. They could, therefore, arrest on mere suspicion and with Teutonic throughness, sought safety in numbers.

2. *Referat* IV B4.

History: This *Referat* had a chequered history. On the outbreak of war, the German frontiers were closed to all traffic and were only re-opened when an organisation had been set up to control the minimum of necessary traffic. In the first instance *Gruppe* I A(b) was set up under the original *Amt* I with *Ministerialrat* Krause as *Gruppenleiter*, acting as a reference department to which all issuing authorities of visas were obliged to refer before a visa could be granted. The chief issuing authorities involved were the *Auswärtiges Amt* [German Foreign Office], the OKW, and the *Wirtschaftsministerium* [Economics Ministry]. The organisation however became far too unwieldy and subsequently became decentralised. In early 1941 the *Zentralsichtvermerkstelle* was transferred to *Referat* IV C1 while the *Pass- und Sichtvermerkswesen* passed to *Amt* II as *Gruppe* II B. *Gruppe* II B was the responsible authority for the issue of visas for all types of civilian travel apart from the Foreign Office issue of visas to its own personnel and to civilians travelling on its behalf. The whole position of frontier control in Germany was one of extreme complexity, as at the same time there existed the *Grenzpolizei*, and later *Gruppe* IV G (qv).

In the autumn of 1943 *Gruppe* II B was transferred to *Amt* IV to form a new *Gruppe* IV F, the breakdown of which is shown at Appendix III. It will be noted that in this reorganisation the *Zentralsichtvermerkstelle* was transferred from *Referat* IV C1 to become *Referat* IV F5. With the major reorganisation in the summer of 1944, *Referat* IV B4 took over the question of visas as dealt with by *Referate* IV F2, F3, F4 and F5, while *Referat* IV F1 eventually found its way to the new *Gruppe* IV G through IV A3c.

Hilfsreferat IV B4a: This department dealt with general questions of the issue to civilians of passports and visas, liaising in this capacity with the OKW and the Foreign Office. The word 'liaison' is perhaps a misnomer.

Hilfsreferat IV B4b: This section had more restricted functions in that it was specially concerned with the passage backwards and forwards of foreign workers, and with questions of internment in cases of infringement of regulations.

Hilfsreferat IV B4c: This was the *Zentrale Sichtvermerksstelle* (Central Office for the authorisation of visas), and in the last few months of the war also dealt with 'Sippenhaftung', i.e. the arrest of the relatives in Germany of prominent persons working abroad against the *Reich*.

Every visa-issuing authority in Germany had to submit requests for permits to travel abroad to the local *Stapo(leit)stellen*. These in turn forwarded them to *Referat* IV B4c, where, after the *Gestapo* central card index had been consulted, the final decision was given by IV B4c who, however, were not competent in the case of members of the *Wehrmacht* and civilians travelling on military business, who were issued with special military passes by a department of the QMG in Berlin, or for official journeys or those undertaken on behalf of the Party, for which visas were issued by the Visa Department of the *Auswärtiges Amt*. It also appears that leave journeys of foreign workers, the regulations for which were worked out in *Referat* IV B4b, were not referred to the *Zentrale Sichtvermerkstelle*. Prior to the re-organisation in 1944 the *Zentrale Sichtvermerkstelle* was known as *Referat* IV F5.

The *Zentrale Sichtvermerkstelle* was transferred to *Amt* IV from *Amt* II in 1941, when Müller took advantage of Best's forced resignation as head of *Ämter* I and II to bring it under his own control. It had been formed in December 1939 as a security measure, and was part of the *Abteilung 'Pass- und Sichermerkwesen'* of *Amt* II. At that time Embassies and Consulates abroad also had to refer back to the *Zentrale Sichtvermerkstelle* before granting entry visas to Germany, and it is not clear whether this practice continued after the transfer to *Amt* IV.

C. Special Sections of *Amt* IV.

In addition to the two main *Gruppen* A and B, *Amt* IV had several special sections working more or less independently of the *Gruppen* and normally directly subordinated to the *Amtschef* himself. By far the most important of these special departments was *Dienststelle* IV N, which is dealt with in detail in Part III (below). The following departments also existed outside of the *Gruppen*.

1. IV ZABP.
The *Zentral Auslands Brief Prüfungsstelle*, formerly dealt with by *Abteilung* III N of the *Abwehr*, was taken over by *Amt* IV at the time of the major reorganisation. It existed for a short spell as *Hilfsreferent* IV A3d, but was soon set up as an independent *Dienststelle* in the *Amt* under the title of ZABP.

The absorption of this department from the *Abwehr* did not materially affect its working methods or organisation, still less its personnel. The function of the ZABP was the censoring of civilian mail leaving and entering the country, extracting information of value and passing it to the ministry concerned. The organisation was extended to include supervision of mail in occupied territory, after the military successes of 1940–42.

The organisational structure of the ZABP consisted of a central office in Berlin with a series of eight subordinate offices in the Reich (Berlin, Cologne, Frankfurt, Hamburg, Hof, Königsberg, Munich and Vienna) to which were added stations in occupied territory (Lyons, Nancy, Oslo, Paris and Sonderburg). The central office was divided into three *Abteilungen*, the third dealing with matters of policy. The subordinate offices, the ABPs, had the following internal organisation:

Gruppe I	Postal section; collection and return of mail.
Gruppe II	Examination section.
Gruppe III	Chemical section; treating mail for secret inks.
Gruppe IV	Private mail censorship section.
Gruppe V	Commercial and economic mail censorship.
Gruppe VI	Censorship of publications and circulars.
Gruppe VII	Evaluation section; receiving material from *Gruppen* IV to VI and distributing to ZABP.
Gruppe VIII	Telegram censorship.

Of the above *Gruppen*, *Gruppe* VII was formed only at the time of the re-organisation. Originally under *Abteilung* III N of the *Abwehr* there existed an *Auslandstelegrammprüfstelle* (ATBPs) analogous to the ZABP, but as the volume of traffic had become slight by 1944, the department was merged in IV ZABP, and a corresponding *Gruppe* created at the ABPs.

The ABPs passed their intercepts to the ZABP, which was responsible for distributing to the *Amt* or Ministry concerned. When the intercept reflected on the political reliability of an individual it was passed by the ZABP direct to the *Stapostelle* concerneed.

The ZABP came under the direction of SS-*Ostubaf* Müller, former KdS Lublin, with SS-*Stubaf* Wipper, former *Polizei Attache* at Sofia, as his deputy. SS-*Ostuf* Bergemann was the *Amt* III representative and liaison officer in the organisation.

3. *Dienststelle* IV G (*Dienstelle des General Grenzinspekteurs*).

(a) Creation of IV G in 1944: IV G came into existence only in the autumn of 1944, after the ZGS (*Zollgrenzschutz*), the part of the Customs Service of the German Finance Ministry which was responsible for actually patrolling the border, manning official crossing points and carrying out searches, had been handed over by the Finance Ministry to Himmler, who appointed Müller *Generalgrenzinspekteur*, and entrusted him with the direction of all ZGS Matters. It is to be noted that IV G had equal status with *Gruppen* A and B, and was referred to as *Gruppe* IV G.

Müller centrolled IV G personally, at least when it was first formed, with Somann under his command as *Chef* of the *Dienststelle*. Control of civilian frontier traffic was then in the hands of the *Grenzpolizei* and the ZGS, and Somann's task was to bring about a unified control (*Grenzschutzkorps*). He was in charge of the organisation and financial administration of the department, and, in addition to his journeys to the frontier posts, etc., was in frequent contact with the Finance Ministry. In October 1944 the pay books of the ZGS personnel were stamped to the effect that they had been *Sipo* personnel since July, and a directive later issued by the CdS and SD provided for the administration of the VGAD (reinforced auxiliaries recruited on the outbreak of war) to be placed under the control of the *Sipo*; the local *Sipo* authorities were to take over the Customs Staff engaged on the administration of personnel, supplies and economic matters. However, the ZGS, a solid clique of ex-regular soldiers, which Himmler had unsuccessfully attempted to penetrate and break, resisted to the last, and at the time of the collapse the absorption was still incomplete.

When *Dienststelle* IV G was formed, *Referat* IV A3c, in which matters dealing with the actual work of the *Grenzpolizei* had been mainly concentrated, ceased to exist. (In this connection some confusion had been caused by the later formation of a new *Referat* which had no connection with the *Grenzpolizei* with the same designation; see paragraph 3). Prior to the re-organisation in 1944 *Grenzpolizei* matters were the province of *Gruppe* IV F, *Referat* IV F1 and IV F2, which dealt respectively with illegal and legal border traffic.

(b) Formation and functions of the *Grenzpolizei*: A decree of 8 May 1937 vested the ultimate responsibility for the control of the frontiers, which had hitherto been the responsibility of the Customs Section of the Finance Ministry and the local *Schupo* or *Gendarmerie*, with the Ministry of the Interior. As a result the *Grenzpolizei* (*Grepo*) was established by the Chief of *Sicherheitspolizei* as a branch of the *Gestapo*. The control of the frontier was thereafter shared between the Customs and the *Grenzpolizei*, though the decree of 1937 gave the *Grepo* the right to call on other branches of the service for assistance and so, on paper at least, the *Grepo* was the senior formation.

The main function of the *Grepo* was to supervise all persons crossing the international frontiers of Germany and to establish their identity by checking passports and other identity papers. It did not normally carry out personal searches nor did it deal with wanted persons after arrest. Suspects would be searched by Customs Control officials who reported the results to the *Grenzpolizei* who, if necessary, took action and handed them over to the *Kripo* or *Gestapo*, according to the circumstances.

The *Grepo* operated through *Grenzpolizei-Kommissariate*, situated at key points along the *Reich* borders, as well as along such borders as those between Germany and the Government General. These *Grekos*, which were on the same level as *Stapo Aussendienststellen*, were controlled by the nearest *Stapo(leit)stelle*, which had a special section (IV 3c, known under the old numbering system as III C) dealing exclusively with the *Grenzpolizei*. The *Grekos*, in turn, established their own branch offices at roads and railways along the frontier within the area of their jurisdiction. These were known as *Grenzpolizeiposten*. Some *Grekos* are also known to have formed special units, called *Fliegende Kommandos* (flying squads).

(c) Relations between the *Gestapo* and the ZGS: When the *Grenzpolizei* was instituted as the senior formation on the border, a bitter quarrel began. The ZGS regarded itself as the rightful frontier guards and obstructed and refused to co-operate with the *Gestapo*. They in turn wrote reports on the lack of cooperation, and the quarrel was taken up at the highest level. The *Gestapo* complained bitterly that the ZGS failed to pass information of a security nature which they obtained to the *Grenzpolizei*.

4. RSHA IV N.
This *Dienststelle* is dealt with in detail in Part III.

5. The *Forschungsamt*.
The relationship between the *Forschungsamt* and *Amt* IV was somewhat indeterminate. The *Forschungsamt* had developed as a section of the Air Ministry under Goering, and was responsible for the monitoring of telephone and wireless messages both inside Germany and abroad. It remained a highly secret organisation, and in spite of efforts on the part of *Amt* II, remained under Goering's control. The Home Section of the *Forschungsamt*, however, worked in close liason with *Amt* IV and submitted intercepts to IV A5a for action. Before the final collapse the question of the absorption of the *Forschungsamt* into the RSHA was under active consideration, and although no definite steps were taken, the Home Section had before the end virtually come under the control of *Amt* IV. SS-*Stubaf* Scholz acted as liaison officer between *Amt* IV and the *Forschungsamt*.

6. *Dienststelle* IV B/a A.
This small section dealt with the distribution, allotment and treatment of foreign workers employed in Germany and areas under German control. It came under the control of SS-*Hstuf* Hässler.

7. The *Fahndungstrupp*.
The *Fahndungstrupp* formed administratively part of *Referat* IV A5a. For all practical purposes it represented a small special section coming under the direct control of the *Amtschef* Müller, who used the *Trupp* for special purpose missions. It numbered some fifteen members under the control of *Krim.Insp.* Schäffler.

Part III

The *Gegnernachrichtendienst* and *Dienststelle* IV N

1. Early efforts in 1934.
The *Gestapo* Intelligence Service was established on the initiative of Müller himself from as far back as 1934, when Himmler had already gained effective control of Goering's Prussian *Gestapo*, and he always kept close personal supervision over it. The results attained never satisfied him, and he was continually criticising his

subordinates for lack of initiative and imagination in building up a network of agents.

For the first few weeks it was not organised. The *Sachreferenten* ran their agents as they pleased, and the dissemination of reports was poor. During that period the main activities of the *Gestapo* were directed against the leftists opposition— communists and socialists—a field in which KK Kraus of *Stapoleitstelle* Hamburg played a leading part. On his own initiative he set up his own network of agents and was so successful that his methods became the guiding principles for the organised Intelligence Service which was later set up. Somewhat later the emphasis shifted to reports on church opposition, but swung back to communist activities at the beginning of the war. From 1941 on however illegal activities and sabotage by foreign workers occupied the most important place in the *Gestapo* agents' reports.

2. *Referat* II N in 1937.

It was not until the 1 February 1937 that the *Gestapoamt* issued its first general directive on the centralised control of the domestic intelligence service. This provided for the registration with the *Gestapo* of all important agents attached to the *Stapostellen*. The new central registry was named II N, and by the beginning of 1938 had approximately 500 registered agents. In 1939 when the *Gestapo* became *Amt* IV and was incorporated into the RSHA, II N became *Referat* IV C4 under Halmanseger, as the '*Nachrichtensammelstelle*'.

The first *Stapoleitstellen* to have N-*Referate* were Hamburg, Stuttgart, Karlsruhe, Munich and Vienna. According to Halmanseger, these were established in 1940 or 1941, but a reliable report states that an N-*Referat* was set up at Hamburg and the larger *Stapostellen* as early as 1938. Progress was slow, largely because the *Referenten* were inclined to regard their agents as personal acquisitions and were reluctant to build up the N-*Referate*. At the semi-annual meeting of all *Stapoleiters* to whom these N-*Referate* were directly subordinated, Müller would stress the importance of their separation from the *Gestapo* executive service, but without marked success.

3. The creation of IV N in 1941.

The importance attached by Müller to the growing intelligence service is evidenced by the creation of the special section of *Amt* IV absorbing the old *Referat* IV C4 and renaming it *Dienststelle* IV N, still under Halmanseger. IV N now was an independent department of the *Amt*, and was directly subordinated to the *Amtschef* himself. The intelligence network of *Amt* IV was however still somewhat indeterminate, and the N-*Referate* were not general throughout Germany, and it was not until August 1941 that Heydrich issued his directive determining the respective duties of *Ämter* III, IV and VI in the field of intelligence, and at the same time making much more precise the nature of *Amt* IV's own intelligence network.

B. Formation of the *Gegnernachrichtendienst* in 1941.

1. Extension of the N-*Referat*.
On 4 August 1941 Heydrich issued a detailed directive for the expansion of the *Gestapo* Intelligence Service within the *Reich*, as a result of which all *Stapo(leit) stellen* set up an N-*Referat*. The immediate effect of this decree on *Amt* IV was therefore that its intelligence network was now extended to cover the whole of Germany, and though in effect all *Stapostellen* and until now ran their own agents, the decree marked a definite centralisation of the network and imposed a common system of recruitment and administration of the agents themselves. At the same time the decree distinguished between the intelligence services of *Ämter* III, IV and VI of the RSHA, which were to be known respectively as:

ND—*Nachrichtendienst auf das Lebensgebieten*
(Intelligence Service of *Amt* III covering 'spheres of life')

GND—*Gegnernachrichtendienst*
(Intelligence Service of *Amt* IV working against the opposition)

AND—*Auslandsnachrichtendienst*
(Intelligence Service of Amt VI working against foreign countries)

2. Division of work between the *Ämter*.
The fields of activity and spheres of jurisdiction of these three intelligence services were defined, and the following regulations concerning the exchange of information, transfer of agents, etc, were laid down:

The GND was allowed to run certain agents abroad, provided that they were engaged on *Amt* IV work (*Fahndungsdienst*) and that all important information they might obtain which would be of interest to the AND was passed immediately to the SD-*Leitabschnitt* concerned, which would forward it to *Amt* VI of the RSHA.

Other agents previously run by the *Gestapo* Intelligence Service abroad were either to be transferred to *Amt* IV or the appropriate SD-(*Leit*)*Abschnitt*, or, if the connection was based on personal ties, agreement was to be reached between the departments concerned on the most suitable methods of dealing with them. Direct control, however, was to exercised by the appropriate SD-*Leitabschnitt* of *Amt* VI of the RSHA.

Similarly *Amt* III and *Amt* VI of the RSHA or the SD-(*Leit*)*Abschnitte* might continue to run agents recruited through their respective intelligence services who were in a position to provide information on persons or groups hostile to the State within the *Reich*, provided that the appropriate *Stapo(leit)stelle* and/ or *Amt* IV were always informed at once of all important information, and that the direct control of such agents was exercised by the *Gestapo*. It was the task of the GND to give political guidance and undertake the central evaluation of all material produced by the AND concerning ideological opponents (Freemasons, Jews, religious sects, etc.).

Any *Gestapo* agents who were only able to provide information of a general character on one or more walks of life, i.e. reports on which executive action could not be taken, were to be transferred to the appropriate SD-*Leitabschnitt*. In addition, any information obtained by the GND which would be of interest to *Amt* III was to be passed on to the SD-(*Leit*)*Abschnitt* and *Amt* III (via IV N) of the RSHA.

3. Overlapping between the *Ämter*.

In practice the difference between these three kinds of intelligence was in many cases solely formal, and every ND-*Stelle* whether of the *Stapo* or the SD, worked in all three fields to a greater or lesser extent. For instance, although the collection of *Stimmungsberichte*, showing the reactions and attitudes of the various classes of the population, was a function of the SD (*Amt* III), a considerable number of agents of *Stapoleitstelle* Hamburg were used for the compilation of these reports. There were very many difficulties between the *Gestapo* and the SD regarding competency, and even in the RSHA in Berlin there was continual friction between *Amt* IV on the one hand and *Amt* III and *Amt* VI on the other. Such jurisdictional controversies were settled by the *Amtschefs* at the highest level.

C. The Scope, Functions and Methods of the *Gegnernachrichtendienst* (GND).

1. At *Stapo(leit)stelle* level.

The directive of 4 August 1941 prescribed that all *Stapo(leit)stellen* should set up an N-*Referat*, under an N-*Referent* who was responsible to and chosen by the *Leiter* of the *Stapo(leit)stelle* himself, and who would devote himself exclusively to the expansion of the GND, i.e. he was not at the same time to be *Leiter* of any other *Abteilung* or *Dienststelle*. He could not be transferred to another appointment, even within the *Stapo(leit)stelle* itself, without the express permission being obtained from Heydrich. The *Leiter* himself was made personally responsible for the carrying out of the principles laid down in the directive.

The duties with which the N-*Referent* were charged were as follows:

Administration and central direction of all agents.

The various *Sachreferate* (IV 1–IV 6) ran their own agents, although these had in the main to confine themselves to the actual sphere of work in which the official runnning them was engaged. The N-*Referent* was however responsible for their central direction and for the supervision of the administrative work, all of which was carried out by his *Referat*. This included:

Maintenance of card indexes and personal files.

Index cards had to be made out for all agents and, in the case of those categories registered with the RSHA, duplicate cards forwarded to IV N. For details see Paragraph E. From the personal files it was possible to assess the value of any agent at a glance. They contained full personal particulars, details of payments, and the circumstances in which he was recruited, all reports he submitted (in their original form), and any correspondence with the RSHA IV N. The *Sachreferate* had of course to keep the N-*Referat* fully informed about the agents they ran. Disguised entries regarding all these personal files had also to be kept in the general personal files administration of II F, and all agents were also entered in the II F General Index.

Classification, registration and de-registration of agents with the RSHA IV N.
For details see Paragraph D.

Reporting unreliable agents to the RSHA IV N.
At the *Stapoleiter's* discretion the briefing and handling of agents was done either by the N-*Referent* or the *Sachreferat*, or by the two working in conjunction. *Referat* N also ran its own agents but, unlike the *Sachreferate*, could not take executive action (captures or interrogations) on the reports they submitted. These had to be passed on to the *Sachreferate* and/or the RSHA IV N, which received all information of more than local interest.

Expansion of the GND network.
This was accomplished in close cooperation with the *Gestapo* officers concerned.

Correct distribution of information to RSHA IV N.
Where necessary information was distributed to the local *Dienststellen* of the *Dienststellen* of the ND *auf den Lebensgebieten*, and, in the case of information from abroad, to the SD-*Leitabschnitte*.

All reports for other *Ämter* or *Referate* of the RSHA had to be sent via IV N. (An exception to this rule was laid down in a further decree dated 23 March 1942, which states that reports received from sources other than the GND and only of interest to the AND and ND auf den *Legensgebieten*, should be sent direct to *Amt* VI or *Amt* III respectively).

All correspondence connected with the ND.
This was to be regarded as secret.

Submission of a Progress Report to the RSHA.
Originally the N-*Referent* had to submit a short report, giving a general survey of the ND to date, future plans, etc, every two months. After September 1942 this was amended to twice yearly.

Security.

The decree of 4 August 1941 laid down various security measures (categories of secrecy of correspondence, etc.). These had included the allocation of symbols to agents, which had to be used in all correspondence, and two-digit code numbers to all *Stapo(leit)stellen*. These were used in combinction when reports were submitted to the RSHA IV N. For details see Appendix VI.

2. RSHA *Amt* IV level.
Working mechanism of *Dienststelle* IV N.

RSHA IV N was considered a *Dienststelle* rather than a *Referat*, and as such was directly responsible to the head of *Amt* IV, Müller. It was set up in 1941 as a collating centre for internation for the whole of the GND, and its functions were to keep a central registry of agents affiliated within the *Stapostellen* and to distribute agents' reports to the proper *Referate* of *Amt* IV, and where necessary, to *Ämter* III and VI.

The incoming reports were registered and then usually read by Halmanseger (Müller himself was only shown important information) before being passed along to the *Sachreferat*. Usually if a report dealt with several subjects, IV N would make extract copies and send the proper section to each interested *Referat*. If there was no time it would be sent to the *Referat* mainly concerned which then became responsible for further dissemination.

IV N received reports only on information considered to be *Amt* IV level, such as large illegal organisations and other dangerous opposition elements, particularly important persons or those considered especially dangerous (saboteurs, terrorists, etc.), and matters of particular political interest. Lesser matters were consolidated into a monthly situation report which the *Stapoleiter* sent directly to the head of *Amt* IV. RSHA IV N averaged approximately forty reports daily.

In theory all foreign information of counter-intelligence interest was to have been sent from IV N to *Amt* VI, but this was rarely done. The exact dividing line between the functions of *Amt* IV and *Amt* VI was obscure even to Halmanseger, and when in doubt he would not circulate information to *Amt* VI direct, but would leave that to the discretion of the *Referate* to which it was passed.

RSHA IV N had no agents of its own. It did no13however register the few remaining agents of *Amt* IV *Referate* who were retained after the great bulk had been reluctantly transferred to *Stapoleitstelle* Berlin.

From time to time IV N issued so-called 'Warning Lists' of unreliable agents, which were compiled on the basis of information supplied to them by the various N-*Referenten*, and were circulated to all *Stapo(leit)stellen* and SD-*Leitabschnitte*. These lists sometimes included highly qualified men, who were only dropped as unreliable through the stupidity or intrigue of some official, as well as active agents who were proceeding abroad and whose name was entered solely for reasons of cover.

Evaluation of information and liaison with *Referate*.

The *Referate* were charged with the evaluation of intelligence, and IV N had to consult them if information was required about the credibility of a given report. Liaison between the *Referate* and IV N varied from the fairly close cooperation of IV A1a, to an almost complete lack of liaison with others. In many instances, when there was some query about an agent's report, the *Sachreferat* would take up the matter directly with the *Stapostelle* concerned. If information about an agent was desired, however, the *Referat* had to consult IV N.

Training courses for N-*Referenten*.

These were held at the RSHA under the direction of Müller, every six months. In all cases, however, they only last one or two days, and should be described rather as conferences. Lectures were given by the various *Sachgebietsleiter* of the RSHA, and any shortcomings were pointed out.

3. Territorial jurisdiction of the *Gegnernachrichtendient* (GND).

The activities of IV N were limited to the territory of Germany proper, Austria, the Protectorate, Alsace-Lorraine, Poland (*Generalgouvernement*), Lithuania, Esthonia, Latvia, certain occupied Russian territories (Minsk and Bialystok areas), and also, unofficially, Denmark. Reports from agents in all the regions mentioned above were sent to IV N, but since most of the information was evaluated locally the number of reports was small. Elsewhere in German occupied Europe there were no IV N agents, all the *Gestapo* contacts having been handed over to the *Einsatzkommandos* of the *Sipo* and SD after the arrival of German troops. The reports of these agents were transmitted by the KdS or BdS direct to *Amt* IV.

Although officially IV N was not supposed to cover neutral countries, *Stapo(leit)stellen* in the border areas had some agents who functioned in Sweden and Switzerland. (See Part IV for details of *Gestapo* activities abroad).

4. Functions and working methods of the *Gegnernachrichtendienst* (GND).

The GND covered the intelligence activities of the *Gestapo* in internal political and general police security spheres, i.e. its aims were to track down the enemies of the state, penetrate their organisations, and keep a constant watch on their contacts and activities. The task of its agents was to report specific information, and not to give general situation reports. A principle rarely violated was that they were only to observe and were not to act as provacateurs.

Their primary fields of operations were cities, though factories were favourite targets, since it was there that opposition movements were most likely to form. Although rarely attained five to ten *Gestapo* agents were considered a good ratio in a plant employing 10,000. Even the management did not know the identity of these agents, although some directors of *Arbeitsämter* might have had that knowledge, since agents were planted in factories through the *Arbeitsamt*. They were to receive no preferential treatment, and started out without any specific mission. After watching and observing they were to determine from the workers' attitude whether any opposition groups existed; they then received instructions to join one of these movements, but not to seek leading positions unless they were qualified to hold them. Whenever it was necessary for more than one agent to penetrate the same group, they were not to know each other.

Agents were only used to cover groups or political movements with which they were familiar, and preferably of which they were (or had been) a member. Thus an agent who had been politically active before 1939 could not use old connections. By visiting the restaurants where his old political cronies met he could sound them out to see whether they were still active in political groups, and ascertain their attitude towards the regime.

An example of *Gestapo* methods in combatting communism during the war years is provided by *Stapoleitstelle* Hamburg. A group of agents was formed which worked under the cover of a lending library for periodicals and a soap business, both situated in a working class district. Good relations were maintained by the members of this group with the clients of the reading circle, and as a result communist cells had been formed. Records were kept of all conversations, and it was thus ascertained which persons were engaged in illegal political activities or were likely to become so engaged.

Anti-communist work in connection with the Russian Intelligence Service was centralised under the RSHA, which issued instructions whenever clues pointed to the areas of the *Stapo(leit)stellen.*

Many new problems arose for the *Gestapo* when foreign workers poured into Germany. The recruitment of new agents was not difficult, but few of them were German, which complicated the problem of reporting the information. A '*Meldekopf*' system was therefore introduced. One reliable German speaking foreigner called a '*Meldekopf*', was placed among a group of foreign workers. He recruited his own sub-agents, who were known only to himself, and was responsible for supplying the information required. This system produced excellent results.

The *Länderreferate* (*Gruppe* IV E) of *Amt* IV became interested in the *Meldekopf* system, and eventually set up their own on a national scale, including some mobile units which travelled throughout Germany. Their French agents were at the same time in touch with the Vichy French government office for foreign workers in Berlin, in which a certain Dr Gasbonde is said to have played a leading role.

5. Fields of activity of the GND.

The fields of activity of GND agents and their relative importance, reviewed in the light of the reports which passed through Halmanseger's hands to the various *Sachreferate*, are described below.

Communist and Socialist activities.

One of the most important fields, especially the communist phase. It gained in importance in later years, not only because of German communist activities but also because of similar developments among foreign workers.

Sabotage and Explosions.

The wartime increase in Germany was slight compared with that in Poland. The *Referat* which dealt with these reports, IV A2a, was considered important by Müller and was charged with many special missions, such as '*Rote Kapelle*'. Reports on the latter type of action did not pass through IV N, but circulated directly through channels established by IV A2a.

Rightist Opposition.

Considered dormant for a period, this was a field of renewed activity after 20 July 1944.

Espionage.

Cases of 'pure' espionage were not referred to IV N, the reports it received usually being on espionage undertaken in conjunction with other illegal activities.

Industry and commerce.

A small number of reports were received, mainly on industrial espionage.

Churches.

There was a moderate number of reports, with occasionbal connections to Rome. The *Referat* concerned, IV A4a, frequently ran its own agents without informing IV N.

Jewish Question.

No reports were received during the last few years. *Referat* IV B4 dealt almost exclusively with the Jewish question in *Amt* IV.

Protection of leading personalities.

Only an occasional report on attempted assassinations was submitted.

Foreign workers from the West.

This field grew more important with the increase of resistance movements and communist propaganda. Numerous reports were forthcoming.

England.

No reports of any kind were received by IV N.

Scandinavian countries.

Occasional reports arrived on *Abwehr* matters and emigres from Sweden. Also some reports, received for the most part from *Stapo* Kiel, on Danish resistance movements in Denmark and Danish workers in Germany.

Eastern territories and workers (except Poles).

There were many reports dealing with illegal organisations and communist group.

Poland and Polish workers.

This was the biggest field of activity in recent years. A great number of reports were received on the Polish Underground, communications between groups, sabotage, poisoned foods, insurrection, etc.

Czech Protectorate and Slovakia.

Reports on the Czech resistance movements were received from *Stapo* Prague and Brünn.

Foreign workers from the Balkans.

Occasional reports were submitted on resistance movements among these workers.

Switzerland.

Some reports were received on *Abwehr* matters from *Stapo* Stuttgart and Karlsruhe.

D. The recruitment, classification and administration of IV N agents.

1. Recruitment.

A variety of methods were used in recruiting agents. As a rule greater skill and patience were needed in recruiting German nationals than with foreigners. Many were recruited during interrogations. An arrested person, after being confronted with strong evidence against him, would be released on promising to serve as an agent. Inmates of concentration camps, whose families were trying to obtain their release, sometimes proved to be willing agents when pressure was brought to bear upon the family and the prisoner.

A person who was about to be released from prison after serving a sentence for a political offence would be sounded out on service as a *Gestapo* agent. Failure to cooperate, it would be hinted, might have dire consequences, such as transfer to a concentration camp after 'release'.

Recruiting among churchmen was pursued along somewhat different lines. A favourite method was to threaten to expose the love life of a Catholic priest unless he consented to be an agent. Priests who had separated themselves from the Church were sometimes found to be suitable agents, and occasionally Catholic or Protestant clergy in favour of pan-Germania (though not National Socialists) consented to work for the *Gestapo*.

Among foreign workers those from the East were easiest to recruit, probably because they were the most maltreated. Some volunteered, to get money or additional rations, and others were recruited under pressure during interrogation. Some, such as the Doriot adherents among the French, had already worked in their native countries for German authorities. Since those with 'experience' proved most valuable to the *Gestapo*, the BdS or KdS in the occupied countries were requested to report all V-*Leute* among the workers being shipped into Germany, who were told to report immediately to the local *Stapostelle*. Good results were obtained in this way.

2. Classification and registration with RSHA IV N.
Classification in 1941.

The directive of 4 August 1941 prescribed the following classification of agents:

> V-Persons—V-*Leute*. *Vertrauenspersonen*, agents who, owing to their special contacts in opposition circles, were in a position to obtain important information, but had to operate more or less in disguise.
> W-*Personen*. *Auskunftspersonen*, informants whose special local knowledge, professional standing or personal status enabled them to supply particular information, either voluntarily or on request. Individuals whose work brought them into contact with large numbers of people were quoted as useful W-*Personen*.

All V- and W-*Personen* had to be card indexed at the *Stapo(leit)stelle*, N-*Referat*, and, with the exception only of those of the latter category who worked on a special basis and were of no great importance, registered by the N-*Referat* with RSHA IV N by means of special printed forms and duplicate index cards. Although a decree of 4 September 1942 specified that this had to be done not later than three months after recruitment, according to Halmanseger registration did not take place until an agent had been found reliable over a six month period.

As the *Stapoleiter* himself had been made personally responsible for the expansion of the GND at his *Stapo(leit)stelle* he was accordingly anxious to report as large a number as possible of V- and W-*Personen*. This resulted in many officially registered agents who were utterly incapable of doing the work and who were mostly de-registered again shortly afterwards. Accordingly there was a continual flow of registrations and de-registrations, and in order to prevent this a third group of agents, known as 'Gewährspersonen' (G-*Personen*), was instituted about the beginning of 1942. These were merely registered with the N-*Referat* of the

Stapo(leit)stelle. Only if they were later recruited as V- and W-*Personen* were they registered with RSHA IV N.

Classification in 1944.
    In 1944 the RSHA Amt IV ordered a change in the classification of agents:

V-*Personen* to become G-*Personen* (*Gegner-Personen*)
W-*Personen* to become I-*Personen* (*Informations-Personen*)
G-*Personen* to become A-*Personen* (*Auskunfts-Personen*)

The new G- and I-*Personen*, i.e. the former V- and W-*Personen*, had to be reported as previously to RSHA IV N, while the A-*Personen* merely continued to be registered with the N-*Referat*. Only a few officials of the *Gestapo* were able to differentiate between these designations, the same as there were anyway only a few officials who were capable of carrying out intelligence work at all. In conversation reference was always made to '*Vertrauensleute*'. In reality some of the A-*Personen* were better informants than some of the G- and I-*Personen* registered with IV N. This was due to the fact that during the latter years of the war there was a lot of carelessness in the N-*Referate* and the registration, de-registration and re-registration (e.g. re-registration from A-*Personen* to G-*Personen*) was not carried out with sufficient throughness. It was not therefore always possible to apply a standard on the basis of the designation 'G-', 'I-' or 'A-Person' as should have been the case.

3. Size of GND Network.
It is estimated that the total of G- and I-*Personen* registered with RSHA IV N between 1937, when the central registry was started, and 1945, was between 13,000 and 14,000. Of that total approximately 6,000 were active in the final stages. There were also approximately 4,000 A-*Personen*, i.e. the total number of *Gestapo* agents operating in Germany early in 1945 was some 10,000.
    As a rule a small *Stapostelle* would have between 50 and 80 G- and I-*Personen* (about evenly divided), and a large *Stelle*, located in an industrial area, some 100 to 200, also some 50 to 150 A-*Personen*. *Stapoleitestelle* Hamburg, one of the largest, had a total of approximately 500 G-, I- and A-*Personen* at the time of the [Allied] occupation of Hamburg. These figures exclude agents employed on political security in factories etc. These were appointed and registered by the *Sachreferat* IV 3 of the *Stapoleitstelle*, in collaboration with the military authorities, which ran them at the same time on military work.

4. Payment of agents.
All matters pertaining to the payment of agents were handled by the *Stapo(leit) stellen* with funds requested from and provided by *Amt* II. The guiding principle for the amount of payment was laid down in Müller's '*Leistungs Prinzip*', which

provided that an agent be paid only in accordance with the volume and quantity of his output. A mediocre agent averaged anything from 10 to 100 Reichsmark a month, in addition to expenses. Outstanding agents were paid up to 500 Reichsmark a month. A large number of agents (in the case of *Stapoleitstelle* Hamburg, the majority) were unpaid. Payments were made against receipts, signed by the agent with his cover number and kept by the N-*Referat*.

Early in 1939 the monthly outlay for all *Stapo(leit)stellen* was approximately 50,000 to 60,000 Reichsmark. Later, because of the war, the occupation of larger territories, and the influx of foreign workers, the amount increased tremendously, and by 1944 approached a peak of 300,000 to 400,000 Reichsmark for Germany and certain occupied countries. Not more than one-fifth of this sum ever went to agents engaged on *Abwehr* work. Monthly expenses began declining in 1944 when Germany started to withdraw from foreign territories.

Certain *Stapo(leit)stellen*, such as Berlin, Bremen, Hamburg, Düsseldorf, Vienna, Munich, Stauttgart, Prague and Brünn, because of their great activity and area covered, spent considerably more money on agents than the rest.

Small quantities of tobacco and liquor went to agents in addition to their pay. During 1944 RSHA IV N distributed 500,000 cigarettes, 50,000 cigars, 500 bottles of liquor and a small quantity of supplementary ration cards monthly to the *Stapostellen* in Germany for payment to agents. Application for any supplementary ration cards required had to be made by the N-*Referent* of the *Stapo(leit)stelle* every quarter on a special form.

5. Contact between *Gestapo* officials and agents.

The technique of handling agents differed in each *Stapostelle*. However, a few basic rules were observed by practically all of them. No agent was permitted to come to the *Stapo* office or to the home of a *Stapo* employee. Meetings usually took place in restaurants, outdoors or in offices rented for that purpose and suitably camouflaged.

6. Miscellaneous points.

The decree of 5 August 1941 stipulated this:

> Agents who moved away from the area of their *Stapo(leit)stelle* or who worked in the district of another *Stapostelle* should transfer to the latter, unless there was some special reason to the contrary. In any case the N-*Referat* concerned should be fully informed of the activities of an agent in another *Stapo(leit)stelle* area.
>
> Agents could only be ordered abroad (neutral territories) by express permission of Heydrich.
>
> Correspondence with agents abroad could only be undertaken with permission of the head of the *Stapo(leit)stelle*, and in all doubtful cases RSHA IV N had to be called in.

7. Collaboration with the *Gendarmerie* and State Railways.

During the last two years of the war RSHA *Amt* IV issued instructions for collaboration with the State Railways (*Reichsbahn*) and the *Gendarmerie* on intelligence work. In October 1943 all *Gendarmerie* posts were instructed to recruit agents to strengthen the preventative work of the police. In specially important cases these agents could also be used for *Gestapo* work, and the *Gestapo* was instructed to give the *Gendarmerie* every help in recruiting and running them. Any agents recruited by the *Gendarmerie* who were solely engaged on political work had to be handed over to the *Stapo(leit) stellen* or the KdS. All these agents had to be registered with the local *Stapo(leit) stellen* or KdS, although their particulars were not forwarded to the RSHA.

Little information is available about collaboration between the *Gestapo* and the State Railways. In the case of *Stapoleitstelle* Hamburg no organisation of any importance was ever achieved, although conversations took place frequently with three officials of the administration of the State Railways. The railwaymen detailed for this work had no experience and appeared little suitable. For the most part they ran foreign workers, who were supposed to supply information on cases of sabotage, thefts, etc, as their agents.

8. Work in the final stages of the war.

There is no indication that the work of the GND in any way flagged during the latter stages of the war. On the contrary, as late as January 1945, *Stapostelle* Cologne drew up a highly complicated plan whereby three separate networks of agents were to penetrate the opposition simultaneously. It also provided for the formation of small bands of agents, employed on a full-time basis, to check up on the V-*Personen* already employed, or to be recruited, and to undertake special missions. These groups were to be known collectively as '*Sondereinsatz Komet*' and could if necessary be used by the *Sachreferate* for executive work.

E. Symbols and Card Index system in the GND.

1. Symbols.

As from 4 August 1941 all *Gestapo* agents were given a symbol, which had to be used in all correspondence with the RSHA. This did not preclude the continued use of cover names (e.g. 'Max') in local work.

The regulations governing the allocation of these symbols by the *Stapo(leit) stellen* were as follows:

> Numbers had to be allocated in serial order, not picked at random, e.g. the sixth and tenth agents recruited by a *Stapo(leit)stelle* would be given the symbols 6 and 10 respectively. Later, three digit symbols (001-200) were used, and the category of agent (G, I or A-Person) indicated, e.g. G.010.

The symbol of a 'dead' agent might not be used for a period of at least six months after he had been dropped, but was thereafter to be realloted to a newly recruited agent.

In addition each *Stapo(leit)stelle* was given a two digit basic number (see list below), which was inserted in front of the agent's symbol. The origin of reports, which were always submitted to RSHA IV N on a plain unheaded sheet of paper, could be seen at a glance from these combined figures, e.g. 01 G 132 would indicate that the source was a specific G-Person of *Stapostelle* Aachen.

The basic number of the *Stapo(leit)stelle* might not be divulged to agents who could, however, be told their own symbols and use these when sending in reports.

2. Basic numbers of N-*Referate*.
Germany, Austria and the Protectorate.

In addition to the basic numbers, the list below also indicates, where known, the strength of the N-*Referate* still in existence in the final stages of the war.

Note: in the table below 'dissolved' typically indicates a downgrading to *Aussendienststelle*.

No.	Stapo(leit)stelle	N-Referat (strength)
01	Aachen	dissolved, 1945
02	Allenstein	dissolved, 1943
03	Augsburg	2 persons
04	Berlin	15 persons
05	Bielefeld	dissolved
06	Braunschweig	4 persons
07	Bremen	5 persons
08	Breslau	3 persons
09	Brünn	7 persons
10	Bromberg	7 persons
11	Chemnitz	3 persons
12	Danzig	3 persons
13	Darmstadt	7 persons
14	Dessau	dissolved
15	Düsseldorf	??
16	Dortmund	10 persons
17	Dresden	5 persons
	Elbing	dissolved, before 1941
18	Erfurt	dissolved
19	Frankfurt/Main	2 persons
20	Frankfurt/Oder	??
21	Graz	4 persons

22	Graudenz	dissolved
23	Halle	3 persons
24	Hamburg	7 persons
25	Hanover	3 persons
26	Hildesheim	dissolved
27	Hohensalza	dissolved
28	Innsbruck	3 persons
29	Karlsbad	2 persons
30	Karlsruhe	5 persons
31	Kassel	??
32	Kattowitz	6 persons
33	Kiel	3 persons
34	Klagenfurt	4 persons
35	Koblenz	2 persons
36	Köln	2 persons
37	Königsberg	3 persons
38	Köslin	dissolved
39	Leipzig	3 persons
40	Liegnitz	dissolved
41	Linz	3 persons
42	Lodz	3 persons
43	Magdeburg	3 persons
44	Munich	15 persons
45	Münster/W.	3 persons
46	Neustadt a.d. Weinstraße	dissolved, 1941
47	Nürnberg	5 persons
48	Oppeln	3 persons
49	Osnabrück	dissolved
50	Plauen	dissolved
51	Posen	3 persons
52	Potsdam	3 persons
53	Prague	6 persons
54	Regensburg	1 person
55	Reichenberg	1 person
56	Salzburg	2 persons
57	Saarbrücken	2 persons
58	Schneidemühl	dissolved
59	Schwerin	1 person
60	Tilsit	1 person
61	Trier	dissolved
62	Stuttgart	6 persons
63	Stettin	4 persons

64	Wesermünde	dissolved
65	Weimar	2 persons
66	Wilhelmshaven	dissolved
67	Vienna	6 persons
68	Würzburg	dissolved
69	Zichenau-Schröttersberg	??

Other occupied territories.

19a	KdS Veldes	??
04a	KdS Bialystok	??
45a	KdS Minsk	??
43a	KdS Marburg	??
39a	KdS Lemberg (Lwow)	??
41a	KdS Lublin	??
38a	KdS Krakow	6 persons
53a	KdS Radom	4 persons
64a	KdS Warsaw	??
?	KdS Strasbourg	??
?	KdS Metz	??

3. Card Index system.

At *Stapo(leit)stellen*:

All agents, whether or not they belonged to a category which required registration with RSHA IV N, had to be entered in the following indexes.

Name Index (*Namenskartei*): This was arranged alphabetically according to the agent's true name. The cards also indicated his cover symbol, date and place of birth, field of activity, category, date of recruitment, and the basic number of the *Stapo(leit)stelle* running him. Cards of different colours were used to indicate in which of six fields he was working:

Red   KPD (Communist Party)
Pink   SPD (Social-Democrat Party)
Yellow   *Abwehr* matters
Blue   Church matters
Green   Rightist opposition
White   Miscellaneous

Code Index (*Deckbezeichnungskartei*): The cards of this index contained the same information as those of the Name Index, and were also colour coded. They were arranged according to the agent's symbol.

Local Index (*Kreis-Ortskartei*): This was also a colour coded index of all agents, but was arranged under districts. It provided a constant survey of the geographical development of the GND network in the area of the *Stapo(leit)stelle* concerned.

At RSHA IV N.

The decree of 4 August 1941 stipulated that duplicate cards of all the three above-mentioned indexes should be attached to the registration form when notifying agents to RSHA IV N. As from 4 September 1942, however, Local Index cards were no longer submitted.

'Dead' Index (*Ausgelegte Kartei*): An alphabetical index of cards of agents dropped from the *Gestapo* payroll.

Report Index (*Berichtskartei*): Index on which the reports of each *Stapo(leit) stelle* were entered by agent's number and by date. This allowed for simple checking on the frequency of reports submitted by each *Stelle*.

Case Files: All agents registered with the RSHA had case files.

Usually each agent had a page with his photograph, personnel data and pertinent basic information, such as findings of investigations, change of status, political affiliations, card of dependents, etc.

Fictitious Pass Index (*Deckpass kartei*): This contained copies of applications for fictitious passports arranged alphabetically and using cover names. The information was sent in by *Asts(Aussenstellen)*, *Stapo(leit)stellen* and *Amt* VI, after the issue of fake passports. The real name of the bearer was never used, and this index had no connections with IV N activities.

Part IV

The *Gestapo* outside Germany

General.

By reason of its broad functions, the combatting of persons and groups which might endanger the security of the state, *Amt* IV was largely an internal German security service and had little claim to operate outside the borders of the Reich. Nevertheless, it was the constant ambition of Müller to extend the functions of the *Amt* to cover foreign territory, and in certain directions he was successful in doing so. The work of the *Gestapo* abroad can be classified under two headings—open and covert. In the first instance the *Amt* had gained the right to operate in German occupied territory and to a certain degree in neutral territory by virtue of the *Polizei Attache Gruppe*, and as a result of the Heydrich decree of August 1941 (see Part III, Paragraph B). In addition, however, instances have come to light of *Stapostellen* in Germany operating outside their recognised sphere and sending agents to foreign territory and in some instances to neutral territory—an important development in *Amt* IV work, as the *Amt* as a whole was better trained and better staffed than *Amt* VI in running information networks. These three aspects of *Gestapo* work abroad are dealt with in the following paragraphs. It will be remembered in this connection that on the dissolution of the *Abwehr*, Müller made strenuous efforts to acquire the entire counter-espionage activities of the *Abwehr* for *Amt* IV, but was unable to acquire the right to operate in neutral territory, a function which became the province of the new RSHA *Gruppe* VI Z.

A. The *Gestapo* in Occupied Territory.

1. The BdS and *Einsatzkommandos*.

Little need be said of the *Gestapo* in occupied territory, as the functions performed did not differ in essential features from the work of the *Stapostellen* in Germany, the only differences being the shifting of emphasis to different braches of the work, for example, the combatting of resistance movements, and the supervision of foreign workers and their transfer to Germany.

Organisationally, the *Gestapo* operated through an *Abteilung* forming part of an *Einsatzkommando* or through *Abteilung* IV of a BdS. The organisational structure of such Abteilungen is dealt with in Paragraph D of Part I (above), and it is only necessary to repeat that they followed closely on the organisation of the *Amt* itself.

It is to be noted that the work of the BdS and *Einsatzkommandos* was supervised through the funtional *Referate* of the *Amt* on matters such as communism, resistance movements, and captured W/T operators, and only general summaries of the work were sent to the old *Gruppe* IV E (territorial) and the later IV B, which was responsible for dissemination to other interested sections.

B. Activities abroad of *Stapostellen* in Germany

General.

Stapostellen known to have operated abroad are listed in Paragraph 1 below; it is quite possible that other *Stellen* near the borders of Germany operated in similar fashion, and in order to give some idea of the type of work performed by *Amt* IV in this connection, the activities abroad of *Stapoleitstelle* Hamburg are given in some detail in Paragraph 2, below.

1. *Stapostellen* known to have operated abroad.

The following *Stapo(leit)stellen* are known to have been engaged in intelligence work abroad:

Stapoleitstelle Hamburg possessed the most experience in this field and had some measure of joint control over other N-*Stellen* of the *Gestapo*. It covered Sweden and other countries, of which details are given in Paragraph 2 below.

Stapoleitstelle Karlsruhe likewise held a leading position, and as from January 1943 controlled all activities in Switzerland. The decree in question stipulated that the *Gegnernachrichtendienst* (GND) for the whole of Switzerland should be exclusively in the hands of Karlsruhe, Innsbruck and Munich, also BdS Strasbourg. In addition all *Gestapo Dienststellen* were required to:

> Report to Karlruhe all their agents domiciled in or travelling to Switzerland.
>
> Submit any assignments to be carried out by agents in that country and which were not of a general nature to Karlsruhe first.
>
> Forward to Karlsruhe copies of all reports of any interest for the guidance, formation or expansion of the GND in Switzerland.

They were also in principle only allowed to undertake any sort of ND activity on the German-Swiss frontier in agreement with the *Grenzpolizei Kommissariat* (*Greko*) in question, which would in turn inform Karlsruhe.

Stapostelle Bremen prior to the outbreak of war ran an intelligence service on the 'Bremen' and 'Europa' with functions similar to those of the *Staposteleitstelle* Hamburg organisation (see Paragraph 2 below). It later also covered Sweden.

Stapostelle Kiel covered Sweden.

Stapoleitstelle Stettin covered Russia with other *Stapostellen* in Eastern Germany.

In 1936 and 1937 most of the German engineers and technicians who had gone to Russia returned to Germany, and were interrogated on the eastern frontier exclusively by *Stapo* officials on the lines of a directive issued by the *Gestapo*. They reported on the methods of the NKWD, conditions in Russian concentration camps, and, most important of all, on economic conditions in Russia, the technical side of the armaments industry, and military matters. Reports were sent in duplicate to the *Gestapo*, one copy being passed to the *Abwehr*. The department of the *Gestapa* was II A3.

2. Actvities of *Stapoleitstelle* Hamburg.

General.

Details of the activities of the *Stapo(leit)stellen* are known in only one instance, that of Hamburg. When an N-*Referat* was set up at this *Stapoleitstelle* in 1938 it was planned to extend intelligence work, which had hitherto been confined to combatting opposition in Germany, to other fields, such as counter-espionage, information on German *emigres*, etc., i.e. to set up an '*Auslandsnachrichtendienst*'. Previously information on German *emigres*, foreign politicians working against the Reich, etc, had been obtained through the monitoring of foreign periodicals.

This '*Auslandsnachrichtendienst*' was mainly run by the N-*Referat* itself, although one case is known of an agent being sent to Sweden in 1945 on a mission for one of the *Sachreferate* (IV 5).

A review of the countries in which *Stapoleitstelle* Hamburg worked, or attempted to work, is given below. It will be seen that, where details of the activities of the agents employed are available, these mainly covered *Amt* IV work (counter-espionage, watching German *emigres*, left wing movements, etc.). There were however several exceptions (see paragraphs on Holland, Jugoslavia and Sweden).

Stapoleitstelle Hamburg closed down its intelligence service as soon as any country was occupied by German troops, in accordance with a decree issued by *Amt* IV, which provided for all *Gestapo* agents to be handed over to the responsible *Einsatzkommandos* of the *Sipo* and SD. Thus the information on Belgium, Holland and Jugoslavia refers to work prior to the occupation. In Denmark, however, Hamburg continued to work at any rate up to 1943, and on occasion, travelling agents visited other occupied territories.

U.S.A.

In 1938 agents were appointed on the Hapag steamships *Hamburg*, *Hansa*, *New York* and *Deutschland*, with instructions to look around in New York for any political, especially communist movements which had been founded, and to attempt to contact German *emigres* abroad, and also to find out which members of the crews of German vessels might possibly be in touch with enemy intelligence services or communist organisation. These seafarers, some of whom were arrested during a round-up of a group of agents run by *Abwehrstelle* Hamburg, occasionally obtained useful information in conversation with friends and acquaintances in New York. The only resident was a German, a former OGPU agent, who had been recruited by *Stapoleitstelle* Hamburg in 1944, and later settled in New York.

When war broke out and sea communications were interrupted, this intelligence service was paralysed before it had achieved any successes worth mentioning. Later attempts to establish a link with New York from Genoa failed owing to the lack of suitable communications, and in particular because the N-*Referat* did not receive sufficient powers from RSHA *Amt* IV.

South America.

Shortly before the war broke out members of the crews of vessels proceeding to Buenos Aires, Rio de Janeiro, etc., were recruited with the object of setting up an intelligence service in those towns through their intermediary. Prospects seemed promising, but came to nothing owing to the interruption of sea communications.

Great Britain.

Groups of agents were run from Antwerp in 1938 and 1939 by two German nationals, one a local resident, and the other a Catholic refugee who had offered his services as an agent through a German pastor of the Evangelical Seamans' Mission there. The latter worked through a cut-out (his fiancé), and the information he provided included reports on Catholic organisations and German *emigres* in Antwerp, as well as useful counter-espionage material. He maintained personal contact with Hamburg, travelling on an Esthonian passport. Another German Catholic, recruited through the Catholic Seamans' Mission in Antwerp, was in touch with the British and Belgian intelligence services, and also provided information on the activities of German *emigres* in Belgium. He too reported personally to Hamburg, crossing the frontier illegally.

All of the above eventually became compromised, and transferred their activities to Rotterdam. The above mentioned cut-out, however, remained in Belgium, and was duly transferred (presumably with some of the sub-agents) to the *Einsatzkommando* of the *Sipo* and SD in Antwerp after the occupation (in 1940).

Another German, a very cunning and experienced agent, who was employed full time by *Stapoleitstelle* Hamburg before being transferred to the *Einsatzkommando*, ran a large group of Belgian (mostly Flemish) agents.

Holland.

In addition to the three above mentioned refugee agents from Belgium, *Stapoleitstelle* Hamburg had two highly efficient Dutch agents in Holland, both recruited before the war. One of these, who became known to *Stapoleitstelle* Hamburg through the *Deutsche Fichtebund*, made regular journeys between Amsterdam and Hamburg, producing a large number of reports of a high standard. The other, a resident of The Hague, ran a network of agents covering all the large towns of Holland. His reports covered various fields, and he had extensive connections with members of enemy intelligence services, especially among Mitropa waiters, who collected his reports for transmission to the N-*Referat*. Shortly before the outbreak of war he was engaged in negotiations to obtain the prints of a propellerless aircraft.

Denmark.

Here again *Stapoleitstelle* Hamburg ran some good agents, both before and during the war. These were practically without exception Danish nationals, and included two National Socialists, one of whom was introduced by the *Deutsche Fichtebund*, one a *Volksdeutsche*. They were employed on work against the Social Democrat Party and communists, obtaining information about suspects and wanted persons, etc, and were either resident in Denmark or made trips there from Hamburg.

In addition to these Danes, an Esthonian agent, an employee of the Esthonian Consulate in Hamburg, made several trips to Denmark, both before and during the first years of the war, and set up a group of agents there, from time to time submitting good reports. (Information about his activities lacks precision, and it is possible that these agents were used to penetrate Esthonia from Denmark).

It is not clear whether or not *Stapoleitstelle* Hamburg continued intelligence work in Denmark after 1943, when at least one of the resident agents there, as well as two other Danes hitherto employed on watching Danish workers in Hamburg, and who had returned home, were handed over to the *Einsatzkommando* of the *Sipo* and SD in Copenhagen.

Finland.

One of the Danish national socialists employed by the N-*Referat* in Denmark, who had fled to Finland before the occupation to escape arrest, was used for a time during the war as an agent. He received regular payments through a courier, in return for which he delivered information of a general character.

Sweden.

The agents working in Sweden included three ex-communists, two of whom were Germans. One of these was sent to Sweden in 1938 and submitted rgeular reports by courier until he was arrested by the Swedish police and deported (prior to 1942). The other, a refugee, volunteered his services and sent regular reports on the communist movement in Stockholm and the activities of German *emigres* until July or August 1943, when he ceased work. The third ex-communist, a stateless Finn, trained in Russia and a member of the crew of a German vessel calling at Stockholm, was in contact with the Russian Intelligence Services, and was still working for *Stapoleitstelle* Hamburg in the later stages of the war.

Five other agents, Germans belonging to the German merchant navy, were employed on counter-espionage work, and three are alleged to have been in contact with the British Intelligence Service in Stockholm or Goteborg (Gothenburg). One of these was arrested in Sweden in 1943 and deported after serving a term of imprisonment, since when he did no further work.

Between 1939 and 1942 a *Volksdeutsche*, previously employed in Denmark, and who had been deported by the Danish police, made two trips to Stockholm for the N-*Referat*, on the second of which he was imprisoned by the Swedish police for holding false papers. On his release he returned to Germany.

Reports on the morale of the diplomatic representatives in Stockholm, their views regarding the outcome of the war, etc, were received from a Swedish merchant who was also Consul General for Chile and who communicated with *Stapoleitstelle* Hamburg through a Hamburg merchant with whom he did business.

Switzerland.

As stated above, *Stapoleitstelle* Karlsruhe controlled all activities in Switzerland, and Hamburg merely received some few reports, all of a general character, from casual agents who paid visits there. These included an Iranian, who was recruited in 1942 and obtained visas for Holland, Switzerland, the Protectorate, and occasionally Turkey. Considering the large number of journeys he undertook, the reports he submitted on these countries were unsatisfactory.

Latvia.

A group of agents was set up in Latvia through a Latvian, a hospital doctor with excellent connections, who was recruited shortly before the outbreak of war. Communications were maintained with him by courier, and he submitted good reports on the behaviour of the Russians during the occupation. Contact was broken off after Latvia became incorporated in the USSR.

The Balkans.

Bulgaria.

In 1941 it was planned to build up an intelligence service through several White Russians in Sofia, with whom a leading official of the *Deutsche Fichtebund* was in contact, but this was not approved by RSHA *Amt* IV, ostensibly because they already had adequate contacts in Sofia.

Jugoslavia.

A group of 7–8 pro-German Jugoslav agents was formed early in 1941 by a German agent of *Stapoleitstelle* Hamburg who visited Jugoslavia under cover as a journalist. (These were duly handed over to the *Einsatzkommando* of the *Sipo* and SD after the occupation, 1941). On his return to Germany the above-mentioned German agent submitted a valuable report on the *coup d'état* aginst the Jugoslav government and the pact between the new regime and Soviet Russia.

Occasional reports were received from Hamburg merchants who visited the Balkans, and had some connection with *Stapoleitstelle* Hamburg officially.

(m) Spain.

Here also *Stapoleitstelle* Hamburg had an established intelligence service, but a comparatively larger number of reports were received than from the Balkans. This was due to the fact that the N-*Referat* maintained friendly relations with an officer of *Abwehrstelle* Stettin, who controlled an exceptionally large and reliable network of Spanish agents and submitted some counter-espionage reports to the N-*Referat* when he visted Hamburg from Spain.

(n) Portugal.

A group of agents was set up in Portugal in 1940 by the same German who later established contacts in Jugoslavia (see above). These were dropped in 1941 after *Amt* IV had objected that the RSHA already ran a good intelligence service in Lisbon.

C. The *Polizei Attachés*.

The '*Attaché Gruppe*' under SS-*Stubaf* Zindel came under the direct control of the CdS himself. Nevertheless the organisation had its roots in the *Gestapo*, and was staffed exclusively by *Amt* IV personnel.

The *Gruppe* had its beginnings in 1936 when Heydrich inaugurated a series of 'good-will' visits to foreign police services, leading eventually to a series of congresses in Berlin to discuss matters of mutual interest, at the time mainly the question of communism. Naturally the idea made the greatest development in relation to those countries of ideological tendencies similar to those of Germany. After the *Anschluss*, an 'International Police Commission' was set up in Vienna under the presidency of Heydrich, and, with the creation of the RSHA, the '*Polizei Attaché Gruppe*'. Heydrich's main achievement was in obtaining the right to obtain representation for the *Polizei Attachés* in the various German Legations abroad, an advantage which both Heydrich and Müller were eager to exploit, as it represented an opportunity for extending the scope of *Amt* IV outside the Reich itself. For this reason the *Attachés* received the full support of both Heydrich and Müller, and were accorded an importance out of keeping with their worth, as the personnel chosen had normally little training or ability to suit them to their new tasks. Any value which they might have had for *Amt* VI was largely destroyed by the bad relations existing between Müller and Schellenberg, both jealous of the rights of their own *Ämter*. The *Attachés* were officially given the function of acting as chief representative of the RSHA for all other dependent formations also represented in the country, and by virtue of this, Müller attempted to claim the right for the *Attachés* to not only act in charge of *Amt* VI, a right which was strongly and successfully resisted by Schellenberg, as the chief fault of the *Attaché* was normally that, as a *Gestapo* official, he was a 'marked man' from the date of his appointment. The *Polizei Attachés* varied in quality and in influence, Winzer in Spain being one of the strongest and most efficient, Kappler in Rome being intelligent and a good source for *Amt* VI, while Meisinger in Tokyo was a complete failure.

The only importance to *Amt* VI in the *Attaché Gruppe* lay in the right acquired by Schellenberg to use their courier service, which granted diplomatic privilege. In addition, Schellenberg's right to the exclusive allocation of Foreign Exchange gave him a useful lever against Müller's ambition. The various *Polizei Attachés* and their stations are listed below:

Rome	SS-*Ostubaf* Herbert Kappler
Madrid	SS-*Stubaf* KR Paul Winzer
Tokyo	SS-*Staf Oberst der Polizei* Josef Meisinger
Bucharest	SS-*Hstuf* KR Kurt Geissler
	(then) SS-*Staf Oberst der Polizei* Horst Böhme
	(then) SS-*Stubaf* Gustav Richter

Bratislava	SS-*Stubaf* KR Franz Goltz
Agram	SS-*Stubaf* KR Hans Helm
Belgrade	SS-*Ostuf* KI Hübner
Sofia	SS-*Ostubaf* ORR Adolf Hoffmann
Sweden	SS-*Stubaf* Lothar Neumann
Portugal	SS-*Stubaf* KR Erich Schröder
Istanbul	SS-*Stubaf* KR Bruno Wolff

Part V

Miscellaneous

A. The Role of the *Gestapo* in German Resistance Movements.

1. General.

By virtue of its long experience, the general fanaticism and ruthlessness of its members, its ready made networks in Germany itself, the *Gestapo* organisation in Germany was by far the best suited for the setting up of resistance movements to combat Allied occupation of the country. Its potential value in this respect was somewhat lessened by the eternal conflict within the Party between refusing to acknowledge the possibility of defeat and preparing for all eventualities, as such preparations in themselves would have required an order emanating from some high authority, and no responsible person, not even Himmler, was prepared to risk his reputation and his neck in the eyes of Hitler. Generally speaking, therefore, attempts by the *Gestapo* to organise post-occupational sabotage and resistance networks came too late in the day to be effective, but their efforts were considerably better than the pathetic I-*Netze* on which *Amt* VI had spent so much time and money since 1943.

Nevertheless the capacity for spontaneous resistance in the *Gestapo* was much more marked than elsewhere. The normal *Gestapo* officer had little to gain by surrender to the Allies, and a feature of the arrests made immediately after the collapse was the high percentage of *Amt* VI personnel involved. *Amt* VI, relatively mere amateurs in the field of espionage and intelligence, folded up without a fight, except of course for *Gruppe* VI S. *Amt* IV held out for a considerably longer period, and it was some time before arrests of leading personnel took place. Nor can the incentive to resist had completely disappeared. Faced with the alternative of probable trial under the War Crimes Commission, the *Gestapo* officer must feel the primitive urge of the beast to die fighting rather than surrender to an inevitable fate.

The danger to the [Allied] security authorities in occupation comes therefore much more from the *Gestapo* than from any other direction. It is small consolation that the RSHA as a whole has been liquidated, as the *Gestapo* methods and organisation have, so to speak, a high degree of 'spontaneous combustion'. The personnel themselves have had too long experience in the arts of repression, interrogation, clandestine activity and ruthlessness, not to be able to turn that experience to good account under circumstances, which in their essence resemble those of the early days of the Party. In addition, the twenty years of active control which they have enjoyed has permitted the organisation in Germany of a network, the size and effectiveness of which can be judged from Part III, above. While, therefore, it can be said with certainty that no centralised control remains which is in a position to issue directives to its former branches, the development of local movements, however disconnected they may be, is much more likely to revolve round the elements of the old *Gestapo*, officer and agent, than any other former Nazi organisation. The danger lies in a successful penetration of some organisation promoted and fostered by the Allies themselves; it is easy to develop on the framework of an already existing organisation. The former hardy plant of the *Gestapo* is most likely to reappear as a parasite. The effective safeguard is in the identification of all *Gestapo* personnel and agents, a problem which is largely a local one in the early stages.

It would be unwise, therefore, to underrate the efforts which were made by the *Gestapo* in the period preceding the collapse at resistance in the light of their failure. These efforts are summarised briefly below, no attempt having been made to give details of the local organisation of networks. Three distinct phases can be distinguished in the development of the resistance movements, easily classified under their code names—Nibelungen, Siegrune and Bundschuh.

2. The Nibelungen Scheme.

The first attempts at any stay-behind activities on the part of *Amt* IV came as a result of an order issued by Himmler himself in the autumn of 1944, when he was for a short spell in command of the Army Group fighting in the Upper Rhine area, and realised that the information available to the army in that area was insufficient. As a result of this deficiency he issued a general instruction to *Amt* IV and to the HSSPFs concerned that the *Gestapo* was to organise a stay-behind network to supplement that of *Amt* VI and the *Mil.Amt.* The order was given without any regard to the capacity of *Amt* IV to undertake such a task at short notice, and the resultant preparations were hurried and ineffective. Concrete results as far as organisation is concerned were obtained in two directions only. *Stapostelle* Köln, on receipt of its instructions from the HSSPF West, attempted an ambitious scheme of '*Widerstand und Sabotagegruppen*' (resistance and sabotage groups), controlled through *Referat* IV N of the *Stelle*. Unfortunately for the *Stelle*, documents were captured at an early date giving documentary evidence on the organisation of the scheme and the personnel and agents involved. On paper the *Unternehmen* (operation) was impressive; in practice it was a complete failure, as in many cases the agents scheduled to be used as stay-behind agents showed under interrogation that they were unaware of the fact that they had even been recruited. The network was quickly rounded up.

The second result of Himmler's order was an attempt by *Referat* IV A2b to set up in Western Europe a network of W/T agents, most of whom were arrested Russian agents who had been dropped by parachute in the East. The scheme, however, in common with that undertaken at Köln, was hastily improvised and though some twenty-five agents were trained and equipped only about ten were sent to the Saarbrücken and Koblenz areas of the Rhine with instructions to allow themselves to be overrun and then establish contact by W/T with the main transmitter in Berlin. The scheme failed in two respects, as the central station had to be evacuated and did not have the opportunity of re-establishing itself for any time in any other place, while the agents themselves, seeing which way the wind was blowing, made little effort to carry out their mission.[5]

3. The Siegrune Operation.

While the Nibelungen scheme was hastily organised as a result of orders from Himmler, the Siegrune operation was a conscious effort on the part of *Amt* IV to use its *Stapostellen* throughout Germany for the organisation of an information network based on the already existing networks under the control of the *Stellen*. Instructions for the organisation of the Siegrune network were issued in March 1945, and applied to non-occupied territory at the time. The *Stapostellen* which up till then had not been over run by the Allies were instructed to organise within their areas information networks covering the political and military spheres and, in addition, a sabotage network to operate when the areas were overrun.

Siegrune functioned mostly in the West, as in the East general instructions had already gone out to *Stapostelle* through the IdS that the *Stellen* were to co-operate with *Gruppe* VI C in bolstering up the new shaky *Unternehmen* Zeppelin, now called *Unternehmen* Dessau. Siegrune was prominent in the Weimar area under SS-*Ostubaf* Hans Helmuth Wolff, formerly of *Referat* IV D3, but here again the enterprise was started at too late a date to be effective. It is probable too that the Renndorfer organisation further south came under the Siegrune scheme, though this is as yet unknown.

4. *Aktion* Bundschuh.

Bundschuh marked the third and final stage in the efforts at resistance. The origins of Bundschuh are still a matter of doubt, but it now seems fairly clearly established that the orders emanated from *Amt* I. With the confusion then existing in the RSHA, this fact is less surprising than it might otherwise have been. It seems too that Bundschuh was under consideration by late 1944, but effective orders were not given until April 1945. Bundschuh differed from the previous *Unternehmen* in that it provided for direct action on the part of *Sipo* personnel themselves (that is, the *Gestapo* and the *Kripo*). They received instructions to go underground themselves, their immediate task being to remain effectively in hiding and await further instructions before beginning any activity. There was no suggestion in the Bundschuh scheme that agents should be recruited for the purpose of organising a network. The scheme depended of course on there remaining some centralised German control capable of issuing further instructions. When in fact all effective military resistance ceased in early May 1945, Bundschuh collapsed with it.

B. Special Points.

1. The last stages of RSHA *Amt* IV.

The attempts at resistance which have been described above must be seen against the general background of *Amt* IV from the latter half of 1944 onwards, a period which was marked by confusion in organisation and personnel as a result of compulsory evacuation following on the heavy Allied air-raids on Berlin. Temporary headquarters were set up in Brandenburg under the cover name *Dachs* I and *Dachs* II. This evacuation took place in July 1944, but as a result of the Russian breakthrough, a further move became necessary, and as Berlin itself was under heavy air bombardment at the time, the *Amt* moved as a whole to Hof in Bavaria. As a result of insufficient accommodation, and inevitable breakdowns in communications, the working capabilities of the *Amt* became extremely restricted. In view of this the *Gestapo* in Germany was working largely through the individual efforts of the *Stapostellen*.

The final stage came with the formation of the *Nordstab* and the *Südstab* in the period immediately preceding the final collapse. It was originally planned that the *Nordstab* should remain in Berlin, but this plan was altered, and the group left Berlin to join the general *Nordstab* of the RSHA under Ohlendorf, disintegrating in the north in the early days of May 1945. The *Südstab* meantime had gone south under Isselhorst to join in the general disintegration in the Alpine Redoubt. By early May 1945 RSHA *Amt* IV had ceased to exist as a centralised body.

2. Arrests.

The arrests of *Amt* IV personnel were, in the early stages, very restricted in number. It was only from about September 1945 onwards that leading personalities were roped in, and the position at the moment can be considered as fairly satisfactory. The obvious gap is of course the *Amtschef* himself, Müller, who almost certainly remained in Berlin until the end, but his fate is unknown. The other personnel who have been arrested are shown in Appendix VI. It is again stressed, however, that while *Amt* IV has ceased to exist in its previous form, as a result of which the importance of the arrests of further leading personnel is considerably lessened, the danger from the *Amt* exists throughout its entire echelons, as has been explained in Paragraph A.

3. Sources.

The EDS [Enemy Document Section] Publication, 'The German Police', issued in April 1945 under reference EDS/G/10, contains detailed information on the regional organisation of the *Gestapo* in Germany.

On the *Amt* itself:

> Interrogation of SS-*Stubaf* Horst Kopkow, dated 7 June 1945.
> USFET Consolidated Report No. 9 on *Amt* IV based on interrogations of SS-*Stubaf* Lindow, SS-*Ostubaf* Wolff, SS-*Staf* Isselhorst, SS-*Staf* Mildner and SS-*Hstuf* Halmanseger, dated 15 November 1945.
> Separate interrogation of SS-*Hstuf* Halmanseger on *Dienststelle*, RSHA IV N.

This report was issued by W.R.C.3a, on 7 December 1945.

Appendix I

Organisation of RSHA *Amt* IV (*Gegnerbekämpfung*), 1939–1940

Amtschef: SS-*Oberführer Reichskriminaldirektor* Heinrich Müller.

Gruppe	Referat	Sachgebiet	Referent
Gruppenleiter A: vacant			
Geschäftsstellenleiter: SS-*Stubaf* Zimmermann			
A	1	*Kommunismus, Marxismus, Einheitsfront*, Illegal Propaganda	SS-*Stubaf* Vogt
	2	*Sabotagebekämpfung, Sabotageabwehr, Falschungswesen*	SS-*Ostuf* Geissler
	3	Opposition, *Reaktion, Legitismus, Heimtücke*	SS-*Stubaf* Litzenberg
	4	*Kirchenpolitische Angelegenheiten*	SS-*Ostuf* Roth
	5	*Emigranten*	SS-*Ostuf* Ass Jagusch

Gruppenleiter B: SS-*Stubaf* Dr Rang

B	1	*Parteiangelegenheiten, oppositionalle Jugend, Sonderfälle*	SS-*Stubaf* Stage
	2	*Schutzangelegenheiten, Attentats-meldungen*	SS-*Stubaf* Schulz
	3	*Wirtschaftsangelegenheiten*	SS-*Stubaf* Wolter
	4	*Presseangelegenheiten*	SS-*Stubaf* Dr Rang

Gruppenleiter C: SS-*Hstuf* Dr Berndorff

C	1	*Kartei, Personalakten, Ankunftswesen*	POI Matzke
	2	*Schutzhaftangelegenheiten*	SS-*Hstuf* Dr Berndorff
	3	*Berichterstattung, Ereignismeldungen*	SS-*Hstuf* Pieper
	4	*Nachrichtensammelstelle*	SS-*Hstuf* Halmanseger
	5	*Überwachungen, Sonderaufträge*	SS-*Hstuf* Nippe

Gruppenleiter D: vacant

D	1	*Protektoratsangelegenheiten*	SS-*Hstuf* Dr Jonak
	2	*Gouvernementsangelegenheiten*	SS-*Hstuf* Baatz
	3	*Minderheiten, Vertrauensstellen, Juden*	SS-*Hstuf* Schröder
	4	*Auswanderung*	SS-*Hstuf* Eichmann
	5	*Verkehr mit ausl. Polizei*	SS-*Ustuf* Priebke

Gruppenleiter E: SS-*Brif.* Dr Best
Vertreter: SS-*Stubaf* Schellenberg

E	1	*Allg. Abwehr und Wehrmachts-angelegeheiten*	KD Bläsing
	2	*Auslander*	SS-*Hstuf* Jarosch
	3	*Abwehr – West*	SS-*Hstuf* Dr Fischer
	4	*Abwehr – Nord*	KD Dr Schambacher
	5	*Abwehr – Ost*	SS-*Stubaf* KD Kubitzky
	6	*Abwehr – Süd*	SS-*Ostuf* KR Liska

Appendix II

Organisation of RSHA *Amt* IV, 1941–1943 (Investigation and Combatting of Opponents)

Amtschef: SS-*Brigadeführer und Generalmajor der Polizei* Heinrich Müller.
Adjutant: SS-*Ustuf* Duchstein

Note: Directly subject to the *Amtschef*:
　　　　IV (N) Information-collection office [*Nachrichtensammelstelle*]
　　　　IV (P) Communication with foreign police forces.

General Border Inspector: *Amtschef* IV
Deputy: SS-*Staf* Krichbaum

Geschäftsstelle IV

Leiter: vacant
Deputy: SS-*Hstuf Polizeirat* Pieper
IV Gst.　a) Matter of personnel, *Amt* IV
　　　　　　Internal activity
　　　　　　Plan of distribution of work, Filing plans, Statistics
　　　　　　Need and distribution of space
　　　　　　Business requirements
　　　　　　Secret Registry of *Amt* IV
　　　　　　Official activity of office employees

　　　　　b) Reporting
　　　　　　Announcements of incidents

　　　　　c) Office prison (i.e. in the building)
　　　　　　Permanent service
　　　　　　Identification service

Gruppe	*Referat*	*Sachgebiet*	*Referent*
* *Gruppenleiter* A: SS-*Ostubaf* ORR Panzinger *			
A	1	Communism, Marxism and associated organizations, wartime crimes, illegal and hostile propaganda	SS-*Stubaf* KD Vogt

2	Defence against sabotage, combating of sabotage, commissioners of defensive political police activity, political forgeries	SS-*Hstuf* KK Kopkow
3	Reaction, opposition, *Legitismus*, Liberalism, emigrants, treachery	SS-*Stubaf* KR Litzenberg
4	Protective service, reports of attempted assassinations etc., special guarding jobs, pursuit troop	SS-*Stubaf* KD Schulz

Gruppenleiter B: SS-*Stubaf* Hartl
Deputy: SS-*Stubaf* RR Roth

B	1	Political Catholicism	SS-*Stubaf* RR Roth
	2	Political Protestantism, Sects	SS-*Stubaf* RR Roth
	3	Other Churches, Freemasonry	vacant
	4	Jews and Evacuation	SS-*Stubaf* Eichmann

Gruppenleiter C: SS-*Ostubaf* ORR Dr Rang
Deputy: SS-*Stubaf* RuKR Dr Berndorff

C	1	Evaluation, Main Card Index, Administration of personnel files, A-Card Index, Supervision of foreigners, Central Visa Office	*PolRat* Matzke
	2	*Schutzhaft*	SS-*Stubaf* Dr Berndorff
	3	Press and Literature	SS-*Stubaf* Dr Jahr
	4	Party Matters; Special Cases	SS-*Stubaf* KD Stage

Gruppenleiter IV D: SS-*Ostubaf* Dr Weinmann
Deputy: SS-*Stubaf* RR Dr Jonak

D	1	Protectorate (Bohmen & Moravia), Czechs in the Reich	SS-*Stubaf* Dr Jonak
	2	General Government Matters; Poles in the Reich	*RegAss* Thiemann
	3	Confidential offices, foreigners hostile to the Reich	SS-*Hstuf* RR Schröder
	4	Occupied Territory: France, Luxemburg, Alsace and Lorraine, Belgium, Holland, Norway, Denmark	SS-*Stubaf* RR Baatz

Gruppenleiter E: SS-*Stubaf* RR Schellenberg

E	1	General Defence Matters, supplying of legal opinions in matters of high and state treason	SS-*Hstuf* KK Lindow
	2	General Economic Matters; economic espionage	*RegAss* Sebastian
	3	*Abwehr* – West	SS-*Hstuf* KR Dr Fischer
	4	*Abwehr* – North	KD Dr Schambacher
	5	*Abwehr* – East	SS-*Stubaf* KD Kubitzky
	6	*Abwehr* – South	SS-*Hstuf* KR Dr Schmitz

Appendix III

Organisation of RSHA *Amt* IV, 1943–1944 (*Gegner-Erforschung und -Bekämpfung*)

Amtchef:	SS-*Gruppenführer und Generalleutnant der Polizei* Heinrich Müller.
Adjutant:	SS-*Ostuf* Duchstein
Anmerkung:	*Dem Amtschef unmittelbar unterstellt*: IV (N) *Nachrichtensammelstelle*
Generalgrenzinspekteur:	*Amtchef* IV, SS-*Gruf* Müller
Vertreter:	vacant at this time; function being carried out by SS-*Ostubaf* ORR Huppenkothen

Geschäftstelle IV:

Leiter:	SS-*Stubaf* Amtsrat Pieper

IV Gst.	a) *Personalangelegenheiten des Amtes* IV
	Innerer Geschäftsbetrieb
	Geschäftsverteilungensplan – Aktenplan – Statistik
	Raumbedart und Raumverteilung
	Geschäftsbefdürfnisse
	Geheimregistratur des Amt IV
	Dienstbetrieb der Amtsgehilfen
	b) *Berichterstattung*
	Ereignismeldungen
	Kartei –
	c) *Hausgefängnis*

Dauerdienst

Erkennungsdienst

Zeichenstelle

Gruppe	*Referat*	*Sachgebiet*	*Referent*

Gruppe A: Gegner, *Sabotage und Schutzdienst*

Gruppenleiter A: SS-*Staf* RD Panzinger

A	1	Kommunismus, Marxismus und Nebenorganisationen, Kriegsdelikte, Illegale und Feind-Propaganda	SS-*Stubaf* KD Lindow
	2	Sabotageabwehr, Sabotage-bekämpfung, Politische Falschungswesen	SS-*Hstuf* KR Kopkow
	3	Reaktion, Opposition, Legitimus, Liberalismus, Heimtücke-Angelegenheiten	SS-*Stubaf* Litzenberg
	4	Schutzdienst, Attentatsmeldungen, Überwachungen, Fahndungstrupp	SS-*Stubaf* Franz Schulz

Gruppe B: *Politische Kirche, Sekten und Juden*

Gruppenleiter: vacant

Deputy: SS-*Stubaf* RR Roth

B	1	Politischer Katholizismus	SS-*Stubaf* RR Roth
	2	Politischer Protestantismus, Sekten	SS-*Stubaf* Hahnenbruch
	3	Sonstige Kirchen, Freimaurerei	SS-*Ostuf* Wandesleben
	4	Judenangelegenheiten, Räumungs-angelegenheiten, Einzichung volks- und staatsfeindlichen Vermögens, Aberkennung der deutschen Reichsangehörigkeit	SS-*Ostubaf* Eichmann

Gruppe C: *Personenkartei, Personenaktenverwaltung, Schutzhaft, Presse und Partei*

Gruppenleiter C: vacant

Deputy: SS-*Ostubaf* Dr Berndorff

C	1	Auswertung, Hauptkartei, Personenaktenverwaltung, Auskunftsstelle Auslanderüberwachung	SS-*Hstuf* Witzel

	2	*Schutzhaftangelegenheiten*	SS-*Ostubaf* Dr Berndorff
	3	*Angelegenheiten der Presse und des Schrifttums*	vacant
	4	*Angelgenheiten der Partei und ihrer Gliederungen, Sonderfälle*	SS-*Stubaf* Stage

Gruppe D: *Grossdeutsche Einflussgebiete, Auslandische Arbeiter*
Gruppenleiter D: SS-*Staf* Dr Rang
Deputy: vacant

D	1	*Protektoratangelegenheiten, Tschechen im Reich, Slowakei, Serbien, Kroatien, und die übrigen Gebiete des ehem. Jugoslavien, Griechland*	Dr Lettow
	2	*Gouvernementangelegenheiten, Polen im Reich*	SS-*Stubaf* Thomsen
	3	*Vertrauenssteller Staatsfeindliche Auslander, Emigranten*	SS-*Stubaf* Wolff
	4	*Besetzte Gebiete Frankreich, Belgien, Holland, Norwegen, Dänemark*	SS-*Stubaf* Dr Höner
	5	*Besetzte Ostgebiete*	SS-*Hstuf* Thiemann

Gruppe IV E: *Abwehr*
Gruppenleiter E: SS-*Ostubaf* ORR Huppenkothen

E	1	*Allgemeine Abwehrangelgenheiten, Erstattung von Gutachten in Hoch- und Landesverrats und sonstigen Angelegenheiten gemäss Ziffer 5 der Verschulessachen-Anweisung, Abwehrbeauftragte*	SS-*Stubaf* Renken
	2	*Allgemeine Wirtschaftsangelegen- heiten, Wirtschaftsespionage-abwehr, Werkschutz und Bewachungs-gewerbes, Politisch-polizeiliche Abwehrbeauftragte*	SS-*Stubaf* Quetting
	3	*Abwehr West*	SS-*Stubaf* Dr Schäfer
	4	*Abwehr Nord*	SS-*Hstuf* Clemens
	5	*Abwehr Ost*	SS-*Hstuf* Häussler
	6	*Abwehr Süd*	KR Rauch

Gruppe IV F: *Passwesen und Auslanderpolizei*
Gruppenleiter F: *Ministerialrat* Krause
Deputy: SS-*Ostubaf* ORR Kröning

F	1	*Grenzpolizei*	SS-*Stubaf* Opitz
	2	*Passwesen*	SS-*Stubaf* Dr Baumann
	3	*Ausweisen und Kennkarten*	SS-*Stubaf* Kelbling
	4	*Auslanderpolizei und grundsatz-liche Grenzangelegenheiten*	SS-*Ostubaf* Kröning
	5	*Zentrale Sichtvermerkstelle*	SS-*Hstuf* Jarosch

Appendix IV

Organisation of RSHA *Amt* IV, 1944–1945
(*Gegnerforschung und Bekämpfung*)

Note: The following breakdown is based on interrogations and not on captured documents; absolute accuracy is therefore not guaranteed, especially as the leading *Amt* IV characters seem to be uncertain themselves on the final organisational structure of the *Amt*. Attention is drawn to *Hilfsreferat* IV A3g, which has not been mention in Part II (above).

Amtschef: SS-*Gruppenführer und Generalleutnant der Polizei* Heinrich Müller.
Adjutant: SS-*Ostuf* Duchstein

Den Amtschef unmittelbar unterstellt:

IV N	*Nachrichtensammelstelle*	SS-*Hstuf* Halmanseger
IV ZABP	*Zentral Auslandsbrief-prüfungsstelle*	SS-*Ostubaf* Heller
IV G	*Zollgrenzschutz*	SS-*Obf* Somann
IV B/a A	*Auslandischer Arbeiter*	SS-*Hstuf* Häussler

Geschäftstelle IV:
Leiter: *PolRat* Pieper

IV Gst. a) *Personalangelegenheiten des Amtes* IV
 b) *Bericherstattung, Ereignismeldungen, Kartei*
 c) *Hausgefängnis, Dauerdienst, Erkennungsdienst, Zeichenstelle*

Gruppe Referat Sachgebiet   *Referent*
Gruppe IV A: *Fachabteilungen*
Gruppenleiter A: SS-*Staf* Huppenkothen

A	1	Opposition	SS-*Stubaf* Litzenberg
	1a	*Linksbewegung*	SS-*Hstuf* Pütz
	1b	*Rechtsbewegung*	SS-*Stubaf* Litzenberg
	2	Sabotage	SS-*Stubaf* KD Kopkow
	2a	Sabotage	SS-*Hstuf* Büchert
	2b	*Funkspiele, Gegenabwehr*	SS-*Hstuf* Ampletzer
	3	*Abwehr*	SS-*Stubaf* Quetting
	3a	*Spionageabwehr*	SS-*Stubaf* Schäfer
	3b	*Wirtschaft*	SS-*Stubaf* Quetting
	3c	*Industriesicherung*	KR Tischer
	3g	*Spielmaterial*	RR Engelmann
	4	*Weltanschauliche Gegner*	SS-*Ostubaf* Eichmann
	4a	*Politische Kirchen*	SS-*Stubaf* Hahnenbruch
	4b	*Juden, Emigranten*	SS-*Ostubaf* Eichmann
	5	*Sonderfälle*	SS-*Staf* Dr Rang
	5a	*Schutzdienst*	SS-*Stubaf* Schulz
	5b	*Partei, Presse*	SS-*Stubaf* Sanders
	6	*Karteien, Schutzhaft*	SS-*Ostubaf* Dr Berndorff
	6a	*Kartei, Akten*	SS-*Ostubaf* Dr Berndorff
	6b	*Schutzhaft*	SS-*Stubaf* Witzel
	6c	*Sippenhaft*	*PolRat* Jarosch

Gruppe IV B: *Gebietsabteilungen*
Gruppenleiter B: SS-*Stubaf* Lischka

1	*West-Nord*	SS-*Stubaf* Höner
1a	*Frankreich, Belgien*	SS-*Stubaf* Höner
1b	Holland, England, *Amerika*	SS-*Stubaf* Clemens
1c	*Dänemark, Norwegen, Schweden,* Finland	SS-*Hstuf* Rauch
2	*Ost-Südost*	SS-*Ostubaf* Wolff
2a	*Ostgebiete, Sowjetunion*	SS-*Ostubaf* Wolff
2b	*General-Gouvernement*	SS-*Stubaf* Thomsen
2c	*Protektorat, Slowakei*	SS-*Stubaf* Thiedecke
3	*Süd*	SS-*Ostubaf* Trenker
3a	Balkan, *Turkei, Ferner Osten*	SS-*Hstuf* Ahrens
3b	*Schweiz, Italien, Spanien,* Portugal, *Afrika*	SS-*Stubaf* Hilliges
4	*Pass- und Ausweiswesen*	*Min.Rat* Krause
4a	*Passwesen*	SS-*Stubaf* Baumann

4b	*Ausweiswesen, Ausländerpolizei*	SS-*Ostubaf* Kröning
4c	*Zentralsichtvermerkstelle*	SS-*Hstuf* Jarosch

Appendix V

Organisational development of RSHA *Amt* IV, 1939–1945

Note: This chart is intended to serve merely as a rough guide; absolute accuracy is impossible.

Sachgebiet	1939–40	1941–43	1944–45	1944–45
Kommunismus, Marxismus, illegale Propaganda	IV A1	IV A1	IV A1	IV A1a
Sabotagebekämpfung	IV A2	IV A2	IV A2	IV A2a
Opposition, Reaktion	IV A3	IV A3	IV A3	IV A1b
Kirchenpolitische Angelegenheiten	IV A4	IV B1-B2	IV B1-B2	IV A4a
Emigranten	IV A5	IV D2	IV D3	IV A4b
Parteiangelegenheiten, Sonderfälle	IV B1	IV C4	IV C4	IV A5b
Schutzangelegenheiten, Attentatmeldungen	IV B2	IV A4	IV A4	IV A5a
Wirtschaftsangelegenheiten	IV B3	IV E2	IV E2	IV A3b
Presseangelegenheiten	IV B4	IV C3	IV C3	IV A5b
Kartei, Personalakten, Auskunftsw.	IV C1	IV C1	IV C1	IV A6a
Schutzhaftsangelegenheiten	IV C2	IV C2	IV C2	IV A6b
Berichterstattung, Ereignismeldung.	IV C3	IV Gst b	IV Gst b	IV Gst b
Nachrichtensammelstelle	IV C4	IV N	IV N	IV N
Überwachung, Sonderaufträge	IV C5	IV A4	IV A4	IV A5
Protektoratsangelegenheiten	IV D1	IV D1	IV D1	IV B2a
Gouvernementgen.angelegenheiten	IV D2	IV D2	IV D2	IV B2b
Minderheiten, Vertrauenstellen, Juden (until 1941, transferred to IV B4)	IV D3	IV D3	IV D3	IV A4
Auswanderung, Räumnung Juden (from 1941)	IV D4	IV B4	IV B4	IV A4b
Verkehr mit ausl. Polizeien	IV D5	IV (P)	IV F4	IV B4b
Allg. Abwehr und Wehrmachts-angelegenheiten	IV E1	IV E1	IV E1	-
Auslander	IV E2	?	?	IV B/a A
Abwehr West	IV E3	IV E3	IV E3	IV B1a-b
Abwehr Nord	IV E4	IV E4	IV E4	IV B1c
Abwehr Ost	IV E5	IV E5	IV E5	IV B2
Abwehr Süd	IV E6	IV E6	IV E6	IV B3

Freimauerei	IV B3	IV B3	IV A4b
Besetzte Gebiete (France, Belgium Holland, Norway, Denmark)	IV D4	IV D4	IV B1
Besetzte Ostgebiete		IV D5	IV B2
Grenzpolizei		IV F1	IV G
Passwesen (from *Amt* II, 1943)		IV F2	IV B4a
Ausweisen und Kennkarten (from *Amt* II, 1943)		IV F3	IV B4b
Ausländerpolizei		IV F4	IV B4b
Zentralsichtvermerkstelle (from *Amt* II, 1941)	IV C1	IV F5	IV B4c
Sippenhaft			IV A6c
Spielmaterial			IV A3g

Appendix VI

Alphabetical Index of RSHA *Amt* IV Personnel, 1939–1945

Note: The *Referat* given in column 3 below indicates the *Referat* under the organisational structure of *Amt* IV as given in Appendix IV, except where the date under the 'Remarks' column ante-dates July 1944.

In such cases the old *Referat* is given, as no information has been forthcoming to indicate the new *Referat* of the officer concerned. In most cases however the new *Referat* will be that indicated in Appendix V. Arrested personnel are underlined.

The author has taken the liberty of adding additional information under 'Remarks' and dating it where relevant or important.

Name and Rank	*Referat*	Remarks
Achamer Pifrader, SS-*Obf* Humbert	IV B	to 1945, *Gruppenleiter*; killed in air-raid on Linz, April 1945
Adam, SS-*Hstuf* KK Manfred	IV A3b	
Ahrens, SS-*Hstuf* Hermann	IV B3a	*Referent*
Albrecht, SS-*Ustuf* KS Artur	IV A5b	
Albrecht, SS-*Stuschaf* KS Erich	IV A1b	
Albrecht, SS-*Ustuf* KS Josef	IV E5	Nov. 1943
Altmann, SS-*Stuschaf* KS Hans	IV A1b	
Ampletzer, SS-*Hstuf* KR Thomas	IV A2b	*Referent*, KIA Berlin, Apr. 1945
Anders, SS-*Hstuf Reg.Amtmann* Karl	IV A4b	
Apelt, SS-*Ustuf* POS Erich	IV B3	
Aporius, POS Erich	IV A4a	Arrested British Zone

Arndt, SS-*Ustuf* KOS Heinrich	IV B1b	
Ast, SS-*Hstuf* KOS Erich	IV C4	Nov. 1943
Aubert, ORR	IV A3	Nov. 1943
Baack, KS Erich	IV E5	Nov. 1943
Baader, KS Oskar	IV A5a	
Baatz, SS-*Stubaf* RR Bernhard	IV D	Aug. 1943 posted to BdS Riga
Baberske, POI Johannes	IV D3	Nov. 1943
Backhaus, KS Albert	IV A4b	
Backhaus, PS Gerhard	IV A4b	
Baldin, KS Hugo	IV A3c	
Bandow, KS Max	IV A4a	
Barowski, KS	IV A2a	
Bartel, KS Max	IV A6b	
Bauer, KOS Wilhelm	IV A1a	
Baumann, SS-*Stubaf* ORR Christian	IV B4a	Arrested British Zone
Becker, SS-*Ostuf* PI Becker	IV B4c	
Behrendt, SS-*Ustuf* KOS Ernst	IV B1b	
Berg, KOS Wilhelm	IV A2a	Deputy *Referent*, Apr. 1945
Bernau, KOS Richard	IV E5	Nov. 1943
Berndorff, SS-*Ostubaf* ORuKR Dr Emil	IV A6	*Referent*, Apr. 1945
Berndt, SS-*Hstuf* POI Herbert	IV Gst.	at Hof, Feb. 1945
Best, SS-*Brif* Dr Karl Werner	IV E	*Gruppenleiter*, 1939–1940
Betz, SS-*Ostuf* PI Ferdinand	IV B2	
Beyer, PS Franz	IV B2	
Bielemeyer, KOS Wilhelm	IV A2b	at Hof, March 1945
Bläsing, KS Hermann	IV D1	1939–1940
Blobel, SS-*Staf* Paul	IV A4a	1944–1945, attachment only
Blume, SS-*Staf* Walter	IV C	*Gruppenleiter*, 1945
Bock, SS-*Stuschaf* KS Erich	IV A2a	arrested British Zone
Böhme, KS Karl	IV A2b	at Hof, March 1945
Böhmer, SS-*Stubaf* Amtsrat Hermann	IV G	1944–1945
Bölter, KS	IV B1c	
Bolz, *Büro Angestellter* Karl	IV A6a	arrested British Zone
Bonath, SS-*Hstuf* POI Gerhard	IV A6b	
Bordasch, SS-*Stuschaf* KOS Herbert	IV A1a	
Bosshammer, SS-*Stubaf* RR Fritz	IV B4	Nov. 1943
Brandt, SS-*Hstuf* KR Erwin	IV A1a	
Bräuer, KS Johannes	IV E3	Nov. 1943
Breier, KOS Mathias	IV E3	Nov. 1943
Breitenfeldt, SS-*Ostuf* PI Ulrich	IV B2	
Brenner, SS-*Ustuf* KK Rudolf	IV A2b	at Hof, March 1945
Brestrich, KS Helmut	IV B1a	in south Germany, March 1945

Breuer, SS-*Ustuf* KK Hans	IV B1a	
Brockmeier, SS-*Hstuf* POI Heinrich	IV A5b	to IV Gst., April 1945
Büchert, SS-*Hstuf* KK Karl-Heinrich	IV A2a	*Referent*; at Hof, March 1945
Büchler, ROI Bruno	IV A5b	
Buchmann, SS-*Ostuf* KK Helmuth	IV A5a	
Bucksch, SS-*Ostuf* PI Gustav	IV A6a	
Bunke, SS-*Hstuf* ROI Erich	IV A3b	
Burg, SS-*Hstuf* KR Dr Richard	IV B3a	
Burger, SS-*Ostuf* Anton	IV A4b	
Burghardt, SS-*Ostuf* POI	IV A6a	
Bürjes, SS-*Ustuf* KS Hans	IV B1a	
Carl, PI Walter	IV B1a	
Clemens, SS-*Hstuf* KR Wilhelm	IV B1b	*Referent*; at Schwerin, Apr. 1945
Dann, PI Konrad	IV Gst.	*Geheim Registratur*
Dedio, *Angestellter* Joseph	IV B2b	Russian interpreter
Deppe, PS Heinrich	IV A6a	
Deppner, SS-*Stubaf* RR Erich	IV	1944–1945
Deumling, SS-*Stubaf* RR Joachim	IV D2	1941–1944
de Waal, *Angestellter*	IV B1a	French interpreter
Didier, SS-*Hstuf* POI Richard	IV A6b	
Dorbrandt, PI Karl	IV D1	to 1943
Doring, KOS Erich	IV A5a	
Döring, SS-*Uschaf* Gerhard	IV B	Special courier to *Amtschef*
Drescher, KI Johann	IV A3	
Dresp, KS Kurt	IV A4a	Nov. 1943
Dressel, KOS Paul	IV B1a	
Dubiel, SS-*Hstuf* POI Adolf	IV B2b	
<u>Duchstein</u>, SS-*Ostuf* KK Albert	IV	Adjutant to *Amtschef* Müller; left Berlin, March 1945; arrested in US Zone
Eckerle, SS-*Hstuf* ROI Fritz	IV A1a	
Eder, KOA Anton	IV N	
Eichmann, SS-*Ostubaf* Adolf	IV A4	*Referent*
Eisenschmidt, SS-*Hstuf* KR Gerhard	IV A3b	
Engelmann, SS-*Stubaf* RR Heinz	IV E1	Nov. 1943
Falley, KOS Hermann	IV A5a	
Fehling, KI Fritz	IV A5b	
Feldmann, SS-*Ostuf* KK Erich	IV B1a	
Feussner, ROI Konrad	IV A6b	
Fiene, KS August	IV C4a	Nov. 1943
Findendei, KOS Heinrich	IV A5a	*Fahndungstrupp*, April 1945
Fischer, SS-*Ustuf* Helmut-Joachim	IV	Liaison officer to *Amt* III, 1945

Fischer, PS Herbert	IV A3a	
Fischer, SS-*Ostuf* KOS Karl-Heinz	IV A6b	
Fleger, KS Albert	IV E6	Nov. 1943
Förster, KR Karl	IV A6	Deputy *Referent*; in Prague, 1945
Frank, SS-*Ustuf* KS Rudolf	IV A2b	at Hof, March 1945
Franz, *Amtsrat* Richard	IV C4b	Nov. 1943
Frohwein, PS Waldemar	IV A6b	
<u>Fuhrmann</u>, SS-*Ustuf* KS Erich	IV A2a	arrested British Zone
Fumy, SS-*Stubaf Polizeirat* Rudolf	IV B2a	
Furrer, PS Willi	IV E1	Nov. 1943
Gans, SS-*Stubaf* KD Ernst	IV A3c	
Gärdler, KR	IV A	Nov. 1943; special duties
<u>Gebert</u>, *Büro Angestellter* Arthur	IV A6b	arrested British Zone
Geissler, SS-*Ostuf* KK Kurt	IV A2	*Referent*, 1939–41; with IV D1 as SS-*Stubaf* KD, 1943
Gerber, KOS Paul	IV B1a	
Giedlow, SS-*Hstuf* POI Hermann	IV B4c	
Giering, SS-*Hstuf* KR Hans	IV A2	1939–1941
Giesen, SS-*Ostuf* PI Bruno	IV A6b	
Gogalla, SS-*Ostuf* Wilhelm	IV Gst	supervised the *Hausgefängnis*
Gogolla, SS-*Ostuf* KOS Gustav	IV A2b	
Gohlke, *Ministerial Amtsgehilfe* Rudolf	IV E1	Nov. 1943
Gopfert, SS-*Ustuf* KK Alfred	IV D3	1942–1944
Göpfert, SS-*Ustuf* KK Karl	IV A2b	at Hof, March 1945
Grahn, SS-*Ostuf* KOS Werner	IV A5b	
Grenz, SS-*Ostuf* KS Otto	IV B1a	
Gross, SS-*Hstuf* KR Kurt	IV A2	from 1945, *Referent Amt* VI D4
Grothe, KS Bruno	IV B1b	
Grünberg, *Ministerial Registratur* Gustav	IV A1b	
Gründling, SS-*Hstuf* ROI Georg	IV B2a	
Grunert, SS-*Ustuf* PS Heinz	IV A1a	
Grunert, SS-*Stuschaf* KOS Richard	IV C1b	Nov. 1943
Gudjons, SS-*Hstuf* KK Lothar	IV B3a	
Günther, SS-*Stubaf* RR Rolf	IV A4b	at Salzburg, 30 April 1945
Gutzsche, KS Otto	IV A1a	Nov. 1943
Haak, KS Willy	IV A5a	at Hof, March 1945
Haaker, KI Hermann	IV A3a	
Haase, KOS Ferdinand	IV A4	Nov. 1943
Habecker, *Frau*	IV N	1944–1945
Habecker, KK Walter	IV A2a	
Hagemeister, SS-*Ustuf* KOS Louis	IV B3a	
Hahnenbruch, SS-*Stubaf* RR Erich	IV A4a	at Hof, April 1945

Hahnlein, PI Herbert	IV A6a	
Halmanseger, SS-*Hstuf* KI Leonhard	IV N	*Dienststellenleiter*; arrested in US Zone
Hamel, SS-*Ostuf* POI Erwin	IV A4a	
Hammermeister, SS-*Ustuf* KS Wilhelm	IV E3	1943, posted to KdS Warsaw
Harder, SS-*Ustuf* PS Kurt	IV A6b	
Hartl, SS-*Stubaf* Albert	IV B	1941, *Gruppenleiter*; arrested in US Zone
Hartmann, KOS Karl	IV E5	Nov. 1943
Hartmann, SS-*Ostuf* Richard	IV A4b	
Hasenbank, KOS Gerhard	IV A4a	
Hässler, SS-*Hstuf* KK Rudolf	IV B/a A	*Referent*, at Schwerin, April 1945
Häusler, SS-*Stubaf* RR Josef	IV A3a	
Hauck, KOS Hans	IV C4b	Nov. 1943
Haupt, SS-*Hstuf* KK Richard	IV A2a	MIA Berlin, April 1945
Hauth, SS-*Ustuf* Otto	IV A1a	
Havermann, SS-*Ostuf* PI Otto	IV B1a	
Hayn, SS-*Ustuf* KS Wilhelm	IV B2a	
Hegemann, SS-*Oschaf* POS Erich	IV Gst.	
Hein, KS Kurt	IV B2a	
Hein, SS-*Ostuf* KI Paul	IV A5a	*Fahndungstrupp*, April 1945
Hein, KS Wilhelm	IV D3	Nov. 1943
Heinrichs, SS-*Ostuf* KS Gerhard	IV A2	
Heinrichsohn, SS-*Oschaf* Ernst	IV B1a	
Heise, SS-*Ustuf* KS Ernst	IV A2a	at Hof, March 1945
Heller, SS-*Hschaf* KS Karl	IV A1b	
Heller, SS-*Ostubaf* ORuKR Reinhold	IV A1b	
Hentschel, POS Walter	IV E1	Nov. 1943
Henze, KK Hans	IV A2	died in an air-raid, 22 Jan. 1944
Herold, SS-*Hstuf* POI Richard	IV A1a	
Hilbig, POS Karl	IV E3	Nov. 1943
Hilliges, SS-*Ostuf* PI Heinz	IV Gst.	(brother of Werner Hilliges)
Hilliges, SS-*Stubaf* KR Werner	IV B3b	
Hinze, SS-*Ustuf* PS Bruno	IV C1	Nov. 1943
Höche, KI Wilhelm	IV A3b	
Hofer, ROI Adolf	IV Gst.	1944, posted to *Stapo* Munich
Hoffmann, KS Erich	IV A2	
Hoffmann, KS Friedrich	IV A3b	
Hoffmann, SS-*Ostuf* KI Hugo	IV C4a	Jan. 1945, posted to *Kripo* Berlin
Hoffmann, KS Konrad	IV A2	
Hoffmann, SS-*Stubaf* RR Max	IV B1	
Hoffmann, SS-*Ustuf* KOS Reinhard	IV A1a	

Hofmeister, ROI Adolf	IV A3b	
Holzhauser, KOS Walter	IV E4	Nov. 1943
Höner, SS-*Stubaf* RR Dr Heinz	IV B1a	in Austria, April 1945
Hübner, KS Heinrich	IV A2b	at Flensburg, April 1945
Hunsche, SS-*Hstuf* RR Otto	IV A4b	
Huppenkothen, SS-*Staf* ORR Walter	IV A	*Gruppenleiter*
Huse, SS-*Stuschaf* KS Walter	IV A1a	died Berlin, 28 April 1945
Ibsch, POI Paul	IV A6b	died 1944
Icker, *Angestellter*	IV B2c	
Irrgang, SS-*Ustuf* PS Erich	IV A6a	
Isselhorst, SS-*Staf* Dr Erich	IV B	1945; arrested US Zone
Jacobs, SS-*Ostuf* Emil	IV A4a	at Hof, April 1945
Jacquin, KS Alex	IV B1a	
Jaffke, KS Walter	IV E4	Nov. 1943
Jagusch, SS-*Ostuf RegAss* Dr Walter	IV A5	1939–1940, posted to BdS France
Jahn, SS-*Ostuf* PS Fritz	IV B	1945
Jahr, SS-*Stubaf* RR Dr Ernst	IV A4a	at Schwerin, 26 April 1945
Jänisch, SS-*Hstuf* Rudolf	IV A4b	Eichmann's adjutant
Jarosch, SS-*Hstuf* POI Erwin	IV B4a	left Berlin 21 April 1945
Jeske, SS-*Stubaf Amtsrat* Willy	IV A4b	
Jessel, SS-*Hstuf* ROI Erwin	IV A4a	
Joecks, PS Hermann	IV A2	
John, KI Alfred	IV A3c	
Jonak, SS-*Stubaf* RR Dr Gustav	IV D1	1939–1941
Jungnickel, SS-*Ustuf* POS Helmut	IV A6b	at Prague, 7 May 1945
Kablitz, SS-*Ostuf* KI Emil	IV A5a	
Kablitz, KS Otto	IV N	
Kaleske, SS-*Hschaf* KS Willy	IV A2a	MIA Eastern Front, April 1945
Kaul, SS-*Ustuf* Arthur	IV A6b	
Kelbling, SS-*Stubaf* RR Rolf	IV B4b	1943–1944, *Referent*; then posted
to BdS Brussels		
Keller, SS-*Ustuf* Erich	IV D3	Nov. 1943
Kempel, KS Andreas	IV A1a	at Hof, March 1945
Kendler, SS-*Stuschaf*	IV B2a	
Kettenhofen, *Reg.Amtmann* Felix	IV A6b	near Prague, 7 May 1945
Kienbaum, KS Otto	IV A2	
Kiessel, SS-*Stubaf* RR Dr Georg	IV	June–Dec. 1944; then posted as KdS Bromberg; arrested British Zone
Kirchdorf, KOS Walter	IV A5a	*Fahndungstrupp*, April 1945
Kirsch, SS-*Ustuf* KK Heinrich	IV A2a	1945, drafted into military
Klein, *Amtsgehilfe* Andreas	IV Gst.	courier
Klein, SS-*Obf* RD Georg	IV zbV	1945, special missions

Klein, *Amtsgehilfe* Walter	IV A3	Nov. 1943, messenger of IV E
Klinger, SS-*Hschaf* KS Freddie	IV A2b	at Hof, March 1945
Klude, KOS Wilhelm	IV C4b	Nov. 1943
Knobloch, SS-*Hstuf* KR Dr Günther	IV A1a	
Knuth, SS-*Ustuf* KS Arthur	IV C4a	Nov. 1943
Königshaus, SS-*Hstuf Reg.Amtmann* Franz	IV B4c	at Berlin, April 1945
<u>Kopkow</u>, SS-*Stubaf* KD Horst	IV A2	*Referent*; arrested British Zone
Koppe, POS Paul	IV B4c	
Koschate, ROI Otto	IV B4c	
Kosmehl, SS-*Ustuf* PS Karl	IV A6b	at Prague, 7 May 1945
Kranz, SS-*Stubaf Amtsrat* Richard	IV A5b	at Hof, April 1945
Krappel, SS-*Hschaf*	IV A6b	at Prague, 7 May 1945
Krause, *Ministerialrat* Johannes	IV B4	*Referent*, Berlin, 21 April 1945
Krause, SS-*Stuschaf* RS Karl	IV A6b	
Krause, SS-*Ustuf* KOS Wilhelm	IV Gst.	1945, *Erkennungsdienst*
Kreiser, *Pol.Amtsgehilfe* Johann	IV A5b	
Kretschmann, SS-*Ostuf Min.Reg.* Karl	IV Gst.	1945, *Geheim Registratur*
Krichbaum, SS-*Staf* ORuKR Willi	IV	1941–43 Deputy *Grenzinspekteur*
Kroggel, SS-*Hstuf* KS Erwin	IV A2b	May 1945, severely wounded and in Stolp hospital
Kromm, PS Erich	IV E1	Nov. 1943
Kröning, SS-*Ostubaf* ORR Rudolf	IV B4b	
Krüger, POS Johann	IV A1b	Nov. 1943
Krüger, KS Max	IV B2a	
Krüger, PS Walter	IV C1b	Nov. 1943
Krumbach, SS-*Hstuf* KK Alfred	IV A2a	1945 only
Krumrey, SS-*Hstuf* PI Theodor	IV A6b	at Prague, 7 May 1945
Kryschak, SS-*Hstuf Reg.Amtmann* Werner	IV A4b	
Kubitzky, SS-*Stubaf* Walter	IV E5	1943, transfer to RSHA VI
Kubsch, SS-*Hstuf* POI Paul	IV A6b	at Prague, March 1945
Kufahl, *Amtsrat*	IV B2b	
Kühn, POS Gerhard	IV B2a	
Kuhn, SS-*Ostuf* KK Karl	IV A1b	
Künne, *Reg.Amtmann* Walter	IV A6b	at Prague, 7 May 1945
Kunz, SS-*Hstuf* RR Dr Walter	IV D	
Kunze, SS-*Hstuf* Heinz	IV A4a	at Hof, April 1945
Kunze, SS-*Ostuf* ROI Walter	IV A3b	
Kurpisz, KOS Eduard	IV E5	Nov. 1943
Küster, KS Alfred	IV A2a	
Kutschenreiter, *Amtsgehilfe* Waldemar	IV A6a	

Ladewig, *Amtsrat* Johannes	IV B4b	at Hof, April 1945
Lange, ROI	IV B3a	
Lange, SS-*Ustuf* KOS Gustav	IV A5a	*Fahndungstrupp*, April 1945
Lange, SS-*Hstuf* KR Herbert	IV A1b	
Lange, SS-*Ustuf* KOS Hermann	IV A2a	at Hof, March 1945
Lange, PI Wilhelm	IV A6a	
Langgemach, SS-*Stuschaf* KS Curt	IV A3a	
Lehmann, PI	IV A6a	
Leipold, SS-*Hstuf* Max	IV A4a	
Lenz, PS Willi	IV B4c	
Leppin, PS Walter	IV B2	
Lettow, SS-*Stubaf* RR Dr Bruno	IV D1	*Referent*; March 1944 appointed *Leiter Stapoleitstelle* Karlsbad
Lewe, KS Ewald	IV B2	
Lica, KOS Josef	IV A6b	
Liebenow, KS Wilhelm	IV Gst.	Nov. 1943, *Geheim Registratur*
Liebscher, SS-*Ostuf* Richard	IV A4a	
Liepelt, ROI Hans	IV A4b	
Lietz, KS Paul	IV A6a	
<u>Lindow</u>, SS-*Stubaf* KD Kurt	IV B1a	arrested US Zone
Lischka, SS-*Ostubaf* ORR Kurt	IV B	1944–April 1945, *Gruppenleiter*
<u>Litzenberg</u>, SS-*Stubaf* RuKR Willy	IV A1	*Referent*; arrested US Zone
Lorenz, SS-*Stuschaf* KS Friedrich	IV A2b	at Schwerin, April 1945
Lorenz, PS Gustav	IV A6a	
Lorenz, KOS Hugo	IV C4	Nov. 1943
Lorenz, PS Karl	IV A6a	
Ludewig, SS-*Oschaf* Roland	IV A2a	
Ludwig, POI Wilhelm	IV A5b	
Lux, KS Josef	IV A5b	
Manig, KS Emil	IV A2b	at Hof, March 1945
Marowsky, KOS Kurt	IV A2a	
Martin, *Amtsgehilfe* Adam	IV A3b	
Martin, SS-*Ustuf* Friedrich	IV A4b	
Matthieu, SS-*Ostuf* KK Paul	IV A5a	
Matzke, POI Paul	IV C1	1939–1942; died 1942
Mauch, SS-*Hstuf Reg.Amtmann* Karl	IV A6a	
Mayerhof, KOS Fritz	IV A2a	at Schwerin, April 1945
Mehl, KS Günther	IV A3b	
Meier, PS Ernst	IV A4a	
Mertin, SS-*Ostuf* PI Wilhelm	IV A5b	
Meyer, SS-*Ustuf* KOS Gerhard	IV A1a	
Meyer, POS Hermann	IV A2a	at Hof, March 1945

Meyer, SS-*Hstuf* POI Walter	IV B2	
Mika, SS-*Ustuf* KK Johannes	IV A2b	at Hof, March 1945
Milles, PS Friedrich	IV A6b	
Milo, PS Georg	IV C1d	Nov. 1943
Minnieur, SS-*Ustuf* POS Hermann	IV A4b	
Mischke, *Reg.Amtmann* Alexander	IV A4b	
Mittelstadt, PS Wilhelm	IV A6a	
Möller, SS-*Hstuf* KR Walter	IV B1a	
Moes, SS-*Hstuf* POI Ernst	IV A4b	
Motzkus, *Kriminalangestellter* Max	IV A3b	
Mügge, KOS Paul	IV C4a	Nov. 1943
Müller, KR	IV A5b	
Müller, KS Christoph	IV A5a	*Fahndungstrupp*, April 1945
Müller, SS-*Hstuf* KR Georg	IV C4a	Nov. 1943
Müller, SS-*Hstuf* Hans	IV A2b	at Hof, March 1945
Müller, SS-*Gruf* Heinrich	*Amtschef*	died Berlin, April–May 1945
Müller, SS-*Ustuf* KOS Herbert	IV A5a	
Nack, PI Kurt	IV A6a	
Neubourg, SS-*Ostuf* KR Dr Ludwig	IV B4	arrested US Zone
Neuendorf, SS-*Ustuf* KS Franz	IV C4b	Nov. 1943
Neuhaus, SS-*Stubaf* RR Dr Karl	IV A4a	MIA at Posen, spring 1945
Neumann, KK Herbert	IV E1b	Nov. 1943
Nieburg, KOS Robert	IV A5b	
Nippe, SS-*Hstuf* Eugen	IV C5	1939–1940
Nobelmann, KS Wilhelm	IV A5b	
Nordmann, SS-*Oschaf* KS Hans	IV A2a	
Nosske, SS-*Ostubaf* ORR Gustav Adolf	IV D	1942–1943, *Gruppenleiter*, arrested British Zone
Nothnagel, KOS Wilhelm	IV A2	
Novak, SS-*Hstuf* Franz	IV A4b	
Oberstadt, SS-*Hstuf* POI Reinhold	IV A6b	
Ochs, PS Theodor	IV A6a	
Oetzel, SS-*Ostuf Min. Registratur* Eduard	IV Gst.	at Hof, March 1945
Oetzel, SS-*Stuschaf* KOS Gregor	IV B3a	
Opitz, *Amtsgehilfe* Heinz	IV Gst.	courier
Opitz, SS-*Stubaf* RuKR Paul	IV G	from 1945; previously *Referent* IV A3c
Oppermann, SS-*Hstuf Amtsmann* Ernst	IV B2b	
Ortler, POS Kurt	IV D1	Nov. 1943
Ortmann, SS-*Hschaf* KOS Reinhold	IV A1a	
Pachow, SS-*Ostuf* PI Max	IV A4b	
Pahlke, KS Franz	IV E5	Nov. 1943

Panzinger, SS-*Staf* RD Fritz	IV A	1941–1944, *Gruppenleiter*; then August 1944, RSHA *Amtschef* V
Patzer, KS Hermann	IV A5a	
Paulik, KOA Paul	IV B1	
Peters, SS-*Ustuf* PS Willi	IV A6a	
Pich, SS-*Stuschaf* KS Johannes	IV A2b	at Hof, March 1945
Pichler, SS-*Stuschaf* KS Johann	IV A2a	at Hof, March 1945
Pieper, SS-*Stubaf* RR Hans	IV Gst. Leiter	at Schwerin, April 1945
Pietsch, SS-*Hstuf* POI Erich	IV A1b	at Hof, March 1945
Pilling, SS-*Hstuf* POI Albin	IV B2a	
Pitz, SS-*Schaf* KA	IV A1a	
Plate, KS Emil	IV B1b	
Popischel, KS	IV A1a	
Preisser, SS-*Ustuf* KS Johann	IV N	Nov. 1943
Preuss, PI Paul	IV A4b	
Prochnow, SS-*Hstuf* KR Otto	IV A1b	
Protzner, SS-*Stuschaf* KS Otto	IV A1a	at Hof, March 1945
Przewozny, *Angestellter* Bruno	IV B2a	Russian interpreter
Pukall, SS-*Ustuf* KOS Otto	IV D2	KIA in the East, Aug. 1944
Pütz, SS-*Hstuf* KR Gunter	IV A1a	at Salzburg, 30 April 1945
Quetting, SS-*Ostubaf* ORR Hermann	IV A3	and Acting *Gruppenlieter* IV A, 1945
Radloff, KOS Emil	IV A5a	*Fahndungstrupp*, April 1945
von Rakowski, SS-*Ustuf* KS Johannes	IV A1	
Ramlow, SS-*Ustuf* KS Karl	IV A2a	at Hof, March 1945
Rang, SS-*Staf* RD Dr Fritz	IV A5	1944–1945; arrested British Zone
Rasch, SS-*Stuschaf* KS Paul	IV A1a	
Rauch, SS-*Stubaf* KR Fritz	IV B1c	at Schwerin, 26 April 1945
Rechentin, SS-*Hstuf* PI Wilhelm	IV B2a	
Regnath, KOS Franz	IV N	
Reichenbach, SS-*Hstuf* KK Joachim	IV A1	March 1944 to *Stapo* Danzig
Reimer, PS Hans	IV C1a	Nov. 1943
Rempel, SS-*Mann*	IV B2a	Russian interpreter
Rendel, SS-*Ustuf* PS Walter	IV A6b	
Renken, SS-*Stubaf* RR Walter	IV A3g	Legal expert; Dec. 1944 posted to KdS Kattowitz
Rennau, SS-*Ostubaf* ORuKR Dr Heinz	IV A3b	Personal *Referent* to *Amtschef* Müller; in Sweden, May 1945
Richter, SS-*Hstuf* POI Erich	IV B4a	
Richter, SS-*Stuschaf* KS Waldemar	IV A2b	at Hof, March 1945
Riedel, SS-*Hschaf* KOA Erich	IV A2a	at Hof, March 1945

Rikowski, KK Wilhelm	IV A1a	suicide, Berlin, April 1945
Roggon, POI Richard	IV A2b	
Rohrbach, PS Franz	IV A6a	
Rollenhagen, SS-*Ostuf* Johannes	IV A4a	at Hof, April 1945
Rose, SS-*Hschaf*	IV B2a	
Roth, SS-*Stubaf* RR Erich	IV A4a	1939–1944; then *Stapoleiter* Dortmund
Ruddat, PI Hermann	IV B4a	
Rudolph, *Frau*	IV N	
Sackermann, KS Paul	IV B4b	
Sader, *Stubaf* KR Heinz	IV A1b	
Sadikow, *Angestellter*	IV B2a	Russian interpreter
Samuel, SS-*Hstuf* POI Hermann	IV B1c	
Sanders, SS-*Stubaf* KR Erich	IV A5b	at Schwerin, 21 April 1945
Schäfer, SS-*Stubaf* KD Dr Karl	IV A3a	arrested US Zone
Schäffler, KI	IV A5a	*Fahndungstruppleiter*, April 1945
Schambacher, RuKR Dr Ernst	IV A3a	1940, *Referent* IV E4; 1941, *Gruppenleiter* D; 1942 to BdS Riga
Schau, *Amtsrat* Max	IV B4b	Nov. 1943
Scheffels, POI Albert	IV B1c	
Scheffka, SS-*Oschaf* KA Bruno	IV A2b	arrested British Zone
Scheffler, KI Willi	IV A5a	
Schellenberg, SS-*Gruf* Walter	IV E	1939–1941, *Gruppenleiter*; then *Amtschef* VI; arrested by British
Scheibel, SS-*Oschaf* KS Fritz	IV A1b	
Schiele, SS-*Hstuf* KR Eberhard	IV A5b	
Schilling, KI Konrad	IV E5	1943, to KdS Warsaw
Schilling, KOS Max	IV A5b	at Hof, March 1945
Schlomm, SS-*Stuschaf* KOS Franz	IV A2a	at Hof, March 1945
Schlott, SS-*Ustuf* RS Otto	IV B4c	
Schmauss, SS-*Ustuf* KS Ludwig	IV E6	1943, to *Stapo* Munich
Schmidt, PI Erich	IV E1	Nov. 1943
Schmidt, *Reg.Amtsmann* Walter	IV B2a	at Hof, March 1945
Schmitz, SS-*Stubaf* KD Dr Wilhelm	IV E6	early 1944, to RSHA VI
Schneider, POS Valentin	IV E1b	Nov. 1943
Scholz, SS-*Stubaf* KR Christian	IV A	Liaison Officer – *Forschungsamt*
Schonknecht, KS Arthur	IV E5	Nov. 1943
Schreier, SS-*Stuschaf* KS	IV B2c	
Schröder, SS-*Stubaf* RR Erich	IV D3	March 1941, appointed *Polizei Attaché* at Lisbon
Schulz, KS Erich	IV E5	Nov. 1943
Schultze, SS-*Ustuf* KK Erich	IV A2a	at Hof, March 1945

Schultze, SS-*Hstuf* KR Heinz	IV B2a	
Schulz, SS-*Stubaf* RR Franz	IV A5a	at Schwerin, April 1945
Schulz, KI Hermann	IV A2a	at Berlin, April 1945
Schulz, PI Otto	IV A6b	
Schulz, KOS Otto	IV A1a	Nov. 1943
Schumacher, SS-*Ustuf* KS Heinrich	IV N	1943–1945, and Asst Adjutant to *Amtschef* Müller
Schuster, *Ministerial Rat* Gottfried	IV G2	
Schwalenstöcker, ROI Fritz	IV C1d	Nov. 1943
Schwarzer, *Polizei Amtsgehilfe* Franz	IV A3b	
Schwindt, KOS Bruno	IV E4	Nov. 1943
Seibold, SS-*Hstuf* Fritz	IV B1a	
Seidel, POI Friedrich	IV B1a	
Simmer, SS-*Ostuf* KK Kurt	IV A1a	1944–1945
Simon, SS-*Ostuf* PS Gustav	IV B2	
Sobek, SS-*Ostuf* KK Gerhard	IV A2b	at Berlin, April 1945
Soenderop, KS Heinrich	IV A3b	
Somann, SS-*Obf* Otto	IV G	1945, *Gruppenleiter*
Sonderegger, KK Franz	IV B3	
Sonnemann, KS Harry	IV C4c	Nov. 1943
Span, SS-*Ostuf* KR Hermann	IV ZABP	earlier with IV A1
Späth, SS-*Hstuf* ROI Walter	IV A6a	
Sperling, KS Johann	IV A1a	
Spiecker, SS-*Ostuf* PI Kurt	IV A6b	
Stage, SS-*Stubaf* KD Kurt	IV C4	1939–1942, *Referent*; then appointed KdS Tromso; arrested in Austria
Stahn, KS Hans	IV B3c	
Starck, *Amtsrat* Ernst	IV A4a	pensioned off in 1945, Bavaria
Stark, KS Walter	IV B1a	
Steffen, KI Paul	IV B2a	
Steinert, SS-*Oschaf* KA Helmut	IV A2b	arrested British Zone
Stempel, SS-*Ustuf* KK Erich	IV A2a	
Stiller, SS-*Hstuf* Kurt	IV B2	1944, to BdS Holland
Stobbe, SS-*Ustuf* KS Hans	IV A6b	
Storkebaum, *Reg.Amtsmann* Ernst	IV A3b	Nov. 1943
Strübing, SS-*Ostuf* KK Johann	IV A2b	at Hof, March 1945
Struwe, *Reg.Amtsmann* Artur	IV E2	1943, to *Stapoleitstelle* Berlin
Stuber, SS-*Ustuf* Kurt	IV A6a	
Stuschke, SS-*Ustuf* Franz	IV A4b	
Teufelhardt, POS Franz	IV E1	Nov. 1943
Thiedecke, SS-*Stubaf* Amtsrat Franz	IV B2c	*Referent*; died Berlin April 1945
Thiemann, SS-*Stubaf* RR Dr Jobst	IV B2a	Deputy *Referent*

Tholen, SS-*Hstuf* KR Walter	IV ZABP	
Thomass, PI Kurt	IV C1 (ZS)	1942, to KdS Krakau; returned to RSHA and in 1945, with IV B4c
Thomsen, SS-*Stubaf* RR Harro	IV B2b	*Referent*; arrested British Zone
Tiemann, KS Kurt	IV B3a	
Tiemann, SS-*Stuschaf* KS Walter	IV A1b	1942, to BdS Riga
Tischer, SS-*Stubaf* KR Rudolf	IV A3b	*Referent*; in Flensburg, May 1945
Tischler, SS-*Ustuf* KOS Johannes	IV Gst.	*Zeichnungsstelle*
Torno, KOS Gustav	IV E3	Nov. 1943
Trenker, SS-*Ostubaf* ORR Dr Ottmar	IV B3c	1944–1945, *Referent*
Tscheutschler, KS Heinrich	IV A2a	
Tschirner, SS-*Ostuf* Richard	IV C1d	Nov. 1943
Tunk, SS-*Ustuf* PS Hans	IV A6b	
Usenbinz, KS Wilhelm	IV B2b	at Hof, March 1945
Vogt, SS-*Stubaf* RR Josef	IV A1	1942, *Referent*, then to KdS Veldes; arrested in Austria
Voss, KS Ernst	IV B2	
Voss, SS-*Stuschaf* KS Richard	IV A2b	
Wabnik, KOS Robert	IV E3	Nov. 1943
Wandesleben, SS-*Ostuf* Otto-Wilhelm	IV A4a	
Warzecha, SS-*Ostuf* KA Gerhard	IV E3	July 1943, to BdS Paris
Wassenberg, SS-*Stubaf Amtsrat* Hans	IV E1	Nov. 1943
Wauer, KS Willy	IV A5b	
Weber, SS-*Stuschaf* KS Günther	IV B2a	
Weege, SS-*Hschaf* KS	IV B1a	
Wegener, SS-*Ustuf* PI Fritz	IV A1c	1944, to BdS Hungary; MIA
Weichert, SS-*Ustuf* KS Günther	IV A2a	
Weiermann, KOS Johann	IV A5b	at Hof, March 1945
Weiler, SS-*Hstuf* KR Mathias	IV B2b	
Wellhöner, SS-*Hstuf* Karl	IV C12	1945, with RSHA VI F
Wendorff, KS Wilhelm	IV A2	died 1943
Wenzel, SS-*Ustuf* KS	IV B1c	at Hamburg, April 1945
Wernicke, KOS Erich	IV E1	Nov. 1943
Werth, SS-*Hstuf* KK Herbert	IV A2b	
Westermann, SS-*Ostuf* KK Wilhelm	IV A1a	
Wieczorek, KOS Niklaus	IV A1a	
Wieschendorf, SS-*Hstuf* ROI Bodo	IV A4a	
Wilke, SS-*Stubaf* RR Wilhelm	IV B4b	1943–1945; at Schwerin, April 1945
Wille, KOS Albert	IV B3b	
Winzer, SS-*Hstuf* KK Rudolf	IB V2	
Wipper, SS-*Stubaf* KD Alwin	IV C5	1942, appointed *Polizei Attaché* Sofia

Witt, SS-*Ustuf* KS Erich	IV E6	Nov. 1943
Witzel, SS-*Stubaf Amtsrat* Johannes	IV A6a	1945, *Referent*
Wodtke, KOS Gustav	IV A1a	
Wöhrn, SS-*Hstuf Reg.Amtsmann* Fritz	IV A4b	
Wolansky, SS-*Stuschaf* KS Kurt	IV B2a	
Wolf, KS Hermann	IV A2	
Wolf, SS-*Hstuf* ROI Wilhelm	IV A4a	
Wolf, SS-*Ustuf* KS Willy	IV B2a	
Wolff, SS-*Hstuf* PI Detlev-Malte	IV A4a	
<u>Wolff</u>, SS-*Ostubaf* ORR Hans Helmuth	IV B2	1943–1945, *Referent*; then KdS Weimar; arrested in US Zone
Wolter, SS-*Stubaf* Willi	IV B3	1939–1940; then to BdS Metz
Wuthe, *Ministerial Registratur* Waldemar	IV A1a	
Zager, SS-*Ustuf* POS Albert	IV A6b	
Zeeck, SS-*Ustuf* PS Paul	IV A6a	
Ziehals,	IV Gst.	courier
Ziethen, KS Hermann	IV A1a	at Hof, March 1945
Zimmat, SS-*Ustuf* POS Fritz	IV B2a	
Zimmermann, SS-*Stubaf* RR Alexander	IV Gst.	Jan.–Feb. 1945, with KdS Posen where KIA, 23 Feb. 1945
Zimmermann, *Pol.Assistent* Herbert	IV B4b	

OKW personnel attached to RSHA *Amt* IV in 1945

Bauermeister, *Hauptmann*	IV A5a	
Haas, *Hauptmann*	IV B1a	
Horsch, *Major*	IV B2a	
Keller, *Oberstleutnant* Hans	IV A3b	
Rohleder, *Oberst* Joachim	IV B	in charge of all OKW personnel assigned to IV B
Saltzinger, *Hauptmann*	IV B2b	

The interrogation report of SS-*Stubaf* Horst Kopkow mentioned in the above CIWR Situation Report on RSHA IV, undoubtedly refers to his lengthy interrogation from 7 June 1945. Kopkow proved to be an invaluable source about the organisation, activities and personnel of RSHA IV and extensively interrogated by British Intelligence. His first interrogation took place at Neumünster and as soon as the British interrogation centre at Bad Nenndorf (CSDIC/WEA) near Hannover became available, Kopkow was taken there and remained for two years. He was interrogated alone and sometimes together with others. It is unlikely that CIWR when preparing Situation Report No. 4 on RSHA IV were able to include new material that came from CSDIC/WEA when three former *Gestapo* officers, SS-*Stubaf* Horst Kopkow, SS-*Stubaf* Harro Thomsen and SS-*Ostubaf* Gustav Adolf Nosske produced Combined Interim Report, IR 47, dated 14 November 1945. This report notes: 'The bulk of the information given below has been provided by Kopkow, since his knowledge of the subject is far more extensive than that of either of the other Prisoners; Thomsen did not join RSHA *Amt* IV until May 1943, while Nosske was in the Amt only from Feb 42 to Aug 43.'

However, Kopkow and Thomsen gave conflicting departmental descriptions for the years 1941–1944, whilst Nosske's input is barely mentioned. Their shared descriptions are limited outside their particular spheres of work and bear little resemblance to the RSHA organisation listing dated 1 May 1941 as an example. To avoid discrepancies between their personal views and the organisation listing, the Interim Report has been confined to the development of the *Gestapo* in its early stages and how it re-organized in 1944 after the loss of much formerly occupied territories.

Combined Interim Report, IR 47, 14 November 1945, BAOR, CSDIC/WEA.

1. History of Organisation
Introductory

2. Kopkow suggests that the organisation of the *Gestapo Amt* and of the *Stapoleitstellen* and *Stapostellen* subordinate to it can be divided into four phases:

A. The development of the *Gestapo* from its foundation as a Prussian State organisation in 1933 until 1936–37, by which time it had become a Reich organisation.
B. Further development under Dr Best and Müller until the spring [*sic*—summer] of 1939.
C. The incorporation of the *Gestapo* into the RSHA as *Amt* IV in the spring [*sic*—summer] of 1939 (at this stage, Dr Best left the *Gestapo* and Müller became *Amtschef*).
D. The final re-organisation of *Amt* IV which, Prisoner states, must have started in the winter of 1943 and have been completed by mid-1944.

A. PHASE 1

3. Kopkow states that he has no first-hand knowledge of the changes at HQ during the early years, as he himself only entered the service in 1934 and until 1938 was at *Stapostelle* Allenstein, East Prussia. He considers, however, that the sequence of events must have been approx. as follows:

4. The Prussian Secret State Police was founded by a decree of 1933 and had as its first head *Ministerpräsident* Göring. The leading personalities of this early organisation were first Patschowsky and later Diels, both of whom were members of the '*Preussische Innenverwaltung*' until 1934. During this same period, in Bavaria and other states outside Prussia, development was on the following lines:

5. Shortly after the assumption of power by the NSDAP, Himmler became *Polizeipräsident* of Munich and under him, as head of the Political Dept at the Munich *Polizeipräsidium*, was Heydrich.

6. During the years 1933–1934, Himmler gradually became head of all the political police forces in all the remaining non-Prussian states of the *Reich*. Finally, in 1934, Himmler became chief of the Prussian Secret State Police, still, however, under Göring.

7. In 1935 followed the fusion of the political police forces of all the German States into one force for the whole of the *Reich*; at this stage Göring relinquished his position as head of the Prussian *Gestapo* and Himmler became head of the *Staatspolizei* for the whole of the *Reich*. He appointed Heydrich to direct the '*Sicherheitspolizei*', which covered both the *Stapo* and the *Kripo*. At this time Himmler was nominally under the Minister of the Interior Frick, but was in actual fact quite independent as '*Reichefführer-SS und Chef der deutschen Polizei im Reichsministerium des Innern*'. When this fusion took place, the various provincial '*Polizeiämter*' in the States became '*Staatspolizeileitstellen*'.

8. When Himmler went to Berlin he took with him not only Heydrich but a number of other officials from the Bavarian Political Police, all of whom secured for themselves leading positions in the *Gestapo* from 1935 onwards.

Organisation (1935–1939).

9. The *Gestapo* from this period up to the time when it became RSHA *Amt* IV in the summer of 1939 was divided into three main departments:

a) Abt I—Administration and Legal
b) Abt II—Measures against Internal Opposition (*Innernpolitik*)
c) Abt III—Counter-espionage

Both Abt I and Abt III were under the control of *Ministerialrat* Dr Best, whilst Abt II was at first run by SS-*Hstuf* Flesch, who had come from Munich with Heydrich; within two years, however, Flesch had to relinquish this post owing to failing health and it was given to Müller, who had also come from Munich.

10. As regards the organisation of a *Stapostelle* at that time, Kopkow gives the following account:

The *Stapostelle* had two active departments:

Abt II—Measures against Internal Opposition
Abt III—Counter-espionage.

There was also an Abt I, which was responsible for administrative matters, but this was not of any great importance.

11. The *Leiter* of a *Stapostelle* or *Stapoleitstelle* was usually the Political *Referent* of the staff of the permanent *Regierungspräsident* and was stationed in the town which was the seat of the *Regierung*. However, certain other large towns also had *Stapostellen*, which helped their local police authorities.

12. A feature of the *Stapostellen* and *Stapoleitstellen* was the frequent changing of the *Leiter*, who was often recalled to HQ in his other capacity of Political *Referent* and replaced by a new man. In the early years there was a paucity of leading executive officials, and departments were being run by minor '*Bezirkssekretären*'. In the years 1935–1936 the officials who had been trained on the first courses at the '*Führerschule der Sicherheitspolizei*' became available, and Abt II and III were put under *Kriminalkommissäre*. The medium-grade executive officials were almost without exception *Kriminalbeamten* transferred from the State *Kripo* and from Ia Political Police Depts at the *Polizeipräsidium*.

13. Abts II and III worked quite independently and officials in one department were not allowed to interfere with the affairs of the other. Abt III had a strong working connection with the military *Abwehr*, the latter at the time having certain supervisory and advisory powers in matters of counter-espionage.

14. The individual *Stapostellen* were all independent units and each had one or more wireless links with the *Gestapo* in Berlin; they used a secret cipher. The establishment of *Stapoleitstellen* had very little influence on the *Stapostellen*; the small advisory powers within their own provincial area, which the *Stapoleitstellen* had over the *Stapostellen*, disappeared entirely when Inspectors of the *Sipo* and SD [IdS] were appointed later....

D. Phase 4.

23. This is the final phase.... The history of the organisational changes in RSHA *Amt* IV would not, however, be complete without a reference to the time when

this re-organisation took place; the motives which were behind it are dealt with in Section II below.

24. Kopkow states that this final re-organisation must have started about the end of 1943 or beginning of 1944, because when the *Abwehr* was taken over in Jan [*sic*] 1944, the framework of the new organisation was already in existence. Kopkow believes, however, that whilst orders for the taking over of the *Abwehr* were issued in Jan [*sic*] 1944, the actual process dragged on, so that RSHA *Amt* IV was not fully organised until mid 1944.

II. Reasons for changes in organisation

25. Kopkow maintains that it is necessary to differentiate between the organisational changes in the *Gestapo* during 1933–1943 and the final re-organisation of RSHA *Amt* IV in 1943–1944.

26. As a result the first ten years, the changes were all made for sound objective reasons, *viz*:

a) The organisation had to be adjusted to meet changes in the relative importance of the various subjects with which it dealt.
b) The organisation had to take into account the territorial changes which occurred during the war.
c) The organisation had to cope with the change-over from peace to war conditions.
d) The organisation had at all times to keep pace with any movements regarding political feeling within the Reich.

27. Particular examples of changes which left their mark on the organisation are:

a) Communism, which from 1933 to 1935 had been of first-rank importance, gradually diminished in importance, until it had once again became a field of very important activity during the war.
b) Marxism was in time so greatly reduced that counter-measures against it disappeared as an independent problem and became a mere sideline.
c) Methods of dealing with sabotage had to be reconsidered on the outbreak of war—in peacetime anti-sabotage activity had been confined to certain specified fields.
d) In wartime counter-espionage became of greater importance, as it had to cope with the greater effort of the enemy intelligence services.
e) Industrial questions could not be dealt with without organising a system of industrial intelligence, and this resulted in industrial matters being passed to the Counter-Intelligence Department.

f) The importance of the '*Kirchenreferate*' (dealing with Evangelists, Catholics, Sects etc) at first increased owing to the '*Zweiter Kulturkampf*' movement, but diminished again when that movement had been suppressed. Finally, these *Referate* could be merged.

g) The problem of immigrants gradually fell into the background and eventually disappeared altogether.

h) Owing to the fact that espionage organisations and resistance movements worked hand in hand, counter intelligence was no longer able to carry on independently, but had to be re-organised to work in a more co-operative manner with other sections of the *Amt*.

i) *Dienststellen* to deal with the Occupied Territories had to be established. A very large number of political police questions arose which were new and had not previously appeared as part of the *Stapo*'s work.

j) A section had to be created to deal with the large number of foreign workers.

k) The guarding of frontiers increased in importance during the war.

l) The protection of industry was seen in a new light in the later stages of the war. At first considered purely as a 'safety-first' measure which was to be looked after by the anti-sabotage dept, it was later looked upon as a problem directly affecting armament production (especially in view of the ever-increasing employment of foreign workers).

28. The reasons which lay behind the final re-organisation of RSHA *Amt* IV in 1943–mid-1944 were entirely different, as this was mainly concerned with the transfer of the '*Geheimer Meldedienst*'—practically, that is, the whole of OKW *Amt Ausland/Abwehr*—into the RSHA. This change was no longer an 'objective' one but represented, more or less, a trial of strength between Himmler and Canaris and should not have been necessary, especially at that stage of the war.

29. Thomsen makes no distinction between the changes in organisation which occurred in 1933–1943 and the final re-organisation in 1943–1944. The reasons he gives for the changes which took place are the same as those given by Kopkow, except that Thomsen adds that the considerable losses of the *Sipo* in the war and the enforced dismissal of corrupt *Stapo* officials in the occupied territories (especially France) led to essential work being neglected in these countries; this, he points out, also had its effect on the organisation of *Amt* IV and the *Stapostellen*.

III. Effects of changes in organisation

30. Kopkow, while agreeing that any change is bound to have its effect on the smooth working of an organisation, maintains that the changes in first ten years, since they were justified by circumstances or events, did not result in any undue

stress on the organisation or unnecessary confusion at HQ and regional level. As for the final re-organisation, however, he states that, as almost the whole of the year 1944 was taken up with this 'regrettable' question, it did have a bad effect on the work.

31. Thomsen considers that the changes which were made were necessary and correct, but that their execution was not supervised strictly enough. He points out that the changes were not understood at all *Stapostellen*, especially the significance of IV B in *Amt* IV, which had no representative at the *Stapostelle*. He does NOT [stress in original] agree that the confusion which resulted from these changes was very great, but admits that some confusion did arise and that personal rivary very often contributed to it.

32. Kopkow concludes by stating that, unfortunate as this re-organisation was, it did have one good effect on the work concerned from the point of view of security. He claims it was ascertained on several occasions that the re-organisation had so confused both the British and the American Intelligence Services that, in spite of their admitted efficiency, they were unable to ascertain the system

Although it had an issue date of 7 December 1945, the CIWR report on RSHA IV indicates they were aware of the results of the US Intelligence interrogation of SS-*Hauptsturmführer Kriminalkommissar* Leonhard Halmanseger. His interrogation report by USFET is dated 3 October 1945 and gives more detailed information on section RSHA IV N, under the control of Halmanseger who reported directly to RSHA *Amtschef* IV Müller. RSHA IV N operated the network of *Gestapo* informers and informants through the various *Gestapo* offices across Germany and the occupied territories.

USFET Counter-Intelligence Intermediate Interrogation Report (CIIIR) No. 24 dated 3 October 1945: Prisoner—SS-*Hstuf* KK Leonhard Halmanseger:

CONTENTS

1. References.
2. Reason for Report
3. Report
   a. Introduction
   b. Life history
4. Conclusion
5. Comments and Recommendations

ANNEXES

I. The *Gestapo* Intelligence Service (IV N)
   1. History
   2. Organisation and Administration
      a. At *Stapostelle* and *Leitstelle* level
      b. At RSHA IV level
   3. Functions
      a. General
      b. Fields of Activity
   4. Agents (*V-Leute*)
      a. General
      b. Recruiting
      c. Payment
      d. Commitment
   5. List of N-*Referate* in Germany
II. Personality List.
....

3. Report.

a. Introduction.
Halmanseger was a German civil servant for 32 years. He had direct dealings with agents between 1919 and 1933. Subsequently, however, he became engaged in the administration and registry of agents and thereby lost touch with operational problems. He is well versed in the rules and regulations governing the administration of IV N, but tends to overlook the fact that the actual running of agents often deviates from the prescribed pattern. As a typical German civil servant, his thinking lacks the imagination and flexibility otherwise in keeping with a good background. This report should be read with that limitation in mind.

b. Life History.
Halmanseger, who was born in 1892, finished school in 1911 and subsequently had two years of military training. He joined the Munich police force in 1914 and during that same year entered the army, in which he served with a border protection unit till 1918. The following year (1919) he was assigned to the Bavarian Political Police to help organise a political intelligence service set up by Dr Frick. Halmanseger eventually became an authority on the activities of left-wing parties because the Bavarian government, for many years dominated by the Catholic Peoples Party, was greatly interested in that subject. Halmanseger attended communist and socialist rallies, and also used V-*Leute*. From 1921 on he was in contact with Müller (later head of *Amt* IV RSHA) who at that time was an interrogation officer at Munich.

The Nazification of the Bavarian Political Police took place under Heydrich (1933) with Müller in charge of the department. The following year (1934) Halmanseger was transferred to Berlin where Müller was building up the *Gestapoamt*. Here he was assigned to assist ORR Heller in building up an intelligence service, and also to act as liaison man for Heydrich. In 1936 Halmanseger returned to Munich where he resumed his former job, but two years later (1938) he was transferred back to Berlin to become head of the central agents' registry. He held this post until the end and saw the department's name progressively changed from II-N to IV C4 and eventually to IV N.

Halmanseger joined the SS in 1938, and the NSDAP in 1941.

4. Conclusions.

Halmanseger states that he is a practicing Catholic and was forced to keep his religious activities secret so as not to be denounced as a church-goer.

He is a civil servant, ergo he has no political convictions and served his government no matter who runs it. With this type of mentality it is still difficult for him to understand why he should be locked up after 'having served his country faithfully for thirty-two years.' Imagination is certainly not one of Halmanseger's attributes, but he has given an account of his work to the best of his ability....

Annex I

The *Gestapo* Intelligence Service (IV N).

1. History.

The *Gestapo* Intelligence Service (*Der innenpolitische Nachrichtendienst*) was always a favorite of SS-*Gruf* Heinrich Müller, head of RSHA *Amt* IV. He took the initiative to establish this intelligence agency when he founded the *Gestapo* (1933), and he always kept close personal supervision over it. The results attained never satisfied Müller, who kept criticizing his subordinates for lack of initiative and imagination in building a net of *Gestapo* agents.

In the first years of its activities the *Gestapo* was mainly concerned with its enemies from the left—communists and socialists. Somewhat later the emphasis shifted to reports on church opposition, but swung back to communist activities at the beginning of the war. From 1941 on, however, illegal activities and sabotage by foreign workers occupied the most important place in the *Gestapo* agent's reports.

Agents were handled without much unified control till 1937. The *Gestapo* specialist *Referenten* ran their agents as they pleased, and dissemination of information was poor. On 1 February 1937 the *Gestapoamt*, then *Amt* II [of the *Hauptamt Sicherheitspolizei*], issued its first general directive on the centralized control of the domestic intelligence service. This provided for the registration with

Amt II of all important V-*Leute* attached to the *Stapostellen*. The new central registry was named II-N, and by the beginning of 1938 had approx. 500 registered agents.

Progress was slow, according to Halmanseger, largely because the *Referenten* were inclined to regard their V-*Leute* as personal acquisitions and were reluctant to build up the N-*Referate*. At the semi-annual meetings of all *Stapoleiter*, Müller would stress the importance of N-*Referate* being separated from the *Gestapo* executive service, but without marked success. The first *Stapoleitstellen* to have N-*Referate* (1940–1941) were Hamburg, Stuttgart, Karlsruhe, Munich and Wien.

When *Amt* II became RSHA *Amt* IV … II-N became known as IV C4 and was included in the *Geschäftsverteilungsplan* (distribution lists).

A new directive on the domestic intelligence service was issued on 4 August 1941. In it the three German intelligence services were defined as:

GND: *Gegnernachrichtendienst*, the function of RSHA *Amt* IV
AND: *Auslandsnachrichtendienst*, the function of RSHA *Amt* VI
ND: *auf den Lebensgebieten*, the function of RSHA *Amt* III

The directive also set forth the objectives and functions of the GND, gave instructions on the recruiting and handling of agents, the keeping of agents registers, etc. It directed the formation of N-*Referate* in all *Stapostelle* and emphasised the importance of registering agents with RSHA *Amt* IV. (IV C4 was renamed IV N, but its functions remained unchanged.)

Handling of agents by the specialist *Referenten* was not explicitly prohibited by the directive, provided these agents were registered with RSHA IV-N through the IV-N of their respective *Stapostellen*. Because of this and certain technical difficulties, the terms of the directive went into effect slowly and were not executed by all *Stapostellen* till early in 1942. On the basis of this information it is possible to explain statements made in other interrogations by member of IV-N *Referate* that some of their V-*Leute* were handled directly by the specialist *Referenten*.

The *Gestapo* Intelligence Service reached its maximum expansion in 1944 when the *Stapostellen* in Germany utilized some 10,000 V-*Leute*.

Halmanseger claims that no orders for stay-behind activities passed through his office. He has no knowledge on this subject other than having heard about such activities from an N-*Referat*. Orders for stay-behind activities came directly from RSHA *Amt* IV to the individual *Stapostellen*, by-passing RSHA IV-N.

2. Organization and Aministration.

a. At *Stapostelle* and *Stapoleitstelle* level.
The directive of 4 August 1941, basis of the *Gestapo* Intelligence Service, prescribed that all V-*Leute* of a *Stapostelle* be registered with its *Referat* IV-N. It lays down a broad policy but leaves the *Stapoleiter* directly responsible for its execution. At the

Stapoleiter's discretion, the briefing and handling of V-*Leute* was to be done either by the N-*Referent* or the *Sach-Referent*, or by the two working in conjunction. In any event, the N-*Referent* was responsible for all administrative and financial matters pertaining to V-*Leute*, and for the proper dissemination of information. Usual dissemination of information was to be respective *Referate* of his *Stapostelle*, but whenever the information had wide ramifications it was also sent to RSHA IV-N. The N-*Referent* was directly responsible to his *Stapoleiter*.

The rise of N-*Referate* varied between three and fifteen persons. Usually there were two scheduled conferences a year which all N-*Referenten* in Germany would attend for instruction. At these two-day conferences, Müller would usually lecture on the internal political situation, the specialists of RSHA IV would speak on the various fields of illegal activity, and Halmanseger would discuss the correct methods of registration and reporting. The last conference took place in Weimar, June 1944.

b. At RSHA *Amt* IV level.
(1) Working mechanism of RSHA IV-N.
RSHA IV-N was considered a *Dienststelle* rather than a *Referat*, and as such was directly responsible to the head of RSHA *Amt* IV, Müller. Its functions were to keep a central registry of agents affiliated with the *Stapostellen*, and to distribute agents' reports to the proper *Referate* of *Amt* IV. When an agent had been recruited and found reliable over a six-month period, a set of cards containing his personal data was sent to RSHA IV-N by the *Stapostelle*, and the cards were incorporated into the proper index.

When the *Stapostellen* sent their reports in, agents' names were replaced by identifying numbers. The incoming reports were registered and then usually read by Halmanseger before being passed along to the proper *Sach-Referat*. (Müller received reports only on important matters.) Usually, if a report dealt with several subjects, IV-N would make extract copies and send the proper section to each interested *Referat*.

IV-N received reports only on information considered to be RSHA *Amt* IV level, such as matters of sabotage, widespread illegal organizations, etc. Lesser matters were consolidated into a monthly situation report which the *Stapoleiter* sent directly to RSHA *Amtschef* IV. RSHA IV-N averaged approx. 40 reports daily.

RSHA IV-N had no agents of its own. However, it did register the few remaining agents of *Amt* IV *Referate* who were retained even after the great bulk had been reluctantly transferred to *Stapoleitstelle* Berlin.

(2) Evaluation and liaison with *Referate*.
The *Referate*, not IV-N, were charged with the evaluation of intelligence. Liaison between these and IV-N varied from the fairly close co-operation of IV A1a [dealing with communism, Marxism] to the almost complete lack of liaison with other *Referate*. In many instances, when an agent's report raised further questions, the *Sach-Referat* would take up the matter directly with the *Stapostelle* concerned.

If information about a V-*Mann* was desired, however, the *Referat* had to consult RSHA IV-N. The reverse was true if IV-N was seeking such information as the credibility of a given report.

(3) Files and Card Indexes.
In 1943 the card and file indexes of IV-N were moved to Prague, and in 1944 to Wulkow (near Küstrin/Oder), the evacuation center of RSHA *Amt* IV. Part of the files were burned there (January 1945) and the rest removed to Hof (Bavaria). During February and March 1945, these card and file indexes were transferred to a village outside Hirschberg (Thuringia), and from there to Salzburg (Austria) where they were burned by KOS Franz Regnath who was then in charge. Regnath is now at the Third US Army Interrogation Center.

V-Leute, for the purpose of filing, were divided into three categories, namely:

> G: *Gegnermann*
> I: Informator
> A: *Auskunftsperson*

The first and most important section, <u>G</u>, was reserved for those V-*Leute* who were either inside or in direct contact with an illegal organisation. Section <u>I</u> was for those V-*Leute* who had only indirect contact with illegal organisations, and <u>A</u> was used for the unpaid, occasional informers. The first two categories only (G and I) had to be registered with RSHA IV-N.

RSHA IV-N kept the following indexes and files:

<u>*Namenskartei*</u>: Agents' card index, arranged in alphabetical order according to the agent's true name.

Column 'Stapo' was to be filled in with a two digit number designating the *Stapostelle* handling the agent. No name was used. (*Stapostelle* Aachen, for purpose of illustration, had the code number 01.) The agent's cover number was a three digit affair between 001 and 200 which appeared under '*Deckbezeichnung*'. These two numbers plus the agent's category (G or I) were combined to identify a V-*Mann* in his report, thus: 01 G 127, a specific *Gegnermann* from *Stapostelle* Aachen.

These index cards were further color-coded to indicate in which of six fields of activity the V-*Mann* was working. The colors were:

> Red: KPD (German Communist Party)
> Pink: SPD (German Socialist-Democrat Party)
> Yellow: *Abwehr* matters
> Blue: Church matters
> Green: Rightist opposition
> White: Miscellaneous

Deckbezeichnungskartei: Code Index, containing the same information as the *Namenskartei* on the same type of color-coded cards. This index was arranged according to the *Stapostelle*, and within each *Stapostelle* according to the agent's number.

Ausgelegte Kartei: Dead file into which an agent's card was transferred after being dropped from the *Gestapo* payroll; arranged similarly to active index file.

Berichtskartei: Report Index on which the reports of each *Stapostelle* were entered by agent's number and by date. This allowed for simple checking on the frequency of reports submitted by each *Stapostelle*.

Sachakten: Case file for all agents registered with RSHA IV-N. Usually each V-*Mann* had a page containing photograph, personal data, and pertinent basic information. Any additional information concerning the individual agent was also to be found there, such as: findings of investigations, change of status, political affiliations, family support, etc.

Deckpasskartei: Fictitious Pass Index, containing copies of applications for fictitious passports arranged alphabetically and using cover names. The information was sent in by *Aussenstellen*, *Stapostellen*, and RSHA *Amt* VI, after delivery of false passports. The real name of the bearer was never used, and this index had no connection with IV-N activities.

3. Functions.

A. General.

The *Gestapo* Intelligence Service was charged with uncovering any group, organization, or activity directed against the state, and the finding of such persons who constituted a danger to the state within its borders. Agents were employed to do this job. Their task was to report specific information, not to give general situation reports (*Stimmungsberichte*).

The collection of '*Stimmungsberichte*', showing the reactions and attitudes of the population in various spheres of life, was a function of the SD (RSHA *Amt* III). V-*Leute* were generally briefed not to bring in this type of information. If this type of information did come in, however, the *Stapostellen* were instructed to pass it on to the SD-*Abschnitte* and *Leitabschnitte*, and thereafter RSHA IV-N would relay it to RSHA *Amt* III.

The activities of RSHA IV-N were limited to the territory of Germany proper, Austria and the Czech Protectorate, and the following areas (set forth in directive dated 4 August 1941): Alsace-Lorraine, Poland (General Government), the Baltic countries of Lithuania, Eastonia and Latvia, certain occupied Russian territories

(Minsk and Bialystok areas), and also, unofficially, Denmark. Reports from V-*Leute* in all the regions mentioned above were sent to RSHA IV-N, but since most of the information was evaluated locally, the number of reports was small. Elsewhere in German-occupied Europe there were no IV-N agents. Whatever agents were employed there reported to the KdS or BdS who in turn relayed this information directly to RSHA *Amt* IV.

Though neutral countries were not to be covered by IV-N officially, *Stapostellen* in the border areas had some V-*Leute* who functioned abroad. During the war, the only countries covered were Switzerland and Sweden. (*Stapostellen* for Switzerland were Stuttgart, Karlsruhe, Munich and Innsbruck; for Sweden, Hamburg, Bremen and Kiel.) In theory, and according to instructions, all foreign information of counter-intelligence interest was to have been sent from IV-N to RSHA *Amt* VI, but this rarely was done.

The exact dividing line between the functions of RSHA *Amt* IV and RSHA *Amt* VI was obscure even to Halmanseger. When in doubt, he would not disseminate information to *Amt* VI, but would leave that to the discretion of the *Referate* to whom the information was disseminated. For purposes of illustration: A German sailor, who is a V-*Mann* run by *Stapostelle* Kiel, establishes contact in Sweden with German *émigré* communists. They ask him to furnish information on German armament production. At least three *Referate* in *Amt* IV would be interested in this report, namely: IV A3a (*Abwehr*), IV A1a (Communists) and IV B1c (Scandinavian countries).

According to Halmanseger, there were no standard procedures to cover such a situation. It there was time, he would make extracts and disseminate to all three *Referate*; otherwise, he would send the report to the *Referat* concerned with the V-*Mann's* special assignment, e.g. *Abwehr* man etc. Further dissemination then became the responsibility of that *Referat*.

Whenever RSHA *Amt* IV became involved in a jurisdictional controversy with *Ämter* III or VI, it was settled by their *Amtschefs* at the highest level.

B. Fields of Activity.
Below is a review of the principal fields of activity for *Gestapo* V-*Leute*. Also, mention is made of the *Referate* of RSHA *Amt* IV which would deal with each specific type of report and where IV-N would disseminate information. The name of the person given in parentheses is the *Referent* or *Sachbearbeiter* with whom Halmanseger usually was in contact.

(1) Communist and Socialist activities.
One of the most important fields, especially the communist phase. This field gained in importance in later years, not only because of German communist activities but also because of similar development among foreign workers. Reports to *Referat* IV A1a (KR Puchta).

(2) Sabotage, Explosions.

Wartime increase in Germany was slight compared with that in Poland. Reports to *Referat* IV A2a (KK Büchert). This *Referat* was considered important by Müller, and was charged with many special missions, such as '*Rote Kapelle*'. Reports on the latter type action did not pass through IV-N but circulated directly through channels established by IV A2a.

(3) Rightist Opposition.

Considered dormant for a period, it was a field of renewed activity after 20 July 1944. Reports to *Referat* IV A1b (ORR Litzenberg).

(4) Espionage.

Usually that undertaken in conjunction with other illegal activities. Cases of 'pure' espionage were not referred to IV-N. Reports to *Referat* IV A3a (KD Schäfer).

(5) Industry and Commerce.

A small number of reports, mainly on industrial sabotage. Reports to *Referat* IV A3b (RR Quetting).

(6) Churches.

Moderate number of reports with occasional connection to Rome. Reports to *Referat* IV A4a (SS-*Hstuf* Kunze), which frequently ran its own V-*Leute* without informing IV-N.

(7) Jewish Questions.

No reports during the last few years.

(8) Protection of Leading Personalities.

Only an occasional report on attempted assassinations. Reports to *Referat* IV A5b (RR Schulz).

(9) Foreign Workers from the West.

A field which grew more important with the increase of resistance movements and communist propaganda. Numerous reports to *Referat* IV B1a (KR Seybold).

(10) England.

No reports to *Referat* IV B1b (KR Clemens). When the British radio denounced persons in Germany as *Gestapo* informers, Clemens would check with IV-N to find whether these names were on the registers. Halmanseger does not recall one instance where a name could be traced.

(11) Scandinavian Countries.

Occasional reports on *Abwehr* matters and *emigres* from Sweden. Also, some reports on Danish resistance movements in Denmark and among Danish workers in Germany, reported, for the most part, by *Stapostelle* Kiel. Reports to *Referat* IV B1c (KR Rauche).

(12) Eastern Territories and Workers (except Poles).

Dealt with illegal organizations and communist groups. Many reports to *Referat* IV B2a (KR Schulze and KR Fumy).

(13) Poland and Polish Workers.

Was biggest field of activity in recent years. Resistance movement, Polish underground, communications between groups, sabotage, poisoned foods, insurrection, etc. A great number of reports to *Referat* IV B2b (RR Thomsen).

(14) Czech Protectorate and Slovakia.

Reports on the Czech resistance movement from *Stapoleitstelle* Prague and Brünn, to *Referat* IV B2a (ORR Lischka).

(15) Foreign Workers from the Balkans.

Occasional reports on resistance movements among these workers to *Referat* IV B3a (KR Dr Burg).

(16) Switzerland.

Some reports on *Abwehr* matters from *Stapoleitstellen* Stuttgart and Karlsruhe, to *Referat* IV B3b (KR Hilliges).

(17) *Forschungsamt.*

Halmanseger states that the *Forschungsamt* monitored telephone conversations but had no connection with IV-N. It had a liaison office (*Verbindungsstelle*) in RSHA *Amt* IV, under RR Scholz, who employed two others besides a secretary. The only dealings IV-N had with that agency were occasional requests for information by Scholz who wanted to know whether a given person was a V-*Mann* run by IV-N. Halmanseger presumes these were persons mentioned over the telephone as *Gestapo* informers.

4. Agents (V-*Leute*).

A. General.

Halmanseger estimates the total of G and I agents registered with RSHA IV-N between 1937 (beginning of the central registry) and 1945 somewhere between thirteen and fourteen thousand. Of that total, approx. 6,000 were active in the final stages. There were also approx. 4,000 A-*Personen* (run, by the *Stapostellen*) who were not registered, so the total number of *Gestapo* agents in Germany early in 1945 came to approx. 10,000, according to Halmanseger.

As a rule, a small *Stapostelle* would have 50–80 V-*Leute*, and a larger *Stelle*, located in an industrial area, 100–200. G and I personnel were about evenly divided, and a *Stapostelle* would also have 50–150 A-*Personen*.

B. Recruiting.

Recruiting of agents was done in many different ways. As a rule, recruiting among German nationals required greater skill and patience than it did among others.

Many agents were recruited during interrogations. An arrested person, after being confronted by strong evidence against him, would be released on the promise to serve as an agent.

Inmates of concentration camps, whose families were trying to obtain their release, sometimes proved to be willing agents when pressure brought upon the family and the prisoner.

A person who was about to be released from prison after serving a sentence for a political offence would be sounded out on serving as a *Gestapo* agent. Failure to co-operate, it would be hinted, might have dire consequences, such as being transferred to a concentration camp after 'release'.

Recruiting among churchmen was pursued along somewhat different lines. A favorite method of the *Gestapo* was to threaten to expose the love life of a Catholic priest unless he consented to be a V-*Mann*. Priests who had separated themselves from the church were sometimes found to be suitable agents. Catholic or Protestant clergy in favor of pan-Germanic (though not National Socialist) sometimes consented to act as V-*Leute*.

Among foreign workers those from the East were easiest to recruit, probably because they were most mistreated. Some volunteered, to get money or additional rations; others were recruited under pressure during interrogation. Some, such as the Doriot adherents among the French, had already worked in their native countries for German authorities. Since those with 'experience' proved most valuable to the *Gestapo*, the BdS or KdS in the occupied countries was requested to report all V-*Leute* among the workers being shipped into Germany. These agents were told to report to the local *Stapostelle* immediately. Good results were obtained this way.

C. Payment.

All matters pertaining to the payment of agents were handled by the *Stapostellen* with funds requested from and provided by RSHA *Amt* II. The guiding principle for amount of payment was laid down in Müller's 'Leistungs Prinzip', which provided that a V-*Mann* be paid only in accordance with the volume and quantity of his output. A mediocre agent might average anywhere from 10 to 100 RM a month in addition to expenses. Outstanding agents were paid up to 500 RM a month. Payment was made against a receipt signed by the agent with his cover number. Receipts were kept by the N-*Referat*.

Early in 1939 the monthly outlay for all German *Stapostellen* and *Stapoleitstellen* was approx. 50,000–60,000 RM. Later, because of the war, the occupation of larger territories and the influx of foreign workers, the amount increased tremendously and by 1944 approached a peak of 300,000–400,000 RM for Germany and certain occupied countries. (Not more than one-fifth [20 per cent] of this sum ever went to agents involved in *Abwehr* matters.) Monthly expenses began declining in 1944 when Germany started to withdraw from foreign territories, and in the following year, 1945, no figures were submitted to Halmanseger.

Certain *Stapostellen* and *Stapoleitstellen*, because of their great activity and area coverage, spent considerably more money for agents than the rest. Halmanseger mentioned several of these: Berlin, Bremen, Hamburg, Düsseldorf, Wien, Munich, Stuttgart, Prague and Brünn.

Small quantities of tobacco and liquor went to V-*Leute* in addition to their pay. During 1944, RSHA IV-N distributed monthly to the *Stapostellen* in Germany for payment to agents: 500,000 cigarettes, 50,000 cigars, 500 bottles of liquor, and a small quantity of supplementary ration cards.

D. Commitment.

The technique of handling V-*Leute* differed in each *Stapostelle*. However, a few basic rules were observed by practically all of them. No agent was permitted to come to the *Stapo* office or to the home of a *Stapo* employee. Meetings with agents usually took place in restaurants, outdoors, or in offices rented for that purpose and suitably camouflaged. A V-*Mann* was only to cover groups or political movements with which he was familiar, and preferably one of which he was (or had been) a member. Another principle rarely violated was that agents were only to observe and were not to act as provocateurs.

Cities were the primary field of operation for agents. Factories, because they were most apt to breed opposition movements, were favorite targets for V-*Leute*. Although rarely attained, 5–10 *Gestapo* agents were considered a good ratio in a plant employing 10,000. Even the management did not know the identity of these agents, although some directors of *Arbeitsämter* might have had that knowledge because V-*Leute* were set up in factories through the *Arbeitsamt*. They were to receive no preferential treatment, and started out without any specific mission. After watching and observing, they were to determine from the workers' attitudes whether any opposition groups existed; they then received instructions to join one of these movements. V-*Leute* were further cautioned not to seek leading positions in the groups unless qualified to hold such offices. Whenever it was necessary for more than one agent to penetrate the same group, the agents were not to know of each other.

A V-*Mann* who had been politically active before 1933 would use old connections. By visiting the restaurants where his old political cronies met, he could sound them out to see whether they were still active in political groups, and what their attitude towards the regime was.

Many new problems arose for the *Gestapo* when foreign workers poured into Germany. Arranging for new V-*Leute* was not difficult, but few of these recruited knew German, and that complicated the problem of reporting information. A system of '*Meldekopf*' (message centers) was introduced. One reliable, German-speaking foreigner, called a '*Meldekopfe*', would be placed among a group of foreign workers. He would recruit his own agents, who would be known only to himself, and would be responsible for turning in the information desired. This system produced excellent results.

The *Länder Referate* (RSHA *Gruppe* IV B) became interested in the *Meldekopf* system and eventually set up their own on a national scale, including some mobile units which travelled throughout Germany. The Frenchmen in this organization were at the same time in touch with the Vichy French government office for foreign workers in Berlin. A certain Dr Gasbonde is said to have played a leading role in that activity.

A Russian police officer from Kiew named Maikowski was a *Meldekopf* for *Stapoleitstelle* Berlin, and he is supposed to have obtained particularly good results.

5. List of N-*Referate* in Germany.

Below are listed all *Stapostellen* and *Stapoleitstellen* in Germany, Austria and the Czech Protectorate. Names of IV-N *Referenten*, as remembered by Halmanseger, are included. The number designations (*Grundziffern*) given in the first column are those which appeared in agent's reports forwarded to RSHA IV-N (see B S2, above), and are reasonably accurate, though Halmanseger admits some error might exist. (Asterisks indicates a *Stapoleitstelle*.)

No.	Location	Referent	Strength	Remarks
01	Aachen			dissolved
02	Allenstein	KS Zimmermann		dissolved 1943
03	Augsburg	KS Walter	2	
04	Berlin*	KK Kalies (to 1944)	15	
		KS Kusin (asst.)		
05	Bielefeld			dissolved
06	Braunschweig	KI Scharfe	4	
07	Bremen	KK Schultz	5	
08	Breslau	KK Leiser (?)	3	
09	Brünn*	KR Taudt		
10	Bromberg			

11	Chemnitz	KS Fetzner	3	
12	Danzig	KS Schnak	3	
13	Darmstadt			
14	Dessau			dissolved
15	Düsseldorf*			
16	Dortmund	KS Gutzeit (asst.)	10	
17	Dresden	KR Wagner	5	
		KS Riedl (asst.)		
--	Elbing			dissolved, 1940
18	Erfurt			dissolved
19	Frankfurt/Main	KOS Datz (?)	2	
20	Frankfurt/Oder			
21	Graz	KK Otto Müller	4	
22	Graudenz			dissolved
23	Halle	KS Wedow	3	
24	Hamburg*	KS Mathiessen	7	
25	Hannover*	KOS Mikusch	3	
26	Hildesheim			dissolved
27	Hohensalza			dissolved
28	Innsbruck	KS Beringer	3	
29	Karlsbad	KOS Burz	2	
30	Karlsruhe*	KK Kraut	5	
		KOS Nagel (asst.)		
31	Kassel			
32	Kattowitz*	KR Magwitz	6	
33	Kiel	KS Schmidt	3	
34	Klagenfurt	KOS Sedlak	4	
35	Koblenz	KK Simmer	2	
36	Köln	KI Mayer	2	
37	Königsberg*	KI Langfried	3	
38	Köslin			dissolved
39	Leipzig	KK Michelis	3	
40	Liegnitz			dissolved
41	Linz	KI Müller	3	
42	Litzmannstadt (Lodz)	KS Bayer	3	
43	Magdeburg	KI Bennewitz	3	
44	Munich	SS-*Ostuf* Wuchner	15	
		KI Blümlhuber (asst.)		
45	Münster/W.	KOS Kruschwitz	3	
46	Neustadt a.d.W.			dissolved, 1941
47	Nürnberg*	KK Rudorf	5	
48	Oppeln	KS Steinhard	3	

49	Osnabrück			dissolved
50	Plauen			dissolved
51	Posen*	KOS Wetzel	3	
52	Potsdam	KK Gubalke	3	
53	Prague*	KR Schulz	6	
54	Regensburg	KS Siegert	1	
55	Reichenberg	KS Gluck	5	
56	Salzburg	KS Würzel	2	
57	Saarbrücken	KOS Rebohle	2	
58	Schneidemühl			dissolved
59	Schwerin	KS Bülow	1	
60	Tilsit	KS Mittag	1	
61	Trier			dissolved
62	Stuttgart*	KI Jahn	6	
63	Stettin*	KK Gutmann	4	
64	Wesermünde			dissolved
65	Weimar	KS Jahn	2	
66	Wilhelmshaven			dissolved
67	Wien*	KI Leutgeb	6	
68	Würzburg			dissolved
69	Zich.-Schröttersburg			dissolved

Occupied Territories

19a	KdS Veldes		
04a	KdS Bialystok	KK Schmid	
45a	KdS Minsk		
43a	KdS Marburg	KK Burholz	
39a	KdS Lemberg		
41a	KdS Lublin	KK Schneider	
38a	KdS Krakau	KR Weissmann	6
		KI Schulz (asst.)	
53a	KdS Radom	KR Fuchs	4
64a	KdS Warschau	KR Spilker	
--	KdS Strasbourg	KI Leber	
--	KdS Metz	KOS Bader	

(Note: the *Stapostellen* noted as dissolved, were typically downgraded to *Stapo Aussenstelle* and *Stapo-Aussendienststelle*.)

Annex II

Personality List

BAYER, *Krim.Insp.*, N-*Referent Stapo* Lodz, 1941–1945.
Born 1905; lives Lodz; slender build; brown hair; brown eyes.

BERINGER, *Krim.Sek.*, N-*Referent Stapo* Innsbruck, 1941–1945.
Born 1900; lives Innsbruck; 1.70m tall; stocky build; brown hair; brown eyes; married.

BLÜMLHUBER, *Krim.Insp.*, *Mitarbeiter* (Asst.) IV-N *Stapo* Munich.
Born 1895; lives Munich; 1.70m tall; slender build; brown hair; brown eyes; married.

BÜLOW, *Krim.Sek.*, *Mitarbeiter* IV-N *Stapo* Schwerin to 1944, and IV-N *Referent* 1944–1945.
Born 1905; lives Schwerin; 1.80m tall; muscular build; brown hair; brown eyes; married.

BURZ, *Krim.Ob.Sek.*, N-*Referent Stapo* Karlsbad, 1941–1945.
Born 1895; lives Karlsbad; 1.70m tall; slender build; brown hair; brown eyes; married.

DATZ, *Krim.Ob.Sek.*, *Mitarbeiter* IV-N *Stapo* Frankfurt/Main, to 1941, then N-*Referent*, 1941–1945.
Born 1900; lives Frankfurt/Main.

DENNEWITZ, *Krim.Insp.*, *Mitarbeiter* IV-N, *Stapo* Magdeburg, to 1941, the N-*Referent*, 1941–1945.
Born 1894; lives Magdeburg; 1.72m tall; muscular build; brown hair; brown eyes; married.

FETZER, *Krim.Ob.Sek.*, *Mitarbeiter* IV-N, *Stapo* Chemnitz, to 1941, then N-*Referent*, 1941–1945.
Born 1900; lives Chemnitz; 1.78m tall; slender build; blond hair; married.

GLUCK, *Krim.Sek.*, *Mitarbeiter* IV-N, *Stapo* Reichenberg, to 1941, then N-*Referent*, 1941–end 1944.
Born 1900; lives Reichenberg; 1.70m tall; slender build; blond hair; brown eyes; married.

GUBALKE, *Krim.Komm.*, N-*Referent*, *Stapo* Potsdam, 1941–1945.
Born 1908; lives Potsdam; 1.65m tall; slender build; blond hair; blue eyes; married.

GUTMANN, *Krim.Komm.*, N-*Referent*, *Stapo* Stettin, 1944–1945.
Born 1895; lives Stettin; 1.70m tall; stocky build; black hair; brown eyes; wears glasses, speaks Russian; married.

GUTZEIT, *Krim.Sek.*, *Mitarbeiter* IV-N, *Stapo* Dortmund.
Born 1905; lives Dortmund; 1.70m tall; stocky build; brown eyes; married.

JAHN, *Krim.Insp.*, N-*Referent*, *Stapo* Stuttgart, 1941–1945.

Born 1890; lives Stuttgart; 1.75m tall; muscular build; brown hair; brown eyes; married.

KALIES, *Krim.Komm.*, N-*Referent, Stapo* Berlin, 1943–1944.

Born 1905; lives Berlin; 1.70m tall; frail build; blond hair; married.

KRAUT, *Krim.Komm.*, N-*Referent, Stapo* Karlsruhe, 1941–March 1945.

Born 1905; lives Karlsruhe; 1.70m tall; slender build; brown hair; brown eyes; married.

KRUSCHWITZ, *Krim.Insp.*, *Mitarbeiter* IV-N, *Stapo* Münster/W., to 1941, then N-*Referent*, 1941–44.

Born 1890; lives Münster/W.; 1.70m tall; muscular build; bald; blue eyes; married.

KUSIN, *KrimSek.*, *Mitarbeiter* IV-N, *Stapo* Berlin.

Born 1905; lives Berlin; 1.68m tall; slender build; black hair; brown eyes.

LANGFRIED, *Krim.Insp.*, *Mitarbeiter* IV-N, *Stapo* Königsberg, to 1943, then N-*Referent*, 1943–1945.

Born 1892; lives Königsberg; 1.70m tall; slender build; grey hair; brown eyes; wears glasses.

LEBER, *Krim.Insp.*, N-*Referent*, KdS Strasbourg.

Lives Strasbourg; stocky build; brown hair; brown eyes; married.

LEISER, *Krim.Komm.*, N-*Referent, Stapo* Breslau, 1944–1945.

Born 1905; lives Breslau; 1.72m tall; slender build; blond hair; blue eyes; married.

LEUTGEB, *Krim.Insp.*, N-*Referent, Stapo* Wien.

Born 1900; lives Wien; 1.75m tall; strong build; black hair; brown eyes; married.

MAGWITZ, Guido, *Krim.Rat.*, to end 1944, *Referatsleiter, Stapo* Kattowitz, end 1944–1945, N-*Referent, Stapo* Kattowitz.

Born 1900; lives Kattowitz.

MATHIESSEN, *Krim.Sek.*, *Mitarbeiter* IV-N, *Stapo* Hamburg, 1941–1945.

Born 1900; lives Hamburg; 1.70m tall; stocky build; blond hair; blue eyes; married.

MAYER, *Krim.Insp.*, *Mitarbeiter* IV-N, *Stapo* Aachen, to 1943; N-*Referent, Stapo* Köln, 1943–1945.

Lives Köln; married.

MICHALIS, *Krim.Komm.*, N-*Referent, Stapo* Leipzig, 1944–1945.

Born 1905; lives Leipzig; 1.70m tall; slender build; blond hair; blue eyes; married.

MIKUSCH, *Krim.Ob.Sek.*, N-*Referent, Stapo* Hannover.

Born 1900; lives Hannover; 1.70m tall; stocky build; brown hair; brown eyes; married.

MITTAG, *Krim.Sek.*, N-*Referent, Stapo* Tilsit.

Born 1905; lives Tilsit; 1.75m tall; strong build; brown hair; brown eyes.

MÜLLER, *Krim.Insp.*, *Mitarbeiter* IV-N, *Stapo* Linz, to 1941; N-*Referent*, 1941–1945.

Born 1895; lives Linz; 1.75m tall; slender build; black hair; brown eyes; married.

MÜLLER, Otto, *Krim.Komm.*, *Referatsleiter, Stapo* Graz, to 1944; N-*Referent*, end 1944–1945.

Born 1896; lives Graz; 1.68m tall; slender build; brown hair; brown eyes; married, one child.

NEUGEBAUER, *Krim.Sek.*, N-*Referent*, *Stapo* Kattowitz, 1941–1944; *Mitarbeiter* IV-N, 1944–1945 (under Magwitz).

Born 1900; lives Kattowitz; 1.70m tall; slender build; brown hair; brown eyes; married.

REBOHLE, *Krim.Ob.Sek.*, *Mitarbeiter* IV-N, *Stapo* Saarbrücken, to 1941; N-*Referent*, 1941–1944.

Born 1892; lives Saabrücken; 1.70m tall; slender build; brown hair; brown eyes; wears glasses; married

RIEDL, *Krim.Sek.*, *Mitarbeiter* IV-N, *Stapo* Dresden to 1943; N-*Referent*, 1943–1945.

Born 1900; lives Dresden; 1.75m tall; slender build; brown hair.

RUDORF, *Krim.Komm.*, *Mitarbeiter* IV-N, *Stapo* Nürnberg, to 1943; N-*Referent*, 1943–1945.

Born 1905; lives Nürnberg; 1.80m tall; slender build; brown hair; brown eyes; married.

RUMPLER, *Krim.Sek.*, N-*Referent*, *Stapo* Graz, 1943–end 1944; *Mitarbeiter* IV-N, *Stapo* Graz, end 1944–1945.

Born 1900; lives Graz; 1.75m tall; slender build; brown hair.

SCHARFE, *Krim.Insp.*, N-*Referent*, *Stapo* Braunschweig, 1941–1945.

Born 1900; lives Braunschweig; 1.75m tall; stocky build; brown hair; blue eyes; married.

SCHMIDT, *Krim.Sek.*, N-*Referent*, *Stapo* Kiel, 1941–1945.

Born 1898; lives Kiel; 1.70m tall; stocky build; brown hair; brown eyes; married.

SCHNAK, *Krim.Sek.*, N-*Referent*, *Stapo* Damzig, 1941–1945.

Born 1904; lives Danzig; 1.80m tall; slender build; black hair; brown eyes; married.

SCHNEIDER, *Krim.Komm.*, N-*Referent*, KdS Lublin, 1944.

Born 1907; lives Lublin; 1.70m tall; slender build; brown hair; brown eyes; wears glasses.

SCHULTZ, *Krim.Komm.*, *Referatsleiter*, *Stapo* Bremen, before 1944; N-*Referent*, *Stapo* Bremen, 1944–1945.

Born 1905; lives Bremen; 1.80m tall; slender build; blond hair; married.

SCHULZ, *Krim.Insp.*, Deputy N-*Referent*, KdS Krakau, to 1944.

Born 1892; born Krakau; 1.75m tall; strong build; bald; brown eyes; wears glasses; married.

SCHULZE, *Krim.Rat*, *Referatsleiter*, *Stapo* Prague, to 1944; N-*Referent*, *Stapo* Prague, 1944–1945.

Born 1900; lives Prague; 1.70m tall; slender build; brown hair; brown eyes; married.

SEDLAK, *Krim.Ob.Sek.*, N-*Referent*, *Stapo* Klagenfurt, 1941–1944; *Mitarbeiter* IV-N, *Stapo* Klagenfurt, end 1944–1945.

Born 1894; lives Klagenfurt; 1.70m tall; stocky build; brown hair; brown eyes.

SIEGERT, Johann, *Krim.Sek.*, *Mitarbeiter* IV-N, *Stapo* Regensburg, to 1941; N-*Referent*, *Stapo* Regensburg, 1941–1945.

Born 1900; lives Regensburg; 1.70m tall; slender build; brown hair; brown eyes; married.

SIMMER, *Krim.Komm.*, N-*Referent, Stapo* Koblenz, 1941–end 1944; then with RSHA IV A1a, Berlin, end 1944–1945.
Born 1905; lives Koblenz; 1.70m tall; slender build; blond hair; blue eyes; wears glasses; married.

SPILKER, Alfred, *Krim.Rat, Referatsleiter,* KdS Krakau, to 1943; then N-*Referent* with BdS Krakau then BdS Warschau, 1943–1945.
Born 1905; lives Warsaw; 1.75m tall; stocky build; brown hair; brown eyes; married.

STEINHARD, *Krim.Sek., Mitarbeiter* IV-N, *Stapo* Oppeln, to 1941; then N-*Referent, Stapo* Oppeln, 1941–1945.
Born 1900; lives Oppeln; 1.70m tall; slender build; brown hair; grown eyes; married.

TAUDT, *Krim.Rat, Referatsleiter, Stapo* Brünn, to 1941; then N-*Referent, Stapo* Brünn, 1941–1945.
Born 1900; lives Brünn; 1.90m tall; slender build; blond hair; married.

WALTHER, *Krim.Sek., Mitarbeiter* IV-N, *Stapo* Leipzig, to 1944; then N-*Referent, Stapo* Augsburg, end 1944–1945.
Born 1900; lives Leipzig; 1.70m tall; stocky build; bald; married.

WEDOW, *Krim.Sek., Mitarbeiter* IV-N, *Stapo* Halle, to 1944; the N-*Referent, Stapo* Halle, 1944–45.
Born 1900; lives Halle; 1.80m tall; muscular build; blond hair; blue eyes; married.

WEISMANN, *Krim.Rat, Referatsleiter,* KdS Krakau, to 1943; then N-*Referent,* KdS Krakau, 1943–Jan 1945.
Born 1900; lives Krakau; 1.70m tall; stocky build; brown hair; brown eyes; married.

WETZEL, *Krim.Ob.Sek., Mitarbeiter* IV-N, *Stapo* Posen, to 1941; then N-*Referent, Stapo* Posen, 1941–1945.
Born 1894; lives Posen; 1.80m tall; slender build; brown hair; brown eyes; married.

WÜRZEL, *Krim.Sek.*, N-*Referent, Stapo* Salzburg, 1943–March 1945.
Born 1900; lives Salzburg; 1.70m tall; slender build; black hair; brown eyes; married.

On 1 March 1941, the RSHA issued an Organisational Plan (*Geschäftsverteilungsplan*) listing each *Referat*, with a description of its responsibilities and its *Referatsleiter*:

Amt IV: *Gegnererforschung und Bekämpfung.*
Amtschef: SS-*Brigadeführer und Generalmajor der Polizei* Heinrich Müller
<u>*Gruppe* IV A</u>
Gruppenleiter: SS-*Ostubaf* ORR Fritz Panzinger

Referat IV A1: *Kommunismus, Marxismus und Nebenorganisationen, Kriegsdelikte, Illegale und Feindpropaganda.*
Referatsleiter: SS-*Stubaf* KD Josef Vogt

Referat IV A2: *Sabotageabwehr, Sabotagebekämpfung, Politisch-polizeiliche Abwehrbeauftragte, Politisches Falschungswesen.*
Referatsleiter: SS-*Hstuf* KK Horst Kopkow

Referat IV A3: *Reaktion,* Opposition, *Legitismus, Liberalismus, Emigranten, Heimtücke-Angelegenheiten.*
Referatsleiter: SS-*Stubaf* KD Willy Litzenberg

Referat IV A4: *Schutzdienst, Attentatsmeldung, Überachungen Sonderaufträge, Fahndungstrupp.*
Referatsleiter: SS-*Stubaf* KD Franz Schulz

Gruppe IV B
Gruppenleiter: SS-*Stubaf* Alfred Hartl
Vertreter: SS-*Stubaf* RR Erich Roth

Referat IV B1: *Politischer Katholizismus.*
Referatsleiter: SS-*Stubaf* RR Erich Roth

Referat IV B2: *Politischer Protestantismus, Sekten.*
Referatsleiter: SS-*Stubaf* RR Erich Roth

Referat IV B3: *Sonstige Kirchen, Freimauerei.*
Referatsleiter: unoccupied at this time.

Referat IV B4: *Judenangelegenheiten, Räumungsangelegenheiten.*
Referatsleiter: SS-*Stubaf* Adolf Eichmann

Gruppe IV C
Gruppenleiter: SS-*Ostubaf* ORR Dr Friedrich Rang
Vertreter: SS-*Stubaf* R.- u. KR Dr Emil Berndorff

Referat IV C1: *Auswertung, Hauptkartei, Personenaktenverwaltung, Auskunftstelle, A-Kartei, Ausländerüberwachung, Zentrale Sichtvermerkstelle.*
Referatsleiter: *Pol.Rat* Paul Matzke
Referat IV C2: *Schutzhaftangelegenheiten.*
Referatsleiter: SS-*Stubaf* R.- u. KR Dr Emil Berndorff

Referat IV C3: *Angelegenheiten der Presse und des Schrifttums.*
Referatsleiter: SS-*Stubaf* RR Dr Ernst Jahr

Referat IV C4: *Angelegenheiten der Partei und ihrer Gliederungen.*
Referatsleiter: SS-*Stubaf* KR Kurt Stage

<u>*Gruppe* IV D</u>
Gruppenleiter: SS-*Ostubaf* Dr Erwin Weinmann
Vertreter: SS-*Stubaf* RR Dr Gustav Jonak

Referat IV D1: *Protektoratsangelegenheiten, Tschechen im Reich.*
Referatsleiter: SS-*Stubaf* RR Dr Gustav Jonak

Referat IV D2: *Generalgouvernement, Polen im Reich.*
Referatsleiter: SS-*Hstuf* Dr *Reg Ass* Jobst Thiemann

Referat IV D3: *Vertrauensstelle, Staatsfeindliche Ausländer.*
Referatsleiter: SS-*Hstuf* KK Erich Schröder

Referat IV D4: *Besetzte Gebiete*: Frankreich, Luxemburg, Elsaß *und* Lothringen, Belgien, Holland, Norwegen, Dänemark.
Referatsleiter: SS-*Stubaf* RR Bernhard Baatz

<u>*Gruppe* IV E</u>
Gruppenleiter: SS-*Stubaf* RR Walter Schellenberg

Referat IV E1: *Allgemeine Abwehrangelegenheiten, Erstattung von Gutachten in Hoch- und Landesverratssachen, Werkschutz und Bewachungsgewerbe.*
Referatsleiter: SS-*Hstuf* KK Kurt Lindow

Referat IV E2: *Allgemeine Wirtschaftsangelegenheiten, Wirtschafts-spionage-Abwehr.*
Referatsleiter: *Reg Ass* Karl Sebastian

Referat IV E3: *Abwehr West.*
Referatsleiter: SS-*Hstuf* KR Dr Herbert Fischer

Referat IV E4: *Abwehr Nord.*
Referatsleiter: KD Dr Ernst Schambacher

Referat IV E5: *Abwehr Ost.*
Referatsleiter: SS-*Stubaf* KD Walter Kubitzky

Referat IV E6: *Abwehr Süd.*
Referatsleiter: SS-*Hstuf* KR Dr Wilhelm Schmitz

The CIWR Situation Report No. 4 used at the beginning and also the statement by SS-*Stubaf* Horst Kopkow both mention that by late 1944, the RSHA organisation had stream-lined due to the military situation and losses of occupied territories. RSHA IV cut back and three of its original five *Gruppen* had disappeared in the last RSHA organisation plan dated 1 December 1944 when just two *Gruppen* were left, and it acquired a third:

Amt IV:
Amtschef: SS-*Gruppenführer und Generalleutnant der Polizei* Heinrich Müller
Geschäftsstelle IV: SS-*Stubaf* Hans Pieper

Gruppe IV A
Gruppenleiter: SS-*Gruf* Heinrich Müller

Abteilung IV A1: *Rechtsbewebung*
Leiter: SS-*Stubaf* Willy Litzenberg.

Abteilung IV A2: *Sabotageabwehr, Sabotagebekämpfung, Funkspiele*
Leiter: SS-*Stubaf* Horst Kopkow

Abteilung IV A3: *Industriesicherung*
Leiter: SS-*Stubaf* Hermann Quetting

Abteilung IV A4: *Weltanschauliche Gegner, Judenangelegenheiten*
Leiter: SS-*Ostubaf* Adolf Eichmann

Referat IV A5a: *Schutzdienst, Sonderaufgaben*
Leiter: SS-*Stubaf* Franz Schulz

Referat IV A5b: *Partei- und Presseangelegenheiten*
Leiter: SS-*Stubaf* Erich Sanders

Abteilung IV A6: *Schutzhaft, Kartei, Akten*
Leiter: SS-*Ostubaf* Dr Emil Berndorff

Gruppe IV B
Gruppenleiter: SS-*Ostubaf* Kurt Lischka

Abteilung IV B1: *Protektorat, Slowakei*
Leiter: SS-*Ostubaf* Kurt Lischka

Abteilung IV B2: *Ost- und Südostgebiete*
Leiter: SS-*Ostubaf* Kurt Lischka

Abteilung IV B3: Balkans, *Ferner Ost*
Leiter: SS-*Staf* Dr Friedrich Rang

Abteilung IV B4: *Pass- und Ausweiswesen*
Leiter: *Ministerialrat* Johannes Krause

Gruppe G—Grenzinspekteur—SS-*Oberführer Oberst der Polizei* Otto Somann

To fill in the bare bones of RSHA IV organisation in the last stages as noted above, a more fulsome account came in the USFET interrogation of five former RSHA officers: Counter Intelligence Consolidated Interrogation Report (CICIR) No. 9 dated 15 November 1945, on the subject of RSHA *Amt* IV.

This report deals with the functions, organization, and personalities of *Amt* IV RSHA and its satellite agencies.

CONTENTS

1.   Sources of Information
2.   Report
     a. Introduction
     b. Size of *Amt* IV RSHA
     c. *Forschungsamt* and *Forschungsstellen*
     d. Organization, Functions and Personalities of *Amt* IV RSHA.
3.   Conclusions
4.   Comments and Recommendations
...

1.   Sources of Information
     a. SS-*Stubaf* KD Kurt Lindow, RSHA IV B1a.
     b. SS-*Staf Oberst d.Pol.* Dr Rudolf Mildner, KdS Wien and Niederdonau.
     c. SS-*Ostubaf* ORR Hans Helmut Wolff, *Stapoleiter* Dresden.
     d. SS-*Staf* Erich Isselhorst, RSHA IV, *Südstab* at Hof.
     e. SS-*Hstuf* KK Leonhard Halmanseger, RSHA IV N.

2.   Report

a. Introduction

The primary purpose of this report is to give as detailed a list as possible of personnel and their position in *Amt* IV RSHA. Like all other agencies during the last stages of the war, *Amt* IV underwent a number of sudden confusing changes; consequently, individuals named and located by above sources may have been transferred unknown to them during the last few weeks of the war. It seems certain that with the exception of a few transferred to local *Stapo* offices, most of the changes and transfers were within *Amt* IV RSHA.

b. Size of *Amt* IV RSHA

Amt IV RSHA employed about 800 people of whom approx. 400 were women assigned to routine clerical work. None of these women was affiliated with the SS. According to SS-*Stubaf* Lindow, the shortage of help became so acute towards the end, that cleaning women were often taken from their jobs of sweeping and dusting and put to work filing and typing as best they could. Sources estimated the male strength of *Amt* IV as approx. 400 at the close of the war, of whom 220 are accounted for in this report. It is reasonably certain that all important members have found their correct places on this list and that those who do not appear below were very minor clerks.

c. *Forschungsamt* and *Forschungsstellen*

The *Forschungsamt*, an agency which worked in very close co-operation with *Amt* IV, was a part of the Air Ministry and under the command of *Reichsmarschall* Göring. Its central office was in the Air Ministry building. The *Amt* and its subordinate units, *Forschungsstellen* A and D, the only ones permitted to tap [telephone] wires; evidence collected in such a manner was not submitted in court because the very existence of the office was supposed to be closely guarded from the knowledge of all but a few.

The *Forschungsstelle*, which organized in the large towns, consisted of departments A and B. In a supervised office, A for telephones and B was in charge of telegraphic communications. Requests by local *Stapostellen* for such services were able to contact a local *Forschungsstelle* for action.

The tapping of wires was done from a chamber set aside in the local Post Office where an employee of the *Forschungsstelle* was on duty 24 hours a day. Nobody except the individual on duty within the room and no outsider was supposed to know of its existence or the information so obtained forwarded to the *Forschungsamt* who maintained close liaison with *Amt* IV through SS-*Stubaf* RR Scholz, a close friend of *Amtschef* Müller.

As soon as information was received at the *Forschungsamt*, it was forwarded to *Referat* IV A5a to be acted upon: thus it came about that the *Forschungsamt*, which was really an agency of the Air Ministry, worked directly with Müller and subsequently took orders from him.

d.   RSHA *Amt* IV organization

Amtschef RSHA *Amt* IV	SS-*Gruf* Heinrich Müller
Adjutant	SS-*Ostuf* KK Albert Duchstein
Asst Adjutant	SS-*Ustuf* KS Heinrich Schumacher
Stenographer	*Fräulein* Barbara Helmuth
Stenographer	*Fräulein* Eva Schmidt

The above were part of Müller's office staff and worked in the same building with him.

zbV Officer	SS-*Obf* Georg Klein
	Special missions for Amtschef IV
Liaison Officer	SS-*Stubaf* RR Christian Scholz
	Liaison with *Forschungsamt*. Is said to have escaped with Müller and may be hiding with him
Liaison Officer	SS-*Ustuf* Fischer
	Liaison with RSHA *Amt* III
Gruppenleiter IV A	SS-*Staf* Walter Huppenkothen
	Succeeded Panzinger; worked directly under Müller
Gruppenleiter IV B	SS-*Ostubaf* ORR Paul Lischka
	Succeeded Pifrader; worked directly under Müller.

RSHA *Gruppe* IV B had a large number of military personnel assigned to work for it, including a high ranking officer detached from the OKW. Whether RSHA *Gruppe* IV A also had an officer assigned is not certain.

Attached to IV B	*Oberst* Rohleder
	In charge of all military personnel assigned to IV B
Adjutantur Gruppe IV B	SS-*Ustuf Pol.Ob.Sek.* Fritz Jahn
Special Courier	SS-*Uschaf* Gerhard Döring

Amt IV *Geschäftsstelle* (Administrative HQ)
This organization was directly under *Amtschef* Müller and consisted of five sub-sections:

1.   *Geschäftsstelle* proper
2.   *Geheime Registratur* (secret registry officer)

3.   *Erkennungsdienst* (photo identification of arrested persons)
4.   *Zeichnungsstelle* (drafting section)
5.   *Polizeigefängnis* (Stapo prison)

The *Leiter* of the entire *Geschäftsstelle* was SS-*Stubaf* RR Hans Pieper. Personnel of the *Geschäftsstelle* proper, included:

> SS-*Hstuf* Polizeirat Herbert Berndt
> SS-*Hstuf* POI Heinrich Brockmeier
> SS-*Ostuf* PI Heinz Hilliges
> SS-*Ostuf* POI Eduard Oetzel
> SS-*Oschaf Pol.Ob.Sek* Erich Hegemann
> Heinz Opitz, courier
> Andreas Klein, courier
> Ziehals, courier

a.   *Geheime Registratur*
        Pol.Insp. Konrad Dann (not a SS member)
        SS-*Ostuf* PI Alfred Kretschmann

b.   *Erkennungsdienst*
        SS-*Ustuf* KOS Wilhelm Krause

c.   *Zeichnungsstelle*
        SS-*Ustuf* KOS Johannes Tischler

d.   *Polizeigefängnis*
        SS-*Ostuf* Oberverwalter Wilhelm Gogalla

Abteilung IV A1
Leiter: SS-*Stubaf* ORuKR Willy Litzenberg; succeeded SS-*Obf.*
    Panzinger late 1944 and also kept position of *Referatsleiter*, IV A1b.

Referat IV A 1a
    Dealt with communists and civilians who had crossed existing frontiers.
Leiter: SS-*Hstuf* KR Günther Pütz (succeeded by SS-Stubaf KD Lindow, January 1945);
Asst: SS-*Bewerber* KK Wilhelm Rikowski
        SS-*Bewerber* KOS Wilhelm Bauer
        SS-*Bewerber* KOA Herbert Bordasch
        SS-*Hstuf* KR Erwin Brandt
        SS-*Hstuf* Reg.Amtsmann Fritz Eckerle
        Erhard Haupt, clerk, not an SS member

SS-*Ustuf* KOS Reinhard Hofmann
KS Walter Huse, not an SS member
KS Andreas Hempel, not an SS member
SS-*Hstuf* KR Dr Günther Knobloch
SS-*Ustuf* KOS Gerhard Meher
SS-*Hschaf* KOS Reinhold Ortmann
SS-*Schaf* KA Pitz
SS-*Bewerber* KS Paul Rasch
KOS Fritz Schmidt, not an SS member
SS-*Ostuf* KK Kurt Simmer
KS Johann Sperling, not an SS member
SS-*Ostuf* KK Wilhelm (Willi) Westermann
KOS Gustav Wodtke, not an SS member
KS Nikolaus Wieczorek, not an SS member
Ministerial-Registratur Waldemar Wuthe, not an SS member)

Referat IV A1b
This *Referat* handled all reactionary movements such as 'National Opposition', '*Legitimisten*' (Austrian movement), '*Bayrischer Monarchismus*' (Bavarian monarchism), '*Separatismus*', 'Schwarz Front' and violations of radio control.
Leiter: SS-*Stubaf* ORuKR Willy Litzenberg
Asst: KR Hans Sader, not an SS member
         KS Hans Altmann, not an SS member
         KS Karl Heller, not an SS member
         SS-*Hstuf* POI Erich Pietsch
         SS-*Hstuf* KR Otto Prochnow
         SS-*Oschaf* KS Fritz Scheibel
Note: the names of a number of female employees who served as file clerks, etc., but who were not connected with the SS are not available.

Abteilung IV A2
Leiter: SS-*Stubaf* KD Horst Kopkow

Referat IV A2a
Combatted espionage in Germany.
Leiter: SS-*Hstuf* KK Karl-Heinrich Büchert
Asst: KOS Willi Berg, not an SS member
         SS-*Ostuf* KS Gustav Gogolla
         KK Walter Habecker, not an SS member
         SS-*Ustuf* KOS Hermann Lange
         KS Kurt Marowsky, not an SS member
         KOA Paul Schulz, not an SS member
         KS Heinrich Tscheutschler, not an SS member

Referat IV A2b

Known as the *Funkspiel Sachgebiet*. Induced enemy agents apprehended in Germany to send back false reports and to maintain communications with their respective countries. Information received by these agents was used by the *Referat*.

Leiter: SS-*Hstuf* KR Thomas Ampletzer

Asst: SS-*Hstuf* KK Hans Müller
          KOS Wilhelm Bielemeyer, not an SS member
          SS-*Ostuf* KK Rudolf Brenner
          SS-*Oschaf* KS Erich Fuhrmann
          SS-*Hstuf* KK Richard Haupt
          SS-*Bewerber* Freddie Klinger
          SS-*Hstuf* KK Johann Strübing

Note: IV A2 is reported to be a small office. It is likely that additional but unimportant personnel can be named by Kopkow (held by British authorities) and by Klinger (now held at 3rd US Army Interrogation Center).

Abteilung IV A3

Leiter: SS-*Stubaf* Hermann Quetting, who replaced Huppenkothen when the latter was given the post of Acting *Gruppenleiter* (under Panzinger who later left *Amt* IV for a position with RSHA *Amt* V. Quetting, in addition to being *Abteilungsleiter*, kept his position as *Referatsleiter* IV A3b

Referat IV A3a

Handled counter-espionage cases and cases of treason against the State.

Leiter: SS-*Stubaf* KD Dr Karl Schäfer (this was formerly Huppenkothen's *Referat*.)

Asst: *Hauptmann* Bauermeister (detached from OKW)
          KI Hacker, not an SS member
          SS-*Stubaf* RR Dr Heinz Engelmann
          SS-*Stubaf* KD Josef Häusler
          KS Curt Langgemach, not an SS member

Referat IV A3b

Industrial security (i.e. planting of V-*Leute* in big plants and keeping check on certain potential threats to security), corruption in industries and political police. Personnel:

Leiter: SS-*Stubaf* Hermann Quetting

Asst: KS Hoffmann
          Oberstltn. Keller, detached from OKW
          PI Kunze
          Krim.Angestellter Max Motzkus
          SS-*Stubaf* KR Rudolf Tischer
          SS-*Hstuf* KK Gerhard Eisenschmidt
          KD Ernst Gans, not an SS member

Referat IV A3c
This *Referat* (*Leiter*—SS-*Stubaf* RuKR Paul Opitz) was dissolved and taken over by RSHA IV G (November 1944).

Abteilung IV A4
Leiter: SS-*Ostubaf* Adolf Eichmann
Asst: SS-*Stubaf* Rolf Günther
Both also were in charge of *Referat* IV A4b.

Referat IV A4a
Handled church matters. A specialist was assigned to handle each faith (Catholic, Protestant, etc.) and sect matters.
Leiter: SS-*Stubaf* RR Erich Hahnenbruch
Asst: SS-*Staf* Paul Blobel
         SS-*Stubaf* Dr Ernst Jahr (formerly worked in Press Affairs with RSHA *Amt* IV but after his return about March 1945 from the east (Tilsit) he is believed to have been assigned to Hahnenbruch)
         SS-*Hstuf* Jakobs
         SS-*Hstuf* Erich Kunze
         SS-*Stubaf* RR Dr Dr Karl Neuhaus (spring 1945 to KdS Posen)
         SS-*Hstuf* POI Franz Novak
         KOS Gerhard Hasenbank, not an SS member

Referat IV A4b
The activities of this enemy were centered around affairs of Jews and lodges, such as Freemasons. Personnel:
Leiter: SS-*Ostubaf* Adolf Eichmann (reported to have done extensive travelling)
Asst: SS-*Stubaf* Rolf Günther
         SS-*Hstuf* Reg.Amtmann Karl Anders
         SS-*Hstuf* Reg.Amtmann Fritz Wöhrn
Note: Sources indicate that there were many more persons in *Abteilung* IV A4 and especially in *Referat* IV A4b, but these persons are not known by name. Mildner has given a list of possible hide-outs which Eichmann may be using. (List forwarded through channels.)

Abteilung IV A5
Leiter: SS-*Staf* RD Dr Fritz Rang. Rang succeeded Dr Mildner (one of the sources) who claimed that his position was left vacant upon his release [from RSHA]. However, it seems likely (as borne out by other sources) that SS-*Staf* Rang, whose rank called for a better position, was transferred out of IV A6 (where his usefulness was limited) and put in charge of IV A5. His old job was given to Trenker.

Referat IV A5a
a.   *Schutzdienst* for personnel (security for personnel)
b.   *Attentatsmeldestelle*: Handled attempted assassinations or plans for such which were discovered through monitoring of telephone conversations. Routed reports from the *Forschungsamt* go to higher echelons.
Leiter: SS-*Stubaf* RuKR Franz Schulz
Asst: SS-*Ostuf* KI Emil Kablitz
        SS-*Ostuf* KK Paul Matthieu

Referat IV A5b
This *Referat* dealt with Party member affairs, and sought to prevent corruption within the organization. Its task was made difficult by favoritism and intrigue within Party ranks. Information from Halmanseger and Lindow indicates that Press Matters were also handled by this office.
Leiter: SS-*Stubaf* KR Erich Sanders (formerly Samierski)
Asst: KK Fehling, not an SS member
        KR Müller
        SS-*Stubaf Reg.Amtmann* Richard Kranz (Press specialist)
Note: Organization of this office was fluid, and lack of names of additional personnel may be attributed to this fact.

Abteilung IV A6
Leiter: SS-*Ostubaf* ORuKR Dr Emil Berndorff
Asst: KR Karl Förster, not an SS member

Referat IV A6a
Protective Custody [*Schutzhaft*]. (As defined by sources, this title refers not to individuals but to the safety of the government.) Actions of this *Referat* are treated in a separate report now being compiled at this Center. IV A6a had purely administrative functions and did not make any arrests.
Leiter: SS-*Ostubaf* ORuKR Dr Emil Berndorff
Asst: SS-*Hstuf* POI Gerhard Bonath
        SS-*Hstuf* POI Richard Didier
        POI Bruno Giessen, not an SS member
        POI Paul Ibsch, not an SS member (died 1944)
        Reg.Amtmann Felix Kettenhofen, not an SS member
        Reg.Amtmann Walter Künne, not an SS member

Referat IV A6b
Kept principal files (*Hauptkarteien*) on matters handed throughout Germany by the *Gestapo*.
Leiter: SS-*Stubaf Amtsrat* Johannes Witzel

Asst: PI Lehmann, not an SS member
          SS-*Hstuf* Pol.Rat Karl Mauch
          SS-*Ustuf* POS Albert Zager
          PS Heinz Grunert, not an SS member

Abteilung IV B1
Leiter: SS-*Stubaf* ORR Dr Heinz Höner; also *Referatsleiter* IV B1a

Referat IV B1a
Dealt with political matters in France and Belgium.
Leiter: SS-*Stubaf* ORR Dr Heinz Höner
Asst: SS-*Stubaf* KD Kurt Lindow
          SS-*Ustuf* KS Hans Hans Breuer
          SS-*Ustuf* KS Hans Bürjes
          Major Dr Brunner, detached from OKW
          KI Drexel (or Drexler), not an SS member
          SS-*Ostuf* KK Erich Feldmann
          SS-*Ustuf* PI Walter Carl
          KOS Paul Gerber, not an SS member
          SS-*Ustuf* KS Otto Grenz
          Hauptmann Hass, detached from OKW
          SS-*Ostuf* PI Otto Havemann
          SS-*Uschaf* *Kriminalangestellte* Erich Heinrichsohn
          SS-*Hstuf* KK Walter Möller
          SS-*Hstuf* KR Fritz Seiboldt
          POI Friedrich Seidel, not an SS member
          de Waal, interpreter, not an SS member
          SS-*Hschaf* KS Weege

Referat IV B1b
Supervised activities in Great Britain, Netherlands and the USA.
Leiter: SS-*Stubaf* KR Wilhelm Clemens
Asst: SS-*Ustuf* KOS Heinrich Arndt

Referat IV B1c
Concerned with Norway, Sweden, Denmark and Finland.
Leiter: SS-*Hstuf* KR Fritz Rauch
Asst: SS-*Hstuf* POI Hermann Samuel
          KS Wenzel ('Not certain of this employee')
          SS-*Ustuf* KOS Ernst Behrendt
Note: IV B1b and IV B1c were small departments. It is therefore possible that not
many more persons were employed.

Abteilung IV B2
Leiter: SS-*Ostubaf* ORR Hans Helmuth Wolff. Although transferred to *Stapo* Dresden in February 1945, he should be listed as chief of this *Abteilung*, since his influence persisted even after his departure. Fumy succeeded him as *Abteilungsleiter*.

Referat IV B2a
Handled matters concerning Russia.
Leiter: SS-*Ostubaf* ORR Hans Helmuth Wolff
Asst: SS-*Stubaf* KR Rudolf Fumy
          SS-*Stubaf Reg.Amtmann* Jobst Thiemann
          Reg.Amtmann Walter Schmidt, not an SS member
          SS-*Hstuf* KR Heinz Schultze
          SS-*Hstuf* POI Albin Pilling
          SS-*Hstuf* POI Wilhelm Rechentin
          SS-*Ustuf* KS Wilhelm Hayn
          KOS Kurt Hein, not an SS member
          Major Horsch, detached from OKW
          SS-*Hstuf* POI Georg Gründling
          KI Paul Steffen, not an SS member
          SS-*Ustuf* KS Willy Wolf
          SS-*Stuschaf* KS Kurt Wolansky, interpreter
          SS-*Stuschaf* KS Günther Weber
          SS-*Stuschaf* Walter Kändler
          SS-*Ustuf* KS Rose
          SS-*Ustuf* POS Fritz Zimmat
          POS Kühn, not an SS member
          Joseph Dedio, clerk, interpreter
          Zimmermann, clerk, interpreter
          SS-*Mann Kriminalangestellter* Rempel, interpreter
          Kriminalangestellter Wirsing, not an SS member
          Bruno Przewozny, clerk, interpreter, not an SS member
          POS Johann Krüger, not an SS member
          Sadikow, interpreter, not an SS member

Referat IV B2b
Handled matters pertaining to Poland
Leiter: SS-*Stubaf* RR Harro Thomsen
Asst: *Amtsrat* Kufahl
          SS-*Ostuf* KK Heller
          SS-*Hstuf Amtmann* Ernst Oppermann
          SS-*Hstuf* ROI Adolf Dubiel
          SS-*Hstuf* KR Mathias Weiler
          Hauptmann Saltzinger, detached from OKW

Referat IV B2c
Dealt with Czechoslovakia. SS-*Stubaf* Manfred Schöneseiffen the former *Leiter*,
left for the front in early 1945. Below personnel as of last known listing:
Leiter: SS-*Stubaf Amtsrat* Franz Thiedecke
Asst: SS-*Stuschaf* KS Schreier
          Icker, not an SS member
Note: Above list of names of IV B2a is believed complete except for the names
of two minor employees. In addition to all listed male employees, there were
approx. 50 women employed as typists, file clerks, etc., but none held responsible
or confidential positions.

Abteilung IV B3
SS-*Ostubaf* ORR Othmar Trenker (formerly known as Trnka) succeeded SS-
Staf RD Dr Fritz Rang as *Abteilungsleiter* late in 1944. Rang was sent to IV A5.
Trenker's duties are not known to sources. They believe that he also assumed
charge of IV B3c.

Referat IV B3a
Handled activities in Spain and Portugal.
Leiter: SS-*Hstuf* KR Hermann Ahrens
Asst: SS-*Hstuf* KK Lothar Gudjons
          SS-*Ustuf* KOS Louis Hagemeister
          ROI Lange, not an SS member

Referat IV B3b
Supervision of Italy and Switzerland.
Leiter: SS-*Stubaf* KR Werner Hilliges

Referat IV B3c
Handled activities in Balkan countries.
Leiter: SS-*Ostubaf* ORR Dr Othmar Trenker
Asst: SS-*Hstuf* KR Dr Richard Burg
          KS Hans Stahn, not an SS member
Note: The list of names is believed incomplete; efforts are being made to secure
further information about *Abteilung* IV B3.

Abteilung IV B4
Leiter: *Ministerialrat* Johannes Krause, not an SS member

Referat IV B4a
Passport matters.
Leiter: SS-*Stubaf* ORR Christian Baumann

Referat IV B4b
Central office for Immigrants (*Einwanderer Zentralstelle*)
Leiter: SS-*Ostubaf* ORR Rudolf Kröning
Asst: KS Paul Sackermann, not an SS member

Referat IV B4c
Visa and permits for travel abroad.
Leiter: SS-*Hstuf* Pol.Rat Erwin Jarosch
Asst: PI Becker, not an SS member
         SS-*Hstuf Reg.Amtmann* Franz Königshaus
         ROI Otto Koschate, not an SS member
Note: Baumann, now in US custody, should know more names.

Several special agencies were at the disposal of RSHA *Amtschef* IV, Müller, and although these agencies worked independently, as was the case with the Special Investigation Squad (*Fahndungstrupp*), they were for administrative purposes placed under an *Abteilung* of RSHA *Amt* IV.

Dienststelle IV B/aA. Foreign Workers (*Ausländische Arbeiter*).
Dealt with distribution, allotment, and treatment of foreign workers employed in Germany and areas under German control.
Leiter: SS-*Hstuf* KK Rudolf Hässler.
    Other personalities not known so far. It is believed that there was only one other co-worker.

Gruppe IV G. Border Control (*Zollgrenzschutz*).
This agency, concerned with the checking of traffic and mail, was taken over from the Finance Department, in October 1944.
Leiter: SS-*Obf* Otto Somann
Asst: SS-*Staf* Dr Walter Blume
         SS-*Hstuf* RR Paul Opitz

Dienststelle IV—ZABP. Central Censorship Office (*Zentrale Auslands Briefprüfungsstelle*).
Taken over in April 1944 from the *Abwehr* and placed under the command of SS-*Ostubaf* Johannes Müller who was later replaced by Heller and dismissed from the service for alleged inability to find billets in Hof for RSHA *Südstab Gruppe*.
Leiter: SS-*Ostubaf* ORR Reinhold Heller
Asst: SS-*Stubaf* RR Josef Vogt
         SS-*Ostuf* KR Hermann Spann
         SS-*Hstuf* KR Walter Tholen

Fahndungstrupp, Special Investigation Squad.
The *Fahndungstrupp* was under *Amtschef* Müller's personal supervision, although administratively attached to IV A5a. Its members (approx. 15) were sent on special missions.
Leiter: KI Schäffler.
Asst: SS-*Ostuf* KI Paul Hein
      SS-*Ostuf* KOS Walter Kirchdorff
      KOS Heinrich Finkendel, not an SS member
      SS-*Ustuf* KOS Gustav Lange
      SS-*Ustuf* KS Christoph Müller
      KOS Emil Radloff, not an SS member

Referat IV N.
IV N Berlin was the file and message center where all records of agents and V-*Leute* working with *Stapostellen* in various localities were kept. All reports to the various *Referate* were channelled through this office.
Leiter: SS-*Hstuf* KK Leonhard Halmanseger
Asst: KOS Franz Regnath, not an SS member
      SS-*Ostuf* KI Otto Kablitz
      KOA Anton Eder, not an SS member
      Frau Rudolph, secretary
      Frau Habecker, file clerk

5. Conclusions
None.

6. Comments and Recommendations
It is believed that the sources have given the names of all the important members of RSHA *Amt* IV. Interrogation of Albert Duchstein, SS-*Gruf* Müller's chief adjutant, should reveal specific details about Müller's activities and plans.

Notes

* The National Archives, Kew, KV 3/109, CIWR Situation Report No. 4 on RSHA IV.
* The National Archives, Kew, KV 2/1501, Combined Interrogation Report IR 47 of Horst Kopkow, Harro Thomsen and Gustav Adolf Nosske; this report is available at US National Archives & Records Administration, College Park, RG 498 Box 16.
* The National Archives, Kew, WO 311/174, Interrogation Report, USFET CI-IIR No. 54, of Leonhard Halmanseger.
* Nuremberg document L-185, Organisation Plan of RSHA dated 1 March 1941.

* The National Archives, Kew, KV 3/104, Organisation Plan of RSHA IV dated 1 December 1944.

* US National Archives & Records Administration, College Park, RG 65, Entry A1-136P, Box 191, Interrogation Report CICIR No. 9 of Lindow, Mildner, Wolff, Halmanseger and Isselhorst.

1 The National Archives, Kew, KV 2/1500, Interrogation Report, 030/8/64/2 dated 7 June 1945, of Horst Kopkow.

2 From this paucity of information about the role Adolf Eichmann in RSHA IV and his department dealing with Jews, little was explored by Allied interrogators.

3 In May 1943 this *Referat* employed 376 persons, 218 of them women, who operated the vast Card Index system.

4 Foot, M.R.D., *SOE in France*, (1966), pp 304-318.

5 See Note 1.

4

Organisation of the German Police (up to 1938)

A report by Counter-Intelligence War Room on RSHA V (*Kriminalpolizei*) has not so far been declassified. Such a report may not have been produced and, instead, reliance placed on knowledge of the *Kriminalpolizei* provided by a document translated and issued by the Prisoner of War Interrogation Service from the London District Cage in September 1944.

Part I

Reichspolizei

I.   Development of the *Reichspolizei*, its central command, departments and general organisation.
Section 1: Development
Section 2: Central—and the highest command of the *Reichspolizei* office.
Section 3: General organisation of the *Reichspolizei*.

II.   *Ordnungspolizei*.
Section 1: Organisation of the *Ordnungspolizei*
Section 2: *Hauptamt Ordnungspolizei*
Section 3: *Verwaltungspolizei*
Section 4: *Schutzpolizei*
Section 5: *Gendarmerie*
Section 6: *Schutzpolizei der Gemeinde*
Section 7: *Feuerlöschpolizei*
Section 8: *Technische Nothilfe* (TENO)
Section 9: *Ordnungspolizei* on the territory of former Austria

III.   *Sicherheitspolizei.*
       Section 1: Organisation *Sicherheitspolizei*
       Section 2: *Hauptamt Sicherheitspolizei*
       Section 3: *Kriminalpolizei*
       Section 4: *Geheime Staatspolizei*
IV.   The relationship and co-operation of the *Reichspolizei* with State and other institutions and auxiliary police organs (*Hilfspolizei*).
       Section 1: Relationship and co-operation of the *Reichspolizei* with State and other institutions
       Section 2: *Hilfspolizei*
V.   Conclusions.

Appendices to Part I.
       1. General organisation *Reichspolizei*
       2. *Ordnungspolizei. Organization Kommandoamt.*

Part I: Development of the Reichspolizei, Its Central High Command, Departments and Its General Organization

Section 1: Development.

The Reconstruction-Act of the *Reich*, dated 30 January 1934, is also a stepping-stone in the endeavour to re-organise the German police. When this law came into force a thorough purge of the *Reichspolizei* followed, particularly among officers. The resulting gaps had to be filled with reliable members of the NSDAP, particularly out of the ranks of the SS. In Prussia alone almost 10,000 members of the *Waffen*-SS were taken over. Similar changes took place in other provinces.

A great number of unionist police organizations, very often mutually conflicting were banned and a sole organization created—'*Kameradschaftsbund Deutscher Polizeibeamten*'. A high ranking SS officer was put in command of this organization. A rigid discipline was enforced and the police corps had to be educated in the National Socialist political ideology.

A law for police officials was passed; only one uniform was permitted, the pay, leave and other questions were solved. The Police officer got his serge-uniform back, the low-ranking police a bayonet, the police units received their colours. The rubber-truncheon was done away with. Musical police platoons, orders, badges of honour and military regulations were introduced and a correct military relationship between the officers and the other ranks of the police corps was established.

On the whole, the position of the police units was strengthened.

The armament underwent significant change as great attention was paid to the re-equipment, i.e. re-arming of the police with modern light and heavy infantry weapons and great care was taken of *Offiziers-Anwärter* [officer candidates].

Finally, in 1936, three important police-laws came into force. The first law regulated the equal scale of allowances and enforced equal nomenclature for police officials in all provinces.

Under the second law, the employees of the *Vollzugspolizei*, i.e. protective police [*Schutzpolizei*], *Gendarmerie*, Criminal and Secret State police (*Polizeiverwaltungsbeamte*) continued to be included in the enforced barracking and budget of the particular provinces.

The third law divided the members of the police into four service-years, formulated marriage regulations, established a service age-limit (up to 51–60 years) and arranged the possibility of transfer of individual cases into the category of the ordinary police (*Schutzpolizei-Gemeinde*), i.e. transfer of the ordinary policeman to other activities.

Gradually, the police became the unique prerogative of the *Schutzstaffeln—SS*. Just as the army was given as its task the defence against the external enemy, so the police merged with the SS was given the task of defence against the enemy at home. The State Police was merged with the Party Police NSDAP (SS) and amalgamated into one corps—*Staatsschutzkorps*. An external expression was given to this interior fusion by way of a regulation dated January and July 1938, according to which all members of the SS accepted by the police were to be allowed to wear the SS badge on the police uniform (in Runic letters). All members of the uniformed and un-uniformed police who, up to 30 January 1933, were members of the NSDAP and its *Waffenkorps* [*Waffen-SS*], or subscribing members of the SS, or all those who served in the police for at least three years under the command of the *Reichsführer-SS*, are automatically incorporated into the SS organisation where they receive the equivalent police rank. The administrative sectors of the newly appointed superior SS and, of the police commands coincide throughout with sectors of the respective SS-*Oberabschnitte*.

Section 2: The Central Office and highest command of the *Reichspolizei*.
The Central Office of the *Reichs*-police (*Reichspolizei*) is the *Reichs* and Prussian Ministry of the Interior (R.u.Pr. *Ministerium des Innern*).

The chief of the *Reichs*-police and also the permanent deputy of the Minister of the Interior, to whom he is immediately subordinate, is the *Reichsführer-SS* and *Chef der deutschen Polizei im Reichsministerium des Innern*, at present Heinrich Himmler.

His official status is between that of the State Secretary and the *Reichsminister*. During debates in police matters, he takes part in the sittings of the *Reichskabinett*.

In June and July 1938, superior commands of the SS and Police (*Höhere SS- und Polizeiführer*) were nominated. The service sectors of these functions coincide numerically, in boundaries and designations with the sectors of the SS-*Oberabschnitte*. This new arrangement is another step towards a complete fusion of the police and the SS into one State Corps (*Staatsschutzkorps*).

Section 3: General Organization of the *Reichspolizei.* **(see Appendix 1)**
By a decree of the *Reichs* Chancellor [Hitler], dated 17 July 1936, the police, *Gendarmerie* and the fire service were unified into the *Reichs*-police (*Reichspolizei*), and is organised as follows:

> *Ordernungspolizei,* i.e. general order, uniformed police
> *Sicherheitspolizei,* i.e. protective un-uniformed (civil) police

Part II: *Ordnungspolizei* **(General Order Police)**

Section 1: Organization.
1. *Hauptamt Ordnungspolizei* (highest command and central office)
2. *Verwaltungspolizei* (police administration)
3. *Schutzpolizei* (protective police—*Schupo*)
4. *Gendarmerie*
5. *Schutzpolizei—Gemeinde* (community police)
6. *Feuerlöschpolice* (Fire Service by professionals and volunteers)
7. *Technische Nothilfe*—TENO (auxiliary police corps of technical emergency assistance).

Section 2: *Hauptamt Ordnungspolizei.*
This is the highest command, controlling and central department of the *Ordnungspolizei.*
Commander: *Chef der Ordnungspolizei* and also Deputy Chief of the *Reichspolizei* (at present SS-*Gruppenführer* Gen Maj Kurt Daluege).
    This office was set up at the beginning of July 1936 and is organised as follows:

The Adjutant's Department
Press Department
Inner command with the Director of the Departments.

    The executive and the Departments of the *Hauptamt Ordnungspolizei:*

1. *Amt für Verwaltung und Recht*
2. *Kommandoamt*
3. *General Inspekteure*
4. *Inspekteure*
5. Police and *Gendarmerie* officers attached to high police Departments
6. Political Departments of various degrees.

Amt für Verwaltung und Recht.

Has the authority of an administration and legal office.

Kommandoamt.

Deals with problems or organization, personnel, training, tactical, technical, hygiene and veterinary matters. For organisation see Appendix 2.

General Inspekteure.

Controls departments for the Protective Police, *Gendarmerie*, Police Schools and the Fire Service.

Among the functions of the *General Inspekteure* of the Police is the co-ordination of all problems of basic nature (personnel, organisation, technical, supply, tactical, education).

Inspekteure.

These are higher ranking police officers, posted to departments of the Interior administration. Their function is to supervise police training, preparton of police defence in the appropriate area and to supervise the civilian police administration departments.

Police and *Gendarmerie.*

At higher police departments are police and gendarmerie officers of the General Staff, posted to Regional Governments (*Höhere Verwaltungsbehörde*) who assume the function of technical advisors.

Police Departments of various sizes.

Mittelstelle (Departments of medium size only in larger regions. In Prussia there are *Landespolizeibehörden*).

Kreispolizeibehörden (*Bezirkspolizeibehörden*, i.e. police administration of *Bezirke–Kreise*).

Ortspolizeibehörden (local, public communal police administrations).

The <u>State Police</u> is established in more important districts and in approx 104 larger towns.

In towns where there is the State Police (*Polizeipräsidium* or *Polizeidirektionen*) the Commander of the *Schutzpolizei* (protective police) takes part in the police administration.

There is one *Gendarmerie-Obermeister* attached to regional departments (*Untere Verwaltungsbehörde*) with the function of a technical advisor

In towns (*Kreisfrei Stadt*) without the State Police, the local police is under command of a *Polizeidirektor*, chief inspector or *Polizeimeister*.

The organisation of the *Ordnungspolizei* is quite complicated and although it is being simplified it has not been completed in all provinces as yet.

One of the main factors contributing to the establishment of a unified organisation was the incorporation of the executive police into the budget of the *Reich*, the establishment of equal small scale allowances and equal designations of ranks and uniforms.

Moreover, in all localities with less than 5000 inhabitants, the communal police is being gradually merged with the *Gendarmerie*.

Section 3: *Verwaltungspolizei.*
This is an administration police machine comprising of all groups of employees of the Q and A [Quality and Assurance] branches, technical etc. One of these groups consists of technical officials of the police administration, technical police inspectors and technical police secretaries of the State Secret Police.

Section 4: *Schutzpolizei (Schupo).*
This is a State Police establishment in larger towns and has the following functions: Supervising of all traffic, maintenance of general order and security, protection of individuals and their property, detect and pursue offences for preliminary examinations of the case and the handing over of the persons concerned to the department of the Criminal Police. They also carry out checking of passports, supervise registration and the civilian *Luftschutz*.

Organisation of the *Schutzpolizei*

Non-barracked police (*Schutzpolizei—Revierpolizei*)
Barracked police (*Schutzpolizei—Hundertschaften*)
Mounted Police (*Polizei Reitstaffeln*)
Motorized police for traffic control (*Motorisierte Verkehrsbereitschaften*)
River Police (*Wasserschutzpolizei*)

Non-barracked police
    To this belongs all members of the *Revierpolizei* who perform their police duty individually.

Barracked police
    To this belong police units organized in Companies (*Hundertschaft Kompanie*) or in raid-departments (*Überfallskommando*). These units vary in strength according to the size and importance of a town and are permanently barracked for tasks where large and combined effort is needed. They are partly or fully mechanized and trained in military and police tasks.
    The nucleus of the barracked units was formed out of 8,000 to 10,000 members of the former corps of *Feldjäger* (FKJ) who, in 1936, were incorporated into the *Schutzpolizei*. They remained, however, in compact groups and serve today as a

permanent corps of instructors for the training of the barracked police units. The *Hundertschaften* form the main body of the barracked police, consisting of the OR [other ranks] of the *Schutzpolizei* with less than 4 years service.

The garrisoning, methods of training, the several years service, particularly however the organization of the Machine Gun Companies, communication units and administration sections indicate that the organization of barracked formations is of an assault character and can be brought quickly into action.

Location of *Schutzpolizei* and of garrisoned units:

Polizeipräsidium Königsberg

Polizeidirektion Tilsit

Polizeipräsidium Elbing

Polizeipräsidium Berlin

Polizeipräsidium Potsdam

Polizeipräsidium Frankfurt/Oder

Polizeipräsidium Stettin

Polizeidirektion Schneidemühl

Polizeipräsidium Breslau

Polizeipräsidium Waldenburg

Polizeidirektion Oppeln

Polizeipräsidium Gleiwitz

Polizeipräsidium Magdeburg

Polizeipräsidium Halle

Polizeipräsidium Weissenfels

Polizeipräsidium Wittenberg

Polizeipräsidium Erfurt

Polizeidirektion Suhl

Polizeipräsidium Flensburg

Polizeipräsidium Kiel

Polizeipräsidium Lübeck

Polizeipräsidium Hannover

Polizeidirektion Augsburg

Polizeidirektion Würzburg

Polizeidirektion Regensburg

Polizeidirektion Ludwigshafen

Polizeidirektion Kaiserslautern

Polizei Amt Speyer

Polizei Amt Zweibrücken

Polizeipräsidium Stuttgart

Polizeidirektion Esslingen

Polizeidirektion Heilbronn

Polizeidirektion Cuxhaven

Polizeipräsidium Münster/W.

Polizeipräsidium Recklinghausen

Polizeipräsidium Bochum

Polizeidirektion Hamm

Polizeipräsidium Kassel

Polizeidirektion Hanau

Polizeipräsidium Wiesbaden

Polizeipräsidium Frankfurt/Main

Rheinpolizei Koblenz

Polizeipräsidium Koblenz

Polizeipräsidium Düsseldorf

Polizeipräsidium Duisburg

Polizeipräsidium Oberhausen

Polizeipräsidium Essen

Polizeipräsidium Wuppertal

Polizeipräsidium Gladbach-Rheydt

Polizeipräsidium Köln

Polizeipräsidium Aachen

Polizeipräsidium München

Polizeipräsidium Nürnberg-Fürth

Polizeidirektion Hof

Polizeipräsidium Dresden

Polizeipräsidium Leipzig

Polizeipräsidium Chemnitz

Polizeipräsidium Plauen

Polizeipräsidium Zwickau

Polizeipräsidium Braunschweig

Polizei Amt Ludwigsburg

Polizei Amt Heidenheim

Polizei Amt Tuttlingen

Polizei Amt Karlsruhe

Polizeidirektion Ulm	*Polizeidirektion* Baden-Baden
Bezirks Amt Rastatt	*Polizeidirektion* Pforzheim
Bezirks Amt Bruchsal	*Polizeipräsidium* Wien
Bezirks Präsidium Mannheim	*Polizeidirektion* Linz
Bezirks Direktion Heidelberg	*Polizeidirektion* Salzburg
Bezirks Direktion Freiburg i.Br.	*Polizeidirektion* Graz
Bezirks Amt Lörrach	*Polizeidirektion* Innsbruck
Bezirks Amt Waldshut	*Polizeidirektion* Klagenfurt
Bezirks Amt Villingen	*Polizeidirektion* Eisenstadt
Bezirks Direktion Darmstadt	*Polizeipräsidium* Hamburg
Bezirks Direktion Offenbach	*Polizeipräsidium* Altona-Wandsbk.
Bezirks Direktion Rauheim	*Polizeipräsidium* Harburg-Wilmbg.
Bezirks Direktion Friedberg	*Polizeidirektion* Bremen
Bezirks Direktion Mainz	*Polizei Amt* Bremerhaven
Bezirks Präsidium Weimar	*Polizeipräsidium* Gera
Bezirks Direktion Jena	*Polizeipräsidium* Dessau
Bezirks Direktion Gotha	*Polizeipräsidium* Saarbrücken
Bezirks Direktion Altenburg	*Polizeidirektion* Wilhelmshaven
Bezirks Amt Zella-Mehlis	*Polizeiverwaltung* Rostock

Mounted Police

The Mounted Police is an addition to the *Schutzpolizei*, and is located in larger towns. The basic unit of the Mounted Police, irrespective of the material strength, is the *Reitstaffel* which, according to necessity, are either combined into mounted detachments or into combined detachments with the police (on foot). The complete detachments are as follows:

Mounted detachments stand-to (*Bereitschaften*) in Berlin, Königsberg, Stettin, Breslau and Gleiwitz, where there are always three detachments combined under command.

Mixed *Bereitschaften* in Frankfurt/Main, Bochum, Düsseldorf, Halle, Magdeburg. Composition: two-thirds mounted, one-third foot police.

Mixed *Bereitschaften* in Tilsit, Elbing, Schneidemühl, Oppeln, Erfurt, Kassel, Koblenz, Aachen. Composition: one-third mounted, two-thirds foot police

Mixed *Bereitschaften* in Wiesbaden, composed of one-half mounted and one-half foot police.

The supply of horses for the Mounted Police come mainly from East Prussia, Hannover, Holstein, Brandenburg, Pommern and Westfalen.

Motorized Police for the regulation of traffic (*Motor Verkehrsbereitschaften*)

New police units, formed in August 1937, located in 51 larger towns on the whole territory of Germany and old Austria. The units, 11–48 men strong, are fully motorized and equipped for first aid. They control and regulate the street-traffic in larger towns (above 200,000 inhabitants) and render first aid in traffic accidents. These units were successfully employed during the occupation of Austria, especially of Vienna. Locations of the motorized police for the regulation of traffic are as follows:

Königsberg	Kiel	Köln
Elbing	Hannover	Aachen
Berlin:	Recklinghausen	Münster/W.
Gruppe Mitte	Bochum	München
Gruppe Ost	Dortmund	Nürnberg
Gruppe Süd	Kassel	Augsburg
Gruppe West	Frankfurt/Main	Ludwigshaven
Gruppe Nord	Wiesbaden	Würzburg
Potsdam	Koblenz	Leipzig
Stettin	Essen	Dresden
Breslau	Wuppertal	Chemnitz
Gleiwitz	Oberhausen	Plauen
Magdeburg	Düsseldorf	Stuttgart
Halle	Duisburg	Mainz
Erfurt	Gladbach-Rheydt	Darmstadt
Mannheim	Hamburg:	Saarbrücken
Karlsruhe	*Gruppe Ost*	Dessau
Freiburg i.Br. *Gruppe West*	Rostock	
Heidelberg	Bremen	Wien
Lübeck	Braunschweig	

River Police (*Wasserschutzpolizei*—SW).

This is established on rivers, lakes and in coastal regions for the defence of its installations and for the co-operation in customs control. By the 1936 decree the River Police was transferred from the *Gendarmerie* to the *Schutzpolizei* and by a 1937 decree it was re-organised and its strength was increased by the following additions: The state police of the Rhine, the police of the Bodensee [Lake Konstanz], the coastal police, the river police and the police of the river Danube.

The *Wasserschutzpolizei* consists, according to the size of the appropriate areas of:

SW—*Gruppe* (SWG)
SW—*Abschnitt* (SWA)
SW—*Kommando* (SWK)
SW—*Revier* (SWR)
SW—*Station* (SWS)
SW—*Wach* (SWW)
SW—*Posten* (SWP)

The organisation is similar to that of the *Schupo*, however, with being modified according to its peculiar type of conditions and employment.

The locations of the *Wasserschutzpolizei* are as follows:

Tilsit (SWR)	Berlin (SWA)
Podrizeny: subordinate	Baumschulenweg (SWR)
Labiau (SWS)	Spandau (SWR)
Kloken (SWW)	Küstrin (SWW)
Königsberg (SWR)	Fürstenberg (SWW)
Pillau (SWS	Oranienburg (SWP)
Lötzen (SWW)	Wernsdorf (SWP)
Dresden (SWR)	Potsdam (SWR)
Riesa (SWW)	Brandenburg (SWW)
Bad Schandau (SWW)	Rathenow (SWW)
Magdeburg (SWR)	Recklinghausen (SWR)
Wittenberg (SWW)	Essen-Dellwig (SWW)
Wittenberge (SWW)	Heinrichenburg (SWW)
Hitzacker (SWW)	Münster/W. (SWW)
Elbing (SWR)	Bewergern (SWW)
Breslau (SWR)	Minden (SWW)
Cosel (SWS)	Duisburg-Ruhrort (SWP)
Glogau (SWW)	Hamburg (SWG)
Stettin (SWA)	3 SWA
Stettin (SWR)	10 SWR
Swinemünde (SWS)	1 SW
Stralsund (SWS)	Brunsbüttelkoog (SWS)
Fiddichow (SWW)	Köln (SWS)
Cuxhaven (SWR)	Düsseldorf (SWW)
Rostock (SWR)	Bonn (SWW)
Lübeck (SWR)	Duisburg (SWS)
Travemünde (SWS)	Emmerich (SWW)
Kiel (SWR)	Bodensee (SWW)
2 SW	Friedrichshafen (SWS)
Flensburg (SWR)	Konstanz (SWS)
Bremen (SWA)	Lindau (SWS)
2 SWR	Koblenz (SWK)
1 SW	Karlsruhe (SWS)
Bremerhaven (SWR)	Ludwigshafen (SWW)
Wesermünde SW	Mainz (SWS)
Emden (SWR)	Koblenz (SWS)
Elafloth (SWW)	Bad Salzig (SWW)

SW—Linz for the Danube region on the
territory of late Austria from Passau to Hainburg

<u>*Schutzpolizei*:</u>

General points—

Strength: *Schupo* consists of approx 3,500 officers, 70,000 *Wachmeister* (policemen, including the Mounted Police) and is located in approx 104 towns.

Motorisierte Verkehrsbereitschaften is approx 1,400 strong.

Wasserschutzpolizei is approx 2,200 strong.

Re-inforcements in peace and war—

a) <u>Police officers.</u>

In peace-time the re-inforcements of the officers corps of the police come solely from the qualified men from the two schools for the education of the SS (SS-*Junkerschule*) All qualified men from the SS-*Junkerschule* have to do six months service with the police (even if they are not accepted by the police) and after its successful completion they receive the rank of a police officer on the reserve.

SS-Officers (SS-*Führer*) transferred to the *Ordnungspolizei* continue to remain members of the SS. They wear, however, the police uniform, the cord of honour and the SS badges on the left side of the coat. They are subject to the police (criminal) jurisdiction, in marriage and overseas leave matters. However, they continue to be subject to the *Reichsführung*-SS.

b) <u>Other Ranks.</u>

The reinforcements in Other Ranks of the police come in peace-time from the SS-*Verfügungstruppe* and SS-*Totenkopfverbände*. Also from NCOs of the Army reserve.

In wartime, police re-inforcements come through a continuous rotation, i.e. exchange of officers and Other Ranks of the SS-*Verfügungstruppe* with the officers and Other Ranks of the police. It is the SS-*Totenkopfverbände* brought up to the strength of 30 special police units (SS-*Totenkopfsondersturmbänne*) who are supposed to provide the replacements for the vacancies of the police (approx. 25,000 men) resulting from the transfer of the conscripted personnel to the *Wehrmacht*. These SS-*Totenkopfsturmbänne* will form the police and military nucleus and the attack-force for the control of the hinterland.

<u>The ranks in the *Schutzpolizei*.</u>

Officers:	Other Ranks:
General	*Schutzpolizeiinspektor*
Oberst	*Pol.Obermeister*
Oberstleutnant	*Pol.Meister*
Major	*Pol.Hauptwachtmeister*
Hauptmann	*Pol.Revieroberwachtmeister*
Inspektor der Schupo	*Pol.Oberwachtmeister*

Oberleutnant   Pol.Wachtmeister
Leutnant

Dress: Greenish uniform, light green gorget patches, straps and black boots. Walking out dress: Shako with white plume, silver bandoleer with cartridge-box and a silver-belt.

Wasserschutzpolizei wear a uniform of the Navy. Dark-blue colour.

Equipment:
    Light and heavy infantry weapons, police armoured cars of a modern type. The police armouries (*Waffenmeisterei* each for 1,000 policemen) are responsible for the maintenance and repair of the equipment, except for the *Gestapo* equipment.
    In 1937, the *Reichspolizei* had approx 58 *Waffenmeistereien* for the use of *Stapo* police administrations, including the Rhineland police, the *Gendarmerie* (including motorized *Gendarmerie* Companies and the Communal Police).
    ...

Part III: *Sicherheitspolizei* (Civilian)

Section 1: Organization.
a) *Hauptamt Sicherheitspolizei* (highest command and its central office).
b) *Kriminalpolizei—Kripo.*
c) *Geheime Staatspolizei—Gestapo* (Secret State Police).

Section 2: *Hauptamt Sicherheitspolizei.*
This is the highest command and the central office of the *Sicherheitspolizei.*
    Commander: *Chef d. Sicherheitspolizei* (at present SS-*Gruppenführer* Reinhardt Heydrich).
    The office was set up at the beginning of July 1936. On 1 October 1936, *Inspektorate der Sicherheitspolizei* for Prussia and other States were set up and the heads of the departments are *Inspekteure der Sicherheitspolizei.* The role of the *Inspekteure* is close co-operation with the central office of the public and interior administration the Lands and Provinces, with the *Gauleiter* of the NSDAP and with the departments of the *Wehrmacht.* They are at the same time, subordinate officials (*Referent*) under the respective *Regierungspräsident* or Minister of the respective State in political and police matters.

Section 3: *Kriminalpolizei* (*Kripo*).
The *Kripo* is a civilian security corps of detectives who co-operate with the *Ordnungspolizei* and the *Gestapo.*

<u>Organization:</u> The *Kripo* is divided into the directive-branch and executive branch.
a) *Reichskriminalpolizeiamt [RKPA]:* This is broadly subordinate to the *Chef d. Sicherheitspolizei* who is responsible for the technical policy of the *Kripo* in all German States. He is also responsible for co-ordination in criminal matters with all other police, for the organization and policy in instruction and training, he deals with questions of equipment of the police etc.

The *Reichskriminalpolizeiamt* is the only office authorized to liaison and co-operate with foreign countries. Exceptions are being made where necessary and as a result of experience from local contact at the frontiers.

The executive organs of the *Kripo*:
Reichszentralstellen (Reich technical control stations)
Kriminalpolizeileitstellen
Kriminalpolizeistellen
Kriminalabteilungen

Reichszentralstellen—twelve in number, are immediately subordinate to the *Hauptamt der Sicherheitspolizei.*

Kriminalpolizeileitstellen—are central regional criminal offices which replaced the *Landeskriminalämter* or *Stellen* and are situated in larger towns. Their locations coincide in general with those of the analogous branches of the *Gestapo*. They are in charge of several *Kriminalpolizeistellen* and assume their function in their own district.

Kriminalpolizeistellen—are lower departments and several of them are subordinate to the *Kripoleitstelle*. They supervise the criminal services and the criminal service of the *Gendarmerie* and the *Gemeindepolizei* in this own district. The *Kripostellen* remain to be attached to the present state police administration and the locations are analogous to those of the *Gestapo*.

For the organization of the *Kripo* see Appendix 1.

Kriminalpolizei in general.

Ranks:

        at lower level: *Kriminal Assistentanwärter*
                Kriminal Assistant
                Kriminal Oberassistent
                Kriminal Sekretär
                Kriminal Obersekretär
                Kriminal Inspektor

        at higher level: *Kriminal Kommissaranwärter*

> *Kriminal Kommissar*
> *Kriminalrat*
> *Kriminal Direktor*
> *Regierungs- u. Kriminalrat*
> *Oberregierungs- u. Kriminalrat*
> *Regierungs- u. Kriminal Direktor*
> *Reichskriminal Direktor*

Identity papers & badges:

The officials and employees of the *Kripo* possess an identity card (green colour) with an oval badge made of yellow metal bearing the inscription:

Beamter der Kriminalpolizei, the serial number and the *Hoheitsabzeichen*.

Women in the *Kripo*:

Kripo employs women. The selection, schooling and appointments of women fall under the competence of the *Chef der Kripo*.

Appendix 1

General Organization of the *Reichspolizei*

Reichs- und Preussische Ministerium des Innern
|
|
Reichsführer-SS und Chef der Deutschen Polizei
|
|
|_____ *HAUPTAMT ORDNUNGSPOLIZEI*
| |
| |_____*Amt für Verwaltung und Recht*
| |
| |_____*Kommandoamt*
| |
| |_____*General Inspekteure*
| |
| |_____*Inspekteure*
| |
| |_____ *Verwaltungspolizei*
| |
| |_____*Schutzpolizei, Wasserschutzpolizei, Not.Verkehrsbereitschaft*

```
|     |
|     |_____Gendarmerie, Not.Gendarmeriebereitschaft
|     |
|     |_____Gemeinde Schutzpolizei
|     |
|     |_____Feuerlöschpolizei, Technische Nothile (TENO)
|
|
|_____HAUPTAMT SICHERHEITSPOLIZEI
         |
         |_____Kriminalpolizei (Kripo)
         |        |
         |        |_____Kriminalpolizeileitstellen
         |                 |
         |                 |_____Kriminalpolizeistellen
         |                          |
         |                          |_____örtliche Kriminalabteilungen
         |
         |
         |_____Geheime Staatspolizei (Gestapo)
                  |
                  |_____Staatspolizeileitstellen
                           |
                           |_____Staatspolizeistellen
                                    |
                                    |_____Grenzpolizeikommissariate
                                    |
                                    Grenzpolizeiposten
                                    Grenzdienststellen
                                    Grenzpolizeiposten
```

After the war the Allied occupying forces did not regard the *Kriminalpolizei* to be a criminal organization and was not indicted as such at the Nuremberg Trials. This did not stop the Allies from interning some *Kripo* officers as security suspects, and employing others in a new criminal police force in their respective zones of occupation. Undoubtedly more *Kripo* officers and officials would have been interned had the Allies looked more earnestly for organisation lists.

The organisation lists of RSHA *Ämter* dated 1 March 1941 and 1 October 1943, show little change in the functions of RSHA V departments in Berlin:

Chef des Amtes V (*Verbrechensbekämpfung*)
Amtschef: SS-*Brif. und Generalmajor der Polizei* Artur Nebe, to July 1944

Amtschef: SS-*Obf* RD Friedrich Panzinger, from August 1944–April 1945

Geschäftsstelle des Amtes V
Leiter: SS-*Stubaf* RuKR Walter Hasenjaeger (1940–1942)

V   A   *Kriminalpolitik und Vorbeugnung*
            Gruppenleiter: SS-*Stubaf* ORuKR Werner

            A1   *Rechtsfragen, internationale Zusammenarbeit und Kriminal-*
                   forschung
                   (*Leiter*: RuKR Dr Wächter)
            A2   *Vorbeugnung*
                   (*Leiter*: SS-*Stubaf* RR Dr Riese)
            A3   *Weibliche Kriminalpolizei*
                   (*Leiter*: KD Wieking)
            A4   *Polizeiliche Melde- und Registerwesen*
                   (*Leiter*:

V   B   *Einsatz mit den Reichszentralen des Reichskriminalpolizeiamtes*
            (RKPA)
            Gruppenleiter: RuKR Galzow

V   B1   *Kapitalverbrechen*
             (*Leiter*: RR Hans Lobbes)
      B2   *Betrug*
             (*Leiter*: KD Rassow
      B3   *Sittlichkeitsverbrechen*
             (*Leiter*: KD Gerhard Nauck)

V   C   *Fahndung, Diensthundewesen, Auskunftserteilung*
            Gruppenleiter: ORuKR Wolfgang Berger (1941)
            Gruppenleiter: Dr Richard Schulze (1943)
            Deputy: KD Dr Baum (1941)
            Deputy: SS-*Stubaf* KR Kurt Amend (1943)

            C1   *Reichserkennungsdienstzentrale*
                   (*Leiter*: SS-*Stubaf* KD Müller, 1941)
                   (*Leiter*: SS-*Stubaf* KR Kurt Amend, 1943–1945)
            C2   *Fahndungszentralen*
                   (*Leiter*: KD DR Baum
            C3   *Diensthundewesen*
                   (*Leiter*:

V   D   *Kriminaltechnisches Institut* (KTI)
           Gruppenleiter: SS-*Stubaf* ORuKR *Dr Ing* habil. Heess
           Deputy: SS-*Hstuf*/*Stubaf* KR *Dr Ing* Walter Schade

           D1   *Spurenidentifikation*
           (*Leiter*: SS-*Hstuf*/*Stubaf* KR *Dr Ing* Walter Schade)
           D2   *Chemische und biologisch-naturwissenschaftliche*
                  Untersuchungen
           (*Leiter*: SS-*Ustuf Dr Ing* Widmann)
           D3:   *Urkundenprüfung* (in 1941, department re-organised by 1943)
           (*Leiter*: KR *mag.chem.* Wittlich)
           D3   *Herrnskretschen*: *Kriminalmedizinisches Zentralinstitut*
                  (being established in 1943)
           D W   *Werkstätten, Lichtpauserei*
           (*Leiter*: vacant)

V   F   *Wirtschaftsangelegenheiten, Sonderbeschulung und Ausrüstung*
           der Kriminalpolizei
           Gruppenleiter: ORuKR Wolfgang Berger, 1939–1942

V   Wi   Investigations into SS corruption

Because CIWR did not compile a liquidation or situation report for RSHA V there
is no extent Personalities List of its personnel. The list below has been compiled
from various postwar Allied interrogation reports of *Kriminalpolizei* officers
available in UK and US National Archives:

RSHA V

Alphabatical List of RSHA personnel

Name and Rank	*Sachgebiet*	Remarks
Altenloh, SS-*Stubaf* RR Dr Wilhelm	V A	from Sept. 1944, with a Dezernat '*Korruption in den obersten Reichsbehörden*'
Amend, SS-*Stubaf* KR Kurt	V C1	*Referent* and Deputy *Gruppenleiter* V C
Andexer, KD Kurt	V A2	V B1, 1940; died 1942
Ballhause, SS-*Ostuf* KK Werner	V D1	1944–1945
Baum, KD Dr Karl	V A1	V C2, 1941, then to BdS Strasbourg
Becker, SS-*Ustuf* KOS Kurt	V A2	1939-1945
Bender, KR Hans	V B1c	1943, *Hilfsreferent*
Berger, ORuKR Wolfgang	V C and F	*Gruppenleiter* V C and V F, 1939–1942, then to *Kripoleitstelle* Hamburg
Bergohse, PI Otto	V F2	1943
Beuys, SS-*Hstuf* KR Werner	V D1b	1939–1944
Blees, KR Josef	V A2	1943
Bleymehl, SS-*Ostuf* KK Otto	V C2	1944–1945; KIA, Feb. 1945, Oder front
Boening, SS-*Ostuf* KD Wihelm	V B1	1941–1944, then to RSHA VI S
Böhlhoff, SS-*Hstuf* KD Heinrich	V A2	1941–1945, *Referent*
Bonse, SS-*Ustuf* KOS Bernhard	V A2	
Braschwitz, SS-*Ostubaf* ORuKR Gün.	V C	1945
Britz, KR Paul	V A2	1943–1944
Busch, KS	V D1a1	1943–1945
Class, SS-*Stubaf* RuKR Friedrich	V	1943
Cornely, SS-*Ostuf* KK Hans	V Wi 2a	1943–1945
Dardaillon, SS-*Ustuf* KK Georg	V D3b	1943; earlier in V C1, 1940
Dennerlein, SS-*Ostuf* KK Hans	V B1d	to 1943; then with V Wi
Diemer, KK Georg	V B2c	1943
Drescher, SS-*Hstuf* KR Heinz	V D1b1	to 1943; 1943–1944, V Wi
Eichberger, KI Josef	V B	1940–1945 (*Zigeunerbekämpfung*)
Engelmann, SS-*Hstuf* KR Heinz-Gün.	V	Adjutant to *Amtschef* Nebe, 1941–1944
Erdmann, KK i.R. Albert	V A2b	1943 (when 70 years of age)
Essner, KR Gerda	V A3	from 1941
Fähnrich, KR Kurt	V B1	1943–1943, *Hilfsreferent*

Felgenhauer, SS-*Hstuf* KR Erwin	V A1	from 1943
Fleischer, KR Willy	V A2	to 1940, then to KdS Krakau
Freytag, SS-*Hstuf* RR Dr Günter	V Wi 2	to Dec. 1943, Deputy *Abt.Leiter*
Frosien, SS-*Hstuf* KR Hans	V B2b	1942–1944
Fuchs, SS-*Ostuf* KK Herbert	V C2a	1943, then to *Einsatzgruppe* B
Galzow, ORuKR Georg	V C	*Gruppenleiter*, 1940–1941
	V B	*Gruppenleiter*, 1941–1942, then retired
Garnickel, SS-*Ostuf* KK Werner	V A2	to 1943, then to *Kripoleitstelle* Berlin
Grahnel, KI Karl	V A2	1943
Hamann, PI	V D1b2	1943
Hasenjaeger, SS-*Stubaf* RuKR Walter	V A2	from 1943, previously *Geschäftsstelle*
Hauke, SS-*Stubaf* RuKR Dr Walter	V Wi	V B2a to Jan. 1945, then *Abt.Leiter*
	V Wi	
Heess, SS-*Staf* ORuKR Dr Walter	V D	*Leiter* KTI, 1939–1945
Herber, KK Franz	V A2b	1943
Hirsemann, SS-*Ostuf* KK Johannes	V Wi	1944–1945
Hochgräbe, SS-*Hstuf* KR Hans-Joach.	V D1	1939–1945
Hoffmann, SS-*Stubaf* Dr Helmut	V D2c	KTI, from 1941
Horn, SS-*Hstuf* KK Dr Rudolf	V F2	1940–1942
Hünten, SS-*Hstuf* KK Friedrich	V Wi 1b	1944–1945
Jacob, SS-*Hstuf* KR Erich	V B3d	1943–1944
Junge, SS-*Ostuf* KK Herbert	V C1b & B2	1942–1944
Kapell, SS-*Ustuf* KI Otto	V D1b1	1939, 1943
Keller, SS-*Ustuf* KOS Willi	V C	1942–1945
Kiehne, SS-*Stubaf* KD Karl	V B2d	1941–1944
	V Wi 2	Jan.–April 1945, *Referatsleiter*
Kosmehl, SS-*Hstuf* KR Erwin	V B3c	1942–1945
Kozik, SS-*Ustuf* KS Robert	V B1a	1943
Krause, KR Herbert	V B1d	1940–1945
Krupke, SS-*Ustuf* KS Helmut	V B1d	1937–1945
Lange, KK Otto	V B2a	1941–1943
Lobbes, SS-*Ostubaf* ORuKR Hans	V C1	to 1941, *Referent*
	V B and	1941–1944, *Referent* and Deputy
	V B1	*Gruppenleiter* V B.
Lüdcke, SS-*Stubaf* RuKR Dr Karl	V C3	1939–1940
Maly, SS-*Stubaf* KR Dr Hans	V D3	1942–1945
Martin, SS-*Stubaf* RuKR Dr Otto	V D1a2	1940–1945
Matzke, KK a.W.	V B1d	to 1944, then retired
Menke, SS-*Stubaf* RuKR Dr Josef	V A1	1940–1945
Merten, SS-*Hstuf* KR Dr Hans	V C1b	1942–1944, *Referent* V C1b and Deputy *Referent* V B2

Mohr, SS-*Ustuf* KK Peter	V C2	1944–1945
Moritz, SS-*Stubaf* KR Kurt	V C2	to 1945
Mühlpforte, SS-*Ostuf* KI Wilhelm	V D1b1	1939–1943, then to *Kripoleitstelle* Berlin
Müller, SS-*Stubaf* KD Helmut	V D1	1940–1941; 1941–1942, V C1
Nauck, KD Gerhard	V B3	1941–1944, *Referent*; 1944–1945, V D3
Otto, KR Herbert	V A2b	1942, 1943
Paar, SS-*Hstuf* KR Anton	V Wi	1945
Pietsch, SS-*Hstuf* KR Erich	V A3	1943
Pokorny, SS-*Stubaf* RuKR Dr Hans	V	1940–1941
Rassow, SS-*Stubaf* RuKR Dr Ernst	V B2	1941–1944
Ratzesberger, RuKR Dr Karl	V	1943–1944
Rickrath, SS-*Stubaf* RR Eduard	V A2	1939–1945
Riese, SS-*Stubaf* RR Dr Friedrich	V B	1940–1941, Gruppenleiter
	V A2	1941–1942, *Referent*
Schade, SS-*Stubaf* RuKR Dr Walter	V F3	1940
	V D1	1941–1945, and Deputy *Gruppenleiter*
Schäfer, KR Hans	V F3	1940; V Wi 2b, 1942–1945
Schefe, SS-*Stubaf* RR Dr Robert	V C	Oct. 1941–March 1943, *Gruppenleiter*
Schmidt-Till, SS-*Hstuf* KK Arnold	V Wi	1944–1945
Schulz, SS-*Ostuf* KK Karl	V B2	1939–1941, 1943–1944
Schulze, SS-*Ostubaf* ORuKR Dr Rich.	V C	1943–1945, *Gruppenleiter*
	V Wi	1945, *Gruppenleiter*
Sommerfeld, SS-*Ostuf* KR Dr Herb.	V B3	1940, *Referent*
	V A1c	to 1943, *Referent*
Steinbach, SS-*Ostuf* KK	V B2	1943, also with V C1c and V C2d
Struck, SS-*Ostuf* KK Bodo	V B2	1942–1945, also with V C1b1
Supp, SS-*Ostuf* KK Wilhelm	V A2b	1942–1943
Wächter, RuKR Dr Franz	V D	1939–1941, *Gruppenleiter*
	V A	1941–1942, *Gruppenleiter*
Wehner, SS-*Hstuf* KR Dr Bernhard	V B1a	1939–1945
Werner, KK Dr Albrecht	V D1a	1941–1943
Werner, SS-*Stubaf*-SS-*Obf* Paul	V A	1939–1941, *Gruppenleiter*
	V	1943-1944, Deputy *Amtschef* to Nebe
	V A and V B	1944–1945, *Gruppenleiter*: SS-*Obf*
Widmann, SS-*Stubaf* Dr Albert	V D2	1941–1945
Wied, SS-*Hstuf* KK Dr Heinz	V C2b	1942–1943
	V B3c	1943–1945

Wieking, *Frau* KD	V A3	1940–1945, *Referent*
Wiszinsky, SS-*Hstuf* KK Albert	V A2b	1941–1945
Wittlich, RuKR Dr Felix	V D3	1941–1945
Wolter, SS-*Ustuf* KS Fritz	V D3b	1943–1945
Wulf, SS-*Hstuf* KK Walter	V C3	1942–1945
Zach, SS-*Hstuf* KR Willy Zach	V B1	1941–1943, then V Wi, 1943–1945
Zander, SS-*Hstuf* KR Max	V Wi	1945
Zaucke, KR Dr Richard	V B2	1940–1941

Notes

* The National Archives Kew, WO 208/3648, report LDC 333, report on the German Police to October 1938.
* Nuremberg document L-185, Organisation Plan of RSHA dated 1 March 1941.
* Nuremberg document L-219, Organisation Plan of RSHA dated 1 October 1943.

5

Liquidation Report No. 6:
Amt VI of the RSHA—*Gruppe* VI A

INDEX

1   The Organisation of *Gruppe* VI A in 1939–40
2   The Organisation of *Gruppe* VI A in early 1941
3   The Period 1941–43
4   The Period after Sandberger's appointment in 1944
5   VI *Kult*—its Functions and Development
6   The Difficulties facing VI *Kult* in its work
7   The *Zentral-Büro*
8   Wirsing and the Egmont reports
9   The Re-organisation of RSHA *Gruppe* VI A in 1945
10 Miscellaneous Notes on the *Referate* of *Gruppe* VI A

Appendix I: The Distribution of Work in RSHA *Amt* VI from 1940–45
Appendix II: The Organisational Chart of *Gruppe* VI A in 1940
Appendix III: The Organisational Chart of *Gruppe* VI A in early 1941
Appendix IV: The Organisational Chart of *Gruppe* VI A in 1944–45
Appendix V: Index of Personalities in *Gruppe* VI A
RSHA *Gruppe* VI A

Preamble

Throughout the history of RSHA *Amt* VI, *Gruppe* VI A has remained the organisational section of the Amt and as such has not the same importance as the other *Gruppen*. Its development is of interest however in so far as it reflects from time to time the efforts of the *Amtschef* to make the *Amt* function smoothly; this aspect is most noticeable in the later stages where Schellenberg made a last effort at the proper co-ordination of the work of the *Amt*. The history of the *Gruppe* previous to 1944 is largely of historical and reseach interest only.

1

The Original Organisation of RSHA *Gruppe* VI A in 1939–40

The earliest existing document showing the organisation of RSHA *Amt* VI is dated January 1940 and represents probably the first settled arrangement of the division of work between the various *Gruppen*. In this organisation *Gruppe* VI A came under the control of SS-*Ostubaf* Filbert; the breakdown of the *Gruppen* is shown fully at Appendix II. It will be seen from this chart that the scope of the original *Gruppe* was rather more that mere organisation and apparently aimed at some degree of co-ordination of work between the remaining *Gruppen*. The *Gruppe* included the five *Beauftragter* with geographical divisions of interest corresponding roughly at the division of territory between the *Gruppen*. (See also Appendix II.)

It would seem too that the organisation was ambitious rather than practical as several of the *Referate* are not known to have functioned. Thus RSHA VI A3 under Seidel had very few 'VM in Ausland' to look after, and Seidel did in fact merely continue his previous duties as head of the *Abteilung* III/3 of the old SD-*Hauptamt*, the roots of the new RSHA *Amt* VI. These duties were control of personnel matters in the *Amt*. Similarly VI A, VI A5 and VI A8 were liaison *Referate* which did not long survive, while VI A6 and VI A7 apparently attempted to carry out functions which were soon taken over by the *Gruppen* themselves, each *Gruppe* looking after its own territory as far as foreign broadcasts and foreign press were concerned. The de-centralisation of the functions of VI A into the *Ländergruppen* of the *Amt* was probably due to the weakness of Jost himself who was not strong enough to counter the ambitions of the *Gruppenleiter*. But it is noticeable that Schellenberg in his final conception of the most efficient organisation of the *Amt* did in fact return to a high degree of co-ordination between the *Gruppen* centralised in *Gruppe* VI A. But between 1941 and 1944, RSHA *Gruppe* VI A tended more and more to mere administrative duties, while the *Ländergruppen* became more and more self-contained to the general detriment of the efficiency of the *Amt* as a whole.

2

The Organisation of
RSHA *Gruppe* VI A in early 1941.

The Organisational Chart of the *Gruppe* in January 1941 is shown at Appendix III. It will be seen that under this scheme *Gruppe* VI A was in fact a co-ordination section with the *Referent* controlling the SD-*Abschnitte* from which offensive operations against the territories outside the *Reich* were planned. Matters affecting the organisation and personnel of the *Amt* have in fact passed to the Administrative office under SS-*Ostuf* Sauer. This organisation of RSHA *Amt* VI, shown in a document dated January 1941 (for details see Appendix III) is somehat puzzling and the division of work it shows is so different from what went before and what came after that it is doubtful whether in fact it was ever put into practice. In any case it is certain that before the end of the year the organisation was again on the lines of the first chart and *Gruppe* VI A now represented the Administrative Gruppe of the *Amt* with the *Referent* Filbert as *Gruppenleiter*, Seidel in charge of personnel matters and Sauer transferred from the *Geschäftsstelle* back to the *Gruppe*. Bernhard and Lehmann by the end of the year had joined the *Ländergruppen* in which they were interested while Salisch, Thiemann and Lapper have disappeared from the scene. The *Gruppe* was still responsible for liaison with the SD-*Abschnitte* but the importance of the SD-*Abschnitte* in terms of offensive action against foreign territory had by now greatly decreased and did in fact disappear when Schellenberg finally recalled the *Amt* VI representatives as SD-*Abschnitte* in 1942.

3

The Period 1941–1943

This period marks the stage in the development of RSHA *Gruppe* VI A when it was of least importance, functioning very largely as a mere administrative section of five *Referate* covering personnel, pay, etc. The *Gruppenleiter* by 1943 was SS-*Stubaf* Herbert Müller. By the end of the year however Schellenberg had decided that not only was *Gruppe* VI A inefficient on the work it had to do, but that the whole work of the *Amt* was in need of overhaul and the *Amt* would require a re-organisation to bring it into line with his ambitious plans for a wholly co-ordinated intelligence service. The fundamental conceptions of Schellenberg were selectivity, independence and co-ordination, and in this scheme of things he attached much greater importance to *Gruppe* VI A, in which *Gruppe* the necessary co-ordination of work would be established. His first task was to find an efficient *Gruppenleiter* and he found his answer in SS-*Staf* Sandberger, who had already made a name for himself in RSHA *Amt* I in the early stages of the RSHA and subsequently in Esthonia and Verona [Italy].

4

**The Period after Sanderberger's Appointment
and the Absorption of the *Abwehr***

As the re-organisation of the *Gruppe* was so complete after the *Abwehr* was absorbed, little need be said about this intervening period. The number of *Referate* under RSHA *Gruppe* VI A however, was extended to seven. Of the new *Referate* the most important was VI A7, which dealt with the evaluation of non-secret material. It was this *Referat* which later developed into the *Zentralbüro*. VI A6, the other new *Referat*, absorbed the new department which had been created in RSHA *Amt* VI by Schellenberg—VI *Kult*. Both of these new developments are discussed at some length below.

5

**RSHA VI *Kult*:
Its Functions and Development**

It was Schellenberg's conception that his brain-child, the *Geheim-Meldedienst*, should obtain its information about foreign countries from all available sources and not simply through the RSHA VI representatives in the various foreign countries. He would have liked the closest possible liaison with the other *Reich* Ministries whose functions extended beyond the *Reich*'s frontiers—the Foreign Office, the Auslands Organisation, the Propaganda Ministry, etc., side by side with a centralisation of information within the *Reich* itself—information from *Ämter* III, IV and VII. Information about foreign countries need not necessarily be obtained from that country—it might indeed be obtained from within Germany itself. It was because of this realisation that sources within Germany useful to RSHA *Amt* VI in its work were untapped that Schellenberg created the new VI *Kult* in late 1942. The function of this department was to establish contact with cultural circles in the *Reich*—not with the purpose on the circles themselves (that would have been the function of RSHA *Amt* III and became the province of *Gruppe* III G in late

1944) but because such circles were most likely to provide the type of information RSHA *Amt* VI required. The contacts were not however direct—at least not in the early stages. Liaison was established with the other *Reich* Ministries of which the following were involved:

The Foreign Office
Propaganda Ministry
Ministry of Education
Ministry of Transport
Postmaster General's Department
Ministry of Labour
Ministry of Justice
Auslands Organisation

The functioning of the new department through the liaison officers attached to these various ministries was a simple one. The Ministry of Education, for example, would inform the Liaison Officer that a Professor had returned from Sweden and was available for questioning on matters of interest to RSHA *Amt* VI. Or alternatively that a professor was about to leave for neutral territory and was available for special briefing for *Amt* VI. Similarly the other Ministries mentioned were through their normal functions in a position to obtain information for their own purposes from foreign countries. The Laision Officer of VI *Kult* would be informed when information of interest to RSHA *Amt* VI was ontained through these channels.

6

The Difficulties Facing
RSHA VI *Kult* in its Work

The functions of VI *Kult* as outlined above are clear and admirable. Things did not however run smoothly for the new department, which functioned independently for a short time before being absorbed by RSHA *Gruppe* VI A as *Referent* VI A6. The difficulties facing the department were obvious and immediately raised the old problems of inter-departmental jealousies. RSHA *Amt* III was hostile, as it felt that German territory was its field and not that of the *Auslandsnachrichtendienst*. Co-operation from the Ministries varied, due both to open hostility to a suspected infringement of their own sphere of work and to a lack of understanding of what was required. The opposition was of course most pronounced from the Foreign Office and from the Auslands Organisation, both of which departments had ambitions regarding their own information services abroad. Opposition from Goebbels and his Propaganda Ministry was no less strong. And side by side with these difficulties was the equally eternal problems facing Schellenberg in his new enterprises—that of finding personnel of sufficiently good calibre to carry the work through successfully in spite of the difficulties. In the initial stages RSHA VI *Kult* was badly managed under SS-*Stubaf* Möller assisted by SS-*Hstuf* Amthor. Möller in 1944 went to Budapest and Amthor was dismissed. SS-*Stubaf* Wadel was then in charge until the end of 1944 but he too was a failure and was transferred to the *Waffen*-SS. Finally VI *Kult* in December 1944 was given to SS-*Stubaf* Carstenns. (The other officers and agents in the department are listed at Appendix V). This Carstenns is <u>not</u> identical with SS-*Stubaf* Friedrich Carstenn of VI D. By the end however VI *Kult* was working more smoothly and was justifying its existence.

7

The *Zentralbüro* (ZB)

While RSHA VI *Kult* was a manifestation of Schellenberg's desire to extend the field of RSHA *Amt* VI by liaison with other Government departments, the *Zentralbüro* was the outcome in the later stages of his attempt at coordination within the *Amt* itself. It is important to realise that the ZB did not reach any final and definite form. It was in process of evolution and its structure remained until the end loose and indefinite.

Side by side with the idea of coordination of work must be put as a contributing factor of Schellenberg's efforts at a stricter personal supervision of the work of the *Amt*. For this purpose Schellenberg gradually assembled a kind of personal cabinet composed of those officers in the *Amt* whom he could trust and in whose ability he had full confidence. Schellenberg did not at any time appoint a deputy *Amtschef*—he had not sufficient faith in any one single person to do so. His small 'cabinet' (which has been referred to as VI *Verwaltung*, though 'VI V' was never really recognised as a section of RSHA *Amt* VI) took the place of the deputy. Through it he established a personal contact with the *Gruppen* of *Amt* VI and with the *Mil Amt* when the *Abwehr* was absorbed in the summer of 1944. It would be inaccurate to say that 'VI V' became the *Zentralbüro*. VI V did not in fact ever exist; but the tendency was that the dual purpose of personal contact with the *Ländergruppen* and effective collation of the work of the *Amt* became centralised in the ZB which department did not progress beyond the embryonic stage.

The *Zentralbüro* evolved out of *Referat* VI A7 which had been placed under SS-*Stubaf* Schindowski of RSHA VI D in the summer of 1944. VI A7 had been given the task of collecting non-secret information for further distributon to the various *Gruppenleiter*. Such material was obtained through the press, the news agencies and the Radio News Service. By the end of the year VI A7 as such ceased to exist and became the *Zentralbüro* with much extended functions. The sources of information available to the *Zentralbüro* were extended from non-secret to top secret material. The main sources were now the daily political reports from the OKW Chi—the decoding section of the OKW—which that department had obtained from the deciphering of foreign diplomatic messages. These reports numbered from 30 to 80 per day. The range also extended from mere political matter to military, economic and technical reports. The liaison officers to the various Ministries made their contribution and material still continued to come from the Press agencies.

The *Zentralbüro* collated and evaluated these Daily Reports and prepared its own report which was distributed originally to Himmler only, but later given wider distribution to Hitler, Himmler, Fegelein, Hewel of the Foreign Office, General Winter, and Admiral Dönitz.

8

Wirsing and the Egmont Reports

To the rather intangible organisation of the *Zentralbüro* and 'VI V' must be added an account of the '*Egmont Berichte*' with which the Daily Report of the *Zentralbüro* was closely connected. It must be borne in mind that the essential conception of Schellenberg's intelligence service was the preparation by RSHA *Amt* VI of a properly coordinated summary of political intelligence from all available sources; and Schellenberg to achieve that end did not hestitate to go beyond the recognised organisation of *Amt* VI. VI *Kult* is one example of his efforts within the existing framework of the *Amt*. His association with SS-*Stubaf* Eggen as his personal agent in Switzerland was an example of his circumvention of an inefficient official representative through whom reports would normally be received whether good or bad. Another striking example is his use of Dr Wirsing in the preparation of the Egmont Reports. Dr Wirsing was a journalist and author of note whose grasp of political affairs Schellenberg much admired. He was however in no sense a RSHA *Amt* VI officer or agent. But Schellenberg, recognising his ability decided that Wirsing with his wide knowledge of political affairs and in his training as a political writer was better fitted for the task he had in mind than any *Amt* VI officer, and did not hesitate to invite Wirsing to prepare reports on political matters for *Amt* VI. The remarkable feature is that Wirsing was given access to all *Amt* VI material likely to be of assistance to him. With this material at his disposal Wirsing prepared reports on various aspects of political importance which were in turn passed to the *Zentralbüro* for further distribution as the '*Egmont Berichte*'. Schellenberg had calculated in this way to have these reports, which attempted to be a true assessment of a deteriorating situation, passed through Himmler to Hitler with the hope that the foreign policy of the *Reich* would be framed to meet realities which Hitler would not face. It should be noted that this effort by Schellenberg had full support from Himmler.

While therefore the *Egmont Berichte* were made available to the *Zentralbüro*, the real situation was that evaluation and collection of RSHA *Amt* VI political reports was done by a person not even a member of the *Amt* and passed back to the *Amt* in final form.

9

The Re-organisation of RSHA *Gruppe* VI A in 1944

The absorption of the *Abwehr* in the summer of 1944 marked the final re-organisation of the *Gruppe*. Properly speaking RSHA *Gruppe* VI A was amalgamated with *Abteilung Mil* A of the *Mil Amt* with a new *Gruppenleiter*, SS-*Staf* Sandberger. Only the *Amt* VI side however is treated in this paper and a final form of the *Gruppe* is shown at Appendix IV. It should be noted however that between the re-organisation in mid-1944 and the final collapse several readjustments within the *Gruppe* took place due to the influence of Sandberger, who tended, if anything, to over-organise.

10

Miscellaneous Notes on Appendix IV

(a) *Referat* VI A2.

This was a new *Referat* introduced on the orders of Kaltenbrunner who instructed Spacil, RSHA *Amtschef* II, to place an *Amt* II representative in the organisational section of RSHA *Amt* VI A in order to supervise the financial administration of *Amt* VI. The officer chosen was SS-*Hstuf* Schuler, previously of *Amt* II, who then became *Referent* VI A2 acting as Spacil's representative in the financial matters of *Amt* VI. The reason for this appointment was Kaltenrbunner's fear that Schellenberg would attempt to make RSHA *Amt* VI self-sufficient and independent. The move was however a failure as Sandberger was able to give Schuler so much other work to do that he had very little time to take any active interest in the financial matters of RSHA *Amt* VI.

Previous to this appointment VI A2 had been the administrative *Referat* of RSHA VI A, while VI A3 had been the financial *Referat* under SS-*Ostuf* Wiesinger. Schuler's appointment as *Referent* VI A2 meant that the former VI A2 merged into VI A1 to form an organisation section, while VI A3 became the new VI A2. The new VI A3 under SS-*Stubaf* Reinhardt was concerned with questions of personnel.

(b) *Referat* VI A4.

This *Referat* was from Schellenberg's point of view an important development. He had considered that until the creation of this new *Referat* insufficient attention had been made to the training of officers in *Amt* VI and in the *Mil Amt*, and under the auspices of VI A4 courses of training were inaugurated for all branches of RSHA *Amt* VI work, including that of the *Mil Amt*. Sandberger himself took a very close interest in VI A4. This training *Referat* however never progressed beyond the initial stages. Schellenberg had envisaged courses of instruction for Ic [Intelligence] officers attached to the Army and Military *Attachés* for which the *Wehrmacht* had made no provisions. The courses for beginners in *Amt* VI were held at Baruth [in Schloss Baruth, 53 km/33 miles south of Berlin] under the general supervision of *Oberfeldrichter* Schön. The instruction given included a general review of the work of *Amt* VI, the enrolment and handling of V-men [confidential informants] and lectures on the life, customs, and history of the various countries to which *Amt* VI officers were likely to be sent. The courses, however, began at too late a date to be effective, and the Baruth Camp which began in January 1945 was hastily evacuated before the end of February.

The Situation Regarding Post-War Arrests

The arrest of the *Gruppenleiter*, SS-*Staf* Sandberger, and the detailed information which he has given on the *Gruppe* make further arrests of personnel in *Gruppe* VI A of little interest; in addition, the *Zentralbüro* can be considered fully covered by the arrest of SS-*Ostuf* Schüddekopf and Dr Wirsing. The only remaining gap is in VI *Kult* as SS-*Stubaf* Carstenn has not yet been apprehended. While the functions of VI *Kult* are known, information is still lacking on the agents it employed. Sandberger has stated that in addition to liaison work with the various Ministries, VI *Kult* also ran its own agents of whom only three are known—SS-*Stubaf* Hartl (now arrested), Mattes, and Schappel, of whom details are lacking. Carstenn therefore is the last *Referent* of VI *Kult*, should be in a position to give the necessary information and the identity of any remaining agents controlled directly by VI *Kult.* Other arrests are shown in Appendix V. These are still comparatively few in numbers.

Sources of information on RSHA *Gruppe* VI A:

SS-*Staf* Sandberger	*Gruppenleiter*
SS-*Ostuf* Schüddekopf	*Zentralbüro*

Sources of information on RSHA VI *Kult* and the *Zentralbüro*:

SS-*Brif* Schellenberg	*Amtschef* VI
SS-*Staf* Sandberger	*Gruppenleiter*
SS-*Stubaf* Dr Höttl	RSHA VI E
SS-*Ostuf* Schüddekopf	*Zentralbüro*
Dr Giselherr Wirsing	(The Egmont Reports)

This report was distributed by W.R.C.3a on 9 October 1945.

Appendix I

Chart of Distribution of Work in RSHA *Amt* VI from 1939–1945

	1939–1940	Early 1941	Mid 1941–42	1942–1944	1944–1945
VI A	Administration etc.	General Intelligence Tasks Abroad (? Sections)	Administration etc.	Administration etc.	Administration etc.
VI B	Technical Section	Europe Africa Near East (10 sections)	Slovakia Hungary Roumania Jugoslavia Greece Turkey Iraq, Iran Afghanistan	France Low Countries Switzerland Spain Portugal	France Low Countries Switzerland Spain Portugal Italy (from 1944)
VI C	Russia Baltic States Far East	Russia Far East (11 sections)	Russia Japan China Finland Baltic States	Russia Near East Far East (13 sections)	Russia Near East Far East (4 sections by mid 1944)

VI D	Hungary Slovakia Jugoslavia Roumania Bulgaria Greece Turkey	Anglo-American sphere (9 sections)	Gt. Britain British Empire USA S. America Sweden Norway Denmark	Anglo-American sphere (3 sections)	Anglo-American sphere & Scandinavia (from summer 1944)
VI E	Italy Spain Portugal Central & Southern America	Ideological Enemies abroad (6 sections) (previously VI H)	France Low Countries Spain Portugal Italy Switzerland	Central-Europe Balkans Italy Scandinavia	Balkans
VI F	France Low Countries Switzerland Luxemburg	Technical Section	Technical Section	Technical Section	Technical Section
VI G	Gt. Britain British Empire USA Norway	-	Ideological Enemies abroad	Research (from August 1944)	Research
VI H	Ideological Enemies abroad	-	-	-	-

Appendix II

Organisational Chart of
RSHA *Gruppe* VI A in 1940

RSHA *Gruppe* VI A—Organisation and Administration
Gruppenleiter—SS-*Ostubaf* Dr Filbert

> *Beauftragter* I (*West*)—SS-*Ostubaf* Bernhard
> *Beauftragter* II (*Nord*)—SS-*Stubaf* Dr Lehmann
> *Beauftragter* III (*Ost*)—SS-*Stubaf* von Salisch
> *Beauftragter* IV (*Süd*)—SS-*Stubaf* Lapper
> *Beauftragter* V (*Mitte*)—SS-*Ostubaf* Thiemann

Referat	*Sachgebiet*	*Referent*
VI A1	*Allgemeine Organisation des Nachrichtendienstes*	-
VI A2	*Verwaltung der Nachrichtenmittel*	-
VI A3	*Betreuung der VM im Ausland*	SS-*Hstuf* Seidel

VI A4	*Nachrichtendienst. Zusammenarbeit*	SS-*Ostuf* Vorauer
	mit staatl. u. polit. Organisationen	
VI A5	*Nachrichtendienstliche Zusammen-*	SS-*Ostuf* Westergaard
VI A6	*Fundbeaobachtung*	SS-*Ostuf* Gottlob
VI A7	*Pressespiegel des Auslands*	SS-*Stubaf* Dr Siebert
VI A8	*Verbindung zur Nachrichtenschule*	-

Appendix III

Organisational Chart of
RSHA *Gruppe* VI A in January 1941

RSHA *Gruppe* VI A—General Intelligence Abroad
Gruppenleiter—SS-*Ostubaf* Dr Filbert
Verterer—SS-*Stubaf* Finke

The *Beauftragter* of *Amt* VI for examination of all intelligence connections including the assurement of routes of contact and couriers and of the employment of intelligence means of *Amt* VI at home and abroad.

Sachbebiet	*Referent*
Beauftrager I (*West*) for the SD-*Leit-Abschnitte*: Münster/W., Aachen, Bielefeld, Dortmund, Köln, Düsseldorf, Koblenz, Kassel, Frankfurt/Main, Darmstadt, Neustadt a.d. Weinstrasse, Karlsruhe, Stuttgart.	SS-*Ostubaf* Bernhard
Beauftrager II (*Nord*) for the SD-*Leit-Abschnitte*: Bremen, Braunschweig, Lüneburg, Hamburg, Kiel, Schwerin, Stettin, Neustettin	SS-*Ostubaf* Lehmann
Beauftrager III (*Ost*) for the SD-*Leit-Abschnitte*: Danzig, Königsberg, Allenstein, Tilsit, Thorn, Posen, Hohensalza, Litzmannstadt, Breslau Liegnitz, Oppeln, Kattowitz, Troppau and Generalgouvernment	SS-*Stubaf* von Salisch
Beauftrager IV (*Süd*) for the SD-*Leit-Abschnitte*: Vienna, Innsbruck, Linz, Salzburg, Munich, Nayreuth, Prague	SS-*Stubaf* Lapper

Beauftragter V (*Süd*) for the SD-*Leit-Abschnitte*:   SS-*Ostubaf* Thiemann
Berlin, Dresden, Leipzig, Weimar, Magdeburg,
Karlsbad

Appendix IV

Organisational Chart of
RSHA *Gruppe* VI A in 1945

RSHA *Gruppe* VI A—Organisation and Administration
Gruppenleiter—SS-*Staf* Sandberger

Referat	*Sachgebiet*	*Referent*
VI A1	Organisation	SS-*Stubaf* Reichert
VI A2	Finance	SS-*Hstuf* Schuler
VI A3	Personnel	SS-*Stubaf* Reinhardt
VI A4	Training	*Feldwebel* Schoen
VI A5	Travel Arrangments	SS-*Ostuf* Geppert
VI *Gesellschäft* (mail, files, etc.)		SS-*Hstuf* Hartmann
VI *Kult*	Contact with cultural circles	SS-*Stubaf* Carstenns
VI A7	*Zentralbüro* (Collection and dissemination of Reports)	SS-*Stubaf* Turowski
VI *Promi*	Liaison to Propaganda Ministry	SS-*Stubaf* Ulenberg
VI A/SO	Billets and Lodgings	SS-*Stubaf* Herbert Müller
VI *Abw*	Internal Security	SS-*Stubaf* Otten
VI AR	Legal Matters	Dr Herzlieb
VI AR/I	Discipline	*Oberstrichter* Gramatzky
VI AR/II	Private legal matters	*Min Rat* Dr Studnitz
VI AR/III	V-*Mann* legal matters	Dr Schoen

Appendix V

Alphabetical Index of Personalities in RSHA *Gruppe* VI A, 1939–1945

Post-war arrested personalities are underlined

Rank & Name	*Referat*	Remarks
SS-*Hstuf* Heinz Amthor	VI *Kult*	Dismissed late 1944
SS-*Hstuf* Ferdinand Baus	VI A2	Was VI B; left VI A late 1944
SS-*Ostubaf* <u>Heinrich Bernhard</u>	VI A	Beauftragter West 1940–41; *Referent* VI B2 from 1942
SS-*Hstuf* Walter Buchmann	VI A2	Left VI A late 1944
SS-*Stubaf* Friedrich Carstenn	VI *Kult*	*Referent* VI *Kult* since late1944
SS-*Hstuf* Georg Demski	VI A2	1945; previously RSHA II
SS-*Hstuf* Walter Dierksheide	VI A2	Nov. 1943
SS-*Stubaf* Dr Karl-August Eckhardt	VI A4	1945
SS-*Stubaf* Dr Heinrich Fesel	VI A	Dec. 1939; then VI F
SS-*Ustuf* Erich Feldmann	VI Kult	1945
SS-*Ostubaf* Dr Alfred Filbert	VI A	*Gruppenleiter*, 1939–1941
SS-*Hstuf* Dietrich Fitte	VI A5	Nov. 1943
SS-*Ostuf* Ewald Geppert	VI A5	1945
SS-*Ostuf* Joseph Gottlob	VI A6	1940; with VI F, 1941–1943
SS-*Hstuf* Erich Grundmann	VI A2	1945
SS-*Stubaf* <u>Albert Hartl</u>	VI *Kult*	1945; arrested US Zone
SS-*Hstuf* Hans Hartmann	VI A2	1945
Ministerialrat Herzlieb	VI AR	1945
SS-*Stubaf* Gerhard Hoins	VI A3	1945
SS-*Ustuf* Rudolf Hoppe	VI A2	1945
SS-*Ostuf* Heinz Horn	VI A4	Nov. 1943
Sonderführer Hübbe	VI ZB	Liaison Officer to Ministry of Economics
SS-*Ostuf Pol.Inspektor* Paul Jantzen	VI A2	Nov. 1943
SS-*Hstuf Pol.Ob.Insp.* Rudolf Kaiser	VI A2	Nov. 1943
SS-*Ustuf* Fritz Krause	VI *Kult*	Nov. 1943
SS-*Stubaf* Anton Kriegbaum	VI ZB	Lision Officer to *Standarte*'Kurt Eggers'
SS-*Stubaf* Hermann Lapper	VI A	*Beauftragter Süd*, 1940–1943
SS-*Hstuf* Fritz Langlotz	VI *Kult*	1945; previously VI E
SS-*Stubaf* Dr Hermann Lehmann	VI A	*Beauftragter Nord*, 1939–40

SS-*Stubaf* Erich Möller	VI *Kult*	1943
SS-*Stubaf* Herbert Müller	VI A	*Stellv.Gruppenleiter*, then *Gruppenleiter* 1941–1943
SS-*Ostuf* Heino Naumann	VI A3	left *Gruppe* in 1944
SS-*Stubaf* Friedrich Otten	VI A	1945: Internal Security
SS-*Ustuf* Herbert Pahnke	VI A2	1945, came from BdS Paris; in charge of Transport Pool
SS-*Stubaf* Waldemar von Radetzky	VI ZB	Liaison Officer to *Standarte*'Kurt Eggers', 1945
SS-*Stubaf* Fritz Reichert	VI A1	1945, *Referent*
SS-*Stubaf* Heinz Reinhardt	VI A3	1945, *Referent*
SS-*Stubaf* Rudolf Oebsger-Röder	VI ZB	Liaison Officer to Foreign Office, 1945
SS-*Stubaf* Karl-Otto von Salisch	VI A	*Beauftragter Ost*, 1939–40
SS-*Staf* Martin Sandberger	VI A	*Gruppenleiter*; arrested in US Zone
SS-*Ostuf* Dr Otto-Ernst Schüddekopf	VI ZB	was VI D; arrested in US Zone
SS-*Hstuf* Eugen Schuler	VI A2	was *Amt* II
SS-*Stubaf* Dr Hans Schindowski	VI ZB	*Referent* ZB from 1944
SS-*Ustuf* Schröder	VI A2	1945
SS-*Stubaf* Rudolf Seidel	VI A3	1941; arrested US Zone
SS-*Stubaf* Dr Klaus Siebert	VI A7	1940
SS-*Hstuf* Heinrich Spiegelhauer	VI *Kult*	1945, Liaison Officer to Auslands Organisation
SS-*Ostuf* Günter Tabbert	VI ZB	1945
SS-*Ostubaf* Karl Thiemann	VI A	*Beauftragter Mitte*, 1939–40
SS-*Stubaf* Dr Erst Turowski	VI ZB	1945
SS-*Stubaf* Alfred Ulenberg	VI ZB	1945, Liaison Officer to Propaganda Ministry
SS-*Ostuf* Dr Egon Vorauer	VI A4	1940
SS-*Stubaf* Hans Wadel	VI *Kult*	1940; joined *Waffen*-SS '44
SS-*Hstuf* Herbert Wellendorf	VI *Kult*	Nov. 1943
SS-*Ostuf* Julius Westergaard	VI A5	1940
SS-*Hstuf* Walter Wiesinger	VI A3	1945

Note

* The National Archives, Kew, KV 3/112, Liquidation Report No. 6, on RSHA VI A.

6

Liquidation Report No. 7:
Amt VI of the RSHA—*Gruppe* VI B

INDEX

Part I: The Historical Development of *Gruppe* VI B
Part II: *Referat* VI B1 and its Activities against Italy
Part III: *Referat* VI B2 and its Activities against France and the Low Countries
Part IV: *Referat* VI B3 and its Activities against Switzerland
Part V: *Referat* VI B4 and its Activities against the Iberian Peninsula
Part VI: Miscellaneous

Appendix I: The Distribution of Work in RSHA *Amt* VI from 1939–45
Appendix II: *Gruppe* VI Personnel at RSHA
Appendix III: *Referat* VI B1 Personnel at Outstations
Appendix IV: *Referat* VI B2 Personnel at Outstations
Appendix V: *Referat* VI B3 Personnel at Outstations
Appendix VI: *Referat* VI B4 Personnel at Outstations
Appendix VII: Alphabetical Index of RSHA *Gruppe* VI B personnel, 1939–1945
RSHA *Gruppe* VI B and Western Europe

Preamble

It is merely a matter of convenience to treat the history of Western Europe und RSHA *Amt* VI in terms of the activities of *Gruppe* VI B such as it existed at the time of the German collapse; for it has to be remembered that in the various re-organisations of *Amt* VI, especially in the early part of its history, the section designated as *Gruppe* VI B was not throughout competent for Western Europe, nor were the territorial divisions between the various *Gruppen* without frequent modification. In Part I of this paper therefore, which deals roughly with the years 1939–1941, care is taken to refer to Western Europe rather than to *Gruppe* VI B; the remaining Parts dealing with the work of the *Referate* against the various countries, however, are dealt with in terms of *Gruppe* VI B as if the organisation of the *Gruppe* had remained unchanged throughout, unless where specific points require clarification.

This treatment is somewhat inaccurate, but not seriously so. RSHA *Amt* VI activities against Western Europe fell into two well defined parts, as does indeed the history of the *Amt* as a whole—the periods before and after the appointment of Schellenberg as *Amtschef*. Schellenberg's accession in late 1941 marks a turning point in RSHA *Amt* VI, a change in organisation, in personnel and in policy. The result of *Amt* VI activities in the time of Jost were meagre, in the case of Western Europe almost negligible. Parts II–V deal in fact very largely with the Schellenberg period from early 1942 onwards, by which time *Gruppe* VI B was finally established with only minor subsequent changes. Part I therefore serves as a historical background to the remainder of the paper.

A further complication to be noted is that caused by the military campaigns themselves, broadly speaking RSHA *Amt* VI as the *Auslandsnachrichtendienst* dealt with foreign territory, while RSHA *Amt* III as the *Inlandsnachrichendienst* dealt with the home territory. Occupied territory, however, became a source of friction between the two *Ämter*, and no well defined policy seems ever to have been established. The 1940 campaign in the West and the subsequent occupation of the Low Countries and part of France led to a re-orientation of *Amt* VI policy against these countries. The change however was ill defined, as is evidenced by the strong *Amt* III representation in Holland and Belgium as against the equally strong *Amt* VI representation in the BdS Frankreich. This factor is of importance in dealing with Holland and Belgium.

The main purpose of this paper is to give an account of the development of RSHA *Amt* VI activities against Western Europe and the attempt to assess the degree of success which attended its efforts to obtain through its representatives in the countries under review the information it desired. In this assessment two points must be borne in mind. Firstly all the necessary evidence is not available since some leading representatives have not yet been arrested and interrogated. Secondly, this paper deals only with the SD and its personnel; any advantages which the absorption of the *Abwehr* in 1944 bestowed on *Gruppe* VI B do not form any part of the scope of this review. The first defect is however not serious and further information is not likely to modify this interim assessment. The reservation however must still be made.

Part I

The Historical Development of RSHA *Gruppe* VI B

A. Western Europe.

1. The original Organisation

When the RSHA was created on the outbreak of war, *Amt* VI of this new organisation under SS-*Brif* Jost in effect broke new ground and the SD which until then had not officially concerned itself with the Ausland. The organisation of the new *Amt* therefore in the early stages could only be tentative and would naturally be subject to modification in the light of experience. Such in fact was the case and the *Amt* underwent drastic re-organisation on at least two occasions before the end of 1941. By January 1940 it had lettered *Gruppen* up to the letter H. Under this organisation Western Europe was divided between two *Gruppen*— *Gruppe* VI E and *Gruppe* VI F

Gruppe VI E under SS-*Stubaf* Rossner dealt with Italy, Spain, Portugal and South America, while *Gruppe* VI F under SS-*Hstuf* Bielstein controlled France, Luxemburg, Belgium, Holland, and Switzerland. Roughly therefore, Western Europe was divided into North-West and South-West groups, while the appearance of South America in the South-West group is explained by the fact that penetration of that country was envisaged from the Iberian Peninsula.

2. The *Beauftragter*—Jost's first appointments.

Side by side with this central organisation in Berlin was the appointment by Jost to the various countries listed above of RSHA *Amt* VI representatives whose function it was to provide the *Amt* with the information it had been set up to obtain. In Western Europe these appointments were the following: SS-*Ostuf* Dr Peter was sent to Switzerland, SS-*Stubaf* Plath to Spain, Fast to Portugal, and Dr Erb to Holland. No appointment was made to Italy, as in accordance with the *Führerbefehl*, no espionage activities were to be carried out in that country. No representatives were sent to France and Belgium before the occupation of these two countries in 1940 and indeed Dr Erb in Holland was not a permanent appointment. Erb merely travelled on several occasions to Holland and in the course of his other duties acted on behalf of *Amt* VI.

Generally speaking, the *Beautragter* were badly chosen, ill-trained, and given no clear instructions on their duties. They were given commercial cover, as the Foreign Office opposed giving diplomatic cover to such intruders on its own sphere. They were charged with providing their respective RSHA *Gruppen* with political information regarding the countries to which they were sent, but had in general to find their own contacts, spurned as they were by the Foreign Office, and in some cases had to find their own channels of communication. In these unfavourable circumstances the *Beauftragter* achieved little in the way of results. The development of these original appointment abroad are dealt with in the Parts dealing with the activities of the *Referate* of RSHA *Gruppe* VI B.

3. The Reorganisation of RSHA *Amt* VI in early 1941.
The first major re-organisation of RSHA *Amt* VI took place in January 1941. In this change an entirely new system seems to have been envisaged, but it is doubtful if it was ever in fact put into operation. The number of *Ländergruppen* was decreased, and in particular a new *Gruppe* VI B came into being, having under its control the whole of Europe, Africa, and the Near East. The *Gruppe*, having such a wide territory to cover, had the unusually high number of ten *Referate*, but there is no indication of the territorial division between these *Referate*; nor are the names of the *Gruppenleiter* or *Referent* available. This organisational structure however was obviously an unwieldy one, and it not surprising that before long it was abandoned in favour of a decentralisation of territorial control. The existence of this *Gruppe* VI B must have been very short lived.

4. Jost's final Organisation.
By the summer of 1941 Jost had finally decided on the organisation of his new *Amt*. The *Gruppen* were again seven in number, but the territorial divisions and the lettering of the *Gruppen*, Western Europe went to *Gruppe* VI E which represented in fact an amalgamation of *Gruppe* VI E and *Gruppe* VI F on 1940 as the countries controlled by the new Groups were Holland, Belgium, France, Spain, Portugal, Switzerland and Italy. South America however passed to VI D. The new *Gruppenleiter* was SS-*Hstuf* Bielstein, the *Gruppenleiter* of the 1940 VI F.

5. The personnel under Jost.
Mention has been made in Paragraph 2 above of the poor quality of the *Beauftragter* chosen by Jost as RSHA *Amt* VI representatives abroad; the personnel in the *Amt* itself did not present a very much brighter picture. Jost, the weakest of the *Amtschefs* in the new RSHA, both in personality and in status, was not in a strong position in choosing the personnel of his new *Amt*, and *Gruppe* VI E was little better than any other *Gruppe*. The original *Gruppenleiter* was SS-*Hstuf* Bielstein who was replaced in early 1942 by SS-*Stubaf* Freise. Neither was competent. The main source of recruitment open to Jost was the personnel of *Abteilung* III of the old SD-*Hauptamt* of which *Abteilung* Jost has been Leiter. But the work of that department was an inadequate training ground for the new duties assigned to *Amt* VI. The main weakness was that few of the officers had any knowledge of the countries which now came under their control, a weakness which they shared with the *Beauftragter* who had been sent as representatives to these countries. It is of interest to note that of the original officers chosen for Western Europe in

1939, two survived until the end. They are SS-*Ostubaf* Bernhard and the then SS-*Ostuf* Zschunke, who later became respectively *Referent* for France and for Belgium. As the following history of RSHA *Gruppe* VI B will show, Zschunke can claim to be not only one of the original members but the last officer of the *Gruppe* to be operationally active. The remaining original officers, however, had almost entirely disappeared by 1942 as a result of the efforts of Schellenberg to improve the work of the *Gruppe*.

B. Western Europe under Schellenberg

1. Re-organisation under Schellenberg.

It is with the advent of Schellenberg as *Amtschef* in the latter half of 1941 that RSHA *Amt* VI took its final shape. The *Amt* subsequently merely expanded and apart from minor readjustments of territory between the new *Gruppen*, the organisation of the *Amt* remained substanially the same until the end. The fate of Western Europe in this re-organisation is easy to follow. VI E as created by Jost became *Gruppe* VI B, its final designation. The territory controlled by the new *Gruppe* suffered only one adjustment as Italy passed to the new VI E which dealt with the Balkans; but even this change was only a temporary one as in later 1944 Italy returned to *Gruppe* VI B to become *Referat* VI B1. Between 1942 and 1945 however there were readjustments in the *Referate* of the *Gruppe*. It is under the final internal organisation of the *Gruppe* however that its activities will be considered. This organisation is as shown at Appendix II.

2. Schellenberg's efforts to improve personnel.

Changing the organisation of RSHA *Amt* VI was the least of Schellenberg's troubles. Much more important from his point of view was the necessity of improving the standard of personnel both in the *Amt* itself and abroad. *Gruppe* VI B was no exception in this reform, but here as in the other *Gruppen*, Schellenberg was limited in his plans by the very restricted field available to him for further recruitment. By 1942 Schellenberg had decided to recall the *Amt* VI representatives from SD *Stellen* in Germany where they served very little useful purpose, in the hope that the personnel thus available would strengthen the position in Berlin. Among the leading personnel Bielstein was the first to go, being replaced by SS-*Stubaf* Freise. The latter however did not meet Schellenberg's requirements as a *Gruppenleiter*, and in the Spring of 1943 he in turn was replaced by Schellenberg's final choice, SS-*Staf* Steimle. Steimle had previously been *Amt* VI representative in the SD-*Abschnitt* Stuttgart, where he had worked against Switzerland. Steimle was ambitious and capable and remained in charge until the end.

As a *Referent* for France and the Low Countries, Schellenberg chose SS-*Ostubaf* Bernhard, who also remained in that position until the collapse, though even he has been described by Schellenberg as an 'altogether negligible person'. SS-*Hstuf* Neubourg became *Referent* for the Iberian Peninsula. The personnel problem remained however until the end, and Schellenberg was faced with the everlasting problem of whether to send his reliable men to the outstations to improve the work there at the expense of the *Amt*, or strengthen the *Amt* at the expense of the outstations.

The results of Schellenberg's efforts are discussed in Parts II–V.

Part II

Referat VI B1 and its Activities against Italy.

A. The period before the Italian Armistice.

1. The *Führerbefehl*.

As has been mentioned in Part I, Jost in 1939–40 sent no *Beauftragter* to Italy, as in accordance with the instructions laid down by Hitler himself, no espionage activities were to be carried out in that country. RSHA *Amt* VI therefore had no representation in the country until 1942 when attempts were made to circumvent the *Führerbefehl*. By that time of course Italy's own position in the war had seriously worsened and Hitler's decree made it extremely difficult for *Amt* VI to be well informed on the state of Italian morale and the trend of political thought in official Italian circles. The only existing source of information (apart of course from the Foreign Office and its official channels) was in the person of SS-*Ostubaf* Kappler, the *Polizei Attaché* in the German Embassy in Rome.

2. Kappler's work as *Polizei Attaché*.

Kappler had been appointed to Rome as early as 1939 as *Polizeiverbindungsführer*, later to become *Polizei Attaché*. In this capacity he carried out his normal functions as political adviser to the Embassy and liaison officer with the Italian Police, and was not an *Amt* VI representative. Kappler did, however, submit regular but unofficial reports through the Havel Institute on Italian politics and morale: these reports were proved by subsequent events to be sound, but being sound were not highly popular. Kappler in the main relied on official contacts for his sources of information and was in fact the political observer on the spot. He did however succeed in tapping the Vatican as a source through the medium of an employee in the Vatican Library.

3. Attempts to circumvent the *Führerbefehl*.

By 1942 the *Führerbefehl* had become too awkward to be strictly obeyed. Italy presented great advantages for RSHA *Amt* VI work, and with the changing war situation attempts were made to increase activities in the country, but such attempts had of course to be camouflaged. The first step was the appointment of SS-*Stubaf* Looss as assistant to Kappler, with the specific assignment of using this cover to collect information on general political matters. Looss, who had to establish his own contacts, was largely ineffective. Side by side with this appointment was that in late 1942 of SS-*Hstuf* Gröbl who was sent to Rome under cover as an employee of a German travel agency with the specific assignment of preparing a post-occupational network in the Rome area. Gröbl was to work independently of Kappler and contact between the two was to be avoided. By March 1943 instructions from Schellenberg became more specific: Kappler was now charged with the preparation of a post-occupational network in Sicily, while Gröbl was to be responsible for South Italy. These preparations did not get beyond the initial stages and from the point of view of results, both Kappler and Gröbl failed completely.

The failure however was confined to the organisation of the networks; the political reports from both Kappler and Gröbl continued to be an accurate reflection of opinion, but especially after the fall of Mussolini in July 1943 when an accurate picture reflected the strong existing anti-fascist feeling, the reports were ignored as running counter to official German policy. In Italy, as elsewhere, it was difficult to report objectively and at the same time meet with favour.

B. The period after the Italian Armistice.

1. BdS Italien and the *Aussenkommando* Rome.
The collapse of Italy and the altered situation created by the Badoglio armistice led to a modification in policy regarding Italy as a theatre of espionage operations. The previous restrictions were removed and indeed both Himmler and Kaltenbrunner, quite irrespective of Schellenberg, gave full encouragement to espionage activity, as it was realised that a territory where contact could be made with so many nationalities serving under the Allies, could prove to be a valuable source of information regarding Allied morale and the degree of co-operation or non-cooperation which existed between the Allies themselves. Functionally, SS-*Gruf* Harster was appointed BdS Italy, while Kappler remained in Rome as head of an *Aussenkommando* there. Gröbl meantime had been killed by partisans almost immediately after the armistice.

2. *Aussenkommando* Rome and its Post-Occupational plans.
Between the setting up of the *Aussenkommando* Rome in September 1943 and the fall of Rome in June 1944, the task of preparing a post-occupational network in the Rome area and in Southern Italy fell on the *Abteilung* VI representative in Rome under the command of SS-*Stubaf* Hass. Hass had taken part in the liberation of Mussolini and stayed on in Rome as a replacement of Looss; he had as his second-

in-command, SS-*Ostuf* Schubernig. Hass took over one of Gröbl's agents whom he sent to Naples to allow himself to be overrun and act as a contact for further agents to be sent to the area; the agent (Kallmeyer) was never heard from after his departure. Two further attempts were made, using a cloister and a bee farm as cover, but these too came to nothing. By May 1944 Hass had some five or six groups prepared for operations, while independently of these groups which were to work together, Hass had brought from The Hague the female agent Ten Kate Brouwe to remain in Rome. The network was a complete failure and the fall of Rome in June 1944 made other arrangements necessary.

C. The period after the fall of Rome.

1. Re-organisation in the North.
With the fall of Rome and the dissolution of the *Aussenkommando* there, the *Aussenkommandos* of BdS Italien based in Verona in the North assumed greater importance, and the preparation of stay-behind networks were made through them. The growing seriousness of the position led to further attempts by *Amt* VI to improve the situation.

SS-*Stubaf* Huegel, a competent officer at the *Amt*, was sent as representative to the BdS Verona, while SS-*Stubaf* Wolff (later to become *Leiter* of the *Leitstelle* Siegfried under RSHA VI B2) was given the special assignment of organising the post-occupational networks in Northern Italy. By October 1944 the *Aussenkommandos* had been given their clear instructions and by April 1945 networks had been established in eight different areas in Northern Italy—Genoa, San Remo, Milan, Como, Trieste, Venice, Bologna and Fiume.

2. The Failure of the Networks.
The networks however were not set up without the usual difficulties. There was the problem of finding suitable material and having found it, the question of training prescribed further complications. The training had to be carried through under rushed conditions owing to the pressure of time, and as a result was generally inadequate, especially on the W/T side. The language difficulty itself was a hindrance to speedy training, and the provision of W/T sets capable of overcoming the geographical conditions presented by the Alps was an added problem. On technical grounds alone, therefore, the I-Netze were doomed to failure. But even had these technical difficulties been overcome, and even if sufficient personnel had been available on the German side to train in time a sufficient number of reliable agents, the networks would not have been able to rise above the sequence of events. They were essentially post-occupational networks; no provision had been made to operate them as post-defeat networks. The general surrender in Italy therefore rendered them quite ineffective.

3. *Einheit* Ida.

While the *Aussenkommandos* in the North were preparing their stay-behind networks, the former *Aussenkommando* Rome which had operated under Kappler dispersed on the fall of the city to re-form as a separate unit with its headquarters near Parma. The unit, known by the cover name of *Einheit* Ida, came under the command of SS-*Stubaf* Hass with SS-*Ostuf* Schubernig still as his deputy. *Einheit* Ida did not prepare post-occupational networks but trained its agents for line-crossing missions. The agents were given W/T instruction and the mission given included the obtaining of information on both political and military matters. By October 1944 at least six agents trained by the unit had been arrested and were able to give sufficient information on the personnel of the unit, other agents in training, and even its intended line of withdrawal, to make it a comparatively easy target for counter espionage. The unit achieved very limited success.

4. *Unternehmen* Bertram and Tosca.

Although this enterprise operated from Northern Italy, it was in fact under the control of VI B2 and directed against France. It is therefore discussed in Part III.

D. RSHA *Amt* VI work against the Vatican.

1. SS-*Ostubaf* Elling and his mission.

When Italy was still dealt with by RSHA *Gruppe* VI E in 1943, there existed a *Referat* VI E1 (Vat) under SS-*Ostuf* Reissmann which became VI B1 (Vat) when Italy was transferred from VI E to VI B in late 1944. Reissmann carried on his work against the Vatican in VI B; he is reported to have died in December 1944. By May 1943 RSHA *Amt* VI had decided that the existing channel for obtaining information on the Vatican through Kappler was insufficient. A special representative was therefore chosen in the person of SS-*Ostubaf* Elling. Elling had had a long career in the RSHA concerned with research in church matters and had seen service in that connection with both RSHA *Amt* III and RSHA *Amt* VII. Elling therefore was given a period of training in *Amt* VI under Reissmann preparatory to being sent on his mission.

2. Elling's work at the Vatican.

The usual difficulties were experienced to trying to obtain for Elling proper Consular cover through the Foreign Office. So long was the delay indeed that Elling was finally sent in November 1943 to the *Aussenkommando* at Rome under Kappler to familiarise himself with his new territory pending the granting of his Consular cover into the Vatican itself. It was not until January 1944 that Elling finally succeeded in establishing himself in the German Embassy under Ambassador Weizsäcker. In his comparatively short stay there, Elling succeeded in making only limited contacts, which enabled him to submit reports on the Vatican finances, its relations with Russia, and the Vatican attitude of the war and Germany. The appointment however was made too late for any results of real value to be forthcoming.

3. Attempts at Post-Occupational work.
When it became apparent that Rome would be occupied sooner or later by the Allies, an attempt was made to install Elling in the Vatican as a post-occupational agent. For this purpose a W/T operator was chosen to work with him, but the arrangements were made too late to be effective. Elling in any case was not himself an enthusiastic supporter of the plan which led to nothing. Elling in fact was interned with the other members of the Embassy staff who remained in Rome after its fall.

E. Conclusion.

It is not difficult to reach the conclusion that RSHA *Amt* VI work in Italy was a failure. The *Führerbefehl* had of course deprived it of what in the early stages of the war should have been a profitable ground for its activities in view of the many official contacts which could have been exploited. It deprived the *Amt* too of a suitable base for operations against North Africa. The removal of the restriction came too late for any effective work to be done. The reports received from Kappler and through VI E1 (Vat) and later VI B1 (Vat) were good and accurate but, as has been explained above, official policy did not welcome reports which showed its policy to be wrong. The one great success of RSHA VI S in restoring Mussolini was a false success in that the restoration of the *Duce* was against the recommendation of the reports received through VI B1. The lack of coordination in RSHA *Amt* VI policy is nowhere better illustrated.

Part III

Referat VI B2 and its Activities against France and the Low Countries

A. The period before the French Armistice.

1. Zschunke as *Referent*.
The first *Referent* for France chosen by Bielstein, *Gruppenleiter* of the original RSHA VI F, was SS-*Ostuf* Zschunke, to whom was assigned the task of preparing

V-Men for despatch into that country. Zschunke had no easy task, since prior to the outbreak of war the SD had not even attempted to install agents in France, nor was there, as in Eastern Europe, any pro-German minority in France which could be exploited to advantage. In addition, little background material regarding France was available to the *Gruppe*, so that Zschunke had virtually virgin territory to exploit. The SD-*Abschnitte* in the West had nothing to offer in the way of agents, and Zschunke's efforts at recruitment met with failure.

2. The Lorenz Enterprise.

There was however one exception; in November 1939 Zschunke took over a prospective *Abwehr* agent, SS-*Ostuf* Lorenz, who had been destined for a mission in Paris. Zschunke was successful in providing Lorenz with false papers of sufficiently high standard to enable him to get to Paris through Italy in March 1940, armed with three W/T sets and sabotage material. Lorenz was a failure in his mission, but on his return in April claimed to have obtained through a telephone operator in Paris details of a conversation between Reynaud and Chamberlain regarding the dispositions of Weygand's Near East armies. The story was an invention on the part of Lorenz, but was accepted on its face value and passed direct to Hitler himself. The story was given great prominence in the German Press for propaganda purposes, and was the first success claimed by RSHA *Amt* VI. It was a success of a rather ominous quality.

B. The period after the French Armistice.

1. Early difficulties.

When the French campaign began Zschunke passed what little material he had on France to RSHA *Amt* III as occupied territory was considered by that *Amt* to be its concern. The fall of France and the occupation of Paris however opened up new possibilities for RSHA *Amt* VI, but contrary to what might have been expected, there was no coordinated plan for such an eventuality. Filbert, *Gruppenleiter* RSHA VI A, but in effect directing the work of the *Amt*, sent both Zschunke and Lorenz to Paris to carry on their work there. Their stay did not exceed a fortnight as SS-*Staf* Knochen, the new BdS Frankreich, had his own ideas, and sent them quickly packing. The conflict between *Amt* III and *Amt* VI on occupied territory was an added complication. It was not an auspicious start. Soon two lines of development emerged—the steady growth of *Abteilung* VI in the Paris *Dienststelle* with Knochen as BdS and SS-*Hstuf* Nosek as *Leiter* of *Abteilung* VI, side by side with the despatch by the *Amt* itself of individual representatives to different parts of France.

C. The Activities of BdS Frankreich.

1. Knochen and Nosek.

Of the two tendencies mentioned in the previous paragraph the more considerable was the strong development in *Amt* VI work from Paris; it also yielded least results. Knochen, the BdS, was ambitious and jealous of his reputation, largely based on the Venlo incident; he personally undertook to send reports on France and Vichy direct to the CdS, thus circumventing RSHA *Gruppe* VI B. This relationship, continued when Kaltenbrunner became CdS. Meanwhile Nosek developed his VI *Abteilung*, but on lines hardly profitable to RSHA *Amt* VI. The results achieved under the Jost regime were negligible. By the end of 1941 however Schellenberg had become *Amtschef*, and some attempt at improvement was made, though it is to be noted however that Schellenberg had little faith in *Amt* VI work carried on under a BdS, normally ignorant of what secret intelligence meant and unsympathetic towards it, especially when it dealt with political matters.

2. The Situation in 1942.

SS-*Ostubaf* Bernhard was appointed by Schellenberg as *Referent* for France in January 1942. By now the Paris *Dienststelle* had grown to the extent of having its own *Abteilungen*. It became indeed the largest *Dienststelle* under RSHA *Amt* VI in Europe. It extended its interests beyond the borders of France itself, and thus we find an *Abteilung* VI B responsible for France, *Abteilung* VI C under SS-*Hstuf* Alisch collecting information on the Iberian Peninsula, *Abteilung* VI D under SS-*Hstuf* Zuchristian working against England, and the USA (Zuchristian was in fact a *Gruppe* VI D officer), and a section under SS-*Hstuf* Döhring responsible for North Africa. This section was later to become VI B 4 (Parseval). This organisation however was impressive rather than effective. No results of any importance were achieved and the *Dienststelle* was more concerned in combatting Resistance Movements than in collecting political information. Nosek in July 1942 was replaced by SS-*Stubaf* Hagen, who showed himself equally Resistance minded. Bernhard's attempts at improvement of a rapidly deteriorating situation failed, and the failure was due to the everlasting problem of finding personnel of sufficient ability to carry out the work.

3. The position in 1943—Nosek and the PPF.

Further attempts at improvement were made in the course of 1943. An added impetus was the order to prepare I-*Netze* in the event of an Allied invasion of France, which preparations are dealt with in the following paragraphs. By April 1943 Hagen, whose conception of *Amt* VI work continued to be on operations against the Underground, became Personal *Referent* to the HSSPF Frankreich, and was replaced by SS-*Staf* Bickler who remained in command until the evacuation of Paris. In the same month SS-*Ustuf* Bourjeau took over from Nosek who was given the special assignment of concentrating on Vichy, and North Africa, for which purpose he exploited the PPF. In this work Nosek employed as a specialist Leopold Völker (later despatching officer for agents at *Leitstelle* Siegfried). A certain amount of success was achieved, especially through contact with those PPF delegates who attended the conference in Paris in 1943.

4. Preparations for the I-*Netze*.

A serious start on the preparation of the stay-behind organisation in the event of an Allied invasion was begun by March 1943. For the purpose additional staff was sent to Paris, the actual task of preparing the networks being in the final instance given to SS-*Ustuf* Reissmann. Later SS-*Hstuf* König, SS-*Stubaf* Lang and SS-*Hschaf* Zuang were sent, and a training school established at Rue Desbordes-Vallmore. SS-*Ustuf* Zach of RSHA VI F became the W/T experts at the school. By June 1944 agents had been placed with W/T sets at Rennes, Paris, Bordeaux, Montpelier, Marseilles, and Toulouse. The proportion of agents rejected in training had however been exceptionally high and the comparatively small number of agents ready by June 1944 was a small return for more than one year's work. It is to be noted too that apart from this activity, the Paris *Dienststelle* as an *Amt* VI station had almost ceased to function, the chief contributing factors being the continued poor quality of officers and the attitude of Knochen of himself. The *Dienststelle* therefore had its last chance of justifying its existence.

5. The invasion and the fall of Paris.

The I-*Netze* in fact failed completely; soon after the break-through in Normandy [of the Allied armies] the first of the stay-behind agents was arrested in the second week of August [1944]. Before the end of the month five more were picked up, and the faults in training were now apparent. Little attempt had been made to segregate agents in training, close contact between the agents and the officers themselves had been allowed, the agents themselves were unreliable and easily swayed by the fortunes of battle; the inevitable result was that before the end of August [1944] an almost complete list of agents in training together with the names, functions, and ranks of the officers responsible for the organisation of the network was available to the counter-espionage forces of the Allies. The liquidation of the network became comparatively simple. When Bernhard visited Paris just before the evacuation two W/T links were still available while three more agents could be reached by courier. By February 1945 one W/T set in Montpelier (Margaud) was still operating but on Margaud's arrest the network ceased to function. The information achieved by the network had been negligible.

6. The retreat from Paris.

Early in August 1944 the BdS Paris split up and retreated into Germany in sections. *Abteilung* VI withdrew to St Die and then to Strasbourg where it underwent re-organisation. After some initial confusion it was decided to set up a new organisation to work against France from Germany making use of the subversive elements which had withdrawn from France—the Doriot and Darnand groups. The organisation was placed under the command of SS-*Staf* Bickler and was known as *Leitstelle* Walter.

7. The *Leitstelle* Walter Organisation.

Leitstelle Walter set up its headquarters in Baden-Baden in October 1944. The personnel was largely composed of the personnel of *Abteilung* VI of the BdS Paris, while SS-*Stubaf* Hubig from the *Amt* was sent as Bickler's second-in-command. The *Stelle* was divided into some nine *Kommandos*, each *Kommando* recruiting its agents from one or other of the French subversive organisations; each *Kommando* having a cover name. These *Kommandos* were as follows:

I-BAER under Nosek recruiting from the PPF.
I-IGEL under Moro recruiting from the PPF.
DACHS under Detering recruiting from the Milice.
FUCHS under Bourjeau recruiting from mixed sources.
MARDER under Moritz recruiting from Groupe Collaboration.
HIRSCH I and II under Kunze as the central W/T school.
BIBER under Wild recruiting from the Breton Group.
ELCH under Wenzel recruiting from mixed sources.

The *Stelle* recruited both for line-crossing and parachute operations. The Moritz Kommando concentrated on sending its agents through Switzerland, while Nosek worked in collaboration with SS-*Stubaf* Gohl in Milan. In March 1945, Döhring of VI B4 (Parseval) also joined the unit.

8. The failure of *Leitstelle* Walter.

The results achieved by *Leitstelle* Walter were meagre in the extreme; of the line-crossing operations about a 20% degree of success was achieved in agents reporting back. The parachute operations were a dismal failure; one plane crashed on the take-off, another left but missed its course, a third dropped its agents who were immediately arrested. At the end a further batch of eight agents was ready for despatch but no planes were available. Eventually the *Stelle* itself was overrun by the speed of the Allied advance and instructions were given to the remaining officers and agents to disband. The *Stelle* evacuated from Baden-Baden to Horalberg and finally to Heiligenberg, where it dispersed. This dispersal brought to an end the history of the *Dienststelle* in Paris, the end of five years of continuous failure.

D. Other Activities against France.

1. The individual Representatives.

It was noted in Paragraph B(1) above that the growth of the *Dienststelle* in Paris was one development of *Gruppe* VI B activities against France from 1940 onwards. The other independent development was the despatching of individual representatives to different parts of France reporting directly to the *Amt* and not through a BdS. This development had its beginnings with Zschunke in 1940, not because Zschunke considered such a method superior to working through the BdS, but because no other method was open to him since Knochen had regarded control of his work by the *Gruppe* as unnecessary. By the time Schellenberg took command however in late 1941, the system became a matter of policy and not of convenience, as Schellenberg considered that *Amt* VI work such as he envisaged it was much more likely to succeed through the activities of a single well-trained officer working under proper cover than by a large and self-advertising *Dienststelle*. The trouble as ever, however, was to find the competent well-trained officers.

2. Zschunke's first agents—Reiche at Vichy.

It is to Zschunke's credit that he was instrumental in recruiting the most successful VI B officer to operate in France in the person of SS-*Ostuf* Dr Reiche. In the autumn of 1940 Zschunke sent Reiche to Vichy under cover as the representative of the German Embassy in Paris. Soon after his arrival in Vichy in October 1940 Reiche was given a W/T operator through whom his reports were sent to RSHA *Amt* VI. Reiche was successful in making good contacts in official Vichy circles, and until his departure in 1942, was able to submit reports of a consistently high standard on political trends in Vichy. Reiche had only one paid agent—a Swiss newspaperman. His information was obtained almost entirely through social and diplomatic channels. Reiche left Vichy in 1942 and was transferred to the Eastern Front where he was killed in action. He was replaced by SS-*Hstuf* Schmidt, whose work was not of the same high standard.

3. SS-*Ostuf* Gross at Biarritz.

Zschunke's other venture was hardly so successful. SS-*Ostuf* Gross (alias 'Grande') was sent as an ordinary civilian to Biarritz armed with a W/T set. He did not have Reiche's advantages of any kind of official cover. Gross was quite unsuccessful in his work, falling foul of the *Abwehr*, in the first instance his W/T set, of which the *Abwehr* had had no notification, being taken to be an enemy set, and secondly becoming involved in a drunken brawl, which led to his recall early in 1941.

4. Schellenberg's efforts to improve the work against France.

As explained in Paragraph 1 above, Schellenberg was not long in deciding that proper RSHA *Amt* VI work through the BdS in Paris was not to be hoped for, and his efforts were concentrated on finding single officers of suitable ability for work at outstations. The following officers were given special assignments:

a) SS-*Ostubaf* Schneider: was sent in the spring of 1942 to Strasbourg with the task of exploiting Corsicans circles. Schneider was a failure in his work and achieved nothing. He was eventually recalled in the autumn of 1943 and dismissed from the *Amt*.

b) SS-*Stubaf* Freise: the *Gruppenleiter* before Steimle was appointed at the end of 1942, did little to redeem his past failures. He was sent to Portugal in 1943 but was expelled before the end of the year. On Schneider's recall from Strasbourg, Freise went as replacement. Freise attempted liaison with the Paris *Dienststelle*, but only succeeded in arousing the jealousy and suspicion there. His work achieved nothing and he too was recalled in 1944 to be transferred eventually to RSHA *Amt* IV. His assistant, *Kriminalrat* Uhring, was arrested on the fall of Strasbourg.

c) SS-*Hstuf* Senner at Marseilles: was a more serious effort. Senner was sent under consular cover to Marseilles early in 1942. He succeeded in recruiting a network of some 20–30 agents, finding his material among the Groupe Collaboration. The Senner network covered the south of France and extended into Spain. The results achieved however were negligible owing to the very poor standard of agent available. Senner remained in Marseilles until the retreat, and after his return to Germany was sent to Milan to work with Gohl in the *Unternehmen* Bertram (see Paragraph 5, below).[1]

d) SS-*Stubaf* Fanelsa: at Metz is the last of the group. Fanelsa was a complete failure and it is only necessary to record his name.

5. *Unternehmen* Bertram and Tosca.

Senner returned to Germany from Marseilles in August 1944. He had not attempted any stay-behind network before the invasion. It was decided by Steimle to send Senner to Milan in order to operate against his former territory of Southern France from the Italian side of the border. Senner accordingly established himself at San Remo in October 1944 and made tentative plans to utilise subversive French groups for frontier-crossing operations into France. These efforts came to nothing; by the end of the year SS-*Stubaf* Gohl was sent to San Remo to become head of espionage activities against France and the enterprise now became the *Unternehmen* Bertram and Tosca. Senner's function was to organise the crossings into France either direct through Switzerland or by sea. The agents were sent to him from Berlin already briefed for their missions. The agents chiefly from the PPF groups. In all Senner had nine agents to despatch; the majority were arrested soon after reaching French territory, Senner himself surrendered to the French soon after the collapse.

E. Activities against the Low Countries.

1. Relations with RSHA *Amt* III.

The part played by RSHA *Gruppe* VI B in the Low Countries was a minor one throughout the five years of occupation. The chief factor was that the territory came under the control of RSHA *Amt* III as occupied territory and it was *Abteilung* III of the BdS both in Holland and in Belgium whose responsibility it was to submit reports on political trends and public opinion in the two countries. *Amt* VI activity was as a result very limited though some effort was made to use the Low Countries as a base for operations against the U.K. These efforts in the first three years of the occupation were very limited and quite futile, but in 1943 Steimle made some efforts at improvement, while the preparation of I-*Netze* in 1944 gave the *Stellen* in Brussels and The Hague a somewhat more important part to play.

2. BdS Brussels in 1940–42.

The early history of *Gruppe* VI B activities in Belgium can be very summarily dealt with. The original appointment to BdS Belgium was SS-*Hstuf* Löchelt who attempted nothing and achieved nothing. He was succeeded in 1941 by SS-*Hstuf* Baus whose activities were limited to employing minor agents to submit reports on France, a futile field in view of the existence of the large *Dienststelle* in Paris engaged on the same work. When Bernhard became *Referent* VI B2 in January 1943 the inefficiency of the work in the Low Countries caused him some concern; at that time Belgium and Holland in the *Gruppe* were dealt with by the *Referat* for France. Bernhard therefore decided to set up a new *Referat* dealing with Belgium and Holland with SS-*Hstuf* Lawrenz as *Referent*. To improve the work at the outstations he was instrumental in having recalled from the Eastern Front SS-*Ostuf* Zschunke, previously *Referent* for France, who had been sent there in disgrace at the end of 1941 after a quarrel with SS-*Stubaf* Rossner. Zschunke therefore was sent to Brussels in September 1942 to replace Baus.

3. Zschunke's Activities in Belgium.

Zschunke spent approximately one year in Brussels. His early work was largely concerned with clearing up the chaos left by Baus. Later some effort was made to recruit suitable agents for missions to England, but this ended in failure. An added impetus to such attempts however was given by a visit in May 1942 by Steimle, the new *Gruppenleiter*, who also recommended that efforts should be made to penetrate underground movements controlled from the U.K. with a view to obtaining information on the date of the Allied invasion. No success was achieved in these attempts. Zschunke was eventually sent once again to the Eastern Front in September 1942, having again brought disgrace upon himself, this time through having married a Belgian woman.[2]

4. Activities in Holland.

The story in Holland was even more dismal from the RSHA *Amt* VI point of view; in Holland the *Amt* III representative was especially strong and the original *Abteilung* VI representative, SS-*Hstuf* Müller, was *Abteilung* VI in title only. His work had been entirely controlled by SS-*Staf* Knolle, *Leiter* of *Abteilung* III, and until the middle of 1943 no *Amt* VI work of any kind was carried out in Holland. Müller eventually left the service altogether about mid-1943 and advantage was taken of his resignation by Bernhard in an attempt to set up an independent *Gruppe* VI B representative. The choice of officer however was not a happy one; SS-*Hstuf* Ahrens, previously employed in VI B3, from which department he was dismissed for inefficiency, was sent to Holland in November 1943 to set up his independent *Stelle*. Knolle however insisted on Ahrens working for him, and it was not until early 1944 that Ahrens finally established his independence.

5. Ahrens' work in Holland.

The task assigned to Ahrens was that of obtaining economic and political information about the U.K. and of establishing a stay-behind network in the event of invasion. He also had the job of organising line-crossing missions in the event of a partial occupation of Holland. In these tasks SS-*Hstuf* Hinckfuss assisted in the preparation of the I-*Netze*, and SS-*Ustuf* Egidy in the despatching of line-crossers. Ahrens was a complete failure. No information about the U.K. was obtained, three line-crossers were despatched without success, while the I-*Netze* failed completely. The latter subject is dealt with more fully in paragraph 6.

6. The I-*Netze* in Holland and Belgium.

The preparation of the I-*Netze* in the Low Countries was a combined operation between Hinckfuss, Ahrens and Lawrenz, who had replaced Zschunke on the latter's posting to the Eastern Front. W/T training was carried out in the Seehof School. The preparation was begun too late to stand any chance of success. By July 1944 eight links had been established in Belgium, but the network was almost immediately liquidated by the surrender of one of the main agents to the Allies soon after Belgium was occupied. In Holland six links were prepared, but no contacts were established after the liberation. The faults in the training of agents mentioned in connection with the I-*Netze* in France applied with equal force in the Low Countries.

7. *Leitstelle* Siegfried.

Side by side with the setting up of *Leitstelle* Walter in the South was the creation on very similar lines of *Leitstelle* Siegfried in the North. The *Stelle* had it headquarters at Marburg an der Lahn and was set up to provide agents for line-crossing and parachute operations against Holland, Belgium and North France. As in the South, the supply of agents was from the subversive groups—the Rexists, Flamands, the Degrelle organisation, etc. The *Leiter* of the *Stelle* was SS-*Stubaf* Wolff, with SS-*Hstuf* König and most of the personnel of BdS Belgium and Holland as staff. Zschunke, recalled from the East in March 1945, also joined the staff as the expert on Belgium. About 100 agents underwent training, of whom 30 were trained in W/T. The speed of the Allied advance however prevented the training being completed and *Leitstelle* Siegfried was disbanded before any operations had been undertaken.

8. Zschunke's last effort.

Zschunke together with the rest of the staff of *Leitstelle* Siegfried withdrew to the Munich area. With the approval of Bernhard, Zschunke suggested that he should return to Belgium posing as a D.P. [displaced person], and re-establish contact with his former agents in Belgium. The plan was successfully put into operation, and Zschunke returned to Brussels, where in June 1945 he made contact with one of his former W/T agents. The effort was however purely an individual one and was not symptomatic of any organised attempt by VI B to maintain post-defeat activity. In any case Zschunke's real motive was to get back to Belgium with his Belgian wife. Zschunke was arrested soon after his arrival.

Conclusion.

The history of *Referat* VI B2 is a long record of failure; with the exception of Reiche in Vichy, no sources of information were established which yielded any results of any value whatever. The reasons for the failure are many and are not peculiar to *Referat* VI B2 alone—incompetent officers, lack of coordination in policy, personal ambitions and jealousies, lack of cooperation with other RSHA *Ämter*, lack of security in training of agents. Much sound and fury which signified nothing.

Part IV

Referat VI B3 and its activities against Switzerland

A. The period under Jost.

1. SD activities against Switzerland before 1939.

The old SD-*Hauptamt*, *Abteilung* III/3, under Jost had met with some success in its work against the countries on Germany's eastern frontier prior to the setting up of the RSHA. There were good reasons why work in the East should have been more successful than in the West. In Austria, Czechoslovakia, and in the Polish Corridor there were very active German minorities and the constant stream of travellers crossing these frontiers provided a ready found source of information. In the West such favourable conditions did not exist except in the case of Switzerland and there only to a lesser degree. Nevertheless Switzerland represented the only country in Western Europe where the new RSHA *Amt* VI could build on the already existing work of the SD-*Abschnitte*. Operations against Switzerland had been directed from the SD-*Leitabschnitte* at Stuttgart, Karlsruhe, München and Innsbruck in close collaboration with the old SD-*Oberabschnitt Süd West* at Stuttgart under SS-*Hstuf* Dr Peter and his assistant, SS-*Hstuf* Gutekunst.

2. The First Efforts of RSHA *Amt* VI.

The work of the old SD-*Abschnitte* had of course its obvious limitations in that all the work was directed from outside Switzerland and not from inside the country itself. The extended scope of RSHA *Amt* VI as compared with the SD-*Hauptamt* required direct representation within the country itself. For this reason therefore Jost chose as his *Beauftragter* in Switzerland Dr Peter of Stuttgart who was duly installed under cover of the German Legation at Berne in early 1940. Dr Peter however did not long survive as Jost soon came up against a difficulty which not only hampered him but was to be one of the chief stumbling blocks facing Schellenberg in his strenuous efforts between 1942 and 1945—the reluctance on the part of the Swiss authorities to allow the SD to develop its activities within the country. Peter had to be recalled after only a few months. A similar fate befell SS-*Ostuf* Reiche in the German Consulate at Geneva. Reiche too was recalled at the request of the Swiss authorities. (This Reiche is identical with the Vichy representative mentioned in Part III, above). An attempt was made to install SS-*Hstuf* Gröbl as Reiche's successor, but this too met with no success. Gröbl was recalled and acted for a time as *Referent* for Switzerland before being sent in 1942 to Rome, where he was killed after the fall of Rome.

3. The Position by the end of 1941.

By the autumn of 1941 therefore Jost had failed in his attempts to establish a permanent respresentative in Switzerland. The failure was a partial one, as the SD-*Abschnitts* still continued their work from inside Germany, obtaining information on Switzerland itself from the many German and Swiss nationals travelling backwards and forwards between the two countries. The pro-Nazi Swiss elements were also exploited.

The partial failure was however a serious one, as the war situation by the end of 1941 was such that Switzerland was one of the very few remaining countries in Europe where contact could be made with British and American elements, and where much needed information on the U.K. and the U.S.A. could be obtained. By the end of the year Schellenberg had become *Amtschef* [replacing Jost], and the second phase began.

B. The Period under Schellenberg.

1. The Change of Policy.
Schellenberg was not slow to appreciate the potential value of Switzerland to RSHA *Amt* VI and its work; he fully realised the opportunities that neutral territory offered, and his conception of how Switzerland should be exploited led to a complete change in *Amt* VI policy regarding that country. Two essential changes were necessary. Firstly, to establish a permanent station within the country itself instead of operating from the outside, and secondly, to improve the standard of personnel in the *Amt* controlling operations against Switzerland. This meant that the officers operating from the SD-*Abschnitte* became available to the *Amt* where sweeping changes in personnel too place. The problem of installing an *Amt* VI officer in Switzerland was however not to easy to solve.

2. Daufeldt's appointment.
Schellenberg's choice was SS-*Ostubaf* Daufeldt. Daufeldt had a long record of service in the SD where he had operated under Jost in the old SD-*Hauptamt*. He had been for a period of two years *Gruppenleiter* of VI D where he had been in charge of operations against the U.K. and the U.S.A. It was presumably because of his knowledge of the U.K. where he had studied before the war and of his expertise in VI D that Schellenberg chose him for the important task to looking after *Amt* VI interests in Switzerland. The choice was however a bad one, as Daufeldt's record of success was not commensurable with his length of service. His work in VI D had been quite unsuccessful in face of considerable difficulties. But his failure in VI D was accountable not only by the difficulties he faced, but by his own incompetence. Daufeldt has been variously described as a playboy, a nincompoop, and a fool. The subsequent course of events in Switzerland largely revolves round the personality of Daufeldt.

3. Daufeldt's activities in Switzerland.
Daufeldt took up his appointment in the summer of 1942 as Vice Consul at Lausanne. His assignment was to establish contacts in Switzerland with a view to obtaining information on the Allies with particular reference to the sounding of Allied morale and the volume of economic trade between Switzerland and the Allies; further to assess the attitude of neutral countries towards the war, as well as that of the two German allies, Japan and Italy; to supervise diplomatic travel and to report on German emigres in Switzerland. Of these objectives the most important was of course the first, and that objective was one that would require direct contact with Allied circles in Switzerland. It was just such contact that Daufeldt was careful to avoid, as his first concern was to avoid expulsion from Switzerland, which too active operations might have entailed. Daufeldt's sources were therefore second rate, and such sources, together with the neutral press, formed the bulk of his reports, which reports were voluminous rather than

valuable. The position therefore by the beginning of 1943 was that Schellenberg had succeeded in establishing a permanent representative, but the representative was not taking full advantage of his position.

4. Further efforts to exploit Switzerland.

By the spring of 1943 the war situation was already turning against Germany and the opportunities for exploiting Switzerland were becoming correspondingly less favourable. RSHA *Amt* VI work was therefore intensified and further determined efforts were made by Schellenberg to improve the situation. SS-*Staf* Steimle, previously *Leiter* of the SD-*Abschnitt* Stuttgart, and therefore familiar with the Swiss situation, and now become *Gruppenleiter*, and its is significant that he appointed as his *Vertreter* SS-*Stubaf* Huegel, who at the same time fulfilled the function of *Referent* for Switzerland. Renewed activity developed along two lines.

Firstly Daufeldt himself was instructed to organise a post-occupational network over the frontier in France through which contact could be maintained with Switzerland. For this purpose he was to liaise with the BdS Paris and with Reiche's successor in Vichy, Dr Schmidt. These efforts came to nothing.

The main effort was of course an attempt to increase the number of *Amt* VI representatives within the country itself. In this attempt Schellenberg sought the cooperation of those Reich Ministries which had stations already established within the country with a view to exploiting the cover they afforded. The plan failed as the degree of cooperation between RSHA *Amt* VI and these Ministries—the Foreign Office, the Ministry of Economics, and the *Auslandsorganisation*—was never at any time very high. Relations with the Foreign Office in particular were far from harmonious. An added difficulty was the scarcity of suitable personnel. The general situation therefore by early 1944 had not improved; Daufeldt still remained the sole representative.

5. Developments in 1944.

The year 1944 brought fresh hope to Schellenberg, as two factors now operated in his favour. The *Abwehr* was aborbed in the spring, and as Schellenberg now had control over the *Mil Amt* as well as *Amt* VI, he envisaged the possibility of replacing *Abwehr* representatives already established within the country by RSHA *Amt* VI officers. The scheme however proved impracticable; *Amt* VI could not find the right material and the *Abwehr* was strongly opposed to the idea. Secondly, the changed situation in Italy where the *Führerbefehl* was no longer operative, made it possible to work against the country from the Italian side of the frontier. SS-*Stubaf* Huegel, the former *Referent*, had now become *Leiter* of the *Abteilung* VI of the BdS Italien, and was therefore familiar with the general situation.

Operations from Italy met with a limited amount of success under Huegel's direction, but only one of his agents was able to provide reports of any real value on economic matters. Indeed it was significant by this time that activities against

Switzerland were directed not so much with a view to obtaining information about the Allies, but in order to contact Allied authorities in Switzerland for the purpose of initiating unofficial peace discussions—a plan directed of course by Schellenberg and not reflecting the official German policy.

6. Daufeldt's expulsion and subsequent events.

The situation in Switzerland deteriorated rapidly with the changing war situation. By March 1945 the Swiss authorities had requested the removal of Daufeldt himself and *Amt* VI representation within the country itself ceased. There was however a replacement in the person of Graf Dönhof who was appointed to the Consulate in Zurich. Surprisingly enough, Dönhof's appointment was possible as a result of the benigh cooperation of the Foreign Office, an event which did not however reflect any closer cooperation between RSHA *Amt* VI and the Foreign Office, but which was due to Dönhof's own close personal friendship with Steengracht of the Foreign Office. Dönhof had had only a short period of training with VI D before his departure and was the officer responsible for the final mission of the notorious [British agent] Seth. It need hardly be said of course that this unexpected assistance from the Foreign Office was too late to be effective. Dönhof, who had in any case very little idea of what his functions were to be, was expelled soon after his arrival.

7. The *Sonderlinien.*

There remains one aspect of RSHA *Amt* VI work in Switzerland to be dealt with which is of importance, not so much for the results it achieved, but as a reflection of Schellenberg's conduct of *Amt* VI affairs. Schellenberg did not allow himself to be bound by recognised channels, and when the official reporting channels of *Amt* VI fell short of his standards, Schellenberg established where possible his own sources of information. These contacts have been referred to as his '*Sonderlinien*'. Such a link existed in Switzerland in the person of SS-*Hstuf* Eggen, and the establishing of the contact was a reflection on the inability of Daufeldt to produce the desired results. Eggen travelled frequently to Switzerland in the course of his business and was exploited by Schellenberg to establish contacts within the country; these contacts were on a high level and it was mainly through Eggen that Schellenberg maintained relations with the Swiss Intelligence Service. The extent to which this contact proved valuable to Schellenberg is still a matter of doubt but the mere contact itself was a considerable achievement. Eggen was also responsible for arranging Schellenberg's visits to Switzerland.

This method of penetrating Switzerland was also adopted by Steimle, the *Gruppenleiter* who attempted to exploit Dr Gardemann as a personal agent. Gardemann had previously been employed in the German Embassy in Madrid, where he had acted as a personal informer for Ribbentrop. Steimle's effort was however unsuccessful as it was not found possible to persude the Swiss authorities to allow Gardemann to enter the country.

The personal contact arrangement was further in evidence when Sonnenhol, a professional diplomat who had seen previous service in France, was sent to Switzerland late in 1944. Sonnenhol was not an *Amt* VI representative in the true sense of the term, but through a personal agreement with Steimle, provided the latter with excellent political reports on Switzerland. These in any case would have gone to the Foreign Office and were not the product of the Secret Service, but were symptomatic of the strained relations existing between the Foreign Office and RSHA *Amt* VI.

8. Conclusion.

It will be seen from the above review that RSHA *Amt* VI failed to exploit what should have been a fertile field. The failure was not due to any lack of appreciation on the part of Schellenberg regarding the importance of Switzerland as a field of operations, but due to the difficulties which faced him in his efforts to improve the situation. There was of course the general difficulty of finding suitable personnel; had Daufeldt been more competent or more enthusiastic the story might have been different. But there was no way of remedying this original mistake, as the subsequent difficulties proved insuperable—lack of cooperation from the Foreign Office and other ministries, the opposition of the *Abwehr* even after it had been absorbed, and, also of importance, the attitude of the Swiss authorities to any attempted development of SD espionage, especially when the general war situation from 1943 onwards turned against Germany.

Part V

Referat VI B4 and its Activities
in the Iberian Peninsula

(Note: Part V of this report must not be considered in any way as a liquidation report. The *Amt* VI representatives in Spain and Portugal have not yet been expelled from those countries so that it is not possible to assess with any accuracy the success which attended *Referat* VI B4 and its work in the Iberian Peninsula. The following review therefore necessarily contains many gaps and inevitably several inaccuracies, which gaps and inaccuracies can only be remedied when some of the leading personalities in the Peninsula have been repatriated and interrogated. It is for this reason that this publication has been issued as a situation report only, though the first four Parts can be treated as Liquidation Reports.)

A. General.

1. The importance of the Peninsula.

The importance of neutral territory to RSHA *Amt* VI work in Western Europe has already been mentioned in dealing with *Referat* VI B3 and Switzerland. This importance was considerably greater in the case of the Iberian Peninsula. Switzerland, though neutral, was surrounded by countries entirely under German domination; further, Switzerland attempted to maintain strict neutrality and was not disposed to grant any special facilities to Germany. In both these aspects the Peninsula offered much greater facilities; it had a seaboard, and the number of contacts which could be established with the outer world was thereby greatly increased. Moreover, agents earmarked for despatch to enemy territory, or to other neutral territories abroad, could be sent through Spain, while actual entry into Spain had been greatly facilitated after the French armistice, when German occupied France and Spain had a common frontier of a few miles near the Atlantic coast. Spain also offered an important observation post in the western Mediterranean, and a base for operations against North Africa in view of the Führerbefehl operative in Italy. Secondly, unlike Switzerland, Spain, though a neutral country, was closely bound to Germany, and its exploitation thereby considerably facilitated.

Spain therefore occupied a unique position among the neutral countries in the war as Sweden, the only remaining neutral country in Europe apart from Switzerland (and of course, Eire) was greatly restricted in its communications with the outside world, and in any case it normal volume of trade did not cover the same wide field as that covered by the Iberian Peninsula. It is not surprising therefore that Spain became the cockpit of espionage in the course of the war, and the fruits would fall to that country able to exploit its possibilities to the best advantage. It is hardly necessary to point out that this advantage lay very heavily on the German side; but even then the course of RSHA *Amt* VI activity in the Iberian Peninsula, especially in the initial stages, was not altogether smooth.

2. The *Polizei Attaché*.

The roots of German activity in Spain go back to the Spanish Civil War. The Condor Legion which took part in that campaign contained elements of the GFP [*Geheime Feldpolizei*], and several of the subsequent *Amt* VI representatives in Spain had seen service with the Condor Legion, a typical example being SS-*Stubaf* Mosig. Jost during his period of service as *Leiter* of *Abteilung* III/3 of the SD-*Hauptamt* had paid official visits to Spain in 1938 to foster liaison between the Spanish and German police services, and it was under this liaison that RSHA *Amt* VI developed its first penetration of the Peninsula. The facilities afforded however were not entirely favourable to *Amt* VI. The best cover would of course have been through the Foreign Office, but that department was throughout hostile to *Amt* VI activities in Spain, as elsewhere. It was therefore *Amt* VI which held chief sway in Spain through the powerful position of the *Polizei Attaché*, who, though not officially acting as an *Amt* VI representative abroad, was in fact recruited from RSHA *Amt* IV, as were most of his staff. In Spain the *Polizei Attaché* from 1939 until late 1944 was *Kriminalrat* Winzer.

The position of Winzer in Spain was especially strong; he had been attached to the German Embassy in Madrid as early as 1936-37, and returned to the capital in 1939 where he enjoyed the special support of Heydrich himself. He remained throughout a special protégé of Müller, RSHA *Amtschef* IV, as Müller regarded the *Polizei Attachés* as an extension of his functions into foreign territory. Winzer was on very good terms with the Spanish police and with the Falange, and in the circumstances was not likely to welcome any activity on the part of the new RSHA *Amt* VI into territory over which he ruled in the interests of the RSHA. Winzer was killed in an air crash over French territory in September 1944 and was replaced by *Kriminalkommissar* Hammes, who had until then worked in Barcelona as an *Amt* VI representative under Winzer.

3. The complexity of RSHA *Amt* VI activities.

The pattern of *Amt* VI activities in Spain differs from that in other countries because of its comparative complexity. There was latterly no single *Amt* VI station through which *Amt* VI conducted its affairs. As explained Paragraph 2, the *Polizei Attaché* remained the chief RSHA representative in Spain and the *Amt* VI official representation functioned under his control. This system had disadvantages for *Amt* VI, and in 1943 Mosig was sent under camouflaged cover in the Sofindus firm so as to work independently of the *Polizei Attaché*—the Grille organisation. Thirdly, the '*Sonderlinien*' of Schellenberg operated in Spain as in Switzerland (see Part IV, Paragraph 7) in the persons of von Hohenlohe and Gräfin Podewils. Finally, SS-*Oberführer* Bernhardt, the most important figure in Spain for *Amt* VI, was neither an *Amt* VI officer nor agent but worked both for *Amt* VI and the *Abwehr*, and his activities covered economic as well as intelligence spheres. These separate developments were of course a gradual evolution.

B. The Jost Period (1939–41).

1. Plath in 1939–40.

While the German Intelligence Services (GIS) started with an enormous initial advantage in Spain, this was not true of RSHA *Amt* VI, which entered too late into the field. In Spain, as in other countries, the same difficulties were encountered. The Foreign Office was resentful and unsympathetic, the *Abwehr* suspicious and uncooperative, while an added complication was the strength of the *Polizei Attaché*, Winzer, who considered himself the sole representative of the RSHA and covering the interests of the SD. The general weakness of Jost and the poor quality of his

Beauftragter were not likely to triumph over such difficulties, and the first period of RSHA *Amt* VI activities was, as elsewhere, a failure.

Jost's first appointments to the Iberian Peninsula were SS-*Hstuf* Plath to Spain and SS-*Hstuf* Fast to Portugal. Plath took up his appointment in Madrid shortly before the outbreak of war, where he soon came into conflict with Winzer, who insisted that Plath could only work under him and submit his reports through him. This early did the *Polizei Attaché* impose his ascendancy over *Amt* VI, an ascendancy which was maintained nominally until the end. Plath was a failure and was recalled in the spring of 1940 before being sent to the Eastern Front (in company with Zschunke of VI B2), where he was killed in action. Plath was in turn succeeded by SS-*Hstuf* Pfisterer, who remained a short spell before being transferred to RSHA VI F. Pfisterer was replaced in 1941 by SS-*Ostuf* Singer who remained until the end.

C. The Schellenberg Period (1942–45).

1. Changes of personnel in the *Amt*.

It was with the advent of Schellenberg that RSHA *Amt* VI activities in Spain and Portugal developed along vigorous lines. The importance of the Peninsula was not lost on Schellenberg and his changes involved both the *Referat* and the representatives in the countries themselves. The changes in personnel in the *Amt* were not of course confined to the Spanish *Referat*; Schellenberg's general policy was to introduce into RSHA *Amt* VI some of the officers with whom he had been connected in RSHA *Amt* IV. Among these were SS-*Stubaf* Mosig, who served for a spell as *Referent* for Spain before going there in September 1943 on a special assignment. He had replaced SS-*Ostuf* Keinert, and on his departure to Spain was in turn replaced for a short spell by SS-*Ostuf* Neubourg. Neubourg was succeeded by SS-*Stubaf* Fendler who remained as *Referent* until the final collapse.

2. SS-*Oberführer* Bernhard and Sofindus.

Side by side with these changes within the *Amt* itself was Schellenberg's intensified direction of activity within Spain itself. The most important development was his relationship with SS-*Oberführer* Bernhard. Bernhard was a prominent shipyard owner in Germany who lost most of his money in the early 1930s. Later he established contact with Franco in Morocco and acted as intermediary between Franco and Göring regarding the provision of transport planes for Franco's troops. Thanks to this early and invaluable service to Franco, Bernhard subsequently became the most influential German contact between the German government and Franco's government, and personally enriched himself as head of the Sofindus firm. This firm represented the controlling agency of all German economic interests in Spain, arranging in particular for the import to Germany of valuable raw materials such as wolfram and tungsten. The facilities for espionage offered by Sofindus were obvious, and the firm was exploited both by the *Abwehr* and by the SD. It was only with the advent of Schellenberg as RSHA *Amtschef* VI, however, that VI B exploited Sofindus to any extent.

The relationship between Bernhard and Schellenberg has been reported as a close and personal one though this has not been confirmed; in any case it is certain that Bernhard extended the facilities offered by Sofindus to RSHA *Amt* VI, whether on a personal or official basis. Bernhard's personal contacts were of course invaluable. It was through Bernhard that contact was established with Suner, Franco's Minister for Foreign Affairs until 1943. Suner was a most important source on the political trends of the Franco government itself. Other valuable high-level contacts established through Bernhard were Carcellar, the Spanish Minister of Economy, Bau, the former Minister of Commerce and Shipping, and Munos Grandez, Franco's adjutant and former commander of the Blue Division. Another good source of information, though to a great extent an unwitting one, was General Aranda, the leader of the Spanish opposition party. Bernhard covered of course a very wide field in intelligence and economics and Schellenberg soon realised that Sofindus offered better scope for *Amt* VI work than did the official representative who was subordinated to the *Polizei Attaché*, SS-*Ostuf* Singer.

3. Singer in Madrid.

Plath had been eventually replaced by the permanent representative, SS-*Ostuf* Singer, probably by the end of 1941. Singer's connections in Spain had gone as far back as the Civil War, when he had been a member of the Condor Legion. He took up his appointment as a member of the German Consulate in Madrid where he was attached to the *Polizei Attaché*, Winzer, but the hold of Winzer over Singer was however not so strong as it had been over Plath. Singer was responsible to Winzer on matters of discipline only and his reports were sent direct to the *Amt*. Singer's assignment was to maintain contact with those members of the Spanish police and the Spanish Foreign Office with whom contact had been established by RSHA *Amt* VI, while he likewise acted as paymaster and communications officer for *Amt* VI agents in Spain.

Singer has as his assistant SS-*Hstuf* Krüger, who acted independently and was responsible for recruiting and running the important agent, Schwarz von Berg, who specialised in Spanish military circles. Singer in his capacity was able to make contact with minor officials in the Spanish Foreign Office from whom details of records in the Spanish Foreign Office were obtained. These records contained accounts of visits from foreign representatives.

He also succeeded in contacting the Spanish police and the Spanish Military Intelligence Service.

4. Mosig's appointment—The Grille Organisation.

The disadvantage in Singer's work from the point of view of Schellenberg was his continued subordination to Winzer. The position in the first place was too open, and secondly *Amt* VI activities were by the nature of things known to the *Polizei Attaché*. In order to circumvent these two difficulties, and at the same time to exploit more fully the facilities afforded by Bernhard and his Sofindus organisation, Schellenberg sent Mosig in September 1943 on a special assignment to Spain. Mosig together with three or four agents recruited from the Lehr-Regiment Kürfürst set up their organisation in Madrid known as the 'Organisation Grille', having its own W/T station controlled by Mosig's secretary, *Fräulein* Brückner.

The special assignment given to the Organisation Grille was the exploitation of the Sofindus firm in social and commercial circles, and further to maintain the contacts initiated by Bernhard, and enumerated in Paragraph 2 above. Mosig's subordinates in this work were Lackner, Holting, Ewald Kruse, Hans Weiss, Erich Dietel, Paul Anger, and Franz Staudinger, all with appointments in various branches of the Sofindus organisation. In this way RSHA *Amt* VI was able to operate independently of Winzer.

5. Schellenberg's *Sonderlinien* in Spain.

The third line of development in RSHA *Amt* VI activities in Spain was through Schellenberg's personal '*Sonderlinien*'. These were two in number, Prinz von Hohenlohe and Gräfin Podewils. Hohenlohe was an influential businessman in Spain with extensive and excellent contacts in Spanish social circles. His reports, which were passed to Schellenberg via Singer, represent his own summary of political trends in Spain based on his contacts in political, business or military circles. Gräfin Podewils also had good social connections and was friendly with Suner. Her reports dealt with the results of her conversations with representatives of foreign missions in Spain.

6. Developments in 1944.

By 1944 the change in the general war situation enabled the Allies to bring pressure to bear on the Spanish government regarding the expulsion of German nationals known to be carrying on espionage activities in the country. Owing to the influence of Bernhard only a few minor personalities were expelled, but it became apparent to Schellenberg that provisions would have to be made to meet a threatening situation. Attempts were made therefore to send more RSHA *Amt* VI officers to the Peninsula in case Allied pressure on the Spanish government should become effective. It is uncertain whether in fact any new replacements were sent though it is known that Gumprecht, who joined VI B4 later in 1944 did go to Spain soon afterwards; he returned however after a short stay. It is believed that Gumprecht returned however to Spain early in 1945 in company with SS-*Hstuf* Krüger, Singer's assistant, and a certain SS-*Hstuf* Schumann who is otherwise unknown.

7. The I-*Netze* in Spain and Portugal.

Arrangements were likewise made in 1944 for the organisation of I-*Netze* in Spain and Portugal. Spain offered of course favourable conditions through the Sofindus organisation especially in the transfer of sufficient funds to maintain the I-*Netze* for some time. Arrangements were left to Mosig, but details of his work in this connection are still unknown. In Portugal, Vollbrecht and Nassenstein failed to achieve any results, though the latter is thought to have succeeded in penetrating a Brazilian firm for the purpose. Both in Spain and Portugal, however, one overriding consideration prevailed; the I-*Netze* had been planned on the assumption that some form of central authority would remain functioning in Germany itself, and as this condition was nullified by the German collapse, the I-*Netze*, even if they were successfully organised, were organised to little purpose.

Probably connected with the organisation of the I-*Netze* was the mission entrusted in the autumn of 1944 to a certain Meyer, who had previously been the W/T technician for RSHA *Amt* VI in Tangiers. Meyer was sent under cover of the *Allgemeine Elektrische Gesellschaft* to recruit Spanish born W/T operators. The network was meant to operate in the event of a diplomatic break between Spain and the Allies or when Allied pressure succeed in having German representatives expelled from Spain. It is not thought however that Meyer met with any success in his mission as it was undertaken at too late a date. Gumprecht too, who has been mentioned in Paragraph 6 above, had been given the assignment of recruiting some fifty Spaniards from a Spanish camp in the Tyrol, who were meant to be sent to Spain as intelligence agents. The agents were in fact recruited, but training was not undertaken owing to the speed of the Allied advance. The selected agents were assigned in the end to fighting units.

D. Other RSHA *Amt* VI activities in Spain.

1. Arnold in Madrid.

Karl Arnold worked independently in Madrid through Singer. Although stationed in the Peninsula, Arnold was in fact a RSHA *Amt* VI D representative and operated on behalf of that *Gruppe* in the organisation of a courier service to South America. His activities together with those of Maywald, also a VI D representative, are dealt with in the War Room Publication on *Gruppe* VI D.

2. Activities in Tangiers.

Early activity against Tangiers had come under the control of SS-*Hstuf* Schmuck alias Schmiedow, who was attached to the German Consulate in Tetouan[4] in 1940. Schmuck's special assignment was to submit reports on public opinion in French Morocco, for which purpose his chief agent was the notorious John Dollar. Schmuck remained in Tangiers until January 1942 when he returned to Germany, being eventually sent to Portugal in February 1944 to work under Schröder. Subsequent activity in Tangiers were under the control of SS-*Ustuf* Schulze with his assistant, *Kriminal Assistent* Seidel. Schulze established contact with the Arab nationalist leader, Yassani, from whose entourage he claimed to have recruited some fifty agents for operations in Spanish Morocco. Schulze made extravagant claims regarding his operations, and when the Consulate in Tangiers was closed in May 1944, he had great difficulty in explaining away the large amounts of money which had been expended by him for so little results. He was eventually dismissed from the *Amt* and later worked for the DNB. His assistant, Seidel, was expelled at the same time from Tangiers and later worked in Seville.

The exploitation of French North Africa after the Tangiers expulsion devolved on the newly formed RSHA *Amt* VI B4 (Parseval).

3. Döhring and *Unternehmen* Parseval.
Döhring has already been referred to under VI B2 in his capacity as a member of the *Dienststelle* of BdS Frankreich. In Paris, Döhring had specialised in French North Africa, a subject of which Nosek too had shown considerable interest. During his period of service in France Döhring had made several visits to Spain with a view to establishing a channel through Spain for the despatch of agents into French Morocco. His plans for a network however were cut short by the invasion, and after the retreat from France, *Referat* VI B4 (Parseval) was formed with Döhring as *Referent*, and having as his assistants SS-*Ostuf* Wiedemann, SS-*Oschaf* Schnell and Hans Seidel, referred to in Paragraph 2 above. Details of enterprises undertaken by Parseval are still lacking. In the early part of 1945 however Döhring was attached to *Leitstelle* Walter (Part III, C, Paragraph 7 above).

4. Miscellaneous Representatives.
SS-*Ostuf* Kallab had the important assignment of acting as VI B4 representative at Hendaye on the Franco–Spanish frontier, where he carried out his work under cover of the Sofindus organisation. Kallab's function was to facilitate the passage of VI B agents from France into Spain, as well as documents and equipment which could not be sent openly to the country. He was assisted in this type of work by Paul Anger who specialised in the smuggling of important material such as tungsten out of Spain.

E. Activities in Portugal.

1. The main representatives.
Information on RSHA *Amt* VI activities in Portugal is even less complete than that on its activities in Spain. Jost's first representative in Portugal was SS-*Ostuf* Fast who is almost certainly identical with Waldemar Fast, the RSHA *Amt* VI C representative in Turkey, at present under arrest. Fast was replaced in 1941 for a

short spell by SS-*Ostuf* Schönbeck who had previously been *Amt* VI representative in Finland. Latterly under Schellenberg the two *Amt* VI representatives were SS-*Stubaf* Nassenstein and SS-*Stubaf* Vollbrecht.

2. *Polizeiverbindungsführer* and RSHA *Amt* VI.
The general situation in Portugal differed from that in Spain in two respects. Firstly there was no *Polizei Attaché* as SS-*Stubaf* Schröder, who took up his appointment in Portugal in October 1941, was only recognised as a *Polizeiverbindungsführer*. His position was not so strong as that of Winzer in Spain, but nevertheless his relations with *Amt* VI representatives were never cordial. Secondly the general attitude of the Portuguese government was not so well disposed towards Germany as that of the Spanish government.

3. Later RSHA *Amt* VI representatives.
During the period 1942–43 Kurt Förster has acted in the interests of *Amt* VI, but was expelled in March 1943 as a result of an unfortunate attempt at recruitment of an agent which ended in failure. Förster was replaced by Vollbrecht, who remained in Portugal from August 1943 onwards.

Nassenstein acted in the dual capacity of VI B4 and VI D representative as his duties involved specialisation on South American matters. It is not possible on available evidence to assess the work of Vollbrecht and Nassenstein: it is significant however that Schellenberg considers both as complete failures in their work.

Part IV

Miscellaneous

A. General Summary.

In assessing the work of RSHA *Gruppe* VI B in the six years of its history it should be remembered that it is more than a little inaccurate to say that RSHA *Amt* VI evolved out of the old SD-*Hauptamt* III/3. The extension of SD activity from security operations to offensive operations and from the domestic to the foreign field was in fact a step which broke new grounds. It was really only in Eastern Europe that the old SD-*Hauptamt* laid any good foundations for the work of the new RSHA *Amt* VI. *Gruppe* VI B, there, dealing with Western Europe, was faced with a difficult task, as only in the case of Switzerland was there any previous SD work which it could further exploit. For the *Gruppe* to have been successful therefore in its initial stages it would have required both energetic direction from the RSHA *Amtschef* combined with sympathetic cooperation from other organisations. Neither of their conditions were in fact fulfilled in the first two years of RSHA *Amt* VI activities in the west. Generally speaking therefore *Gruppe* VI B did not succeed in overcoming the difficulties with which it was faced. It failed almost dismally in France, Holland and Belgium: it did not achieve the success if might have done in the case of Switzerland, while Italy represented a case of lost opportunity, but for reasons not attributable to the *Gruppe* itself. But the failures in these countries were due not only to the opposition of other *Ämter* in the RSHA, to the hostility of the Foreign Office, nor to the lack of cooperation with the *Abwehr*, but also to the inefficiency and lack of imagination on the part of most of the leading personnel in the *Gruppe*. The results achieved were meagre in comparison with the effort expended. Only in the case of the Iberian Peninsula is it likely that the final assessment will reflect favourably on the work of the *Gruppe* VI B, and while the final assessment is not yet possible in this connection, it would not seem that RSHA *Amt* VI took full advantage of the very favourable circumstances which existed in Spain.

B. Post-war arrests.

Apart from Spain and Portugal, from which countries RSHA *Amt* VI representatives have not yet been expelled, the situation regarding arrests of personnel of RSHA *Gruppe* VI B can be considered as very satisfactory. The arrested personnel are shown in Appendix VII, and it is not likely that further interrogations will add much that is useful to the general picture of *Gruppe* VI B activities in France, Holland, Belgium and Italy. In the case of Switzerland the details are still lacking regarding the sources used by Daufeldt, but his final interrogation report should complete this gap.

Main Sources for the information in this report.

a) On the general work of the *Gruppe*:
    SS-*Brif* Schellenberg   RSHA *Amtschef* VI
    SS-*Stubaf* Huegel   *Referent*, VI B3

b) *Referat* VI B1:
    SS-*Stubaf* Huegel   BdS Italy, Abt VI
    SS-*Ostubaf* Kappler   *Polizei Attache* Rome
    SS-*Stubaf* Höttl   *Abt* VI E
    Otto Lechner   Secretary to Kappler
c) *Referat* VI B2:
    SS-*Ostubaf* Bernhard   *Referat*, VI B2
    SS-*Hstuf* Zschunke   *Abt* VI B2

	SS-*Hstuf* Ahrens	BdS Holland, *Abt* VI
	SS-*Hstuf* Senner	*Abt* VI B2
	SS-*Hschaf* Zuang	*Abt* VI B2

d) *Referat* VI B3:

	SS-*Stubaf* Huegel	*Referent*, VI B3
	SS-*Stubaf* Daufeldt	VI Representative in Switzerland

e) Referat VI B4:

	SS-*Ostuf* Neuburg	*Abt* VI B3
	John Dollar	*Abt* VI B4 agent

This report was issued by W.R.C.3a on 17 October 1945.

Appendix I

Chart of Distribution of Work in RSHA *Amt* VI from 1939–1945

		1939–1940	Early 1941	Mid 1941–42	1942–1944	1944–1945
VI A		Administration etc.	General Intelligence Tasks Abroad (? Sections)	Administration etc.	Administration etc.	Administration etc.
VI B		Technical Section	Europe Africa Near East (10 sections)	Slovakia Hungary Roumania Jugoslavia Greece Turkey Iraq, Iran Afghanistan	France Low Countries Switzerland Spain Portugal	France Low Countries Switzerland Spain Portugal Italy (from 1944)
VI C		Russia Baltic States Far East	Russia Far East (11 sections)	Russia Japan China Finland Baltic States	Russia Near East Far East (13 sections)	Russia Near East Far East (4 sections by mid 1944
VI D		Hungary Slovakia Jugoslavia Roumania Bulgaria Greece Turkey	Anglo-American sphere (9 sections)	Gt. Britain British Empire USA S. America Sweden Norway Denmark	Anglo-American sphere (3 sections)	Anglo-American sphere & Scandinavia (from summer 1944)

VI E	Italy Spain Portugal Central & Southern America	Ideological Enemies abroad (6 sections) (previously VI H)	France Low Countries Spain Portugal Italy Switzerland	Central- Europe Balkans Italy Scandinavia	Balkans
VI F	France Low Countries Switzerland Luxemburg	Technical Section	Technical Section	Technical Section	Technical Section
VI G	Gt. Britain British Empire USA Norway	-	Ideological Enemies abroad	Research (from August 1944)	Research
VI H	Ideological Enemies abroad	-	-	-	-

Appendix II

Gruppe VI B personnel at RSHA

<u>Note:</u> The location and function of personnel as given in these Appendices is roughly as at 1st January 1945. Several formations however which disappeared before then have been included owing to their importance; e.g. *Abt* VI BdS Frankreich. As a result some personalities may appear twice under different formations. Arrested personnel are underlined.

Gruppenleiter	SS-*Staf* Steimle
Vertreter	SS-*Stubaf* Reichle

<u>*Referat* VI B1 (Italian *Referat*)</u>

Referent	*Oberleutnant* Hohmann
	Oberleutnant Hansen
	SS-*Ostuf* John
	SS-*Ustuf* Möller
	Krim.Assistent Brinkmann
VI B1 (Vatican)	SS-*Hstuf* <u>Reissmann</u> (dead)

<u>*Referat* VI B2 (France and Low Countries</u>

Referent	SS-*Ostubaf* <u>Bernhard</u>
	SS-*Hstuf* Ernst

SS-*Hstuf* Martschke (1944)

SS-*Hstuf* Zschunke (Belgium)

SS-*Hstuf* Haux

SS-*Ostuf* Vernunft

SS-*Ustuf* Crome (1943)

SS-*Ustuf* Tengler

SS-*Ustuf* Schöffler

SS-*Ustuf* Börde

SS-*Hschaf* Meinel

SS-*Hschaf* Richter

SS-*Uschaf* Hübner

Angestellter Mahlis

Angestellter Gerspack

Referat VI B3 (Switzerland)

Referent   *Oberleutnant* Hohmann

SS-*Hstuf* Raden

SS-*Hstuf* Wurdig (1943)

SS-*Ostuf* Felfe

SS-*Ostuf* Urbanek

Krim.Ob.Assistent Pörschke

Angestellter Krohne

Angestellter Lappe

Referat VI B4 (Spain and Portugal)

Referent   SS-*Stubaf* Fendler

SS-*Hstuf* Baus (1943)

SS-*Hstuf* Langbehn (1943)

SS-*Hstuf* Alisch

SS-*Ostuf* Wiedemann

SS-*Ostuf* Engemann

SS-*Ostuf* Dr Neubourg

SS-*Ostuf* Wulffen

SS-*Hschaf* Seitz

SS-*Oschaf* Volt

SS-*Stuschaf* Speck

Dr Schaarschmidt

Angestellter Prauser

Angestellter Gumprecht

Angestellter Rottmann

Angestellter Godefroy
Angestellter Metzger
Angestellter Benz

Referat VI B4 (*Unternehmen* Parseval)
    SS-*Hstuf* Döhring
    SS-*Hstuf* Wenkhausen

Appendix III

Referat VI B1 personnel at Outstations

BdS Italy	SS-*Stubaf* Huegel
	SS-*Hstuf* Schönpflug
	SS-*Ostuf* Ried
	SS-*Ustuf* Didinger
	SS-*Ustuf* Maier
	SS-*Ustuf* Bandorf
	SS-*Ustuf* Lechner
	SS-*Oschaf* Giffey
	SS-*Hschaf* Müller
	Fräulein Wentzky
	Fräulein Weilbacher
Einheit Ida (in Italy)	SS-*Stubaf* Hass
	SS-*Ostuf* Schubernig
	SS-*Oschaf* Ebner
	SS-*Hschaf* Agostini
	SS-*Hschaf* Gasteiner
	SS-*Schaf* Böhm
	SS-*Schaf* Dapra
	SS-*Schaf* Ringold
Aussenkommando Bologna	SS-*Ostuf* Ernst Müller
Aussenkommando Merano	SS-*Ustuf* Zirnbaumer
Aussenkommando Milan	SS-*Ostuf* Zimmer

Aussenkommando Genoa	SS-*Ustuf* Michelsen
Aussenkommando San Remo	SS-*Rotf* Schoffreger
Aussenkommando Rome	SS-*Hstuf* Gröbl (1942) (dead)
	SS-*Stubaf* Looss
BdS Adriatic Coast (Trieste)	SS-*Ustuf* Wolff

Appendix IV

Referat VI B2 personnel at Outstations

BdS Paris (1944)

SS-*Stubaf* Hagen (1942)	SS-*Ustuf* Bourjeau
SS-*Stubaf* Bickler	SS-*Ustuf* Reissmann
SS-*Stubaf* Nosek	SS-*Ustuf* Wild
SS-*Stubaf* Lang	SS-*Ustuf* Gerhard Preil
SS-*Hstuf* Detering	SS-*Ustuf* Hermann Dobritzsch
SS-*Hstuf* Alisch	SS-*Ustuf* Rahe
SS-*Hstuf* Zuchristian	SS-*Ustuf* Zach
SS-*Hstuf* Gutekunst	SS-*Oschaf* Müller
SS-*Hstuf* Kunze	SS-*Oschaf* Schnell
SS-*Hstuf* König	SS-Hschaf Zuang
SS-*Ostuf* Gerardin	*Sonderführer* Kley
SS-*Ostuf* Loba	Dr Keller
SS-*Ostuf* Schmidt	*Angestellter* Völker

BdS Brussels

SS-*Hstuf* Zschunke (1942)	SS-*Ustuf* Eckert (1943)
SS-*Hstuf* Lawrenz	SS-*Ustuf* Alliger (1942)
SS-*Hstuf* Baus (1942)	SS-*Ustuf* Polonyi (1942)
SS-*Hstuf* Löchelt (1941)	SS-*Oschaf* Henze
SS-*Ustuf* Kratz	

BdS Holland (The Hague)

SS-*Hstuf* Ahrens	SS-*Ustuf* Egidy
SS-*Hstuf* Hinckfuss	SS-*Ustuf* Jarl
SS-*Hstuf* Felfe	SS-*Uschaf* Asbach (W/T)
SS-*Hstuf* Müller	SS-*Stuschaf* Ulbrich

KdS Vichy
>SS-*Hstuf* Reiche (1942) (dead)   SS-*Hstuf* Schmid (1944)

KdS Metz
>SS-*Stubaf* Fanelsa

BdS Strasbourg
>SS-*Stubaf* Freise   *Kriminalrat* Uhring
>SS-*Stubaf* Schneider

KdS Marseilles
>SS-*Hstuf* Senner

Unternehmen Bertram and Tosca
>SS-*Stubaf* Gohl   SS-*Hstuf* Senner
>SS-*Hstuf* Werner Neisser

Leitstelle Walter
>SS-*Staf* Bickler (and staff of BdS Paris above)
>SS-*Stubaf* Hubig   SS-*Ostuf* Moritz
>SS-*Hstuf* Wenger   SS-*Ostuf* Eschelböck
>SS-*Ostuf* Hermann   SS-*Ustuf* Westenberger
>SS-*Ostuf* Moro   Odendahl (W/T)

Leitstelle Siegfried
>SS-*Stubaf* Wolff   SS-Stuschaf Katzbach
>SS-*Hstuf* Lawrenz   SS-*Stuschaf* Schütz
>SS-*Ostuf* Einfeld   SS-*Uschaf* Krohne
>SS-*Ostuf* Franke   SS-*Uschaf* Pollmann
>SS-*Hschaf* Baake   *Angestellter* Völker
>SS-*Hschaf* Vierck

Appendix V

Referat VI B3 personnel at Outstations

Representatives in Switzerland
>SS-*Ostubaf* Daufeldt
>*Graf* Dönhof
>Adolf Sonnenhol (Consular staff)

<u>Representatives in SD-*Stellen* working against Switzerland</u>

SD Stuttgart	SS-*Ostuf* Bauer (1944)	
	SS-*Hstuf* Onuszeit	
	SS-*Ustuf* Ehmann	
	SS-*Oschaf* Eisele	
	Dr Hess	
	SD-*Aussenstelle* Lörrach	SS-*Ustuf* Becker
SD-*Ast* Mühlhausen	SS-*Stubaf* <u>Blecher</u> (suicide)	
SD-*Ast* Friedrichshafen	SS-*Hstuf* Buchele	
SD-*Leitabschnitt* Munich	SS-*Ostuf* Dauser	
	SS-*Ustuf* Hierl	
SD-*Ast* Waldshut	SS-*Ostuf* Kemmet	
SD-*Leitabschnitt* Karlsruhe	SS-*Ostuf* Wandhoff	

<u>Miscellaneous</u>

Schellenberg's personal agent	SS-*Stubaf* Eggen
Steimle's personal agent	Dr Gardemann

Appendix VI

Referat VI B4 personnel at Outstations

<u>Representatives in Spain</u>

(a) <u>Subordinated to *Polizei Attache* Winzer:</u>

      SS-*Ostuf* Singer

      SS-*Hstuf* Krüger

      SS-*Ustuf* Kulas

      SS-*Hstuf* Arnold (for *Referat* VI D4)

(b) <u>The Grille Organisation under cover of SS-*Oberführer* Bernhard:</u>

      SS-*Stubaf* Mosig

      Fritz Lackner

      Fräulein Brückner

      SS-*Hschaf* Holting (W/T)

      Ewald Kruse (Pieles Fur Company, Madrid)

      Hans Weiss (Pieles Fur Company, Madrid)

      Erich Dietel (Sofindus, Madrid)

      Paul Anger (Marion Transport Company, Madrid)

Franz Staudinger (Minerales Mining Company, Madrid)

SS-*Ostuf* Kallab (Sofindus, Hendaye)

(c) Representatives in Tangiers:

SS-*Hstuf* Schmuck (Tangiers, 1940–41)

SS-*Ustuf* Schultze (Tangiers until May 1944)

Hans Seidel (Tangiers until May 1944)

SS-*Oschaf* Lechner

Representatives in Portugal

SS-*Ostubaf* Schröder (Polizeiverbindungsführer)

SS-*Ostubaf* Nassenstein

SS-*Stubaf* Vollbrecht

Kurt Förster (until March 1943)

Sumbeck

SS-*Ostuf* Fast (1939–40)

SS-Hstuf Schmuck (previously Tangiers)

Representative at SD-*Leitabschnitt* Munich

SS-*Hstuf* Schwarz

Appendix VII

Alphabetical list of
RSHA *Gruppe* VI B personnel

(Post-war arrested peronnel are underlined)

Rank and Name	Referat	Remarks
SS-*Hschaf* Manfred Agostini	VI B1	*Einheit* Ida, Italy
SS-*Hstuf* Heinrich Ahrens	VI B2	BdS Holland; British Zone
SS-*Hstuf* Ernst Alisch	VI B2	also with VI B4
SS-*Ustuf* Franz Alliger	VI B2	BdS Brussels, 1943; transfer to VI E; held in US Zone
SS-*Hstuf* Karl Arnold	VI B4	VI representative in Madrid; also in VI D4
SS-*Uschaf* Asbach	VI B	
SS-*Hschaf* Wilhelm Baake	VI B2	*Leitstelle* Siegfried
SS-*Ustuf* Dr Herbert Bandorf	VI B1	BdS Italien

SS-*Ostuf* Jakob Bauer	VI B3	VI representative at SD-LA Stuttgart
SS-*Hstuf* Ferdinand Baus	VI B2	transfer to VI A2 in 1944
SS-*Ustuf* Friedrich Becker	VI B3	
Angestellter Benz	VI B4	
SS-*Ostubaf* Heinrich <u>Bernhard</u>	VI B2	*Referent* VI B2; held in US Zone
SS-*Oberführer* Johannes Bernhardt	VI B4	Sofindus Company, Madrid
SS-*Staf* Hermann Bickler	VI B2	*Leiter, Leitstelle* Walter
SS-*Hstuf* Hermann <u>Bielstein</u>	VI B	*Gruppenleiter* 1939–40; arrested in Denmark
SS-*Stubaf* Heinrich <u>Blecher</u>	VI B3	VI representative at SD-*Ast* Mühlhausen; suicide
SS-*Schaf* Böhm	VI B1	*Einheit* Ida, Italy
SS-*Ustuf* <u>Börde</u>	VI B2	
Krim.Assistent Karl Brinkmann	VI B1	
SS-*Hstuf* Fritz Buchele	VI B3	VI representative at SD-*Ast* Friedrichshafen
SS-*Ustuf* Adolf Crome	VI B2	
SS-*Schaf* Hugo Dapra	VI B1	*Einheit* Ida, Italy
SS-*Ostubaf* Dr Hans <u>Daufeldt</u>	VI B3	VI representative in Switzerland; held US Zone
SS-*Ostuf* Josef Dauser	VI B3	VI representative at SD-LA Munich
SS-*Hstuf* Heinz Detering	VI B2	*Leitstelle* Walter
SS-*Ustuf* Josef Didinger	VI B1	BdS Italien; officially with *Abt* IV (*Gestapo*)
SS-*Ustuf* Dobritsch	VI B2	BdS Paris
Graf <u>Dönhof</u>	VI B3	VI representative in Switzerland; arrested Italy
SS-*Hstuf* Erhard Döring	VI B4	*Unternehmen* Parseval
SS-*Oschaf* Ebner	VI B1	*Einheit* Ida, Italy
SS-*Ustuf* Eckert	VI B2	BdS Holland, 1943
SS-*Stubaf* Hans-Wilhelm <u>Eggen</u>	VI B3	Arrested Italy
SS-*Ustuf* Egidy	VI B2	BdS Holland
SS-*Ustuf* Adolf Ehmann	VI B3	VI representative at SD-LA Stuttgart
SS-*Ostuf* Heinz Einfeld	VI B2	*Leitstelle* Siegfried
SS-*Oschaf* Eisele	VI B3	with VI representative at SD-LA Stuttgart
SS-*Ostubaf* Georg <u>Elling</u>	VI B1	VI representative at the Vatican; arrested in Italy
SS-*Ostuf* Hans Endemann	VI B4	
SS-*Hstuf* Ernst	VI B2	
SS-*Ostuf* Eschelböck	VI B2	*Leitstelle* Walter
SS-*Ostuf* Heinrich Fanelsa	VI B2	VI representative at SD Metz

SS-*Hstuf* Waldemar <u>Fast</u>	VI B4	VI representative in Portugal and later with VI C; arrested in British Zone
SS-*Ostuf* Heinz <u>Felfe</u>	VI B2	BdS Holland; held in British Zone
SS-*Stubaf* Lothar Fendler	VI B4	Referent VI B4
SS-*Ostuf* Karl von Förster	VI B4	VI representative in Madrid
SS-*Ostuf Pol.Inspektor* Paul Franke	VI B2	*Leitstelle* Siegfried
SS-*Stubaf* Dr Emil Freise	VI B2	*Gruppenleiter* 1942–43; then VI representative in Strasbourg
SS-*Hschaf* Otto Gasteiner	VI B1	*Einheit* Ida, Italy
SS-*Ostuf* Gerardin	VI B2	*Leitstelle* Walter
Angestellter Alfred Gerspack	VI B2	
SS-*Oschaf* Giffey	VI B1	BdS Italien
Angestellter Godefroy	VI B4	
SS-*Stubaf* Helmut Gohl	VI B2	*Unternehmen* Bertram
Angestellter Hans Gumprecht	VI B4	
SS-*Hstuf* Paul Gutekunst	VI B2	*Leitstelle* Walter
SS-*Stubaf* Herbert Hagen	VI B2	BdS Paris, *Leiter* VI, 1942
SS-*Ostuf* KK Ernst Hammes	VI B4	VI representative in Barcelona
SS-*Stubaf* Dr Karl Hass	VI B1	*Leiter, Einheit* Ida, Italy
SS-*Hstuf* Haux	VI B2	
Dr Hess	VI B3	VI representative at SD-LA Stuttgart
SS-*Ostuf* Walter Hermann	VI B2	*Leitstelle* Walter
SS-*Ustuf* Anton Hierl	VI B3	VI representative at SD-LA Munich
SS-*Hstuf* Armin <u>Hinckfuss</u>	VI B2	BdS Holland; held in British Zone
Angestellter Holting	VI B4	W/T operator in Madrid
SS-*Stubaf* Dr Klaus <u>Huegel</u>	VI B1	BdS Italian, Leiter VI; arrested in Italy
SS-*Stubaf* Hermann Hubig	VI B2	*Leitstelle* Walter; previously with VI C Z
SS-*Uschaf* Wilhelm Hübner	VI B2	
SS-*Ustuf* Jarl	VI B2	BdS Holland
SS-*Ostuf* Hans-Ulrich John	VI B1	
SS-*Ostuf* Hermann Kallab	VI B4	VI representative on Franco-Spanish border at Hendaye
SS-*Stuschaf* Heinrich Katzbach	VI B2	*Leitstelle* Siegfried
SS-*Ostuf* Heinrich Kemmet	VI B3	VI representative at SD-*Ast* Waldshut
Sonderführer Kley	VI B2	BdS Italien
SS-*Hstuf* Fritz König	VI B2	BdS Paris
SS-*Ustuf* Herbert Kratz	VI B2	BdS Brussels
SS-*Uschaf* Krohne	VI B2	*Leitstelle* Siegfried
SS-*Hstuf* Herbert Krüger	VI B4	VI representative in Madrid
SS-*Ustuf* Siegfried Kulas	VI B4	VI representative in Madrid
SS-*Hstuf* <u>Kunze</u>	VI B2	*Leitstelle* Walter; arrested in French Zone

SS-*Stubaf* Rudolf Lang	VI B2	BdS Paris
SS-*Hstuf* Bruno Langbehn	VI B4	
Angestellter Lappe	VI B3	
SS-*Hstuf* Kurt Lawrenz	VI B2	BdS Brussels
SS-*Oschaf* Lechner	VI B4	with VI representative in Tangiers, 1944
SS-*Hschaf* Otto Lechner	VI B1	Secretary to Kappler (Rome) arrested in Italy
SS-*Ostuf* Kurt Loba	VI B2	*Leitstelle* Walter
SS-*Hstuf* Karl-Heinz Löchelt	VI B2	BdS Brussels, 1941
SS-*Stubaf* Helmut Looss	VI B1	*Aussenkommando* Rome
SS-*Hstuf* Lorenz	VI B2	VI representative in France, 1939
Angestellter Mahlis	VI B2	
SS-*Ustuf* Dr Maier	VI B1	BdS Italien
SS-*Hstuf* Gerhard Martschke	VI B2	
SS-*Hschaf* Arno Meinel	VI B2	
Angestellter Metzger	VI B4	
SS-*Ustuf* Fritz Michelsen	VI B1	BdS Italien, *Aussenkdo* Genoa; arrested Italy
SS-*Ostuf* Ernst Möller	VI B1	BdS Italien, *Aussenkdo* Bologna
SS-*Ustuf* Heinz Möller	VI B1	
SS-*Ostuf* August Moritz	VI B2	*Leitstelle* Walter
SS-*Ostuf* Moro	VI B2	*Leitstelle* Walter
SS-*Stubaf* Walter Mosig	VI B4	VI representative in Madrid
SS-*Oschaf* Adalbert Müller	VI B2	BdS France
SS-*Hstuf* Dr Georg Müller	VI B2	BdS France
SS-*Hschaf* Theo Müller	VI B1	BdS Italien
SS-*Stubaf* Cecil Adolf Nassenstein	VI B4	VI representative in Lisbon
SS-*Hstuf* Werner Neisser	VI B2	BdS Paris; later with VI S; arrested in French Zone
SS-*Ostuf* Ludwig Neubourg	VI B4	arrested in US Zone
SS-*Hstuf* Roland Nosek	VI B2	*Leitstelle* Walter; arrested in French Zone
SS-*Schaf* Odenthal	VI B2	W/T operator, *Leitstelle* Siegfried
SS-*Hstuf* Max Onuszeit	VI B3	VI representative at SD Stuttgart
SS-*Hstuf* Dr Ernst Peter	VI B3	VI representative in Switzerland, 1939–40
SS-*Hstuf* Alfred Pfisterer	VI B4	VI representative in Spain
SS-*Hstuf* Karl-Julius Plath	VI B4	VI representative in Spain; KIA in Ukraine, 1943
Krim.Oberassist. Wilhelm Pörschke	VI B3	
SS-*Uschaf* Pollmann	VI B2	*Leitstelle* Siegfried

SS-*Ustuf* Hans <u>Polonyi</u>	VI B2	BdS Brussels, 1943; then transfers to VI E
Angestellter Prauser	VI B4	
SS-*Ustuf* Gerhard <u>Preil</u>	VI B2	*Leitstelle* Walter; arrested in Italy
SS-*Hstuf* Robert Raden	VI B3	
SS-*Ustuf* Walter Rahe	VI B2	*Leitstelle* Walter
SS-*Hstuf* Dr Hans-Ullrich <u>Reiche</u>	VI B2	VI representative at Vichy; KIA in Russia
SS-*Stubaf* Hans Reichle	VI B	Deputy Gruppenleiter
SS-*Hstuf* Alfred <u>Reissmann</u>	VI B1 (Vat)	died December 1944
SS-*Hschaf* Johannes Richter	VI B2	
SS-*Ostuf* Walter Ried	VI B1	BdS Italien
SS-*Schaf* Ringold	VI B1	Einheit Ida, Italy
Angestellter Rothmann	VI B4	
Dr *Schaarschmidt*	VI B4	
SS-*Ostuf* Schönebeck	VI B4	VI representative in Lisbon
Krim.Assistent Otto Schmuck	VI B4	VI representative in Madrid; used alias Schmiedow in Tangiers, 1940–42
SS-*Hstuf* Schmid	VI B2	VI representative in Vichy
SS-*Ostuf* Schmidt	VI B1	BdS Italien
SS-*Ostubaf* Wilhelm Schneider	VI B2	VI representative in Strasbourg, 1943
SS-*Oschaf* Schnell	VI B2	BdS France
SS-*Hstuf* Egon <u>Schonpflug</u>	VI B1	BdS Italian; arrested Italy
SS-*Ustuf* Erwin Schöffler	VI B2	
SS-*Rotf* Schoffreger	VI B1	*Aussenkmdo* San Remo
SS-*Stubaf* Erich Schröder	VI B4	*Polizeiverbindungsführer* Lisbon
SS-*Ostuf* Wilhelm <u>Schubernig</u>	VI B1	*Einheit* Ida; arrested Austria
SS-*Stuschaf* Schutz	VI B2	*Leitstelle* Siegfried
SS-*Ustuf* Schultze	VI B4	VI representative in Tangiers to 1944
SS-*Hstuf* Schwartz	VI B4	VI representative in SD-LA Munich
SS-*Hschaf* Hans Seidel	VI B4	VI representative in Tangiers using alias Seitz, to1944; then *Unternehmen* Parseval
SS-*Ostuf* Heinz Singer	VI B4	VI representative in Madrid
SS-*Hstuf* Hans Sommer	VI B2	*Unternehmen* Bertram; used alias Senner
Consul <u>Sonnenhol</u>	VI B3	VI representative in Switzerland; arrested Italy
SS-*Stuschaf* Speck	VI B4	
SS-*Staf* Eugen Steimle	VI B	*Gruppenleiter*
Angestellter Sumbeck	VI B4	Assistant to Vollbrecht in Lisbon
SS-*Ustuf* Willy Tengler	VI B2	

Kriminalrat Alfons Uhring	VI B1	VI representative in Strasbourg; arrested in French Zone
SS-*Stuschaf* Ulbrich	VI B2	BdS Holland
SS-*Ostuf* Herbert Urbanneck	VI B3	BdS Holland, *Abt* III and VI
SS-*Ostuf* Dr Wallfried Vernunft	VI B2	arrested in US Zone
SS-*Hschaf* Karl Vierck	VI B2	*Leitstelle* Siegfried
Angestellter Völker	VI B2	*Leitstelle* Siegfried; arrested in US Zone
SS-*Stubaf* Dr Hans Vollbrecht	VI B4	VI representative in Portugal
SS-*Oschaf* Volt	VI B4	
SS-*Ostuf* Oswald Wandhoff	VI B3	
SS-*Hstuf* Erich Wenger	VI B2	*Leitstelle* Walter
SS-*Ostuf* Karl Wenkausen	VI B2	
SS-*Ostuf* Wiedemann	VI B4	
SS-*Ustuf* Georg Wild	VI B2	*Leitstelle* Walter
SS-*Ustuf Krim.Komm.* Arno Wolf	VI B1	BdS Trieste
SS-*Stubaf* Reinhard Wolff	VI B2	*Leiter, Leitstelle* Siegfried; arrested in US Zone
SS-*Ostuf* Dr Werner Wulffen	VI B4	
SS-*Hstuf* Walter Würdig	VI B3	KIA, October 1944
SS-*Ustuf* Alfons Zach	VI B2	BdS Paris
SS-*Ostuf* Guido Zimmer	VI B1	*Aussenkommando* Milan
SS-*Ustuf* Dr Heinz Zirnbauer	VI B1	*Aussenkommando* Merano
SS-*Hstuf* Marcel Zschunke	VI B2	Arrested in British Zone
SS-*Hschaf* Jean Zuang	VI B2	*Leitstelle* Walter; arrested in French Zone
SS-*Hstuf* Walter Zuchristian	VI B2	BdS Paris

Notes

* The National Archives, Kew, KV 3/114, Liquidation Report No. 7, on RSHA VI B.

1 Hans Senner was the *nom de guerre* of SS-*Ostuf* Hans Sommer. After the war Sommer was in French then US captivity then released. In 1950 Sommer joined the Gehlen Organisation and in 1954 recruited by the East German secret police, the *Stasi*, as a double agent. He was uncovered in 1960.

2 SS-*Ostuf* Marcel Zschunke was twice posted to Russia. The first occasion for the period October 1941–July 1942, with *Sonderkommando* 4b; the second occasion with KdS Bialystok, responsible for SD activities, October 1943–September 1944.

3 Ronald Seth, a British agent of SOE was parachuted into Estonia in 1942 and captured on arrival Thereafter he was in the hands of the SD. It is claimed he was 'turned' by them which Seth always denied.

4 Tетuan is a town on the Mediterranean coast of Morocco, 40 miles/60 kms east of Tangiers.

7

Situation Report No. 8:
Amt VI of the RSHA—*Gruppe* VI C

INDEX

Part I: The Development of *Gruppe* VI C, 1939–45
Part II: *Gruppe* VI C and Russia—*Unternehmen* Zeppelin
Part III: *Gruppe* VI C and the Near East
Part IV: *Gruppe* VI C and the Far East

Appendix I: The Distribution of Work in RSHA *Amt* VI between 1939–45
Appendix II: Organisational changed in *Gruppe* VI C, 1939–45
Appendix III: Alphabetical Index of *Gruppe* VI C Personnel 1939–1945

Preamble

RSHA *Gruppe* VI C has certain unique features among the *Ländergruppen* of RSHA *Amt* VI; it was the only *Gruppe* to retain the same designation throughout its history, suffering in addition less territorial modification than any other *Gruppe*, as it was since its creation responsible for the Far East and the USSR, the only changes being that it surrendered the Baltic States to RSHA *Amt* III in the course of 1941, balanced by the absorption in the same year of the Near and Middle East from the then RSHA *Gruppe* VI D. The *Gruppe* covered the widest sphere of all the *Ländergruppen* and from the start of the Russian campaign was the most important in the *Amt* for immediate operational purposes. As a result of the changing fortunes in the war on the Eastern Front, the *Gruppe* underwent frequent internal re-organisation, especially in the last year of its existence when the changes were so frequent and so sweeping as to be difficult to unravel. Nor is it surprising that as its sphere of interest offered so few points of contact with the Western Allies except in the Middle East, comparatively little was known of the *Gruppe*, even in the final collapse. What is now known of the activities of RSHA *Gruppe* VI C in Eastern Europe and in the Far East has been learned only since the surrender, and that information is largely confined to the later years with the result that there are still many gaps in our present knowledge, which gaps are not likely to be filled to any great extent. The following review of the development of RSHA *Gruppe* VI C must therefore be read with these reservations in mind.

Part I

The Development of RSHA *Gruppe* VI C 1939–45

A. The Situation at the outbreak of war.

1. The general position of RSHA *Amt* VI.
Overriding any particular considerations which affected the course of *Amt* VI activity in the different territories under review has been pointed out in the Liquidation Report on RSHA *Gruppe* VI E that only in the case of that *Gruppe* was there any previous activity on the part of the old SD-*Hauptamt* which lent itself to immediate development in the creation of the new *Amt*. It must ever be borne in mind that the *Auslandsnachrichtendienst* [Foreign Intelligence Service] was a new venture on the part of the SD, and prior to the outbreak of war no groundwork had been established in any theatre in Europe or outside it, apart from Eastern and especially South-Eastern Europe. The *Amt* began its work therefore under enormous initial disadvantages, which were in no way alleviated by the attitude of the *Abwehr* and the Foreign Office, nor by the weakness of the first *Amtschef*, Jost. An added complication was the shortage of personnel with the necessary background and knowledge of foreign countries—a factor of special importance in dealing with RSHA *Gruppe* VI C in so far as it dealt with countries such as Japan, China, the Dutch East Indies, Turkey, Syria, etc. In approaching the question of *Amt* VI operations in such territory therefore, one must not look for any prepared plan at the outbreak of war; such plans simply did not exist. The German principle of concentrating on one point at a time applied equally well in its intelligence as in its military operations. The *Schwerpunkt* in the first years of the war was remote from the Far and Middle East, and it was not until the summer of 1941 that *Gruppe* VI C became important as a result of the Russian campaign. Characteristically enough the main effort of the *Gruppe* was concentrated on '*Unternehmen* Zeppelin'. When that effort failed it was too late to exploit other territory such as Persia and Turkey to remedy the deficiency.

2. The creation of RSHA *Gruppe* VI C in 1939.

The original *Gruppe* VI C which was a small one had a simple internal organisation on the following lines:

Gruppenleiter   -   SS-*Stubaf* Vietinghoff-Scheel

Referat		*Referent*
VI C1	Russia	SS-*Hstuf* von Westernhagen
VI C2	Baltic States	SS-*Ostuf* Fölkersam
VI C3	Far East	SS-*Hschaf* Hinney

The *Gruppe* had few personnel and had no *Beauftragte* outside of Germany, for reasons which are self-evident, in view of the territory alloted to it. Little is known of its activities at this early stage, but it is not difficult to appreciate the situation with which the *Gruppe* was faced. It is to be noted that Turkey and the Near East did not come under the control of the *Gruppe* but were dealt with at that time by RSHA *Gruppe* VI D. (see Appendix I)

3. *Referat* VI C1 and Russia.

In Russia the Foreign Office under Ribbentrop had just brought off its greatest triumph in the signing of the non-aggression pact which had temporarily removed the threat from the East and allowed the Army to concentrate on Poland. Ideologically speaking, however, the two countries were still diametrically opposed, and the situation was generally delicate enough for the Foreign Office to take a strong line against any attempt by the new and much scorned RSHA *Amt* VI to indulge in any activity which might jeopardise an uneasy truce. In any case the purely physical barriers imposed by the strict Russian security measures made it virtually impossible for Jost to introduce any representatives into the country under any cover, apart from diplomatic, which could only have been obtained with Foreign Office approval, and in that connection it is safe to say that it would have been easier for Jost to pass a camel through the eye of a needle. RSHA *Amt* VI therefore had no direct lines into Russia itself, an achievement it shared with the *Abwehr* at the time, as at a meeting between the SD and *Abwehr* representatives held at Prague in early 1940, it was stated that not one single source of information was available to the German Intelligence Services in Russia itself. It should be noted however that before and after the creation of the RSHA, the *Gestapoamt* had been active in its security functions against the USSR.

Early RSHA *Amt* VI work against Russia was therefore conducted entirely from outside the country, and in the original organisation of *Amt* VI was not directly controlled by *Gruppe* VI C. It has been explained in the Liquidation Report on *Gruppe* VI A that under that *Gruppe* in the period 1939–40 were the *Beauftragte* controlling the *Amt* VI *Referenten* in the SD-*Abschnitte* through Germany. SS-*Stubaf* von Salisch held the position of *Beauftragte* III *Ost*, and in this capacity controlled the following *Amt* VI *Referenten* at their respective SD-*Leitabschnitte*:

SD-*Leitabschnitt* Danzig	SS-*Hstuf* Brohs
(later *Beauftragter* Finland)	
SD-*Leitabschnitt* Memel	SS-*Ustuf* Kurmis
(later of *Unternehmen* Anton in Iran)	
SD-*Leitabschnitt* Kattowitz	SS-*Ustuf* Matysiak
SD-*Leitabschnitt* Königsberg	SS-*Ustuf* List
SD-*Leitabschnitt* Posen	SS-*Ustuf* Weirauch
(later *Referent*, VI C4)	
SD-*Leitabschnitt* Breslau	SS-*Hstuf* Kleinert
(later with *Gruppe* VI A)	
SD-*Leitabschnitt* Krakau	SS-*Hstuf* Kipka
(later with KdS Lemberg, *Abt* VI)	

The function of these *Referenten* was the collection of information regarding Russia from the interrogation of travellers and merchant seamen passing between the two countries; their reports were sent to RSHA *Amt* VI with copies to von Salisch at Bromberg. The *Referenten* maintained close liaison between themselves and held regular conferences at Bromberg under von Salisch. This activity continued until September 1940 when von Salisch was relieved of his position (von Salisch later became *Polizeipräsident* in Bromberg and was shot by the Germans in February 1945 as a result of his desire to surrender Bromberg to the Russians), and thereafter the *Referenten* acted independently and more positively by attempting to establish their own contacts with suitable personalities in commercial, industrial, and scientific circles. It need hardly be said of course that operations of this type did not produce much intelligence of any value.

4. *Referat* VI C2 and the Baltic States.

Little is known of the work of *Referat* VI C2; it is to be presumed however that this *Referat* based its work on the former activity of the *Blockstelle* Tilsit which had been created in 1938 when the first attempts as an *Auslandsnachrichtendienst* were made. The *Blockstelle* had been under the command of SS-*Stubaf* Gräfe who was to become *Gruppenleiter* RSHA VI C by 1941 and the most important figure in the history of the *Gruppe*. It is to be noted however that Jost did not appoint any *Hauptbeauftragter* to the Baltic States, again no doubt owing to the chief influence of Russia, whose interest in that sphere had become most direct after the Polish campaign and the resulting partition in Eastern Europe. The exception was the posting of SS-*Hstuf* Schönebeck to Finland, later to be replaced by SS-*Stubaf* Brohs. Finland however eventually passed to RSHA *Gruppe* VI D as a Scandinavian country, and the activities of Brohs there are dealt with in the Liquidation Report on that *Gruppe*.

5. *Referat* VI C3 and the Far East.

Japan, as one of the Tripartite Powers, was in a position similar to that of Italy, where the *Führerbefehl* prevented any open RSHA *Amt* VI activity until the Italian collapse. Espionage activities against Japan were therefore not officially encouraged, but even apart from that major consideration the position of *Amt* VI as far as the Far East was concerned was one where the normal difficulties facing the other *Ländergruppen* were greatly accentuated. The SD had no previous activity or even interest in that sphere which *Amt* VI could develop, while the personnel problem itself was insuperable. If it was difficult for the much more immediately important *Gruppe* VI D (VI C at the time under review) to find officers with sufficient background knowledge of the U.K. and the U.S.A. to set about its task with any competence, *Gruppe* VI C had little chance of improving on that state of affairs. Indeed it was not until the major reorganisation of the *Gruppe* in the summer of 1944 that any specialists in the Far East were introduced into the *Gruppe*. The liaison between the two Allies was at the best an official one, and the racial and ethnological differences between them was such as to create a lack of interest except in the military sphere. In any case the Far East was too remote from Germany for any special effort to be directed in that direction. Information on the Far East, including China and the Dutch East Indies, was obtained through official channels from the Japanese; no *Amt* VI representatives were sent to that theatre, the only RSHA representation being through the appointment in 1942 of the *Polizei Attaché*, Meisinger, a Bavarian friend of Müller, and quite incompetent from the intelligence point of view. It is significant that at this early stage, the *Referent* for the Far East was a mere SS-*Unterscharführer* [Corporal].

6. Changes before the summer of 1941.

Before the major change in the *Gruppe* that took place with the start of the Russian campaign in June 1941, there were several changes of a minor character, with however only slight significance. *Vietinghoff-Scheel* had been replaced by SS-*Ostubaf* Vollheim as *Gruppenleiter*, Vollheim later to be involved in the alleged financial scandal round Jost, which was to be used for an excuse for the latter's removal from RSHA *Amt* VI by the summer of the year. The Far-Eastern *Referat* had been strengthened by the appointment of SS-*Ostuf* Weirauch as *Referent*. Apart from these changes, the general character of the *Gruppe* remained unchanged, though the preparations for the Russian campaign had promoted some identification of effort against that country, but mainly through the *Abt* VI *Referat* of the SD-*Leitabschnitt* Wien [Vienna], which had succeeded in establishing certain contacts with Hungary and Roumania as bases. The situation however changed entirely in the summer of 1941.

B. Developments after the beginning of the Russian campaign.

1. Re-organisation of the *Gruppe*.

The turning point in the history of RSHA *Gruppe* VI C came in the summer of 1941 as a result of several independent factors. There was of course the Russian campaign which resulted in a concentration of effort against that country, and which led to the creation of *Unternehmen* Zeppelin, the most intense and coordinated effort undertaken by any *Ländergruppen* of RSHA *Amt* VI. The *Gruppe* for that reason alone became the most important in the *Amt*, and the degree of coordination of work between RSHA *Amt* VI and the armies in the field reached a level which was not paralleled in any other theatre of war. The *Unternehmen* Zeppelin, which is dealt with in Part II (below), had certain novel features not met with elsewhere in the *Amt*. Almost simultaneous with the beginning of the campaign was the virtual accession of Schellenberg as *Amtschef* with the resultant clearing out of Jost's 'Old Brigade', which in *Gruppe* VI C involved the dismissal of Vollheim and the appointment of Gräfe. A further important feature was the assimilation of Turkey and the Near East from RSHA *Gruppe* VI D and *Gruppe* VI E, while with the rapid occupation of the Baltic States, that territory passed over to the control of RSHA *Amt* III, though the *Gruppe* still retained interest.

2. The influence of Gräfe.

The effect of Gräfe's appointment as *Gruppenleiter* was greater than that of Schellenberg as *Amtschef*. Gräfe had been *Leiter* of the *Blockstelle* Tilsit in 1938, and was subsequently head of the SD-*Unterabschnitt* there until 1940, but it is not clear what his position was in RSHA *Amt* VI prior to his appointment as *Gruppenleiter* VI C. It is known that in 1940 he had been connected with the then RSHA *Gruppe* VI G, acting for a spell as *Referent* for the U.K., and even as *Gruppenleiter* in place of the incompetent Daufeldt soon after Schellenberg's arrival. His interest however was in the East, and with his appointment as *Gruppenleiter* VI C that interest was granted full scope. Gräfe was a man of considerable ability and enterprise and it was chiefly due to his direction that the *Gruppe* developed considerably in the course of the following year, especially in the *Unternehmen* Zeppelin. His main effort was directed against Russia, and to a lesser extent in the Near East as a base for further activity against that country. His pet plan was the creation of a decentralised German control in the Ukraine, an enterprise which met with little support in the Foreign Office. The subsequent development of RSHA *Gruppe* VI C revolves very largely round the personality of Gräfe.

3. Organisation in 1941.

The *Gruppe* before the end of the year 1941 was re-organised on the following lines:

Gruppenleiter	-		SS-*Stubaf* Gräfe

Referat		Referent
VI C1	Russia & Baltic States	SS-*Hstuf* RR Girgensohn
VI C3	Ukraine	SS-*Hstuf* Dressler
VI C4-6	Japan	-
VI C7-8	China	-
VI C9	Manchukuo & Mongolia	SS-*Hstuf* Weirauch
VI C10	Thailand & French Indo-China	-
VI C11	Dutch Indies & Phillipines	-
VI C12	Turkey, Afghanistan & Iran	SS-*Hstuf* Schuback
VI C13	The Arab Countries	*Angestellter* Em

It will be noted that VI C1 and VI C2 were merged together, while Gräfe's interest in the Ukraine was manifest by the creation of a special *Referat* VI C3 to deal with that territory. The many sub-divisions in the Far-Eastern territory did not however indicate any increased activity in that sphere, as is evidenced by the fact that the *Referat* had a common *Referent*.

4. The Near East prior to RSHA *Gruppe* VI C control.
(a) The general position at the outbreak of war.
No special importance had been attached to the Near and Middle East as a theatre of espionage activity by RSHA *Amt* VI in the early days of the war, inspite of the obvious advantages offered by Turkey as a neutral country from which special efforts could be directed against the fertile field that the Arab speaking countries offered for espionage and subversion. There was no subtle reason for this lack of interest, and it is not necessary to go any further than the general weakness and inefficiency of the *Amt* as a whole to appreciate the situation. There was no well defined RSHA *Amt* VI policy regarding the Near East and the difficulties of personnel, training and background must always be borne in mind. It was not until the summer of 1940 that the *Amt* made its first efforts at penetration in the Near and Middle East, and these efforts bore all the hallmarks of Jost's haphazard and normally futile methods, though curiously enough in this theatre the developments turned out better than *Amt* VI direction of affairs warranted.

(b) Moyzisch and Duplitzer in Turkey.
Moyzisch arrived in Ankara as *Amt* VI representative in June 1940, being followed shortly afterwards by Duplitzer who took up his appointment at Istanbul. By early 1941 Moyzisch had succeeded in establishing himself in the country with good relations existing between himself and the Foreign Office representative there, in itself no mean feat. His activities however were confined to Turkey itself on which country he was required to submit regular political reports. There had been no

question of using the country as a base of operations against the neighbouring Arab countries. For reasons explained in Part III below, Moyzisch adopted a policy of caution in his affairs in Turkey, which in the absence of any precise instructions from Langlotz, then *Referent* VI D4 controlling Turkey, was in fact the best policy possible in the circumstances and which was to bear fruit in the ensuing years. Duplitzer however had acted more in the normal fashion of the *Amt* VI *Beauftragte* with the usual results of friction and bad feeling.

(c) <u>Gamotha and Mayr in Persia.</u>
The circumstances surrounding the recruitment, training and despatch of Gamotha and Mayr to Persia, where they arrived in October 1940, are dealt with in some detail in Part IV below, as they are characteristic of the method or lack of method adopted by RSHA *Amt* VI in its early work. Little need be said of this early work, for the inefficiency of which they had every valid excuse in the circumstances. By the time both Schellenberg and Gräfe had taken over their new appointments, the Russian campaign had begun, the abortive Arab revolt took place soon afterwards, an almost immediate consequence of which was the occupation of Syria and later Persia by British and Russian troops, an event which took the German colony there completely by surprise, including Mayr and Gamotha. As far as *Amt* VI was concerned, the event brought to an end their representation there, and with the main effort of *Gruppe* VI C now directed towards the Eastern Front, the fact was accepted with resignation and without any alternative plan, a lack of foresight which hardly merited the windfall of Mayr's somewhat dramatic message through Tokyo more than a year later. By the end of 1941 Mayr and Gamotha were just 'missing' as far as *Gruppe* VI C was concerned.

(d) <u>The Near and Middle East by the end of 1942.</u>
On the re-organisation of RSHA *Gruppe* VI C in 1941 therefore *Referat* VI C 12 had a fairly strong outpost in Ankara and a weak one in Istanbul, two ill-trained but enthusiastic agents in Iran who were soon to disappear, and no plans for the further exploitation of the two countries. *Referat* VI C 13 competent for the Arab countries had neither representatives nor plans. The potential advantage that Vichy-occupied Syria had offered had disappeared on the occupation of the country by Allied forces in June 1941. Efforts were made however under Gräfe's direction to improve the situation. It was planned at first to instruct Moyzisch to extend his sphere of interest beyond the borders to Turkey, but on the latter's protests, Gräfe finally sent SS-*Ostuf* Fast to Ankara to operate under Moyzisch, but with the specific assignment of using Ankara as a base for penetration into the neighbouring Arabic countries.

The other development of note was the appointment of SS-*Hstuf* Schuback as *Referent* for VI C 12. Schuback was subsequently to become closely identified with all further RSHA *Amt* VI efforts in the Near and Middle East.

C. The development of RSHA *Gruppe* VI C, 1942–43.

1. Development of *Unternehmen* Zeppelin in 1942.
The main feature of RSHA *Gruppe* VI C development during 1942 and 1943 was the expansion of *Unternehmen* Zeppelin, which became a vast enterprise covering the whole Russian Front. Being essentially an operational enterprise the *Unternehmen* developed in the original stages independently of *Gruppe* VI C under the denomination of VI C (Z), coming however under the direct supervision of Gräfe himself with SS-*Stubaf* Hengelhaupt as assistant, the latter being by this time *Referent* of the new combined *Referate* VI C 1-3. The actual commander of VI C (Z) was SS-*Ostubaf* Oebsger-Röder, later liaison officer under RSHA *Gruppe* VI A with the Foreign Office. With the war in the East developing along very favourable lines after the beginning of the German spring offensive in 1942 and with deep penetration into Russia territory itself, little attempt was made at any exploitation at this stage into the USSR from other bases such as Turkey and Scandinavia. It was not until later in 1943 that efforts were made to infiltrate Georgian agents into the Caucasus through Turkey with Turkish connivance. With the German armies outside Stalingrad by the autumn and Rommel driving into Egypt in the summer of 1942, it looked as if the comparative neglect of the Middle East would be justified.

2. Developments in the Near and Middle East.
With the main effort of the *Gruppe* itself still concentrated in VI C (Z), developments in the Middle and Near East were comparatively minor in character. Notable, however, was the despatch of SS-*Stubaf* Wolff to Istanbul in June 1942 to operate there on behalf of RSHA *Amt* VI in equal status with Moyzisch in Ankara. Wolff was a RSHA *Amt* IV [*Gestapo*] officer and had considerable experience in that *Amt*; his assignment reflected the development of *Amt* VI policy in Turkey as part from the normal *Amt* VI functions he was instructed to make special efforts to establish close working relations with the Turkish Intelligence Service. This assignment had the special interest of both Schellenberg and Gräfe, both of whom saw possibilities in exploiting Turkey's fear of Russia to the advantage of *Amt* VI. Another appointment of interest was that of SS-*Hstuf* Mohr, previously of RSHA *Gruppe* VI D, to Ankara to evaluate for *Amt* VI the reliability of the PASHA and REMO organisation, which were the main sources of information to the *Amt* on the Near East. These organisations, which however were <u>not</u> *Amt* VI enterprises, are dealt with in Part III below.

There are still however, apart from the work of SS-*Ostuf* Fast in Ankara of which little is known, no great effort to exploit the Near East and the Arabic countries, and there is no indication from any source that Fast was in any way successful in whatever activity he was engaged in. The two Arab subversive leaders, the Grand Mufti and Raschid Ali, whose escape from Turkey was engineered by Moyzisch, were not to become prominent until 1943.

3. '*Unternehmen* Otto' and the Middle East.

Reference has already been mde in the Liquidation Report on RSHA *Gruppe* VI F to the creation in August 1943 of the special *Referat* VI F/O in *Gruppe* VI F to be known as *Unternehmen* Otto. This *Referat*, with executive functions over a wide sphere cutting across the *Ländergruppen*, reflects the confused policy of RSHA *Amt* VI at the time in the Near East. SS-*Hstuf* Mandl was *Referent* for the *Näheres-Ost Referat*, and it was under this ill-conceived organisation that the first signs of agent-missions made their appearance in the Near East. This however was not manifest until the summer of 1943, with the despatch of agents through the VI F/O subordinate formations in Greece—*Dienststellen* 2000 and 3000.

4. The crisis in late 1942.

The crisis of the war for Germany was in the late autumn of 1942 with the failure to take Stalingrad and the success of the Allied counter-attack at El Alamein. That crisis affected RSHA *Gruppe* VI C in a most immediate sense, as both these theatres were under the control of the *Gruppe*, like the German High Command, had virtually staked everything on the success of these military operations. The failure found the *Gruppe* forced to improvise where improvisation should not have been necessary. The neglect of the Near East in 1939–42 was to tell in 1943. Of the Far East it need only be said that it continued to play its unimportant role.

5. Mayr's bolt from the blue.

A ray of hope in the critical closing months of 1942 came from Tokyo, whence arrived by a most circuitous route in August 1942 the message from Mayr, 'lost' in Persia since 1941, informing the *Gruppe* that both he and Schulze, the former *Abwehr* I-*Luft* representative in Persia, had been actively engaged in preparing the ground in that country for further exploitation provided speedy help was forthcoming. The importance of this independent activity of Mayr and Schulze in Iran cannot be minimised when it is examined in the light of the general war situation in August 1942. The German armies were fighting in the foothills of the Caucasus and at the gates of Egypt. Had either Army been able to break through, all the elements which precipitated the rapid fall of Norway, France and the Low Countries in 1940 were operative in Iran, the vital link between Russia and the Western Allies. The success of the Fifth Column prepared by Mayr in the north and Schulze in the south depended either on the success of the military operations or on speedy help by parachute operations. As events turned out, the autumn of 1942 saw the turning point in the military sphere which was not balanced by effective action by either RSHA *Amt* VI or the *Abwehr* in Iran. Nevertheless, Mayr's message offered an opportunity, and in 1943 the attempt began to take advantage of it.

6. Developments in 1943.

(a) The Jablon Camp

1943 saw the emphasis on VI C (Z) lessened, and the efforts to find alternative scope in the Near and Middle East. In June 1943 Mandl sent two agents to Syria through *Dienststelle* 3000 with the vague mission of carrying out sabotage and moral subversive activities, a mission which failed completely. In the following months, Swedkowicz, a Pole, was sent from the same source to the Middle East with instructions to pass himself off as a Polish refugee with a view to being recruited into the Polish forces in that theatre, thereafter to carry out subversive propaganda—a mission which met the same fate as the first.[1] Soon afterwards VI F/O ceased to exist, and the subordinate formations, *Dienststellen* 2000 and 3000, came under the control of RSHA *Gruppe* VI E, with the subsidiary assignment of acting as springboards on behalf of *Gruppe* VI C for the despatch of agents to the Middle East. It was under this modified organisation that the famous [*Kriminalkommissar*] Merz, who had been recruited by Mandl for *Amt* VI in May 1943, was eventually despatched to Syria in October of the same year with alleged instructions to organise sabotage activities in Iraq and Iran, although the exact purpose of the mission still remains doubtful, for which scheme he was to recruit Poles already in the Middle East. Merz was given Moyzisch in Ankara as an advance base and collaborator. This mission too was a failure, and a costly one, as it was through the interrogation of Merz that much valuable information was obtained for the first time on the structure, personalities and activities of RSHA *Gruppe* VI C.[2]

(b) Attempts to exploit the situation in Iran:

The critical sphere in the Middle East was however in Iran where much depended on the attempts to take advantage of the situation offered to the Amt by Mayr and Schulze. There, one immediate danger from the Allied point of view had been removed by the capture of some of Mayr's documents by the security authorities, which documents had had the inestimable value of allowing the Allied authorities to know the enemy with whom they had to contend. Nevertheless the situation was still dangerous, and was in the event rendered less dangerous by the incorrect interpretation of the situation on the part of both RSHA *Gruppe* VI C and the *Abwehr*. The co-operation that had existed between the SD and the *Abwehr* in Persia had forced a corresponding degree of co-operation on the part of the same authorities in Berlin and the operations carried out to exploit the situation were joint efforts. In this case however union was far from being strong, as the traditional rivalry could not be oversome. In addition, the situation lent itself to political exploitation, a fact which Mayr did not fail to stress, but which was not appreciated. To RSHA *Amt* VI, Iran was a supply line to Russia and that supply line called for sabotage. The failure to exploit Iran lay primarily in the divergence of view between Mayr and *Gruppe* IV C, and Mayr, the man on the spot, was best qualified to know.

In the event, the '*Unternehmen* Franz' expedition, which landed in Persia in April 1943, was a sabotage mission, as was the '*Unternehmen* Anton' expedition in the south in July 1943. While Mayr was successful in modifying the purpose of the 'Franz' expedition to suit his interpretation of the situation, he failed to impress the ambitious and impetuous SS-*Hstuf* Kurmis, leader of the 'Anton' expedition in the south. The situation in Iran as a result of these conflicting interests rapidly deteriorated, a further contributing factor being the changing war situation which was now going against Germany, the effect of which on the potential Fifth Column constituted by tribes can be imagined. A Fifth Column thrives only on the certainty of success, and the attitude of the tribes cooled appreciably, which was evident by that fact that Schule and the Kurmis group spent the following winter under virtual arrest in the tribes they had intended to exploit. In the north the situation collapsed with the arrest of Mayr himself in August 1943.[3]

(c) The situation by the end of 1943:
By the end of the year the writing was already on the wall. VI C (Z) was meeting with increasing difficulties with the continued success of the Russian counter-attack, the opportunity offered in Persia had not been seized, and while efforts were now being made in the course of 1943 to exploit the Grand Mufti group, members of which were undergoing training in Germany, these efforts could not produce any results until 1944, when the situation had already irretrievably deteriorated. The Mufti enterprises themselves had developed too late to be effective, and even there the real driving force had not come from the *Amt* itself, but from the efforts of Lorch of RSHA *Gruppe* VI G and his nephew Wieland of the '*Unternehmen* Atlas' expedition in 1944. Arab activity in 1943 centred round SS-*Stubaf* Beisner and SS-*Ostuf* Kohlhaas, both of whom had had previous experience in handling Arabs during their activity with *Einsatzkommando* Tunis in late 1942 and early 1943.

There was however one important exception to this general state of affairs in the CICERO material, which by the end of the year was becoming available from Ankara. This source was unquestionably the most important in the history of RSHA *Amt* VI and represented the greatest single 'scoop'. But even then it was not as fully exploited as it should have been.

(d) Organisation of RSHA *Gruppe* VI C in late 1943:
The organisational structure of the *Gruppe* had not changed much during the year, being on the following lines:

Gruppenleiter	-		SS-*Ostubaf* Gräfe
Referat			*Referent*
VI C 1-3	Russia		SS-*Stubaf* Hengelhaupt
VI C (Z)	*Unternehmen* Zeppelin		SS-*Ostubaf* Oebsger-Röder

VI C 4-6	Japan	-
VI C 7-8	China	-
VI C 9	Manchukuo & Mongolia	SS-*Hstuf* Weirauch
VI C 10	Thailand, French Indo-China	-
VI C 11	Dutch Indies & Phillipines	-
VI C 12	Turkey, Afghanistan	SS-*Hstuf* Schuback
VI C 13	Arab Countries	*Angestellter* Em

D. Developments in 1944–45.

1. Death of Gräfe.

The year 1944 opened badly for RSHA *Gruppe* VI C with the death of its *Gruppenleiter* in early January 1944 as a result of a motor car accident. The *Gruppe* had now lost its driving force, and until the appointment of SS-*Staf* Rapp at the end of the year, lacked the direction it had previously enjoyed. SS-*Stubaf* Hengelhaupt acted as temporary *Gruppenleiter* until the summer when SS-*Stubaf* Tschierschky was appointed, an appointment which proved to be of short duration, as Tschierschky was dismissed for inefficiency before the end of the year, and was transferred to the *Dienststelle* Prützmann. Meanwhile the situation on the Russian front continued to deteriorate with the inevitable consequences for VI C (Z) which began to show signs of disintegration.

2. Creation of *Referat* VI C 14.

In the course of 1943 SS-*Hstuf* Gamotha, the representative who had been sent to Iran in 1940 and who had escaped after the occupation of the country in August 1941 by Allied forces, returned to Germany in a blaze of publicity and glory as a result of his adventures in makiing good his escape. Recognised as an 'authority' on Iran, he was given the assignment of preparing an operation to that country to be known as the '*Unternehmen* Norma' expedition, an enterprise which did not materialise probably because Gamotha had no intention of returning to the country. In January 1944 however Gamotha was appointed *Referent* of the new *Referat* VI C 14, competency for Iran, a *Referat* which concentrated its efforts in the course of the year on the formation within Germany of a Quisling Iranian government, an enterprise which eventually led to the arrest of Gamotha himself in October 1944 as a result of the inevitable jealousies between all parties concerned in the affair, including Schuback, who opposed Gamotha's nominee for the position of Prime Minister in the new government. The *Referat* was not responsible for any mission to Iran.

3. Operations in the Near East.

By the summer of 1944 the efforts of Beisner and Kohlhaas during the previous year began to take concrete form. Kohlhaas was stationed in Athens acting there as the forwarding agency for agents sent to the country from Beisner in Berlin. In July 1944 Letay was sent to Syria to establish himself there and await further instructions from RSHA VI G, instructions which did not reach him as he was arrested immediately on arrival. An effort was made to strengthen the chain between Berlin, Athens and the Middle East by the establishing of a further link in Istanbul in the person of the Greek, Emanuel, whose function was to act as liaison officer between Kohlhaas and missions sent by the latter to the Middle East through Turkey. Emanuel met the same fate as Letay. In September 1944 the 'Chacun' group including one Arab of the Mufti organisation was despatched to Syria only to join Letay in captivity.

The story of failure in these Near East enterprises was continued in the 'Atlas' expedition, which, after much preparation under RSHA VI C, Wieland and the Mufti, much wrangling between the Mufti and VI C as to who should be in charge of the expedition on landing, and many technical difficulties in equipping and despatching the mission, was finally despatched on the 5th October 1944 to Palestine, enjoying eleven days' liberty before being arrested by the Allied authorities. The Mufti proved to be a costly failure. The only other operation to Arab territory involving the use of his followers was the '*Unternehmen* Telafar' expedition which landed in Iraq in November 1944. This operation consisted of four Arabs without any German in charge, the Arabs being members of the Mufti groups which had undergone training at The Hague sabotage school the previous year. The enterprise had been directed by the Mufti himself and not by VI C, though of course the latter were aware of its nature. The group was provided with W/T, and had the mission of organising armed bands to attack Jews and Jewish interests in Iraq and Palestine. Two of the party were arrested a few hours after landing.

With the failure of the 'Atlas' expedition RSHA VI C activity in the Near and Middle East came to an end apart from the lone mission of Rizos, who had been trained from July 1944 by Kohlhaas and arrived in Turkey in February 1945 to be detained immediately on arrival. The nature of his mission remains obscure, but in any case the enterprise was a failure.

4. Re-organisation of the *Gruppe*.

The *Gruppe* now underwent a major re-organisation in September 1944. The *Gruppe* was reduced to four *Abteilungen*, each with its own *Referate*, the structure of the *Gruppe* now being:

Gruppenleiter	-	SS-*Staf* Rapp

Referat		*Referent*
VI C 1 }		SS-*Stubaf* Lumm
with }	The Soviet Union	
VI C 2 }		SS-*Stubaf* Hengelhaupt

| VI C 3 | The Near East | SS-*Hstuf* Schuback |
| VI C 4 | The Far East | SS-*Stubaf* Weirauch |

The development of interest was the increased attention now paid to the Far East, as it was now apparent that information on that theatre was badly lacking and the attitude towards the Japanese themselves was now hardening, even in official circles. Specialists with the necessary background were now introduced into the *Abteilung* and plans made for the despatch of agents to the Far East, but again the change came to loo late a date to be effective. The subsequent development of *Abteilung* VI C4 is dealt with in Part IV below.

The subsequent changes in RSHA *Gruppe* VI C have no other significance than to indicate the growing confusion on all fronts, but especially in the East. In November 1944 the whole *Gruppe* was instructed to concentrate on Russia only, only small sections being left in *Abteilungen* VI C3 and C4.

The officers of these *Abteilungen* were sent to the various BdS offices in the East to act on behalf on '*Unternehmen* Zeppelin'; meanwhile efforts were made through the Scandinavian countries to infiltrate agents into Russian occupied territory in the north, the *Sonderkommando Nord* under SS-*Stubaf* Brohs of RSHA VI D3 being set up under the joint command of VI D and VI C. These desperate measures were only manifestations of growing disintegration and the *Gruppe* collapsed with the others on the general surrender in May 1945.

Part II

RSHA *Amt* VI and Russia: *Unternehmen* Zeppelin

1. Early activity.
Little need be added to the remarks made in Part I, Paragraph A (3), regarding the early efforts of RSHA *Amt* VI in its work against Russia. It can be said that *Gruppe* VI C in this theatre was no better and no worse than any other *Ländergruppe* at this early stage of RSHA VI development, with the exception of *Gruppe* VI E. The work against Russia had been conducted under the ill-conceived organisation of the regional *Beauftragte* of the original *Gruppe* VI A: there were no direct sources of information within the country itself, and such information as was obtained was through the *Amt* VI representatives attached to the various SD-*Abschnitte* in eastern Germany. That information was of little value. The situation was to change however by the summer of 1941 under the combined effects of the triple change—Schellenberg as *Amtschef*, Gräfe as *Gruppenleiter*, and the beginning of the war with Russia.

2. *Unternehmen* Zeppelin.

The whole weight of the subsequent efforts of RSHA *Gruppe* VI C became centred on an enterprise known as '*Unternehmen* Zeppelin': it is almost certain that RSHA *Amt* VI work against Russia in any other direction either did not exist or was of very little consequence. There was a certain amount of activity directed by VI C through Turkey, employing Kedia's Georgian circles, and towards the end, an effort to penetrate into Russia through the Scandinavian contacts: The Kedia enterprise was of some value but the Scandinavian effort was merely an indication of the collapse of *Unternehmen* Zeppelin on the Eastern Front in early 1945 and had no other significance. The idea was to exploit the *Sonderkommando Nord* under Cellarius and Brohs (see Situation Report of RSHA *Gruppe* VI D).

Unternehmen Zeppelin was indeed a unique feature of RSHA *Amt* VI work and does not find any parallel in other *Ländergruppen*. It represented an enormous organisation with extensive ramifications throughout the Eastern Front: it is not surprising that its development bore close relationship to the varying fortunes of war on that front a consequence of which is that it presents a comprehensive picture on broad lines, but a very confused picture in detail. Information on the organisation has only been forthcoming since the collapse of Germany as previous to that only its existence was known, nothing of its internal structure, aims, methods and successes. The evidence at present available serves only to provide a general picture, as there are many contradictions in detail: for the purpose of this publication therefore, nothing more will be attempted than to provide the broad lines of its origins and development from 1941 onwards.[4]

3. Origins of *Unternehmen* Zeppelin.

It seems probable that at the beginning of the Russian campaign, RSHA *Gruppe* VI C had some representation in the *Sipo* and SD *Einsatzkommandos* which moved forward with the Armies:[5] nothing however succeeded like success on the Eastern Front—by the end of the year over a million Russian prisoners had been taken and it was from this enormous pool that RSHA *Gruppe* VI C developed its Eastern Front organisation. Many of the Russian prisoners offered their services to the German Intelligence Services and as a tactical expedient small *Kommandos* of such volunteers were formed under the direction of a German officer or senior N.C.O. in order to exploit their language knowledge and to help in the interrogation of further batches of prisoners of war. These *Kommandos* passed under the control of *Gruppe* VI C, as it was realised that there was such good material in prisoner of war Cages for espionage purposes.

4. Creation of *Unternehmen* Zeppelin in 1942.

The early exploitation of Russian prisoners of war had been largely confined to tactical purposes: the first check to the German advance in the winter of 1941 and stabilisation of the front lessened considerably the emphasis on tactical exploitation and in the spring of 1942, chiefly due to the vigorous and far seeing policy of Gräfe, it was decided to concentrate the work of RSHA *Gruppe* VI C against Russia in developing the work of the small *Kommandos* mentioned in the previous paragraph, enlarging the scope of these *Kommandos* and making available to the new organisation all other sources of information about Russia available to RSHA *Amt* VI; mainly those provided by the various overt research institutes dealing with the East. In this way the new organisation, henceforth to be known as '*Unternehmen* Zeppelin' was created, probably some time during the early summer of 1942.

5. Main characteristics of *Unternehmen* Zeppelin.
The new organisation had some notable features: it enjoyed a high degree of independence, and had at first only slight connection with the central office of RSHA *Gruppe* VI C in Berlin. It operated primarily as a self-contained field unit working in close co-operation with the armies in the field. Gräfe as a *Gruppenleiter* took of course a very direct interest in the development of the *Unternehmen* but his personal interest did not prevent his encouraging a high degree of de-centralisation from Berlin. A very small directing staff only was maintained in Berlin under Gräfe, the main work of training and recruitment being carried out from the camps set up under the *Hauptkommandos* of *Unternehmen* Zeppelin in the field.

In addition to the independent status of the new organisation, the other most noteworthy feature was the high degree of concentration. The scheme was directed towards obtaining economic and political information regarding Russia from all possible sources, though mainly through the exploitation of prisoners of war. The information thus obtained was to be handled by specialists on those subjects, a principle which entailed a high degree of collaboration with other institutions, mainly the Research Institute on Russia which operated overtly before the war. A result of this was that RSHA *Gruppe* VI G under SS-*Hstuf* Dr Krallert co-operated more closely with *Gruppe* VI C that with any other *Ländergruppe*. It is not surprising therefore to find that during the period of its most effective work, the obtaining of information, its evaluation, and collation with other information available reached a higher standard in *Unternehmen* Zeppelin than in any other *Gruppe*.

The weakness of the system lay in its close dependence on military developments: when the German armies began their retreats, the effectiveness of *Unternehmen* Zeppelin was correspondingly greatly decreased.

6. Methods of *Unternehmen* Zeppelin.
The basic method employed by *Unternehmen* Zeppelin in its task of obtaining all manner of information concerning Russia was in the handling of prisoners of war. The POW camps provided not only agent material but other necessary information for the training and briefing of agents—equipment, identity papers, local conditions, etc. The prisoners were subjected to an elaborate screening

process, the first stages of which provided general information, at the same time sending out those prisoners who seemed suitable for espionage work, these candidates being sent to a series of camps for further training. The standards set in the earlier days of the enterprise were high—sabotage training lasted three weeks, while espionage training took as long as three months: the combined sabotage-espionage course lasted six months. It was a rule that agents recruited had to be volunteers for the work.

The original policy adopted was to recruit and train masses of prisoners of war, counting only on a certain percentage of returns. This procedure had however to be modified when the tide turned against Germany, and mass deployment of agents was dropped and a higher percentage of successes was looked for.

7. Organisation of *Unternehmen* Zeppelin.

Both the internal and external organisation of *Unternehmen* Zeppelin underwent such violent changes as a result of the ebb and flow on the Eastern Front, that there is little point in indicating anything more than its broad organisational lines. In the early stages *Unternehmen* Zeppelin acted almost independently of RSHA *Gruppe* VI C, being loosely controlled through *Referat* VI C1. By late 1943, it became known as *Referat* VI C/Z having its own internal organisation on the following lines:

Referatsleiter	-	SS-*Ostubaf* Oebsger-Röder
VI C Z 1	-	Organisation
VI C Z 2	-	Administration
VI C Z 3	-	Operations
VI C Z 4	-	Recruiting and Training

The main emphasis of the organisation lay however in its external structure: the original small *Kommandos* which had been formed in late 1941 developed into a much more complex organisation of which the basic idea was that each Army Group operating on the Eastern Front had attached to it a *Hauptkommando* of *Unternehmen* Zeppelin. There were normally three such Army Groups—*Nord*, *Mitte* and *Süd*, but these groups were subject to much modification, especially in the final stages before the collapse. The *Hauptkommandos* in turn controlled a series of *Aussenkommandos*, which in their turn might control dependent *Nebenkommandos* according to operational needs. Each *Hauptkommando* was self-contained in its operations and training establishments.

In the summer of 1944, VI C/Z disappeared and came under the control of the new *Abteilung* VI C1: but owing to operational conditions, a further re-organisation took place in November 1944 when the internal structure was on the following lines:

Abteilung	VI C 1	Administration
	VI C 1/Z	Training
	VI C 1/Z	Interrogation
	VI C 1/Z	Operations
	VI C I/Z (org)	Organisation and Supplies
Abteilung	VI C 2	Soviet Union
	VI C 2a	*Erfassung* (Collection)
	VI C 2b	*Auswertung* (Evaluation)
	VI C 2c	Poland

Under this scheme the information obtained by RSHA VI C1 was passed to VI C2 for evaluation. The *Referat* VI C2c was formed as late as March 1945 with the purpose of organizing the Polish National Movement set up to combat communism, and to avoid any signs of Nazi sponsorship.

The external organisation underwent similar changes, the most notable being the creation of Army Group Weichsel, under which VI C (Z) directed two operations known as '*Unternehmen* Wellenbrecher' and '*Unternehmen* Dessau'. The changes during the latter stages were of course considerable: the entire *Gruppe* VI C concentrated on Russia except for small sub-sections of VI C3 and VI C4, the personnel of the *Gruppe* being despatched to the various BdS offices on the Eastern Front, the BdS themselves now receiving instructions to subordinate themselves to *Gruppe* VI C. The VI C representatives were placed in charge of hurriedly prepared *Meldehauptkommandos* with subordinate *Meldekommandos* which were responsible for passing back to *Gruppe* VI C all information obtained through the *Dienststellen* [offices] of the *Sipo* and SD in their areas. In this way, SS-*Stubaf* Weirauch was posted to Hungary and SS-*Hstuf* Heyer to Slovakia.

In this general confusion in the days preceding the surrender, the whole organisation disintegrated and *Unternehmen* Zeppelin came to an end.

8. Camps controlled by *Unternehmen* Zeppelin.
The following is a summary of the chief camps under *Abteilung* VI C (Z) control, together with a brief summary of their functions:

i) The Sandberge Training School:
Sandberge was the main central training establishment of the advance training of agents recruited in the various POW camps and who had undergone preliminary training under the *Hauptkommandos*. The training at Sandberge lasted between four and six months and covered all aspects of espionage work, including W/T and sabotage. The camp had its own workshop for the preparation of false documents and was amply stocked with Russian equipment of all kinds. It is significant of the scope of *Unternehmen* Zeppelin that at the height of its activity the Sandberge

camps catered for as many as 2,000 agents at a time. In the later stages the strength of the camp varied between 900 and 1,000 agents.

The camp leader was originally SS-*Hstuf* Schönemann, replaced early in 1943 by SS-*Ustuf* Rasch who remained in charge for a few months only. Rasch was now succeeded by SS-*Hstuf* Sakuth who held the position until the end of 1943. His successor was SS-*Stubaf* Kurreck who controlled not only Sandberge but on the re-organisation of RSHA VI C (Z) under SS-*Staf* Rapp in late 1944, became Inspector of all camps under the control of *Unternehmen* Zeppelin.

Sandberge was evacuated in late 1944 as a result of the Russian advance and the main training school set up at Tepl in the Sudetenland.

ii) The Sachsenhausen Camp.

This camp was a small one and catered only for specialized training of groups already trained at Sandberge. The strength of the camp did not exceed 30 men. (see also Situation Report No. 11 on RSHA *Gruppe* VI F).

iii) The Pleskau Camp.

Pleskau was the main training camp under *Hauptkommando Nord* which specialised in the training of agents from the northern territories, the Baltic States and White Russia. Owing to the long distance involved, the Pleskau camp enjoyed a high degree of independence and the planning and execution of operations were carried out by the *Kommando* itself. Only enterprises of great importance were referred back to Berlin.

The camp was evacuated latterly to Kahlberg on the Friesen peninsula. (*Leiter*: SS-*Stubaf* Otto Kraus).

iv) Training Camps on *Hauptkommando Mitte.*

Owing to the force of operational conditions, *Hauptkommando Mitte* did not long remain independent; but passed under the control of *Hauptkommando Nord*. In the early part of 1944 the *Kommando* became 'Unternehmen U.H.U.' under *Hauptkommando Nord*. The camps were reportedly changed but when *Hauptkommando Mitte* was re-created towards the end of 1944, a training camp for the *Kommando* was established near Kolin, east of Prague. The camp commander was SS-*Stubaf* Hans Kraus, brother of Otto Kraus of *Hauptkommando Nord*.

iv) The Tepl Camp.

Reference has already been made in i) above to this camp, which replaced the former Sandberge camp: Tepl was set up early in 1945 and as a result of the rapid Russian advances was never completely organised. The camp commandant was SS-*Stubaf* Lumm who set up his headquarters near Marienbad, the main camp being at Tepl with subsidiary camps in the neighbourhood as follows:

Camp	Leiter
Hofstein	SS-*Ostubaf* Körting
Jägerhein	SS-*Oschaf* Schrader
Glatzen	SS-*Hschaf* Scharnelli
Königswart	SS-*Ostuf* Jakubovitch
Markusgrün	SS-*Ustuf* Barbovitch

An interesting feature was the school at Königswart which catered for the training of girls only, an indication of the thoroughness of the whole organisation. It is to be noted that the trainees included French speaking girls, destined to be sent to France.

vi)

This camp was the original training school of *Hauptkommando* Mitte. The camp was closed in the autumn of 1942 as the result of a bombing attack. The special feature of Jablon was that it catered also for the training of purely military units under a Russian colonel, the enterprises going under the code names of 'Drushina I', 'Drushina II' and 'Drushina III'.

vii) The Auschwitz Camp.

This camp under SS-*Ostuf* Huhn dealt only with the training of Caucasians. The camp was disbanded early in 1944.

viii) The Legionowo Camp.

The Legionowo Camp in the suburbs of Warsaw was reserved for the training of Turkestans only. Very few Turkestans were eventually used for *Unternehmen* Zeppelin operations, the majority of the trainees being transferred to the Turkestan Legion for military operations. The camp, which was under the command of SS-*Stubaf* Zinke, was liquidated in the latter half of 1943, the trainees sent to the Sandberge camp.

ix) Camp of *Hauptkommando Süd.*

Little is known of the training camps of *Hauptkommando Süd*: the *Kommando* had its headquarters in late 1942 in the Crimea near Jewpatoria, and the training camps, under SS-*Stubaf* Kurreck, SS-*Stubaf* Oebsger-Röder (the original *Leiter* of the whole *Unternehmen* Zeppelin) and SS-*Stubaf* Kleinert. The *Kommando* withdrew in the general German retreat but details of its locations and operations are lacking.

x) *Sonderlager 'T':*

Sonderlager 'T' was a special camp set up at Breslau-Oswitz where Russian volunteer technicians were enabled to carry on their research and construction work under favourable conditions. The enterprise yielded such good results that it was decided to extend its scope, the result being the formation of *Sonderlager* 'L'.

xi) *Sonderlager* 'L':

Sonderlager 'L' represented an extension of the activities of *Sonderlager* 'T' to include research into economic and statistical matters relating to the U.S.S.R. In this way valuable statistics, maps, charts, and information on the Russian communications system were made available to VI C (Z) for use in their projected operations. In early 1944 the camp was transferred to Blamau in the Niederdonau area [Austria], as a result of the Russian advances and in order to establish closer liaison with the *Forschungsdienst Ost* at St Lamprecht and with the Wannsee Institute at Plankenwarth [both having been evacuated from Berlin].

9. Special Enterprises of *Unternehmen* Zeppelin.

i) The *Einsatz* General Bessanow:

General Bessanow was a Russian POW who was chosen by VI C (Z) as the leader of an operation involving the dropping by parachute of hundreds of trained agents in the Archangel area where large POW camps and concentration camps were situated. The scheme planned in early 1943, aimed at setting free the German POWs and inciting the internees in the concentration camps to revolt. For this purpose a special camp was set up in the Troppau area of Sudetenland. The operation was never carried into effect owing to a suspicion of Bessanow himself who was eventually sent to a concentration camp himself.

ii) *Unternehmen* Ulm:

Unternehmen Ulm was a large-scale sabotage enterprise under taken by RSHA *Gruppe* VI C in the latter half of 1943: its objective was to lessen the productive power of Russian factories in the Urals area by attacking the electric power circuits supplying the factories. A group of some sixty Russians with the necessary local knowledge was formed under the leadership of a Russian refugee from Belgrade, SS-*Hstuf* Semjenov. The training was carried out at the *Sonderlager* 'L' (see above), which was responsible for the provision of all the necessary technical information.

Owing to delays caused by the lack of aircraft the original scheme had to be abandoned and only part of the group was employed against alternative targets in the Volga area. No information is available on the results of the enterprise. The remaining trainees were subsequently used for sabotage operations in Croatia.

iii) *Unternehmen* Mainz:

The leading figure in *Unternehmen* Mainz was the Georgian, Michael 'Sascha' Kedia, a cheese merchant in Paris, who offered his services to the German Intelligence Services. Kedia claimed to have many contacts in the Caucasus area from whom information on Russia could be obtained. Kedia's offer was accepted by RSHA

Himmler and Heydrich whispering. (*Max Williams's collection*)

Reichsführer-SS and Chief of the German Police Heinrich Himmler. (*Max Williams's collection*)

SS-General Reinhard Heydrich,
RSHA Chief 1939–1942.
(*Max Williams's collection*)

SS-General Dr Ernst
Kaltenbrunner, RSHA Chief 1942–
1945. (*Max Williams's collection*)

Prinz Albrecht Palais, Berlin;
headquarters of the RSHA Chief.
(*Max Williams's collection*)

Office of the RSHA Chief,
Prinz Albrecht Palais, Berlin.
(*Max Williams's collection*)

Sipo-Schule Prague, 1942;
Heydrich with RSHA *Amtschef*
I (Streckenbach), right, and the
later *Amtschef* (Erwin Schulz),
left. (*Max Williams's collection*)

Dr Karl Werner Best, RSHA I
Amtschef (1939–1940).
(*Max Williams's collection*)

Erich Ehrlinger, RSHA I *Amtschef* (1944–1945). (*Max Williams's collection*)

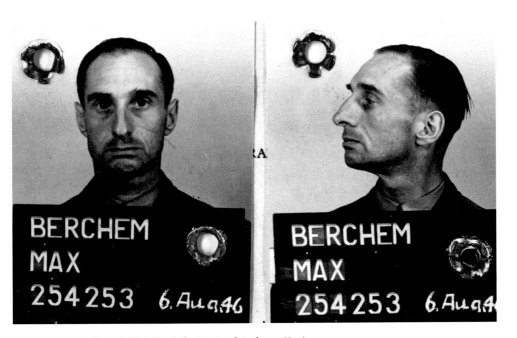

Max Berchem, RSHA I D. (*The National Archives, Kew*)

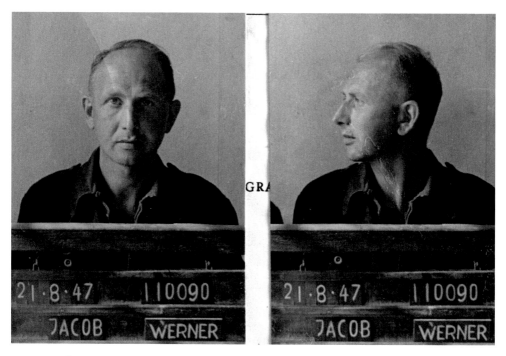

Werner Jacob, RSHA I A2. (*The National Archives, Kew*)

Prague 1939: Heydrich with Walter Hoonoch (in spectacles), RSHA I D. (*The National Archives, Kew*)

Hans Nockemann, RSHA
Amtschef II, 1939–1941.
(*Max Williams's collection*)

Josef Spacil, RSHA *Amtschef* II,
1944–1945. (*Berlin Document
Center, courtesy John P. Moore*)

Walther Rauff, RSHA II, *Gruppenleiter*. (*Max Williams's collection*)

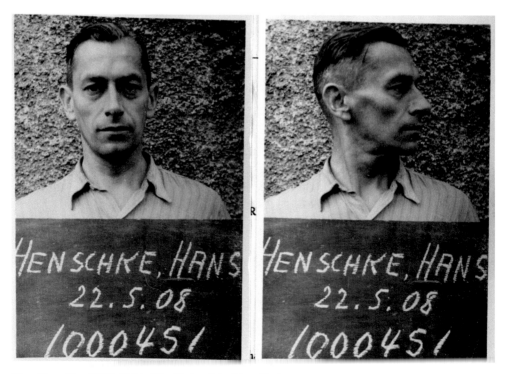

Hans Henschke, RSHA II C4. (*The National Archives, Kew*)

Otto Ohlendorf, RSHA *Amtschef* III (1939–1945). (*Max Williams's collection*)

Dr Hans Ehlich, RSHA III, *Gruppenleiter*. (*Max Williams's collection*)

Willi Seibert, RSHA III,
Gruppenleiter.
(*Max Williams's collection*)

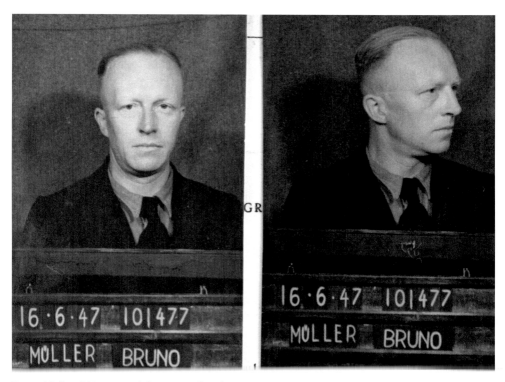

Bruno Müller, RSHA III B. (*The National Archives, Kew*)

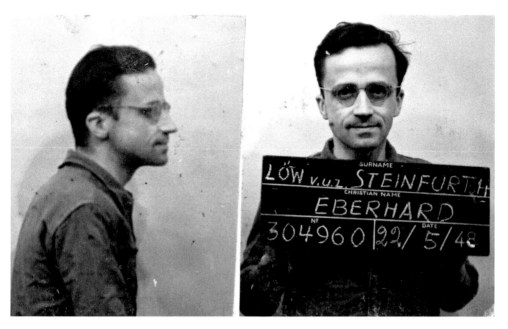

Freiherr Erberhard Löw von Steinfurt, RSHA III B5. (*The National Archives, Kew*)

SD officers on the balcony, Prinz Albrecht Palais, (Schellenberg, second right). (*Max Williams's collection*)

Heinrich Müller, RSHA *Amtschef* IV (1939–1945). (*US NARA, Berlin Document Center, SSO*)

Fritz Panzinger, Deputy *Amtschef* IV (1939–1944). (*Max Williams's collection*)

Walter Huppenkothen, Deputy
Amtschef IV (1944–1945).
(*Max Williams's collection*)

Prinz Albrecht Strasse 8, Berlin; headquarters building RSHA IV. (*Max Williams's collection*)

Albert Duchstein, Adjutant of *Amtschef* IV Müller. (*Max Williams's collection*)

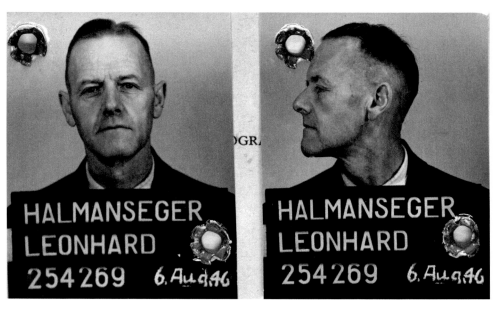

Leonhard Halmanseger, RSHA IV N (1939–1945). (*The National Archives, Kew*)

Horst Kopkow, RSHA IV A2. (*US NARA, Berlin Document Center, SSO*)

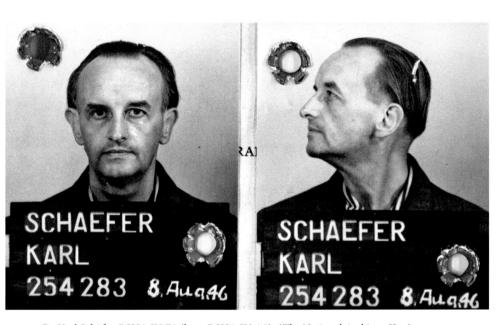

Dr Karl Schäfer, RSHA IV E3 (later RSHA IV A3). (*The National Archives, Kew*)

Kurt Lischka, RSHA IV B, *Gruppenleiter*. (*Max Williams's collection*)

Georg Kiessel, RSHA IV A1 (1944). (*The National Archives, Kew*)

Funeral procession of Heydrich, Berlin, 9 June 1942; *front row*: RSHA *Amtschefs* Artur Nebe, Bruno Streckenbach and Heinrich Müller; *following behind, from left*: Max Thomas, Otto Rasch, Walter Haensch, Oberg. (*Max Williams's collection*)

Dr Achim Ploetz (RSHA *Polizei Attaché* service). (*Max Williams's collection*)

Helmut Knochen
(*Attaché* France).
(*Max Williams's collection*)

Herbert Kappler
(*Attaché Italy*).
(*The National Archives, Kew*)

Bruno Wolff (*Attaché* Turkey). (*The National Archives, Kew*)

Artur Nebe, RSHA *Amtschef* V (1939–1944). (*Max Williams's collection*)

Heydrich and Nebe with a Spanish police delegation visiting Berlin. (*Max Williams's collection*)

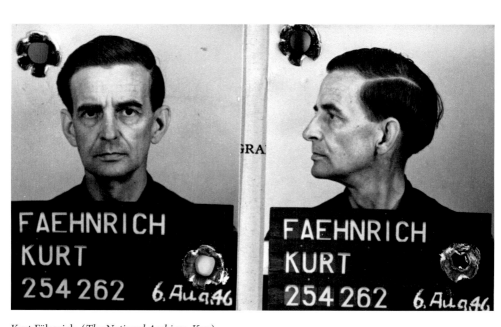

Kurt Fähnrich. (*The National Archives, Kew*)

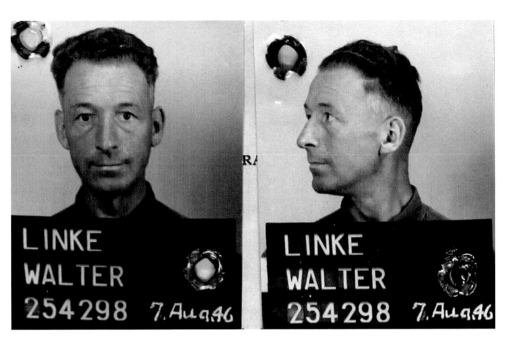

Walter Linke. (*The National Archives, Kew*)

Dr Hans Schumacher.
(*The National Archives, Kew*)

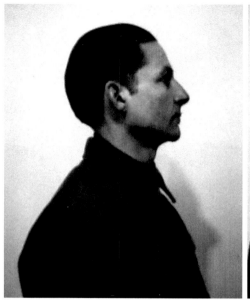

Dr Friedrich Schulze. (*The National Archives, Kew*)

Heinz Jost, RSHA *Amtschef* VI
(1939–1942). (*The National
Archives, Kew*)

Walter Schellenberg, RSHA
Amtschef VI (1943–1945).
(*The National Archives, Kew*)

Berkaerstrasse, Berlin;
headquarters building of RSHA VI.
(*Author's collection*)

Martin Sandberger, RSHA VI A
Gruppenleiter. (*Max Williams's collection*)

Werner Göttsch, RSHA VI B
Gruppenleiter. (*The National Archives, Kew*)

Alfred Naujocks, RSHA VI B.
(*The National Archives, Kew*)

Otto Skorzeny, RSHA VI S
Gruppenleiter. (*US NARA,
Berlin Document Center, SSO*)

Franz Mayr (Iraq).
(*The National Archives, Kew*)

Ludwig Moyzisch (Turkey).
(*The National Archives, Kew*)

Karl Haas (Italy).
(*The National Archives, Kew*)

Siegfried Becker (Argentine).
(*The National Archives, Kew*)

Führerschule der Sipo u.d. SD, Berlin-Charlottenburg. (*Author's collection*)

Otto Hellwig, Commander, *Führerschule der Sipo u.d.* SD, Berlin-Charl. (*Max Williams's collection*)

Grenzpolizeischule Pretzsch. (Author's collection)

Johannes Thummler, commander,
Grenzpolizeischule Pretzsch.
(*Max Williams's collection*)

Site of RSHA building, Prinz Albrecht Strasse, Berlin, in 1972. (*Author's collection*)

Entrance to the *Reichskriminalpolizeiamt* (RSHA V), Werderscher markt, Berlin. (*Max Williams's collection*)

SS-*Stubaf* Friedrich
Bosshammer, RSHA IV B4.
(*US NARA, Berlin Document
Center, SSO*)

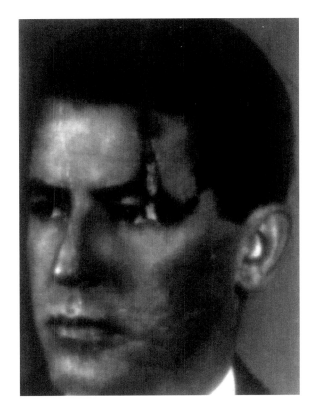

SS-*Stubaf* Walter Dillersberger,
RSHA *Untersuchungsführer*.
(*US NARA, Berlin Document
Center, SSO*)

SS-*Stubaf* Harro Thomsen, RSHA IV B2. (*US NARA, Berlin Document Center, SSO*)

SS-*Staf* Karl Tschierschky, RSHA IV and WERWOLF. (*US NARA, Berlin Document Center, SSO*)

Gruppe VI C (it is known that Kedia was also connected in some way with *Abwehr* II at one time) and was eventually installed at Batum on the Turkish frontier. Through small groups of agents crossing the frontier, Kedia passed weapons, sabotage and propaganda material into Russia and in return obtained quantities of printed material, books and periodicals of all kinds, most of which was made available to the research departments of *Unternehmen* Zeppelin.

The operation ceased to yield results after the spring of 1944 owing to the difficulty of maintaining contacts.

Conclusion.

The above brief notes serve only to give some idea of the scope and comprehensiveness of *Unternehmen* Zeppelin: there is so far little indication of what measures of success attended RSHA *Gruppe* VI C for the enormous expenditure of time, training and agents involved in the scheme. It can, however, be said that *Unternehmen* Zeppelin was a far better conceived operational enterprise than any other undertaken by RSHA *Amt* VI, probably owing to the enterprise and enthusiasm of the *Gruppenleiter*, Gräfe. The *Unternehmen* lost much of its effectiveness after his death, and was unable to stand the strain of the Russian advances in 1944. There are also indications that the Russians themselves were active in counter-espionage work against VI C (Z), with what all-round success is unknown, as only isolated cases of the results of their work have been mentioned.[6]

Part III

RSHA *Gruppe* VI C and the Middle East

1. Controlling *Referate*.

In 1939–40 Turkey and the Near East came under the control of RSHA *Referat* VI D5 under SS-*Hstuf* Hagen, *Gruppe* VI D at that time being responsible for the 'Süd-Ost', embracing the Balkan States and Greece as well as the territory of VI D5. In this organisation therefore it was obviously the intention that penetration of the Near East should be carried out from Greece, in support of which theory there is the fact that Moyzisch in 1940 was briefed for his mission to Turkey by SS-*Hstuf* Langlotz, *Referent* VI D4 covering Bulgaria and Greece. The territory remained under the same *Gruppe* when it was renamed RSHA *Gruppe* VI B in 1940–41. In 1941 Turkey, the Near and Middle East finally passed to *Gruppe* VI C, VI C 12 being competent for Turkey, Iran, and Afghanistan, under SS-*Hstuf* Schuback, while VI C 13 dealt with the Arab countries under *Angestellter* Em. This organisational structure continued until January 1944 when the new *Referat* VI C 14 was created under SS-*Hstuf* Gamotha to deal with Iran. Finally in September

322   RSHA: Reich Security Main Office—Organisation, Activities, Personnel

1944, *Abteilung* VI C3 became competent for the whole area under SS-*Hstuf* Schuback. The sub-division of the *Abteilungen* are so far unknown.

2. Prominent personalities.
Apart from the *Gruppenleiter*, SS-*Ostubaf* Gräfe (now dead), the most prominent personality concerned with the Near East was SS-*Hstuf* Schuback, *Referent* VI C 12 since 1941, and later *Leiter Abteilung* VI C3. The other RSHA VI C officers closely identified with the preparation and despatch of missions were SS-*Stubaf* Beisner, the so-called Arab expert of *Amt* VI who joined the *Gruppe* in 1943 after a period of service in dealing with Arabs in the *Einsatzkommando* Tunis. With him was SS-*Hstuf* Kohlhaas also of *Einsatzkommando* Tunis, Beisner acting as *Referent* VI C 13 and Kohlhaas being stationed in Greece as the despatching agency from the territory. Kohlhaas had replaced SS-*Ustuf* Tappenböck and SS-*Hstuf* Eylitz in the capacity. SS-*Hschaf* Lengling acted for a short period as *Referent* VI C 13 in 1943 before being arrested for fraud. Schuback's deputy was SS-*Ostuf* Belling. It is worth noting that so far none of these personalities have been arrested.

3. Turkey.
(a) <u>Moyzisch in Ankara:</u>
The first RSHA *Amt* VI efforts at the exploitation of the Middle East as a field of operations did not take place until the summer of 1940, when Moyzisch was sent to Ankara by Langlotz, then *Referent* VI D4. Moyzisch took up his appointment as assistant Commercial *Attache* in the German Embassy in June 1940, being followed shortly afterwards by Duplitzer, who took up a similar appointment in Istanbul.

Moyzisch possessed no special qualifications for the post he had to fill, but in his case certain factors operated in favour of RSHA *Amt* VI resulting in Moyzisch proving to be one of the more successful *Hauptbeauftragte* chosen by Jost. There was no well organised policy behind the appointment of Moyzisch and there was very little connection behind the more impressive paper organisation of RSHA *Amt* VI in 1939–40 and the actual work carried out by it. Moyzisch however had the misfortune in German eyes of having Jewish blood in his veins, and in consequence welcomed the appointment to neutral territory where he would be reasonably safe from any action taken against him because of his suspected Jewish parentage. His subsequent activity in Ankara was dependent on two considerations—his concern not to indulge in any activity that would either lead him to fall foul of the Foreign Office representative or which would promote bad relations between himself and the Turkish authorities, either of which eventualities might lead to a request for his recall to Germany, together with his equally great concern to give sufficient satisfaction to *Amt* VI in order that his recall would not come from that direction. Moyzisch therefore pursued a policy of caution, one which suited *Amt* VI well, as the normal *Hauptbeauftragte* appointed in the early days, sharing Moyzisch's lack of training and background, had not tarried in establishing bad relations all round.

(b) SS-*Stubaf* Duplitzer in Istanbul.
The contrast was well marked in Istanbul where SS-*Stubaf* Duplitzer, young, untrained, and erratic, soon got himself into the bad graces of the German Consul, with the result that his recall was frequently urged both by the Consul and by Moyzisch himself. Duplitzer, however, stayed put and was the only representative in Istanbul until the arrival of Wolff in 1942.

(c) Influence of Gräfe in 1941.
The original assignment given to Moyzisch had been simply to submit regular reports on the political situation in Turkey, without any suggestion of using the country as a base for operations against neighbouring territory. The value of Turkey as such a base was not lost on Gräfe when he took over as *Gruppenleiter* in 1941, as was evidenced by his instructions to Moyzisch to extend his functions to cover the Near East. Eventually it was decided to allow Moyzisch to carry on in Ankara and to supplement him by the appointment of SS-*Ostuf* Fast, whose specific assignment was to work independently of Moyzisch and working from Ankara, to recruit agents for penetration into the neighbouring Arabic countries.

(d) The appointment of Wolff in 1942.
The major development of note in 1942 was the appointment of SS-*Stubaf* Regierungsrat Wolff as Vice Consul in Istanbul, a position he took up in June 1942. Wolff, curiously enough, and a RSHA *Amt* IV officer, his previous experience having been confined to conducting special investigations on behalf of *Amt* IV in Norway and the Low Countries. While therefore untrained in RSHA *Amt* VI work, Wolff had had considerable experiences in his own police duties and was well fitted for the assignment he was given. This assignment was that of establishing close and personal relations both with the Turkish Police and Turkish Intelligence Services in order to exploit the possibility of working with them, while in addition he had the tasks, more in keeping with his previous experience, of supervising consular and diplomatic circles in Turkey with a view to checking any attempts on the part of these circles to contact the Allies, and also to discover whether any channels of communications existed through Turkey between resistance organisations in German occupied territory and their headquarters outside the country.

(e) Relations with the Foreign Office representative in Turkey.
A notable feature of RSHA *Amt* VI work in Turkey was the relationship between the *Amt* VI representative and Ambassador von Papen, the Foreign Office representative. The customary relationship between these two services in other spheres was never cordial and the reasons for the state of affairs in Turkey was due not only to Moyzisch's conciliatory and cautious attitude, but to the fact that von Papen himself did not see eye to eye with Ribbentrop and found Moyzisch useful at times for circumventing normal channels. The exchange of information

between the two departments was free, a fact which enhanced the reputation of Moyzisch in the eyes of RSHA *Amt* VI. von Papen on occasions passed reports through RSHA *Amt* VI rather than through his own channels, especially when these reports contained recommendations contrary to Ribbentrop's own policy regarding Turkey, with the hope that they reach Himmler through Schellenberg.

(f) <u>Relations with the Turkish Intelligence Services.</u>
With the re-organisation of the *Gruppe* in the summer of 1941 and the joint appointment of Gräfe and Schellenberg as *Gruppenleiter* and *Amtschef* respectively, there started a series of attempts to establish collaboration between RSHA *Amt* VI and the Turkish Intelligence Services. At that time and during the course of the following year, the general war situation was very much in favour of Germany and the time seemed opportune to woo the Turkish authorities from their official standing with the Western Allies. The hope of success in this venture lay not only in the generally favourable situation, but also in the fact that Turkey, while seeking friendship with the Allies, had also a deep-seated fear of the Soviet Union.

Gräfe himself visited Ankara soon after his appointment to urge Moyzisch to take the first steps and in early 1942 a meeting took place between Moyzisch, von Papen and Perkel, the head of the Turkish Intelligence Service, a meeting which however produced no results. The efforts were continued during the next year and Schellenberg himself visited Turkey in July 1943 for a similar purpose but again without success.

The importance attached to this matter by RSHA *Amt* VI was evidenced by Wolff's appointment to Istanbul in June 1942, one of his specific assignments being to establish contact with the Turkish Intelligence Service. The official meetings between the two services were, however, arranged only through Moyzisch in Ankara, Wolff confining himself to establishing contact with a certain Ferruh, working for the Turkish Intelligence Service, a contact which in any case did not materialise until early 1944.

The efforts of RSHA *Amt* VI in this direction were a failure in the essential points, as no working arrangement was every agreed to; the Turkish attitude was of course conditioned by the developments on the fighting fronts, her early policy being to maintain a balance between Germany and Britain without committing herself to either side, but after the Russian successes from 1943 onwards, her concern was to act as intermediary between the two powers with a view to strengthening her position against Russia. In the circumstances, therefore, it was never Turkey's policy to compromise her intelligence services with Germany, while at the same time making unofficial contacts for immediate benefit to herself.

(g) <u>Contacts with the Turkish Intelligence Services.</u>
The result of this manoeuvring on both sides was that from 1942 onwards both Moyzisch and later Wolff had established contacts with the Turkish Intelligence

Services without any definite policy being agreed on. Moyzisch on his side had established relations from an early date with Bayramoglu, who was connected with the Turkish Intelligence Service and through whom various approaches were made by that service on matters involving both Turkish and German foreign policy in the Mediterranean, especially regarding the status of the Dodecanese Islands under Italian control. It was Bayramoglu too who acted as intermediary between von Papen and Perkel prior to their meeting in early 1942, while after the break in Turkish-German relations in the summer of 1944, he again approached Moyzisch with an offer that he should act as an intermediary between Berlin and the Western Allies with a view to inaugurating peace-talks, a move which would have suited Turkey's foreign policy. This approach was abortive. Throughout their association, however, Bayramoglu furnished Moyzisch with information on diplomatic matters of interest to Germany.

The approach of Wolff in February 1944 through Ferruh had similar motives, and after preliminary discussions, Ferruh gave more definite indications of good faith by supplying Wolff with information on the imminence of the *Vermehren volte-face* and subsequent information on the efforts of Germans in Turkey to seek the right of Turkish asylum. Again, in May 1944, the Turkish authorities connived at, and even assisted in the passage of Georgian agents of *Abwehr* II over the Turco–Russian border, under the leadership of the Georgian minority leader, Kedia. The approach took concrete form immediately prior to the formal severance of relations between Turkey and Germany with the suggestion from the Turkish side that the German representatives should remain in contact by W/T with Ferruh to whom a W/T set was provided for the purpose, in order that a link should be maintained between Wolff and Berlin. Through this means Wolff and Stiele, the Consul, kept in intermittent contact with Berlin until January 1945.

(h) Other contacts in Turkey.

Apart from a few paid agents of minor importance, the contacts for information purposes established by Moyzisch were in journalistic circles such as the Transocean and DNB services and in business circles, most of whom were Germans established in Turkey with good connections. In addition, he collaborated closely with Aoki, a Japanese diplomat in the country politically well informed, who also supplied Moyzisch with Russian newspapers for onward transmission to Berlin, and with Wiitanen, the Finnish military *attaché* in Ankara, who offered in August 1944 to send information on behalf of Moyzisch to Berlin as well as to Helsinki in the event of the latter being unable to maintain contact in view of the impending break in Turco-German relations. This arrangement was left in the hands of Moyzisch's W/T assistant Patek for technical details.

In Istanbul Wolff established contact with the representatives of the Bulgarian Intelligence Service, who supplied information on the general political situation, and with an agent of the Czech Intelligence Service which however represented an attempt at penetration by that service. A more notable contact in view of subsequent events was that with Urlatiano of the Roumanian Intelligence Service. From early 1943 onwards Wolff was in close contact with Urlatiano who supplied information on the internal Roumanian political situation. When Urlatiano was relieved of his position as Consul in May 1944, steps were taken by Schuback to recruit him as a stay-behind agent in Turkey; this recruitment is dealt with under the 'Mob' organisation below.

(i) <u>The 'Mob' Organisation.</u>

The 'Mob' organisation was the name given to the stay-behind network to be set up by RSHA *Amt* VI in Turkey in accordance with the general instructions to all *Amt* VI representatives in neutral and occupied territory to prepare I-*Netze* and R-*Netze* in the event of Allied invasion or expulsion from neutral territory. Instructions for the preparation of the network were given to both Wolff and Moyzisch in the course of 1943, but while the scheme was regarded with a certain amount of enthusiasm in Berlin, it received a very luke-warm reception from both *Amt* VI representatives in Turkey. In Istanbul, Kröger, the W/T operator at the Consulate General, was recruited for the purpose, but though agreeing to the assignment, had no intention of carrying it out. Wolff for his part pleaded a lack of trained personnel, pointing out that only Urlatiano was equipped for such a task. It was for this purpose therefore that Schuback visited Turkey to contact Urlatiano personally and to make arrangements. The other links in the Istanbul sector were provided by *Gruppe* VI C. Marion Graib arrived in Turkey in November 1943 as a link, but left for Germany again in August 1944 on the instructions of Wolff himself, as he considered him completely blown with the Turks. At about the same time Schuback sent a Swiss, Louis Müller, to act in a similar capacity, but the link did not operate. Finally, an Italian named Genovesi arrived in February 1944 to set himself up with the help of Duplitzer. Genovesi, however, destroyed his [W/T] set as he considered the mission too dangerous. The main hope in Istanbul was Urlatiano; the link operated for a short time only, but his activities were known to the Turkish Intelligence Services, as Ferruh revealed in making his approach to Wolff in January 1945.

If the success of the 'Mob' organisation was very limited in the Istanbul area, the position in Ankara was still weaker as a result of the attitude of Moyzisch, who took steps to ensure that the scheme would not work. Two agents were recruited on instructions from Berlin, but in one case Moyzisch gave no instructions to the agent concerned, in the other case altered the final instructions from Berlin regarding the date on which contact was to be established in order that the link would not become effective.

In the circumstances therefore it is not surprising that the attempts at a network in Turkey were a complete failure.

(j) <u>The break in Turkish relations with Germany.</u>

The break with Turkey came in August 1944; as a result the German representatives in the country were interned, including all the RSHA *Amt* VI personnel. Operations came to an end, except for the link which was preserved through the Turkish Intelligence Service, as explained in Paragraph (g) above and for the offer of Wiitanen mentioned in Paragraph (h) above, the results of which are unknown.

(k) <u>The CICERO material.</u>

The CICERO case represents the greatest scoop of the part of RSHA *Amt* VI in any theatre of their operations. From November 1943 until March 1944, Moyzisch in Ankara was successful in establishing a source of information which provided material of consistently high importance obtained from direct access to secret documents relating to British interests in the Middle East. The material thus obtained was passed immediately back to *Amt* VI [in Berlin]; but it is somewhat ironical feature of the CICERO material that its importance was such that in the eyes of *Amt* VI it was treated with reserve, as it was suspected of being in the nature of an Allied plant. Intelligent use of the material might have given the Germans invaluable information on the Second Front. In addition to this military information, the document provided high grade political information. The source stopped completely in March 1944.

(l) <u>The REMO organisation.</u>

The exact nature of the PASHA and REMO organisations is still one of the unexplained points in the Middle East, and it is only possible at the moment to indicate the broad lines of the available evidence.

The leading personality was a certain Dr Reichert who was the Near East representative of the *Deutsche Nachrichtenbüro* [DNB] in Cairo before the outbreak of war. Reichert was deported as an undesirable alien, and from the end of 1940 continued his work in Turkey, where he remained until the beginning of 1942. Through his connections with the DNB, Reichert was instrumental in building up a well-organised information service with sources probably in Cairo itself. The organisation was not directed either by RSHA *Amt* VI or by the *Abwehr*, but the information obtained by Reichert was made available to these two departments according to its nature. In addition Reichert also supplied information to the Embassy, the Propaganda Ministry, and the Foreign Office. His chief assistant in this activity was an Italian journalist, named Zamboni.

The information supplied by Reichert's organisation which went under the name of PASHA in the *Abwehr* and REMO in RSHA *Amt* VI, was of sufficiently high quality to make Schellenberg suspicious of its authenticity. It was for this reason that SS-*Hstuf* Mohr was sent to Istanbul in 1942 with the assignment of working with Reichert in order to establish whether or not the information obtained through these sources was genuine or smoke.

The sources of the PASHA and REMO organisations are still unknown, and unfortunately Reichert himself cannot supply the answer as he was killed in an accident early in 1943. Zamboni returned to Italy in July 1943 when the network ceased to operate. Zamboni himself was arrested in Rome and sent to Berlin for interrogation, as the Germans themselves were still uncertain as to the reliability of Reichert's organisation.

Zamboni is now under [post-war] interrogation at AFHQ [Allied Forces Headquarters, in Italy], and the results of his interrogation may be instrumental in clearing up the outstanding points in the REMO organisation. The other personality who should be treated as a priority target in connection with this still outstanding problem is SS-*Hstuf* Mohr himself, who returned to Germany some time in 1944, and was last reported in April 1945 at Reuthe in southern Germany.

4. Persia.

(a) <u>Recruitment of Mayr and Gamotha:</u>

The first efforts of RSHA *Amt* VI at exploiting Persia as a sphere of operations were indeed half-hearted, but made a good illustration of the working methods of the *Amt* at that early date. Early in 1940 Ramon Gamotha and Franz Mayr volunteered for service in the Middle East and were accepted by Jost as prospective *Beauftragte* for the *Amt* in Persia. Neither of the new recruits had any background experience of the country whatever, nor was their knowledge of the language on any higher level: their qualifications were likewise nil. Nor could they in the position in which they found themselves look to RSHA *Amt* VI for guidance and training as the *Amt* had nothing to offer them. There was no *Referat* at that time competent for the country and the best that Jost could do for them was to attach them for a spell to the then *Gruppe* VI H under SS-*Staf* Knochen (later BdS Paris) which purported to specialise in such subjects as Freemasonry, Semitism, etc. outside Germany, the connection between that RSHA *Gruppe* and Iran not being too clear. Nevertheless the two agents spent a short spell there virtually wasting time, although the *Amt* did rise on occasion to the provision of a few books on Persia itself. Jost meantime was engaged in his normal difficulties of trying to persuade the Foreign Office to grant the necessary visas.

Tired of waiting both Mayr and Gamotha applied to be returned to the Army, a request which was granted. Eventually however the visas were ready by August 1940, and after a false start which took them as far as Moscow before returning to Berlin because of further complication with the Foreign Office, the two *Beauftragter* finally left for Persia in October 1940.

(b) <u>Mission of Mayr and Gamotha:</u>

In reality, their troubles now only began, not however by reason of the complexity of the mission assigned to them, which consisted merely of making themselves acquainted with the country and their surroundings pending the receipt of further instructions from Berlin. They were inevitably fated to come into conflict with the Foreign Office representatives. Their position on arrival therefore was that they were both untrained in intelligence and in W/T, had received no instructions in sabotage methods, had been unable to obtain any accurate information on the country itself prior to their departure, were given no connections already existing in the country which they could profitably exploit, had been given no channel of communications apart from the Foreign Office, which facilities were promptly refused them and last but not least, had been given no specific instructions on the nature of their mission. It is hardly surprising therefore that the success or otherwise of their stay in Iran would depend entirely on the intelligence and enthusiasm which they themselves displayed and not on any guidance from RSHA *Amt* VI.

(c) <u>The Allied occupation of Iran in August 1941:</u>
As events turned out their official stay in the country was destined to be of short duration. In August 1941, Russian and Allied troops occupied the country following on the attempted Arab revolt, an event which took the German colony completely by surprise and which caused both Mayr and Gamotha to seek their own way of escape. Gamotha succeeded after a hazardous journey in reaching Turkey where he was interned for a spell before returning to Germany in 1943 while Mayr sought refuge among the tribes with whom he had established contact. The results achieved by the two during their stay had of course been negligible, except for the contacts which Mayr had made among the tribes, a factor which was to prove of importance later. Mayr remained in hiding throughout the winter during which time of course he was out of contact with RSHA *Amt* VI who were unaware of his whereabouts.

(d) <u>Schulze at Tabriz:</u>
During Mayr's stay in Tehran he had contacted Dr Schulze, the *Abwehr* I-*Luft* representative at Tabriz, northern Persia. Schulze had arrived there in May 1941 to carry out normal *Abwehr* functions. In August 1941 Schulze attempted to escape into Afghanistan but was arrested near the border and returned to Tehran, where he was successful in obtaining sanctuary in the German Legation, claiming diplomatic cover. While negotiations were proceeding for his transfer to Allied authorities, Schulze succeeded in escaping and remained in hiding in the Tehran area for some eight months, in company with his wife. The situation therefore during the winter of 1941–42 was both RSHA *Amt* VI and the *Abwehr* had representatives in hiding in Persia without however either service being aware of their location or being able to make contact with them. The subsequent events in Persia depended entirely on the personal initiative of these two representatives.

(e) <u>Developments in February 1942:</u>
Mayr for his part remained politically inactive during the winter months in the Tehran region and it was not until early in 1942 that he felt safe enough to restart

his activities. By this time Mayr had got the 'feel' of the country, and had already conceived himself in the role of a second 'Lawrence of Arabia', this time however on behalf of Germany. His early first steps were to create and foster an effective 'fifth column' among the Persian tribes which offered good scope for such work. In February he was successful in re-establishing contact with Schulze by means of one of his couriers, Vaziri, while at the same time he visited the Japanese Legation in Tehran to discuss the situation with the Japanese there. Meantime a meeting was arranged between Mayr and Schulze, when it was mutually arranged that the two should agree to a functional division of interest in Persia. Mayr to concentrate on the fostering of a fifth column and the organisation of a political espionage system, while Schulze would deal with military matters. In April, Mayr again contacted the Japanese Legation now due for expulsion and at this meeting the Legation bequeathed Mayr with five old W/T sets, while Mayr gave the Japanese a message to be sent to Berlin via Ankara and Tokyo giving an account of the situation and suggesting a code which might be used if Mayr were successful in getting his W/T sets to work.

The following month Schulze's position in Tehran became too difficult owing to the arrest of one of his couriers. It was then decided that the division between Mayr and Schulze should be geographical and not functional, Mayr to remain in the north, while Schulze would be responsible for all activities in the south. Schulze therefore left for the Qashgi territory establishing good relations by promise of delivery of arms and ammunition from Germany, maintaining at the same time contact with Mayr in the north by means of the courier system. Schulze also set about the preparations of a landing ground for the expected expedition from Germany. At the same time he had been provided with one of Mayr's W/T sets to attempt to establish contact with Berlin.

(f) Attempts to contact Berlin:
The major weakness in the situation was of course that neither Mayr nor Schulze had found it possible to contact Berlin, and the continual success of their operations depended on help being provided from this quarter in order to keep the tribes in good humour. In August 1942, Mayr sent a courier to contact the German Embassy in Ankara carrying with them a letter signed on behalf of Schulze which requested the despatch of a W/T operator from Berlin and of course, money. The letter also suggested a code which should be used in sending any reply.

It is interesting to note the method suggested by Mayr for receiving messages from Berlin, a method he had already proposed in the message given to the Japanese in Tehran in April. The suggestion was that the Germans should send their reply quite openly through the '*Kameradschaftdienst*' broadcasts to German forces, using at the same time the simple code proposed by Mayr. It was in fact by this method that Mayr learned in the course of August 1942 that the message given to the Japanese in Tehran had reached Berlin via Ankara and Tokyo: in October

1942 a similar message was received through the same channel confirming the arrival of the courier in Ankara and promising that a courier was on the way to Mayr with a message, a false ray of hope for Mayr as when the courier did in fact arrive with a message in the shape of a small pill wrapped in paper, it was beyond even the ingenuity and resource of Mayr to discover what message the pill or paper contained. Nothing daunted, Mayr sent a further courier in January 1943 to Ankara, this time with much more definite and business-like proposals, giving three alternative landing-grounds for projected parachute operations and a code whereby the type of mission and the landing ground to be used would be indicated. In February 1943 a reply was received that operations were in course of preparation.

(g) Events in Berlin:

After the occupation of Persia in August 1941 both the *Abwehr* and RSHA *Amt* VI were completely unaware of the fate of their representatives in the country and were as a result quite ignorant of the activities of Mayr and Schulze during the winter of 1941–42. Until Mayr's message was received from Tokyo therefore, both services had been pursuing independent lines for further operations in the country, the *Abwehr* on their side making some effort to use the Persian colony in Germany for the purpose, while RSHA *Amt* VI had taken no more vigorous action than the sending of Fast to Ankara with instructions to exploit the Middle East territory. No specific plans were therefore in course of preparation, though it is to be remembered that in the course of 1942 the German armies were already penetrating deep into Russian territory, and *Gruppe* VI C presumably did not attach too great importance to Persia in the expectation that they would enter the country by military operations. The expected and much-heralded success in the East would make everything else quite simple.

The arrival of the first message from Tokyo preceded by a few weeks only what was to prove the turning point in the war: in September 1942 both Stalingrad and Cairo seemed about to fall, by October the Allies were counter-attacking in the desert and Stalingrad remained uncaptured and a Russian counter-attack was on the way. Interest in Persia therefore increased as that country represented a slender link between the two powers. At the time therefore when the importance of Persia in the general pattern of the war became apparent both the *Abwehr* and the SD suddenly became aware that they had active and enterprising representation in the country, and both services set about exploiting the unexpected windfall.

(h) Preparation for Expedition:

The collaboration between Mayr and Schulze presented problems to Berlin, as both the *Abwehr* and RSHA *Amt* VI claimed that exploitation of the situation was their affair. Finally it was agreed that any missions sent in reply to the appeals of Mayr and Schulze should be under joint control, a factor which in fact was greatly to weaken the effectiveness of the operations. In addition neither service was inclined to be guided by the recommendation of Mayr, whose specific request was for a W/T operator, money and arms. To the SD however, Persia represented a supply line to Russia, and their main interest was to sabotage that supply line. The expedition therefore which was sent to Persia in the course of the following year failed to exploit the situation to the best advantage and a potentially dangerous situation for the Allies did not fully materialise. The expeditions were ill-conceived and rendered ineffective the good work of both Mayr and Schulze during the long period in which they had operated alone.

(i) The Franz Expedition:

The Franz expedition consisted of six agents, SS-*Ustuf* Bluhm, SS-*Oschaf* Rockstroh, SS-*Oschaf* Holzapfel, SS-*Uschaf* Grille, *Obergefreiter* Köndgen and *Obergefreiter* Korel. The SD personnel of the above had been in training at the Oranienburg Camp where their training had commenced at the end of 1942. The importance attached to their mission by RSHA *Amt* VI is evidenced by the fact that the party was invited to a party at which Kaltenbrunner, Schellenberg and Gräfe were all present. Of the *Abwehr* personnel Köndgen and Korel, Köndgen had been a member of the Brandenburg Division while Korel had previous experience in Persia itself where in fact he had already met Mayr in 1941. The *Abwehr* party therefore would have suited Mayr's purpose, but *Gruppe* VI C insisted on representation with the result that the final party of six was eventually despatched landing at Persia in the first days of April 1943, the party soon being reduced to five as a result of the death of Korel.

The nature of the mission given to the Franz expedition in so far as it invovled sabotage did not meet with Mayr's approval but in this instance he was successful in persuading the party to abandon their mission and conform to his ideas. The party split into two groups, Bluhm and Köndgen going south to the 'Dora' expedition, with whom contact was maintained by W/T, the 'Dora' group being unable to contact Berlin directly. In addition a courier system was maintained. It is to be noted that early in August 1943 the 'Dora' group received further arms and ammunition from Germany by parachute.

(j) The Anton Expedition:

Meanwhile Schulze in the south was finding it increasingly difficult to maintain good relations with the Qashgai tribes as his repreated promises of help from Germany were not materialising. When Schulze therefore learned by courier of the safe arrival of the 'Franz' expedition for his territory in the south, a request which Mayr duly passed and to which there came the ominous reply that plans were already underway without however any indication of the nature of the expedition or its personnel. Mayr's fears that again the expedition would be wrongly planned and conceived were only too well founded: Mayr's conception was still that the situation in Persia lent itself to political exploitation while Berlin thought only in terms of sabotage. On July 16th 1943 the 'Anton' expedition landed in the south consisting of four agents under the leadership of SS-*Ustuf* Kurmis and Kurt Piwonka, Kurt Harbers as W/T operators and a Persian interpreter, Farzad. Though the party was primarily SD, *Abwehr* II had collaborated in the training and preparation, Farzad having been an *Abwehr* agent prior to joining the expedition. The choice of personnel was unfortunate as Kurmis showed no intention of either acting under Mayr or even co-operating with him being the typical Nazi fanatic, young, impetuous and intransigent. Kurmis had been in 1940 *Leiter* of *Abteilung* VI of the SD-*Abschnitt* Memel.

(k) <u>Deterioration in the situation:</u>
It is a curious and significant feature of events in Persia at this time that where Mayr and Schulze had met with no little success in establishing good relations with the tribes and fomenting a potentially dangerous fifth column within the country during the period in which they acted singly without help from Berlin, the situation generally deteriorated when they succeeded in their primary object of establishing contact with Berlin. The main reason of course lay in the fact that the policy adopted by Berlin did not agree with that which had been in operation for over a year in Persia.

In the space of five months three expeditions had been successfully carried out—the 'Franz' expedition in the north, the reinforcement operation for the 'Dora' group, and the 'Anton' expedition in the south, though the 'Bertha' operation which was planned to reinforce 'Franz' did not materialise.

In spite of these operations however the situation was not improved: apart from the lack of cohesion in policy between Berlin and Persia itself, there was the additional factor that with the war situation now going against Germany, the tribes themselves were less disposed to co-operate, especially in the south where Schulze had been living on unfulfilled promises. Indeed Schulze's and Kurmis's group remained virtual prisoners throughout the winter of 1943 and were unsuccessful in making any W/T contact with Berlin. Meanwhile the Qashgai brothers themselves were under arrest in Cairo and negotiations were opened up for an exchange of personnel. Finally in March 1944 Schulze and three others were handed over to the British authorities, Kurmis however avoided capture by committing suicide.

The situation in the north had come to a head even more rapidly. In August 1943 a Persian army officer was arrested and admitted having been in contact with Mayr. Through this lead Rockstroh was arrested with his W/T set on the 14th August 1943, Mayr himself the following day, and Holzapfel on the 16th. The arrest of Grille, the other member, was not long delayed. The 'Dora' group was liquidated soon afterwards. Thus by October 1943 the Mayr/Schulze enterprise had been virtually ended.

5. Syria, Iraq, Palestine.

(a) General:

The general picture giving the background of RSHA *Amt* VI activity in these countries has already been given in Part I above. There was of course no direct representation in any of these countries and exploitation of the territory was variously carried out from Turkey under Fast and Duplitzer, under the '*Unternehmen* Otto' in 1941–43 and directly by RSHA *Gruppe* VI C in 1943–45. The following paragraphs therefore merely summarise the missions which were directed by these various controlling agencies, in chronological order.

(b) The Papadopoulos mission:

The Papadopoulos mission in June 1943 represented the first attempt by *Dienststelle* 3000 under RSHA VI F/O to penetrate the Middle East, the mission given to Papadopoulos and his companion Lavrentiades being one of sabotage and moral subversion. The mission was a failure although Lavrentiades was eventually released after interrogation and made his way to Cairo. The operation was an unimportant one, except that it was the first sign of any RSHA *Amt* VI activity in the Middle East theatre.

(c) The Swedkowicz mission:

Stanislaw Swedkowicz was a Pole employed from 1940 in the Organisation Todt until his recruitment in December 1942 by the SD-*Abschnitt* Klagenfurt. That *Stelle* then handed Swedkowicz over to RSHA *Amt* VI where VI F/O recruited him for a sabotage and subversion mission. The '*Unternehmen* Otto' had only recently been created under the order of Himmler (see Liquidation Report on RSHA *Gruppe* VI F) and the *Näheres Ost Abteilung* came under the control of SS-*Hstuf* Mandl, later of RSHA *Gruppe* VI E. Swedkowicz was trained in sabotage, handling of weapons, and cypher, but not in W/T as his channel of communication was to be by letter to a cover-address in Prague. After about five months of intermittent training Swedkowicz was finally despatched early in July 1943 via Austria, Jugoslavia and Greece to proceed through Turkey to either Palestine or Syria with instructions to join the Polish Forces or obtain employment in some capacity with the Poles, posing as a refugee. Once established he was to communicate through his cover-address giving details of his location, when steps would be taken to contact him through another agent. Swedkowicz crossed the Turkish frontier on Juy 20th 1943 and gave himself up to the Turkish police, but was soon broken under interrogation.

(d) The Merz mission:

The Merz mission remains still uncertain as to its exact purpose: *Kriminaloberassistent* Hans Merz had been a member of the German *Kripo* (Criminal Police) since 1935, who in the course of 1943 had been active on behalf of *Gruppe* IV D of RSHA *Amt* IV in Poland combatting Polish resistance movements.

In the course of this work Merz became acquainted with the leader of a Polish movement who openly suggested a rapprochement between the movement and the Germans, also suggesting that contact should be made with the Polish forces in the Middle East with a view to presenting a united Front against the Russians. The suggestion did not meet with official approval but later when Merz had been transferred to the *Sipo* Hamburg he was summoned to RSHA *Amt* VI through the recommendation of SS-*Ostuf* Eylitz of RSHA VI C whose acquaintance he had made a few months before at a *Kriminalkommissar's* course and who was aware of his Middle-East plan. It was now suggested that the plan be put into operation under RSHA *Amt* VI control. The subsequent events leading up to the actual mission are complicated in the extreme and irrelevant to the purpose of this publication. In October 1943 Merz was sent on a mission similar to that given to Swedkowicz, that is to establish contacts in the Middle East with Polish circles, and once these contacts had been established, RSHA *Amt* VI could exploit them to its own advantage. It was intended in due course to organise a sabotage network working against the supply lines through Iraq and Iran. The sabotage side of this mission came under Mandl of RSHA VI F/O, while the espionage aspect was dealt with by RSHA VI C 13. Merz was broken, and then not completely, only after long and detailed interrogation. His mission was of course a failure.

(e) The Emannuel case:

The Emannuel case represented the first attempts of RSHA VI C 13 in the course of 1943 to strengthen its links from Berlin to the Middle East through Athens and Turkey. Since the end of 1942, VI C 13 had had representatives in Athens firstly through Eylitz, subsequently through Tappenböck and finally through Kohlhaas, their function being to facilitate the passage of agents into the Middle East. To strengthen this chain still further Emmanuel, a Greek, was sent to Turkey in April 1944, to contact Duplitzer in Istanbul and assist the passage of agents through Turkey. Emmanuel was arrested in Turkey on arrival.

(f) The Chacun group:

The Chacun group consisted of Raymond Chacun, his wife and a Tunisian Arab, a member of the Mufti group: Chacun had been recruited for his mission through the *Dienststelle* in Paris following on his arrest in southern France early in 1944, after it had been learned that he had a knowledge of Syria. After a short stay in Berlin under VI C 13, Chacun and his wife were sent in the first stage of their mission to Athens where they were looked after by Kohlhaas and where they were introduced to their W/T operator Slama, who had received his training with the Mufti group at The Hague and Lehnitz. The mission given to the Chacun group was to organise a political espionage network in the Damascus area. The party was arrested on landing on the Turkish coast, August 1944.

(g) <u>The Letay mission:</u>

The Letay mission closely resembled that of the Chacun group: Letay was recruited at the end of 1943 By VI C 13 through SS-*Stubaf* Höttl of RSHA VI E, after Gamotha had failed to persuade him to join the still-born 'Norma' expedition. It had been planned that Letay would be despatched to Syria through Kohlhaas in Athens and Emmanuel in Turkey but this arrangement fell through and only after considerable delay was Letay finally sent on his mission late in August 1944. Letay surrendered on arrival and confessed to the nature of his mission.

(h) <u>The Rizos case:</u>

The Rizos mission was the last effort of RSHA VI C in the Middle East. Rizos had been active on behalf of the Italian intelligence service as early as 1941 and was responsible for the recruitment of several agents despatched to the Middle East from Italy. On the collapse of Italy he was contacted by the Germans and questioned about the agents for whom he had been responsible. Quite contrary to fact Rizos succeeded in persuading Tappenböck of VI C 13 that a network still existed and suggested that he be sent to revive it in the interests of RSHA *Amt* VI. In July 1944 Kohlhaas became case officer for the enterprise and Rizos was sent to Berlin for final training. He was sent on his mission in February 1945 and was arrested in Turkey on arrival and handed over to the British authorities. A noteworthy feature of the mission was the large sum of £50,000 carried by Rizos.

(i) <u>The Atlas expedition:</u>

The Atlas expedition to Palestine in October 1944 was the only effort on the part of RSHA *Gruppe* VI C to exploit the Mufti group, which for nearly two years had been a source of considerable expense to the *Amt*. During the course of 1943, the Mufti group of agents had been training in sabotage and W/T but no clear picture for their use seems ever to have been established by VI C. In point of fact the Atlas expedition was conceived in its initial stages by Dr Lorch of RSHA *Gruppe* VI G (*Forschungstelle* Orient) who submitted to Gräfe late in 1943 a detailed plan which he entitled the '*Unternehmen* Elias' setting out a comprehensive course of action to be adopted by RSHA *Amt* VI to exploit the Arab situation. Lorch's nephew, *Oberleutnant* Wieland, formerly of the *Lehrregiment* Brandenburg offered his services for a mission on Palestine both to *Abwehr* I and II before being accepted by RSHA *Amt* IV. Wieland now took over the 'Elias' expedition, renaming it 'Atlas', at the same time making use of the *Lehrregiment* Brandenburg to suitable material for personnel. From this source he finally recruited Ltn. Frank and *Oberfeldwebel* [Senior Sergeant] Deininger. Liaison was established with the Mufti group from which two further agents were recruited, Abdul Laitif and Hassan Slama. Preparations for the expedition occupied the greater part of 1944, involving much discussion with the Mufti regarding the control of the mission, it being finally decided that the technical preparations should be in the hands of Wieland and RSHA *Gruppe* VI C, but that on landing the German part of the group should merely act as a link between the Arab part and the Mufti. The mission given to the exploitation was likewise in two parts, the Arabs to organise guerilla bands to work against Jews and Jewish interests in Palestine and control them, the German party to provide the W/T communication and act as technical advsiers in the training of the guerilla bands. It was agreed that the German party would not undertake any independent action.

The expedition finally started in October 1944 after some delay, Wieland, Frank and Laitif being arrested eleven days after landing.

(j) <u>The Iraqi expedition:</u>
The Iraqi parachute expedition which landed in Iraq in November 1944 consisted of four agents of the Mufti group who had undergone sabotage and W/T training at The Hague and Lehnitz. The training and planning of the operations were much more under the control of the Mufti than in the case of 'Atlas' and it is noteworthy that no Germans were included in the party. The mission given to the group was that of organising armed bands to fight the Jews both in Palestine and Iraq so that in substance the mission had an aim similar to the 'Atlas' expedition. Of the party, two were arrested almost immediately, the other two, including the leader of the party Abu Salih managing to escape. It is not known what success or otherwise was obtained by the two agents remaining at liberty.

Part IV

RSHA *Gruppe* VI C and the Far East

1. Controlling Referate:
In the original organisation of RSHA *Amt* VI, *Referat* VI C3 under SS-*Hschaf* Hinney and *Reg.Assistent* Wullweber (who died in late 1940) was the competent *Referat* for the Far East, this remaining in force until the expansion of the *Gruppe* in 1941 when the Far East was spread over *Referat* 4–11, with the following subdivisions:

Referat VI C 4-6	-	Japan
Referat VI C 7-8	-	China
Referat VI C 9	-	Manchukuo, Inner & Outer Mongolia
Referat VI C 10	-	Thailand & French Indo-China
Referat VI C 11	-	Dutch East Indies & Phillipines

The next organisational change occurred at the time of the general re-organisation of RSHA *Gruppe* VI C in September 1944 when the *Gruppe* was divided into *Abteilungen*, each *Abteilung* having its internal *Referate*. The Far East now came under the control of *Abteilung* VI C 4, having the following internal organisation:

Referent:	SS-*Stubaf* Weirauch

Referat VI C 4a	-	Intelligence: *Angestellter* Kirfel
Referat VI C 4a I	-	Recruiting and briefing of agents: *Angestellter* Wilkering
Referat VI C 4b	-	Scientific analysis: SS-*Ostuf* Leo
Referat VI C 4b I	-	Press & Journals: *Angestellter* Klingenberg
Referat VI C 4c	-	Evaluation: *Angestellter* Classen
Referat VI C 4c I	-	Preparartion of reports: *Angestellter* Weinert

2. Personalities.

The RSHA *Amt* VI personalities concerned with the Far East were few in number and contained few specialists until the creation of *Abteilung* VI C 4 in September 1944. From 1940 until 1944, the leading personalities were SS-*Hstuf* Weirauch, SS-*Hstuf* Heyer, SS-*Ostuf* Leo and SS-*Hschaf* Hinney. The former *Referent* Weirauch had no specialist qualifications for the post he held, his chief virtue being his industry and conscientiousness. Heyer had been in charge of Indo-China but was transferred to *Abteilung* VI C3 (The Near East) in October 1944. Of these early personalities only SS-*Ostuf* Leo had any specialist qualifications. He had been the former director of the Propaganda Office of the *Reichsbahnweberzentrale* on Tokyo, and had studied in Japan for many years, received his doctorate there. His knowledge of Japan was therefore extensive.

On the creation of *Abteilung* VI C4, several new personalities with considerable qualifications were introduced into the *Abteilung*, the most outstanding being *Angestellter* Kirfel and SS-*Ostuf* Classen, both of whom had considerable Japanese background. (Classen had previously been in RSHA *Gruppe* VI C in 1941, but had spent the years 1942–44 in active service at the Front). The other newcomers, *Unteroffizier* Klingerbey and Wilkering had no special qualifications.

3. Representatives abroad:

RSHA *Gruppe* VI C had no representatives in the Far East: the only representation on behalf of the RSHA was through the *Polizei Attaché* Meisinger, a Bavarian friend of Müller (RSHA *Amtschef* IV) who was quite unsuited to his task and produced no results. Meisinger had assistants in Bangor (*sic*—Bangkok?) and Shanghai. In 1940 a Dr Werner Köln had gone to Japan to study there and was contacted by RSHA *Amt* VI with a view to working for them, an enterprise which led to nothing. Köln was a member of the SS-*Mannschaft* Häuser who limited his Far Eastern activity to mild liaison with Meisinger.

4. RSHA *Amt* VI and the Japanese:
Until the creation of *Abteilung* VI C4 in September 1944 *Amt* VI activity in the Far East had been on a very restricted scale as a result of official policy which regarded Japan as an ally to be trusted, falling into the same category as Italy, where the *Führerbefehl* had forbidden espionage activities of any kind. It was considered that a true picture of the situation in the Far East could be obtained through official channels and through the various Japanese representatives in Berlin itself. The official attitude to Japan was a friendly one, but Weirauch did not display the same confidence in their ally. There was however no recognised link between the intelligence services of the two countries though to a lesser extent contact had been established through Onodera in Stockholm and through a contact of Moyzisch in Ankara.

5. Activities after the creation of *Abteilung* VI C4:
The official attitude continued to exist until the end but with the creation of *Abteilung* VI C4 in September 1944 the unofficial attitude underwent a marked change. Personnel with the necessary qualifications were introduced into the *Gruppe* and the work of *Abteilung* VI C4 was henceforth directed towards providing the authorities concerned with a true picture of the Far Eastern situation based on its own sources of information and not on the official Japanese statements. In support of this policy steps were taken to recruit V-*Männer* for the *Abteilung* and in addition missions were planned for the despatch of agents to the Far East itself. The recruitment of V-*Männer* was in order primarily to conduct espionage operations against the Japanese in Europe. This activity met with no little success as the specialists in the *Gruppe* already had well established contacts in Japanese circles and in a short time the *Abteilung* not only issued a monthly report giving a general picture of the Far Eastern situation but also issued an appendix to the report forecasting the trend of future events. This type of work against the Japanese was greatly facilitated by the attitude of the *Abteilung* itself which tended to be anti-Japanese in contrast to the official policy. This development in VI C4 activity however was of short duration as by the end of the year all VI C activity was devoted to the situation on the Russian Front.

6. Sources of *Abteilung* VI C4:
The main sources of VI C4 were of two kinds—through direct intelligence from the Far East through Meisinger and through exploitation of Japanese circles in Europe itself. (Meisinger proved to be a complete failure and it was mainly due to this that steps were taken to set up an independent network in the Far East by the despatch of V-*Männer* by submarine from Germany). This latter move was rendered inoperative owing to the deterioration in the general war situation.

7. Organisation of *Abteilung* VI C4:

The organisation of the new *Abteilung* has already been given in Paragraph 1 above. The *Abteilung* was divided into three *Referate*, one concerned with *Erfassung* [Collection], one with analysis and the third with evaluation. VI C4a, the *Erfassungsreferat* received all reports which it classified and passed to VI Cc for final evaluation, that *Referat* being responsible for the preparation of the consolidated final report for presentation to the higher authorities such as the *Amtschef*, the CdS, the Foreign Office and the Ministry of Propaganda. Reports were also passed by VI C4a to VI C4b which acted as the link between the *Abteilung* and the Ostasien Institute under RSHA *Gruppe* VI G. *Referat* VI C4b was also responsible for the maintenance of a card index on East Asiatic personalities in public life.

8. Sources available to *Abteilung* VI C4:

a) V-*Leute*

Mainly through Classen and Kirfel, the following V-*Leute* were at the disposal of the *Abteilung*, most of them having connections with Japanese circles in Germany:

Admiral Förster	Director of the Deutsch-Japanese *Gesellschaft* in Berlin
Legationsrat Braun	Far East Department, Foreign Office
Dr Jakob	Assistant to Braun
Herr Schabbel	Liaison Officer for the Japanese Embassy to the Press Department
Fräulein Alla Meyer	Chief Secretary in the Manchurian Legation
Herr Vogler	Chief Secretary to the Japanese Military *Attaché*
Herr Eberhardt	Secretary in the Manchurias Legation
Frau Dr Herzfeld	Scientist with East-Asian connections
Herr von Hopfgarten	Chief of the Indo-Chinese Colony, Berlin
Dr Richter	Head of Germano-Manchurian Economic Union

b) German sources:

Abteilung C 4 of OKW	Provided intercepts of Far Eastern W/T traffic
Seehausdienst	The W/T listening station of the Foreign Office
'Roland' *Referat*	Based in Hamburg, reported to have provided information of value from a source known as 'Boris', details of which are lacking

The Ostasien Institute of RSHA *Gruppe* VI G under Prof. Donath

Deutsche Nachrichtenbüro (DNB)

'Transocean' Information Büro

c) Outsides sources:

The *Polizei Attaché*—Meisinger in Tokyo.

9. RSHA *Abteilung* VI C4 and its projected plans in the Far East:

a) <u>Despatch of agents:</u>

It was planned by *Abteiling* VI C4 to set up its own network to operate in the Nanking area. For this purpose it was proposed to send Dr Kirfel as adjutant to the Air *Attaché* there to work under cover as an interpreter, having as his chief agents Indo-Chinese Tram van Trong, van Muc and van Waw, who would respectively be placed with auxiliary W/T sets at Shanghai, Indo-China and Kalgan. The agents were given W/T training through RSHA VI F. The scheme was abandoned owing to the imminence of the German collapse.

b) <u>Liaison with the Japanese:</u>

It was also proposed to set up an *Abteilung* VI C4 liaison post with Onodera in Stockholm but this project did not materialise. The general relations of RSHA *Gruppe* VI C with the Japanese have already been dealt with, and they can be briefly described as being of mutual distrust and suspicion. The Stockholm project was an isolated one and was not indicative of any general improvement between the two countries.

10. Conclusion:

It is not difficult to arrive at the conclusion that the work of *Abteilung* VI C4 was a failure: the reasons for this failure have been aptly summarised by the *Referent* himself, Weirauch, who has pointed out the lack of co-operation from the Foreign Office, lack of qualified personnel, the enormous distances involved, lack of direction from higher levels, and the general lack of interest in Far Eastern matters. The *Abteilung* had no independent sources of its own and was hardly competent to handle what information it did receive from other sources, mostly overt.

Postwar arrests:

There is still a serious gap in arrests affected among personnel of RSHA *Gruppe* VI C as far as the Middle East is concerned. So far all the information obtained on RSHA *Amt* VI activities against the Middle East has been obtained chiefly from captured agents themselves or from members of RSHA *Amt* VI not directly concerned with such activity. The target personalities concerned are the following:

SS-*Ostuf* Belling	-	RSHA VI C3
SS-*Stubaf* Beisner	-	RSHA VI C3
SS-*Hstuf* Gamotha	-	RSHA VI C3
SS-*Hstuf* Matysiak	-	RSHA VI C2
SS-*Hstuf* Mohr	-	RSHA VI C 12
SS-*Stubaf* Schuback	-	RSHA VI C 12

Any of the above personalities under arrest should be interrogated on the identity of RSHA *Amt* VI agents despatched to and employed in the Middle and Near East.

It is not considered necessary to interrogate any further on the organisation and personalities of the *Gruppe* itself.

This report was issued by W.R.C.3. on 28 February 1946.

Appendix I

Chart of Distribution of Work in RSHA *Amt* VI from 1939–1945

	1939–1940	Early 1941	Mid 1941–42	1942–1944	1944–1945
VI A	Administration etc.	General Intelligence Tasks Abroad (? Sections)	Administration etc.	Administration etc.	Administration etc.
VI B	Technical Section	Europe Africa Near East (10 sections)	Slovakia Hungary Roumania Jugoslavia Greece Turkey Iraq, Iran Afghanistan	France Low Countries Switzerland Spain Portugal	France Low Countries Switzerland Spain Portugal Italy (from 1944)
VI C	Russia Baltic States Far East	Russia Far East (11 sections)	Russia Japan China Finland Baltic States	Russia Near East Far East (13 sections)	Russia Near East Far East (4 sections by mid 1944
VI D	Hungary Slovakia Jugoslavia Roumania Bulgaria Greece Turkey	Anglo-American sphere (9 sections)	Gt. Britain British Empire USA S. America Sweden Norway Denmark	Anglo-American sphere (3 sections)	Anglo-American sphere & Scandinavia (from summer 1944)
VI E	Italy Spain Portugal Central & Southern America	Ideological Enemies abroad 6 sections) (previously VI H)	France Low Countries Spain Portugal Italy Switzerland	Central-Europe Balkans Italy Scandinavia	Balkans

VI F	France Low Countries Switzerland Luxemburg	Technical Section	Technical Section	Technical Section	Technical Section
VI G	Gt. Britain British Empire USA Norway	-	Ideological Enemies abroad	Research (from August 1944)	Research
VI H	Ideological Enemies abroad	-	-	-	-

Appendix II

Organisational Changes in RSHA *Gruppe* VI C, 1939–45

1. Organisation 1939–41

Gruppenleiter -   SS-*Ostubaf* Vietinghoff-Scheel

Referat	*Sachgebiet*	*Referent*
VI C 1	Russia	SS-*Hstuf* Westernhagen
VI C 2	Baltic States	SS-*Ostuf* Fölkersam
VI C 3	Far East	SS-*Hschaf* Hinney

2. Organisation 1941–42

Gruppenleiter -   SS-*Stubaf* Gräfe

Referat	*Sachgebiet*	*Referent*
VI C 1-2	Russia & Baltic States	*Regierungsrat* Girgensohn
VI C 3	Ukraine	SS-*Hstuf* Dressler
VI C 4-6	Japan	}
VI C 7-8	China	}
VI C 9	Manchukao & Mongolia }	SS-*Hstuf* Weirauch
VI C 10	Thailand & French Indo-China	}
VI C 11	Dutch East Indies & Phillipines	}
VI C 12	Turkey, Iran & Afghanistan	SS-*Hstuf* Schuback
VI C 13	The Arab Countries	*Angestellter* Em

3. Organisation 1942–44

Gruppenleiter   -   SS-*Ostubaf* Gräfe

Referat	*Sachgebiet*	*Referent*	
VI C 1-3	Russia, Baltic States & Ukraine	SS-*Stubaf* Hengelhaupt	
VI C (Z)	*Unternehmen* Zeppelin	SS-*Stubaf* Oebsger-Röder	
VI C 4-6	Japan	}	
VI C 7-8	China	}	
VI C 9	Manchukuo & Mongolia	}	SS-*Hstuf* Weirauch
VI C 10	Thailand & French Indo-China	}	
VI C 11	Dutch East Indies & Philippines	}	
VI C 12	Turkey, Iran & Afghanistan	SS-*Hstuf* Schuback	
VI C 13	The Arab Countries	SS-*Hstuf* Beisner	
VI C 14	Iran (after Jan 1944)	SS-*Hstuf* Gamotha	

4. Organisation late 1944–45

Gruppenleiter   -   SS-*Staf* Rapp

Abteilung	*Sachgebiet*	*Abteilungsleiter*
VI C 1	Administration	SS-*Stubaf* Lumm
VI C 2	*Russlandabteilung*	SS-*Stubaf* Hengelhaupt
VI C 3	*Näh-Ost Abteilung*	SS-*Hstuf* Schuback
VI C 4	*Fern-Ost Abteilung*	SS-*Stubaf* Weirauch

Appendix III

Alphabetical Index of RSHA VI C personnel, 1939–45

(Note: The *Referat* after the summer of 1945 is shown only when definitely known. Postwar arrested personnel are underlined.)

Rank and Name	*Referat* to June 1944	1944–1945	Remarks
SS-*Hstuf* Arthur Augsburg	VI C Z		brother of Dr Augsburg & later with VI Wi
SS-*Stubaf* Dr Emil Augsburg	VI C Z	VI C2	previously *Amt* VII; deputy head Wannsee Inst
SS-*Uschaf* Franz Autrata			
SS-*Hstuf* <u>Alfred Backhaus</u>	VI C Z	VI C 1	arrested British Zone (1943–44)
SS-*Sturmmann* Baer	VI C 1		
SS-*Ustuf* Barbowitsch		VI C Z	Director, Training School Markusgrün, 1945
SS-*Rotf* Dominik Bayer	VI C Z		
Angestellter Prof. Beck			Training in Persia
Angestellte Dorothea Beinze	VI C Z		
SS-*Stubaf* Wilhelm Beisner	VI C 13	VI C 3	reported Italy, 1945
SS-*Ostuf* Bruno Belling	VI C 12	VI C 3	reported Innsbruck, 1945
SS-*Hstuf* Bellinghaus	VI C Z	VI C 2p	dealt with Polish volunteers for VI C Z
Angestellter Berger	VI C Z	VI C 1	
Angestellter Werner Berndt	VI C 4-11		
SS-*Ustuf* Blumberg		VI C 3	dismissed end 1944
SS-*Oschaf* <u>Bobach</u>	VI C 1		dead
SS-*Uschaf* Boekee	VI C Z		
SS-*Ustuf* Erich Boes	VI C Z		*Meldehauptkdo Süd*
Angestellte Fräulein Boldt	VI C		
Kanzleiangestellte Boscheinen	VI C 12		transfer to Istanbul, 1942
SS-*Ostuf* Hans-Jürgen Bosse	VI C		
Angestellte Angela Braun	VI C Z		
SS-*Hschaf* Paul Brecht	VI C		Sandberge Training Sch.
SS-*Ustuf* Hermann Brose		VI C 2p	
SS-*Hstuf* Walter Buchmann	VI C Z		Zeppelin *Kdoführer*
SS-*Ostuf* Karl <u>Burmeister</u>	VI C 2		dead

Name			
SS-*Stubaf* Bernhard Christensen	VI C	VI C	*Führer, Meldehauptkdo Nord* to March 1945, then Weichsel, Mar-Apr 1945
SS-*Stubaf* Prof Wilhelm <u>Classen</u>		VI C 4	arrested British Zone
Angestellte Fräulein Cord	VI C 13		discharged 1944
SS-*Stubaf* Dieter		VI C 1 Z/bg	head of POW section
SS-*Hstuf* Karl-Benno Ditges		VI C 3	
SS-*Hstuf* Karl Dittrich	VI C 1		
SS-*Hstuf* Hans-Eugen <u>Dressler</u>	VI C Z		Deputy *Führer, Meldehauptkdo Süd*; dead
Angestellte Frau <u>Dressler</u>	VI C 3		dead
SS-*Ustuf* Bruno Dulckeit		VI C 2a	
SS-*Stubaf* Emil <u>Duplitzer</u>		VI C 3	arrested British Zone
SS-*Hstuf* Eckhard	VI C 3		Swede, now reported to be in Sweden
SS-*Hstuf* Dr Eder	VI C 12		
SS-*Hstuf* Richard Engelmaier		VI C	VI C representative at BdS Krakau
Angestellter Dr Anton <u>Em</u>	VI C 13		dead
SS-*Stuschaf* Franz Everhardt	VI C Z		
Krim.Kommissar Herbert Eylitz	VI C 12		
SS-*Ostuf* Waldemar <u>Fast</u>		VI C 3	representative in Turkey; arrested British Zone
SS-*Hstuf* Faust	VI C Z		
Krim.Ob.Sekretär Hans Felten	VI C 12		
SS-*Hstuf* Heinz Fenner	VI C Z		*Hauptkdo Süd*, 1941
SS-*Hschaf* Oswald Fettköther	VI C Z		
SS-*Uschaf* Gerhard Feuersenger	VI C Z		*Meldehauptkdo Süd*
SS-*Uschaf* Fleischer	VI C Z		to Havel Institute, 1944
SS-*Ostuf* Adrian von Fölkersam	VI C 2		dead
SS-*Ostuf* Wolfgang Gabeler		VI C Z	Security Officer
Angestellter Gallmeister		VI C 4	
SS-*Hstuf* Ramon Gamotha	VI C 12	VI C 3	reported deserted to Russians, Vienna, 1945
SS-*Hstuf* Theodor <u>Girgensohn</u>	VI C Z		dead
SS-*Ostubaf* Dr Heinz <u>Gräfe</u>	VI C		*Gruppenleiter*; dead
SS-*Hstuf* Ernst Gramowski	VI C 12	VI C 3	transfer to *Stapo*, 1944
SS-*Ustuf* Georg Greife	VI C Z		
SS-*Stubaf* Alfred Grün	VI C Z		Liaison Officer with *Hauptkommando Süd*
Angestellter Grüning	VI C 12	VI C 3	

SS-*Hstuf* Dr Hans Handrack		VI C 2b	
SS-*Ostuf* Walter Hanisch	VI C Z		
Angestellte Fräulein Hart		VI C 1	
SS-*Ostuf* Dr Richard Hasselbach	VI C Z		with Wannsee Institute
SS-*Stubaf* Emil Haussmann		VI C 1	Deputy *Leiter* VI C 1945
SS-*Hstuf* Paul Heimann	VI C Z		
SS-*Uschaf* Hellwig-Larsen	VI C 12		
SS-*Stubaf* Hermann Hubig	VI C 1-3	VI C 2	reported Tegernsee 1945
Angestellter Henkmann		VI C 3	
SS-*Stuschaf* Richard Hentschke	VI C 12	VI C 3	
SS-*Ostuf* Otto Heyer		VI C 4	tranfer to Slovakia as VI representative, 1945
SS-*Ustuf* Günther Hinney	VI C 4		
SS-*Stubaf* Gerhard Hoins		VI C Z	head of Training School, *Hauptkommando Nord*
SS-*Ostubaf* Karl Hönscheid	VI C Z		*Meldehauptkdo Süd*, 1944
SS-*Hstuf* Herbert Hösselbarth		VI C 13	earlier BdS Athens
Kriminalrat Hoffmann	VI C		Havel Institute, 1944
SS-*Sturmmann* Eugen Horak	VI C 12		arrested Vienna, 1945
SS-*Stubaf* Hermann Hubig	VI C Z		
SS-*Ustuf* Dr Erwin Hübner	VI C Z	VI C 2b	
SS-*Uschaf* Erwin Hübner		VI C 1	
SS-*Hstuf* Guido-Horst Huhn	VI C		Deputy head, Training School Tepl, 1945
SS-*Ustuf* Bruno Inser		VI C 2a	
SS-*Schütze* Kurt Jacke	VI C Z		
SS-*Ustuf* Jakubovitsch		VI C Z	Head of Training School at Königswarthe
Polizeisekretär Richard Janthur	VI C Z		
SS-*Ustuf* Karl Jobke	VI C 12		
SS-*Hstuf* Hans Jörgens		VI C 1	
SS-*Hstuf* Karl Jung	VI C Z		left U Z, Oct 1942
SS-*Stubaf* Werner Kämpf	VI C 2		chief of *Dienststelle* Franken, Markt Redwitz
Angestellte Fräulein Keitel		VI C 4	secretary of Weirauch
SS-*Sturmmann* Friedrich Kern	VI C Z		
Angestellter Dr Harald Kirfel		VI C 4	arrested British Zone
SS-*Ostuf* Wilhelm Kirotar	VI C Z		Esthonian; head of *Aussenkdo* U Z
SS-*Stubaf* Johannes Kleinert	VI C Z		*Leiter, Aussenkdo* U Z
SS-*Uschaf* Alois Kleinhaus	VI C		specialist – Turkestan activists

SS-*Ustuf* Georg Klindworth	VI C 2	
SS-*Stubaf* Waldemar	VI C Z	arrested British Zone
Klingelhöfer		
SS-*Ostuf* Dr Erich Körting	VI C Z	Head, Hofstein School;
		arrested by Czechs
SS-*Rotf* Koslowski	VI C 12	at Ankara, 1942-43
SS-*Ostuf* Arkadayi	VI C1	1941-42
von Kotschoubey		
SS-*Stubaf* Hans Kraus	VI C Z	Chief, *Hauptkdo* Mitte1942–
		end 1944
SS-*Stubaf* Otto Kraus	VI C Z	U Z *Kommando Nord*
SS-*Ostuf* Erich Krause	VI C 12	chief, W/T station in Turkey,
		1942
SS-*Hschaf* Paul Krocker	VI C Z	
SS-*Hstuf* Martin Kurmis	VI C 12	parachuted into Iran and
		arrested; suicide, 1943
SS-*Stubaf* Walter Kurreck	VI C Z	to Italy, Feb 1945
SS-*Ustuf* Kuschin	VI C Z	Führer, espionage school
		at Teichwaldunder, U Z
		Kommando Nord, 1944
SS-*Uschaf* Theodor Langner	VI C Z	
Angestellter Lautenbach	VI C 2	arrested US Zone
SS-*Hstuf* Egon Lengeling	VI C 13	involved in fraud and arrested,
		May 1944
SS-*Ostuf* Jörn Leo	VI C 4	Japanese expert
SS-*Ostuf* Klaus von Lepel	VI C 2	
SS-*Ostuf* Emil Liebenschel	VI C Z	from U Z to VI A, 1943
SS-*Hstuf* Karl-Heinz Löchelt	VI C Z	earlier VI B and VI F; reported
		Salzburg, 1945
SS-*Hschaf* Losch	VI C Z	
SS-*Stubaf* Hermann Lumm	VI C 1	in charge of U Z agent training
Krim.Kommissar Mach	VI C 12	
SS-*Uschaf* Karl Marschke	VI C Z	
SS-*Hstuf* Hanns Matysiak	VI C 12 VI C 2	
SS-*Hstuf* Mayr	VI C 12	parachuted into Iran and
		arrested Teheran 1943
SS-*Hstuf* Mehlert	VI C Z	prepared U Z agent i.ds.
SS-*Ustuf* Günter Mehring	VI C Z	Security Officer U Z
SS-*Uschaf* Menebrücker	VI C Z	
SS-*Hstuf Pol.Ob.Inspektor*	VI C	arrested US Zone
Paul Metz		
SS-*Hstuf* Karl-Heinz Mohr	VI C 12	

Angestellter Dr Paul von Mollik		VI C 3	
SS-*Stubaf* Ludwig <u>Moyzisch</u>	VI C 12		representative in Turkey; arrested British Zone
SS-*Hstuf* Erich Nähler		VI C 1	liaison with VI F
SS-*Ostuf* Ekkehardt Neumann-Reppert	VI C 12		to *Amt* VII, 1944
SS-*Ostubaf* Rudolf Oebsger-Röder	VI C Z		later with VI A
SS-*Hstuf* Reiner Olzscha		VI C 2	head, Turkestan Institute
Angestellte Fräulein Opitz		VI C 2b	
Angestellter Viktor <u>Patek</u>	VI C 12		in Ankara, 1941
SS-*Ostuf* Dr Peter Paulsen	VI C		
SS-*Hstuf* Heiner Paust	VI C 1	VI C 1	to *Heeresgruppe* Schörner in 1944
Angestellte Fräulein Plöger		VI C 2a	
SS-*Hstuf* Alfred Pfisterer	VI C 12		1942, Tunisia; 1943, to Greece for VI; later VI F
SS-*Hschaf* Anton Pfitzner	VI C 12		1943, to VI F
SS-*Rotf* Willy Preuss		VI C 3	
SS-*Ostuf* Adolf Prieb	VI C 1		
SS-*Ustuf* Werner Prösdorf	VI C		
SS-*Ostuf* Günther Quoos	VI C		later to VI F
Angestellte Fräulein Rademacher		VI C 2a	
SS-*Stubaf* Waldemar von Radetzky	VI C		later BdS Slovakia, *Abt* VI and Liaison Officer in Vlassov Committee
SS-*Staf* Albert Rapp		VI C	*Gruppenleiter*, 1944–45
SS-*Ustuf* Erich Rasch	VI C Z		head, Sandberge Camp
SS-*Stubaf* Rohrig (sic)	VI C Z		U Z *Hauptkommando*; later VI representative in Prague
SS-*Hstuf* Dr Wilhelm Rohrmann	VI C Z		
SS-*Oschaf* Horst Rosenmüller	VI C Z		
SS-*Ustuf* Rouleau	VI C 13		
SS-*Ustuf* Viktor von Sadowsky	VI C Z		
SS-*Hstuf* Edwin Sakuth	VI C 3		head, Sandberge camp after Rasch, Nov 1943
SS-*Staffelmann* Michael Salzmann	VI C Z		
SS-*Hschaf* Scharnelli		VI C Z	head, Glatzen School
SS-*Stubaf* Dr Hans Schindowski	VI C Z		U Z *Kommandoführer*
SS-*Stubaf* Heinrich Schönemann	VI C Z		head, Sandberge Camp until Jan 1943
SS-*Oschaf* Schrader		VI C Z	head, Jagerheim School
SS-*Ustuf* Schröder		VI C	Deputy for Reichert

SS-*Stubaf* Kurt Schuback	VI C 12		
SS-*Hstuf* Dr Wilhelm Schroer	VI C 1-3		later Liaison Officer to Vlassov
SS-*Hschaf* Schultz	VI C 13		
SS-*Hstuf* Schulz	VI C Z		*Meldehauptkdo Süd*; came from VI B
SS-*Ostuf* Schumacher	VI C 10		
Angestellter Schwartzkopf		VI C 1	in Flensburg, June 1945
SS-*Hstuf* Nikolay Semenov	VI C Z		head, *Unternehmen* Ulm
SS-*Hschaf* Sielinski		VI C 2	
SS-*Ostuf* Wilhelm Spiekermann	VI C 12		dismissed early 1945
Angestellter von Staden	VI C 1		VI C 2a
Angestellter Staisch		VI C 3	interpreter; Iran 1943; Berlin, 1945
SS-*Ostuf* Erwin Steinbach	VI C Z		*Meldehauptkdo Süd*
SS-*Ostuf* Karl Steinberg	VI C 12		to Istanbul, 1943
SS-*Hstuf* Dr Emil Steudle		VI C 2a	arrested US Zone
SS-*Stuschaf* Alfons Stinauer		VI C 1	
Angestellte Fräulein Stiglmayer		VI C 1	
SS-*Hschaf* Alfred Stoltze	VI C Z		
SS-*Uschaf* Alexander Szonn		VI C Z	
SS-*Hstuf* Dr Gerhard Teich		VI C 2b	arrested British Zone
SS-*Sturmmann* Bruno Tappenböck	VI C 13		
SS-*Uschaf* Karl Thom	VI C Z		
SS-*Ostuf* Karl Tschierschky	VI C		*Gruppenleiter* from May1944; then to *Dienststelle* Prützmann
SS-*Hstuf* Heinz Unglaube	VI C		head of Training Camp for *Unternehmen* Uhu in 1944
SS-*Hschaf* Ludwig Udet	VI C Z		
Angestellter Ungern-Sternberg	VI C		*Sachbearbeiter*
SS-*Hstuf* Günter Vieth	VI C Z		
SS-*Stubaf* Paul von Vietinghoff-Scheel	VI C		*Gruppenleiter*, 1940
SS-*Ostubaf* Friedrich Vollheim	VI C		*Gruppenleiter*, 1941
Angestellter Dr Hans Vorndran	VI C 12	VI C 3	arrested US Zone
SS-*Stubaf* Peter Weirauch	VI C 4-11	VI C 4	Dec 1944 transfer to BdS Hungary, *Leiter* VI; arrested US Zone
SS-*Ostuf* Hans-Joachim Weise	VI C 13		
SS-*Hstuf* Karl-Georg Wellhöner	VI C 12		arrested British Zone
SS-*Oschaf* Friedrich Werner	VI C Z		
SS-*Hstuf* Heinz von Westernhagen	VI C 1		

SS-*Ostuf* Dr Wieck	VI C 2b	
SS-*Rotf* Wilkerling	VI C 4	
SS-*Oschaf* <u>Winalli</u>	VI C Z	arrested by Czechs
SS-*Stubaf* Bruno <u>Wolff</u>	VI C 12	*Amt* VI representative in Istanbul; arrested by British
SS-*Ostuf* Franz Wondrak	VI C 1	
SS-*Ustuf* Hans-Heinrich Worthmann	VI C Z	*Meldehauptkdo Süd*
Reg.Assessor <u>Wullweber</u>	VI C 3	died late 1940
SS-*Stubaf* Theodor Zinke	VI C Z	to *Amt* VI S, 1944

Notes

* US National Archives, RG 263, CIA Name File: Emil Duplitzer, Situation Report No. 8, RSHA VI C.

1 The National Archives, Kew, KV 2/1161, MI 5 Name File: Stanislaw Swedkowicz.

2 The National Archives, Kew, KV 2/203-206, MI Name Files: Hans Merz.

3 For an uptodate examination of RSHA VI C and *Abwehr* activities in the Middle East, see: Adrian O'Sullivan, *Nazi Secret Warfare in Occupied Persia (Iran)*, Palgrave Macmillan, 2014.

4 Either by omission or lack of knowledge, but Bletchley Park interception and decryption centre in Britain, had decoded almost 2,000 German messages in relation to *Unternehmen* Zeppelin between 1942 and 1945.

5 No personnel of the *Einsatzgruppen* A-D and their *Sipo* and SD *Einsatzkommandos* in 1941–1942 had personnel among their staffs doing *Amt* VI tasks.

6 An interesting view of Soviet Intelligence and the *Unternehmen* Zeppelin operations can be found in, Pavel & Anatol Sudoplatov, *Special Tasks: The Memoirs of an Unwanted Witness – a Soviet Spymaster*, Little Brown, 1994.

8

Situation Report No. 9:
Amt VI of the RSHA—*Gruppe* VI D

INDEX

Part I: The Organisational Development of *Gruppe* VI D
Part II: The Functional Development of *Gruppe* VI D
    A. The Period under Jost 1939–41
    B. The Period under Schellenberg 1941–45
Part III: *Referat* VI D1 and the USA
Part IV: *Referat* VI D2 and the United Kingdom
Part V: *Referat* VI D3 and Scandinavia
Part VI: *Referat* VI D4 and South America

Appendix I: The Distribution of Work in RSHA *Amt* VI between 1939–45
Appendix II: Organisation and Personnel of *Gruppe* VI D 1944–45
Appendix III: Alphabetical Index of *Gruppe* VI D Personnel 1939–1945
RSHA *Gruppe* VI D

Part I

The Organisational Development of RSHA *Gruppe* VI D

1. *Gruppe* VI G in 1939–40.
In the orginal organisation of RSHA *Amt* VI in 1939, Great Britain, and USA, and Northern Europe came under the control of *Gruppe* VI G, the *Gruppenleiter* being SS-*Stubaf* Daufeldt, previously active in the SD-*Hauptamt*, *Abteilung* III/3, under Jost, RSHA *Amtschef* VI. The *Gruppe* had only three *Referate*, the actual breakdown being as follows:

RSHA *Gruppe* VI G
Gruppenleiter   –   SS-*Stubaf* Daufeldt

Referat		*Referent*
VI G1	Great Britain & British Empire	SS-*Ostuf* Zuchristian
VI G2	USA	-
VI G3	Northern Europe	-

It will be noted from the above that South America was not dealt with by *Gruppe* VI G; that country formed one of the *Referate* of the original *Gruppe* VI E competent for Southern Europe, the reason for its inclusion in that *Gruppe* being that exploitation of the country was best effected through the Iberian Peninsula.

The only two officers in the new *Gruppe* VI G were SS-*Stubaf* Daufeldt as *Gruppenleiter*, and SS-*Ostuf* (later SS-*Hstuf*) Zuchristian as *Referent* for the UK. Daufeldt was one of the few officers available to Jost who had previous knowledge of Great Britain, where he had resided for a time before the war. Zuchristian had only a slight knowledge of English; he was later sent to *Abteilung* VI, BdS Paris, where he concentrated on English and American matters, and was also responsible for the recruitment of Georgian agents for *Gruppe* VI C. There were no officers at that time suitable as *Referent* for the USA.

2. The Re-organisation in 1941.

By January 1941 a new organisation of RSHA *Amt* VI was envisaged whereby the Anglo-American sphere became the province of *Gruppe* VI D, with Daufeldt still *Gruppenleiter*. Details of the organisation of the *Gruppe* are lacking, but it is known that it had nine *Referate*; it is probable therefore that the *Gruppe* continued to be competent for the Scandinavian countries, and probably also included South America. Before the end of the year the *Amt* was further re-organised, though *Gruppe* VI D remained comparatively unaffected, being competent for the Anglo-American sphere including South America, together with the Scandinavian countries, with the exception of Finland. Daufeldt still remained as *Gruppenleiter*, though during the latter half of 1941 it is known that SS-*Stubaf* Gräfe, *Gruppenleiter* VI C, also acted as *Gruppenleiter* in a supervisory capacity and as *Referent* for England. SS-*Hstuf* Maywald had now become *Referent* for the USA, Zuchristian still remaining as *Referent* for the UK. SS-*Hstuf* Grönheim was the *Referent* for Scandinavia. SS-*Ostuf* Reimers, who had had a long period of residence in the USA, was also now employed in the American *Referat*. SS-*Ostuf* Geppert was *Referent* for South America.

3. The re-organisation in 1942.

The re-organisation which took place in the summer of 1942 was a reflection on the reforms introduced by Schellenberg, now in command as RSHA *Amtschef* VI.

Scandinavia now passed to the the the control of *Gruppe* VI E, where it became *Referat* VI E6 under SS-*Hstuf* Grönheim. The number of *Referate* was now reduced to three, the USA now having SS-*Hstuf* Carstenn as *Referent*, SS-*Ostuf* Schüddekopf as *Referent* for the UK, while Geppert was relieved of his appointment as *Referent* for South America. Both Carstenn and Maywald in turn acted as *Referent* in his place until the appointment of SS-*Hstuf* Gross in 1943. The most important change was the appointment of SS-*Stubaf* Paeffgen as *Gruppenleiter* in succession to *Kriminalkommissar* Schambacher, who had acted in that capacity for a few weeks only. Schambacher had been introduced to the *Amt* from RSHA *Amt* IV, as were many of Schellenberg's new recruits. Paeffgen had been *Referent* in RSHA *Gruppe* I B2 of *Amt* I in 1940, and was latterly on the staff of KdS Bialystok.

Other important organisational changes late in 1942 and early in 1943 involved the despatch of SS-*Hstuf* Maywald and SS-*Hstuf* Arnold on special assignments to Spain, where they acted on behalf of RSHA *Gruppe* VI D. SS-*Hstuf* Zuchristian, former *Referent* for the UK, now joined the BdS Paris, while Daufeldt was sent as RSHA *Amt* VI representative to Switzerland.

The structural organisation of RSHA *Gruppe* VI D at this time is still a matter of some doubt. It appears certain that the number of *Referate* was considerably expanded, but evidence on the relationship between countries and numbered *Referate* is very conflicting. VI D7 was probably at one time competent for the UK, while VI D 1–4 covered the USA.

4. Further re-organisation in 1944.

The last major re-organisation in this *Gruppe* came in the summer of 1944, a re-organisation which this time was a reflection on the work of the *Gruppe* itself. Scandinavia returned to the *Gruppe* from VI E, which had at that time moved to Vienna. The *Gruppe* now took this internal structure:

RSHA *Gruppe* VI D

Gruppenleiter	–	SS-*Ostubaf* Paeffgen

Referat		*Referent*
VI D1	America	-
VI D2	UK	SS-*Ostuf* Schüddekopf
VI D3	Scandinavia	SS-*Hstuf* Grönheim
VI D4	South America	SS-*Hstuf* Gross

SS-*Hstuf* Carstenn was now posted to Finland to serve under SS-*Hstuf* Brohs, the representative there. The American *Referat* now practically dissolved, as VI D4 took on the *Erfassungsabteilungen* of VI D1 and VI D2 owing to the lack of success of these two *Referate*. SS-*Ostuf* Rudolph of RSHA *Amt* VII, however, supervised the work of *Referat* VI D1. Schüddekopf too was soon to leave the *Gruppe*, being posted to the *Zentral-Büro* in December 1944, his place being taken by his deputy SS-*Ostuf* Niklas. Grönheim was sent on a special assignment to Oslo [Norway] late in the year, his deputy SS-*Hstuf* Bussinger acting as *Referent* in his absence. SS-*Hstuf* Daufeldt, brother of the former *Gruppenleiter*, joined the *Gruppe* from RSHA VI F/O (*Unternehmen* Otto) in late 1943, and in this re-organisation was sent to Denmark on a special assignment, where he was joined before the end of the year by Carstenn after the latter's return from Finland on the evacuation of that country by the Germans. The *Gruppe* continued under this organisational structure until the dissolution of the *Amt* in May 1945.

Part II

The Functional Development of RSHA *Gruppe* VI D

A. The Period under Jost 1939–41.

1. The SD-*Hauptamt* and the Anglo-American sphere.
The Situation Report on RSHA *Gruppe* VI E has pointed out that the strong position which that *Gruppe* held among the *Ländergruppen* of RSHA *Amt* VI was due to the fact that only in South-Eastern Europe, and to a lesser extent in Switzerland, had *Abteilung* III/3 of the SD-*Hauptamt* developed any previous activity on which the new RSHA *Amt* VI could base its work. *Amt* VI was very much the Cinderella of the new *Ämter* of the RSHA, and the difficulties which faced Jost as RSHA *Amtschef* VI were considerable indeed—difficulties which were not eased by the comparative indifference of Heydrich to the *Amt*. Jost had no solid foundations on which to build, few officers with experience in the work he was to undertake whom he could recruit and he met with little support from these departments most fitted to help him abroad—the Foreign Office, the *Auslandsorganisation*, etc.

The general difficulties varied in intensity in accordance with the different territories allotted to the *Ländergruppen*; they were most marked in the case of the original RSHA *Gruppe* VI G, which dealt with the Anglo-American sphere, as the SD-*Hauptamt* had not in any way been active in that territory prior to the outbreak of war.

2. *Gruppe* VI G and its difficulties.
The new RSHA *Gruppe* VI G had in fact almost virgin territory to explore. In the case of the United Kingdom, there were no agents already placed within the country before the war to be active there after its outbreak, nor were there any subversive minorities which lent themselves to exploitation, apart from the possible exception of the British Union of Fascists. There in any case, however, two difficulties would

have had to be faced; firstly, that the members of that organisation were already well known to the British authorities and appropriate action under the Defence Regulations could be taken whenever circumstances warranted it, and secondly any contact had to be established in face of considerable difficulties, as no effort had been made at exploitation before the war. The USA presented a similar problem, although the many varying nationalities in that country, including the active *Deutscher Bund*, offered greater potential scope than did the UK. But again the difficulty of establishing contact was greater than in the case of the UK owing to geographical factors.

3. Difficulties regarding Representatives.
The normal procedure in the case of the other *Ländergruppen* was to despatch representatives under suitable cover to the various countries to act as *Amt* VI representatives. In the case of Britain this was of course impossible, while the severance of diplomatic relations with the USA made such a procedure there almost equally difficult. The only other way open would have been the despatch of agents by covert means, either by parachute, by submarine, or through neutral shipping facilities. All three methods were possible as far as Britain was concerned, but it must be borne in mind that the *Amt* had no firmly established connections with the other agencies involved in such operations, and as the central office itself was merely in a state of evolution, any such attempts in the early months of the war were virtually impossible. This factor of course allowed the development of the counter-espionage and security organisations of the UK to meet any attempts made at a later date.

The mere distances involved in the case of the USA were a serious deterrent; only submarines and neutral shipping were available as means of despatch, and the factors mentioned in connection with the UK were equally operative. In any case, interest in the USA was not great in the early stages of the war, as apparently the German High Command had not the foresight to appreciate the political importance of the USA as the war developed, a neglect which was to prove costly by 1942. South America of course offered greater scope in view of the neutral countries making up that continent.

4. Difficulties in personnel.
But Jost's primary difficulties were to arise much nearer home. He had to find somewhere officers with some background knowledge of the UK and the USA, and such personnel were hard to come by, even if Jost had been granted full freedom in recruitment. The strong nationalist spirit which the Party had developed within Germany during the years prior to the war served its purpose in essential directions, but had had the effect of cutting Germany off from the Western Hemisphere and from Britain. It was difficult to be the perfect Nazi and know the outside world, and in this case 'what could they know of the Ausland, who only Germany knew?'

There were, generally speaking, few Germans who were in a position to appreciate the outlook of either the UK or the USA, who understood the workings of these two countries, or who were well informed about them politically or economically, all of which were essentially qualifications for any persons who sought to conduct intelligence operations against these countries. In any case Germans possessing such qualifications were not likely to be found among the ranks of the SD, and the employment of non-SD personnel in the *Amt* was not encouraged, a failing which Schellenberg was quick to appreciate in 1942.

Jost's difficulties did not end there; while the general resources of recruitment were thus intentionally restricted, he was in no position to choose freely from the material that was available. His position relative to the other RSHA *Amtschefs* was a weak one, and the latter were not disposed to release competent officers to *Amt* VI. Jost had to rely mainly for his personnel on the members of his former *Abteilung* III/3 of the SD-*Hauptamt*, which offered little in the way of officers with any qualifications in the Anglo-American sphere.

5. RSHA *Gruppe* VI G in 1939–40.
The *Gruppe* VI G which was set up in 1939 was made competent for Scandinavia as well as for the Anglo-American sphere. It is significant that Jost was able to find only two officers from the SD-*Hauptamt* who possessed any qualifications for the *Gruppe* VI G. The *Gruppenleiter* was SS-*Stubaf* Daufeldt who had spent rather more than a year in England studying at the London School of Economics in 1936-37. He was at that time already a member of the SD, and it was he who was placed in charge of the *Blockstelle Hof* when the first attempts at an *Auslandsnachrichtendienst* was made in 1938. Daufeldt therefore had some background, but his qualifications are deceptive. He has been variously described as a nincompoop, a playboy and a fool—a judgment which, in view of his later record, would not seem to be too severe.

The other original member of *Gruppe* VI G was SS-*Ostuf* Zuchristian, who had only a fair knowledge of English. There was no one at all available for the position of *Referent* for the USA.

To have overcome the difficulties which have been enumerated in Paragraphs 2–4 above would have required energetic direction both on the part of the *Amtschef* and of the *Gruppenleiter*, combined with sympathetic cooperation from other departments. But the *Amtschef* was weak, the *Gruppenleiter* inefficient, while the *Amt* as a whole received scant consideration from other Ministries and departments. It is hardly surprising therefore that during the first two years of the existence of the *Gruppe* practically nothing was achieved in the way of results.

6. RSHA *Gruppe* VI G Representatives Abroad.
Only in the case of Scandinavia was it possible for the *Gruppe* to have direct representation in the countries over which it had control. Dr Wagner was sent

to Sweden, where he remained until 1942. SS-*Ostuf* Schönebeck was posted to Finland, where he established good connections with Finnish Nationalist circles; he remained there only until the end of 1940, when he was transferred to Portugal to replace Fast. Schönebeck was succeeded by SS-*Hstuf* Brohs, who remained in Finland until his evacuation by the Germans in 1944. The remaining appointments were quite ineffective and need only be recorded. SS-*Stubaf* Knab spent only a few days in Norway before that country was invaded [1940], when it became the province of RSHA *Amt* III, and direct *Amt* VI representation ceased. A similar fate befell Pahl in Denmark, in which country he had a spell of a few months before the invasion [1940], whereupon he was transferred from the Amt to the Police Service of the Civil Administration in Denmark.

7. Sources available to RSHA *Gruppe* VI G.

In face of the inability to obtain direct representation in either the UK or the USA, and the difficulties in the early stages of despatching agents to these countries, the *Gruppe* was obliged to look elsewhere for sources of information. The best expedient would have been to establish representation in neutral territory controlled by the other *Ländergruppen*, especially in the Iberian Peninsula and in the Middle East, but the *Gruppenleiter* concerned were opposed to any such intrusion by *Gruppe* VI G into their territory. Jost was of course too weak to impose his will in such matters; as a result therefore the remaining *Ländergruppen* merely passed to *Gruppe* VI G any information relative to VI G territory obtained through their sources. Deprived of other sources, Daufeldt was forced to rely on the foreign press received through neutral countries, which material, needless to say, was of very poor standard.

8. The situation at the end of the Jost regime.

Jost ceased before the end of 1941 to exercise any effective direction of the *Amt*, Schellenberg acting as *Amtschef* for a period of several months before his actual appointment was confirmed. By the middle of 1941 the *Gruppe* had become VI D, its final designation, losing Scandinavia to *Gruppe* VI E, and taking over South America from the original *Gruppe* VI E. This *Gruppe* which Schellenberg inherited had a sorry record; no direct sources of information had been opened up in either the UK or in the USA. Daufeldt made efforts to enlist the services of the *Stapoleitstelle* Hamburg, at which port neutral seamen offered some hope, but the *Stapoleitstelle* did not show any desire to cooperate. No representatives had been installed in neutral territory on behalf of the *Gruppe*, and as the other *Ländergruppen* were themselves in rather poor shape, apart from *Gruppe* VI E, the information which they passed to *Gruppe* VI G was not only restricted, but of poor quality. The only bright feature was the South American *Referat* which the *Gruppe* had inherited from *Gruppe* VI E. There Geppert, the *Referent*, had been instrumental in recruiting for the *Gruppe* Siegfried Becker as representative in the

Argentine, the beginning of what was to prove a most energetic and resourceful network. As will be seen, the South American *Referat*, later VI D4, was to become the focal point of practically the whole activities of the *Gruppe*.

Regarding personnel, the situation was hardly any brighter; Daufeldt himself was incompetent, and so great was the dearth of capable officers that Gräfe, *Gruppenleiter* VI C, acted as *Referent* for England, and virtually as *Gruppenleiter*, SS-*Ostuf* Reimers, who had lived for some time in the USA, had by now been recruited for the American *Referat*, while Thost, formerly correspondent of the *Völkische Beobachter* in London, had joined the English *Referat*, his task being the evaluation of Press reports contained in the foreign Press. The period 1939–41 in the history of RSHA *Gruppe* VI D has been described by Schellenberg as 'rank dilettantism'—an assessment justified by the record of the *Gruppe*.

B. The Period under Schellenberg 1941–45.

1. Schellenberg's 'Problem Child'.
Schellenberg therefore had no easy task to face in any attempt to improve the work of *Gruppe* VI D. In other *Ländergruppen* his line of reform was in three directions—change in organisation, change in personnel, and change in policy. The first of these was a comparatively simple matter, while the remaining two were met with to a certain extent by the withdrawal of *Amt* VI representatives in SD-*Abschnitte* in Germany to the *Amt* itself in order to work more effectively against the countries with which they were concerned, while in addition, Schellenberg with some difficulty succeeded in introducing into the *Amt* some of the more competent officers with whom he had been acquainted during his service as *Gruppenleiter* IV E. But in the case of VI D the number of officers he could find with any qualifications necessary for that *Gruppe* was very small, while it was extremely difficult to improve the working methods of the *Gruppe* in view of the peculiar difficulties with which it was faced. *Gruppe* VI D therefore became Schellenberg's 'problem child'—his own description.

2. Changes in personnel.
The most urgent need was to find a *Gruppenleiter* with the necessary qualifications combined with sufficient ability to redirect the work of the *Gruppe* along better lines. This change however was not easy to effect owing to the shortage of suitable personnel, and from approximately the middle of 1941 until the latter half of 1942 the position of *Gruppenleiter* VI D was one of uncertainty. Daufeldt himself remained nominally in charge during the latter half of 1941, but was in effect posted to the SD-*Abschnitt* Königsberg, from which he was appointed to Switzerland in 1942 as *Amt* VI representative there for *Gruppe* VI B. Meanwhile, Gräfe, who had combined his duties as *Gruppenleiter* VI C with those of *Referent* VI D2, worked for

a spell as *Gruppenleiter* in 1941. It was, however, to RSHA *Amt* IV that Schellenberg looked for his solution, and his choice was *Kriminalkommissar* Schambacher, who acted for a short spell as *Gruppenleiter* in 1942, before a breakdown in health made it necessary to find a replacement. Schellenberg finally chose SS-*Ostubaf* Paeffgen who had studied for a period at Edinburgh University in 1929–30, and had a fair knowledge of English and the UK though not a profound one. He was industrious and conscientious but not of great ability. He formed, however, one of the 'Swabian Group' in *Amt* VI around Schellenberg, as opposed to the 'Austrian Group' round Kaltenbrunner and Waneck, *Gruppenleiter* VI E.

Recruitment of other suitable personnel remained difficult. SS-*Hstuf* Maywald became *Referent* for the USA in 1941, and on his special assignment to Spain in late 1942, he was replaced by SS-*Hstuf* Carstenn. In September 1942 SS-*Ostuf* Schüddekopf, who had worked for a few months in the American *Referat*, was appointed *Referent* for the UK, then *Referat* VI D7, soon to become VI D2. The South American *Referat*, the only really active *Referat* in the *Gruppe*, remained under SS-*Ostuf* Geppert until June 1942 when Geppert was transferred to RSHA *Gruppe* VI A. Nominally, both Maywald and Carstenn in turn acted as *Referent* in his absence, but the actual direction of the *Referat* passed to SS-*Hstuf* Gross who joined the *Gruppe* in the latter half of 1943.

3. Changes in organisation and policy.

It was not until Paeffgen's appointment as *Gruppenleiter* that Schellenberg made any serious attempts to improve the work of the *Gruppe*, which now had only three *Referates*, as Scandinavia had passed to VI E. The organisational changes were minor in character, and much more important was the effort to modify existing policy. Schellenberg's chief effort was to endeavour to obtain for the *Gruppe*, direct representation in neutral territory to replace the existing system whereby the *Ländergruppen* merely passed relevant information to VI D. In this Schellenberg was in the main unsuccessful, as the other *Gruppenleiter* continued to resent any encroachment on their territory. As Sweden now came under *Gruppe* VI E, the situation was that, apart from *Referat* VI D4 which had Becker in the Argentine, *Gruppe* VI D had no representatives of any kind outside of Germany, and still depended on the remaining *Ländergruppen* for its material. It was not until the end of the war that this situation was changed to any degree.

4. Changes in Representatives abroad.

At the end of 1942 Karl Arnold, who had been active on behalf of the *Gruppe* earlier in the year in contacting interned South American diplomats awaiting repatriation, was sent to Spain to act on behalf of the South American *Referat*, and to a lesser extent for *Gruppe* VI D as a whole. This enterprise, which went under the name of '*Unternehmen* Kolumbus' was to assume considerable importance in the course of 1943 and 1944, and is dealt with in more detail in Part VI, dealing with *Referat* VI D4. In the spring of 1943 Maywald, former *Referent* for America, was likewise despatched to Spain to act on behalf of both VI D1 and VI D2, this enterprise going under the name of '*Unternehmen* Ohio' (see Part III). Much less important was to the posting of SS-*Hstuf* Zuchristian to BdS Paris. These changes were of importance to *Referat* VI D4 and the position of the UK and USA *Referate* was not greatly affected.

5. The situation by mid-1944.
The success or otherwise of these changes introduced by Schellenberg can only be judged in the light of the achievements of the *Gruppe* by the summer of 1944 when a further reorganisation took place. *Referat* VI D4 continued to be active and enterprising, but the major weakness in the *Gruppe*—activities against the UK and the USA—was the real test. By the summer of 1944 both *Referate* VI D1 and VI D2 had made efforts to send agents to their respective territories. VI D1 had met with dismal failure in the Kenny/O'Reilly operation, while Carstenn as *Referent* VI D1 had spent considerable time on the '*Unternehmen* Roesl', which proved to be stillborn. *Referat* VI D2 had recruited various agents with connections in neutral territory, but the results had been meagre, while the material obtained from the remaining *Ländergruppen* was of little consequence apart from the 'Nero' material from VI E. The situation had therefore not improved as the essential weakness still remained—*Gruppe* VI D had no agents in the UK or the USA, a failing which resulted among other causes from the very restricted field for recruitment of suitable agent material. Repatriated Germans returning from America had too wholesome a respect for the FBI to wish to risk returning to that country as German agents, while renegade Irishmen did not make ideal agents.

The failure to exploit Eire was a notable one; the causes lay in the fact that no pre-war attempts had been made to place agents in the country under suitable cover, and primarily in the strong opposition of the Foreign Office, which resented any interference by RSHA *Amt* VI in that territory. Indeed, the Foreign Office in association with the *Veesenmayer-Büro*, had prepared its own plan for the landing of agents in Eire—the '*Unternehmen* 1000', which did not get beyond the preparatory stage.

By the summer of 1944, therefore, RSHA *Gruppe* VI D had failed apart from the South American *Referat*. A further re-organisation took place, and the nature of that re-oganisation was a confession of this failure.

6. The re-organisation of the *Gruppe* in summer 1944.
The final re-organisation was a significant one. Both *Referate* VI D1 and VI D2 abandoned any further pretence at independent *Einsatze*, and the need for an *Erfassungsabteilung* within the *Referate* themselves disappeared. As a result, *Referat* IV D4, the South American *Referat*, undertook the despatch of missions for *Referat* VI D1, while VI D2 did not attempt any further missions. Carstenn was now

despatched to assist Brohs in Finland, SS-*Ostuf* Rudolph of RSHA *Amt* VII acting as temporary *Referent* VI D1, while Schüddekopf transferred before the end of the year to the *Zentral-Büro*. At the same time, Scandinavia returned to the *Gruppe* to become *Referat* VI D3 under Grönheim.

7. New Departures in *Gruppe* VI D activity.

The dissolution of the *Erfassungsabteilungen* of both VI D1 and VI D2 brought changes in the type of work undertaken by these *Referate*. Several of the officers were sent to POW camps to interrogate British and American prisoners of war, to sound them on British and American morale, and also to exploit that field for possible agent recruitment. SS-*Hstuf* Lange was sent to the *Stalag* [*Dulag*] at Oberursel, while Thost of VI D2 was instrumental in recruiting an English Major due for repatriation—a mission which was to prove quite futile. It need hardly be said that this activity was likely to improve the work of the *Gruppe*, and the enterprise served mainly the purpose of finding redundant officers something to do.

8. Conclusion.

RSHA *Gruppe* VI D was responsible for two of the major enemies of Germany, and for this reason alone it might have been expected that RSHA *Amt* VI efforts would have been concentrated on this *Gruppe* at the expense of the others. In point of fact, apart from VI D4 and South America, *Amt* VI activity against the UK and the USA was an almost complete failure. The reasons for this failure have already been dealt with in the preceding paragraphs. Although allowance can be made for the difficulties which faced the *Gruppe* in its work, the ultimate reasons for the dismal record of the *Gruppe* lie in the fact that its controlling officers were incompetent and completely incapable of surmounting the difficulties with which they had to contend. In the case of South America, where they were officers of some ability and enterprise, there was a different story to tell.

Whatever the reasons for the failure of RSHA *Gruppe* VI D to exploit Eire as a base for operations against the UK may have been, the failure remains the most striking in all *Amt* VI activity. It is difficult to make excuses for VI D2 in this connection when the Kenny/O'Reilly case stands against its name—a mission which must serve as a model of how not to recruit agents, how not to train them, and how not to send them on their task—a mission which had a fitting conclusion when its chief agent was able to buy himself a hotel after the war with the funds given him by RSHA *Amt* VI.

Part III

Referat VI D1 and the USA

1. Personnel.

Referent:	SS-*Hstuf* Maywald (1941–42)
	SS-*Hstuf* Carstenn (1942-January 1944)
	SS-*Ostuf* Rudolph (January 1944–April 1945 as Acting *Referent*)
Other personnel:	SS-*Hstuf* Mohr (1941–1945)
	SS-*Oschaf* Denker
	Angestellter Burmann

2. Representatives Abroad.

Karl Arnold	Spain (*Unternehmen* Kolumbus)
SS-*Hstuf* Maywald	Spain (*Unternehmen* Ohio)
SS-*Hstuf* Mohr	Turkey (based in Istanbul)

3. Sources of Information.

(a) <u>*Unternehmen* Kolumbus</u>
Details of the activities of Karl Arnold in Spain, where he worked primarily on behalf of *Referat* VI D4, are given in Part VI dealing with that *Referat*.

(b) <u>*Unternehmen* Ohio</u>
In the early part of 1943 SS-*Hstuf* Maywald, *Referent* for VI D1 from 1941, was sent to Madrid to open there a dress salon. Maywald's confederates in this enterprise were a certain *Herr* Schmidt, whom Maywald had previously known in Paris, and Maywald's girlfriend, Anna de Pompo. The three duly opened up a shop named 'Casa de Pompo' (for which they received a first payment of 25,000 dollars) with the intention of establishing good contacts in the social life of Madrid. Schmidt had a criminal record as a swindler—a reputation which he preserved in his new enterprise as the shop failed owing to his embezzlement of the funds. RSHA *Gruppe* VI D however restarted the enterprise, but Schmidt and his girlfriend, who was also involved in the affair, returned to Paris in disgrace towards the end of 1944.

The results of this enterprise were on the whole a failure, though Maywald has been reported as having established contact with representatives of Badoglio in Madrid. The primary object, however, which had been to obtain information on the USA through contacts in Madrid, was not achieved.

(c) <u>SS-*Hstuf* Mohr in Istanbul</u>
Mohr had been employed in both the American and English *Referate* under Daufeldt, with whom he was not on good terms owing to the latter treating him

as a child. In 1943 he was sent to Istanbul to obtain information on American matters in that territory. Mohr established contact with the REMO organisation which functioned in the Middle East, his assignment being to check on the validity of reports coming from that source, as they were considered suspect by RSHA *Amt* VI. The REMO organisation is dealt with in the Liquidation Report on RSHA *Gruppe* VI C. Mohr was unsuccessul in his mission as in his other assignment of submitting reports on America through contacts in Istanbul.

(d) Other Sources

In the absence of any direct sources of information on America itself, VI D1 was forced to rely on third-hand reports from neutral countries received through the other *Ländergruppen*, on radio intercepts, and on the Press. The chief source covering these was Arnold of *Referat* VI D4 (see Part VI), and to a lesser extent from Nassenstein in Portugal. American newspapers were received from neutral countries about one month old, and were useful only in summarising technical matters, this side being dealt with by RSHA VI Wi/T under SS-*Stubaf* Ogilvie.

Late in 1942 some results were received from the monitoring of transatlantic telephone calls between America and the UK. The leading personality in this work was *Oberpostrat* Vetterlein of the *Reichspost*, who had set up a station near Eindhoven in Holland which succeeded in monitoring radio-telephonic conversations between Washington and London. The results obtained from this source were meagre, as, even though it was possible to get the text of the conversations, it was not possible to divine the various cover names and code words used in them.

4. Missions undertaken by *Referat* VI D1.

(a) *Unternehmen* Roesl.

This enterprise was undertaken by Carstenn during his period as *Referent* VI D1. In the summer of 1943 a certain Sievers, a German merchant seaman who had spent a long time in the USA, offered his services to RSHA *Gruppe* VI D as a potential agent stating that he was prepared to be sent to America to organise an espionage network there. At the same time he submitted the names of others who would form the basis of the projected network, an offer which was accepted by Carstenn. Two of the recruits were sent to RSHA *Gruppe* VI F for W/T training, but were found unsuitable and were dropped. Sievers however found a replacement, a certain Rasch, to complete the party, which now numbered three, the other being by name Steckmesser. Carstenn spent the better part of a year in preparing the mission, which involved several journeys to Copenhagen to arrange transport. It was finally decided however to despatch the party by submarine from Lorient [France], the mission being sent on its way in the spring of 1944. The submarine was however sunk in the Bay of Biscay, and it was as a result of this failure that VI D4 undertook the organising of any further missions to America on behalf of VI D1.

(b) *Unternehmen* Elster.

This mission was in its early stages the concern of *Referat* VI D1, but owing to the failure of *Unternehmen* Roesl and the subsequent re-organisation of the *Gruppe*, was undertaken by VI D4. The agents involved were Gimpel and Colepaugh, the former having originally been destined to form part of the *Unternehmen* Remo in company with Zuhlsdorf and Schneemann (see Part VI). Gimpel was an engineer who had spent some time in the USA, and during his period of training with Zuhlsdorf and Schneemann, he introduced Colepaugh to Gross. Colepaugh having jumped his ship at Lisbon, where it had arrived from America, and suggested that they should be sent on a separate mission to North America. The two were then trained as a team, receiving instruction in W/T and secret inks. Gimpel was to set up a network, but his own W/T equipment in the USA, and in addition to establishing contact with Germany itself, was to attempt contact with the 'Jolle I' and 'Jolle II' teams in South America (see Part VI). The mission was despatched by submarine in August 1944, and the agents were safely landed, only to be arrested soon after by the FBI. As a result of their arrest, the names of Schneemann and Zuhlsdorf were published in the American Press to the discomfiture of VI D4.[1]

Part IV

Referat VI D2 and the United Kingdom

1. Personnel.

Referent:	SS-*Hstuf* Zuchristian (1939–41)
	SS-*Stubaf* Dr Gräfe (1941, Acting *Referent*)
	SS-*Hstuf* Carstenn (1941–42; in addition was *Referent* VI D1)
	SS-*Ostuf* Schüddekopf (Dec 1942–Dec 1944)
	SS-*Ostuf* Niklas (Dec 1944–Apr 1945, as Acting *Referent*)
Other personnel:	SS-*Hstuf* Giese
	SS-*Hstuf* Pretzsch
	SS-*Ostuf* Reimers
	SS-*Ostuf* Gaede
	SS-*Hstuf* Mohr (1941–42)
	SS-*Hstuf* Dr Lange
	Angestellter Dr Thost

2. Representatives Abroad.

SS-*Hstuf* Zuchristian (BdS Paris, 1942–44)

3. Sources of Information.
In the absence of direct representation, *Referat* VI D2 had to rely on the other *Ländergruppen* for most of its material. The most important sources were the CICERO material obtained from RSHA *Gruppe* VI C, and the NERO material from RSHA *Gruppe* VI E.

(a) The CICERO material.
This source, which existed in Turkey, is dealt with in the War Room Liquidation Report on RSHA *Gruppe* VI C.

(b) The NERO material.
The NERO material was passed to VI D through SS-*Stubaf* Höttl of RSHA *Gruppe* VI E. Höttl had established connections with the Military Intelligence department of the Hungarian General Staff, whose lines into Lisbon and Madrid were the source of information on Great Britain. This material was considered of great importance by RSHA *Gruppe* VI D and represented their main source, but was treated with reserve as the material was suspected of being '*Spielmaterial*' [deception material].

Apart from these two sources, VI D2 and VI D1, had to depend on the Press obtained in neutral countries, and on any relevant information obtained from RSHA VI Wi, and RSHA VI Kult. RSHA *Gruppe* VI G was used for reference purposes. In addition, the Vetterlein station was used (see Part III, Paragraph 3 (d)). In the final stages, after the dissolution of the *Erfassungsabteilungen*, SS-*Hstuf* Dr Lange was sent to Oberursel to interrogate POWs as a possible source of information on the UK. This activity was a failure, through a British Major was recruited in this way, being given the half-hearted assignment of 'putting in a good word for Germany' on his return to the UK. This PW reported his mission to the proper authorities immediately on repatriation.

(c) Dr Kraemer in Sweden.
Kraemer was originally an *Abwehr* I-*Luft* agent in Sweden under cover of the German Legation in Stockholm. In this capacity he submitted reports both to Daufeldt, then *Gruppenleiter* VI D, and to *Abwehr* I-*Luft* until January 1943. The reports were of doubtful reliability and for this reason were dropped by VI D. From December 1944 onwards reports were again received from this source through RSHA *Mil Amt* C, the reports covering the labour situation in England and questions of British home and foreign policy.

4. Agents employed by *Referat* VI D2.
Referat VI D2 employed several agents of an allegedly high level type with connections in neutral territory to make up for the absence of direct representation both in the UK and in neutral territory. These agents were listed below.

(a) <u>Vilma Varga.</u>
Varga was a professional dancer who at one time worked for the Istanbul branch of the American Office of War Information in 1942. She was expelled from Turkey in 1943 and was contacted by Schüddekopf in Berlin as a possible agent for *Referat* VI D2 for an assignment in Lisbon. The project eventually fell through after she had been on the *Referat* VI D2 payroll for several months.

(b) <u>Arthur Pfauss.</u>
Pfauss was a member of the Fichtebund who claimed to have contacts with leading members of the IRA, through a Catholic priest in Paris. The project was taken up by SS-*Hstuf* Niklas but dropped as more concrete results were by that time expected from the O'Reilly/Kenny operation.

(c) <u>Arthur Gold.</u>
Gold had been a trainee in RSHA *Gruppe* VI E under '*Unternehmen* Otto', and on the dissolution of that *Referat* in August 1943 was transferred to VI D2. He was despatched to Spain mid-1943 to obtain a Polish passport through penetration of a Polish underground movement. It was intended to use this passport to sign on a neutral ship in Lisbon and bound for the UK, and there obtain specimens of identity cards and other documents urgently required by RSHA *Amt* VI. Gold was however unable to obtain a visa to enter Portugal, and on a second attempt reached Spain where he remained without attempting to get any further.

(d) <u>Dr Ludwig Weissauer.</u>
Dr Weissauer was a former personal representative of Ribbentrop, and later liaison officer of the *Ostministerium* to the *Heeresgruppe Nord* [in the Russian campaign]. He had good connections in Finland and Finnish circles in Berlin, and on behalf of *Referat* VI D2 attempted to establish an espionage service in the UK through the Finnish General Staff and the Swedish Military and Naval Attaches in Stockholm and London, a project which led to nothing. Weissauer travelled abroad frequently, and submitted reports on political matters which were considered to be of value. Weissauer was on friendly terms with a *Frau* Wiedemann, who accompanied him on most of his journeys. *Frau* Wiedemann had at one time been an agent for *Referat* VI D1, but was dropped, though she later in 1942 offered her services again to Daufeldt for a mission to Sweden or Spain.

(e) <u>Professor Volz.</u>
Volz was a former college lecturer in Atlanta, USA, who had returned to Europe via Portugal. There he had contacted SS-*Stubaf* Gottlob (previously of RSHA *Gruppe* VI F) acting in Lisbon as 'broadcasting' attache. Gottlob introduced Volz to *Gruppe* VI D as a prospective agent, and he was eventually sent to Davos-Platz in Switzerland with the assignment of procuring American newspapers and periodicals. No reports of any value were received from this source.

(f) <u>Collins.</u>

Collins, like Gold (see above), was a trainee of *Referat* VI F/O, who had been made available to the new RSHA *Gruppe* VI S at the end of 1943. Skorzeny however dropped him as unsuitable, and he was taken on by *Referat* VI D2. Collins received W/T training at Lehnitz on behalf of VI D2, but was never used.

(g) <u>Gräfin Knyphausen.</u>

Gräfin Knyphausen's father was a Norwegin plenipotentiary in Helsinki, who was sent to Stockholm on behalf of *Referat* VI D2 after a period in Switzerland as an agent for *Referat* VI B1. In Stockholm she established contacts with high social circles and submitted reports based on conversations in these circles through Finke in Sweden. The reports were not of a high standard, and Finke was unsuccessful in persuading her to untertake more important work.

(h) <u>Viggo-Jensen.</u>

Viggo-Jensen was a Danish journalist employed by *Referat* VI D2 in September 1942 after a spell as an agent for *Referat* VI D1, for whom he had operated in Lisbon. Efforts were made to send him to Finland or Sweden, but his reputation as a collaborator made this impossible. He was dropped by VI D2 in the autumn of 1943.

5. Missions undertaken by *Referat* VI D2.

(a) <u>The Kenny/O'Reilly Case.</u>

This mission was the only one directly undertaken by *Referat* VI D2 and was meant to exploit what should have been the fertile field of Eire. O'Reilly was a former member of the IRA [Irish Republican Army], who had been interned in Jersey after the Germans occupied that island in 1940. He was subsequently released from internment to work for *Abwehr* Ast Bremen, but in the early summer of 1943 he was recruited by Schüddekopf through a *Frau* O'Mara for a projected operation in Eire. O'Reilly suggested that a former fellow-internee in Jersey, Kenny (an uneducated person of peasant-like intelligence) should join him on the mission, and in October 1943 O'Reilly travelled to Jersey with Paeffgen to bring Kenny back. O'Reilly had been trained in W/T by *Abwehr* Ast Bremen, and continued his training with RSHA VI F. During their stay in Berlin, both agents mixed freely with the renegade population there, and spoke rather freely of their impending mission, a fact of which both Schüddekopf and Paeffgen were warned. Nevertheless in December 1943 Schüddekopf and Niklaus accompanied the two agents to an airfield in Rennes, O'Reilly being dropped in the first flight (it was discovered at the last moment that the plane could not accommodate two passengers), Kenny being dropped the following night as O'Reilly's despatch. This mission was a complete failure, both agents being arrested soon after they landed.

(b) <u>The Seth Case.</u>
Ronald Seth was a British agent [of Special Operations Executive, SOE] who had been parachuted into Esthonia in 1941. After service with the *Abwehr*, he was contacted by Graf Dönhof, *Leiter* of *Referat* VI B3, and submitted reports from the POW Camp where he was interned, which reports were sent to RSHA *Gruppe* VI D as they were of interest to that *Gruppe*. At the end of 1944 it was intended by *Referat* VI B3 that Seth should go to Switzerland to act as a V-*Mann* there on their behalf, but Dönhof had developed the idea of sending him back to England—a project which he discussed with Schüddekopf. Seth surrendered to the British authorities immediately on entering Switzerland.

(c) <u>Mission to Iceland.</u>
In April 1944 two agents landed in Iceland, and proved under interrogation to have been recruited by RSHA *Amt* VI. Although this mission came within the territory of *Gruppe* VI D, the agents had actually been recruited and trained under the organisation '*Unternehmen* Otto' of RSHA *Gruppe* VI F in 1942-43 (see Liquidation Report on *Gruppe* VI F). SS-*Hstuf* Daufeldt, later of VI D3, was responsible for the mission, which aimed as obtaining reports on the weather and Allied troop movements. The agents were badly trained and the mission organised with the customary SD inefficiency, the agents themselves nullifying any success by jettisoning their W/T apparatus and codes.

Part V

Referat VI D3 and Scandinavia

1. The controlling *Referate*.
Scandinavia was under *Referat* VI G3 of the original *Gruppe* VI G in 1939–41. In 1941 it passed to RSHA *Gruppe* VI E to become *Referat* VI E6, returning to *Gruppe* VI D in the summer of 1944 to form *Referat* VI D3. It should be noted that until 1942 the Baltic States and Scandinavia were treated separately, *Gruppe* VI C being competent for the Baltic States including Finland until 1942. After 1942 the Baltic States—Esthonia, Lithuania and Latvia—were under the control of RSHA *Amt* III as occupied territory, but Finland joined the Scandinavian group to become the province of *Gruppe* VI E, later *Referat* VI D3. Similarly, Norway and Denmark passed to RSHA *Amt* III control until the summer of 1944 when *Gruppe* VI D sent direct representation to that country.

2. Personnel.
Referent: SS-*Hstuf* Grönheim (1940–summer 1944)
SS-*Hstuf* Bussinger (summer 1944–April 1945)

3. Other Personnel.

     SS-*Hstuf* Döhring

     SS-*Hstuf* Zöllner

     SS-*Ostuf* Wahlstab

4. Representatives Abroad.

Sweden:	SS-*Stubaf* Finke (1942 to late 1944)
	SS-*Ustuf* Schiller
	Angestellter Dr Krüger
	SS-*Oschaf* Pioch
Finland:	SS-*Hstuf* Schönebeck (1940–41)
	SS-*Hstuf* Brohs (1941–44)
	SS-*Hstuf* Carstenn (1944, formerly *Referent* VI D1, later in Denmark)
Denmark:	SS-*Hstuf* Paul (1940)
	SS-*Stubaf* Seiboldt (1943–44, later *Gruppe* VI S)
	SS-*Hstuf* Daufeldt (1944, formerly RSHA VI F/O and later RSHA I)
	SS-*Hstuf* Carstenn (formerly in Finland)
Norway:	(a) *Abteilung* VI, BdS Oslo
	SS-*Stubaf* Knab (1940)
	SS-*Stubaf* Berg (1940–41)
	SS-*Hstuf* Seiboldt (1941–43)
	SS-*Ostuf* Schopp (1943–44)
	SS-*Stubaf* Grönheim (autumn 1944)
	SS-*Ostuf* Laqua
	SS-*Ustuf* Bialwons
	SS-*Ustuf* Stotz
	Angestellter Mothes
	SS-*Oschaf* Rönnfeldt
	SS-*Oschaf* Strauss
	(b) KdS Oslo
	SS-*Ostuf* Krause
	SS-*Ostuf* Stätterau
	(c) *Aussendienststelle* Kristiansand
	SS-*Hstuf* Kerner
	SS-*Ustuf* Evers
	(d) KdS Trondheim, *Abteilung* VI
	SS-*Hstuf* Döhring
	(e) KdS Bergen
	SS-*Hstuf* Zöllner (1945)

5. Activities in Norway.

(a) <u>General</u>

SS-*Stubaf* Knab was sent by Jost to Norway as *Amt* VI representative, but he arrived only a short time before the invasion in 1940, after which the country became the province of RSHA *Amt* III. Knab subsequently joined *Abteilung* VI of the BdS set up under SS-*Oberführer* Stahlecker, later becoming KdS Lyons. As a result of this ascendancy of *Amt* III, *Amt* VI activity in the country was on a very reduced scale, and the only representative in Norway was SS-*Ostuf* Krause, *Leiter Abteilung* VI at BdS Oslo (later KdS Oslo). Previously SS-*Stubaf* Berg and later SS-*Hstuf* Seiboldt had held the position, but Seiboldt had really worked under *Amt* III supervision. Seiboldt later went to Denmark, and finally joined RSHA *Gruppe* VI S as a SS-*Stubaf.*

(b) <u>Early RSHA *Amt* VI work in Norway.</u>

Until the summer of 1944 it was considered that Norway could be used by RSHA *Gruppe* VI D as a base of operations against the UK, it being contemplated that use could be made of the considerable refugee traffic escaping from Norway to Britain. This plan, however did not meet with any success owing to the difficulty of finding recruits among the Norwegians themselves, and in any case such refugees were almost certain to finish up in the Norwegian Forces in England—not a suitable base for intelligence operations. As a result, *Abteilung* VI in Oslo confined itself to obtaining information from businessmen travelling backwards and forwards to Sweden. The information obtained in this way was of little value.

(c) <u>Renewed activity in 1944.</u>

In the summer of 1944 a much more determined effort was made to use Norway as a base for operations. SS-*Stubaf* Grönheim, *Referent* for Scandinavia, was sent to Oslo to organise the *Abteilung* there with specific objects in view. These may be summarised thus:

(i)   Infiltration of agents into Sweden and Finland.

(ii) To exploit Northern Norway as a base for operations against Russia.

(iii) The organisation of an I-*Netze.*

(iv) The organisation of a courier service into Sweden in view of the possibility of the severing of diplomatic relations between Sweden and Germany.

(d) <u>The organisation of *Abteilung* VI in Oslo under Grönheim.</u>

Grönheim was an officer of considerable ability, and during his comparatively short stay in Norway, he organised an *Abteilung* VI on very workable lines. The structure was as follows:

Abteilungsleiter		SS-*Stubaf* Grönheim
Referat VI A	Organisation	SS-*Ustuf* Bialwons (Referent)

VI A1	Registration Files	*Angestellter* Mothes
VI A2	Card Index	*Fräulein* Hirschmann
VI A3	Liaison Section	SS-*Ustuf* Bialwons
VI A4	Censorship	SS-*Ustuf* Bialwons (Material)
Referat VI B		SS-*Ostuf* Krause (*Referent*)
VI B1	The UK	-
VI B2	North & South America	-
VI B3	USSR, Near and Far East	-
VI B4	European countries exc. Scandinavia	-
Referat VI C		
VI C1	Sweden	SS-*Ustuf* Stotz
VI C2	Finland	SS-*Ostuf* Laqua
Referat VI D	W/T Training	SS-*Oschaf* Rönnfeldt
VI D1	W/T training	SS-*Oschaf* Strauss
VI D2	W/T equipment	SS-*Oschaf* Strauss

There was in addition an outpost at Kristiansand under SS-*Hstuf* Kerner and SS-*Ustuf* Evers, charged with the provision of shipping reports.

(e) The I-*Netze.*

The above organisation was ambitious rather than a reflection on the work undertaken by the *Abteilung*, but although the organisation did not get much beyond the paper stage, it was a reflection on the energy with which Grönheim tackled the task. More important were the actual efforts made at organising the I-*Netz*; some twenty-five agents were trained in W/T, all Norwegians except one Italian and two Finns. Agents were placed at Hammerfest and Alten und KdS Tromso, having direct communication with Berlin, while another two parties were sent to Kirkenes and Varanger peninsula under the control of a W/T set at Narvik. These two operations were meant to cover the Russian occupation in the north. Other agents were despatched into Sweden, including the Italian who was installed in Stockholm. The network was of course rendered invalid by the surrender on May 7th [1945].

(f) Activities of *Referate* VI B and VI C of *Abteilung* VI.

In addition to the I-*Netz* which was organised and trained under SS-*Oschaf* Rönnfeldt of *Referat* VI D, agents were despatched by VI C into both Finland and Sweden. The agents despatched to Finland were instructed to contact a Major Patsalo of the Finnish Intelligence Service who was actively engaged in organising commando raids behind the Russian lines in Finland. This operation was under the control of SS-*Ostuf* Laqua. As far as *Referat* VI B was concerned the section was dissolved after a short time as it had no hope of fulfilling the function it was supposed to.

(g) <u>Additional VI D postings to Norway.</u>
In addition to the despatch of Grönheim to Oslo, VI D took further steps to reinforce their representation in the country. SS-*Hstuf* Döhring was sent in March 1945 to cooperate with Grönheim, he himself being posted as *Leiter Abteilung* VI of the KdS Trondheim. Döhring's assignment of organising a network was far too late to be effective. Similarly, SS-*Hstuf* Zöllner of VI D3 was sent to Bergen, but he too more or less arrived just in time to be arrested on the general surrender in early May [1945].

6. Activities in Sweden.
(a) <u>Finke as Representative.</u>
SS-*Stubaf* Finke had joined RSHA *Amt* VI on its inception and had become *Referent* VI A2 in the original RSHA *Gruppe* VI A, his colleagues at that time in 1940 including SS-*Hstuf* Wossagk as *Referent* VI A1 and SS-*Hstuf* Neufert as *Referent* VI A4. Finke was one of the few original RSHA *Amt* VI officers to survive until 1942 when Schellenberg took over, Wossagk and Neufert both joining the fighting forces in 1941, while SS-*Ostuf* Westergaard, the *Referent* VI A5, left the *Amt* altogether. Finke himself was due for similar treatment, but was saved in April 1942 as Schellenberg had wrung the concession out of the Foreign Office that an *Amt* VI representative should be attached to the Legation in Stockholm. Schellenberg however had no officer ready with the necessary qualifications, and rather than risk any change of Foreign Office policy until a suitable officer could be found, decided to send Finke to Stockholm. Finke therefore arrived in Stockholm in May 1942 with an indifferent record of service behind him and with no language or other qualifications for the post he had to take over.

(b) <u>Finke's Failure.</u>
From Schellenberg's point of view the choice was doubly unfortunate, as Sweden as neutral territory represented a potentially important outpost for RSHA *Amt* VI activities against such countries as Russia, Britain the USA. In this respect Finke was a complete failure, and his reports were vague and of little value. Finke did not succeed in making any important direct contacts, his agents being largely recruited among journalists, mainly of the *Folkets- Dagblatt*, and while these contacts were instrumental in providing occasional good reports on the internal conditions in Sweden, such reports were of secondary importance. It was not Sweden itself which really mattered, but the opportunities which the country offered as a base of operations extending much farther afield. A further difficulty was the increasingly

strained relations which existed between Germany and Sweden, especially in the course of 1944, relations which finally led to Finke's expulsion in February 1945.

(c) Attempts at an I-*Netze.*
The worsening situation in 1944 made it necessary to make provisions for the possible rupture of relations between Germany and Sweden. For this eventuality, four Swedes were trained in W/T, and Finke, with the help of SS-*Ustuf* Schiller, arranged to have the sets installed near Stockholm. The network was prepared in collaboration with the political movement connected with the *Folkets-Dagblatt.*

In addition to the organisation of a network in Sweden itself, steps were taken to penetrate the country from Norway. SS-*Stubaf* Grönheim being sent to Oslo to make the necessary arrangements. Grönheim's activities have been dealt with in Paragraph 5 above. The Swedish network itself collapsed when Finke was expelled.

(d) Finke's contacts.
Finke's contacts and agents were few in number; he relied mainly on the *Folkets-Dagblatt* circle under its editor, Johannson, while among the German journalists in Sweden his principal contact was Dr Penzlin of *Das Reich.* Other contacts were Gossler of the *Reichsbahnwerbezentrale,* and von der Goltz, a banker. Finke was also in contact with Gräfin Knyphausen mentioned in Part IV, Paragraph 4(g) above.

In the Legation itself Finke had close contact with Bauersfeld of the *Kulturabteilung,* while in the latter stages before his expulsion he worked in close collaboration with Dankwort, Counsellor of the German Embassy. Finke had discussed with the latter on how best to set up a stay-behind organisation on behalf of the *Auswärtiges Amt*—a project which came to nothing.

7. Activities in Finland.
(a) Brohs as Representative.
SS-*Stubaf* Brohs was recruited by Jost early in 1940 as a possible representative in Sweden, but having no experience at the time it was decided to send him to the SD-*Leitabschnitt* Dresden as *Referent Abteilung* VI. In March 1941 he was sent to Finland to replace SS-*Hstuf* Schönebeck, working there under cover of the *Reichsbahn-Zentrale* in Helsinki. Ostensibly Brohs was head of a small travel agency under the control of the *Deutschen-Amerika-Linie.* He remained in Helsinki until the withdrawal in September 1944.

Brohs proved himself to be an agent of considerable ability and recruited his agents among personal acquaintances with anti-communist feelings, his chief assignment in Finland being to study the influence of Russian propaganda on the Finns. The reports submitted by Brohs from these sources were considered by *Gruppe* VI D to be of high quality.

(b) The I-*Netze.*

Brohs was instrumental in recruiting a certain Kyrre to function as a stay-behind agent after the German withdrawal, he remaining in Helsinki to act as a technical adviser to the Russians. Although only one link had been established, Brohs left behind five W/T sets with Kyrre with the intention to despatching additional agents to join Kyrre and thus extend the network, it being planned to set up outstations in Lapland and Northern Finland. Reports were received from the Kyrre link until January 1945. These reports were based on intelligence received by Kyrre through the Finnish undergound movement with which he was in clloose touch through its leading members. Kyrre was presumably arrested by the Russians in January 1945 as a Press report dated March 1945 announced that he had escaped from prison in Helsinki.

(c) The *Sonderkommando Nord.*

At the end of September 1944 Cellarius, the former *Abwehr* representative in Finland who had been forced to withdraw from the country, was ordered by Schellenberg to set up a *Sonderkommando Nord* whose function it would be to recruit Finns to return to Finland to contact the undertground intelligence organisation which Cellarius had left behind. In December 1944 this enterprise was extended to cover *Gruppe* VI D interests, and Brohs was given instructions to work in liaison with Cellarius. Brohs recruited his agents from the Finnish Resistance Movement. In this work he was assisted by SS-*Ostuf* Wassermann who has been reported as having been killed in an air-raid in Copenhagen, being replaced by a certain SS-*Ostuf* Laurel. The enterprise collapsed by February 1945 owing to the poor material available, and to the lack of time in preparing the agents for this mission. Nevertheless Laurel left with his small *Kommando* of twelve agents in early 1945 with instructions to contact Grönheim in Oslo, the agents themselves receiving instructions to make their way to Finland from Oslo.

It should be noted that the *Sonderkommando Nord* came under the general control of both RSHA *Gruppe* VI C and *Gruppe* VI D, as the former *Gruppe* was at that time anxious to exploit the Scandinavian countries for the purpose of infiltrating agents into Russian territory. Brohs himself was arrested soon afterwards.

8. Activities in Denmark.

Little need be said of RSHA *Amt* VI activities in Denmark. After the occuption of that country in 1940 the territory came under the complete control of RSHA *Amt* III and no RSHA *Amt* VI work of any kind was carried out apart from a short and ineffective visit by SS-*Stubaf* Seiboldt in 1943. Seiboldt later joined RSHA *Gruppe* VI S. It was not until the organisation of the I-*Netze* throughout occupied territory was contemplated that *Amt* VI showed any further interest in Denmark, but the effort was much too late for any results to be achieved. SS-*Hstuf* Daufeldt, who had been *Leiter* of the *Abteilung Nord* in the '*Unternehmen* Otto' in 1943, was sent to Denmark in the latter half of 1944 with the assignment of organising a stay-behind network, but was a complete failure. He was recalled in December 1944 and transferred to RSHA *Amt* I. After Carstenn's withdrawal from Finland, he too was sent to Denmark to assist Daufeldt, but with no greater measure of success. Carstenn was arrested in Denmark after the surrender.

Part VI

Referat VI D4 and South America

A. Historical Development of the South American *Referat*.

1. The importance of *Referat* VI D4.
The general difficulties which faced RSHA *Gruppe* VI D, and which have been elaborated in Part II above, did not apply in the same degree to South America as to North America. The whole South American continent was neutral territory, which lent itself to exploitation, and the regular traffic between that country and the Iberian Peninsula was an added advantage. Nevertheless, while the conditions in South America were more favourable than in any other part of the Western Hemisphere, the general difficulties which faced the *Amt* as a whole in the early stages applied with equal force to the South American continent. The *Referat*, however became one of the most successful in RSHA *Amt* VI, if success is to be measured in vigour and enterprise. *Referat* VI D4 became before the end the only operationally active *Referat* covering the Anglo-American sphere.

2. Early history.
It will be seen from Part I above, that South America was originally covered by RSHA *Gruppe* VI E, the *Referent* being SS-*Ostuf* Geppert, who operated for a time under cover from Rome and from the Iberian Peninsula. Geppert himself was a hard worker and ambitious, but not extremely talented in intelligence work, as is evidenced by his transfer for inefficiency in June 1942 to RSHA *Gruppe* VI A, where he eventually became *Referent* VI A5. Nevertheless, Geppert was responsible for the recruitment of Siegfried Becker, who was sent as representative to the Argentine on behalf of RSHA *Amt* VI. The importance of this recruitment cannot be minimised, as the subsequent development of the work of the *Referat* centres very largely round the enterprise and resource shown by Becker in his work. Geppert at the same time recruited Heinz Lange to accompany Becker.

The only other achievement of note to Geppert's credit was his exploitation of the Brazilian Embassy in Berlin, of which details are given in Paragraph C (4) below.

3. Transfer to RSHA *Gruppe* VI D.

The *Referat* was transferred to RSHA *Gruppe* VI D in the summer of 1942 as *Referat* VI D4. By this time the Becker organisation was well under way, and developing favourably, and it seemed opportune to Schellenberg to exploit this comparative success to the full. Geppert was transferred to *Gruppe* VI A, the *Referent* being in turn SS-*Hstuf* Carstenn of VI D1 and SS-*Hstuf* Maywald of VI D2.

The important developments under Schellenberg took the form of giving the *Referat* direct representation in the Iberian Peninsula. This was not achieved without opposition from RSHA *Gruppe* VI B who resented any intrusion into their territory, but Schellenberg prevailed in the end, and Karl Arnold was sent to Spain to act on behalf of VI D4 and as a liaison with the South American networks and as a springboard for further operations against that continent. Arnold was conscientious, hard-working, and a good organiser.

4. Gross as *Referent*.

In August 1943 SS-*Hstuf* Kurt Gross was appointed *Referent* VI D4. Gross had at one time resided in the Argentine, had served in the Spanish Civil War in the Condor Legion, and on the creation of RSHA *Amt* VI in 1939 was chosen by Zschunke, then *Referent* for France, as an *Amt* VI agent in Biarritz, a mission which was short lived and unsuccessful (see Liquidation Report on *Gruppe* VI B). After a period with RSHA *Amt* IV he was re-transferred to *Amt* VI as *Referent* VI D4. Gross was an energetic type of considerable imagination and resource. As *Referent* VI D4 he assumed considerable authority in the direction of the *Referat*, a characteristic which brought him into conflict with Paeffgen from time to time.

5. The position of *Referat* VI D4 in 1944–45.

The occasional clashes between Gross and Paeffgen were of little significance; much more important was that from the end of 1943 *Referat* VI D4 had an enterprising and energetic *Referent*, a chief representative in South America of considerable resource who had developed and organised a network which functioned, and between the two a conscientious and intelligent go-between in Spain who had succeeded in organising, among other things, a courier service to South America which also functioned. It is not surprising therefore that VI D4 continued to thrive, nor is it to be wondered at, that VI D1 and VI D2 in their dismal failures, handed over the running of all enterprises against the Anglo-American sphere to VI D4.

The success of course of a *Referat* is not in the last analysis measured in terms of its energy and enterprise, but by the concrete results achieved. The activities of VI D4 and the results of these activities are summarised in Part B below.

B. The Activities of *Referat* VI D4.

1. Siegfried Becker and the '*Unternehmen* Bolivar'.
(a) <u>Early history and development.</u>
Siegfried Becker had been in the Argentine at the outbreak of war and returned to Germany early in 1940. During his stay in Germany he contacted Geppert and was recruited together with Heinz Lange with a view to being sent back to the Argentine on a sabotage mission. The point is an important one, as the subsequent development of the Becker network was not the result of carefully given instructions from RSHA *Amt* VI, but a reflection on Becker's own enterprise and energy. The South American network expanded in spite of *Amt* VI in the early stages.

(b) <u>First mission to the Argentine in 1940.</u>
Becker and Lange were duly despatched to the Argentine in the summer of 1940 with vague instructions to carry out sabotage operations against Allied shipping in Buenos Aires. This original mission had, however, to be cancelled as the Foreign Office learned of its nature, and as a result of their protests, the assignment of Becker was limited to the general one of obtaining any information on the United States and Britain. In this early stage, no W/T was provided, Becker maintaining contact with Berlin by means of a post-box operated through a commercial cover firm.

Becker was however successful in procuring for himself through his own efforts a W/T transmitting set, and by early 1941 had established contact with RSHA *Gruppe* VI F, using both this means of communication together with the post-box, his letters now being sent in code or treated with secret ink. At this time Becker was operating from Sao Paulo in Brazil, as it had become dangerous to pursue operations in the Argentine.

The results achieved by this time were to little consequence as far as information was concerned; the important feature was that Becker had already shown charactistic enterprise, which promised well, and by the summer of 1941 it seemed that the South American field was ready for exploitation.

(c) <u>Strengthening of the network.</u>
In the course of 1941 agents were sent from Germany to reinforce the growing Becker network. The most important feature was the despatch of Utzinger of RSHA *Gruppe* VI F in August 1941 as he was an experienced radio engineer whose presence in the Becker organisation was becoming increasingly necessary. Utzinger became responsible not only for the maintenance of the W/T equipment but also for the training of further agents recruited in South America itself. Other agents sent about this time included Engling, who was sent to Brazil in June 1941 with considerable funds for the network, and also with supplies of secret ink material, and Hartmuth, who was originally recruited by VI D2 for despatch to the USA

via South America, but remained with the Becker group on arrival in Brazil. The only other agent of the network at this time who had been sent from Germany (the network had already recruited in South America itself) was a German journalist, von Merk, who had gone to Brazil as a representative of the *Völkische Beobachter* newspaper, but who had been contacted by Geppert prior to his departure unknown to the newspaper, and requested to work on behalf of RSHA *Amt* VI. On arrival in Brazil he too contacted Becker and henceforth worked for him. von Merk later worked with Nassenstein in Portugal after his repatriation in 1942.

(d) <u>Becker's return to Germany.</u>
By the end of 1941 Becker had a fairly well organised network which had been created largely on his own initiative. It is characteristic that Becker decided to return to Germany off his own bat and without prior consultation. On his retun he was officially appointed as leader of all RSHA *Amt* VI espionage activity in South America (it should be remembered that Becker had merely been sent in the first instance as a sabotage agent). His return was delayed owing to transport difficulties until March 1943, and again characteristically, he smuggled himself across to the Argentine at a time when the *Amt* had decided that he should return to Berlin and abandon the idea of returning. During his stay in Spain, Becker was in close contact with Arnold, and between them the basis of the subsequent courier system was worked out.

(e) <u>Dispersal of the Brazil network and subsequent re-organisation.</u>
During Becker's absence in Germany the network he had left in Brazil was forced to flee to Paraguay owing to the danger of arrest in Brazil. On Becker's return, the network was re-established on new lines, he himself setting up his headquarters in Buenos Aires, while Hartmuth was left in Paraguay and Lange was sent to Chile. Both Hartmuth and Lange were provided with W/T sets. Becker now set about organising a network of his own in the Argentine, Utzinger being charged with the W/T training of agents recruited. Becker also established contact with the German Embassy in Buenos Aires, with the Argentine Government, and with the Integralist movement in Brazil. A further recruit for the network had been sent from Berlin early in 1942 in the person of SS-*Oschaf* Schorer-Stolle, who was sent with funds and cipher equipment, the latter however being jettisoned en route as Stolle was afraid of detection during routine security examination at Trinidad.

(f) <u>The arrests in January 1945.</u>
In January 1944 the Argentine Government took action against the Becker organisation, which resulted in the arrest of several members, including Schorer-Stolle. Becker and Utzinger however escaped and managed to re-establish contact with Berlin after a period. The network had of course been seriously disrupted and Becker's messages were confined largely to requests for more W/T equipment,

technical material and money. At this time Gross was *Referent* VI D4, and he took energetic steps to meet Becker's requirements.

(g) The 'Jolle I' Project.

Gross conceived the plan of sending the requested material to Becker with the assistance of the the RSHA *Mil Amt*, as that department had already been active in sending its agents to South America through the Schuchmann organisation. The RSHA *Mil Amt* agreed to give the required assistance and Gross proceeded with the training of two agents, Hansen and Schröll, who were to take the necessary equipment to Becker, though the agents themselves were under instructions to make their way northwards after completing the first part of their task and establish themselves, one in Mexico, and the other in the USA, where they would develop their own networks on their own initiative, acting together as a team, (by this time VI D4 had taken over all *Einsatze* against the USA from VI D1). The cutter eventually left in April 1944 with considerable quantities of technical material, and succeeded in landing the two agents on the Argentine coast where contact was established with Becker. The success of the mission was short lived; Becker's last message to Berlin was to acknowledge the safe arrival of Hansen and Schröll, for soon afterwards Utzinger was arrested by the Argentine authorities, and the network was completely broken up. The arrest of Becker himself followed soon afterwards.

(h) Assessment of the Becker Group.

It is easy to overrate the value of the Becker network; there is no doubt that its development and organisation was a personal triumph for Becker, and the group was the most enterprising controlled by RSHA *Amt* VI. But, as previously stated, an espionage organisation can only be judged in the light of the practical successes achieved in the transmitting of information to the parent organisation. Viewed in this light the Becker organisation was only a moderate success, and the great volume of messages transmitted to Berlin were largely concerned with the organising of the network itself and with matters of administration, payments, etc. The quality of political information received from Becker was not of an exceptionally high standard; and its quantity was not considerable. The main virtue of the Becker organisation was the trouble it caused to the counter-espionage forces of the Allied and Argentine authorities to detect it and break it up. If, however, the success of the Becker network was largely a negative one, it was a considerable negative one.

(i) The liquidation of the Chile Network.

Meantime Heinz Lange in Chile had been engaged in the organisation of his own network. In this he cooperated closely with the *Abwehr* representative in Santiago, von Bohlen. Lange met with very little success in his efforts, and in November 1943 his activities came to an end in Chile as a result of action taken by the Chilean

Government in arresting several members of the network, though Lange himself succeeded in escaping to the Argentine where he re-established contact with the Becker group. Lange returned to Europe on board the 'Jolle I' in company with two other agents, Imhoff and Sievers. Lange evaded internment on arrival in Portugal, and made his way to Germany and joined RSHA *Gruppe* VI D at its evacuation quarters at Burg Lauenstein. Meantime Hartmuth, who on his escape from Brazil had remained in Paraguay as the chief agent of the Becker network there, died in that country in February 1944.

2. Karl Arnold and the '*Unternehmen* Kolumbus'.

(a) Functions of the '*Unternehmen* Kolumbus'.

The primary object behind the despatch of Arnold to Spain was the organisation of a courier system to South America to liaise with the Becker organisation there. In this capacity Arnold was to operate as a RSHA *Gruppe* VI D representative and would only be subordinated to Singer, the *Gruppe* VI B representative in Madrid, in matters of administration and communications, Arnold's messages to Berlin being sent through Singer's channels. This procedure was only established in face of opposition from *Gruppe* VI B. The actual arranging of the courier system was facilitated by the conversation Arnold had with Becker during the latter's stay in Spain in 1942, when he was awaiting transport back to South America. Side by side with the courier organisation, Arnold developed independent activity in Spain itself.

(b) The courier system.

Arnold recruited his agents for the courier system on an ideological basis, searching for his material among seamen of strong anti-communist sentiments, in this way obtaining the collaboration of men who did not seek payment for their services, and who were likely to prove reliable. Arnold recruited normally one seaman per ship, the man being given a different code word for each operation, the code word being transmitted to Becker by W/T. The normal procedure was for Becker to inform *Gruppe* VI D by W/T that a courier would be arriving by such and such a ship, which information was passed through Singer to Arnold, who in turn contacted the shipping company concerned to learn the date and port of arrival. This information was then passed to Arnold's contact man in Spain who met the ship on arrival and received the package from the courier on production of the code word. The reverse procedure operated for outgoing traffic.

(c) The value of the courier system.

The system which operated from early 1943 in full vigour until early 1944 when the arrest of two couriers by the British authorities dampened the ardour of the others and decreased the volume of traffic, had its limitations. Information received from South America in this way was inevitably out of date by the time it reached RSHA *Gruppe* VI D, and its value correspondingly diminished. Its positive value was its use in sending to Becker materials of which he had need, a value which must not be underrated. The system continued to operate on a reduced scale until the break-up of the Becker organisation.

(d) Other activities or Arnold.
During his stay in Madrid, Arnold was instrumental in establishing other contacts of value to *Referat* VI D4.

At the end of 1942 he recruited an employee of the Brazilian Embassy in Madrid through whom he received copies of all despatches sent out by the Brazilian Ambassador, though the material contained in these messages did not turn out to be of any great value. Similarly contacts were established in the American Embassy in Madrid, through which a considerable amount of material of low-grade quality was received. To assist him in his work Arnold was given the help of several assistants at various times, including *Angestellter* Hink and *Angesteller* Hertel, neither of whom were of any great use.

C. Other Agents and Activities of *Referat* VI D4.

1. Exploitation of South American diplomats.
Early in 1942 Arnold was given the assignment of contacting interned South American diplomats awaiting repatriation with a view to developing these contacts for future use in South American espionage activities. This enterprise did not yield any results, mainly because the *Abwehr* were already busy on the same project, so that Arnold's field was considerably restricted. A second attempt was made in the spring of 1943 when *Frau* Sommer, an employee of *Referat* VI D4, was sent to Bad Godesberg where South American diplomats previously stationed in France were awaiting repatriation. This activity yielded no results, this time because of the disinterested attitude of *Frau* Sommer herself, and owing to lack of direction from VI D4 where at that time Carstenn was Acting *Referent*.

2. Nassenstein in Portugal—'*Unternehmen* Hidalgo'.
In addition to the outpost in Spain under Arnold, *Referat* VI D4 was successful in establishing a similar outpost in Lisbon under SS-*Stubaf* Nassenstein, who, like Arnold, worked under RSHA *Gruppe* VI B supervision. Nassenstein fulfilled two main functions, that of establishing contact with the Brazilian Integralist Group under Salgado, and of lesser importance, the procurement of a steady supply of South and North American publications of all kinds. Nassenstein was not of the same ability as Arnold, and the results obtained from this source were not high.

3. The '*Unternehmen* Remo'.

This enterprise was the last to be undertaken by the South American *Referat*. Schneemann, who had originally been scheduled to go on the '*Unternehmen* Elster', was joined in this mission by two other agents, Zuhlsdorf and Wilms. Zuhlsdorf was a German repatriated from America in 1942, and who had been recruited by the *Abwehr* in July 1943, but who volunteered his services to RSHA *Amt* VI in May 1944, being accepted by *Referent* VI D4. Schneemann too had been repatriated from America. Zuhlsdorf, Schneemann, Colepaugh and Gimpel were trained at the Seehof School together, and the arrest of Gimpel and Colepaugh after this landing in America led to the warning notice in the American Press. By the time the news of the arrest was received in Berlin in February 1945, both Zuhlsdorf and Schneemann were at Kiel ready to depart; the trip was hurriedly cancelled. Gross now attempted to arrange for submarine transport for the agents, arrangements being made at the same time to alter their forged documents to meet the new situation. The 'Remo' undertaking now became the '*Unternehmen* Omer' (Remo in reverse). This enterprise however had finally to be abandoned owing to the deteriorating war situation, the capitulation of Germany concurring while both agents were in Spain awaiting transport to South America. Zuhlsdorf, however, anxious to get out of Europe, succeeded in stowing away on board a ship bound for South America, but was arrested by the British authorities in Trinidad as a result of the information given by Gimpel and Colepaugh.

4. Hochheimer in Chile.

The circumstances surrounding the activities of Hochheimer in Chile are still not clear. It is known that a certain Hochheimer, who had been employed at some time in the Chilean Embassy in Amsterdam, went to Chile some time probably late in 1943, agreeing to work there on behalf of the BdS in The Hague on the understanding that his wife and family would not be sent to a concentration camp on account of their Jewish blood. From early 1944 onwards Hochheimer submitted long reports to RSHA VI D which were considered of high quality.

It is not clear how Hochheimer's reports were routed from Chile to RSHA *Amt* VI, though it is believed that they were sent through Switzerland for onward transmission to The Hague. In the summer of 1944 action was taken by the *Gestapo* against Hochheimer's family, and as RSHA *Amt* VI was unable to have this action prevented, the reports from Hochheimer ceased.

Hochheimer showed remarkable adaptness in reporting the political and economic developments in the Western Hemisphere, particularly in Chile and the United States. His analysis of current happenings and his forecast of the trend of future events proved to be very accurate.

5. The penetration of Embassies.

In the course of 1941 Geppert was successful in establishing a contact in the Brazilian Embassy in Berlin in the person of the Ambassador's valet. The valet is reported to have had access to the Ambassador's safe from which documents were extracted and photostated before being handed over to Geppert. In addition Geppert obtained the Brazilian diplomatic code from the same source and was thereby able to have fill knowledge of all incoming and outgoing [radio] traffic between Germany and Brazil. This source continued uninterrupted until the rupture of relations between Brazil and Germany in January 1942.

In February 1944 Gross for a short period made a successul penetration of the Argentine Embassy in Berlin from which certain documents and official stamps were obtained. This source was however cut short by the rupture of relations between the Argentine and Germany.

6. Attempts at exploitation of South American diplomats.

On two occasions VI D4 attempted to exploit South American diplomats interned in Germany and awaiting repatriation. In February 1944 Arnold himself went to Baden-Baden to attempt to recruit some of the South American diplomats for the benefit of RSHA *Amt* VI, but was unsuccessful. A similar attempt was made in February 1943 by *Frau* Sommer, an employee of VI D4, to establish contact with South American diplomatic representatives at Bad Godesberg who had been interned in France and were waiting to return to South America. This effort too was unsuccessful, due to the disinterested attitude of Frau Sommer herself, and the lack of intelligent direction from Carstenn, who was Acting *Referent* VI D4 at the time.

Outstanding Points.

It is unlikely that any further interrogation of RSHA VI D personnel will add anything to the present knowledge of VI D activities against the UK and the USA. A possible exception is the case of SS-*Hstuf* Daufeldt who, during his service as *Referent* VI F/O, *Abteilung Nord*, was responsible for the training and despatch of agents in the Anglo-American sphere. So far only the two agents who landed in Iceland in 1944, mentioned in Part VI, are known to have been trained in this way, but it is possible that Daufeldt was responsible for the training of other agents whose indentity is still unknown.

In the Scandinavian countries it appears that nothing further remains to be known of RSHA *Amt* VI activities in Norway and Denmark, and the interrogation of Finke and Brohs should cover adequately Sweden and Finland.

The outstanding gaps are naturally concerned with VI D4, and while the Becker network in South America has been effectively liquidated, not enough is known of the activities of Arnold in Spain and his contacts in that country. Similarly, the case of Hochheimer in Chile remains unsatisfactory, and the sources of his information and the method employed in the routing of his reports are still unknown.

Sources of information for this Report.

SS-*Ostuf* Schüddekopf	*Referent* IV D2
SS-*Ostubaf* Paeffgen	*Gruppenleiter* VI D
SS-*Stubaf* Grönheim	*Referent*, VI D3
Frau Sommer	*Angestellte*, VI D4

This report was issued by W.R.C.3a on 23 November 1945.

Appendix I

Chart of Distribution of Work in RSHA *Amt* VI from 1939–1945

	1939–1940	Early 1941	Mid 1941–42	1942–1944	1944–1945
VI A	Administration etc.	General Intelligence Tasks Abroad (? Sections)	Administration etc.	Administration etc.	Administration etc.
VI B	Technical Section	Europe Africa Near East (10 sections)	Slovakia Hungary Roumania Jugoslavia Greece Turkey Iraq, Iran Afghanistan	France Low Countries Switzerland Spain Portugal	France Low Countries Switzerland Spain Portugal Italy (from 1944)
VI C	Russia Baltic States Far East	Russia Far East (11 sections)	Russia Japan China Finland Baltic States	Russia Near East Far East (13 sections)	Russia Near East Far East (4 sections by mid 1944
VI D	Hungary Slovakia Jugoslavia Roumania Bulgaria Greece Turkey	Anglo-American sphere (9 sections)	Gt. Britain British Empire USA S. America Sweden Norway Denmark	Anglo-American sphere (3 sections)	Anglo-American sphere & Scandinavia (from summer 1944)

VI E	Italy Spain Portugal Central & Southern America	Ideological Enemies abroad (6 sections) (previously VI H)	France Low Countries Spain Portugal Italy Switzerland	Central-Europe Balkans Italy Scandinavia	Balkans
VI F	France Low Countries Switzerland Luxemburg	Technical Section	Technical Section	Technical Section	Technical Section
VI G	Gt. Britain British Empire USA Norway	-	Ideological Enemies abroad	Research (from August 1944)	Research
VI H	Ideological Enemies abroad	-	-	-	-

Appendix II

Organisation and Personnel of RSHA *Gruppe* VI D

(Note: Locations are given as at approximately January 1945. Personnel known to be arrested are underlined.)

Gruppenleiter	SS-*Ostubaf* Paeffgen
Adjutant	*Kriminalassistent* Prassdorf
Secretary	*Fräulein* Fricke

Referat		*Referent* and other personnel
VI D1	U.S.A.	(vacant)
		SS-*Ostuf* Rudolph (Acting Ref.)
		SS-*Hstuf* Lange
		SS-*Oschaf* Denker
		Angestellter Burmann
	Spain (VI representatives)	SS-*Hstuf* Maywald
		Angestellter Arnold
VI D2	British Empire	(vacant)
		SS-*Ostuf* Niklas (Acting Ref.)
		SS-*Hstuf* Pretzsch
		SS-*Ostuf* Giese

		SS-*Ostuf* Reimers
		SS-*Ustuf* Gaede
		Angestellter <u>Thost</u>
VI D3	Scandinavia	SS-*Hstuf* Bussinger
		SS-*Ostuf* Wahlstab
	Sweden	SS-*Stubaf* <u>Finke</u>
	(VI representatives)	SS-*Ustuf* Schiller
		SS-*Oschaf* Pioch
		Angestellter Dr Krüger
	Finland	SS-*Hstuf* <u>Brohs</u>
	(VI representative)	
	Denmark	SS-*Hstuf* Daufeldt
	(VI representatives)	SS-*Hstuf* <u>Carstenn</u>
	Norway	
	BdS Oslo	SS-*Stubaf* <u>Grönheim</u>
	(VI representatives)	SS-*Ustuf* <u>Bialwons</u>
		Angestellter Mothes
	KdS Oslo	SS-*Ostuf* <u>Krause</u>
	(VI representatives)	SS-*Ostuf* Stötterau
		SS-*Ostuf* Laqua
		SS-*Oschaf* Rönnfeldt
		SS-*Oschaf* Strauss
	KdS Trondheim	SS-*Hstuf* <u>Döhring</u>
	(VI repr.)	
	KdS Bergen	SS-*Hstuf* <u>Zöllner</u>
	(VI representative)	
	at *Aussendienststelle*	SS-*Hstuf* Kerner
	Kristiansand	SS-*Ustuf* Evers
VI D4	South America	SS-*Hstuf* Gross
		SS-*Ostuf* Grosse
		SS-*Ustuf* Hamann

Angestellter Wilkens
Angestellter Harcks
Angestellter Hinze

Spain   *Angestellter* Arnold
(VI representative)

Argentine (VI repr.)   SS-*Hstuf* Becker

Appendix III

Alphabetical Index of RSHA *Gruppe* VI D personnel, 1939–1945

(Post-war arrested personnel are underlined)

Rank & Name	*Referat*	Remarks
Angestellte Fräulein Ahrens		VI D4
Angestellter Karl Arnold	VI D4	Representative in Spain under RSHA VI B
SS-*Hstuf* Siegfried <u>Becker</u>	VI D4	Chief representative in South America; arrested in Argentine
SS-*Ustuf* Otto Bialwons	VI D3	BdS Oslo, *Abt* VI
SS-*Ustuf* Kurt Böhme	VI D4	
SS-*Hstuf* Alarich <u>Brohs</u>	VI D3	VI representative in Finland; arrested in British Zone
Angestellter Burmann	VI D1	
SS-*Hstuf* Gottlieb Bussinger	VI D3	Acting *Referent*, VI D3, from late 1944
SS-*Hstuf* Friedrich <u>Carstenn</u>	VI D1	*Referent* 1942–44; 1944 in Finland; end 1944 Denmark; arrested British Zone
SS-*Ostubaf* Dr Hans <u>Daufeldt</u>	VI D	*Gruppenleiter* 1941–42; then VI B3 representative in Switzerland; arrested US Zone
SS-*Hstuf* Helmut <u>Daufeldt</u>	VI D3	VI F/O, 1943; late 1944 in Denmark, VI B3 representative
SS-*Oschaf* Denker	VI D1	
Kanzleiangestellter Dörksen	VI D	
SS-*Hstuf* Erhard <u>Döhring</u>	VI D3	early 1945, KdS Trondheim; arrested Norway

Kanzleiang. Fräulein Dressendorfer	VI D4	
SS-*Ustuf* Evers	VI D3	ADS Kristiansand
SS-*Stubaf* August <u>Finke</u>	VI D3	1939–42, *Referent* VI A2; Representative in Sweden, 1942–45; arrested Denmark
Angestellte Fräulein Finzek	VI D2	
SS-*Hstuf* Wolf <u>Franczok</u>	VI D4	alias Utzinger; W/T expert in Becker network
Kanzleiange. Fräulein Fricke	VI D	Secretary to Paeffgen
SS-*Ustuf* Hans-Joachim Gaede	VI D2	
SS-*Ostuf* Ewald Geppert	VI D4	*Referent*, 1940–42; *Referent* VI A5, 1942–45
SS-*Ostuf* Hermann Giese	VI D2	
SS-*Stubaf* Artur <u>Grönheim</u>	VI D3	*Referent* 1940–44; BdS Oslo *Abt.Leiter* BI, 1944–45; arrested in Norway
SS-*Hstuf* Kurt Gross	VI D4	VI B2, 1940; *Referent* VI D4, 1943–45
SS-*Ostuf* Kurt Grosse	VI D4	
SS-*Ustuf* Friedrich Hamann	VI D4	
Angestellter Hanke	VI D4	
Angestellter Harcks	VI D4	
Angestellter Hedrich	VI D	
Angestellter Rudolf Hinze	VI D4	
Kanzleiange. Fräulein Holland	VI D	
Angestellte Fräulein Horsch	VI D2	
Angestellter Hans-Ulrich John	VI D2	
SS-*Hstuf* Rudolf Kerner	VI D3	ADS Kristiansand
Angestellte Fräulein Doris Kochs	VI D	
SS-*Ostuf* Werner <u>Krause</u>	VI D3	KdS Oslo; arrested Norway
Angestellter Dr Krüger	VI D3	Assistant to Finke
SS-*Hstuf* Dr Heinz <u>Lange</u>	VI D1	Arrested US Zone
Angestellter Heinz Lange	VI D4	Representative in Chile, 1941–44; then returned to Germany
SS-*Ostuf* Willy <u>Laqua</u>	VI D3	KdS Oslo
SS-*Rotf* Johann Lindinger	VI D4	
Angestellter Lutzenschreiter	VI D4	
Angestellte Fräulein Maede	VI D4	
SS-*Hstuf* Martin Maywald	VI D1	*Referent*, 1941–1942; in Spain, 1942–45
SS-*Hstuf* Karl-Heinz Mohr	VI D1	Posted to Istanbul, 1942
Angestellter Mothes	VI D3	BdS Oslo, *Abt* VI
SS-*Ostuf* Kurt Niklaus	VI D2	Acting *Referent* from Dec 1944
Angestellte Fräulein Otto	VI D4	

SS-*Ostubaf* Theodor <u>Paeffgen</u>	VI D	*Gruppenleiter*, 1942–45
SS-*Oschaf* Günther Pioch	VI D3	Assistant to Finke
Krim.Sekretär Fritz Prasdorf	VI D	Secretary to Paeffgen
SS-*Hstuf* Waldemar Pretzsch	VI D2	
SS-*Ostuf* Max Reimers	VI D2	
SS-*Oschaf* Karl Rönnfeldt	VI D3	KdS Oslo
SS-*Ostuf* Hans-Wilhelm Rudolph	VI D1	Acting *Referent* from summer 1944; formerly with RSHA VII
Angestellter Alexander Runge	VI D4	
Angestellte Felicitas Schäfer	VI D	
Krim.Rat Dr Ernst Schambacher	VI D	Formerly with RSHA IV; *Gruppenleiter* VI D, 1942
Angestellte Fräulein Schettek	VI D	
SS-*Ustuf* Hans Schiller	VI D3	Assistant to Finke; sent to Norway early 1945
SS-*Oschaf* Schorer-Stolle	VI D4```	

Notes

* The National Archives, Kew, KV 3/113: Situation Report No. 9, on RSHA VI D.
1 William Colepaugh and Erich Gimpel were landed by U-Boat on the coast of the US State of Maine on 29 November 1944. They made their way via Boston to New York where they were eventually arrested by the FBI. Convicted of conspiracy by US military court in February 1945, both were sentenced to be hanged; sentence commuted to life imprisonment. Colepaugh was released on parole in 1960, and died in Pennsylvania, aged 86 years in 2005. Gimpel was released on parole in 1955, he died in Brazil aged 100 years in 2010.

Situation Report No. 10:
Amt VI of the RSHA—*Gruppe* VI E

INDEX

Part I: SD Activities in South-Eastern Europe prior the creation of the RSHA
Part II: The Period after the creation of the RSHA
  A: The Period under Jost
  B: The Period under Schellenberg
Part III: The Structure and Working Methods of *Gruppe* VI E
Part IV: *Gruppe* VI E and its Activities in South-Eastern Europe

Appendix I: Chart of the distribution of work *Amt* VI from 1939–1945
Appendix II: The organisational changes in *Gruppe* VI E, 1939–45
Appendix III: Organisation and Personnel of *Gruppe* VI E in 1945
Appendix IV: Personnel of *Gruppe* VI E at Outstations
Appendix V: Alphabetical Index of *Gruppe* VI E Personalities

Preamble

Gruppe VI E holds a unique position among the *Ländergruppen* of RSHA *Amt* VI: it was unquestionably the strongest *Gruppe* in the *Amt* throughout its history, being the only one to function effectively in the early days under Jost. It came to be closely identified with the history and development of *Amt* VI, especially from the end of 1942 onwards when Kaltenbrunner succeeded Heydrich as CdS. The *Gruppe* became the focal point of *Amt* VI policy in the latter stages before the final collapse as directed by Kaltenbrunner, as against the policy in the north-west as pursued by Schellenberg. To appreciate these subsequent developments in the history of VI E it is necessary to trace the origins of the *Gruppe*, which go far back in SD history. These origins form the subject matter of Part I of this publication.

Part I

SD activities in South-East Europe prior to the creation of the RSHA

1. The Origins.

The *Sicherheitsdienst* [SD] was created in 1933 by Heydrich as the intelligence service of the NSDAP. In the early stages the SD did not operate completely independently of the Party as its early functions tended to overlap with those of other sections in the Party, which did not welcome its creation. The following account therefore of the development of SD activities tends to be misleadingly simplified, and this factor should be borne in mind. It is only at a much later date that the SD as an intelligence service became clearly defined and separated from the other activities of the Nazi Party.

By 1934 Jost, later to become RSHA *Amtschef* VI, had been given the task of setting up what became *Abteilung* VI of the SD-*Hauptamt*, an *Abteilung* whose function was essentially a security one and was concerned solely with the security of German industry. In this capacity it worked in close collaboration with *Abteilung* III of the *Abwehr* and with the *Gestapoamt*. The *Abteilung* developed gradually, and by 1937 became, in the re-organisation of the SD-*Hauptamt*, *Amt* III. This new *Amt* III was itself subdivided into three sections of which *Abteilung* III/3 contained the germ of the subsequent *Amt* VI of the RSHA.

2. The development of the work of *Abteilung* III/3.

Amt III functioned in its early stages through the then existing SD organisations of *Oberabschnitte* and its subordinate formations throughout Germany. The development of its work was most marked in Eastern Europe where it gradually assumed a more positive role in German industry, acting latterly as a positive espionage service as against a security service, and was able to provide the SD-*Hauptamt* with a fairly clear picture of German industry and its productive capacity. This development of *Amt* III work was a general one throughout Germany, but in the East a further line of development was taking place as early as 1937. The SD-*Oberabschnitte* in Eastern Germany began to act as collecting centres of information on political trends in those countries sharing a common frontier with Germany in the East, especially Czechoslovakia and Austria, where the large pro-German minority groups served as a source of information through the constant passage backwards and forwards across the frontiers.

3. The first attempts as an *Auslandsnachrichtendienst*.

It was these two tendencies in the work of *Abteilung* III/3, its ability to act as an espionage rather than a security service, and the readiness with which it could extend its interest from Germany itself to territory outside the Reich, which interested Heydrich to the extent of instructing Jost to prepare the foundation of a proper *Auslandsnachrichtendienst* on the basis of the work of *Abteilung* III/3. In this, Jost was merely given his general instructions without any clearly defined policy, the original conception being that Jost should exploit the industrial connections to establish good contacts in business circles and to develop the facilities which the SD-*Oberabschnitte* near the German frontier provided for espionage activities outside the Reich.

4. The *Anschluss*.

The factor however which had been chiefly instrumental in influencing Heydrich's decision to attempt an *Auslandsnachrichtendienst* was the part played by the SD in the *Anschluss* with Austria in March 1938. The role of the SD was a prominent one, though the direction of its activities had been from a very much higher level than Jost as *Leiter* of *Abteilung* III/3. The SD had functioned as the liaison between the underground Nazi Party in Austria and the governmental authorities in Germany, but the importance of the *Anschluss* to the future of the SD was that it represented the first offensive operation undertaken by it, and the significance of this success was not lost on Heydrich. Equally important, though the importance was not immediately apparent, was the effect of the *Anschluss* on the subsequent history of *Gruppe* VI E. Prominent among the figures who had played a leading part in the underground movement in Austria prior to the *Anschluss* were Kaltenbrunner and Neubacher, both of whom were to be closely identified with the work of VI E subsequent to Kaltenbrunner's appointment as CdS in succession to Heydrich late in 1942. In addition, the SD-*Leitabschnitt* which was set up in Vienna immediately after the *Anschluss* had among its personnel some officers who were to become leading members of VI E. It was in fact the *Anschluss* which gave birth to the 'Austrian Group' which was to play an important part in the subsequent history not only of *Gruppe* VI E, but in the development and dissolution of *Amt* VI.

5. The *Blockstellen*.

The fundamental change of policy which this new departure involved was that the new service should work quite independently of the existing SD-*Oberabschnitte*, which would confine themselves to their normal SD functions. In their place it was proposed to set up the so-called *Blockstellen* to act as the focal points from which the envisaged espionage activities could be directed. In point of fact only three such *Blockstellen* were created—at Hof under SS-*Hstuf* Daufeldt (later to become *Gruppenleiter* VI D), at Tilsit under SS-*Hstuf* Gräfe (later *Gruppenleiter* VI C), and at Vienna under SS-*Hstuf* Gröbl (later employed by *Amt* VI as its representative in Switzerland and subsequently in Rome). But even these three *Blockstellen* had been set up only in the face of considerable opposition from the *Leiter* of the SD-*Oberabschnitte*, who regarded themselves as the proper channel for SD reports, irrespective of the extended scope of the new stations. The *Blockstellen* were not destined by the subsequent course of events to have a long history, but they played an important part in the events leading up to the creation of RSHA *Amt* VI.

6. The work of the *Blockstellen*.
The value of the *Blockstellen* in the turbulent history of 1938 and 1939 was considerable; the Hof *Stelle* under Daufeldt became the centre of activity against Czechoslovakia in the period preceding the occupation of that country in the Spring of 1939, and it was to the SD and the facilities which it afforded that Ribbentrop turned to exploit the growing tension in Czechoslovakia in order to engineer the political *coup d'état* which was to precede the occupation. While Hof played the part of the intelligence centre, it was the *Blockstelle* in Vienna under Göttsch which played the more operational role, as both Göttsch and his assistant Kraus were seconded for special duty to Vessenmayer, the Czech specialist in the Foreign Office.

7. Göttsch and the Czech crisis.
It was Göttsch who acted as the intermediary between the Foreign Office and Tiso in accordance with the plan previously conceived by Ribbentrop for the political crisis. The information received through the *Blockstelle* at Hof, where Daufeldt had been working in collaboration with SS-*Stubaf* Rossner, to whom the Czech affair had been given as a special assignment, showed that by February 1939 a more active participation by the Germans was possible. Göttsch and Kraus operated under the orders of the Foreign Office, while the whole enterprise was directed from Vienna where Stahlecker had become Leiter. Göttsch and Veesenmayer now established contact with the Slovaks themselves, and it was Göttsch to whom Tiso sent his letter addressed to Hitler requested German intervention in order to maintain Slovak independence. Apart from the importance which the success of the enterprise had on the history of the SD, the incident is of note as it represents one of the very few occasions on which Ribbentrop not only asked for the help of the SD, but took the advice it offered. The same measure of collaboration between the Foreign Office and the SD was singularly lacking after the creation of RSHA *Amt* VI in 1939.

8. Rossner and the *Unternehmen* Tannenberg.
Unternehmen Tannenberg was the name given to the incident preceding the Polish crisis leading to the outbreak of war. The *Unternehmen* was not directed by *Amt* III, but came under the direct supervision of Heydrich. SS-*Stubaf* Rossner however was again employed in the scheme and worked with SS-*Stubaf* Hellwig (later to become SSPF Bialystok) in the recruiting and preparation of special

SS *Kommandos*. SS-*Hstuf* Reissmann, later of RSHA VI B1 (Vatican), was also prominent in the preparations leading up to the crisis. The SS *Kommandos*, who in the actual operation were placed under the command of SS-*Gruf* Müller (later RSHA *Amtschef* IV), were let loose to carry out their 'acts of provocation' at the end of August [1939], and the outbreak of war soon followed.

9. The position at the outbreak of War.
The creation of the RSHA coincided with the actual outbreak of hostilities: Heydrich now assumed command of the *Gestapo*, the *Kripo* and the SD-*Hauptamt*, which services now became separate *Ämter* of the new organisation. This major change was the opportune moment for creating the new *Auslandsnachrichtendienst* based on Jost's *Abteilung* III/3, the new service becoming *Amt* VI. The creation of RSHA *Amt* VI was in fact a recognition of the work of the old *Amt* III in the preceding year; the security functions of *Amt* III passed to the new *Amt* IV and *Amt* VI became an offensive and not a defensive service. But this change, coupled with the enormous extension of spheres of activity, gave the new *Amt* little on which to build; only in South-Eastern Europe had the SD-*Hauptamt* given the new RSHA *Amt* VI any basis for further work.

Part II

The Period after the Creation of the RSHA

A. The early period under Jost.

1. The general position in the early stages.
It will be appreciated from the account given in Part I that of the new *Gruppen* formed under RSHA *Amt* VI, that dealing with South-Eastern Europe was in the most favourable position for beginning the new tasks assigned to the *Amt*; the *Ländergruppen* dealing with the Far East, the Near East, Western Europe and the Western Hemisphere, had virtually to begin from scratch, while the *Gruppe* responsible for the Balkans had the advantage of experience in the type of activity it was to develop, had at its disposal personnel of a certain amount of experience in the work, and, probably most important of all, the territory which it had to exploit lent itself to exploitation in view of the active subversive groups already in existence in the Balkan States. The general effect of this position was that while the other *Ländergruppen* of RSHA *Amt* VI in the early stages spent the first months of their existence in efforts to establish a suitable working basis, work in the Balkans continued under the original impetus of previous SD work based mainly

on the activities of the SD-*Leitabschnitt* Vienna. This previous activity had now to conform itself to the general organisation of RSHA *Amt* VI with the installation of the directing *Gruppe* in Berlin and the despatch of special representatives to the various countries. For a time in the Balkans the two systems worked together side by side, the SD-*Leitabschnitt* Vienna pursuing its former activity side by side with the creation of the central office in Berlin.

2. Organisational changes.

The original organisation of RSHA *Amt* VI gave the control of South-Eastern Europe to *Gruppe* VI D with SS-*Stubaf* Göttsch as *Gruppenleiter*. The *Gruppe* had the following internal structure:

Referat		*Referent*
VI D1	Hungary and Slovakia	SS-*Hstuf* Friedrich Hanke
VI D2	Jugoslavia	vacant
VI D3	Roumania	SS-*Ostuf* Wilhelm Waneck
VI D4	Bulgaria and Greece	SS-*Ostuf* Fritz Langlotz
VI D5	Turkey and Near East	SS-*Hstuf* Herbert Hagen

It will be noted that in this organisation *Gruppe* VI D was also competent for Turkey and the Near East.

The RSHA *Amt* VI was re-organised in 1941 when *Gruppe* VI E was renamed VI B with SS-*Stubaf* Rossner as *Gruppenleiter*, and the *Referent* including such officers as SS-*Stubaf* Hanke, SS-*Stubaf* Kraus, SS-*Stubaf* Waneck, SS-*Stubaf* Göttsch, SS-*Stubaf* Beisner, SS-*Hstuf* Höttl, SS-*Hstuf* Gröbl and SS-*Hstuf* Bolschwing. Details of the breakdown of this *Gruppe* VI B are lacking, but it is known that the *Gruppe* was still responsible for Turkey and the Near East. Of the above mentioned *Referent*, it is almost certain that SS-*Stubaf* Beisner was the officer competent for the Near East.

Comparison of the personnel in the period 1939–1941 with those still working under VI E at the end shows that the *Gruppe* maintained a remarkable degree of continuity of personnel. This continuity was singularly lacking in the other *Gruppen* of *Amt* VI, the major changes taking place when Schellenberg took over effective control of the *Amt* at the end of 1941. This factor is a reflection on the working efficiency of *Gruppe* VI B during the early stages, and from the end of 1942 onwards reflected also the influence of Kaltenbrunner on the *Gruppe*, an influence which forms the subject matter to Paragraph B (below).

3. The *Hauptbeauftragte*.

In keeping with the generally favourable position in South-Eastern Europe in the early days of the *Amt*, the *Hauptbeauftragte* chosen by Jost for that territory were more successful than those chosen in the countries in which the SD was to operate for the first time. The most outstanding representative was SS-*Hstuf*

Bolschwing in Roumania, and although the remaining *Hauptbeauftragte* did not reach the same high standard, advantage was taken of the favourable situation prevailing for good and effective contacts to be established in the Balkan States. The remaining *Hauptbeauftragte* including SS-*Hstuf* Kienast and SS-*Stubaf* Urban in Hungary, SS-*Stubaf* Glass in Bulgaria, and SS-*Stubaf* Kraus in Jugoslavia. The development of their early work is dealt with in Part III.

4. The role of the SD-*Leitabschnitt* Vienna.

Reference has already been made in Paragraph 1 to the independent activity of the SD-*Leitabschnitt* Vienna. It was this *Stelle* which was responsible for the despatch of SS-*Hstuf* Goldschmidt to Bratislava in 1939 on his own initiative. Slovakia was soon destined to become the concern of RSHA *Amt* III, a right which that *Amt* maintained until 1944, but during his stay in Bratislava, Goldschmidt reported both to Vienna and to Berlin. This operation is symptomatic of the independence of the *Dienststelle* Vienna in the early stages, an independence which was built on the earlier activity of the old SD-*Oberabschnitt* Vienna and the *Blockstelle*.

During the period from 1939 to the Spring of 1942 SS-*Stubaf* Höttl was *Leiter* of *Abteilung* VI in the SD-*Leitabschnitt* Vienna, and in that time organised his own networks in Hungary, Jugoslavia, Roumania, Bulgaria, Albania, Montenegro and Turkey. This independence of Vienna remained in force until the end of 1941, when the leading personnel of the *Abschnitt* were transferred to RSHA *Gruppe* VI E and the *Amt* succeeded in centralising all activity in Berlin. It should be noted, however, that Höttl's own network did not pass to VI E until he himself became *Referent* VI E in 1943, when he reactivated his own network. This network therefore operated independently of that set up by the *Hauptbeauftragte*.

5. The situation at the end of 1941.

By the end of 1941 Jost had ceased to have any controlling influence over RSHA *Amt* VI, as Schellenberg had virtually taken command. The general position of *Amt* VI at that time was one of weakness, and the lack of success in the work of the *Amt* had even endangered its further existence. Jost had not been able to overcome the many difficulties which he was faced with in the first few years of the *Amt's* existence, and it was only due to the energetic work and reforms introduced by Schellenberg in the early part of 1942 that it could manage to survive. The impact of Schellenberg's reforms was most marked on the remaining *Ländergruppen*, and in some cases caused a complete upheaval in personnel and organisation. The two *Gruppen* least affected were *Gruppe* VI C, which underwent only moderate changes, and *Gruppe* VI B (i.e. the forerunner of VI E), which remained almost unscathed. The chief contributing factor was of course the relatively strong position of *Amt* VI in South-Eastern Europe, and the degree of success which *Gruppe* VI B had by this time achieved. Schellenberg directed his efforts at the then weak *Ländergruppen*, and did not greatly interfere with RSHA *Amt* VI work in South-Eastern Europe, but a stronger influence which was to contribute to the comparative independence of South-Eastern Europe under the control of Schellenberg, was seen to emerge at the end of 1942 in the person of Kaltenbrunner who succeeded Heydrich as CdS.

B. The Period under Schellenberg.

1. The formation of *Gruppe* VI E in 1942.

As has been mentioned in the preceding paragraph, Schellenberg's main effort in RSHA *Amt* VI in the first months of his control of the *Amt* had been directed towards replacing the inefficient personnel of the *Amt*. This was in general a difficult problem and one which Schellenberg never effectively solved. The sources available were very restricted, but one source tapped by Schellenberg was the recall of *Amt* VI representatives in SD-*Abschnitte* in Germany, the results of this move being on the whole meagre, except in the case of VI E, as did the SD-*Leitabschnitt* Vienna provided personnel with a knowledge of the territory in which they operated and familiar with the general situation in South-Eastern Europe. The most important result of Schellenberg's re-organisation to VI B came in 1942 when the *Ländergruppen* of the *Amt* were re-lettered with changes in territorial control. RSHA *Gruppe* VI B now became VI E with SS-*Ostubaf* Hammer as *Gruppenleiter*. The *Gruppe* however had a considerably extended field to cover as it was now competent for Scandinavia and Italy, as well as for South-Eastern Europe. Details of the internal structure of the *Gruppe* are shown at Appendix II. Generally speaking, the *Gruppe* was not greatly affected by the coming of Schellenberg; it was not until the end of the year that new developments took place with the appointment of Kaltenbrunner as CdS.

2. The influence of Kaltenbrunner in 1943.

The most important influence in the subsequent history of VI E was Kaltenbrunner himself; he had been active in Austria before the *Anschluss*, for which efforts he had been rewarded by being appointed as HSSPF for Austria. Before the end of 1942 Kaltenbrunner had been nominated by Himmler as the CdS designated to succeed Heydrich, being actually confirmed in office in January 1943. His appointment was to have a profound effect on the subsequent history of RSHA *Amt* VI, due not only to differences of outlook and temperament which soon became manifest between himself and Schellenberg, but also to his political ambitions.

Kaltenbrunner considered himself above all as a politician to the extent of having designs on the Foreign Office itself, but his political outlook was coloured entirely by his Austrian background. His aim was not the independence of Austria, but rather towards a re-orientation of German policy towards South-Eastern Europe. His interest in RSHA *Amt* VI therefore centred round VI E.

3. The Austrian Group.

It was from the time of Kaltenbrunner's appointment and as a result of his Austrian complex that two lines of development became apparent in RSHA *Amt* VI. The relations between Kaltenbrunner and Schellenberg were never friendly, the former holding the latter in a certain degree of respect but never cooperating with him, and always more than a little afraid of his ambitions, the latter never entertaining anything but a strong feeling of revulsion for the former. The difference only grew with the passage of time, and finished by being a chasm. Kaltenbrunner's attitude to RSHA *Amt* VI was largely one of indifference in so far as the actual working organisation of the *Amt* was concerned, his interest being purely a geographical one. His only concern therefore was to ensure that in those departments of the *Amt* which interested him there should be a strong Austrian flavour by the appointment of his favourites, and his main interest was IV E. To a lesser extent he was attracted by VI G because of his fascination for maps and statistics, and later he was to be the strongest supporter of VI S because of the nature of its work. The *Gruppenleiter* was in each case an Austrian, and the effect on *Amt* VI was that the *Amt* divided into two groups—the 'Austrian Group' centred round VI E and VI S, and the 'Western Group' around Schellenberg, sometimes referred to as the 'Swabian Group', as its chief exponents, apart from the *Amtschef* himself, were Paeffgen and Steimle, both of whom came from Württemburg.

4. The development of the Groups.

It is not possible to estimate what the ultimate result of the division in RSHA *Amt* VI would have been had the general war situation developed in Germany's favour. One can only speculate. But in point of fact the deteriorating situation by the end of 1943 gave this development a new orientation. Schellenberg by that time had no illusions as to the ultimate result of the war, and was already seeking lines of approach to the Western Allies. The Austrian Group on the other hand became identified with the 'bitter enders', with Kaltenbrunner and Skorzeny as the prominent figures. The division in the *Amt* reached its final stage shortly before the collapse, with Schellenberg arranging his surrender to the Western Powers in the North, while in the South Kaltenbrunner was appointing Waneck as RSHA *Amtschef* VI and Skorzeny in charge of the *Mil Amt*.

5. The transfer of RSHA *Gruppe* VI E to Vienna.

It was only natural, of course, that Kaltenbrunner's political ambitions and his Austrian outlook should become centred on *Gruppe* VI E. By 1943 Hammer was replaced as *Gruppenleiter* by Waneck, whose relations with Kaltenbrunner were very close. Before the end of the year the growing independence of VI E became manifest by the transfer of the *Gruppe* from Berlin to Vienna—a move which was strongly resisted by Schellenberg, on whom the purpose of the transfer was not lost. In December 1943 VI E set up its headquarters in Vienna, leaving only a liaison officer in the *Amt* in Berlin. From that date Schellenberg's control of the *Gruppe* became increasingly less, the W/T communications with the Balkans from Berlin being restricted to one link in Roumania, while both Waneck and Höttl had the right to report direct to Kaltenbrunner, this circumventing Schellenberg himself. The Austrian Group now had its own headquarters in Austria itself.

6. The re-organisation of RSHA *Gruppe* VI E in 1944.
Organisationally there is one further development to be noted: in the summer of 1944 a further re-organisation of territorial divisions between the *Ländergruppen* took place, the effect of which was to confine the scope of VI E to South-Eastern Europe only. The Scandinavian *Referat* passed to *Gruppe* VI D to become *Referat* VI D3, while the Italian *Referat* passed to *Gruppe* VI B to become *Referat* VI B1. At the same time Slovakia, which had for the previous three years been the province of RSHA *Amt* III, now came under the control of *Amt* VI to become *Referat* VI E1. These changes involved an internal re-organisation of *Gruppe* VI E, details of which are given in Appendix II. It is under this final form that the work of VI E will be dealt with in Part IV, Scandinavia and Italy being dealt with under the *Gruppen* to which they latterly belonged.

7. The role of RSHA *Gruppe* VI E in the final stages.
The tendencies which were noticeable by 1944 became more marked in the early part of 1945 when the situation became more adverse to Germany. 'Resistance as symbolised by the activities of *Gruppe* VI S under Skorzeny, became increasingly important to the 'bitter-enders', and that *Gruppe* became the most important in the eyes of the CdS'. *Gruppen* VI B and VI D, and to a lesser extent VI C, had become largely ineffective, and Schellenberg was actively engaged in opening up lines of approach to the Western Allies. *Gruppe* VI E, the only *Ländegruppe* to liaise effectively with VI S, was however meeting with growing danger from the East: but even in face of this growing threat the *Gruppe* was able to maintain its networks, with however a purpose in view. *Gruppe* VI E left Vienna in March [1945], evacuating in turn to Steyerling, to Kremsmünster, and finally to Alt Aussee. Now two lines of development emerged—Kaltenbrunner and Skorzeny still actively pursued their 'Redoubt' plans for continued resistance, while VI E became involved in independent approaches to the Western Powers with a view to maintaining its own organisation intact.

8. The VI E approaches.
As early as 1943 Höttl had been actively engaged in making contact with those circles in Austria favouring the independence of Austria from Germany. This contact with the Austrian Freedom Movement had not been without Kaltenbrunner's knowledge, who indeed encouraged it. But, whereas Höttl had the conception of developing these contacts with a view to obtaining for Austria some degree of

favourable treatment when the inevitable end came, Kaltenbrunner, a confirmed 'bitter-ender' who did not depart from his conception of a Gross-Deutschland with its centre of political gravity in the South-East rather than in Berlin, regarded the manoeuvre merely as a penetration of opposition groups within Germany. By March 1945, when the situation was rapidly deteriorating, the first approach to the Allies was made by Höttl—an approach of which Kaltenbrunner was aware, though he instructed that it should be made in order to obtain information only, and without any commitment on the part of Germany.

9. Kaltenbrunner's '*Vollmacht*' and the Austrian Solution.

Kaltenbrunner meantime left Berlin at the end of April [1945] armed with authority granted by Himmler to act as plenipotentiary for Austria, and was responsible for all future resistance in that area, an ambition realised, though rather late in the day. The split in RSHA *Amt* VI now became complete; learning that Schellenberg in the North was already arranging his surrender to the Allies through Sweden, Kaltenbrunner dismissed him from office, and in the subsequent re-organisation of the *Amt*, appointed Waneck as RSHA *Amtschef* VI and Skorzeny as Chief of the *Mil Amt*. The Austrian Group were now in full command, and with Kaltenbrunner officially recognised as plenipotentiary for Austria, the triumph of the Austrian Group was now complete. Events however proved too much for Kaltenbrunner; the rapid advance of the Allies into the Redoubt area made any plans for continued resistance invalid, and some sort of compromise between the 'bitter-enders' and the VI E approaches became necessary, the compromise being Kaltenbrunner's 'Austrian Solution'.

10. The 'Austrian Solution' and the End.

Göttsch and Waneck, now convinced that further resistance was useless, succeeded in persuading Kaltenbrunner that the Höttl approach should be developed, and this time be accompanied by a definite offer. The offer was to take the form of an explanation that the contacts established with the Austrian Freedom Movement had been made with Kaltenbrunner's consent, and that the approach had been in keeping with his long term policy of ultimately establishing an Austria independent of Germany. The Allies were to support this independence movement, and Kaltenbrunner, the anti-Nazi at heart, would become a prominent personality in the New Austria. This 'Austrian Solution' had already been the subject of discussion between Kaltenbrunner and Himmler before the failure of the Redoubt plan, Kaltenbrunner's conception then being that it would be easier to continue resistance from within than from without. Under pressure of events the 'Austrian Solution' became the only one possible to Kaltenbrunner, but it was a solution which, in so far as it involved a general surrender of the leading personalities of VI E, solved only one thing—the task of the Allies in rounding up the *Gruppe*. No other *Gruppe* was so speedily and effectively liquidated. The Redoubt plan became a general '*sauve qui peut*' [every man for himself], and the new RSHA *Amt* VI disintegrated.

Part III

The Structure and Methods of RSHA *Gruppe* VI E

1. The Central Office.

The general background picture of the development of *Gruppe* IV E has been given in Part II. As a result of the personal interest of Kaltenbrunner in the work of the *Gruppe*, VI E developed a working basis which differs from the normal functioning of the other *Ländergruppen*, a tendency which became more marked after the transfer of the central office from Berlin to Vienna later in 1943. A liaison officer only remained in Berlin. The final structure of the *Gruppe* and the leading personnel are given in Appendix III, and it is under this final organisation that the work of the *Gruppe* in the Balkan States will be considered in Part IV. The *Gruppe* maintained liaison officers with the Neubacher and Altenberg *Dienststellen*, these laision officers being directly subordinated to the *Gruppenleiter*. In common with other *Ländergruppen* each *Referat* had a *Referent*, an *Erfasser*, whose duty it was to act as the collecting point of information within the *Referat*, but who in VI E also acted as liaison officer with the outside offices, with which he kept in personal contact, and an *Auswerter* responsible for the evaluation and dissemination of information. In addition there were subordinate *Sachbearbeiter* working under their direction. The *Referate* conducted their operations through the *Hauptbeauftragte* working in the various countries under suitable cover.

2. The outside organisation.

The outside organisation of RSHA *Gruppe* VI E took two forms, as in addition to the *Hauptbeauftragte* mentioned in Paragraph 1 above, the *Gruppe* also had representatives in the various BdS offices set up in the countries of South-Eastern Europe at different times. The BdS normally had a small *Abteilung* VI under the control of a *Sachbearbeiter* if the territory controlled by the BdS was important enough to warrant it. The BdS himself worked more closely in liaison with RSHA *Amt* VI than was the case, for instance, in Western Europe, where the BdS normally showed himself uncooperative and unsympathetic to *Amt* VI work. The reason of course lay in the relatively much stronger position of VI E in South-Eastern Europe compared with the position of VI B in Western Europe. The BdS representation was naturally of minor importance, though, as in the case of Slovakia, the *Amt* VI *Sachbearbeiter* with the BdS might be of greater importance in the absence of a *Hauptbeauftragter* when the country was not of sufficient importance to warrant the presence of a *Hauptbeauftragter*. Examples of such *Sachbearbeiter* were SS-

Stubaf Rexeisen, BdS Serbia, and SS-*Ostubaf* Hammer, the former *Gruppenleiter*, BdS Prague.

3. The *Hauptbeauftragte*.
The *Hauptbeauftragte* themselves were responsible for setting up a cell within the country in which they operated, usually composed of a small number of VI E officers including a W/T operator. The *Hauptbeauftragte* were appointed only to those countries whose importance warranted direct VI E representation. Thus Slovakia, in which VI E began to operate only in the latter half of 1944, did not have a *Hauptbeauftragter*, while Hungary, which was of importance, had both SS-*Stubaf* Höttl and SS-*Stubaf* Urban after the crisis of March 1944. The other *Hauptbeauftragte* in the latter stages were Materna in Montenegro and Albania, Wawrzinowski in Greece, Kob in Bulgaria, and SS-*Hstuf* Gunne and SS-*Hstuf* Auner in Roumania.

4. Channels of communication.
The normal means of communication was of course by W/T, but after the transfer to Vienna, the other common channel used was the couriers of the *Deutsche Lufthansa*. In addition, use was made of the Foreign Office diplomatic pouches, the *Ämter* couriers, and, less often, railway employees. The *Hauptbeauftragte* were also required to visit the central office at least once every two months in order to submit special reports and to attend conferences under the *Gruppenleiter*, and occasionally under Schellenberg. Likewise, the *Referent* also paid frequent visits to the outstations to make personal contact with the more important agents and to keep in touch with the countries themselves. It will be seen from this that the direction of operations from the *Gruppe* itself was much closer in *Gruppe* IV E than in other *Ländergruppen*. The accessibility of the countries of course lent itself to such a procedure.

5. Liaison with other Agencies.
The liaison initiated by *Gruppe* VI E with other agencies operating in the countries within the control of the *Gruppe* was also much closer than in other *Ländergruppen*. The reason for this cooperation lay in the strength of *Gruppe* VI E itself. The tendency was especially marked in the case of the Foreign Office, though this was not due to any official policy laid down by Ribbentrop, but to the personal relationship established with the Foreign Office representatives in the Balkan countries by the VI E representatives themselves. Another important factor was the close relationship between Kaltenbrunner and Neubacher of the Foreign Office, who had been active with Kaltenbrunner in Austria in the days prior to the *Anschluss*. The agencies with which *Gruppe* VI E was in close liaison are listed below.

(a) *Gruppe* III B of RSHA *Amt* III.

In territory occupied by German forces RSHA *Amt* III maintained its interest through *Gruppe* III B which was responsible for the supervision of German minority groups in South-Eastern Europe. The spheres of interest between VI E and III B of course overlapped, and VI E was responsible for passing to III B information concerning such minority groups without giving details of its own intelligence activities within these groups. The most prominent minority groups operating in South-Eastern Europe were the Andreas Schmidt Group in Roumania, the Janko Group in Serbia, the Altgayer Group in Croatia, the Basch group in Hungary, and the Karmasin Group in Slovakia. The conflict between VI E and III B in South-Eastern Europe was not so strong as the rivalry which existed between the two *Ämter*, for example, in the occupied territories of Western Europe.

(b) Liaison with RSHA *Gruppe* VI S.

Similarly there was much closer cooperation between VI E and VI S than existed between VI S and the other *Ländergruppen* of RSHA *Amt* VI, a liaison which had two fundamental causes. Firstly there was the influence of the Austrian Group and Kaltenbrunner's personal interest in the work of both VI E and VI S, the former because of its geographical interest, the latter because of the type of operations in which it specialised. Secondly, *Gruppe* VI S was obliged to recruit from the same material as that available to VI E, and instructions were laid down by Kaltenbrunner himself that in order to avoid friction between the two *Gruppen*, they were to keep each other informed of their projected operations in South-Eastern Europe. This rule applied to [*Abwehr*] *Leitstelle* II *Süd-Ost* for similar reasons. Offical liaison was maintained through the person of SS-*Hstuf* Mandl, who in December 1944 was given the special appointment of *Referent* VI E/S, in which capacity he acted as liaison officer for *Gruppe* VI E to Skorzeny. In the latter stages too, SS-*Hstuf* Gunne in Roumania was responsible for sabotage operations in that country in cooperation with VI S. A special liaison also existed in Greece through *Dienststelle* 3000 under SS-*Stubaf* Begus, details of which are given in Part IV, Paragraph 5.

(c) *Dienststelle* Neubacher.

The liaison with Neubacher, who acted as special Foreign Office representative in the Balkans, was a close one, and was due in the first instance to the close association which had existed between Neubacher and Kaltenbrunner in pre-war days in Austria. Kaltenbrunner had a high opinion of Neubacher's ability and knowledge on Balkan affairs, and the policy was laid down by Kaltenbrunner himself that VI E should cooperate fully with Neubacher, irrespective of the attitude of Ribbentrop. The relations between Ribbentrop and Neubacher were not cordial, as the former was jealous of the latter and afraid of his ability and knowledge. Neubacher had been appointed in mid-1940 as economic emissary of the Foreign Office in Roumania, and by 1942 had been given the appointment of special envoy and plenipotentiary in South-Eastern Europe with the special assignment of dealing with partisan activities in Greece, establishing contact with Mihailovic in Jugoslavia, and suppressing communist elements in the Balkans.

(d) *Dienststelle* Altenberg.

Altenberg had been the Foreign Office representative in Greece until his retirement from that country in November 1943. In September 1944 Altenberg was given the assignment of creating a *Dienststelle* whose special function was liaison with the various exiled Balkan governments, the *Stelle* having its seat in Vienna itself, where it remained until early April 1945. The *Dienststelle* consisted of some eighteen people and had its own W/T set. Altenberg was responsible for the recruitment of volunteer legions of Bulgars and Roumanians in Germany, and for their ideological training. Contact between VI E and the *Dienststelle* was not so strong as that with *Dienststelle* Neubacher. Nevertheless the *Stelle* was a source of information to VI E, to which organisation it passed its reports based on information obtained from prisoners and persons crossing into Austria from the Balkans. SS-*Hstuf* Zeischka was appointed as official liaison officer between the two organisations.

(e) The *Polizei Attachés.*

The *Polizei Attachés* in the Balkans were SS-*Stubaf* Richter in Roumania, SS-*Ostubaf* Hoffmann in Bulgaria, SS-*Ostubaf* Helm in Croatia, and SS-*Stubaf* Golz in Slovakia. The *Polizei Attachés* submitted their reports to the *Attaché-Gruppe* in Berlin, who under normal procedure would pass any information of interest to the *Ländergruppe* concerned. In the Balkans however reports were passed simultaneously to VI E if they were considered of sufficient importance. In those countries where no *Polizei Attachés* existed, liaison was established with the BdS through the *Abteilung* VI representation, if such existed.

(f) Commercial Firms.

Use was also made by VI E of German commercial firms in the Balkans, who submitted reports of interest to VI E by personal contacts, and were also instrumental in supplying suitable cover to agents employed by RSHA *Gruppe* VI E. The principal firms used in this connection, together with the contact with VI E, are listed below.

> Gebr. Schicht (soap manufacturers), Vienna. Supplied contacts for Höttl.
> DDSG (Donau Dampfschiffahrtsgesellschaft); supplied contact with Waneck and Höttl through Director Seeliger in Vienna.
> Vereinigte Chemische Fabriken, Vienna. Supplied contact with Waneck.
> Knorrbremse, Berlin; President Leibrock in contact with Waneck.
> Klöckner-Humboldt-Deutz; President Ludwig in contact with Auner.
> Mannesmann; representative Bauer in contact with SS-Hstuf Pratsch.

AEG, Berlin; representatives and contacts were Brunken in Sofia, Thomashausen in Athens, Tischak in Bucharest, and Bräber in Sofia.
Steyr Works, Vienna; contacts were President Meinl and Director Weidner.
Ferrostahl; Director Langenhahn in contact with Auner.
Alpine Montan Gesellschaft and Steyrische Guss Stahlwerke, Vienna; in contact with Zeischka and the firm Julius Meinl; information sent via Berlin.

Part IV

RSHA *Gruppe* VI E and its
Activities in South-Eastern Europe

(Note: In view of the high degree of continuity in policy and personnel which obtained in *Gruppe* VI E it has not been considered necessary, as in papers dealing with the other *Ländergruppen*, to deal with VI E activities in chronological order. The following notes are therefore listed under convenient subject headings.)

A. *Referat* VI E and Slovakia.

1. Early work under Jost.
As Slovakia was virtually occupied by Germany even by the time the RSHA was set up, the country came to be regarded as the province of RSHA *Amt* III, and RSHA *Amt* VI did not undertake any direct work in the country. However, the SD-*Leitabschnitt* Vienna, acting independently operated in the country at an early date. SS-*Stubaf* Polte, then *Leiter* of the SD-*Leitabschnitt* Vienna, sent SS-*Hstuf* Goldschmidt to Bratislava to act in SD interests. Goldschmidt, a journalist on the staff of the *Völkischer Beobachter*, established contact with the *Hlinkagarda* under Mach, and with the German minority group led by Karmasin and submitted reports both to Berlin and to Vienna on the Slovakian Foreign Minister Durczanski and the anti-German circles which centred round him. Goldschmidt was assisted by SS-*Ostuf* Hahn.

2. The ascendancy of RSHA *Amt* III.
RSHA *Amt* VI was not however greatly interested in Slovakia as a field of operations, and their activities were not of long duration. Slovakia, regarded as occupied territory, passed over to *Amt* III, and by late 1940 *Amt* VI ceased to take active participation in that country. This ascendancy of *Amt* III continued until the greatly altered war situation after early 1943 caused *Amt* VI to take a revived

interest in the country. Difficulties arose however between the two *Ämter* on the general question of the respective spheres of interest, Schellenberg being anxious to establish the adjudication, was not solved to the advantage of *Amt* VI, and only in the case of Slovakia was any concession made.

3. RSHA *Amt* VI Activity in 1944.

The revival of *Amt* VI interest in Slovakia occurred in the latter half of 1944. The country was still not considered of sufficient importance to warrant the appointment of a *Hauptbeauftragter*, and the installation of an intelligence network was assigned to SS-*Ostuf* Ubl, with SS-*Stubaf* Kraus and SS-*Hstuf* Westergaard and SS-*Hstuf* Orglmeister as his assistants. The contacts established were similar to those made by Goldschmidt mentioned in Paragraph 1, and reports were submitted on general political questions, in particular on the attitude of the Tiso Government and on the Hungarian minority groups under Count Esterhazy. Attempts were also made to exploit Slovak contacts abroad, in particular the Slovak ambassador to Switzerland, a plan which was put into operation at too late a date to be successful.

B. *Referat* VI E2 and Hungary.

1. The *Hauptbeauftragte.*

The earliest appointment to Hungary was SS-*Ostuf* Kienast who had worked in the country prior to the outbreak of war. Kienast had concentrated on establishing contacts in Hungarian social and diplomatic circles, but his work proved to be disappointing and led to his recall before the end of 1940. Kienast reappeared on the Hungarian scene in March 1944 when he was appointed to the staff of Winkelmann when the latter became HSSPF on the occupation of the country by German troops.

One of the most efficient of VI E representatives operated in Hungary from the earliest days in the person of SS-*Stubaf* Urban, who remained as *Hauptbeauftragter* from 1940 until the evacuation of the country. Urban had worked before the war as a representative of the *Donau Dampfschiffahrtsgesellschaft* in Vienna, and continued his work for VI E under cover of that firm through which he was successful in establishing good contacts throughout the country. His reports were voluminous and carefully prepared.

2. Contacts established in Hungary.

The VI E penetration of Hungary was considerable, and close contact was established with the various minority groups in the country as sources of information. These, together with other profitable sources, are listed below:

(a) <u>The Arrow Cross Party.</u>
There was close collaboration with Szalassy, the leader of the Party, and his deputy Szoeloessy. When Szalassy gained control of the country in October 1944, his Foreign Minister Kemeny, and the Minister of the Interior, Vayna, both continued their close cooperation with VI E2.

(b) <u>The *Erneurungs Partei.*</u>
Under Bola von Imredy.

(c) <u>The German Minority Group.</u>
Under Dr Basch.

(d) <u>The Hungarian Military Intelligence.</u>
Was also exploited as a source of information, providing details of messages to the War Department from its military attachés abroad. The decoding branch of the War Department also provided information on messages sent by the Allied governments to the representatives in neutral countries.

Until March 1944 and especially from that date until the subsequent Hungarian crisis in October 1944, the above sources were exploited to provide information on Horthy's relations with the Allied governments.

3. VI E and the Hungarian Crisis.
The information obtained by VI E on Hungarian matters was considerable; when it became apparent in early 1944 that Hungary's attitude to the war was wavering, plans were drawn up to cope with the situation. It was proposed by the Foreign Office that the occupation of Hungary should be carried out by Slovakian and Roumanian troops, a plan which was overthrown on the recommendation of VI E, which insisted that such measures would only meet with opposition on the part of the Hungarians. On this advice therefore the country was occupied by German troops only, and no resistance was met with.

The first Hungarian crisis was soon to lead to another in which VI E was to play a prominent part. On the occupation of the country, Winkelmann was appointed HSSPF and SS-*Oberführer* Geschke became BdS. At the same time Höttl, *Referent* VI E2, was sent to Budapest to act as political adviser to the Ambassador, Veesenmayer. There followed a political tug-of-war between the various representatives with Höttl supporting Palfy as Horthy's successor, Urban supporting Szalassy in company with Winkelmann, and Veesenmayer supporting the Imredy group. In this confused situation Kaltenbrunner chose the Höttl solution.

Höttl was responsible for the '*Unternehmen* Maus' by which a VI E agent was sent to make contact with Horthy's son, positing as an envoy of Tito, with the purpose of discovering what Horthy's real intentions regarding the Allies were. As a result of this penetration, Horthy's son was arrested; almost concurrently, however, the crisis came to a head with Skorzeny ready to launch his attack on the citadel. The political manoeuvring was however decided by Hitler, who selected the Szalassy group as the new government, a choice which had Kaltenbrunner changing sides in almost indecent haste, dropping the Höttl plan and maintaining that it was Szalassy that he himself favoured. Soon afterwards Budapest was evacuated as a result of the Russian advance.

4. The BdS Hungary.

As mentioned in Paragraph 3 above, the BdS Hungary was set up in March 1944 when Hungary was occupied by German troops. The BdS was SS-*Oberführer* Geschke, who had under his command a small *Abteilung* VI, of which the original *Leiter* from March until September 1944 was SS-*Stubaf* Oebsger-Röder. Röder was succeeded for a period of a few weeks by SS-*Stubaf* Brandt, he in turn being replaced in November [1944] by Weirauch of VI C. Weirauch remained with the BdS staff until May 1945. The role of *Abteilung* VI of the BdS was a small one, and VI E had strong direct representation in the country in Urban and Höttl, with SS-*Hstuf* Neunteufel and SS-*Hstuf* Deworetzky as his assistants. It was however to the BdS that the task of preparing an I-*Netze* was entrusted.

5. The I-*Netze*.

The I-*Netze* in Hungary were set up under the direction of the BdS, two groups being organised under the leadership of two Hungarian police officials. After the withdrawal from Hungary, contact was established with one of the groups for a short time but the organisation of networks had been faulty, and they failed completely.

Independently of the BdS effort, plans were laid down by Höttl previous to the evacuation to leave his own network in working condition. Three W/T sets were left in Budapest, of which one maintained contact after the withdrawal. Attempts were made at the last moment to reinforce this link by the despatch over the border of a further agent with a W/T set to operate in the Veszpran area, but this attempt failed. Some twenty W/T operators were trained in Hungary during the occupation of the country, of whom only four were available for operations at the last moment. These agents were left with instructions to allow themselves to be overrun, but no subsequent contact was established.

C. *Referat* VI E3 and *Referat* VI E4—Serbia, Croatia, Albania and Montenegro.

1. Jugoslavia—general.

Jugoslavia was overrun by German troops in April 1941, and as a result of the complete subjugation of the country, VI E interest was never very strong, as the territory was regarded as coming within the province of the *Dienststelle* Neubacher, from whom most reports were received by IV E. It was only at a much later date, in 1943–44, that VI E began to take any special interest in the country, as a result of requests from Neubacher himself in view of the changing war situation and the increasing partisan activities within the country. In the first instance, Albania and Montenegro were dealt with by the Serbian *Referat*, but, again at the request of Neubacher, a separate *Referat* was set up at the time of the re-organisation in 1944 to deal with Albania and Montenegro, this *Referat* being VI E4.

2. Serbia.

When the German troops occupied Jugoslavia in April 1941, they were accompanied by by the *Einsatzkommando* Jugoslavien, which remained in existence until the Spring of 1942, when it was replaced by the BdS Serbien, composed largely of the personnel of the *Einsatzkommando*. At the same time came the appointment of SS-*Gruf* Meyszner as HSSPF, while Schäfer became BdS. As a result of pressure from Neubacher, Meyszner was replaced in March 1944 by SS-*Gruf* Behrends. Early work in Serbia was carried out under this set up, with Neubacher as the main source of information through his *Dienststelle*, while the BdS had a small *Abteilung* VI representation on his staff. The original *Leiter* of this *Abteilung* was SS-*Hstuf* Hausding, who was replaced in October 1943 by SS-*Stubaf* Rexeisen. In January 1944 Rexeisen was transferred to the *Einsatzkommando* Hungary and was replaced by SS-*Ostuf* Schwarzenbacher.

The activities of *Abteilung* VI of the BdS Serbia were very restricted. Hausding had organised no network, and Rexeisen did not remain long enough to achieve his object of setting up a network. Rexeisen however was used for the despatching of agents to the Near East, though he himself had no part in the training or recruiting of these agents.

3. Croatia.

The situation in Croatia was very similar to that in Serbia. The territory came very largely under the control of the *Dienststelle* Neubacher, but there was *Hauptbeauftragter* in Agram in the person of SS-*Stubaf* Hayde, with SS-*Hstuf* Kungl as his assistant.

4. Albania and Montenegro.

As mentioned in Paragraph 1, direct IV E activity in Albania was of recent date, the country being adequately covered by the *Dienststelle* Neubacher. VI E interests in the country were carried out through Hausding, previously *Leiter Abteilung* VI in the BdS Serbia, who became BdS Albania after leaving Serbia at the end of 1943. His assistant was SS-*Hstuf* Knösel who became *Referent* was the *Referat* was set up. The *Hauptbeauftragter* in Albania was Materna.

5. Contacts in Jugoslavia.

(a) <u>The Mihailovic Movement.</u> The contact with this organisation was very strong, mainly through Neubacher, who had his own W/T link in the Mihailovic headquarters.

(b) <u>The Serbian Volunteer Corps</u> under Ljiotic.

(c) <u>The Ustachi Group</u> in Croatia.

(d) <u>The Pavelic Group</u> in Croatia.

(e) <u>The Serbian Special Police</u> under Begarevic.

(f) <u>DEVA</u>, the Minister of the Interior in Albania.

6. Efforts to penetrate Jugoslavia after the withdrawal.

The attempts which were made to organise I-*Netze* failed in Jugoslavia. Rexeisen in Serbia had insufficient time to prepare a network, the Ustachi Group in Croatia were wiped out by partisans, while Materna in Albania, who was left behind with his W/T operator Olsen, found himself with insufficient funds to carry out the proposed scheme. After the withdrawal however efforts were made by Mandl, acting on the instructions of Höttl, to re-establish contacts within the country. These attempts are summarised below.

(a) <u>Ringelnatter Operation.</u> Gasparevic, a Serb captain, assisted by SS-*Ustuf* Schwarz, was sent in January 1945, with a group of sixty Serbs to establish contact with the Mihailovic organisation. The group included three W/T operators and the desired contact was established.

(b) <u>Begarevic Operation.</u> Begarevic, the chief of the Serbian Special Police, was destined to be sent into Serbia with a group of forty agents, but as a result of squabbles with Mihailovic and Nedic, the operation was dropped. Begarevic was subsequently sent to Istria to organise a network there to work against Tito.

(c) <u>Janko Operation.</u> Jakubec, a Barat-German, was sent in January 1945 to Belgrade to organise *Anlaufstellen*. No subsequent contact was established.

(d) <u>Dinara Operation.</u> Hasanagic, of the Mohammedan Youth Movement, assisted by Franzosi, was destined to be sent to the Albanian sector to act as despatching officer for agents to be sent into Albania and Montenegro. Hasanagic got as far as Sarajevo, but owing to the retreat retired to Agram [Zagreb]. There he established contact with the Ustachi Group, for whom he was instructed to work, concealing the fact that he was acting on behalf of the Germans.

(e) <u>Dusko Operation.</u> Klopp, a Barat-German, was sent to establish contact with the Mihailovic Headquarters, where he was to act as liaison officer. This operation had previously been arranged by Neubacher. Klopp, a W/T operator, got as far as Agram, when it was impossible to go further as the location of the headquarters was by that time unknown owing to the retreat.

(f) <u>Katkus Operation.</u> Konrad Klaser, a former member of the Austria State Police, was sent to Croatia to establish contact with the Ustachi Group. Klaser had previously been active in Jugoslavia between 1941 and 1945, and had been successful in establishing relations with the Croatian intelligence service as well as with the Ustachi Group. Klaser established himself in Agram.

(g) <u>Mulec Operation.</u> Adalbert Kummel, who had been an SD agent for a long time in Agram, was sent to that city to establish liaison with Djinisic, the Chetnik leader in Montenegro, and with Drijevic, the leader of the Montenegran independence movement and former Prime Minister of Montenegro. Kummel was provided with W/T equipment and was active as late as May 1945.

(h) <u>Erwin Operation.</u> Two Croats, one a W/T operator, were sent to Fiume in order to obtain information on the Tito organisation, which information was to be sent by W/T to Agram. This operation was later changed to one of finding out about communist activities in Istria.

(i) <u>Tela Operation.</u> In collaboration with Schavedeva, who was then in Vienna, an operation destined for Albania was planned under SS-*Hstuf* Tela. The operation consisted of a small *Kommando* of four men, including a W/T operator, and arrangements had been made to have the agents parachuted through the *Kommando* Klara. The operation was abandoned owing to the shortage of aircraft, and Tela eventually left Vienna with three of his men in order to try to get to Croatia through Klagenfurt. The result of this operation is not known.

(j) <u>Other Projects.</u> In addition to the above operations, three further missions were envisaged, but failed owing to various reasons. Ali Draga was destined for Albania in company with a W/T operator, but the operation abandoned. The other operations also destined for Albania were likewise abandoned owing to the lack of W/T operators.

D. *Referat* IV E5 and Activities in Greece.

1. Early activity.
Early activities against Greece had been directed from Bulgaria where SS-*Stubaf* Glass operated under cover of the representative of the Vienna Fair in Sofia. Glass was successful in establishing contacts with Greek Army officers through Saeta, who had his headquarters in Athens. Glass was killed by Greek partisans after the British landing in 1941. His successor was SS-*Ostuf* Wawrzinowsky who had previously seen service with the SD in Bucharest.

2. Work under Wawrzinowsky.
Wawrzinowsky operated from Athens under cover of the *Leiter des Reisebüros des Deutschen Reichsbahn*, through which he was able to establish political connections. Until September 1943 Wawrzinowsky operated independently in Greece, but at the end of 1943 he was instructed to liaise with Dienststelle 3000 which had been set up in Greece under Dr Begus. The cooperation between Begus and Wawrzinowsky

was close, as their political views were very similar—views which brought them into conflict with the BdS Athens under SS-*Staf* Blume, who was anxious to establish a Greek Nazi party as the government in the country.

3. *Dienststelle* 3000.

Dienststelle 3000 was set up in February 1943 under Dr Begus, and was given the main assignment of organising a post-occupational sabotage network in southern Greece. In addition, Begus was instructed to organise routes for the despatch of agents to the Near and Middle East, and before the end of the year received further instructions to collaborate in the organistion of a political espionage network with Wawrzinowsky. A similar organisation, *Dienststelle* 2000, was set up in northern Greece under SS-*Ostuf* Ried. The two *Dienststellen* operated separately until December 1943, when they were placed under the control of *Gruppe* VI E and Begus was given authority to direct the operations of both *Dienststellen*. Begus was replaced as *Leiter* of *Dienststelle* 3000 in June 1944, his successor being SS-*Ostuf* Nebenführ. Begus himself being sent to Italy to continue operations under *Gruppe* VI S4.

The political espionage activities of *Dienststelle* 3000 were directed by Begus himself, who was successful in penetrating EAM, ELAS, and EDES organisations, and in establishing contacts in Athenian society.

4. The I-*Netze*.

The I-*Netze* planned for Greece were also in collaboration with *Gruppe* VI S, groups being set up, which only operated, however, for a short time after the Allied landing in 1944.

E. *Referat* VI E6 and Activities in Bulgaria.

1. Early work under Glass.

As mentioned in Part D, SS-*Stubaf* Glass was the original RSHA *Amt* VI representative in Sofia, from which base he also covered Greece. Glass was successful in establishing good relations with the Bulgarian Police and with the National Revolutionary Party, as well as with Macedonian circles, and journalists. His reports were of a high quality and he gave an up to date and accurate picture of internal conditions in the country. He was instrumental in stealing documents from the British Embassy in Sofia, which documents, however turned out to be of minor importance. Glass disappeared from the scene after the British landing in Greece in 1941, being at the time in hospital in that country. He is believed to have been killed subsequently. His successor in Sofia was SS-*Hstuf* Kob.

2. Contacts in Bulgaria.

(a) <u>The IMRO Organisation.</u> This organisation under Michailov proved to be of considerable value to RSHA *Amt* VI. The organisation was placed at the disposal of the Germans and served as a recruiting ground for W/T agents, who were trained in Germany before being returned to Bulgaria to serve as operators and stay-behind agents. Kob's chief V-*Mann* was Dimitar Tsileff, a member of the organisation, who himself operated the IMRO network and sent his reports to VI E through Kob.

(b) <u>The Ratniks Organisation.</u> This organisation—the Bulgarian Nazi Party— had as its leader Professor Kantarjieff, who himself controlled an intelligence network of high value with ramifications in all strata of Bulgarian life. His special assignment was to report on private conversation of high-ranking officers and leading politicians, as well as providing general reports on Bulgarian public opinion. These reports were excellent and comprehensive.

(c) <u>The Court of King Boris.</u> The Court provided contact through Bureff, who was in charge of the King's private intelligence service during his lifetime.

3. The collapse of the Bulgarian I-*Netze*.

In September 1944 SS-*Hstuf* Kob, Tsileff of the IMRO organisation, and Knöbl, the W/T operator, were ambushed and killed by Jugoslav partisans while attempting to leave Bulgaria. As a result the networks which they controlled collapsed and were no longer operative, most of the members taking refuge in Germany or in the woods in Bulgaria. Attempts were made, however, to revive the networks by the despatch of six agents in October 1944 into Bulgaria through Serbia, but the group was ambushed by partisans and wiped out. A further attempt was made in conjunction with *Abwehr Leitstelle* II *Süd-Ost* to parachute two agents into Bulgaria in the middle of April 1945, but this scheme also failed as a result of the sudden departure of the SD from Vienna. The *Leitstelle* did succeed in launching a further group near Sofia, but the group had a sabotage assignment and could not be used by VI E.

F. *Referat* VI E7 and Activities in Roumania.

1. Early activities under Bolschwing.

The original *Hauptbeauftragter* sent to Roumania in 1939 was SS-*Hstuf* Bolschwing, one of the most capable *Amt* VI representatives in the Balkans. Bolschwing was intelligent and had good social connections, through which he was able to establish good contacts in Roumania, especially in Roumanian Foreign Office circles, through which he received reports emanating from Moscow. Bolschwing himself was an economist and was able to give a clear and up to date a picture of economic conditions within the country. He was also successful in maintaining good relations with other services operating in Roumania, especially with Neubacher of the Foreign Office.

Bolschwing came into violent conflict with the Foreign Office at the time of King Carol's abdication in the autumn of 1940, as he supported Horia Sima of the Iron Guard, a policy which was contrary to that adopted by Ribbentrop, who was anxious to keep on friendly terms with Antonescu, who himself was opposed to the Iron Guard. Sima established official contact with Himmler promising Germany the support of the Iron Guard, but the differing policies came to a head when Antonescu took active measures against the Iron Guard on the outbreak of riots in Bucharest. Bolschwing was instrumental in smuggling Sima into Germany, but as a result of the ensuing quarrel with the Foreign Office and the SD, he was recalled from Roumania on the insistence of Ribbentrop. Bolschwing's successor as *Hauptbeauftragter* was SS-*Stubaf* Auner.

2. The activities of Auner in Roumania.
Auner had been active in Roumania from 1939 and he remained in the country until the withdrawal in 1944. His work was of a high quality, and Auner was responsible for establishing the best intelligence network in the Balkans, the agency employed being on a very high level. The network was carefully chosen, and Auner was successful in withholding the identity of some of his most important agents, even from Waneck himself. Working with Auner in Bucharest was SS-*Hstuf* Gunne who had been a friend of Auner's for many years.

3. Contacts in Roumania.
Auner controlled a number of *Volksdeutsche* who had excellent connections with Roumanians in all walks of life, including prominent political figures in the country. The Roumanian General Staff and the Security Service, the head of which, Christescu, put his own intelligence service at the disposal of the SD, were also used as sources of information, through the *Polizei Attaché* in Roumania, SS-*Stubaf* Richter. In addition, the Neubacher *Dienststelle* had contacts with the oil industry and in Roumanian banking circles, the governor of the National Bank himself being as agent of VI E7.

4. The Roumanian Crisis.
In August 1944 Christescu, the head of the Roumanian Secret Service, reported to RSHA *Amt* VI on the impending crisis in Roumania. Christescu also established contact with Killinger, the Foreign Office representative, and warned him of the possibility of Roumania's defection from the war, but the Foreign Office refused to take the reports seriously. The actual defection therefore took the German government by surprise, and hurried arrangements were made to take counter measures. It was proposed that Horia Sima and Andreas Schmidt, the *Volksgruppenführer* in Roumania, should collaborate, Sima forming a counter-

government and organising a resistance movement, while Schmidt made use of the Iron Guard and the *Volksdeutsche* in his, Schmidt's, group. The proposed plan however met with difficulties owing to the enmity which existed between Waneck and Schmidt, but eventually Schmidt flew to Roumania to establish contact with SS-*Hstuf* Gunne. Schmidt's plane crashed, however, and the fate of the mission is unknown, though it is reported that Gunne actually had Schmidt shot.

6. The I-*Netze*.

SS-*Hstuf* Gunne remained behind in Roumania to maintain the VI E network in the country. The network was still in operation in May 1945, but was in danger of liquidation through lack of funds. An independent I-*Netz* was set up in the Ploesti area, contact with which was lost after the occupation of Bucharest. After the Russian occupation a small network was set up by Fritz Kluess, one of Gunne's agents, but no contact was established.

Arrests.

Most of the leading personalities of RSHA *Gruppe* VI E have already been arrested and the *Gruppe* can be considered as effectively liquidated. While, however, information on the structure, personalities and working of VI E is fairly complete, the Special Agencies [the Allied intelligence agencies] are still interested in more detailed information on the activities of the *Gruppe* within the Balkan countries themselves, for which purpose special briefs may be submitted from time to time. The War Room however does not require anything more than notification of the arrest of any other leading characters.

Sources of Information for this Report.

SS-*Brif.* Walter Schellenberg	RSHA *Amtschef* VI
SS-*Gruf.* Dr Ernst Kaltenbrunner	CdS/*Chef* RSHA
SS-*Stubaf.* Dr Wilhelm Höttl	*Referent*, RSHA VI E1
SS-*Brif.* Heinz Jost	Former RSHA *Amtschef* VI

This report was distributed by W.R.C.3a, 9 November 1945.

Appendix I

Chart of Distribution of Work in RSHA *Amt* VI from 1939–1945

	1939–1940	Early 1941	Mid 1941–42	1942–1944	1944-1945
VI A	Administration etc.	General Intelligence Tasks Abroad (? Sections)	Administration etc.	Administration etc.	Administration etc.
VI B	Technical Section	Europe Africa Near East (10 sections)	Slovakia Hungary Roumania Jugoslavia Greece Turkey Iraq, Iran Afghanistan	France Low Countries Switzerland Spain Portugal	France Low Countries Switzerland Spain Portugal Italy (from 1944)
VI C	Russia Baltic States Far East	Russia Far East (11 sections)	Russia Japan China Finland Baltic States	Russia Near East Far East (13 sections)	Russia Near East Far East (4 sections by mid 1944
VI D	Hungary Slovakia Jugoslavia Roumania Bulgaria Greece Turkey	Anglo-American sphere (9 sections)	Gt. Britain British Empire USA S. America Sweden Norway Denmark	Anglo-American sphere (3 sections)	Anglo-American sphere & Scandinavia (from summer 1944)
VI E	Italy Spain Portugal Central & Southern America	Ideological Enemies abroad (6 sections) (previously VI H)	France Low Countries Spain Portugal Italy Switzerland	Central-Europe Balkans Italy Scandinavia	Balkans
VI F	France Low Countries Switzerland Luxemburg	Technical Section	Technical Section	Technical Section	Technical Section
VI G	Gt. Britain British Empire USA Norway	-	Ideological Enemies abroad	Research (from August 1944)	Research
VI H	Ideological Enemies abroad	-	-	-	-

Appendix II

Organisational Changes in
RSHA *Gruppe* VI E (1939–1945)

Organisational Chart 1939–1941.

> *Gruppe* VI D – *Süd-Ost*
> *Gruppenleiter* – SS-*Stubaf* Werner Göttsch

Referat		*Referent*
VI D1	Hungary & Slovakia	SS-*Hstuf* Friedrich Hanke
VI D2	Jugoslavia	-
VI D3	Roumania	SS-*Ostuf* Wilhelm Waneck
VI D4	Bulgaria & Greece	SS-*Ostuf* Fritz Langlotz
VI D5	Turkey & Near East	SS-*Hstuf* Herbert Hagen

Organisational Chart 1941–1942.

> *Gruppe* VI E – *Süd-Ost*
> *Gruppenleiter* – SS-*Stubaf* Hermann Rossner

Details of internal organisation unknown, but the *Gruppe* was responsible for the same territory as given in Paragraph A above, probably with the same *Referate*.

Organisational Chart 1942–1944.

> *Gruppe* VI E – *Süd-Ost*
> *Gruppenleiter* – (until 1943) SS-*Ostubaf* Dr Walter Hammer (from 1943) SS-*Ostubaf* Wilhelm Waneck

Referat		*Referent*
VI E1	Italy	SS-*Stubaf* Dr Wilhelm Höttl
VI E2	Hungary	SS-*Stubaf* Friedrich Hanke
VI E3	Serbia & Croatia	SS-*Ostuf* Rudolf Schrems
VI E4	Roumania & Bulgaria	SS-*Ostubaf* Wilhelm Waneck
VI E5	Greece	SS-*Ostuf* Kurt Klein
VI E6	Scandinavia	SS-*Hstuf* Artur Grönheim

<u>Organisational Chart 1944–1945.</u>

Gruppe VI E – *Süd-Ost*
Gruppenleiter – SS-*Ostubaf* Wilhelm Waneck

Referat		*Referent*
VI E1	Slovakia	SS-*Hstuf* Dr Wolfgang Wolfram von Wolmar
VI E2	Hungary	SS-*Stubaf* Dr Wilhelm Höttl
VI E3	Serbia & Croatia	SS-*Hstuf* Rudolf Schrems
VI E4	Albania & Montenegro	SS-*Hstuf* Adolf Knösel
VI E5	Greece	SS-*Hstuf* Kurt Pratsch
VI E6	Bulgaria	SS-*Hstuf* Bruno Klaus
VI E7	Roumania	SS-*Hstuf* Kurt Pratsch

Appendix III

Organisation and Personnel of
RSHA *Gruppe* VI E in 1945

Gruppe VI E – Süd-Ost	
Gruppenleiter:	SS-*Ostubaf* Dr Walter Hammer
Deputy:	-
Secretary:	*Fräulein* Franke
Liaison Officers	–
to RSHA VI, Berlin:	SS-*Hstuf* Otto Andernach
to *Dienstst.* Neubacher:	SS-*Hstuf* Theodor Wührer
Radio Operator	*Staffel-Mann* Bättig
Radio Operator	*Staffel-Mann* Herbert Fehland

<u>*Referat* VI E 1 (Slovakia)</u>

Referent	SS-*Hstuf* Wolfgang Wolfram von Wolmar
	SS-*Hstuf* Herrmann
	Regierungsrat Albrecht
	SS-*Hstuf* Wolfgang Wolfram von Wolmar
	Fräulein Horatschek

<u>*Referat* VI E2 (Hungary)</u>

Referent	SS-*Stubaf* Dr Wilhelm Höttl
	SS-*Hstuf* Josef Deworetzky
	SS-*Hstuf* Heinz Fröhlich

SS-*Hstuf* Paul Neunteufel
SS-*Hstuf* Kerber
SS-*Hschaf* Emil Kuderna
SS-*Hschaf* Wendel
SS-*Rotf* Hoffmann
Fräulein Wagner

Referat VI E3 (Serbia & Croatia)
    Referent

SS-*Hstuf* Kurt Wiesenberger
SS-*Stubaf* Friedrich Hanke
SS-*Hstuf* Rupert Mandl
SS-*Hstuf* Rudolf Schrems
SS-*Oschaf* Vosseler

Referat VI E4 (Albania & Montenegro)
    Referent

SS-*Hstuf* Otto Knösel
SS-*Hstuf* Werner Kleber
SS-*Ostuf* Springer

Referat VI E5 (Greece)
    Referent

SS-*Hstuf* Kurt Klein
SS-*Rotf* Johannes Leichtfriend

Referat VI E6 (Bulgaria)
    Referent

SS-*Hstuf* Bruno Klaus
SS-*Ostuf* Gerhard Bollmann
SS-*Ostuf* Franz Dorner
SS-*Hstuf* Viktor Zeischka
SS-*Hschaf* Franz Deixler
SS-*Hschaf* Arno Grässner

Referat VI E7 (Roumania)
    Referent

SS-*Hstuf* Kurt Pratsch
SS-*Stubaf* Kurt Auner
SS-*Hstuf* Theodor Ondrey
SS-*Ustuf* Herrschaft
SS-*Ustuf* Rolf Waber
SS-*Oschaf* Borislav Bavlakovic
Dr Ernst Weissenfeld
Frau Weissenfeld

Appendix IV

Personnel of RSHA *Gruppe* VI E at Outstations

<u>*Referat* VI E1 (Slovakia)</u>

Hauptabeauftragter	SS-*Ostuf* Georg Ubl
	SS-*Stubaf* Karl Kraus
	SS-*Hstuf* Orglmeister
	SS-*Hstuf* Julius Westergaard
Abteilung VI, BdS Prague	SS-*Ostubaf* Dr Walter Hammer
	SS-*Ustuf* Zink

<u>*Referat* VI E2 (Hungary)</u>

Hauptbeauftragter	SS-*Ostubaf* Josef Urban
Deputy *Hauptbeauftragter*	SS-*Ostuf* Rudolf Dienst
	Kriminalsekretär Georg Meindl
	SS-*Rotf* Müller
	SS-*Rotf* Moravzik
	Staffel-Mann Hinkelmann
	SS-*Hschaf* Wendel
	SS-*Oschaf* Morawek
	Angestellter Deak
Abteilung VI, BdS Hungary	SS-*Stubaf* Peter Weirauch

<u>*Referat* VI E3 (Serbia & Croatia)</u>

Hauptbeauftragter Agram	SS-*Stubaf* Ernst Hayde
Deputy *Hauptbeauftragter* Agram	SS-*Ostuf* Kungl
	SS-*Hschaf* Wissel (or Wyssel)
	Staffel-Mann Lamm
Abteilung VI, BdS Serbien	SS-*Stubaf* Hans Rexeisen (until Jan 1944, then SS-*Ustuf* Hermann Schwarzenbacher
	SS-*Ustuf* Berger
	SS-*Ostuf* Schröder
	SS-*Oschaf* Schuster

<u>*Referat* VI E4 (Albania)</u>

Hauptbeauftragter	*Angestellter* Materna
	Angestellter Olsen

Referat VI E5 (Greece)

Hauptbeauftragter	SS-*Ostuf* Friedrich Wawrzinowsky
	SS-*Hstuf* Herbert Hösselbarth
Radio operator	Erich Franz
	Sonderführer Pfann
Dienststelle 3000 and 2000	SS-*Stubaf* Dr Otto Begus (until June 1944, then)
	SS-*Ostuf* Franz Nebenfuhr
	SS-*Ostuf* Walter Ried
	SS-*Ustuf* Kanakis
	SS-*Oschaf* Wilhelm Kröger

Referat VI E6 (Bulgaria)

Hauptabeauftragter	SS-*Hstuf* Rudolf Kob (dead/KIA)
Radio Operator	Adolf Knöbel (dead/KIA)

Referat VI E7 (Roumania)

Hauptbeauftragter	SS-*Hstuf* Roland Gunne
Deputy *Hauptbeauftragter*	SS-*Ustuf* Liebhardt
Deputy *Hauptbeauftragter*	SS-*Ustuf* Steiner
	SS-*Ustuf* Franz Alliger
	SS-*Ustuf* Bergel
	SS-*Oschaf* Hans Polonyi
Radio Operator	*Angestellter* Günther Bauer

Appendix V

Alphabetical Index of RSHA *Gruppe* VI E personnel

(Note: This list does not contain personnel of the Scandinavian and Italian *Referate* who were in the *Gruppe* between 1942 and 1944. Such officers appear in the Liquidation Reports on *Gruppe* VI D and *Gruppe* VI E respectively. Personnel known to be under arrest are underlined.)

Rank & Name	*Referat*	Remarks
Regierungsrat Albrecht	VI E1	
SS-*Ustuf* Franz Alliger	VI E7	Arrested.
SS-*Hstuf* Otto Andernach	VI E	Transferred to *Sipo*, Apr '45

SS-*Stubaf* <u>Kurt Auner</u>	VI E7	Arrested.
Staffel-Mann <u>Bättig</u>	VI E	W/T; arrested.
Angestellter Bauer	VI E7	W/T call, Roumania
SS-*Oschaf* Bavlakovic	VI E7	
SS-*Stubaf* Dr <u>Otto Begus</u>	VI E5	*Leiter, Dienststelle* 3000; transferred to VI S in Italy in June 1944; arrested
SS-*Stubaf* Dr Wilhelm Beissner	VI E	In *Gruppe* VI D, 1939–40; later in VI C.
SS-*Ustuf* Reinhard Bergel	VI E7	Cell, Roumania
SS-*Ustuf* Cletus Berger	VI E	
SS-*Ostuf* Gerhard Bollmann	VI E6	transfer BdS Braunschweig in May 1945
SS-*Hstuf* Otto von Bolschwing	VI E7	*Hauptbeauftragter* Roumania 1939–40
Angestellter <u>Deak</u>	VI E2	Cell, Hungary; arrested
SS-*Hschaf* Franz Deixler	VI E6	
SS-*Hstuf* <u>Josef Deworetzky</u>	VI E6	Arrested.
SS-*Ostuf* Rudolf Dienst	VI E2	Deputy *Hauptbeauftragter*, Hungary
SS-*Ostuf* Franz Dorner	VI E6	
Drewitz	VI E6	
Ecker	VI E4	
Staffel-Mann <u>Herbert Fehland</u>	VI E	Arrested.
Angestellter Franke	VI E	
SS-*Uschaf* Erich Franz	VI E5	Cell, Greece.
SS-*Hschaf* Franzoesky	VI E3	Joined *Einsatz* E/S, 1945
SS-*Hstuf* Heinz Fröhlich	VI E2	transfer *Sipo* Prague, April 1945
SS-*Stubaf* Fridolin Glass	VI E5	Representative in Greece, 1939–40; killed by Greek partisans, 1941
SS-*Ostubaf* <u>Werner Göttsch</u>	VI E	*Gruppenleiter*. Arrested.
SS-*Hschaf* Arno Grässner	VI E6	transferred BdS Halle, '45
SS-*Stubaf* <u>Artur Grönheim</u>	VI E6	*Referat* VI E6 when *Referat* Scandinavia; later IV D3; arrested in Norway, 1945
SS-*Hstuf* Roland Gunne	VI E7	HB Cell, Roumania
SS-*Ostubaf* Dr Walter Hammer	VI E1	*Gruppenleiter*, then Prague
SS-*Stubaf* Friedrich Hanke	VI E3	
SS-*Hstuf* Günther Hausding	VI E3	BdS Serbia; VI E Albania
SS-*Stubaf* Ernst Hayde	VI E3	HB Agram
SS-*Hschaf* Egon Hellermann	VI E3	Joined *Einsatz* E/S, 1945
SS-*Hstuf* Herrmann	VI E1	
SS-*Ustuf* Hans Herrschaft	VI E7	
Staffel-Mann <u>Hinkelmann</u>	VI E2	Cell Hungary; arrested
SS-*Hstuf* Herbert Hösselberth	VI E5	Cell Greece

SS-*Stubaf* Dr Wilhelm Höttl	VI E2	Arrested
SS-*Rotf* Hoffmann	VI E2	to BdS Trieste, 1945
Angestellter Horatschek	VI E1	
SS-*Oschaf* Helfried Jäger	VI E3	Joined *Einsatz* E/S, 1945
Zivilangestellter Sergius Kanakis	VI E5	*Dienstelle* 3000, Greece
SS-*Hstuf* Kerber	VI E2	
SS-*Hstuf* Bruno Klaus	VI E6	Arrested.
SS-*Hstuf* Werner Kleber	VI E4	
SS-*Hstuf* Kurt Klein	VI E5	Discharged to *Stapo* Linz, April 1945
SS-*Oschaf* Stefan Klopp	VI E3	Joined *Einsatz* E/S, 1945.
SS-*Oschaf* Adolf Knöbel	VI E6	Cell Bulgaria; dead/KIA.
SS-*Hstuf* Otto Knösel	VI E4	
SS-*Hstuf* Rudolf Kob	VI E6	HB Bulgaria; dead/KIA
SS-*Stubaf* Karl Kraus	VI E1	Cell Slovakia; arrested
SS-*Oschaf* Wilhelm Kröger	VI E5	*Dienststelle* 3000, Greece
SS-*Hschaf* Emil Kuderna	VI E2	
SS-*Ustuf* Adalbert Kungel	VI E3	Deputy HB Agram; joined *Einsatz* E/S, 1945
Staffel-Mann Lamm	VI E3	Agram
SS-*Hstuf* Fritz Langlotz	VI E5	released for ill-health, '43
SS-*Oschaf* Johannes Leichtfried	VI E5	intended to be left behind at Lunz-am-See
SS-*Ustuf* Samuel Liebhardt	VI E7	Deputy HB Roumania
SS-*Ostuf* Mader	VI E4	
Mandelos	VI E5	W/T, V-Mann cell, Greece
SS-*Hstuf* Rupert Mandl	VI E3	*Einsatz* E/S; arrested
Angestellter Materna	VI E4	HB Cell, Albania
KrimSek Georg Meindl	VI E2	Cell Hungary; transfer to *Stapo* Regensburg, 1945
SS-*Oschaf* Moravzek	VI E2	W/T Cell Hungary; arrested
SS-*Oschaf* Morawek	VI E2	Cell Hungary; arrested
SS-*Rotf* Müller	VI E2	W/T, Cell Hungary
SS-*Ostuf* Franz Nebenfuhr	VI E5	*Leiter, Dienststelle* 3000
SS-*Hstuf* Paul Neunteufel	VI E2	Arrested.
Angestellter Olsen	VI E4	W/T, Cell Albania
SS-*Hstuf* Theodor Ondrey	VI E7	
SS-*Hstuf* Orglmeister	VI E1	Cell Slovakia
Angestellter Ott	VI E3	
Sonderführer Pfann	VI E5	Cell Greece
SS-*Hstuf* Kurt Pratsch	VI E7	
SS-*Oschaf* Hans Polonyi	VI E7	Arrested.
SS-*Stubaf* Hans Rexeisen	VI E3	BdS Serbia, Abt. VI

SS-*Ostuf* Walter Ried	VI E5	*Leiter, Dienststelle* 2000 to June 1944; then RSHA VI E and Dec 1944 to BdS Italy
SS-*Stubaf* Hermann Rossner	VI E	*Gruppenleiter*, 1941
SS-*Ostuf* Scheiber	VI E3	Liaison Cell Albania; death reported in 1944
SS-*Hschaf* Rudolf Schemmel	VI E3	Joined *Einsatz* E/S, 1945
SS-*Hstuf* Rudolf Schrems	VI E3	Transfer to *Stapo* Salzburg in April 1945; arrested
SS-*Ostuf* Schröder	VI E3	BdS Serbia, Abt VI
SS-*Oschaf* Schuster	VI E3	BdS Serbia, Abt VI
SS-*Ustuf* Hermann Schwarzenbacher	VI E3	Arrested.
SS-*Ustuf* Borislov Snidarsic	VI E3	
SS-*Ostuf* Josef Springer	VI E4	
SS-*Ustuf* Steiner	VI E7	Deputy HB Cell Roumania
SS-*Ustuf* Karl Stüwe	VI E3	Joined *Einsatz* E/S, 1945
SS-*Ostuf* Georg Ubl	VI E1	transfer to *Sipo*, April 1945
SS-*Ostubaf* Josef Urban	VI E2	HB Cell, Hungary
SS-*Oschaf* Vosseler	VI E3	
SS-*Ustuf* Rolf Waber	VI E7	
Fräulein Wagner	VI E2	Interpreter
SS-*Ostubaf* Wilhelm Waneck	VI E	*Gruppenleiter* VI E
SS-*Ostuf* Friedrich Wawrszinowski	VI E5	HB Cell Greece
SS-*Stubaf* Peter Weirauch	VI E2	BdS Hungary, *Abt* VI; was *Referent* VI C4
Angestellter Dr Ernst Weissenfeld	VI E7	
Angestellte Frau Weissenfeld	VI E7	
SS-*Hschaf* Wendel	VI E2	Cell Hungary; driver
SS-*Hstuf* Julius Westergaard	VI E1	Cell Slovakia
SS-*Hstuf* Kurt Wiesenberger	VI E3	
SS-*Hschaf* Wissel (or Wyssel)	VI E3	Cell Croatia
SS-*Hstuf* Wolfgang Wolfram von Wolmar	VI E1	
SS-*Hstuf* Theodor Wührer	VI E	Liaison Officer to *Dienststelle* Neubacher
SS-*Hstuf* Viktor Zeischka	VI E6	Arrested.
SS-*Ustuf* Zink	VI E1	BdS Prague, *Abt* VI.

Notes

* The National Archives, Kew, KV 3/101: Situation Report No. 10, RSHA VI E.

10

Situation Report No. 11:
Amt VI of the RSHA—*Gruppe* VI F

INDEX

A. The Organisational Development of RSHA *Gruppe* VI F
  1   The Formation of *Gruppe* VI B in 1939
  2   The Early Enterprises—the Forging of Bank of England Notes
  3   The Dismissal of Naujocks
  4   The Organisation in 1941
  5   Reorganisation in Summer of 1942
  6   Organisational Structure of *Gruppe* VI F in 1942
  7   Reorganisation in September 1943
  8   Absorption of the *Abwehr* in Summer 1944

B. The Functions of RSHA *Gruppe* VI F *Referate*
  1   The Havel Institute
  2   *Unternehmen* Otto (*Referat* VI F/O, 1942–43)
  3   *Referat* VI F 3
  4   *Referat* VI F 4

Appendix I: Distribution of Work in RSHA *Amt* VI, 1939–45
Appendix II: Organisation and Personnel of *Gruppe* VI F, 1944–45
Appendix III: Alphabetical Index of *Gruppe* VI F personnel, 1939–45

Preamble

RSHA *Gruppe* VI F was the technical section of *Amt* VI and was broadly responsible for the provision of technical material for the use of the *Ländergruppen*, and also for the supervision of W/T communications for the *Amt*. At this stage, little information is available on the technical aspects of the *Gruppe* as so far only one prominent member of the *Gruppe*, Dr Schäffner, is under interrogation. It will be appreciated too, that owing to this specialised nature of the work of the *Gruppe*, information from other sources has been only on very general lines. The present summary, therefore, is deficient in many aspects and these deficiencies can only be rectified when more of the leading characters in the *Gruppe* have been arrested and interrogated. The lack of information is confined not to the technical side of the *Gruppe* but also to its organisational development, information of which is still scanty. The main purpose of this publication, therefore, is to give a broad outline of the development and work of the *Gruppe* and a list of the personalities known to have worked at some time for the *Gruppe*.

A

The Organisational Development of RSHA *Gruppe* VI F

1. The formation of RSHA *Gruppe* VI B in 1939:

The origin of the technical department of RSHA *Amt* VI was a somewhat casual affair, and it should be borne in mind that in the original organisation of the RSHA, *Amt* I was responsible for the overall provision of technical equipment for the whole of the RSHA, the competent *Gruppe* being *Gruppe* I G under SS-*Stubaf* Rauff. The new *Amt* VI required of course a W/T station to establish communications with its projected representatives in foreign countries, and for this reason a W/T department was set up providing a central receiving and transmitting station at Berlin-Grunewald. This department was a purely technical one staffed mainly by civilian technicians and was placed under the control of *Gruppe* VI B, set up with Alfred Naujocks as *Gruppenleiter*, the *Gruppe* being described as a technical section of the *Amt*.

It was on Naujock's suggestion that such a section was set up as he foresaw that a department which intended to run its own agents would require a section to provide the necessary materials. It should be remembered too, that the old *Amt* III/3 of the SD-*Hauptamt* had no corresponding section which could provide any basis for expansion, nor had Najocks any technical staff already at his disposal.

The development of the *Gruppe*, therefore, was rather haphazard and it was not until mid-1942 that it was finally established as an important section of the *Amt*, with any established organisation and wholly defined functions.

This does not apply to the W/T side of the *Gruppe* which necessarily had to develop in keeping with the development of the *Amt* as a whole. The W/T section soon transferred from Berlin-Grunewald to Berlin-Wannsee and was to become known as the Wannsee Institute, and owing to its functions can be treated separately from the rest of the *Gruppe*. The development of the Havel Institute, therefore, forms the subject matter of Part B, Paragraph 1 below.

2. The early Enterprises—the forging of Bank of England notes:
The first impetus given to RSHA *Gruppe* VI B came in the shape of a request, or rather a demand, from Heydrich that Naujocks should proceed with the manufacture of forged Bank of England bank notes to be used in the invasion of Great Britain. As can be imagined, however, the *Gruppe* was quite incapable of meeting this demand without considerable preparation as no qualified staff was available. To meet Heydrich's insistent demands, therefore, Naujocks was able to recruit for his department a large staff of civilian assistants mainly through the *Deutsches Arbeitsamt*. The whole energies of the *Gruppe* were directed to this new enterprise not through enthusiasm for the work, but because of Heydrich's intolerant attitude. By the summer of 1940 the notes were in production on some scale, but the results were not of high quality, and moreover, the notes were printed in denominations which made them practically useless for the purpose for which they were intended.

3. The dismissal of Naujocks:
As a result of this failure, Naujocks was dismissed from his position as *Gruppenleiter* in the autumn of 1940. In the first year of its existence, therefore, the *Gruppe* had achieved little of note but the experience gained in the manufacture of the forged Bank notes was to prove of some value when the *Gruppe* turned to the more routine task of preparing false identity documents and passports. The initial work on such forgeries was undertaken by Dr Langer, a technical but eccentric specialist from Vienna, whom Naujocks had recruited when the *Gruppe* was first formed. Meantime, as a result of Naujocks's dismissal, his deputy SS-*Stubaf* Fuhrmann acted as *Gruppenleiter*. The *Gruppe*, however, remained a small one and the period until the summer of 1941 can only be regarded as a period of training for the *Gruppe* itself.

4. The organisation in 1941:
By early 1941 a complete re-organisation of the *Amt* was under consideration and reached the length of being drafted on paper. This paper organisation dated early 1941 shows that RSHA *Gruppe* VI B was destined to become VI F with SS-*Stubaf* Rauff as *Gruppenleiter* and SS-*Stubaf* Fuhrmann as his deputy. Rauff, as

mentioned in Paragraph 1, was the *Gruppenleiter* at that time of RSHA *Gruppe* I G and it is not certain that he ever did in fact become *Gruppenleiter* of VI F. It was not until later in the year that the re-organisation of RSHA *Amt* VI finally took place when *Gruppe* VI B did in fact become VI F with, however, SS-*Stubaf* Dörner as *Gruppenleiter*. The internal organisation of the *Gruppe* at that time is uncertain but it is probable that there were—apart from the W/T section at Wannsee—at least three other sections, one dealing with Administration, the other two dealing with Secret Inks under Dr Schamberger and the other under SS-*Stubaf* Krüger dealing with forged documents. There is little indication, however, the *Gruppe* was either active or efficient in its work at that time, the very opposite is in fact the case if the testimony of Dr Langer can be taken as authentic.

5. Re-organisation in summer 1942:

The first major re-organisation of RSHA *Gruppe* VI F took place in the summer of 1942, the immediate reason being Himmler's direction that the production of sabotage material should be undertaken on more serious lines, and as VI F3 had previously been the source of such material for RSHA *Amt* VI, the new activity was centralised in VI F. Side by side with this increased interest in sabotage material was the creation of a new *Referat*. *Referat* VI F/O (*Unternehmen* Otto) which was created to deal with the actual training of sabotage agents and which was also responsible for their despatch to various countries. *Unternehmen* Otto is dealt with in detail in Part B, Paragraph 2, below. The creation of this *Referat* led to conflict with the *Ländergruppen* as this assignment to VI F had the result that the *Gruppe* cut across the work of the remaining *Ländergruppen*.

At the same time greater attention was paid to the W/T aspect of RSHA *Amt* VI work, as as the *Amt* under Schellenberg with the support of Himmler was at that time taking a new lease of life and greatly extending its activities, more centralised and expanded W/T service became necessary. For this reason the Havel Institute was created, becoming a separate *Referat* known from then on as VI F (H).

6. Organisational structure of RSHA *Gruppe* VI F in 1942:

Details of the organisational structure of RSHA *Gruppe* VI F at this time are not clear, and there appear to have been frequent modifications between 1942 and the end of 1943. The following chart is however probably approximately correct.

Gruppenleiter - SS-*Stubaf* Dörner

Referat	*Sachgebiet*	*Referent*
VI F 1	Administration	SS-*Ostuf* Nötenburg
VI F 2	Radio Broadcasts Monitoring	-
VI F 3	Technical Materials	SS-*Stubaf* Lassig
VI F 4	Forgery of Documents	SS-*Stubaf* Krüger

VI F 5	Technical Assistance (?)	SS-*Hstuf* Weideling
VI F 6	Wireless Interception	SS-*Stubaf* Gottlob
VI F 7	Library	SS-*Stubaf* Fesel
VI F/O	*Unternehmen* Otto	SS-*Stubaf* Dörner
VI F *Hauskapelle*	Security	*Kriminaldirektor* Gans
VI F (H)	The Havel Institute	SS-*Stubaf* Siepen

The connection between VI F2 and VI F6 in the above chart is not clear: SS *Stubaf* Gottlob left the *Gruppe* in the course of 1943 to go on a special mission to Portugal when the *Referat* was probably dissolved. VI F2 was absorbed in August 1943 by VI F (H).

Referat VI F7 was a new departure for the *Gruppe*: the *Referent* SS-*Stubaf* Fesel had been previously *Referent* VI A8, which in the years 1940–42 represented the reference library of RSHA *Amt* VI. In April 1942 this library was transferred to *Gruppe* VI F to become *Referat* VI F7 with Fesel as *Referent* and SS-*Hstuf* Langlotz as his assistant. The library was finally transferred to *Gruppe* VI G under Krallert at the end of 1943.

With this new reorganisation the *Gruppe* considerably increased in personnel, while VI F3 and VI F4 greatly intensified their own branches of work. The activities of these two *Referate* are dealt with in Part B, Paragraphs 3 and 4 below.

7. Re-organisation in September 1943:

The agent training undertaken by *Gruppe* VI F was stopped in September 1943, the sabotage functions passing to the new *Gruppe* VI S. As a result of this change the *Gruppe* underwent a simplification in its internal structure, the breakdown being as follows:

Gruppenleiter   -   SS-*Stubaf* Dörner

<u>*Referat*</u> VI F 1		<u>*Referent*</u>: SS-*Stubaf* Siepen
and VI F 2	Transferred to Havel Institute	
VI F 3	Technical Matters	SS-*Stubaf* Lassig
VI F 4	Forged Documents	SS-*Stubaf* Krüger

Both *Referate* VI F1 and VI F2 was dissolved and were absorbed into VI F (H), VI F 2 becoming VI F (H) 2 under SS-*Oschaf* Herb, while VI F *Hauskapelle* became *Abteilung* VI F (H) 4.

8. Absorption of the *Abwehr* in summer 1944:

In the spring of 1944 SS-*Stubaf* Dörner was posted as Intelligence Officer (Ic) to an SS-*Korps* on the Eastern Front. No *Gruppenleiter* was immediately appointed in his place as the fusion of the *Abwehr* with RSHA *Amt* VI was at that time under consideration. When the absorption did take place *Oberstleutnant* Boening of the *Abwehr* was placed in joint command of *Gruppe* VI F and of *Abteilung Mil* E and *Mil* G, the sections of the *Abwehr* corresponding to *Gruppe* VI F in RSHA *Amt* VI. The organisation of *Gruppe* VI F was not materially affected, VI F1 and VI F2 being responsible for the Havel Institute, VI F3 and 4 continuing their previous functions.

The only subsequent modification was the creation in the spring of 1945 of a new section, *Referent* VI V (BFN), the *Beschäftungstelle für Nachrichtengerät*, a section under SS-*Hstuf* Steckhan whose intended responsibility was the provision of intelligence apparatus to VI F (H) and *Abt. Mil.* E.

B

The Functions of RSHA *Gruppe* VI F *Referate*

1. The Havel Institute:

a) The Wannsee Institute 1939–42:

The Havel Institute was created in September 1942 on the orders of Himmler himself as the general situation of RSHA *Amt* VI W/T communications was unsatisfactory. It became known as *Referat* VI F (H) of RSHA *Gruppe* VI F. Previously the first receiving station of *Amt* VI had been set up in December 1939 at Grunewald in Berlin, at the time the headquarters of *Gruppe* VI B under Naujocks. Early in 1940 the W/T section of VI B transferred to Berlin-Wannsee and became known as the Wannsee Institute, maintaining a comparatively small staff of technicians and nominally under the control of Naujocks. The staff of the Institute under SS-*Oschaf* Werner also had a teleprinter section under SS-*Hstuf* Redlin.

b) Creation of the Havel Institute in 1942:

The new Havel Institute created in 1942 was much extended in functions and personnel: the *Leiter* of the new *Referat* was SS-*Stubaf* Siepen with SS-*Hstuf* Schäffner as his deputy. The section took over a new radio network named '*Netz* B', a national network comprising all the auxiliary W/T stations set up within the *Reich* itself, in addition to the already existing '*Netz* A' which controlled the foreign stations. In addition seven *Abteilungen* were set up within the *Referat* itself, details of which are given below. Siepen remained in command until December 1944 when he was replaced by SS-*Stubaf* Faross, but Schäffner remained as deputy *Leiter*.

c) W/T stations [*Wetterstellen*] in the B-*Netz*:

The following W/T stations in Germany came under the control of the Havel Institute:

Babelsberg	Near Berlin, acting as the alternative station for the Havel Institute itself, but also communicating with outstations in Norway.
Gotenhafen	Near Danzig, communicating with northern Europe.
Kirchsassen	Near Prague and communicating with south-east Europe and the Balkans.
Marienbad	Station in Czechoslovakia communicating with the Balkans.
Vienna	Communicating with the Balkans.
Bamberg	Near Nuremberg, responsible for communications with Italy.
Nickersburg	In Baden, responsible for communications with France and western Europe.

Apart from the recognised B-*Netz* described above, efforts were made at the end of 1944 to set up alternative W/T stations to replace the Wannsee station in case of the evacuation of Berlin. Stations were constructed at Tegernsee in Bavaria and at Hall near Braunschweig. A further station was constructed in 1945 on the instructions of Faross at Grossgeschwenda in Thuringia.

d) Schools controlled by the Havel Institute:
In addition to being responsible for the maintenance of RSHA *Amt* VI W/T communications, the Havel Institute also trained radio personnel and W/T agents of *Amt* VI, to whom it supplied the necessary radio equipment. For this purpose four schools were maintained by the Havel Institute as follows:

> The Lehnitz School, near Potsdam
> The Harzburg School, near Braunschweig
> The Pansdorf School, near Lübeck
> The Wannsee School, in Berlin-Wannsee

In addition to running the above schools under its direct control, VI F (H) also supplied technical staff to the various schools run by the *Ländergruppen* themselves, such as the VI B school at Paris, The Hague, Stuttgart, etc.

e) Organisation of RSHA VI F (H):
The Havel Institute itself was organised into seven sub-sections covering the different functions which the Institute had to perform. Details of this organisation are given below:

Referat VI F (H)   -   *Referent* SS-*Stubaf* Faross

Abteilung	*Sachgebiet*	*Leiter*
VI F (H) 1	*Vorbereitung für technische Einsatz*	SS-*Hstuf* Schäffner
(H) 2	*Funkunterlagen und Betrieb*	SS-*Oschaf* Herb
(H) 3	*Schlüsselwesen*	*Angestellter* Voigt

(H) 4	*Abwehr*	SS-*Hstuf* Müller
(H) 5	*Verwaltung, Werbung*	SS-*Ostuf* Reinhard Dr Hagemeister
(H) 6	*Schulung*	*Angestellter* Faul
(H) 7	*Geräte*	SS-*Ustuf* Simon

f) Evacuation of the Havel Institute, 1945:
The Institute was divided into two parts in April 1945, conforming to the general *Nordstab* and *Südstab* of the RSHA. The *Gruppe Norden* under Faross left Berlin on 10th April 1945 for the alternative station at Lübeck while the *Gruppe Süden* under Schäffner left earlier, on 5th April 1945, for Thuringia, later proceeding to Tegernsee. The *Gruppe Süden* dissolved in the early days of May.

2. *Unternehmen* Otto—*Referat* VI F/O (1943–43).

a) Functions:
Unternehmen Otto or Ottladen was the name given to the special *Referat* of RSHA VI F created in July 1942 on the orders of Himmler. The special function of the *Referat* was the training of sabotage agents, but it is important to note that the *Referat* was responsible for the missions of the agents it trained. In this way *Unternehmen* Otto cut across the activities of the *Ländergruppen* and as a result met with the opposition of the *Gruppenleiter*. The *Referat* also trained its agents in W/T and codes, drawing on the special section of the *Gruppe* for instructors in these subjects—Dr Langer for codes, and the Havel Institute for W/T instructions.

b) Organisation:
The *Referat* VI F/O was organised on a regional basis, there being three geographical sections together with an administrative and training section. The organisation was on the following lines:

Unternehmen Otto (*Referat* RSHA VI F/O

> *Leiter*: SS-*Stubaf* Dörner (also *Gruppenleiter* VI F)
> Deputy: SS-*Stubaf* Lassig

Administrative *Abteilung*:
    SS-*Ostuf* Nötenburg
    SS-*Ostuf* Jansen
    SS-*Ostuf* Möck
    SS-*Hschaf* Liebe

Training *Abteilung*:
    SS-*Hstuf* Dersch
    SS-*Oschaf* Westphal (sabotage)
    Dr Lange (codes)

| *Abteilung Näheres Osten:* | SS-*Hstuf* Mandl (later VI E) |
| | SS-*Ostuf* Bohnhoff |

| *Abteilung Nord:* | SS-*Hstuf* Daufeldt (later VI D) |
| | SS-*Ustuf* Schwarzenbacher (later VI E) |

| *Abteilung* Morocco: | SS-*Hstuf* Schulze (later VI B) |
| | SS-*Hstuf* Weideling (later VI F) |

In addition to the above sections there was a further special section in *Gruppe* VI F which did not come under VI F/O but which performed very similar functions. This was the so-called 'Balkans *Abteilung*' under SS-*Hstuf* Reinel (later *Leiter, Dienststelle* 1000), assisted by SS-*Hstuf* Wandhoff, who later went to SD-*Aussenstelle* Maastricht.

c) Outside organisation:
In February 1943, *Referat* VI F/O extended its scope by the setting up of three dependent organisations through which its activities were to be directed. These were the *Dienststellen* 1000, 2000 and 3000.

(i) *Dienststelle* 1000: This Stelle was set up in Belgrade in March 1943 under SS-*Hstuf* Reinel and was based on the Balkans *Abteilung* mentioned in paragraph b) above. The *Stelle* had the function of organising a stay-behind sabotage and resistance movement in the Belgrade area. *Dienststelle* 1000 however had only a brief period of existence and was soon dissolved.

(ii) *Dienststelle* 2000: This *Stelle* was set up in Salonika under SS-*Ostuf* Ried, with functions similar to that described under *Dienststelle* 1000. The *Stelle* worked in close liaison with *Dienststelle* 3000 below and in fact came under the control of that *Stelle* in December 1943, when both *Dienststellen* were placed under the command of *Gruppe* VI E, *Referat* VI F/O by that time being dissolved.

(iii) *Dienststelle* 3000: *Dienststelle* 3000 was set up in Athens in April 1943 under SS-*Stubaf* Begus. It had its own W/T station and until August 1943 reported directly to VI F. After August the *Stelle* continued to report to VI F, though by that time VI F/O had been dissolved, a state of affairs which continued to exist until December 1943, when VI E became the controlling *Gruppe*. The original functions of *Dienststelle* 3000 had been to organise a sabotage and political espionage network in southern Greece and also to organise routes for the despatch of agents to the Near and Middle East for VI F/O at the same time acting in a similar capacity for other *Ländergruppen* interested in that territory. When VI E assumed command of the *Stelle* in December 1943, these functions were correspondingly modified: the *Stelle* was now instructed to work in liaison and unde the supervision of

Wawrzinowsky, the VI E *Hauptbeauftragter* in Athens, while facilitated the passage of agents to the Middle East would be on behalf of *Ländergruppen* only and not for VI F/O which had been dissolved. The *Stelle* now divided its functions between *Angestellter* Ludwig (previously VI F/O) who organised the sabotage network and Begus himself who was responsible for the espionage side.

d) Activities of *Dienststelle* 3000:
Begus worked in close liaison with the *Geheime Feldpolizei* (GFP) Athens from whom he recruited most of his important agents for political espionage purposes. Begus concentrated on obtaining information on Greek political movements (especially the underground movement), on the Greek Government, on the policy of neutrals through their representatives in Athens and on the work of Allied Intelligence Services in Greece. He was successful in penetrating EAM, ELAS and EDES through agents who held leading positions in these organisations. The leading agents under Begus organised their own networks and submitted consolidated reports to *Dienststelle* 3000. Agents were also established in society circles in Athens. Through these sources Begus was able to pass to VI E through Wawrzinowsky a document containing peace proposals from the Greek Government to the German plenipotentiary in Greece. The penetration of foreign diplomatic circles was also considerable, mainly through the notwork of a certain Burg-Horny.

On the sabotage side Ludewig established cells in Athens, Piraeus, Thebes, Karitse and on the west coast of Greece.

Begus himself was transferred to Italy in June 1944 to work with VI S, his place as *Leiter* being taken by SS-*Ostuf* Nebenführ. Other members of the staff of *Dienststelle* 3000 were SS-*Oschaf* Kronberger—now arrested—SS-*Hschaf* Wolf, *Angestellter* Willsch and *Unteroffizier* Dölle. Willsch, mentioned above, was placed in command of *Dienststelle* 2000 in May 1944 as it was suspected that that *Stelle* had been detected by the Allies and was in danger of attack. SS-*Ostuf* Ried, the *Leiter* of the *Dienststelle*, returned to Germany.

e) Other operations controlled by *Referat* VI F/O:
SS-*Hstuf* Langenbach, *Leiter* of *Abteilung* West was responsible for the training of some 25 foreign Legionaires. 15 of whom were parachuted into Tunis in February 1943 with sabotage missions. Only two of these agents returned, one of whom was Kohlhaas later of RSHA *Gruppe* VI C. Langenbach worked in close cooperation with SS-*Hstuf* Schulze of the *Abteilung* Morocco who had previously been the SD representative in Tangiers.

Daufeldt of *Abteilung Nord* was responsible for the training of a Norwegian called Petersen who was destined to be sent to London via Sweden on a sabotage reconnaissance mission. This enterprise was not successful. Daufeldt himself was later sent to Copenhagen as representative of RSHA VI D 3.

f) Dissolution of *Unternehmen* Otto:

Referat VI F/O was finally dissolved in September 1943 when it became apparent that the effort expended in this enterprise was not yielding satisfactory results. The primary function of the *Referat* had been sabotage which now assumed considerable importance in the eyes of Himmler who ordered the creation of RSHA *Gruppe* VI S under Skorzeny to specialise in that subject. The *Referat* was therefore dissolved, the personnel being posted either to *Gruppe* VI S or to their respective *Ländergruppen*—i.e. Daufeldt to VI D, Mandl to VI E, etc. In addition, as mentioned above, *Dienststelle* 2000 and 3000 came under the control of VI E.

3. *Referat* VI F 3.

Referat VI F 3 was responsible for the preparations of special Intelligence material for the use of other *Ländergruppen* including secret inks and poisons. It had been the competent *Referat* for the production of sabotage materials but with the creation and development of *Gruppe* VI S at the end of 1943 its activity was subsequently greatly reduced.

The *Referat* had sub-divisions, details of which are not available, but it is known that the *Referat* controlled a camp at Friedenthal which dealt with storage of weapons, uniforms and equipment, and also had a small mechanical workshop whose chief function was liaison with VI F4. The workshop dealt with such matters as photographing pictures appearing in technical newspapers, magazines, and books and on occasion pictures of land maps. This section was under the control of *Angestellter* Rau assisted by SS-*Oschaf* Gebhardt and *Angestellter* Paul. Paul's special function being the preparation of plates for counterfeit purposes which were passed to VI F4.

VI F3 also controlled the *Forschungsinstitut* which was located in Marienbad. This Insitute was one of those which Krallert, *Gruppenleiter* VI G, intended to take over and develop for the *Amt* as a whole, but as it was constituted at the latter half of 1944 it represented a small section studying Allied industry, communications and transport for the purpose of preparing plans for sabotage. The staff was a composite one and included in addition to SD personnel, civilians and Army personnel. The Institute also worked in liaison with 'Sonderkommando DORA' and its subordinate functions.

The *Referat* was also responsible for the preparation of secret inks and poisons, the leading personalities in this type of work being SS-*Stubaf* (*sic*) Tauboeck and Dr Schamberger, a former chemist on the staff of I.G.Farben. Little is known of this section of the *Referat*.

4. *Referat* VI F 4.

This *Referat* was responsible for the production of all types of forged documents for the use of agents employed by other *Ländergruppen*. The forging of documents had been undertaken at an early stage in the history of VI F4, but had not been of very high standard, the chief personalities concerned in this work being Dr Langer, and *Angestellter* Rau, later of VI F3. In addition to the manufacture of forged documents, the *Referat* had also been concerned with the attempts at counterfeiting Bank of England notes (see Part A, Paragraph 3). It was not until late summer 1942 that attempts were being made to improve the work of the *Referat* and in particular the forging of Bank notes was undertaken on a much wider scale. The printing shop and workshop for the production of both forged documents and forged notes was set up in August 1942 at the concentration camp at Sachsenhausen. The personnel for this work was largely drawn from skilled technicians interned in other concentration camps in Germany, there being no restriction on the use of Jews.

a) The forging of documents:
Prior to the setting up of the workshop at Sachsenhausen the forging of documents on behalf of *Gruppe* VI F had been largely carried out by private firms having the confidence of the SD. The work thereafter was concentrated at Sachsenhausen under the supervision of SS-*Stubaf* Krüger. Among the documents reproduced were passports, birth certificates, pay books, Red Cross writing paper, identity cards of all kinds, British postage stamps, Dutch receipt stamps, and for propaganda purposes samples of the British Coronation stamp showing the Queen replaced by Stalin, and overprinted with the inscription 'Teheran 2.6.44.' Other British stamps also for propaganda purposes showed King George with a prominent Jewish nose. These stamps were distributed among all *Ländergruppen* of RSHA *Amt* VI, but their subsequent distribution was largely confined to the Iberian Peninsula and the Balkan States.

b) Counterfeit Money—'*Unternehmen* Bernhard':
The production of counterfeit Bank notes which was begun by *Referat* VI F4 was on a much more extended scale than the previous attempt in 1940. The enterprise went under the name of '*Unternehmen* Bernhard' and early in 1944 Kaltenbrunner himself developed a special interest in the matter, the other prominent personality being the notorious SS-*Stubaf* Schwendt alias Wendzio who operated in Italy.

By 1944 the monthly production of forged notes had risen to 650,000 of which some 40% were usable. The production of these notes led to a considerable amount of corruption among the personnel handling the money. By January 1945 the camp at Sachsenhausen was threatened by the advance of Allied troops [i.e. Russian troops] and was forced to evacuate to Austria where finally the camp was over-run, the notes being variously disposed of by burning or by dumping in neighbouring lakes.

The notes which had been produced prior to the evacuation of the camp were collected weekly by Krüger and were probably distributed to German Embassies and Legations abroad.

Postwar arrests:
The number of arrests among leading personnel of RSHA *Gruppe* VI F has been very small: the gap is a serious one, as it is especially desirable that the technical achievements and methods of the German Intelligence Services should be known.

Appended is a list of VI F technicians whose arrest should be notified as soon as effected so that detailed interrogation on technical matters can be arranged.

a) <u>Leading *Gruppe* VI F personalities:</u>

Oberstleutnant Boening	*Gruppenleiter*
SS-*Stubaf* Dörner	Former *Gruppenleiter*
SS-*Stubaf* Lassig	*Referent*, VI F3
SS-*Stubaf* Krüger	*Referent*, VI F4
SS-*Hstuf* Weideling	Administrative Officer
SS-*Stubaf* Faross	*Leiter*, Havel Institute
SS-*Stubaf* Siepen	Former *Leiter*, Havel Institute

b) <u>Technical Experts:</u>

Dr Tauboeck	Specialist on secret inks. Tauboeck should be considered a priority target.
Dr Schambacher	A specialist in chemical matters, formerly on the staff of I.G.Farben. Schamberger should be in a position to give full information on the use of secret inks and poisons.
Fräulein Issek	Trained agents in use of secret inks.
Professor Zapp	Head of the VI F school in micro-photography at Georg-Beer-Strasse No. 1, Dresden. Zapp is of special importance as he is reported to be the inventor of the latest German models of micro-dot cameras.
SS-*Oschaf* Voigt	Photography expert of VI F3.

The importance of these personalities concerned with microfilming is increased by the fact that it has been reliably reported that attempts were made by RSHA *Gruppe* VI F to reproduce *Amt* VI records by this means for concealment. While it is not believed that this attempt was successful but it is important to establish how far *Amt* VI had proceeded with such arrangements.

Sources:

SS-*Hstuf* Mandl	VI F/O
SS-*Stubaf* Naujocks	Former *Gruppenleiter*
Angestellter Grasshoff	VI F (H)
SS-*Hstuf* Schäffner	VI F (H)
SS-*Oschaf* Kronberger	VI F/O and *Dienststelle* 3000
SS-*Stubaf* Begus	*Leiter*, *Dienststelle* 3000
Angestellter Dr Langer	VI F 4

This report was issued by W.R.C.3a. on 9 November 1945.

Appendix I

Chart of Distribution of Work in
RSHA *Amt* VI from 1939–1945

	1939–1940	Early 1941	Mid 1941–42	1942–1944	1944–1945
VI A	Administration etc.	General Intelligence Tasks Abroad (? Sections)	Administration etc.	Administration etc.	Administration etc.
VI B	Technical Section	Europe Africa Near East (10 sections)	Slovakia Hungary Roumania Jugoslavia Greece Turkey Iraq, Iran Afghanistan	France Low Countries Switzerland Spain Portugal	France Low Countries Switzerland Spain Portugal Italy (from 1944)
VI C	Russia Baltic States Far East	Russia Far East (11 sections)	Russia Japan China Finland Baltic States	Russia Near East Far East (13 sections)	Russia Near East Far East (4 sections by mid 1944
VI D	Hungary Slovakia Jugoslavia Roumania Bulgaria Greece Turkey	Anglo-American sphere (9 sections)	Gt. Britain British Empire USA S. America Sweden Norway Denmark	Anglo-American sphere (3 sections)	Anglo-American sphere & Scandinavia (from summer 1944)
VI E	Italy Spain Portugal Central & Southern America	Ideological Enemies abroad (6 sections) (previously VI H)	France Low Countries Spain Portugal Italy Switzerland	Central-Europe Balkans Italy Scandinavia	Balkans
VI F	France Low Countries Switzerland Luxemburg	Technical Section	Technical Section	Technical Section	Technical Section
VI G	Gt. Britain British Empire USA Norway	-	Ideological Enemies abroad	Research (from August 1944)	Research
VI H	Ideological Enemies abroad	-	-	-	-

Appendix II

Organisation and Personnel of
RSHA *Gruppe* VI F, 1944–45

Gruppenleiter	-	*Oberstleutnant* Boening
Vertreter	-	SS-*Stubaf* Lassing
Administration	-	SS-*Hstuf* Weideling

<u>*Referat*</u>	VI F 1 }	<u>*Referent*</u>: SS-*Stubaf* Siepen
	} The Havel Institute	(until Dec 1944
	VI F 2 }	SS-*Stubaf* Faross
		(from Dec 1944)

<u>*Abteilung*</u>		
VI F (H) 1	Technical Preparations	SS-*Hstuf* Schäffner
		Fräulein Funk
VI F (H) 2	W/T Interception	SS-*Oschaf* Herb
		SS-*Ustuf* Wagner
VI F (H) 3	Codes, Cyphers	SS-*Ustuf* Arndt
		SS-*Oschaf* Ellmenreich
		Angestellter Voigt
		Angestellter Mersmann
VI F (H) 4	Security	SS-*Hstuf* Müller
VI F (H) 5	Organisation & Recruitment	SS-*Ostuf* Reinhardt
		SS-*Oschaf* Geisinger
		SS-*Ostuf* Weber
		SS-*Stuschaf* Wiese
		SS-*Hschaf* Weixel
		Angestellter Hagemeister
VI F (H) 6	Training	*Ltn.* Hänel
		Angestellter Paul
VI F (H) 7	Provision of Material	SS-*Ustuf* Simon
		SS-*Ostuf* Krüger

| | *Angestellter* Fröhlich |
| | *Angestellter* Lenner |

Funkleitstelle Berlin   SS-*Uschaf* Voss
                                 SS-*Stuschaf* Grasshoff
                                 SS-*Ustuf* John
                                 Angestellter Grumm

Wetterstelle Babelsberg   SS-*Oschaf* Krischker
                                 SS-*Oschaf* Klaus
                                 SS-*Hschaf* Menger
                                 Angestellter Timmering
                                 SS-*Schütze* Schumacher

Wetterstelle Nickersberg   SS-*Hstuf* Pfisterer
                                 SS-*Oschaf* Maushart
                                 SS-*Schaf* Hofmann
                                 SS-*Sturmmann* Knauff
                                 SS-*Sturmmann* Vollert
                                 SS-*Sturmmann* Eigenmann
                                 Angestellter Schultz
                                 Angestellter Berndt
                                 Polizei Oberwachtmeister Schuhmacher

Wetterstelle Marienbad   SS-*Oschaf* Ruster
                                 SS-*Oschaf* Beer
                                 SS-*Uschaf* Rhen
                                 SS-*Sturmmann* Reichelt
                                 SS-*Sturmmann* Mateschny
                                 Angestellter Florentin
                                 Angestellter Schultze

Wetterstelle Kirchsassen   SS-*Stuschaf* König
                                 SS-*Oschaf* Brantenstein
                                 SS-*Uschaf* Margolus
                                 SS-*Uschaf* Franz
                                 SS-*Rotf* Böhm
                                 SS-*Schütze* Arendt
                                 Angestellter Weiss
                                 Polizei Wachtmeister Erle

<u>*Wetterstelle* Bamberg</u>	SS-*Schaf* Rendel
	SS-*Uschaf* Mehlig
	Angestellter Hallschmidt
<u>*Wetterstelle* Gotenhafen</u>	SS-*Ustuf* Schönmehl
	SS-*Rotf* Könnecke
<u>Wetterstelle Oswitz</u>	Angestellter Brecht
<u>*Wetterstelle* Riga-Assern</u>	SS-*Ustuf* Schönmehl
	SS-*Oschaf* Rummel
	SS-*Sturmmann* Matejka
<u>*Wetterstelle* Wien</u>	SS-*Hschaf* Lucchesi
	SS-*Oschaf* Benz
	SS-*Oschaf* Heinrichs
	SS-*Uschaf* Schreiter
	SS-*Uschaf* Stiner
	Angestellter Bink
	Angestellter Eisenbraun
	Polizei Oberwachtmeister
	Muschack
<u>W/T Station Konstanz</u>	SS-*Hschaf* Hartenstein
<u>W/T Station Lehnitz</u>	*Leiter*: *Angestellter* Siegel (to June 1942)
	SS-*Hstuf* Dersch (to Oct 1943)
	SS-*Stubaf* Ilse (*sic* – to Apr 1945)
	SS-*Hstuf* Janetsky
	SS-*Hschaf* Pollmann
	SS-*Schaf* Odendahl
	Angestellter Teichert
	Angestellter Hochwald
	Fräulein Rottke

<u>*Referat* VI F 3</u>	Weapons. Secret Inks	SS-*Stubaf* Lassig (*Referent*)
	Poisons, Special Equipments	SS-*Hstuf* Faulhaber
	SS-*Oschaf* Hermann	
	SS-*Oschaf* Antwerber	
	Angestellter Schamberger	
	(secret inks)	

SS-*Stubaf* Tauboeck
(secret inks)
Forschungsinstitut, Marienbad   SS-*Hstuf* Wellhöner
SS-*Ustuf* Seifert
SS-*Hschaf* Flemming
SS-*Hschaf* Bill
SS-*Uschaf* Stoltze

Technical Section, Friedenthal   SS-*Hstuf* Nötenburg (-1944)
SS-*Stubaf* Kirchner (-1945)
SS-*Ustuf* Liebe
SS-*Oschaf* Gebhardt
SS-*Oschaf* Westphal
Angestellter Paul
Angestellter Rau

<u>*Referat*</u> VI F 4   Forged Document etc.   SS-*Stubaf* Krüger (Referent)
SS-*Ostuf* Thiele
SS-*Hschaf* Voigt
Angestellter Langer

KL Sachsenhausen   SS-*Ostuf* Hänsch
(Forged Bank Notes)   SS-*Hschaf* Werner
SS-*Oschaf* Janssen
SS-*Oschaf* Hoffmann
SS-*Oschaf* Heizmann
SS-*Uschaf* Bugelmann
SS-*Uschaf* Psoch
SS-*Uschaf* Gebhardt
SS-*Uschaf* Krämer
SS-*Uschaf* Wildfang

<u>*Referat*</u> VI F   *Beschäftungsstelle für*   SS-*Hstuf* Steckhan
Nachrichtengerät (BfN)

Appendix III

Alphabetical index of RSHA *Gruppe* VI F peronnel, 1939–1945

(Postwar arrested personnel are underlined)

Rank & Name	*Referat*	Remarks
SS-*Oschaf* Herbert Antwerber	VI F 3	
SS-*Schütze* von Arendt	VI F (H)	*Wetterstelle* Kirchsassen
SS-*Ustuf* Gerhard Arndt	VI F (H) 3	
Angestellter Heinrich Baltin	VI F 7	Nov. 1943
SS-*Schaf* Bauer	VI F	Nov. 1943
SS-*Sturmmann* Fritz Bauschewein	VI F (H)	
SS-*Oschaf* August Beer	VI F (H)	*Wetterstelle* Marienbad
SS-*Stubaf* Dr Otto <u>Begus</u>	VI F/O	*Leiter Dienstelle* 3000; later VI S arrested in Italy
Angestellter Erich Berndt	VI F (H)	*Wetterstelle* Nickersburg
SS-*Hstuf* Georg Best	VI F	1939–40
SS-*Oschaf* Eugen Bez	VI F (H)	*Wetterstelle* Wien
SS-*Hschaf* Bill	VI F 3	*Forschungsinstitut* Marienbad
Angestellter Bink	VI F (H)	*Wetterstelle* Wien
Angestellter Erich Bischoff	VI F	Nov. 1943
SS-*Rotf* Fritz Böhm	VI F	
SS-*Rotf* Harald Böhm	VI F	*Wetterstelle* Kirchsassen
SS-*Oschaf* Heinz Bobeth	VI F	Nov. 1943
Angestellter Bobzin	VI F	Nov. 1943
SS-*Ostuf* Konrad Bohnhoff	VI F 1	
Oberstleutnant Wilhelm Boening	VI F	*Gruppenleiter* from 1944
Angestellter Hans-Joachim Böttcher	VI F	Nov. 1943
SS-*Oschaf* Brantenstein	VI F (H)	*Wetterstelle* Kirchsassen
Angestellter Paul Brecht	VI F (H)	*Wetterstelle* Oswitz
Angestellter Viktor Bredick	VI F	Nov. 1943
SS-*Sturmmann* Paul Breitsch	VI F	
Angestellter Heinz Buch	VI F	Nov. 1943
SS-*Oschaf* Bugenheim	VI F	Nov 1943
SS-*Hstuf* Helmut Daufeldt	VI F/O	transferred to VI D3, late 1943
SS-*Rotf* Josef Dedy	VI F	Nov. 1943
SS-*Hstuf* Wilhelm Dersch	VI F (H)	*Leiter*, Lehnitz W/T School, 1944
Unteroffizier Dölle	VI F/O	*Dienststelle* 3000

SS-*Stubaf* Hermann Dörner	VI F	*Gruppenleiter*, 1941–44; later Ic officer on Eastern Front
SS-*Sturmmann* Eigenmann	VI F (H)	*Wetterstelle* Nickersberg
Angestellter Emil Eisenbraun	VI F (H)	*Wetterstelle* Wien
SS-*Oschaf* Herbert Ellmenreich	VI F (H) 3	
Polizei Wachtmeister Erle	VI F (H)	*Wetterstelle* Kirchsassen
SS-*Stubaf* Günther Faross	VI F (H)	*Leiter* from Dec. 1944
Angestellter Faul	VI F (H) 6	
SS-*Hstuf* Josef Faulhaber	VI F 3	
SS-*Sturmmann* Herbert Fehland	VI F (H)	W/T operator; to VI E, Wien
SS-*Stubaf* Dr Heinrich <u>Fesel</u>	VI F 7	*Leiter*, VI F Library 1942; later VI G; arrested British Zone
SS-*Hschaf* Flemming	VI F 3	*Forschungsinstitut* Marienbad
SS-*Uschaf* Karl Florentin	VI F (H)	*Wetterstelle* Marienbad
Angestellter Walter Floret	VI F	Nov. 1943
SS-*Sturmmann* Johannes Forster	VI F (H)	
SS-*Hschaf* Albert Fräfel	VI F	Nov. 1943
SS-*Uschaf* Erich Franz	VI F (H)	*Wetterstelle* Kirchsassen
SS-*Sturmmann* Emil Friedrich	VI F	Nov. 1943
Angestellter Anton Fröhlich	VI F (H) 7	
SS-*Stubaf* Rudolf Fuhrmann	VI F	*Gruppenleiter*, 1941
Kriminaldirektor Ernst Gans	VI F	*Referat Hauskapelle*, 1943
SS-*Uschaf* Heinz Gebhard	VI F 4	Sachsenhausen camp
SS-*Oschaf* Gebhardt	VI F 3	Friedenthal camp
Angestellter Kurt Gellert	VI F (H)	
SS-*Uschaf* Karl Gerber	VI F	Nov. 1943
SS-*Oschaf* Giesinger	VI F (H) 5	
Angestellter Johann Gottlieb	VI F (H)	
SS-*Stubaf* Joseph Gottlob	VI F 3	later sent to Portugal
SS-*Sturmmann* Hans <u>Grasshoff</u>	VI F (H)	*Funkleitstelle* Berlin; arrested
Angestellter Gustav Grumm	VI F (H)	*Funkleitstelle* Berlin
SS-*Sturmmann* Karl Haas	VI F (H)	
Ltn Haenel	VI F (H) 6	
SS-*Ostuf* Kurt Hansch	VI F 4	Sachsenhausen camp
Angestellter Hagenmeister	VI F (H) 5	
SS-*Sturmmann* Josef Hahn	VI F	Nov. 1943
Angestellter Hallschmidt	VI F (H)	*Wetterstelle* Bamberg
SS-*Sturmmann* Leo Harlander	VI F	Nov. 1943
SS-*Hschaf* Hartenstein	VI F (H)	W/T Station Konstanz
SS-*Oschaf* Heinrichs	VI F (H)	*Wetterstelle* Wien
SS-*Oschaf* Hans Herb	VI F (H) 2	
SS-*Oschaf* Herrmann	VI F 3	

SS-*Oschaf* Heizmann	VI F 4	Sachsenhausen camp
Angestellter Karl Hielscher	VI F (H)	
Angestellter Bruno Hinz	VI F	Nov. 1943
Angestellter Hochwald	VI F (H)	Lehnitz W/T School
SS-*Oschaf* Robert Hoffmann	VI F 4	Sachsenhausen camp
SS-*Schaf* Fritz Hofmann	VI F (H)	Wetterstelle Nickersburg
Angestellter Erich Hoppe	VI F	Nov. 1943
SS-*Schaf* Karl Ihms	VI F	Nov. 1943
SS-*Stubaf* Ilse (sic)	VI F (H)	*Leiter*, Lehnitz W/T School
SS-*Rotf* Willi Insel	VI F	
Angestellter Heinz Jablinski	VI F 1b	Nov. 1943
SS-*Schaf* Eduard Jäger	VI F	Nov. 1943
SS-*Hstuf* Herbert Janetzki	VI F (H)	Lehnitz W/T School
SS-*Oschaf* Jannsen	VI F 4	Sachsenhausen camp
SS-*Ostuf* Jansen	VI F 1	Nov. 1943
SS-*Ustuf* John	VI F (H)	*Funkleitstelle* Berlin
SS-*Ustuf* Hans-Joachim Kahle	VI F	Nov. 1943
Angestellter Gustav Kanz	VI F	Nov. 1943
Angestellter Kipka	VI F	Nov. 1943
SS-*Uschaf* Leonhard Kind	VI F	Nov. 1943
SS-*Stubaf* Kirchner (*sic*)	VI F 3	Friedenthal camp
SS-*Oschaf* Lorenz Klaus	VI F (H)	*Wetterstelle* Babelsberg
SS-*Sturmmann* Horst Knauf	VI F (H)	*Wetterstelle* Nickersberg
SS-*Hschaf* Kock	VI F	Nov. 1943; photographer
SS-*Stuschaf* König	VI F (H)	*Wetterstelle* Kirchsassen
SS-*Ostuf* Hermann Kohlhaas	VI F/O	later VI C representative in Greece
SS-*Rotf* Hans Könnecke	VI F (H)	*Wetterstelle* Gotenhafen
SS-*Uschaf* Krämer	VI F 4	Sachsenhausen camp
SS-*Hschaf* Karl Krischker	VI F (H)	*Wetterstelle* Babelsberg
SS-*Oschaf* Georg <u>Kronberger</u>	VI F/O	*Dienststelle* 3000; arrested
SS-*Ostuf* Krüger	VI F (H) 7	
Angestellter Artur Krüger	VI F (H)	
SS-*Stubaf* Bernhard Krüger	VI F 4	Referent
Angestellter Günther Kühne	VI F (H)	Nov. 1943
Angestellter Arthur Lachmann	VI F (H)	
SS-*Hstuf* August Langenbach	VI F/O	later at BdS Paris for VI B 4
Angestellter Dr Albert <u>Langer</u>	VI F 3	Cypher specialist;arrested Austria
SS-*Hstuf* Fritz Langlotz	VI F 7	VI F Library, 1942; transferred to VI A
SS-*Stubaf* Rudolf Lassig	VI F 3	*Referent*
Angestellter Oskar Lenner	VI F (H) 7	
SS-*Ostuf* Klaus von Lepel	VI F	Nov. 1943

SS-*Ustuf* Karl Liebe	VI F 3	
SS-*Hschaf* Walter Lucchesi	VI F (H)	*Wetterstelle* Wien
SS-*Hschaf* Paul <u>Ludewig</u>	VI F/O	*Dienststelle* 3000; arrested
SS-*Hstuf* Rupert <u>Mandl</u>	VI F/O	later with VI E; arrested
SS-*Uschaf* Erich Margolus	VI F/H	*Wetterstelle* Kirchsassen
SS-*Sturmmann* Armin Matejka	VI F (H)	*Wetterstelle* Riga-Assen
SS-*Sturmmann* Ernst Mateschny	VI F (H)	*Wetterstelle* Marienbad
SS-*Oschaf* Rudolf Maushart	VI F (H)	*Wetterstelle* Nickersberg
SS-*Uschaf* Erich Mehlig	VI F (H)	*Wetterstelle* Bamberg
SS-*Hschaf* Albert Menger	VI F (H)	Wetterstelle Babelsberg
Angestellter Mersman	VI F (H) 3	
SS-*Ostuf* Helmut Möck	VI F/O	
SS-*Hstuf* Müller	VI F (H) 4	
Pol. Oberwachtmeister Muschack	VI F (H)	*Wetterstelle* Wien
SS-*Stubaf* Alfred <u>Naujocks</u>	VI F	*Gruppenleiter* 1939–40; arrested
SS-*Ostuf* Franz Nebenfuhr	VI F/O	*Dienststelle* 3000
SS-*Hstuf* Kurt Nötenburg	VI F 3	
SS-*Rotf* Walter Nolte	VI F (H)	
SS-*Schaf* Odendahl	VI F (H)	later VI B2
Angestellter Johannes Ohlsen	VI F (H)	
Angestellter Herbert Paul	VI F 3	
SS-*Ostuf* Peters	VI F (H)	
SS-*Hstuf* Alfred Pfisterer	VI F (H)	*Wetterstelle* Nickersburg
SS-*Hschaf* Pollmann	VI F (H)	Lehnitz W/T School; later VI B2
SS-*Sturmmann* Alfred Pörner	VI F (H)	
SS-*Sturmmann* Willi Preuss	VI F (H)	
SS-*Uschaf* Psoch	VI F 4	Sachsenhausen camp
Angestellter Abdul Rahmann	VI F 7	Nov. 1943
Angestellter Artur <u>Rau</u>	VI F 3	arrested US Zone
SS-*Stubaf* Walter <u>Rauff</u>	VI F	*Gruppenleiter*, 1941; later EK Tunis; *Sipo*/SD commander in Milan where arrested
SS-*Hstuf* Walter Redlin	VI F (H)	
SS-*Schaf* Walter Rendel	VI F (H)	*Wetterstelle* Bamberg
SS-*Schaf* Ernst Rehmann	VI F (H)	
SS-*Sturmmann* Josef Reichelt	VI F (H)	*Wetterstelle* Marienbad
SS-*Ostuf* Bruno Reinhardt	VI F (H) 5	
SS-*Hstuf* Walter Ried	VI F/O	*Leiter, Dienststelle* 2000, Greece
Angestellter Heinz Ruddigkeit	VI F	Nov. 1943
SS-*Oschaf* Willi Rummel	VI F (H)	*Wetterstelle* Riga-Assen
SS-*Sturmmann* Franz Rusch	VI F	Nov. 1943
SS-*Oschaf* Heinz-Eugen Ruster	VI F (H)	*Wetterstelle* Marienbad

SS-*Schaf* Walter Schäfer	VI F	Nov. 1943
SS-*Hstuf* Dr Hans Schäffner	VI F (H) 1	arrested
Angestellter Fritz Schamberger	VI F 3	Chemical Specialist
SS-*Ustuf* Hans Schiller	VI F	Nov. 1943
SS-*Ustuf* Dr Fred Schmitthenner	VI F	W/T Section, 1941-42
SS-*Oschaf* Hugo Schneider	VI F	Nov. 1943
SS-*Ustuf* Emil Schönmehl	VI F (H)	*Wetterstelle* Gotenhafen
Angestellter Schoff	VI F	Nov. 1943
SS-*Uschaf* Heinz Schreiter	VI F (H)	*Wetterstelle* Wien
Angestellter Heinz Schremmer	VI F	Nov. 1943
SS-*Hschaf* Eugen Schuler	VI F	Nov. 1943
Angestellter Karl Schultz	VI F (H)	*Wetterstelle* Babelsberg
Angestellter Hermann Schultze	VI F (H)	*Wetterstelle* Marienbad
SS-*Hstuf* Emil Schulz	VI F/O	later VI B 4
SS-*Schütze* Albert Schumacher	VI F	*Wetterstelle* Babelsberg
SS-*Ustuf* Hermann Schwarzenbacher	VI F/O	*Leiter* VI D; arrested Austria
SS-*Stubaf* Fritz Schwend	VI F 4	connected to *Unternehmen* Bernhard
SS-*Ustuf* Seifert	VI F 3	*Forschungsinstitut* Marienbad
SS-*Sturmmann* Friedrich Sieg	VI F (H)	
Angestellter Georg Siegel	VI F (H)	*Leiter*, Lehnitz W/T School
SS-*Stubaf* Peter Siepen	VI F (H)	*Referent*, 1942–44
SS-*Ustuf* Egon Simon	VI F (H) 7	
SS-*Hstuf* Rudolf Steckmann	VI F	*Referent* VI F (BfN)
SS-*Rotf* Wilhelm Stefan	VI F (H)	
SS-*Uschaf* Willi Stiner	VI F (H)	*Wetterstelle* Wien
SS-*Uschaf* Stoltze	VI F 3	*Forschungsinstitut* Marienbad
Angestellter Dr Fritz Tauboeck	VI F 3	Secret Inks specialist
SS-*Hstuf* Taussig	VI F	Nov. 1943
Angestellter Teichert	VI F (H)	Lehnitz W/T School
SS-*Uschaf* Ernst Then	VI F (H)	*Wetterstelle* Marienbad
SS-*Ustuf* Henry Thiele	VI F 4	
Angestellter Georg Timmering	VI F (H)	*Wetterstelle* Marienbad
SS-*Hschaf* Hans Voigt	VI F (H) 3	Photography expert
SS-*Sturmmann* Vollert	VI F (H)	*Wetterstelle* Nickersberg
SS-*Uschaf* Henry Voss	VI F (H)	*Funkleitstelle* Berlin
SS-*Ustuf* Dr Georg Wagner	VI F (H) 2	*Betriebsleiter*
SS-*Oschaf* Helmut Waller	VI F (H)	
SS-*Hstuf* Oswald Wandhoff	VI F	Balkans Section, 1943; transfer to SD-*Ast* Maastricht
SS-*Ostuf* Weber	VI F (H) 5	
SS-*Hstuf* Erich Weideling	VI F	Administrative Officer
Angestellter Weiss	VI F (H)	*Wetterstelle* Kirchsassen

SS-*Hschaf* Weixel	VI F (H) 5	
SS-*Hstuf* Karl-Georg Wellhöner	VI F 3	*Forschungsinstitut* Marienbad
SS-*Oschaf* Albert Wengelnick	VI F	Nov. 1943
SS-*Hschaf* Kurt Werner	VI F 4	Sachsenhausen camp
SS-*Oschaf* Max Werner	VI F	Cypher specialist, W/T section, 1943
SS-*Oschaf* Josef Westphal	VI F 3	
SS-*Stuschaf* Wiese	VI F (H) 5	
SS-*Uschaf* Wildfang	VI F 4	Sachsenhausen camp
Angestellter Willsch	VI F/O	*Dienststelle* 3000, Greece
Angestellter Dr Hans Woletz	VI F	Nov. 1943
SS-*Hschaf* Walter Wolf	VI F/O	Dienststelle 3000, Greece
SS-*Rotf* Herbert Wyschewski	VI F (H)	
Angestellter Alfons Zach	VI F (H)	later W/T instruction with VI B2 at BdS Paris
SS-*Oschaf* Rudolf Zapp		VI F
Angestellter Professor Zapp	VI F 3	Head of Micro-Dot Photography School in Dresden
Angestellter Theodor Zbitek	VI F	transferred to II D1, Nov. 1943
Angestellter Walter Ziedrich	VI F	Nov. 1943

Note

* The National Archives, Kew, KV 3/183: Situation Report No. 11, RSHA VI F.

11

Liquidation Report No. 12:
Amt VI of the RSHA—*Gruppe* VI G

1. The reasons for the founding of RSHA *Gruppe* VI G.

Gruppe VI G is the youngest of *Gruppen* under RSHA *Amt* VI, being created as recently as October 1943. Briefly, it was designed to serve *Amt* VI as a research section and was responsible for providing the *Ländergruppen* of the *Amt* with information concerning foreign countries on geographical matters and on leading personalities. To achieve this end, the *Gruppe* sought to coordinate existing sources of information on these matters and extend them where necessary and thus become a central reference library for RSHA *Amt* VI. This conception of centralisation is the most important feature of the *Gruppe*; the chief weakness in *Amt* VI records prior to the founding of the *Gruppe* was that each *Gruppe* maintained its own reference library and card indices, a weakness which was emphasised by the territorial nature of the division of work between the *Gruppen*. Such territorial divisions are arbitrary, as inevitably the work of one *Gruppe* would overlap into that of another, and is a system ill-conceived to cope with situations created, for example, by the advance of the Russian armies, the concern of *Gruppe* VI C, into the Balkan States, the concern of *Gruppe* VI E.

2. RSHA *Gruppe* VI C and its relations to RSHA *Amt* VII.

Prior to the creation of RSHA *Gruppe* VI G no central reference library of records was maintained for RSHA *Amt* VI; there existed however RSHA *Amt* VII which had been set up since the earliest days of the RSHA to serve as a central library and archives for the whole of the RSHA. Owing to the opposition of the *Amtschefs* however, who wished to maintain their own records within the *Ämter*, *Amt* VII did not develop along the lines envisaged. Nevertheless Schellenberg considered in the early days of his services as *Amtschef* VI making use of *Amt* VII for *Amt* VI purposes, but abandoned the idea by 1942. It was *Gruppe* VI G which eventually fulfilled the functions which might have been centralised in *Amt* VII. The reasons for this abandonment of *Amt* VII in favour of the new *Gruppe* VI G are dealt with in the Liquidation Report (No. 23) on RSHA *Amt* VII.

3. The overt nature of RSHA *Gruppe* VI G.

It is important however to appreciate that *Gruppe* VI G was in fact very largely a coordination of existing research institutions many of which have no real intelligence significance in themselves, speaking in terms of 'Secret Service'. These institutions were overt, and one of the concerns of the *Gruppe* was that they should remain overt but that their information should be readily available to RSHA *Amt* VI, and that their policy and lines of research should be dictated by the wants and desires of the *Amt*. One effect of this is that a detailed study of RSHA *Gruppe* VI G leads imperceptibly from covert to overt organisations; for the purpose of this publication the institutions which figure prominently in the story of VI G will be merely referred to with the purpose of showing where they fit into the general scheme, and no attempt will be made to analyse these institutions in detail.

4. The *Gruppenleiter*.

The history and development of RSHA *Gruppe* VI G is bound up inextricably with the personality of its founder, SS-*Stubaf* Wilfried Krallert. Krallert was a Viennese student of history and geography, and was associated with the Nazi Party since 1933. From his earliest connections with the NSDAP he became one of its historians and was connected with the Intelligence Service of the *Militärstandarte* Vienna as early as 1934. He became a member of the SD-*Hauptamt* in the same year and acted as a research expert on their behalf. He became director of the '*Publikationsstelle* Wien' in 1938, and at the same time a member of '*Blockstelle* Wien', the original format created by RSHA *Amt* VI in the Balkans, later to become the present RSHA *Gruppe* VI E. After a period of service on the Eastern Front, also in a research capacity, he returned to the RSHA in 1943 and was appointed *Gruppenleiter* VI G, which position he held until his arrest in May 1945.

Krallert himself was a man of considerable intelligence and, as will be seen from the above brief account of his career, eminently suited to the task given to him; and allied to his erudition was a conception of the organisation on an intelligence service which might have made him much more dangerous had he been given the chance earlier in his career to organise the resources of RSHA *Amt* VI and coordinate its intelligence material to the best advantage. Even in the short history of VI G, Krallert was successful to an astonishing degree in organising on practical lines the many institutions which were placed under his command and in making the internal organisation of VI G function smoothly. This success was of course only half way. The real value or otherwise of *Gruppe* VI G lay in whether the information it centralised and classified was used to good purpose by the other *Ländergruppen*. RSHA *Gruppe* VI G was in no sense an executive *Gruppe*.

5. Krallert's dual function—the *Kuratorium*.
In addition to his appointment as *Gruppenleiter* VI G, Krallert in the summer of 1943 was also appointed (as the representative of RSHA *Amt* VI) joint director of the *Kuratorium für Volksstum und Landesforschung*, together with Ehlich of RSHA *Amt* III. It is sufficient for present purposes to say that the *Kuratorium* was a centralisation of existing research organisations in the geographical and ethnological field servicing all the state departments, including the Foreign Office, the NSDAP, the Ministry of the Interior, etc., and was responsible among other things for the provision of maps covering the areas in which the various institutions specialised. The *Kuratorium* controlled some eighteen institutes, including the *Publikationsstelle* Wien, of which Krallert himself had been director since 1938. There was no direct link between RSHA *Amt* VI and the *Kuratorium* and the institutes under its control, and though their researches could be made availabel to *Amt* VI, the institutes were in no sense engaged in secret service work. The close liaison between RSHA *Amt* VI and the *Kuratorium* was in the person of Krallert himself.

6. The scope of RSHA VI G and the institutes under its control.
When *Gruppe* VI G was formed it naturally took over the only research institute then servicing RSHA *Amt* VI, the *Wannseeinstitut* (or the *Institut für die Erförschung der Sowjet Union*), which had been under the control of *Amt* VI since 1939. In addition the *Forschungsstelle* Orient had been formed at Tübingen in 1942 under SS-*Stubaf* Lorch, previously of RSHA *Gruppe* VI C, while the *Ostasieninstitut* under Professor Donath, functioning since 1939, was also assimilated. In addition to these existing institutes, several new ones were formed to serve the particular interests of RSHA *Amt* VI. These institutes with their sphere of interest are listed below:

Name	Director	Subject of Research
Institut zur Erforschung der Sowjetunion (formerly *Wannseeinstitut*), 1935	Dr Achmeteli, until Prof Dr Hans Koch took over, begin 1945	The USSR
Forschungsdienst Ost,	SS-*Hstuf Dipl.ing.* Lieben	Industrial research on the USSR
Informationsstelle für Wirtschaft und Technik, 1943		
Forschungsstelle Orient, 1942	Dr Walter Lorch	The Near East
Weltkartenstelle der	SS-*Stubaf* Dr Wilfried	Production of maps for intelligence overprints
Reichsstiftung für Länderkunde, 1944	Krallert	
Ostasieninstitut, 1939	Prof Dr Donath	The Far East
Nordamerikainstitut, 1943	Prof Dr Willmes	Canada and the USA

Arbeitsgemeinschaft *Grossbritannien*, 1944	Prof Dr Lehmann	British Empire
Arbeitsgemeinschaft Turkestan, 1943	SS-*Hstuf* Dr	Turkestan Olzscha
Wirtschaftswissen- schaftliche Institut Ost-Donau, 1940 (?)	Prof Dr Seraphim	Scandinavia and Finland

The personnel employed in these institutes were of course research specialists and not intelligence officers. A high degree of security was effected by camouflaging the connection between the Institutes and RSHA *Amt* VI, which in all communications with the Institutes was refered to as the '*Reichstiftung für Länderkunde*'.

7. The value of RSHA *Gruppe* VI G to *Amt* VI.
There is little indication that the other *Gruppen* of RSHA *Amt* VI availed themselves of the research facilities with VI G placed at their disposal with the important exception of *Gruppe* VI C, and to a lesser degree, *Gruppe* VI S. It will be noted from the list given above that out of the nine institutes under *Gruppe* VI G control, no fewer than five dealt with the Near East and Far East. From its very geographical position it is only natural that Germany was in a position to specialise on these territories rather than on western Europe and the western hemisphere. It will be seen that as early as 1940 the RSHA controlled the *Wannseeinstitut*, which remained of considerable value to *Gruppe* VI C. This close liaison was increased with the creation of RSHA *Gruppe* VI G, and there is no reason to doubt the value of the research of VI G to VI C. So far there has been no opportunity of assessing the worth of the *Nordamerikainstitut* or of the *Gross-Britannien Institut* to *Gruppe* VI D, but it is not likely to have been great; on one occasion only were maps issued to VI D; these maps were of the coast of Venezuela.

RSHA *Gruppe* VI S however did derive benefit from VI G research and records. In general the material provided was in the form of maps of the areas in which VI S had planned operations, though at Appendix II below, is shown a copy of a circular issued by Krallert to the appropriate institutes as a result of a request by *Gruppe* VI S. The circular is of interest as it shows the extent to which VI G could have been of practical value to the *Ländergruppen* had it been created at an earlier date, and also reveals Krallert's conception of the proper functioning of his *Gruppe*.

8. The organisation of RSHA *Gruppe* VI G.
The organisation of the *Gruppe* is a simple one; there were six *Referate* functioning, with an additional two ready to function. These *Referate* with their *Referent* are listed in Appendix I.

9. Main sources.
There exists a most comprehensive interrogation report on Krallert himself, 1 SC/CSDIC/SD 26 issued by No. 1 Sub-Centre, CSDIC, Austria, dated 17th August 1945,

and distributed by the War Room under reference PF.602,288.[1] This report gives full details of the institutes under VI G and those under the *Kuratorium*, and shows in diagrammatical form the liaison which existed between the various institutes themselves, and in particular the functional links between RSHA *Gruppe* VI C and *Gruppe* VI G. This publication represents no more than a summarised version of that report to which reference should be made for those aspects and ramifications of VI G which are not of primary intelligence interest. The publication also incorporates the assessments of VI G which have been given by leading personalities such as Schellenberg, Sandberger and Höttl, and it is issued primarily in order that wider distribution can be given to it than was possible in the case of the Krallert report.

There is also a B.Doc. 9000 preliminary report on Dr Walter Lorch of the *Forschungsstelle* Orient, reference 3962/9000 issued on 19th October 1945.

This report was issued by W.R.C.3A. on 21 October 1945

Appendix I

Organisation of RSHA *Gruppe* VI G

Gruppenleiter   -   SS-*Stubaf* Dr Wilfried Krallert

Referat VI G 1   *Führungsreferat*
Function: organisation and administration. *Kuratorium für Volkstum und Ländesforschung*
Referent: -

Referat VI G 2   *Schriftumsreferat*
Function: this *Referat* was responsible for the policy governing the management of the libraries and institutes and for the supply of all information published in book form to the other *Gruppen* of RSHA *Amt* VI. It kept close liaison with *Gruppe* III C, the *Prüfungskommission* of the NSDAP, the Propaganda Ministry, the *Gesellschaft für Dokumentation*, and with central libraries.
Referent : SS-*Ostuf* Karasek.

Referat VI G 3   *Landkartenreferat*
Function: this *Referat* was responsible for the supply of maps to the other *Gruppen* of RSHA *Amt* VI and to the institutes. It kept close liaison with the map depots of the IKH, the *Reichsamt für Landesaufnahme*, and the *Preussische Staatsbibliothek*.
Referent: SS-*Ustuf* Paulsen.

Referat VI G 4   *Presserefeerat*
Function: This *Referat* was responsible for the organisation of the evaluation activities of the Press section and the coordination of their translation service.
Referent: SS-*Ostuf* Dr von Hehn

Referat VI G 5   *Karteirefeerat*
Function: this *Referat* was responsible for the uniform organisation of the card indices of the institutes and for liaison with the central card indices of the RSHA and of other organisations.
Referent: -

Referat VI G 6   *Militärisches Referat*
Function: this *Referat* advised the institutes on the production of special maps, such as ethnological or administrative maps, for the use of military formations.
Referent: Ltn Dr Stitz.

Referat VI G 7   *Wirtschaftsrefereat*
Function: this *Referat*, which had not started to function, was to have been responsible for liaison with economic research institutes, such as the *Weltwirtschaftliche Institut* at Kiel and Hamburg, and with RSHA *Gruppe* VI Wi/T.
Referent: -

Referat VI G 8   *Wissenschaftsreferat*
Function: this *Referat*, which also had not started to function, was to have taken charge of the editing of the bigger publications of the institutes, and of liaison with scholastic societies, and to have studied the cooperation between research institutes and political, administrative and military agencies abroad.
Referent: SS-*Stubaf* Dr Fesel.

Appendix II

(A translation of instructions given by SS-*Stubaf* Krallert to Institutes controlled by RSHA *Gruppe* VI G, concerning a request for information on areas suitable for guerilla warfare received from RSHA VI S.)

Der Chef der Sicherheitspolizei und des SD
VI G Tgb. Nr. 45 gRs 763344   Berlin-Schmargendorf
        Postfach 6
        den 11.März 1945

Subject: Planning material for guerilla warfare behind enemy lines.

Behind all fronts, particularly in the East, but also in Italy and in the West, resistance movements and rebellions have spring up on their own initiative. For a long time it has been attempted to gain influence on these movements, to coordinate their activities, and finally to direct and extend them so as to provide decisive assistance and relief to out battle on all front.

This plan can only be carried out successfully if considerable own forces are made available for the purpose and if these forces are fully trained and advised by experts. The making available of these forces as well as the planning and directions of guerilla warfare is the task of VI S and *Mil* D.

It is expected that the institutes of *Gruppe* VI G will afford all possible help as regards advice and training. It is therefore requested that the following problems be studied immediately and that short and precise notes be prepared on the following questions.

1. What nations or racial groups, or what political groups, can be considered suitable for the creation or extension of resistance movements and guerilla warfare?
2. What historic examples of a similar nature tend to show a special inclination to guerilla warfare on the part of the various nations?
3. What political or ideological promises, slogans or offers might be particularly effective in the light of historical experience?
4. For what type of resistance do the individual groups appear to be particularly well suited (open rebellion, passive resistance, etc.)?
5. Which areas and regions appear to be best suited in the light of previous experience?
6. Is it possible or impossible to coordinate resistance movements of different origins (e.g. Polish and Ukrainian, or Bulgarian, Serb and Greek)?
7. What are the fundamental rules of behaviour and treatment which the German forces intended for the task must learn for their contact with the people concerned?

I request that these questions be considered immediately and the results laid down in notes. I request furthermore that all other relevant problems which may appear be subjected to a detailed study and the results forwarded to this HQ, so that the problem can also be considered in other sectors.

For the sake of security I request you to call in additional help only after the most careful consideration, and in any case to consult outside collaborators on part-questions only.

In view of the extreme urgency of the matter I would request you to give this question priority ovall all other work, and if necessary to submit preliminary reports to this HQ. It is also intended to discuss the whole problem shortly at a conference, for which I request you to prepare all available material.

Finally I would like to emphasise that voluminous memoranda are not required, but only a short summary of the most important principles and simple and fundamental directives for practical application. Only the collation of the material and the speed of production of these reports, and not their layout and style, is important.

(signed) KRALLERT
SS-*Sturmbannführer und*
Gruppenleiter VI G.

Distribution:
Institut zur Erforschung der Sowjetunion (attention Major Prof Dr Koch);
Publikationsstelle Berlin (attention *Staatsarchivdirektor* Dr Papritz);
Publikationsstelle Wien (attention SS-*Ustuf* Dr Ronneberger);
Publikationsstelle West (attention *Staatsarchivrat* Dr Kothe);
VI *Zentralbüro* (attention *Oberfeldrichter* Dr Schön).

Appendix III

Alphabetical index of RSHA *Gruppe* VI G personnel

Note: This list includes RSHA *Amt* VI officers and the heads of VI G institutes, but not research personnel of the institute. Postwar arrested personnel are underlined.

Rank and Name	Remarks
Prof. Michael Achmeteli	*Institut zur Erforschung der Sowjetunion*
Prof. Donath	*Ostasien Institut*
SS-*Stubaf* Dr Heinrich Fesel	*Referent*, VI G 8 since end of 1944
SS-*Hstuf* Heinz Fenner	VI G since early 1944; with *Publikationsstelle* Wien from mid 1944
SS-*Ustuf* Johann Gusek	VI G 1 from mid 1944
SS-*Hstuf* Ernst Hachmeister	VI G 1 from end 1943
SS-*Ostuf* Dr Herbert Karasek	*Referent*, VI G 8 since mid 1944; earlier *Publikationsstelle* Wien
Major Prof. Dr Koch	*Institut zur Erforschung der Sowjetunion* from beginning of 1945
SS-*Stubaf* Dr Wilfried Krallert	*Gruppenleiter* VI G; arrested Austria
SS-*Hstuf* Krugler	*Forschungsstelle* Orient; arrested French Zone
SS-*Hstuf* Fritz Langlotz	*Forschungsstelle* Orient from end 1944; also in RSHA VI *Kult*, 1945

Prof. Lehmann	*Arbeitsgemeinschaft Gross-Britannien*
SS-*Hstuf* Hans-Henning von Lieben	*Forschungsdienst Ost*
SS-*Hstuf* Walter <u>Lorch</u>	*Forschungsstelle* Orient; arrested French Zone
Dr Mortensen	Expert on Spain and Portugal; with VI G from end of 1944
SS-*Hstuf* Olzscha	*Arbeitsgemeinschaft* Turkestan
SS-*Hstuf* Dr Peter Paulsen	*Referent*, VI G 2 since mid 1943
Prof. Seraphim	*Wirtschaftswissenschaftliche Institut Ober-Donau*
Ltn Dr Stitz	*Referent*, VI G 6 since beginning of 1945
SS-*Hstuf* Dr Gerhard <u>Teich</u>	*Institut für Grenz- und Auslandsstudien*, mid 1943, then with RSHA VI C 1; arrested British Zone
Prof. Willmes	*Nordamerikain Institut.*

Notes:

* The National Archives, Kew, KV 3/115: Liquidation Report No. 12, RSHA VI G.
1 The National Archives, Kew, WO 208/5228: lengthy interrogation report of Dr Wilfried Krallert, 1SC/CSDIC/SD 26 dated 17 August 1945.

12

RSHA *Gruppe* VI S

Gruppenleiter   -   SS-*Staf* Otto Skorzeny

Under SHAEF, Counter Intelligence War Room did produce a "War Room Publication" on the SS-*Jagdverbände* under the title "Operational Units of *Amt* VI S", dated 9 April 1945. It was based on information received from captured men of the Brandenburg Division. The report contains a number of errors and inaccuracies which were soon overtaken by the arrest of Otto Skorzeny and his adjutant, Karl Radl. CIWR did not produce a further report on RSHA *Gruppe* VI S. In its place, they were evidently satisfied by the initial interrogation reports of Skorzeny and Radl produced by the United States Twelfth Army:

1. Interrogation Report CIR 4/6 dated 31 May 1945 by Otto Skorzeny, regarding the Werwolf organization.
2. Intermediate Interrogation Report (IIR) dated 4 June 1945 by Karl Radl, Skorzeny's adjutant, regarding the activities of RSHA VI S, SS-*Jagdverbände* and RSHA *Mil Amt* D.

These two reports were followed by Consolidated Interrogation Report (CIR) No. 4 dated 22 July 1945, produced by US Forces European Theater (USFET) Interrogation Center. This much longer report came from joint interrogations of Skorzeny and Radl on the activities of RSHA VI S.

SECRET

HEADQUARTERS TWELFTH ARMY GROUP

Mobile Field Interrogation Unit No. 4

Counter Intelligence Report

on

WERWOLF

Source: SS-*Ostubaf* Otto Skorzeny, Chief of *Amt* VI S
and *Mil Amt* D, RSHA.

Interrogation Report CIR 4/6 dated 31 May 1945

Preamble

This is the first of a series of tactical reports on Skorzeny, who surrendered to American forces in Annaberg [Austria] on 16 May 1945, and arrived at MFIU No. 4 on 19 May 1945. Skorzeny's interrogation is not completed, and he still may be holding back vital facts.

An Annex of personalities is attached.

CONTENTS

1.   Skorzeny's introduction to WERWOLF
2.   Meetings with Prützmann
3.   Organization
4.   Communications
5.   Supplies
6.   Skorzeny's participation
Annex: Personalities

1. Skorzeny's introduction to WERWOLF.
In September 1944, Skorzeny received a written communication from Himmler's adjutant, Brandt, to the effect that SS-*Gruppenführer* (*sic*) Prützmann was carrying out special orders (*Sonderauftrag*) by Himmler, and that Skorzeny was to assist him.

2. Meetings with Prützmann.

A few weeks later, Prützmann called on Skorzeny in Friedenthal for the purpose of explaining the WERWOLF scheme to him, and formulating the basis for their collaboration.

Altogether, Skorzeny saw Prützmann four to five times between September 1944 and late January 1945. The meetings took place partly at Friedenthal, partly in Prützmann's headquarters, a special train in a brickyard near Königs Wusterhausen [just outside Berlin]. They met once in the Adlon Hotel in Berlin. Prützmann's staff attended a weapons demonstration in November or December 1944 put on by the *Führungsstab* of Skorzeny's SS-*Jagdverbände* on the Potsdam training grounds. Skorzeny did not attend any of Prützmann's staff meetings, but met some of his associates individually (see Personalities).

During one of their meetings Prützmann told Skorzeny that his last refuge would be the Lübeck Bay, as he knew the area well.

3. Organization.

The plan, as outlined by Prützmann, was as follows. He had been ordered by Himmler to build up an organization to work behind enemy lines. It was to be called WERWOLF after the hero of a Loens novel about the Thirty Years' War [Herman Löns, *Der Wehrwolf. Eine Bauernchronik*, published in 1910]. He planned to visit all Gaue to confer with with *Gauleiters*, HSSPFs and other Party leaders on recruiting and organizational problems. One man per *Gau* (preferably a suitable *Wehrmacht* officer, as Prützmann wanted a military core around which to build his essentially civilian organization) was to be charged with the recruiting.

Prützmann also intended to confer with industrialists on the possibility of planting saboteurs in factories which could not be evacuated.

WERWOLF personnel was to operate in *Gruppen* of three or six men directed by a *Gruppenführer*. The number of *Gruppen* to be organized depended on the time available. Prützmann did not state any minimum numbers. He told Skorzeny in October or November 1944, however, that 50–70 *Gruppenführer* from the Rheinland were ready for training. At that time five to six *Gruppen* were operating in East Prussia.

During their second meeting in October 1944, Prützmann told Skorzeny that the organization had operated with some success in East Prussia. He reported difficulties in the Rheinland, however, mainly because the HSSPF could not get along with the *Gauleiter*.

4. Communications.

The plans called for the establishment of an efficient communications net, allowing for all WERWOLF activities to be centrally controlled by *Dienststelle* Prützmann. Targets were to be numbered to simplify the issuing of order by radio. Prützmann told Skorzeny about an underground telephone net in the Rheinland, which was partly out of use. He intended to request the services of a telephone specialist from the *Reichspost Ministerium* to operate it for WERWOLF purposes.

5. Supplies.

Each *Gruppe* was to receive rations for 60 days. Each man was to have two small-arms and 15–20 lbs [6–9 kg] of explosives. Prützmann intended to install underground depots. Skorzeny told him, this could be done in forest areas like East Prussia. He advised against it in inhabited areas, as the danger of betrayal was too great.

6. Skorzeny's participation.

Skorzeny was asked to help train the organization. He states that he offered only limited assistance, as the activation of his SS-*Jagdverbände* was still in progress, forcing him to look after his own interests first.

He offered to train only the *Gruppenführer*. They in turn were to instruct their men.

He was unable to supply Prützmann with rations, and advised him to get explosives directly from the factories (WASAG, Dynamit A.G., Nobel A.G.) and from Army stores. In order to eliminate transportation problems he suggested that as far as possible supplies be drawn near the places where they were to be used. He promised his help in supplying the organization with fuses and captured enemy weapons. (He estimates that 100–150 Stens guns were released by the SS-*Jagdverbände Führungsstab*.).

In October 1944 after his first conference with Prützmann the following steps were taken:

a) He told his I-b (Supply Officer) SS-*Hstuf* Gerhardt (see Personalities) to cooperate with Prützmann's I-b (see Personalities) as much as possible, avoiding extravagant promises. Under no circumstances were *Jagdverband* interests to be jeopardized. In case of special requests (special fuses, weapons with silencers) Skorzeny's consent was to be asked. In no case were more than 10–20% of *Jagdverbände* stocks to be handed out.

b) A teletype message went to all *Mil D Leitstellen*, that Prützmann's representatives were to be assigned as far as possible without jeopardizing own interests. Each *Leitstelle* was to lend one instructor to the WERWOLF organization. A limited amount of equipment was to be released upon request. Skorzeny states that all supply matters were handled by *Mil D/T*, Major Ehrmann in charge.

c) A teletype message was sent to all SS-*Jagdverbände* announcing the arrival of Prützmann's representatives who were to be given limited assistance. No equipment was to be released, as all supply matters were handled centrally through the *Führungsstab*. Each *Jagdverband* was to furnish one instructor to the Prützmann organization. Under no circumstances was their own training to be impeded. All difficulties were to be reported to Friedenthal.

Skorzeny states that reports arrived from all SS-*Jagdverbände* complaining about exorbitant demands by the WERWOLF representatives. His orders were to turn them down.

Skorzeny gives the following details on the participation of his units in the WERWOLF training program:

a) He estimates that 300–400 WERWOLF recruits (10% women) were trained at the *Kampfschule* of SS-*Jagdverband Nord-West* in Neustrelitz between October 1944 and March 1945. The courses lasted five to eight days, and included instruction in shooting, sabotage without equipment, and fundamental facts about explosives. Prützmann complained on several occasions that the training was insufficient, and requested that more details be covered. Skorzeny told him that within the given time limit this was impossible.

b) SS-*Jagdverband Süd-West* sent two instructors on temporary detachment to conduct WERWOLF training in a HJ camp north of Stuttgart.

c) SS-*Jagdverband Süd-Ost* did not participate, as the WERWOLF liaison man could not get along with its Commanding Officer, SS-*Ostubaf* Benesch.

d) He does not know of any participation by SS-*Jagdverband Ost*. The unit was destroyed near Hohensalza in January 1945.

e) FAK 202 or 203, *Hauptmann* Kirn in charge (attached to Army Group *Mitte*) detached one or two instructors to train WERWOLF recruits in Silesia.

Annex

Personalities

A. *Dienststelle* Prützmann.

Schweiger (Schwager?), *Major der Schupo*, I-b, *Dienststelle* Prützmann. Last seen in special train in brick yard near Königswusterhausen (Jan. 1945).

Karl Siebel, SA-*Brigadeführer*, *Dienststelle* Prützmann. Last seen in special train in brickyard near Königswusterhausen (Jan. 1945). Appeared to be liaison man to the SA.

Karl Tschierschky, SS-*Standartenführer*, Dienststelle Prützmann. Last seen as for Schweiger and Siebel.

B. SS-*Jagdverbände*.

Otto Begus, SS-*Stubaf*, Italian Company, SS-*Jagdverband Süd-West*. He was liaison man to Prince Borchese and Italian swimmers.

Arno Besekow, SS-*Hstuf*, in charge of foreign agents, *Führungsstab* SS-*Jagdverbände*. Last seen in barracks at Hof (Bavaria), 1945. Assumed to have gone to Carinthia.

Claus von Bremen, SS-*Ustuf*, SS-*Jagdverband Ost*. Last in Friedenthal, March 1945;

KIA in Austria, April 1945.

(fnu) Gerhardt, SS-*Hstuf*, I-b, *Führungsstab* SS-*Jagdverbände*. Last seen in Friedenthal, early 1945. Believed to have gone into combat on the Oder front before Berlin.

(fnu) Henn, SS-*Ustuf*, explosives expert and teacher for SS-*Jagdverbände Nord-West* in Neustrelitz. Last seen in Neustrelitz during mid March 1945.

Heinrich Hoyer, SS-*Hstuf*, Commander—SS-*Jagdverband Nord-West*. Last seen in Prague hospital, March 1945.

Friedrich Knolle, SS-*Staf*, Commander—*Kampfschule* Heinrichsburg (in Yugoslavia); later with *Dienststelle* Prützmann. Last seen in Berlin during September 1944.

Fräulein Kopfheiser, Secretary, *Führungsstab* SS-*Jagdverbände*. Last seen in Puch near Salzburg, 3 May 1945, intending to make her way back to Reith im Winkel, Germany.

Frau Kovalsky, receptionist, *Führungsstab* SS-*Jagdverbände*. Last seen in Berlin during early April 1945.

Fräulein Elisabeth Krüger, secretary, *Führungsstab* SS-*Jagdverbände*. Last seen in Puch near Salzburg, 3 May 1945, intending to make her way back to Reith im Winkel, Germany.

Fräulein Marie Krüger, secretary, *Führungsstab* SS-*Jagdverbände*. Last seen in Puch near Salzburg, 3 May 1945, intending to make her way back to Reith im Winkel, Germany.

Ronald Lochner, SS-*Ustuf*, SS-*Jagdverbände*, killed in the Ardennes offensive, near Malmedy, 20 December 1944.

Bernt von Mühlen, SS-*Ustuf*, SS-*Jagdverband Ost*. Last seen with Army Group Schörner near Breslau, April 1945.

Gerhard Ostafel, SS-*Ustuf*, SS-*Jagdverband Ost*. Missing since the battle in Hohensalza, January 1945.

Hans Peter, SS-*Ustuf*, *Führer*, 2nd Company, SS-*Jagdverband Mitte*. Last seen in combat in the Warthegau against the Russians, January 1945.

Adrian von Foelkersam, SS-*Hstuf*, Chief of Staff, *Führungsstab*, SS-*Jagdverbände*. Killed 20 Jan 1945 near Hohensalza.

Heinrich Winter, SS-*Hstuf*, Commander—4th Company (School), SS-*Jagdverband Nord-West*. Last seen in Neustrelitz in March 1945; assumed to be in Austria.

Details of seven others not listed as not relevant to RSHA VI S, Werwolf, or SS-*Jagdverbände*.

HEADQUARTERS 12TH ARMY GROUP
INTERROGATION CENTER
APO 655

INTERMEDIATE INTERROGATION REPORT (IIR)

Prisoner: SS-*Stubaf* Karl Radl   Date: 4 June 1945

1. References: None.
2. Reasons for Report: Report contains information believed to be of immediate interest. Final report will be issued later.
3. Report.

Introduction

This is an intermediate report as SS-*Stubaf* Radl, Karl, RSHA *Amt* VI S/2, adjutant of SS-*Ostubaf* Otto Skorzeny. He and Skorzeny surrendered to US troops at Annaberg on 16 May 1945 and arrived at 12th A Gp Interrogation Center on 19 May.

Radl is a lawyer by profession. He joined the Austrian Nazi Party in 1931 and the SS in 1934. Before coming to *Amt* VI S in April 1943, he had worked for the *Gestapo* and *Grenzpolizei* in minor functions.

As Skorzeny's aide he coordinated his chief's different activities loyally and efficiently. He now emphasizes his cooperative attitude, but it is believed that he is still withholding certain facts.

Contents

a. Organizations under Skorzeny.
(1) RSHA *Amt* VI S
(2) SS-*Jagdverbände*
(3) RSHA *Mil Amt* D

b. Sources of Resistance.
(1) *Dienststelle* Prützmann
(2) *Schutzkorps* Alpenland

c. Operations in Foreign Countries.
(1) *Dienststelle* 2000
(2) SS-*Fallschirmjäger* Btl. 600
(3) Agents
(4) Plots

d.   Technical Developments.
(1)   Sabotage
(2)   Special Weapons

a. Organizations under SS-*Ostubaf* Skorzeny.

(1) RSHA *Amt* VI S.
Amt VI S consisted of the *Führungsstab* (Headquarters Staff), six *Abteilungen* and four *Referate*.

a. *Führungsstab*:

Abteilung Chief	SS-*Ostubaf* Otto Skorzeny	Only alias known to Radl is Dr Woll which Skorzeny used during the abduction of Admiral Horthy
	Fräulein Grete Kopfheise	Skorzeny's secretary, decorated with *Kriegsverdienstkreuz* II. *Klasse*
	SS-*Hstuf* Karl Radl	Skorzeny's adjutant
	SS-*Hstuf* von Foelkersam	Chief of Staff; dead
I a	SS-*Hstuf* Werner Hunke	Arrested by CIC
I b	SS-*Hstuf* Reinhard Gerhardt	Supply Officer; formerly *Abwehr* II
I c	SS-*Ostuf* Hans Graalfs	Intelligence Officer
II a	SS-*Ostuf* Wilhelm Gallent	Officers' records; went to 6.SS-Pz. Army
II b	SS-*Hstuf* Weiss	Sent to SS-*Jagd-verband Süd-Ost*
II b	SS-*Ostuf* Arnold Steinlein	EM records; has one leg amputated; he was discharged
III	SS-*Stubaf* Dr Wolfgang Pinder	Judge Advocate; came in Jan. 1945; transfer to 6.SS-Pz.Army in Feb–March 1945; has been arrested by CIC
IV a	SS-*Hstuf* Herbert Urbanneck	Quatermaster; transfer to 6.SS-Pz. Army
	SS-*Ustuf* Ernst Schenkel	Under Urbanneck; has one foot amputated; discharged
IV b	SS-*Hstuf* Dr Wilhelm Wetz	Medical Officer; went home to Oberdonau
	SS-*Hstuf* Heinrich Slama	Medical Officer; went home to Oberdonau
V	SS-*Hstuf* Mahlow	Transport Officer; believed by Radl to have been captured at Teisendorf, Bavaria

	SS-*Ustuf* Köster	Left at Teisendorf
VI	SS-*Staf* Otto Bayer	Special services officer; came from SSFHA; mid Dec 1944 to 6.SS-Pz. Army
	SS-*Ustuf* Konrad Kutschke	
	SS-*Hstuf* Alfred Kallweit	*Leiter*, W/T Station; discharged at Hof
	SS-*Ustuf* Hein	W/T Station; discharged at Hof
	SS-*Hschaf* Gottfried Bitterwolf	Mail clerk

b. RSHA VI S 1, Administration:

SS-*Hstuf* Erwin Schmiel	Went to Hof, joined *Schutzkorps* Alpenland (SKA)
SS-*Hstuf* Hugo Podlech	Went to Hof, where discharged; then at Teisendorf
SS-*Ostuf* Ulrich Breitenfeld	Stayed in Hof
SS-*Ustuf* Max Windhövel	Disappeared from Hof
Fräulein Wolf	Secretary; discharged at Hof
Fräulein Beirich	Secretary; discharged at Hof

c. RSHA VI S 2

SS-*Hstuf* Karl Radl	Skorzeny's adjutant

d. RSHA VI S 3. Supervision of Training Schools
Seehof, Kurhof and Heinrichsburg

SS-*Hstuf* Herbert Bramfeldt	Joined SKA
SS-*Hschaf* Pahlow	Joined SKA
Fräulein Kaulpach	Secretary

e. RSHA VI S 4. Direction of Agent Operations

SS-*Hstuf* Arno Besekow	Joined SKA
SS-*Ostuf* Werner Meyer	Joined SKA
SS-*Ostuf* Franz Nebenführ	Formerly in Greece; wanted to join his relatives in Austria
SS-*Hschaf* Heinecke	Joined SKA
SS-*Stuschaf* Heinz Stöck	Stayed in Hof with his family
Fräulein Annemarie Krüger	} Secretaries; the
Fräulein Liselotte Krüger	} Krüger sisters and
Fräulein Gisela Bölling	} Frl. Bölling were released at Hof or Puch (near Munich)

f. RSHA VI S Locations.

Besides its headquarters at Friedenthal, near Oranienburg, RSHA VI S had one room and an ante-room (No. 113) at the RSHA offices at Berkaerstrasse 32, Berlin. The secretary was *Frau* Gerda Kowalsky, formerly with RSHA *Amt* VI A. She had not been decorated [with a medal] and was released in February 1945. RSHA VI S had no Tarnbüro (cover address) in Berlin, but agents were seen in the *Jagdverband Kartenstelle* in Kalckreuthstrasse.

g. Movements in 1945.
With the exception of Radl and Gerhardt, the *Führungsstab* went to the area of Hof during the period February–March 1945. From Hof they moved to Teisendorf where the members left for either the SKA or 6.SS-Pz.Army. Radio communications between Friedenthal and the *Führungsstab* at Hof and Teisendorf was maintained until 15 or 20 April 1945.

On 1 February 1945 Skorzeny, Gallent, Slama, Pinder, Hunke, Fucker, all of SS-*Jagdverband Mitte*, and *Fallschirm Jäger* Bn 600, and most of SS-*Jagdverband Nordwest*, went to fight the Russians at Schwedt/Oder. About the middle of March 1945, Skorzeny, Slama and Gallent returned to Friedenthal and continued to Teisendorf and Linz, where they established a *Streifendienst* (patrol service, in this case to prevent straggling) at the request of *Gauleiter* Eigruber.

Radl left Friedenthal to meet Skorzeny in Linz the middle of April 1945. They left Linz on 1 or 2 May and went to a headquarters train at Puch, which left the same night for Pongau, where they remained for two days. They then travelled to Klammstein, remaining there two or three days, then to Radstadt for two or three days, and finally to Annaberg and then surrendered to US troops.

h. Reports.
According to Radl, whose function was to supervise office routine and maintain a semblance of order, no regular reports were issued by RSHA *Amt* IV S to higher authorities. When a successful operation had been concluded, Skorzeny sent a written report to Schellenberg. These reports were frequently prepared by Radl as Skorzeny did not like paperwork. Radl remembers having prepared reports for Schellenberg on the following matters:

(a) *Unternehmen* Theodor. See TITO Operation, Para III 4 below.
(b) Discussions between Skorzeny and General Steinmann, of the *Reichsluftfahrtministerium* who was a specialist on electricity generating stations. The discussions concerned power installations in Russia and the possibility of attacking them with one-man suicide weapons; the discussions took place in the latter half of 1944.
(c) KdK organization and activities. Discussions between the *Kriegsmarine* and Hellmers in March 1944.
(d) Operation against Marshall Tito's HQ. According to Radl, RSHA VI S took no part in this operation, and the report to Schellenberg embodied strong objections to the suggestion that this was one of Amt VI S failures. The date was June 1944.

(e) <u>Official trip to return Mussolini's diary to him</u> in June and July 1944.

(f) <u>Conference with *Abwehr* II at Innsbruck</u> in August 1944.

(g) <u>Resistance movements in the Baltics</u> in August 1944.

(h) <u>Combat reports from Schwedt/Oder</u> issued every two or three days from February to March 1945.

(i) <u>Release of SS-*Ostuf* Fucker from the *Oder Korps.*</u> This was a complicated exchange of correspondence between Kaltenbrunner Schellenberg, and Skorzeny, beginning in April 1945.

(j) <u>The Petain episode.</u> Discussed in Para III 4 below.

(k) <u>Plan of RSHA *Amt* VI S 4's work.</u> Prepared by Besekow. Included a map giving the locations of agents; Radl believes it was burned. Date: January 1944.

(l) <u>Bi-monthly reports.</u> These were to be sent to Schellenberg but only one was issued in November 1944.

(2) SS-*Jagdverbände*:

When Skorzeny came to RSHA VI S in April 1943 there was a company of *Waffen-*SS at Oranienburg. This company participated in the liberation of Mussolini on 12 September 1943. It returned to Friedenthal in October 1943 and became *Jäger* Battalion 502. The unit strength was increased to 200 men, all of German nationality. The Commanding Officer was SS-*Hstuf* Jaeckert. In the summer of 1944, Jaeckert was transferred to the front and was succeeded for a few weeks by SS-*Hstuf* Hoyer. Hoyer was followed by SS-*Ostuf* Fucker. At this time various *Streifkorps*, which had been part of the Brandenburg Division before its reorganization, came to Friedenthal and formed the SS-*Jagdverbände*. There were five SS-*Jagdverbände*: *Mitte* (formerly *Jäger* Battalion 502), *Nord West*, *Süd West*, *Ost* and *Süd Ost*.

a. <u>SS-*Jagdverband Mitte.*</u> Formed out of *Jäger* Battalion 502.

Commander	SS-*Ostuf* Karl Fucker	Came in Nov. 1944. Went with 150 men to Hochkönig area in mid April 1945
I a	SS-*Hstuf* Werner Hunke	Arrested by CIC.
I b	SS-*Hstuf* Reinhard Gerhardt	
I c	SS-*Ostuf* Hans Graalfs	

Since SS-*Jagdverband Mitte* was stationed at Friedenthal it utilized the staff of the *Führungsstab* for administrative purposes, in order to economize on personnel.

Sondereinsatz Abteilung: For administrative purposes the *Sondereinsatz Abteilung*, headed by SS-*Ostuf* Klinkert, was formed within SS-*Jagdverband Mitte*. As every German soldier had to belong to a replacement unit, the *Sondereinsatz Abteilung* served that purpose for SS men assigned to KdK, KG 200, and *Kampfschwimmer* schools at Diana Bad, Vienna, and Bad Tölz. It carried the soldiers' records and was responsible for administrative matters arising out of injury or death.

b. SS-Jagdverband Nord-West.

Strength was about 120 men, although Battalion strength had been envisaged. SS-*Hstuf* Hoyer was Commanding Officer. He was wounded on the Oder front in February 1945 and was succeeded by SS-*Hstuf* Dethier. This SS-*Jagdverband* remained at Neustrelitz until April 1945 when it was evacuated to the area of Hof. Eighty to ninety members of SS-*Jagdverband* went to the Oder front.

SS-*Ustuf* Eberhardt Straub	Adjutant, wounded on the Oder front in Feb. 1945
SS-*Ustuf* Karl Egner	Supply and Courts Martial officer; went to Hof
SS-*Hstuf* Dr Emil Görns	Medical Officer, joined SS-Jg. NW in Nov. 1944; later went with SS-Jg. *Mitte* to Austria
SS-*Ustuf* Gerhard Hackler	Platoon commander, KIA on Oder front.
SS-*Ostuf* Heinz Manns	KIA on Oder front, possibly with SS-Jgd. *Mitte*.

A platoon of 20 to 25 Flemmings under SS-*Ustuf* Bachot was part of SS-*Jagdverband Nord-West*. This platoon was at Giessen between January and March 1945.

Kampfschule Neustrelitz: according to Radl this was the name of the sabotage training school at Neustrelitz.

Commander:	SS-*Hstuf* Heinrich Winter	From Brandenburg Div; Commander and sabotage instructor; went to Austria
	SS-*Ostuf* Gustav Steinmetz	Ordnance, Transport and Supplies; poss. went to Hof
	Fräulein Kottscheng	Winter's secretary; released March 1945

c. SS-Jagdverband Süd West.

Radl states that he has little knowledge of this unit. SS-*Hstuf* Hans Gerlach continued to be Commanding Officer when his *Streifkorps Süd*-Frankreich became SS-*Jagdverband Süd-West*. There was a *Kampfschule* at Tiefenthal under SS-*Hstuf* Heinz Deharde, who is believed to have been killed on the Western front. Under him was SS-*Ostuf* Walter Eisenmenger, who went to 6.SS-Pz.Army in mid April 1945 [in Austria]. SS-*Ustuf* Dr Welle, who undertook a special mission in Holland, was also on the staff of SS-*Jagdverband Süd-West*.

The strength of the SS-*Jagdverband Süd-West* was 80 to 90 men, who were all of German nationality, according to Radl.

SS-*Jagdverband Süd-West* maintained W/T communication with Friedenthal until the middle of April 1945.

d. SS-Jagdverband Ost.

Strength approx. 250 men, half of the German and the rest Balts, Russians, and a few Ukrainians. Headquarters was normally at Hohensalza; there was no *Kampfschule*.

While at Hohensalza radio communication was maintained with Friedenthal at an irregular rate. Sometimes were two messages a day, sometimes there were none for several days.

Commander	SS-*Hstuf* Adrian von Foelkersam	In Hohensalza when SS-Jgd. was overrun by the Russians in Jan 1945: KIA
	SS-*Stubaf* Eberhard Heinze	Deputy Cmder; KIA Jan 1945
	SS-*Stubaf* Wolfram Heinze	brother, he escaped from Hohensalza
	SS-*Ostuf* Gerhard Ostafel	KIA
	SS-*Ustuf* Claus von Bremen	Escaped from Hohensalza to Friedenthal; in early Mar. 1945 hospitalized for exposure.

Early in February 1945 SS-*Stubaf* Alexanders Auch succeeded von Foelkersam as Commanding Officer of SS-*Jagdverband Ost*. He was formerly with the Brandenburg Division and had come to Friedenthal in January 1945. SS-*Jagdverband Ost* was re-organized under him, this time to a strength of 80 to 100 men. In April 1945 SS-*Jagdverband Ost* left Friedenthal in the direction of Troppau. The following staff went with Auch:

I a   SS-*Ustuf* Rinne
I b   SS-*Ustuf* Bernt zur Mühlen
I c   SS-*Ustuf* Tietjen

Jagd Einsatz 'Balticum' was a part of SS-*Jagdverband Ost* and was headed by SS-*Stubaf* Dr Manfred Pechau. Pechau first made contact with Besekow in 1941-42 when both were with BdS Riga [*Einsatzgruppe* A]. He went to the Seehof Sabotage School and was transferred to RSHA VI S4 to supervise a group of Baltic agents. In September 1944 he and his group, believed to number about 30 agents, were assigned to SS-*Jagdverband Ost* to operate in the Baltic. *Jagd Einsatz* 'Balticum' was discontinued in February 1945, and a number of its agents went to Sweden. Radl heard that these agents established contact with the British Intelligence Service in Sweden which, he believes, was operating against the Russians in the Baltic States. After the dissolution of *Jagd Einsatz* 'Balticum', Pechau and about 20 members went to the Eastern Front; a few of the Estonian agents went to Copenhagen, purpose unknown.

e. SS-*Jagdverband Süd-Ost.*
The strength was approx. 500 men. It was located at Krems/Donau near Niederdonau, Austria. When Vienna fell to the Russians they moved to the Lower Enns area:

Commander:	SS-*Ostubaf* Benesch	Formerly leader of *Streifkorps* Croatia; Brandenberg Div.
I a	SS-*Hstuf* Emil Steiner	
	SS-*Hstuf* Weiss	Formerly II B on *Führungsstab*; before with Brandenburg Div
	SS-*Ostuf* Kirschner	Earlier, Brandenburg Div.
	SS-*Hstuf* Erich Müller	Responsible for activities in Roumania
	SS-*Ustuf* Rowohl	Earlier, Brandenburg Div; now responsible for activities in Hungary
	SS-*Ostuf* Schlau	Earlier, Streifkorps in Croatia; responsible for activities in Croatia.

(3) RSHA *Mil Amt* D.

a. Headquarters:

In August 1944 *Abwehr* II was incorporated into RSHA *Amt* VI as *Mil Amt* D. *Mil Amt* D under Skorzeny. The Commanding Officer was Major i.G. Naumann, succeeded in March 1945 by Major Roland Loos. Until mid March 1945 the Headquarters was at Birkenwerder, about 15 kms [10 miles] south of Friedenthal. It was moved to Bad Elster and later to Upper Bavaria, possibly to the Traunstein area. There were about 20 officers in *Mil Amt* D. Radl remembers the following:

Hauptmann Eisenberg	HQ Commandant; earlier *Abwehr* II
Hauptmann Lormis	Responsible for Spain, Portugal, Italy, and North Africa
Hauptmann Schönaich	Responsible for France, Belgium, Holland, Denmark (and Norway?)
Oberltn Gambke	Responsible for the Baltic States, Russia, Ukraine, and Finland
Oberltn Ferrid	Responsible for the Balkans
Major Menger	Administration
Hauptmann Zierjaks	Officers' Records/Personnel
Oberltn Hittner	Other Ranks' Records/Personnel
Ltn Paulus	*Luftwaffe* Liaison
Major Ehrmann	*Leiter* II-T; technical HQ at Brandenburg
Ltn Schultze	II-T, technical expert

b. Liaison.

When the RSHA took over the *Abwehr* early in 1944, the *Wehrmacht Führungsstab* relinquished control of the *Mil Amt*, and the FAKs were directly subordinated to RSHA *Amt* VI Mil. The *Führungsstab* insisted, however, that trained military personnel be included in the organization to make purely military information immediately available to the armies in the field. As a liaison agency *Mil Amt* F was formed, headed by *Oberst* Buntrock, former I-c of Army Group Wiessner in the Crimea and Balkans.

c. *Abteilung* II-T.

Marguerre, Mauritius and Major Poser, all of II-T, were dismissed in July 1944 or earlier.

d. *Leitstelle* II-WEST *für Frontaufklärung.*

Headquarters was at Bad Orb at one time but changed frequently. The Commanding Officer was *Hauptmann* Fred Hellmers. Other officers in *Leitstelle* II West were:

Hauptmann Urmann	Transferred to *Leitestelle* II West from *Amt Mil Amt* D
Ltn Frank	Maintained liaison between Darnand and Doriot on the side and Hellmers and RSHA VI S on the other.

e. *Leitstelle* II-OST *für Frontaufklärung.*

The Commanding Officer was *Oberstleutnant* Ernst zur Eickern, a close friend of Freytag von Loringhoven. Radl has never heard of *Sonderlager* Luckenwalde and has no further information about *Leitstelle* II-*Ost* other than that *Oberstleutnant* zur Eickern went to Birkenwerder after Friedenthal was evacuated.

f. *Leitstelle* II-SÜD-OST *für Frontaufklärung.*

The Headquarters was in the old Austrian *Heeres Ministerium* (War Ministry) in Vienna. When the Russians approached the *Leitstelle* was planning to evacuate to Upper Bavaria. Personnel:

Oberstleutnant Flechner	Commanding Officer.
Major Koch	Recently retired.
Leutnant Piff	Radio instructor
Korv./Kapitän Alfons Weiss	

Weiss was in charge of Donau Schutz, a cover name for an intelligence gathering agency aiding in II-missions (sabotage). He was suspected of collaboration with an Allied agent, known as GAZDA, and was later transferred back to the Navy.

b. Sources of Resistance.

(1) *Dienststelle* Prützmann.

Radl's acquaintance with SS-*Gruf* Prützmann and *Dienststelle* Prützmann is based on the following contacts:

a. In June or July 1944, he met Prützmann for the first time in Italy, when the latter was deputy of SS-*Ogruf* Wolff, the HSSPF of Lake Garda.

b. In November 1944, he met Prützmann in the office of SS-*Ostubaf* Malz, adjutant of Kaltenbrunner, at 102 Wilhelmsstrasse, Berlin.

c. In December 1944, following a chance meeting in Kaltenbrunner's outer office, Prützmann and Skorzeny had an impromptu conference, subject unknown. Sometime in December 1944, Skorzeny drove to see Prützmann, who had his HQ in a train in Königs Wusterhausen.

d. In the winter of 1944–45, Skorzeny and Prützmann went to a demonstration of Nipolit explosives held on the Potsdam training grounds. Radl thought the demonstration had been arranged by SS-*Hstuf* Gerhardt I-b of *Führungsstab*, RSHA VI S. Gerhardt, who went with a combat team to the Oder on 15 April 1945, may have information about the supply of sabotage material that he sent to Prützmann.

e. In December 1944, Prützmann had lent Skorzeny four or five SS guards for Friedenthal. A member of Prützmann's staff, SS-*Stubaf* Horst Müller-West, telephoned Radl about their return.

Radl knew (superficially) the following members of Prützmann's staff:

SS-*Staf* Karl Tschierschky
SA-*Brif* Siebel
SS-*Stubaf* Horst Müller-West

SS-*Staf* Tschierschky succeeded SS-*Ostubaf* Gräfe of RSHA *Amt* VI C who was killed in a motor accident. Tschierschky was transferred to *Dienststelle* Prützmann in autumn 1944. He attended the second meeting in Kaltenbrunner's office, mentioned above. Suggestions had been made to transfer Tschierschky from VI C to VI S, but Skorzeny refused considering him him an intriguer.

Radl said that Prützmann, after he became HSSPF, dealt directly with Himmler instead of Kaltenbrunner. This fact, and possibly the personal character or Prützmann, described as 'ice cold', caused difficulties between Kaltenbrunner and Prützmann in March 1945.

(2) *Schutzkorps* Alpenland (SKA).

After the Allies crossed the Rhine, Skorzeny conceived a plan to take five or six groups of people into the Austrian Alps. Each group was to number 400 to 500 men and was to reinforce the *Wehrmacht* at important passes. The groups were consequently organized as the SKA and supplied with weapons, ammunition, plastic and ordinary *Wehrmacht* high explosives, and food. At the end April 1945, however, Skorzeny gave written orders to each of the groups that SKA was to be dissolved.

The text of the order (as far as Radl remembers it) was as follows:

a. All fighting against the Western Allies will cease immediately.

b. Orders of the Anglo-American occupation forces will be obeyed.

c. Members of the SKA are to remain quietly with the local population and will render all possible help, including agricultural work.
d. They will maintain order among the inhabitants, protect them from marauders, and prevent the formation of Bolshevik groups.
e. They will rid the area of non-Austrian elements (foreign workers and diplomats) to ease the food situation.
f. Personnel is to remain at Skorzeny's disposal for further orders.

There were six groups in the SKA. One was under Fucker in the Hochkönig area; one under Girg in the Lofer (Steinberge) area; one under Schuhmann in the Lofer area; one under Benesch in the Ennstal area; one, including Besekow, Winter and Meyer, in the Radstätten Tauern area between Salzburg and Kärnten; and one additional group, leader unknown.

In compliance with Skorzeny's orders, the weapons and ammunition which were at stores at the SKA HQ at Annaberg, were handed over to the local mayor.

c. Operations in Foreign Countries.

(1) *Dienststelle* 2000:
This organization originally belonged to RSHA *Amt* VI E, but was transferred to RSHA *Amt* VI S when VI E failed to furnish the necessary supplies (spring 1944). The Commanding Officer was Dr Begus who later went to Italy to train VI S agents in Verona; from there Begus maintained liaison with *Amt* VI S through the BdS Verona teletype. SS-*Ostuf* Franz Nebenführ of RSHA *Amt* VI S4 succeeded Begus as Commanding Officer. He later joined the SKA but wanted to go to Niederdonau.

(2) *Fallschirmjäger* Bn 600:
This unit under the SS-*Führungshauptamt* (SSFHA) was commanded by SS-*Hstuf* Kurt Rybka in Croatia, and later by SS-*Hstuf* Siegfried Milius in Poland.

In September 1944 it took part in the operation 'Horthy' after which it joined the SS-*Jagdverbände*. Its designation was changed from *Fallschirmjäger* Bn 500 to 600 and it was re-organized in Neustrelitz. On 1 February 1945 the unit was committed at Schwedt/Oder and early in April 1945 it was transferred to an SS Pz Korps under SS-*Ogruf* Steiner. SS-*Hstuf* Milius was decorated with the '*Deutsches Kreuz in Gold*' and was promoted to SS-*Sturmbannführer*. With this transfer all connection between this unit, and RSHA VI S and the SS-*Jagdverbände* ceased.

(3) Agents:
Radl said he know no agents other than NEBEL. He gave the following men as sources of information on that subject:

Dr Begus	for Balkans
SS-*Hstuf* Besekow	
SS-*Hstuf* Bramfeldt	
SS-*Ostuf* Meyer	
Hauptmann Schönaich	for South America

According to Radl, NEBEL alias NEUMANN, had been the only *Amt* VI S agent who passed through the Allied lines and had returned. In the winter of 1943–44, NEBEL had come from RSHA *Amt* VI B to *Amt* VI S, having worked previously for the SD in Strasbourg. *Amt* VI S sent him to Seehof School in The Hague to pass on the reliability of trainees. RSHA *Amt* VI requested him in the summer of 1944 and sent him on a counter-sabotage mission to Montbeliard [France]. He went to Paris for *Amt* VI S4 in September 1944 to organize a group of 'French nationalists' into a resistance movement. He was not heard of again until early 1945 when he returned to Friedenthal and reported that he had failed.

Upon his return he was promoted to SS-*Obersturmführer* and given the EK I, according to Radl, because he had been in the service for a long time and had risked his life twice crossing the Allied lines.

Nebel returned to France in February 1945 on orders of Besekow. At that time the I-c of an SS-*Korps* reported that Nebel was a traitor but Besekow made an investigation and found this to be untrue. Radl thought that Nebel had originally been a refugee from Switzerland and he does not know what happened to him.

Radl knew of only two agents sent to the United States, both of whom were caught immediately. They were William Colepaugh, an American citizen, and Gimpel who had worked for the SD in Spain. RSHA *Amt* VI D trained them in sabotage and W/T operations at A-*Schule West*, The Hague, and sent them out in the spring of 1944.

RSHA *Amt* VI D asked Skorzeny to take Jacob Collins into *Amt* VI S. He was sent to the school in The Hague to assist in the training of Colepaugh. Collins, a British subject, had been a prisoner of war and had previously worked for the *Abwehr*. His conduct at the school was unsatisfactory, however, and he was returned to *Amt* VI D.

Radl stated that India was too large a territory to be handled by RSHA *Amt* VI S. He mentioned that Franz Mayr was an *Amt* VI C agent in Persia. Two agents from *Sonderlehrgang* 'Oranienburg', who had been to an *Amt* VI F W/T school, *Obergefreiters* Harbers and Piwonka, joined Mayr in Persia.

(4) Plots.

a. Projected Tito kidnapping.

The code name for this operation was '*Unternehmen* Theodor'. It started in January 1944, led by SS-*Hstuf* Rupert Mandl, who belonged to *Amt* VI E. He was an Austrian and an expert on the Balkans. He had under him four to five Germans, including SS-*Ustuf* Karl Stüwe, and was in contact with two groups of Croat gangs comprising 300 men, led by Durecic and Djukic.

The undertaking was supervised by RSHA *Amt* VI S4. The plan was that Tito should first be captured by a small unit of Croat signal troops and then to be passed on to a larger unit. Mandl was supplied with arms, money, and W/T sets by RSHA *Amt* VI F and VI S. The Tito operation was a failure because of communication difficulties, Partisan activity, and internal strife among the Croats. It was abandoned in the winter of 1944, but Mandl continued working as a political informant for *Amt* VI E in the Balkans.

There is no connection between this operation and the one directed against Tito's headquarters in June 1944 in which Major Benesch, at that time in *Streifkorps* Croatia of the Brandenburg Division and SS-*Ustuf* Rybka of *Fallschirm* Bn 500, took part.

b. Projected Petain kidnapping.
At the end of 1943 Ribbentrop decided that he wanted Petain's headquarters to be in Paris. As Petain refused to leave Vichy, Skorzeny was instructed by Himmler and Kaltenbrunner to move the Marshal. He took 50 men from the SS-*Führungshauptamt* and 25 to 30 men from *Jägerbattalion* 502 to Vichy, planning to move Petain to Paris in a private car, by force if necessary. After eight or ten days, however, Ribbentrop announced that the matter had been settled through diplomatic channels and Skorzeny returned from Vichy.

There are discrepancies in the accounts of this projected operation by Radl and Skorzeny, and both failed to remember that Nebel, see c.(3) above, was a member of the party.

c. Projected assassination of General Eisenhower.
Radl said that the report of an assassination plot against General Eisenhower was unfounded. He knows that many rumours were circulating among German troops during the Ardennes offensive. The rumour, he maintained, is evidence of the general tendency to exaggerate the importance of Skorzeny and his functions.

D. Technical Developments.

(1) Sabotage.
Radl's knowledge of the technical aspects of sabotage is superficial. He suggested that technical details be obtained from Skorzeny, who is an engineer, and Gerhardt, who was the Supply Officer on the *Führungsstab*.

a. *Hell- und Dunkel Zünder*:
Radl described this as a fuse which functions when light is removed. It was designed by Dr Albert Widmann of the *Kriminal Technisches Institut* (KTI), Berlin, and turned down by Gerhardt although Skorzeny was interested in it. His account, however, does not agree with that of Skorzeny who claimed to have designed it personally and who said that the fuse functioned when the electric battery inside had run down.

b. Nipolit:
This is an invention developed at the explosives factory WASAG, Wittenberg/Elbe. Radl states that Nipolit was never used by the *Wehrmacht* because I.G.Farben had a complete monopoly on *Wehrmacht* supplies and allowed no innovations other than their own. SS-*Hstuf* Gerhardt maintained contact with WASAG who produced Nipolit in long strips, 10cm thick. They were delivered to:

> *Mil Amt* D-T Brandenburg
> KTI Berlin, Dr Widmann
> SS-*Polizei* Academy Research Station, believed to be in Berlin (the Commanding Officer was *Major der Schupo* Hensel)

Mil Amt D had a small workshop in Brandenburg, where the strips were turned into the finished product. Radl is familiar with the two sorts of Nipolit hand grenades (Nipodiscs and Nipocylinders) and belts and shoe-soles made of Nipolit. Models of these were in Gerhardt's museum in Friedenthal.

c. RSHA *Amt* VI F.
Amt VI F was responsible for the production of false papers, passports, secret inks, and sabotage material. They did not work with Nipolit, however, and handled only normal *Wehrmacht* stores which they supplied to *Amt* VI S. SS-*Stubaf* Lassig, Commanding Officer, was alleged to be an expert on bomb fuses and said to be working on a radio-controlled fuse. He was described as incompetent. *Amt* VI F compiled a textbook on sabotage of which only one copy existed and which was sent to the school at The Hague. *Amt* VI F was considered inefficient and unproductive, and when Gerhardt came to the *Führungsstab*, relations between VI S and VI F practically were severed.

(2) Special Weapons.

a. Suicide weapons:

In the summer of 1943, when a German victory could no longer be regarded as likely, Skorzeny began to develop suicide weapons, backed by the *Luftwaffe* and the Speer Ministry. This was against the will of Hitler who did not drop his objections until the spring of 1944. Together with engineer Censche, Skorzeny worked on a V-1 steered by a man. The project had the cover name 'Reichenbach' (or 'Reichenberg'?) but was discontinued because of lack of fuel.

b. Liaison with the Japanese.

Major Naumann of *Mil Amt* D had one meeting with Japanese officials in Berlin in November 1944, at which sabotage was discussed. This had been done without Skorzeny's permission who immediately forbade any further meetings. Radl stated that they had unsuccessfully tried to obtain reports of results of suicide tactics from the Japanese, but that in the field of sabotage they had nothing to learn from the Japanese.

c. Bacterial warfare.

Radl emphasized that this subject had never been discussed, and that Dr Wetz could never have had anything to do with it. (This does not agree with Skorzeny's statements.)

4. Conclusion.

None.

5. Comments and Recommendations.

The recipients of this report are requested to submit special briefs of any subject upon which this prisoner should be interrogated and to indicate the desirable distribution of the resultant report.

Distribution	Copies
SHAEF C-I War Room	16
G-S, SHAEF	3
BGS (1) 21 Army Group	1
G-2, Third US Army	1
G-2, Seventh US Army	1
G-2, Ninth US Army	1
G-2, Fifteenth US Army	1
G-2, US Port Enclave	1
G-2, (CIB) 12th Army Group	5

HEADQUARTERS
US FORCES EUROPEAN THEATER
INTERROGATION REPORT

CONSOLIDATED INTERROGATION REPORT (CIR) NO. 4

SUBJECT: The German Sabotage Service   DATE: 22 July 1945

This report consolidates information on the German sabotage services obtained from SKORZENY and his adjutant, RADL. It is to be read in conjunction with interrogation report CIR 4/6 of 31 May 1945 and HQ 12 Army Group Interrogation Center IIR, dated 4 June 1945.

CONTENTS

1. Sources of information
2. Report
    a. German Sabotage Agencies
        (1) RSHA *Gruppe* VI S
        (2) *Jäger* Btl 502 (mot.)
        (3) The SS-*Jagdverbände*
        (4) Schools
        (5) *Mil Amt* D
        (6) Associated organizations
    b. Sabotage Operations
        (1) Invasion Nets
        (2) Operations by Agents
        (3) Association with foreign Fascists
3. Conclusions
4. Comments and Recommendations

ANNEXES

I. Organization of the SS-*Jagdverbände*
II. Final disposition of the SS-*Jagdverbände*
III. Invasion Nets in Allied Occupied Countries
IV. Individual Operations (Unternehmen)
V. Technical sabotage information
VI. Poison bullets
VII. Plan of Friedenthal as of March 1945
VIII. Personalities.

1. Sources of Information.

SS-*Ostubaf* Otto Skorzeny, head of *Gruppe* VI S, RSHA, the *Jagdverbände* and *Amt Mil* D, arrived at USFET Intelligence Center on 19 May 1945.

SS-*Stubaf* Karl Radl, head of *Referat* VI S2, Skorzeny's Adjutant, arrived at USFET Interrogation Center on 19 May 1945.

A good deal of discrepancy exists between Skorzeny's and Radl's estimates of the size and effectiveness of the sabotage organizations. Radl attributes this to Skorzeny's frequent absence from his Headquarters on active operations. By losing touch with administrative details, he did not realize the wide gulf which existed between his plans and their execution. In addition, his gullibility and enthusiasm led him to believe every dressed-up report submitted by his ambitious inferiors.

Skorzeny's leadership was inadequate, according to Radl. After the successful Mussolini rescue, Hitler and Himmler used him for all sorts of special missions at the expense of the agencies he was supposed to be organizing. This scattering of his interests became absolute early in 1944 when he became chief exponent of the *Sonderkampf* (miracle weapons) idea. He realized that even if there were still any hope for a German victory, it would prove a Pyrrhic one unless the losses at the front could be cut down. He threw himself into the employment of the new weapons, hoping that they would bring victory, hoping that they would prove the answer to the problem.

Radl is more accurate than Skorzeny on detailed information. In his opinion, Skorzeny's sabotage services were bound to fail.

2. Report.

a. <u>German Sabotage Agencies.</u>
The three main sabotage agencies in Germany, all headed by Skorzeny, were:

(1) *Gruppe* VI S of RSHA
(2) The SS-*Jagdverbände*
(3) *Mil Amt* D of RSHA

The lines of distinction between the three organizations were not always clear, and the tendency was towards amalgamation.

In order to place all German sabotage activities under a unified command and to increase the effectiveness, Skorzeny strove to incorporate *Mil Amt* D and VI S completely into the SS-*Jagdverbände* organization. The plan was to absorb VI S and *Mil Amt* D into the central SS-*Jagdverbände Führungsstab*, and all *Mil Amt* D *Leitstellen* and VI S *Aussenstellen* into the *Führungsstäbe* of the four territorial SS-*Jagdverbände*.

The amalgamation was never completed because no officers of sufficient caliber could be found to command the proposed composite units, and because Schellenberg refused to relinquish control of VI S and *Mil Amt* D to the SS-*Jagdverbände*. The latter as essentially military units were subordinate to the SS-*Führungshauptamt* (SSFHA) rather than RSHA. In spite of these limitations, Skorzeny tried to put his plans into operation, effecting a considerable merging of functions and personnel.

In the fifth year of the war his officers came too late. Personnel was selected without regard for suitability. None of the men in leading positions had ever been abroad or spoke any foreign languages. Most of them were too young for the responsibilities they were supposed to assume.

(1) RSHA *Gruppe* VI S.

Gruppe VIS was organised in the Berkaerstrasse, Berlin, in November 1943, moving to Schloss Friedenthal in May 1944.

It consisted of four *Referate* with the following functions:

RSHA VI S 1:   Administration, finance, procurement of foreign currency; contracts, leases, upkeep of real estate; liaison with RSHA *Amt* VI A and RSHA *Amt* II.
    Referent: SS-*Hstuf* Erwin Schmiel.
    In charge of finance sections: SS-*Hstuf* Hugo Podlech.
    In charge of contracts and personnel matters: SS-*Ustuf* Max Windhövel.
RSHA VI S 2:   Adjutant. Incoming correspondence. Contacts with outside agencies.
    Referent and Adjutant: SS-*Stubaf* Karl Radl.
RSHA VI S 3:   Administration of the schools, including procurement of funds and recruiting of personnel; supervision of instruction.
    Referent: SS-*Hstuf* Herbert Bramfeldt.
    Assistant: SS-*Ustuf* Pahlow.
RSHA VI S 4:   Operation of agents, planning, supervision of training.
    Referent: SS-*Hstuf* Arno Besekow.
    Assistant: SS-*Ostuf* Werner Meyer.

Aussenstellen of VI S 4:

France and Belgium	-	SS-*Ostuf* Charles Hagedorn
		SS-*Ostuf* Franz Nebenfuhr (Neumann)
Italy	-	SS-*Stubaf* Dr Otto Begus
Greece	-	SS-*Ostuf* Franz Nebenfuhr [to Sept 1944]
Yugoslavia	-	SS-*Hstuf* Rupert Mandl
Hungary	-	SS-*Ustuf* Schmidt

Skorzeny considers the division into *Referate* to be largely theoretical. It was maintained as a concession to Schellenberg, who wanted to adhere to the existing

RSHA *Amt* VI organization. In practice it was simply a Headquarters staff working in close cooperation.

When RSHA was ordered to evacuate Berlin in January 1945, *Gruppe* VI S went to Hof with the *Führungsstab* of the SS-*Jagdverbände*. The situation deteriorated rapidly, and it became impossible to communicate with RSHA, *Amt* VI or *Mil Amt* F.

Gruppe VI S was dissolved when Skorzeny dismissed all non-essential personnel and moved his Headquarters on a special [railway] train in Austria.

(2) *Jäger* Battalion 502 (mot.)

Skorzeny asserts that from the very beginning his aim was to rid the German sabotage activities of RSHA political control and to turn them into purely military operations. His personal dislike for Schellenberg was also an important factor in this policy. It should be borne in mind, however, that such a policy coincides with his present effort to paint himself as a military rather than a political figure.

With this aim in mind he established contact with the SS-*Führungshauptamt* immediately after taking charge of RSHA VI S, and obtained the authorization to activate *Jäger* Battalion 502 (mot.) in June 1943.

The cadre was provided by SS-*Sonderlehrgang* Oranienburg, which had been founded the year before by RSHA *Gruppe* VI F. It was commanded by SS-*Hstuf* Pieter van Vessem and consisted of approx. 70 non-commissioned officers (NCOs) and 30 other enlisted men, all fanatical SS men who had volunteered for dangerous missions. It had engaged in one operation in 1943, known as '*Einsatz* Franz', when SS-*Ostuf* Günther Blume went to Iran in an attempt to contact insurgent groups. The mission was unsuccessful and ended with Blume's arrest.

In May 1943 the *Lehrgang* was quartered in the Oranienburg SS barracks [presumably those of KL Sachsenhausen]. During the summer it moved to Friedenthal and was renamed *Sonderlehrgang* zbV Friedenthal. The first operation executed under Skorzeny's command was the liberation of Mussolini. In the meantime the authorization to activate *Jäger* Battalion 502 had been granted and the *Sonderlehrgang* was absorbed into the new unit.

As all SS units in the 500 series were probationary troops recruited from convict SS personnel, and the activation order for *Jäger* Battalion 502 specified that the SS-*Führungshauptamt* was not to supply any men or material, considerable difficulties were encountered. Personnel was drawn from the probationary camp in Chlum, Czechoslovakia. Ninety percent proved unsatisfactory and were sent back. Skorzeny then proceeded to recruit volunteers from the army (150), the Luftwaffe (50), and the SS (100). This enabled him to form Headquarters Company and 1. and 2. Companys. Approx. 30 men were sent to the Havel Institute for W/T instruction. The others underwent strenuous infantry training and engineering and motor courses were added later.

In the fall of 1943 1.Company, led by SS-*Hstuf* van Vessem, was sent against the partisans in Croatia. 3.Company was formed in February 1944 with SS-*Hstuf*

Heinrich Hoyer as Commanding Officer. Personnel was mainly Flemish and Dutch. At the same time, 1. and 2. Companys went to *Truppenübungsplatz* Kurmark for four weeks' training and were in combat on the Eastern Front for four to six weeks. Unsuitable officers and men were eliminated to the extent of 10–15%.

The authorized training order called for 1,200 men organized in five Companys but this figure was never reached. The unit's final strength was 700 men, comprising a Headquarters Company and three line Companys. Skorzeny was Battalion Commander. van Vessem remained Commanding Officer of 1.Company and deputy Battalion Commander until his return from Croatia. He was replaced by SS-*Hstuf* Ulrich Menzel, who held the position until April 1944, when SS-*Hstuf* von Foelkersam, the I-a, became Skorzeny's second in command.

Jäger Battalion 502 was dissolved and its personnel absorbed into the SS-*Jagdverbände*, mainly SS-*Jagdverband Mitte*, in September 1944 (see Annex I, below).

(3) The SS-*Jagdverbände*.

The SS-*Jagdverbände* consisted of four territorial *Jagdverbände*, known as SS-*Jagdverband Ost, Süd-Ost, Süd-West, Nord-West*; and two purely German battalions, SS-*Jagdverband Mitte* and *Fallschirm Jäger* Battalion 600. The latter were organized in order to have sufficient German personnel available for special tasks such as parachute or glider operations like the Mussolini rescue. The detailed organization of the various units is discussed in Annex I, below.

In August 1944 the *Wehrmacht Führungsstab* ordered the re-organization of the Brandenburg Division into a Panzer Division. Two months previously the normal combat elements and the special (zbV) elements of Brandenburg Division had been separated when the personnel trained for special missions and acquainted with foreign languages was formed into so-called *Streifkorps*, which were attached to Army Corps for the execution of special missions,

These *Streifkorps* formed the nuclei of the territorial SS-*Jagdverbände* when Skorzeny received the authorization to recruit 800 Brandenburg volunteers late in September 1944. 1,200 were in fact recruited, but only 90% remained after the unfit had been eliminated. Skorzeny also recruited 2,500 men from the *Ersatz Heer* [Replacement Army] during November and December, and was authorized by SS-*Ogruf* Gottlob Berger of the SS-*Hauptamt* to draw volunteers from the foreign SS units.

The territorial SS-*Jagdverbände* were separate battalions drawn from political and nationalist groups in the countries where they were to operate. Plans for their formation were made by Skorzeny and von Foelkersam in May or June 1944, and the battalions were activated in September by orders SS-*Gruf* Hans Jüttner, head of the SS-*Führungshauptamt*. A SS-*Jagdverband* was to be available to the Armed Forces in each theater to carry out special tasks in the tradition of the defunct Brandenburg Division. The final aim was to have all units engaged in sabotage behind the enemy lines under a unified command in theater territory, i.e. the *Führungsstab* of the territorial SS-*Jagdverband*.

In spite of the pressure of time, the organization was to proceed slowly, allowing the units to grow gradually so that mistakes could be recognized and avoided. The mistake made with Brandenburg Division, when irreplaceable personnel with knowledge of foreign languages and countries was committed as ordinary combat troops, was not forbidden. Accordingly the battalions were to remain separate and independent units and not to be organized into regiments or a single division. Both Skorzeny and Radl claim that this independence went so far as to preclude their personal knowledge of organizational details.

(4) Schools.

Originally the 'S' in VI S stood for *'Schulen'* (schools). Skorzeny states that on his initiative all RSHA sabotage activities were taken out of *Gruppe* VI F and VI S was established as the *Amt's Gruppe* in charge of all operations. Besekow's original task was to study foreign sabotage methods and work out training plans on the basis of this research. As the organization of the Skorzeny apparatus progressed, all schools and training programs came under VI S3 (Bramfeldt) and, later under the I-a SS-*Jagdverbände Führungsstab* (Hunke).

There were two types of schools:

The A(genten) *Schulen*
The *Kampfschulen* of the *Jagdverbände*.

a. A-*Schulen*:

The A-*Schulen* were training schools for sabotage agents. Subjects covered were sabotage methods, demolitions, W/T operation, and firing of weapons.

The training schedules were determined by VI S3 in Berlin. Two to four weeks before the beginning of each course the schools received instructions as to the number and nationality of the prospective students, and the purpose and length of the course. The training was designed to be as varied and interesting as possible. Students were given the opportunity to swim, attend movies, engage in sports, and read books in their own language. Their teachers were constantly with them.

Upon completion of each course individual progress reports were issued, determining the students' further employment.

A-Schule West. This school was in the initial phase of its organization when Skorzeny took it over in June 1943. It had been established by *Gruppe* VI F at a country estate between the Hague and Scheveningen.

The school was ready to open in November 1943. As *Jäger* Battalion 502 and VI S4 were not ready to start operations at that time; *Gruppe* VI B, VI C, VI D and VI E were asked to send agents for sabotage and W/T training. Instructors were supplied by VI F.

The staff included:

SS-*Stubaf* Knolle	Commanding Officer and Director of Training
SS-*Stubaf* Dr Pechau	Deputy Director (left the school in May 1944 to join VI S4)
SS-*Hstuf* Winter	Deputy Director
SS-*Hstuf* Faulhaber	Sabotage instructor
SS-*Hstuf* Besekow	Foreign sabotage methods
SS-*Hschaf* Westphal	Explosives

Between November 1943 and June 1944 the following groups of agents were trained in classes lasting 4–6 weeks at the school.

> Approx. 25 Arabs from the Italian-Arabian Legion. Few were ever used as *Amt* VI S and *Jäger* Batl 502 did not take any.
> 60–75 Italians (three classes). Unsatisfactory with the exception of one class.
> 20 Serbia militia. Good material, eager to learn and act.
> Approx. 15 Frenchmen.
> Approx. 10 Belgians

In the spring of 1944 there were several courses of the same length for group leaders of the projected invasion nets, attended by:

> 10–15 German-Roumanians.
> 10–12 Frenchmen, and
> 6–8 Belgians.

A W/T course, lasting several months, was opened in December 1943. The technical direction was in the hands of a Dutch radio engineer. The course was conducted by a German technician from the Havel Institute. The students included:

> 2 Arabs
> 2 Italians, and
> 4 Frenchmen and Belgians.

The Hague school was dissolved in June 1944. SS-*Stubaf* Knolle was relieved of his command and sent to Heinrichsburg [a school in Yugoslavia]. SS-*Hstuf* Winter took the remainder of the personnel to Neustrelitz.

Neustrelitz School. The school was opened at the Neustrelitz barracks in July or August 1944. After the SS-*Jagdverbände* were formed it became 4.Company, SS-*Jagdverband Nord-West*.

The staff included:

SS-*Hstuf* Winter	Commanding Officer and Director of training
SS-*Ustuf* Henn	Deputy, and Explosives expert
SS-*Ustuf* Hein	W/T instructor

A Flemish NCO   Chemical sabotage (from SS-*Jagdverband Nord-West*)

Classes began in September/October 1944. The school was primarily the *Kampfschule* for SS-*Jagdverband Nord-West* (see *Kampfschule*, below). Skorzeny states that few agents were trained. Approx. 10–15 Frenchmen and 6–10 Belgians attended two-week courses with five to six men per course.

From November 1944 to March 1945 the school was devoted almost exclusively to Werwolf training. (see interrogation report CIR 4/6, Paragraph 6.)

<u>Heinrichsburg.</u> Early in 1944 the necessity for an A-*Schule* for the South East became apparent. SS-*Ostubaf* Karl Appell was given the task. He decided to establish it in guerilla territory and selected a tourist hotel at Heinrichsburg in the Fruska Gora, north west of Ruma, Yugoslavia. Inevitable attacks by guerilla bands were to furnish the students with combat experience. (Skorzeny says that the school and the local guerilla bands shared the same doctor, who divided his time between them.)

At his cadre, SS-*Ostubaf* Appel selected a Company of Serbian Moslems, reinforced by a German platoon from *Jäger* Battalion 502.

From July to September 1944, the following personnel was trained:

40 Italians (two classes)
25 Serbs
120 Russians, and
20 Hungarians.

Appel was replaced by SS-*Stubaf* Knolle in July or August 1944. The school had to be abandoned when the Russians approached in September 1944. At the time the Russia class was in progress. The students and the Moslem Company were sent to the front. Knolle was recalled to Berlin. SS-*Stubaf* Hans Zimmer [of SSFHA] took the remainder of the personnel to Mürzzuschlag, Lower Austria, where the school was operated from November 1944 to February 1945 as part of SS-*Jagdverband Süd-Ost*. Some Roumanians and Hungarians were trained.

b. *Kampschulen.*

The *Kampfschulen* were conducted on a much more military basis than the A-*Schulen*. In addition to the necessary fundamentals of sabotage, the students were taught to shift for themselves when left behind the enemy lines singly or in small groups. This implied intensive terrain intelligence training and toughening of courage. W/T instruction was given sporadically.

The *Kampfschulen* were founded by the Brandenburg Division and incorporated into the SS-*Jagdverbände* along with the *Streifkorps* to which they were attached. Their purpose was both the training of military personnel, and agents for sabotage operations. Theoretically each SS-*Jagdverband* was to have one or more schools. However, SS-*Jagdverbände Ost* and *Nord-West* did not receive any Brandenburg contingents. Therefore, SS-*Jagdverband Ost* did not have any school, while A-*Schule* Neustrelitz was largely converted for the purpose by SS-*Jagdverband Nord-West*.

The *Kampfschule* of SS-*Jagdverbänd Süd-West* was located in Freiburg/Breisgau. It was moved with the *Führungsstab* to Kloster Tiefenthal near Wiesbaden in the autumn of 1944. The opening of an advanced school for selected personnel was planned. It was to be established near Heidelberg. Due to the progress of the war, the plan did not materialize.

In SS-*Jagdverband Süd-Ost* training was decentralized. *Jagd Einsatz* Rumänien had a school at Korneuburg. *Jagd Einsatz* Ungarn conducted courses in the former Flak unit barracks at Wiener Neustadt.

c. Swimmers' School, Diane Bad, Vienna.

The school of *Jagd Einsatz* Donau was located in the Diane Bad, Vienna. All swimmers were gathered there in September/October 1944 after being withdrawn from the KdK training camps Valdagno, Bad Tölz and Venice. A requisitioned rowing club on the Danube near Klosterneuburg was to be used for training during the summer.

(5) RSHA *Mil Amt* D.

The general confusion marking the administration of the German sabotage services reigned supreme in *Mil Amt* D. The long struggle for power between the SS and the army is epitomized in its history, and the welter of political rivalries and personal bickerings make it difficult to gain a clear picture of its organization and functions.

The history may best be understood if one examines the history of *Mil Amt* as a whole.

Officially, RSHA wanted to gain control over the *Abwehr*, under the banner of unification of the German intelligence services. Unofficially, *Abwehr* leadership was considered politically unreliable, and RSHA *Amt* VI also wanted to use the *Abwehr* machinery abroad for its own political intelligence service. The inefficiency of Admiral Canaris and his staff helped RSHA in this struggle.

The big opening came in the spring of 1944 when all *Abwehr* personnel in Turkey deserted to the British. In May, Hitler ordered the unification of the German intelligence services under RSHA control. The new overall term was *Geheimer Meldedienst* (GMD) (Secret Report Service). *Abwehr* was attached intact to RSHA as *Mil Amt*. Admiral Canaris was retired; *Oberst* i.G. Georg Hansen, the former head of *Abwehr* II, was appointed head of *Mil Amt*, and *Oberst* i.G. *Freiherr* von Freytag-Loringhoven became the head of *Gruppe* II.

The *Wehrmacht's Führungsstab* was forced to comply with Hitler's order. Nevertheless, it countered with the following moves:

a. Brandenburg Division was removed from the jurisdiction of *Abwehr* II, and subordinated directly to the *Wehrmacht Führungsstab* a few days before the order was published.

b. A new department was formed in the OKH, called *Abteilung für Heerwesen* (Dept for Army). All FAK *Leitstellen* were directed to report to and accept their orders from the newly created department, which was responsible to the *Wehrmacht Führungsstab*. For all practical purposes *Mil Amt* was bypassed except for receiving a copy of all reports. The official reason given was that the interests of the frontline troops would be endangered by an over-complicated chain of command.

When Freytag-Loringhoven was removed from his position as head of *Mil Amt* II because of political conservation, the *Wehrmacht Führungsstab* put him in charge of the *Abteilung für Heerwesen*. Thus his influence was actually increased.

Major i.G. Naumann replaced him as head of *Mil Amt* II. This was the situation until 20 July 1944:

After the abortive assassination attempt against Hitler, Hansen was executed. Schellenberg took over *Mil Amt*, which was reorganized after the RSHA *Amt* VI pattern. The *Amt* VI *Gruppen* heads took charge of the newly created departments. Skorzeny became head of *Mil Amt* and *Mil* D/T. Major i.G. Naumann remained as deputy.

Freytag-Loringhoven committed suicide and the *Abteilung für Heerwesen* was dissolved. A new agency was created by the *Wehrmacht Führungsstab* to take its place, the *Wehrmacht Führungsstab* I-c under *Oberst* i.G. von Süsskind-Schwend. The name was different; the function was the same. Once again *Mil Amt* was bypassed:

Wehrmacht Führungsstab I-c

Wehrmacht Führungsstab   *Mil Amt* *Leitstelle* II with subordinate FAKs and FATs

Schellenberg attempted to counteract these manouevres of the *Wehrmacht Führungsstab* and gain direct control over the FAK *Leitstellen*. His efforts were apparently successful in the fall of 1944, when the *Wehrmacht Führungsstab* agreed to dissolve its I-c department. *Mil Amt* was to control the *Leitstellen*. One condition was made, however. In order to safeguard frontline interest, a new section was to be created within the *Mil Amt* to coordinate all frontline *Abwehr* activities. It was to be known as *Mil* F (*Chef für Frontaufklärung*) (Chief of Front Reconnaissance).

Oberst i.G. Georg Buntrock, formerly I-c with Army Group Wiessner, was appointed head of *Mil* F. From the beginning he was a puppet of the *Wehrmacht Führungsstab*. He immediately demanded exclusive control of all *Leitstellen*. The net result was that the *Mil Amt* section controlling the FAK was an agency of the *Wehrmacht Führungsstab*. All other sections were bypassed as before.

Mil F

Wehrmacht Führungsstab direct connection with *Leitstelle* II	*Mil* F, C, D with subordinate FAKs and FATs	*Leitstellen* II

All FAK personnel matters were handled by the *Heeres* Personnel *Amt*. RSHA could not possibly infiltrate.

The organization and function of *Mil* D must be regarded in the light of these developments. A wide discrepancy existed between its officials and actual status. Officially it was the central controlling agency for all *Leitstellen* II (-*West*, -*Süd-Ost*, and -*Ost*); the FAK (200-299), and FAT (200-299). Actually the *Wehrmacht Führungsstab* never relinquished its control.

(Some confusion may arise from the fact that the official German abbreviation 'FAK' was used in a dual sense:

a. for *Frontaufklärung*, i.e. a generic term *Leitstellen*, *Frontaufklärungkommando*, and *Frontaufklärungtrupps*.
b. for *Frontaufklärungkommandos* only.)

Mil D had three *Referate*, one per *Leitstelle*. *Referat West* was under *Hauptmann* Schönaich, *Süd-Ost* under *Oberleutnant* Ferit, and *Ost* under *Oberleutant* Gambke. They were in control of all FAK sabotage operations in their respective areas. The diagram below shows the official chain of command:

```
WFüStab                    Mil D
|                          |
Army Groups    Leitstelle II West   Leitstelle II Ost    Leitstelle II Ost
|        |          |        |
Armies   three FAK 2--     three FAK 2--      three FAK 2
|        |          |        |
Corps    six FAT 2--       six FAT 2--        six FAT 2
```

There were two types of operations:

a. Those directly behind enemy lines (*frontnähe Einsätze*),
b. Those further to the rear of the enemy (*frontferne Einsätze*)

Category a. actions were supervised by frontline commanders.

Only the general directives were laid down by *Mil* D. A FAK or FAT could suggest an operation to army or corps. The I-c of army or corps in turn could request a

FAK or FAT to undertake one. A complete report on the results was sent to corps, army, and the respective *Leitstelle* II, which in turn referred to it in a monthly report to *Mil* D. Only operations of particular interest were reported separately.

The necessity for operations of category b. actions was determined by army groups, the *Wehrmacht Führungsstab*, or *Mil* D, on the basis of information gathered by RSHA *Amt* VI and *Mil Amt* intelligence source.

Plans for large scale operations involving great difficulties, large sums of money, or possible political implications (such as operations in neutral countries), were worked out by the *Referat* chiefs, and submitted to Skorzeny and Schellenberg for approval. Skorzeny was permitted to authorize expenses up to RM 3,000 in German and RM 1,000 in foreign currency.

The *Leitstellen* received their orders by teleprinter or radio.

Locations.

Mil Amt D was located at Schloss Baruth on the Rangsdorf-Zossen railway, approx 40 kms [25 miles] south of Berlin. In November 1944, it was evacuated to a hostel and two barracks in Birkenwerder between Berlin and Oranienburg. In the middle of February 1945 it was moved to a small boarding house, two kms north of Bad Elster [near the Czech border with northern Bavaria], and in early April 1945 to Reith im Winkel/Upper Bavaria.

Leitstelle II *Süd-Ost* was located at Stubenring 1, Vienna; *Leitstelle* II *West* at Bad Ems [east of Koblenz]; and *Leitstelle* II *Ost* near Lodz. In January 1945 *Leitstelle* *Ost* was moved to Birkenwerder.

A supply depot for *Leitstelle* II *Süd-Ost* was in Melk/Danube. In April 1945, it was moved to vicinity of Ried/Upper Austria.

Caches.

In 1941, *Amt Ausland Abwehr* started burying sabotage equipment in occupied countries in anticipation of an invasion. This task was almost completed when *Mil Amt* was created in 1944.

Equipment and arms were packed ip watertight crates, 40–50 kgs each. Their locations were recorded as follows:

a. In written descriptions.
b. On photographs taken from different angles.
c. On maps (usually 1:25,000) and situation sketches (1;1000 or 1:5000).

They were registered according to contents of crates and number of the location. (e.g. W325 = weapons (*Waffen*) at location # 325).

Three to four copies existed of each record. One copy was on file with the respective *Leitstellen* II. For each operation the agents were instructed to memorize the details about one or more caches. *Mil* D was informed of the corresponding numbers.

In January 1945 Schellenberg issued an order that safeguards be taken against the capture of these records. All copies were withdrawn, packed in crates, and given to the SS-*Jagdverbände Führungsstab*. Skorzeny saw to it that all records which were not essential were burned before he left Hof. The remainder was burned at Salzburg and Annaberg.

(6) Associated Organizations.
a. *Kriminal Technisches Institut* (KTI).
KTI was part of RSHA *Amt* V, which was headed by SS-*Ogruf* Nebe until his flight after the 20 July 1944 incident. SS-*Oberführer* Panzinger then took over *Amt* V. SS-*Staf* Heess, the director of KTI, was an eminent criminologist, well known at international conferences on the subject before the war. SS-*Stubaf* Dr Widmann was in charge of the *Referat* for chemistry and physics.

The principal work of KTI was the use of technical means for the solution of criminal cases. Since it was frequently called upon to investigate acts of sabotage in this capacity, it had amassed a considerable fund of experience, including enemy sabotage methods. In January 1944 a report was made to Skorzeny on the subject.

As part of the KTI facilities were available, Skorzeny persuaded Widmann to work on the first model of an English one-round pistol with silencer. The job was done unofficially because it appealed to Widmann's taste for tinkering. RSHA *Gruppe* VI F and a weapons factory in Czechoslovakia were also working on the project independently. Difficulties arose when Schellenberg objected to the participation of KTI in the work of *Amt* VI.

KTI manufactured 10 to 20 Russian Nagan revolvers with silencers for the SS-*Jagdverbände*, and also parts for the British silencer-equipped Sten gun. In January and February 1945 KTI participated in the development of the Nipolit unit charge (see Annex V, below), and delivered 300 to 400 ampules of hydrocyanic acid to the *Führungsstab* of the SS-*Jagdverbände* for suicide purposes.

b. *Kommando der Kleinkampfverbände* (KdK).
When Germany inherited the remnants of the Italian armed forces in November 1943 it came into possession of the special weapons of the Italian navy, the following types of weapons were taken over:
(1)   *Märes Kämpfer* (swimmers)
(2)   *Schweine* (two-man torpedoes)
(3)   One-man explosive motor boats
(4)   Two-man torpedo boats
The special weapons were first placed under the direction of *Abwehr* but as the military personnel resented having the status of agents, they were transferred to the Navy as the KdK.

Training and technical developments was the responsibility of the Navy, which had retained the Italian personnel. *Jäger* Battalion 502 furnished personnel to be trained for operations. Under this arrangement Admiral Heye, Commanding Officer of KdK and Skorzeny, head of *Jäger* Battalion 502 were on an equal level. *Frig/Kapitän* Frauenheim was Heye's Chief of Staff.

On Himmler's orders only convicted soldiers on probation were used at first. They had to participate in a three to six week screening course at the *Leibstandarte* barracks, Berlin-Lichterfelde, at the end of with 25%, 150 men per course, were selected for KdK training. One NCO from *Jäger* Battalion 502 was placed in charge of each group of six to eight men. Upon Skorzeny's insistence, *Sonder Einsatz Abteilung* zbV was formed to recruit volunteers from all branches of the *Wehrmacht* (see interrogation report IIR on Radl). In its first week it recruited 200 men.

Training was carried out at the following places:

(1) Valdagno. Commanding Officer *Kapitänltn.* Wolk. Beginner's courses for *Märes Kämpfer*, November 1943–August 1944.
(2) Venice. Started May 1944. Personnel from *Jäger* Battalion 502 left in October 1944.
(3) Bad Tölz. Started in February 1944.
(4) Diane Bad, Vienna. From September 1944 to February 1945.
(5) Lake Como and Spezia. Trained personnel for one-man and two-man motorboats.

c. *Kampf Geschwader (KG) 200.*

Skorzeny's first contact with KG 200 dates back to October 1943, when it was called *Staffel Geschwader* zbV, Commanding Officer Major Gartenfeld, and used as an air transport unit for parachute operations. *Oberst* Heigel took command in January 1944 and the unit was renamed KG 200. In April 1944 all special weapons of the *Luftwaffe* became part of KG 200. These included suicide bombs, remote-control bombs, gliders for special purposes, piloted V-1's, and *Mistel Flugzeuge* (pick-a-back planes). A *Fallschirm Jäger* Battalion zbV was also assigned to KG 200. It operated during the invasion and saw action with Skorzeny in Hungary in October 1944 and worked with Panzer Brigade 150 in the Ardennes Offensive.

KG 200 flew missions for *Amt Ausland Abwehr* and subsequently for RSHA *Amt VI*. Deep penetration missions were flown directly by KG 200 while frontline undertakings were carried out by *Luftwaffe* units near the front. KG 200 was composed of two *Staffeln*, the first being the transport unit and also the second incorporating the weapons of the *Luftwaffe*.

Originally Skorzeny was in direct contact with KG 200, which was located west of Berlin. As the fuel shortage grew worse, missions had to be limited and KG 200 assigned a liaison officer to the VI S office in the Berkaerstrasse, Berlin. Each mission had to be carefully planned and in a monthly conference of RSHA *Amt* VI and *Mil Amt*, Schellenberg decided which missions had the highest priority.

The *Luftwaffe Führungsstab* allowed a certain amount of petrol to KG 200 which could be used at the discretion of the Commanding Officer. KG 200 had the right to refuse missions if they were technically impractical. Detailed planning was done directly by the SS-*Jagdverbände* or FAK and the *Gruppen* concerned. These *Gruppen* usually were attached to army groups and reported to Headquarters after completing operations.

b. Sabotage Missions.
(1) Invasion Nets.
In the spring of 1944, RSHA *Gruppen* VI B, VI C, VI E and VI S were each ordered by Schellenberg to organize invasion nets (*Invasionnetze*—I-*Netze*) for the purpose of sabotaging enemy supply lines in the event of an invasion. VI S, lacking personnel for such groups, was to be helped out by the other *Gruppen* of RSHA *Amt* VI.

Radl denies that any invasion nets were formed by VI S. However, early in 1944 *Amt* VI, and VI E in particular, began making plans for nets, primarily to supply them with information in case the Balkans were occupied. Similar nets for sabotage purposes were contemplated by VI S but failed to materialize because of lack of personnel and on account of personal difficulties between Mandl and Benesch (see Annex III, below). All plans were abandoned in January 1945.

A typical instance of incompetence among the leaders is demonstrated by an incident which was mainly the result of Benesch's failure to consult with Mandl. Benesch decided to send sixty Serbs, all Chetniks, into Serbia. He contacted Luburich, the leader of a gang of nationalist Croatian extremists. Luburich claimed to be willing to guide the group to Serbia via Croatia, but in December 1944 he had them all murdered near Zagreb by his men. Mandl would have known that Luburich was not to be trusted.

The operations of the invasion nets in each country are discussed in detail in Annex II, below.

(2) Operations by Agents.
Ninety-Five percent of the operations by agents were initiated by the FATs. Every German army normally had one *Aufklärungs Kdo* II (FAK II) and each of its three corps had one *Frontaufklärungs Trupp* II (FAT II).

The FAK II on the Western front were subordinated to *Leitstelle* II *West für Frontaufklärung*; the situation was similar in the East and South-East. Each FAK and FAT carried on continuous agent operations contingent with the situation. *Trupps* and *Kommandos* trained their own agents. It is estimated that 20 to 25 operations, each comprising one to five agents, were carried out monthly on the Western Front. On the Eastern Front approx. 600 agents were committed during the last half of 1944, and 20-30 per month in the South-East.

Missions.
Agent operations were usually aimed at disrupting the flow of supplies. Targets
such as ammunition depots and vital factories were attacked rarely and only with
good agents.

Some of the operations, especially after June 1944, were aimed at the formation
of resistance groups who could disrupt supply and communications. Resistance
groups were to operate indefinitely, while agents had orders to return immediately
upon accomplishing their missions.

The percentage of returning agents in the East varied according to the tactical
situation from 15 to 50%. In the West the figure was between 30 and 40%.

Employment of Agents.
Important missions using good agents were carried out with the aid of the *Luftwaffe*.
Parachute troops constituted 20 to 30% of the total number of missions.

Less vital missions which involved crossing the front lines and which had their
objectives within 60 kms [36 miles] of the MLR comprised 60 to 70% of the operations.

Stay-behind operations during a general retreat added up to 10 to 20%.

Reports.
Reports of returning agents were carefully studied. The central office, VI Z, was
informed in the case of new developments, such as new systems of police control,
new means of identification, and new currency.

Monthly reports were sent from the *Leitstellen* II to the *Mil Amt* D central office,
which published reports on experience gained through operations and on sabotage
material. Summary reports described the routine operations of FATs and FAKs
by means of statistical tables. Only special operations were reported individually.

Plans for new operations, most of them involving long distances, were submitted
to Berlin where liaison with KG 200 was available. In case there was not enough
fuel on hand, Schellenberg himself decided the priority of the missions.

Payment.
During their period of training agents were paid in accordance with their former
income; on a scale ranging from RM 400 to RM 800 per month. They received
bonuses of RM 2,000 to RM 4,000 per mission after their claims had been proved
correct. For operations they were paid in the currency of the representative country
at the rate of RM 1,000 for each four weeks.

Payments were made either from imprest funds by the *Dienststellen* or by RSHA
Amt II or VI A from special funds authorized by Schellenberg.

Contact Addresses (*Anlaufstellen*).
The majority of these were parts of the I-Nets or stay-behind groups of *Mil Amt* D.
Usually cafes, restaurants, hotels, bicycle stores, and other public establishments

were used. If no contact address was available in an area, operations were initiated for the purpose of establishing one (see Annex IV, below).

(3) Association with foreign Fascists.

a. <u>French.</u>

The French Government with about 1,000 followers moved to Alsace-Lorraine in September 1944 and to Sigmaringen in October 1944. RSHA *Amt* VI maintained contact with it through the *Beauftragter West* of RSHA *Amt* VI B, SS-*Staf* Bickler. SS-*Hstuf* Roland Nosek was appointed liaison officer in the exiled government by VI B.

Skorzeny met Darnand and Doriot for the first time at a conference arranged by SS-*Staf* Steimle, in the SS *Gästehaus* Berlin-Wannsee. Doriot was backed by Himmler while Darnand was favored by Ribbentrop.

Skorzeny himself was impressed by Darnand. The latter claimed to have 4,000 to 6,000 followers at his disposal. They were distributed throughout France, four to ten men in each small town, and were said to possess enough leadership ability to be used as the nucleus for a resistance movement. He offered his supporters as contacts and prepared that some be used as agents but insisted he be kept informed of their activities. It was agreed that no efficient resistance could be built up out of a political organization. Darnand and Doriot were asked to visit groups in training in order to maintain their influence and continued political indoctrination.

Skorzeny met Darnand for the second and last time in January 1945 at a dinner in the Eden Hotel in Berlin. He told Darnand that he would not need more sabotage agents during the next two months. An adequate number, 60 to 80 men, had been obtained from the organization of Darnand and Doriot and from the French *Waffen*-SS Regiment 'Charlemagne'. He wanted Darnand and Doriot to spend the following two months in preparing a thorough political organization among the White Maquis. Future sabotage operations were to be based on this organization.

Doriot, who was killed in an air attack in March 1945, intended to employ his force of 2,000 miliciens as a military organization. His political interests were limited and he preferred the role of an officer. He offered to furnish agents from his group on the condition that he retain control over them. He also requested especially that RSHA VI S and SS-*Jagdverband Süd-West* use only his agents and not German personnel.

The SS-*Jagdverbände* and *Leitstelle* II *West* at Bad Ems, needed French sabotage agents. *Ltn.* Frank of *Leitestelle* II *West* was ordered to keep in touch with Darnand and Doriot for the two agencies and RSHA VI S, working with Bickler and Nosek. They were to select Frenchmen suitable for sabotage and espionage, who were to be sent to screening camps and then to the various SS-*Jagdverbände* and other interested agencies. Some of the volunteers went directly to SS-*Jagdverband Süd-West* and were used for military purposes (see also Annex IV, below).

Difficulties between Gerlach, Commanding Officer of SS-*Jagdverband Süd-West*, and Hellmers, Commanding Officer of *Leitstelle* II *West*, arose when Hellmers used agents.

No reports of activities were received in the *Führungsstab*, according to Radl, because of the semi-independence of *Mil Amt* D and the independent operations of SS-*Jagdverband Süd-West*.

b. Belgian.

Both RSHA *Gruppe* VI S4 and SS-*Jagdverband Nord-West* had connections with Leon Degrelle and in the winter of 1944 sent SS-*Hstuf* Hoyer to confer with him. It was agreed that only people selected by Degrelle would participate in subversive activities in Wallonia and that Degrelle would send a group of his followers to the school at Neustrelitz. Degrelle did not keep the bargain but sent his men into divisions at the front and even drew personnel away from Neustrelitz.

Van der Wiele had been recommended to Himmler in the winter of 1944, Hoyer conferred with him. As a result, only van der Wiele's followers were to be used for operations in Flanders and 30 Flemish women were to be trained as W/T operators by *Gruppe* VI S. They came to Friedenthal but with the exception of four or five proved to be unsuitable and were sent back by Skorzeny.

Since van der Wiele was recognized by only a minority of the Flemish people, no great activity by VI S or the SS-*Jagdverbände* took place in Flanders. One group of approx. 20 people under SS-*Ustuf* Bachot was located near Giessen, prepared to work in Belgium. Due to the rapid Allied advance, they presumably never became active and were probably captured.

Skorzeny and Radl claim not to know whether *Leitstelle* II *West* had connections with van der Wiele or Degrelle.

3. Conclusions.

None.

4. Comments and Recommendations.

None.

For Colonel Philp:
Harry K. Lennon
Captain, Inf
B & E Section

Annex I

Organization of the SS-*Jagdverbände*

1. The Territorial SS-*Jagdverbände*.

The terriorial SS-*Jagdverbände* were subdivided into Companys, known as *Jagd Einsätze*, which were organized on a nationality basis, e.g. *Jagd Einsatz* Ungarn. The ratio of Germans to foreign nationals was supposed to be two to one. It was considered desirable for the German personnel to be able to speak the respective language.

Detailed organization and strength were not strictly defined, and varied according to circumstances.

a. *Führungsstab*.

The central headquarters (SS-*Jagdverbände Führungsstab*) was located at Friedenthal.

Its orders were to cover matters of principle only. The *Führungsstab* was to develop plans for organization and recruiting, which it then submitted to the central *Reich* agencies to obtain the necessary orders and authorizations. The actual recruiting was to be done by each SS-*Jagdverband*. Requests and orders from the *Wehrmacht Führungsstab* were received by the central HQ for dissemination to the SS-*Jagdverband* concerned. This afforded a unified chain of command without limiting the freedom of action necessary for the handling of situations arising at the front.

Organization of the *Führungsstab*.

Commanding Officer:	SS-*Ostubaf* Otto Skorzeny
Adjutant and Liaison Officer:	SS-*Stubaf* Karl Radl
Chief of Staff:	SS-*Hstuf* Adrian von Foelkersam
	from Jan 1945
	SS-*Ostubaf* Karl Walter

(The Chief of Staff had direct control over all departments. He was permitted to issue orders in Skorzeny's name.)

I-a   SS-*Hstuf* Werner Hunke

Deputy I-a	SS-*Ostuf* Kurt Schröter
Administration Officer	SS-*Ustuf* Wichmann
Agent Operations	SS-*Hstuf* Arno Besekow
Agent Operations	SS-*Ostuf* Werner Meyer

two Non-Commissioned Officers
one Draughtsman

(The I-a department had charge of operations of the SS-*Jagdverbände* and *Gruppe* VI S and the training program. It worked on plans for operations suggested by outside sources, e.g. Himmler or the Speer Ministry. It handled W/T and teleprinter messages and papers pertaining to tactical matters.)

I-b   SS-*Hstuf* Reinhard Gerhardt
           Deputy I-b   SS-*Hstuf* Wolfgang Überschaar
           one SS-*Untersturmführer*
           one Weapons NCO
           one Ammunitions NCO
           one Explosives NCO
           one Draughtsman

(The I-b department was responsible for the procurement of weapons and ammunition following Überschaar's arrival at beginning January 1945. It was also responsible for supply and motor transport for the SS-*Jagdverbände* and *Gruppe* VI S. It also furnished *Mil* D with Nipolit. Standard equipment was drawn by the SS-*Jagdverbände* directly from army groups or armies. I-b dealt with *Mil* D/T; the I-b of the BdE, *Befehlshaber des Ersatzheeres*; the AHA, Allgemeine *Heeres Amt*; the Army, *Luftwaffe*, and Waffen-SS ordnance departments; General Buhle, the Quartermaster General (OQu) of *Führerhauptquartier*; and with private firms engaged in the production of clothing, equipment, weapons, ammo, and explosives. Technical departments by Mil D/T, VI F, ordnance departments, and private firms were followed. The issue of equipment to WERWOLF was handled by the department.)

I-c   SS-*Ostuf* Hans Graalfs
           two interpreter NCOs
           one draughtsman

(I-c maintained liaison with the *Wehrmacht Führungsstab* and I-c *Luftwaffe* to keep abreast with the enemy situation. The department evaluated the intelligence received from the *Seehaus Dienst*, an institution of the Foreign Office for the monitoring of foreign broadcasts. Liaison was maintained with *Mil Amt* B and C.)

II-a   SS-*Ostuf* Wilhelm Gallent (also Skorzeny's assistant adjutant).
           Chief responsibility was the recruiting of new officers from the *Wehrmacht* and the *Waffen*-SS. Liaison was maintained with the HPA (*Heeres Personalamt*), General Burgdorf and General Hellermann; the personnel office of the *Waffen*-SS, SS-*Ogruf* von Herff and SS-*Brif* Dr Katz; and the SS-*Hauptamt*, SS-*Ogruf* Berger.

II-b   SS-*Hstuf* Weiss
           Later SS-*Ostuf* Arnold Steinlein
           Responsible for Enlisted Men.

III   SS-*Stubaf* Dr Wolfgang Pinder
           Judge Advocate.

IV-a   SS-*Hstuf* Herbert Urbanneck
Normal tasks were the handling of rations, pay, clothing, and equipment.
Subordinate to I-b for extra equipment.

IV-b   SS-*Hstuf* Dr Wilhelm Wetz
Chief responsibility was the procurement and training of medical
personnel for all SS-*Jagdverbände*. The Training Officer called for two doctors
per SS-*Jagdverband*. A medical kit for special missions was developed. Dr Wetz
observed two sets of experiments conducted by Naval doctors, which were never
completed: A stimulant for personnel engaged in special conditions, containing
Pervitin, Caffeine, and Morphium enabled swimmers to attain a higher, more even
standard of results. A preparation obtained from algae increased night vision power
eight to ten times while another derived from deep sea fish increased it forty times.

V (K)   SS-*Ostuf* Alois Weber from Feb 1945 SS-*Hstuf* Mahlow
V (K) was in charge of the motor vehicle repair shop. For the procurement
of vehicles he was subordinate to I-b. V (K) also was in charge of drivers' training.
Plans were made to train all SS-*Jagdverband* members to drive all types of vehicles.

VI   SS-*Staf* Otto Bayer
NSFO [*Nationalsozialistische Führungsoffizier – Wehrmacht Offizierkorps*]
and special service officer.

b. HQ Units.
The following units were directly under the *Führungsstab*. In March 1945 it was
planned to organize them into a HQ Battalion (*Stabsabteilung*) under SS-*Stubaf*
Ottomar Blumenthal.

HQ Company:
Commanding Officer: SS-*Ostuf* Wilhelm Gallent
                        succeeded in February 1945 by SS-*Hstuf* Driebholz

Composition: *Führungsstab* personnel, a guard Platoon, a dog section and a horse
section. Total personnel 200.

Signals Company:
Commanding Officer: SS-*Hstuf* Streckfuss
Communications Officer   SS-*Hstuf* Alfred Kallweit

Composition: The W/T and telephone operators and teletypists.
Total personnel 250.

Kallweit was responsible for the SS-*Jagdverbände* communications net and the procurement of signals equipment. Primary task was the operation of communications for *Führungsstab*, SS-*Jagdverbände*, RSHA VI S *Aussenstellen*, *Mil Amt* D *Leitstellen*, and the schools. W/T communications with operational groups were handled by the SS-*Jagdverbände*.

Workshop Company:
Commanding Officer: SS-*Ostuf* Alois Weber
Composition: Approx. 98 men, in three platoons.
A weapons workshop was attached.

Service Company:
Commanding Officer: (after 1945) SS-*Ostuf* Staffer.
Total personnel approx. 80 men.
This Company was responsible to the I-b.

c. SS-*Jagdverband Ost*.
Commanding Officer: SS-*Hstuf* Adrian von Foelkersam
Deputy C.O.:   SS-*Stubaf* Wolfram Heinze-Rogee

According to Skorzeny the approximate strength of SS-*Jagdverband Ost* was 800 men composed as follows:

400 Germans	50 Latvians
200 Russians	30 Lithuanians
80 Estonians	50 Poles

Radl estimates the strength of the entire unit as only 250–300 men.

The units stationed in Hohensalza were almost completely destroyed in the Russian attack of 20/21 January 1945. Remnants returning to Friedenthal included approx. 10 Germans. Among them were SS-*Stubaf* Dr Manfred Pechau and SS-*Stubaf* Heinze-Rogee, SS-*Ustufs* Rinne, Tietjen, zur Mühlen, and Müller, besides 40 Russians, and 20–30 men *Jagd Einsatz* Baltikum.

SS-*Stubaf* Auch was charged with the reorganization of the SS-*Jagdverband*. He received as reinforcements 40–50 Russians (probably Vlassov men) and approx. 50 Germans.

Jagd Einsatz Baltikum. Made up of Estonians, Latvians, and Lithuanians, was formed around a nucleus of Baltic V-men whom SS-*Stubaf* Dr Pechau of *Gruppe* VI S4 had gathered while he was with the BdS Riga. Pechau joined SS-*Jagdverband Ost* in October–November 1944.

Einheit Giel. A Russian *Jagd Einsatz* made up of 20–30 Germans and 60–70 Russians (Skorzeny refers to this unit as *Jagd Einsatz Ost* 2). Stationed near

Trautenau (Czechoslovakia). Giel's staff included a female pharmacist who had large stock of narcotics. Skorzeny states they were issued to operational groups.

d. SS-*Jagdverband Süd-Ost.*

Commanding Officer: SS-*Ostubaf* Benesch

The strength of SS-*Jagdverband Süd-Ost* is estimated by Radl at 800 men, by Skorzeny at 2,000 men. Skorzeny analyses its Brandenburg contingent as follows:

Streifkorps Kroatien	80 men
Streifkorps Slowakei	80–100 men
Streifkorps Rumänien	60 men
Misc. Brandenburg personnel	80–100 men

The head of *Streifkorps* Kroatien, *Hauptmann* (now SS-*Ostubaf*) Benesch, became Commanding Officer, SS-*Jagdverband Süd-Ost.* In September 1944, he left Kraljevo for Jaidhof nears Krems/Danube in order to establish his *Führungsstab* there. Part of his *Streifkorps* were with him.

The remainder was organized as *Jagd Einsatz* Kroatien under SS-*Ostuf* Schlau in the vicinity of Zagreb. *Jagd Einsatz* Ungarn, Commanding Officer SS-Ostuf Kirschner and *Jagd Einsatz* Slowakei Commanding Officer SS-*Ostuf* Dr Walter Pawlowsky were organized in the respective countries. *Jagd Einsatz* Rumänien, Bulgarien, and possibly Serbien, were organized and remained in Jaidhof.

Jagd Einsatz Donau, Commanding Officer SS-*Hstuf* Pfriemer (formerly with Donau Schutz). In September 1944 the swimmers of the *Sonder Einsatz Abteilung* were withdrawn from Naval training camps in Bad Tölz, Valdagno, and Venice. Together with 30–40 picked men from the Donau Schutz, a counter sabotage organization of *Leitstelle* II *Süd-Ost* they were formed into *Jagd Einsatz* Donau. Its Commanding Officer, SS-*Ustuf* Walter Schreiber, was in charge of the swimmers.

e. SS-*Jagdverband Süd-West.*

Commanding Officer: SS-*Hstuf* Hans Gerlach

The strength of SS-*Jagdverband Süd-West* is estimated by Radl at 120–130 men, by Skorzeny at 600 men.

Its Brandenburg contingent is analysed by Skorzeny as follows:

Streifkorps Süd-Frankreich	20–40 men
Streifkorps Frankreich	approx. 60 men
Streifkorps Italien	approx. 60 men
Kampfschule Freiburg/Breisgau	approx. 80 men
Misc. Brandenburg personnel	50–60 men

Additional personnel was recruited from army replacements battalions and from foreign *Waffen*-SS units.

Skorzeny and Radl disclaim a detailed knowledge of the organization. For a short time the *Führungsstab* and two *Jagd Einsätze* for operations in France (designation unknown) were stationed in Freiburg im Breisgau. They moved to Kloster Tiefenthal, Wiesbaden, in September 1944. One of the French Companys was commanded by SS-*Ostuf* Honfeld.

Jagd Einsatz Italien, Commanding Officer SS-*Ostuf* Soelder, was stationed in Val Martello near Meran (South Tyrol).

f. SS-*Jagdverband Nord-West.*
Commanding Officer: SS-*Hstuf* Heinrich Hoyer; succeeded in Feb. 1945
                        by SS-*Hstuf* Willy Dethier.

No Brandenburg Division personnel was available for SS-*Jagdverband Nord-West.* Its strength is estimated by Skorzeny at 400 men. Radl states that the unit never got beyond the recruiting stage with an estimated personnel total of 60–70 men.

The *Führungsstab* was located at Neustrelitz. There was a *Jagd Einsatz* Flandern and a *Jagd Einsatz* Wallonien. The activation of *Jagd Einsätze* Holland and Dänemark was also planned.

2. SS-*Jagverband Mitte.*

SS-*Jagdverband Mitte* was stationed at Friedenthal. It was a purely German Battalion kept in readiness for special operations.

(cf. Operation 'Panzerfaust', Annex IV, below). Administratively, the *Sonder Einsatz Abteilung* zbV (which recruited for the KdK) was part of it.

The strength of SS-*Jagdverband Mitte* is given by Skorzeny as 800, by Radl as 400 men. It was organized in three Companys. The nucleus of its personnel was *Jäger* Battalion 502. Its approximate composition was as follows:

> 60% from the Army
> 20% from the *Waffen*-SS
> 15% from the *Luftwaffe*
> 5% from the Navy

SS-*Jagdverband Mitte* became part of Division Schwedt committed under Skorzeny's command on the Oder front on 31 January 1945.

Tk Company. Because of the difficulties he experienced in activating Panzer Brigade 150, Skorzeny decided to have a Tk Company at his constant disposal. Since no foreign nationals were involved it was to be part of SS-*Jagdverband Mitte.*

SS-*Hstuf* Walter Girg activated the Company near Vienna because important tank factories were in the vicinity. Personnel was drawn from the 10. Pz.Div. Replacement Regiment, Mödling.

In early January 1945 when the situation became critical in East Prussia, 50 men from the Company were ordered to be committed. In the middle of January 1945 the remainder was ordered to Friedenthal.

Late in January 1945, Girg departed for East Prussia with a second group of 50 men. He was stopped en route by the Commanding Officer in Danzig and sent on an operation in Poland without Skorzeny's knowledge or consent.

3. SS-*Fallschirm Jäger* Battalion 600.

SS-*Fallschirm Jäger* Btl 500 was commanded by SS-*Hstuf* Siegfried Milius. It had just returned from operations in Yugoslavia, including an unsuccessful parachute attack on Tito's Headquarters, where it had been attached to XIII (?) *Alpenkorps*. It had also been committed for a short time on the Russian front. On Himmler's orders Skorzeny was put in charge in August or September 1944 and the Battalion became part of the SS-*Jagdverbände* organization.

The Battalion was re-organized in Neustrelitz. Its criminal elements were removed, and it was renamed SS-*Fallschirm Jäger* Battalion 600. After unfit personnel was eliminated it had approx. 250 men. New recruits came from the *Luftwaffe*.

Its ultimate strength is estimated by Skorzeny at 900 men, by Radl at 500. It was organized in three Companys. Because of petrol shortage only one Company could be trained as a parachute Company. The other two were glider Companys.

The approx. composition was as follows:

> 40% from the *Luftwaffe* (parachutists)
> 30% from the Army
> 30% from the *Waffen*-SS

SS-*Fallschirm Jäger* Battalion 600 became part of Division Schwedt.

Annex II

Final Disposition of the SS-*Jagdverbände*

Until March 1945 a rapid collapse of the fronts was not anticipated. By that time W/T contact between the *Führungsstab* and the various SS-*Jagdverbände* had become difficult. No stay-behind plans had been made, except in the Balkans, and hasty make-shift preparations became necessary.

The last order from the *Führungsstab* to the territorial SS-*Jagdverbände* stated that:

1. The individual SS-*Jagdverbände* were not to retreat beyond their assigned areas of operations. *Jagd Einsatz* Ungarn, for instance, was to remain in Hungary unless ordered otherwise by the military commander in its sector.
2. They were to let the enemy pass, establish themselves as potential resistance groups, and await further orders.
3. Meanwhile they were to hamper communications and harrass supply lines as long as they remained close to the front.
4. If this order could not be carried out, they were to join regular combat units.
5. The territorial *Führungsstäbe* were not to stay-behind the enemy lines, but were to maintain W/T contact with the stay-behind groups if possible.

Due to the rapid progress of the war, Skorzeny does not know to what extent this order was carried out. The groups which are known to have stayed behind the lines are treated in Annexes III and IV of this report.

The following is the final disposition of SS-*Jagdverband* elements in German territory:

Führungsstab. In the middle of February 1945, the *Führungsstab* was moved to Hof, Bavaria. From there it moved to Achtal near Teisendorf (west of Salzburg) early in April 1945.

On 25 April 1945 the staff was reduced in size, and established in a special train at Puch near Salzburg. The re-modeled HQ included:

Skorzeny	SS-*Ostuf* Hans Graalfs
Radl	*Fräulein* Kopfheiser
SS-*Hstuf* Arno Besekow	The sisters Krüger
SS-*Ostubaf* Karl Walter	signals personnel and guards
SS-*Ostuf* Kurt Schröter	

A I-b department was established in Bischofshofen (Austria). The Service Company and maintenance section under SS-*Stubaf* Ottomar Blumenthal and SS-*Hstuf* Wolfgang Überschaar.

SS-*Jagdverband Mitte* and *Fallschirm Jäger* Battalion 600. Both units were part of Division Schwedt which was committed on the Oder front bridgeheads at Schwedt, Zehden, and Bellinchen. Skorzeny lost contact with them early in April 1945.

SS-*Jagdverband Süd-West.* *Jagd Einsatz* Italien consisting of approx. 120 Germans and 40 Italians was stationed near Brixen in April 1945.

The units stationed in Tiefenthal are assumed to have gone East with the army corps to which they were attached.

SS-*Jagdverband Nord-West.* Headquarters and 3.Company, consisting of approx. 20 Dutch, 20 Danes, 15 Norwegians, 5 Finns and 50 Germans, remained in Neustrelitz at the dispoal of the local Commanding Officer.

1.Company (*Jagd Einsatz* Flandern) under SS-*Ustuf* Bachot was stationed near Giessen in March 1945.

2.Company, under-strength, was with Division Schwedt.

SS-Jagdverband Ost. In the middle of February 1945, SS-*Stubaf* Heinze-Rogee took 60–70 Russians to Berlin-Schönweide, where they remained.

Two groups totaling 140–150 men, led by SS-*Stubaf* Auch and SS-*Ustuf* Riedl respectively, and one group of 20–30 men from *Jagd Einsatz* Baltikum under SS-*Stubaf* Dr Pechau left for Troppau (Czechoslovakia) during the first week of April 1945.

The remainder stayed in Friedenthal when Radl left on 14–15 April 1945. SS-*Hstuf* Gerhardt was to lead them into combat on the Oder front.

Einheit Giel (*Jagd Einsatz Ost 2*) was attached to Army Group *Mitte*, south of Breslau.

SS-Jagdverband Süd-Ost. Headquarters was in Gföhl near Krems/Danube (Austria) in early April 1945.

Jagd Einsatz Slowakei under SS-*Ustuf* Pawlowsky was committed with Tk Corps in early April 1945.

Jagd Einsatz Rumänien under SS-*Hstuf* Müller was committed north of Pressburg [Bratislava].

Schutzkorps Alpenland (SKA). Skorzeny stuck to the following account of the *Schutzkorps.* When he observed the conditions in Upper Austria, where desertions [mainly from German armies] were out of hand and entire units were withdrawing without proper authority, he suggested the organization of a 'stragglers' patrol to *Gauleiter* Eigruber. For this purpose *Schutzkorps Alpenland* was formed. It consisted of the following seven groups with a total strength of approx. 250 men:

Führungsgruppe near Annaberg (Austria). This group included:
Skorzeny
Radl
SS-*Ostubaf* Walter
SS-*Hstuf* Hunke
SS-*Ostuf* Graalfs
SS-*Ustuf* König
SS-*Oschaf* Bönning
SS-*Uschaf* Behr

Gruppe SS-Hstuf Fucker, via Steinersee Meer (Austria). 40–50 men, organized in two or three squads. One squad was probably commanded by SS-*Ostuf* Ludwig.

Gruppe SS-Hstuf Girg, vicinity of Lofer (Austria), 40–50 men organized in two or three squads.

Gruppe SS-Hstuf Streckfuss, near Altenmarkt, 40–50 men.

Gruppe SS-Ostuf Wilscher, near Bischofshofen (Austria). Approx. 30 men.

Gruppe SS-Hstuf Winter, near Mauterndorf (Austria), approx 20 men.

Gruppe SS-Ustuf Schuermann, near Altaussee (Austria), approx. 30 men.

Annex III

Invasion Nets in Allied Occupied Countries

<u>Greece.</u> *Dienststelle* 2000 and 3000, formerly belonging to RSHA *Gruppe* VI F, were placed under SS-*Stubaf* Dr Begus of *Gruppe* VI S. Begus' headquarters were located in a private residence in Athens. He had a W/T operator in Salonica and operated a sailboat for espionage purposes among the Dodecanese islands.

Orders to activate the invasion net were received in spring or summer of 1944 from SS-*Hstuf* Besekow of VI S4 and Begus went to Berlin for instructions. The largest group was organized in Athens comprising 20 to 25 men. Another was located in Salonica with ten men and it is presumed that smaller groups were formed throughout the country, some of them having been taken over from the former *Dienststellen*. It is not known whether political groups were used. The two larger groups were in possession of W/T equipment and the entire system was centrally controlled from Athens, where contact was maintained with the Havel Institut.

In June 1944 Dr Begus was succeeded by SS-*Ostuf* Nebeführ, a former Navy engineer in Italy sent by RSHA *Gruppe* VI A. After the occupation of Greece, W/T contact with the net was established twice. When street battles in Athens began, the initiative came from sources other than the invasion net. It was reported that subsequently a great number of arrests had occurred which handicapped the work of the net. No operations were reported, and later Nebenführ went to Berlin and left only one German NCO in Greece.

<u>Italy</u>. Dr Begus was transferred to Italy in June 1944. He organized an invasion net in the Po Valley known as Operation 'Zypresse' using personnel from Prince Borchese's *Decima MAS* Flotilla (renamed *Decima MAS* Division in the spring of 1944). Skorzeny estimates its size at six to eight groups of two to three men each. They had no radio communications but presumably used the RSHA *Gruppe* VI B espionage net radio facilities. No reports of their activities were received.

Begus also supervised several operations of the Italian swimmers (*Meereskämpfer*). Two operations in Taranto and one in Naples in the autumn of 1944 were directed against enemy supply ships.

In a small village (name unknown) near Verona, a school for agents was established in cooperation with Major Uslar, *Abwehr* II and Commanding Officer of FAK 214 (?). Assistance was also rendered by *Gruppe* VI B's Italian representative, SS-*Stubaf* Dr Huegel, who had three or four officers with him, and *Jäger* Battalion 502 which furnished seven men as instructors and cadre. The school was opened in June or July 1944 and in December 1944 moved to the vicinity of Brixen (South Tyrol).

Courses lasted two to three weeks and consisted of English and American identifications, infiltration tactics, and the handling of explosives. They were attended by five or six men and taught by NCOs. Upon completion of training, the men were used in operations aimed at Allied supply lines in the Appennines and the Po Valley from September 1944 to January 1945, two to three men participating in each operation.

Roumania. Preparations for an invasion net in Roumania began in April 1944 with the recruiting of Germans living in Roumania. SS-*Hstuf* Liebhart and SS-*Hstuf* Müller were in charge of the activities and responsible to SS-*Ogruf* Berger of the SS-*Hauptamt*. Both of them were Roumanian Germans. Müller was a businessman and a native of Bucharest and Liebhart a landowner in Transylvania. They continued in their occupations wearing both civilian clothes and uniform.

Three or four groups of five or six men were organized in the Ploesti oilfield area. Another five or six groups of four to six men each, were formed in Transylvania. Almost all group leaders had been officers in the Roumanian or German army. They were trained at Seehof School (The Hague) and *Gruppe* VI F in Berlin.

Yugoslavia. Skorzeny gives the following picture of the invasion net in Serbia and Croatia. It was organized from elements of the Brandenburg Division under Major Benesch. He had a battalion of approx. 800 Germans at his disposal in the vicinity of Belgrade which in August 1944 was renamed *Streifkorps* Benesch. In May 1944 SS-*Hstuf* Mandl, a member of RSHA *Gruppe* VI F, was sent as liaison man to *Gruppe* VI E and VI S.

The net was to serve simultaneously as the invasion net of RSHA *Gruppe* VI E3 against Tito.

The territory was divided into ten geographical districts. Seven of them were under control of Brandenburg Division, the remaining three under *Gruppe* VI S. In September or October 1944 all these groups came under SS-*Jagdverband* *Süd-Ost* as *Jagd Einsatz* Croatien, Commanding Officer *Oberleutnant* Rowohl.

France. The invasion net had been organized by Benesch in the spring of 1944 when he made approx. three trips there. The task of directing operations was assigned to SS-*Ostuf* Hagedorn in September 1944. He worked in co-operation with the Paris representative of RSHA *Gruppe* VI B, SS-*Staf* Bickler; and with the organization of *Leitstelle* II *West*, consisting of one or two FAKs each having two to three FATs. *Jäger* Battalion 502 sent SS-*Ostuf* Neumann and three French-speaking NCOs. Neumann, a *Feldwebel* from *Abwehr* II, and two *Unteroffiziers* from Seehof School served as instructors.

The invasion nets were centered in Normandy, Brittany, and Paris. Organization 'LIT' furnished 120 men in Normandy and Brittany and 400 in Paris, in groups of four or five men. The group leaders had been trained at Seehof. There were two or three W/T transmitters, one of them in Paris and another in Brittany.

Belgium. The invasion net was organized by *Unteroffizier* Verstraaten and another man. Both had worked in Belgium for the *Abwehr*. The net was concentrated on the coast and near Brussels. Skorzeny knows of at least 20 to 25 men belonging to the net who were trained at Seehof. Radio stations were established in Brussels and Antwerp.

After the invasion two attempts were made by SS-*Jagdverband Nord-West* to establish contact. The operations were carried out by two groups from the Flemish Company, comprising two to three men each (see Operation 'Jeanne' below).

Norway. Preparations for an invasion net in Norway started in October 1944. SS-*Jagdverband Nord-West* furnished three trained Norwegian NCOs, who recruited about 40 men for training. This was done in co-operation with the FAT II operating in Norway. No radio communications existed.

Baltic States. When the invasion nets in the Baltic States were organized, difficulties arose from the request by the prospective members for a certain amount of political independence. With the consent of Alfred Rosenberg [*Reich* Minister for the Occupied Eastern Territories], Skorzeny granted their request, but all privileges were later abolished by *Gauleiter* Koch. This caused great resentment.

The organization was headed by an Estonian army officer, SS-*Hstuf* Arvid Janevics. He was joined in January 1945 by a Latvian and a Lithuanian SS-*Ostubaf*, both political representatives of the SS-*Hauptamt*. A Company of approx. 80 Estonians, 50 Latvians and 30 Lithuanians was trained by SS-*Jagdverband Ost* from October 1944 until January 1945.

The invasion net as it was established in Estonia comprised only 20 to 30 men. At the end of January 1945, after parts of the Baltic States had already been lost, three groups were sent to Estonia, one to Latvia, and one to Lithuania, each composed of two or three men. Janevics remained behind the lines and was last heard from in April or May 1945.

Annex IV

Individual Operations (*Unternehmen*)

1. Operations in the West.

Operation 'PETER'

In December 1943 or January 1944, Hitler told Ribbentrop and Himmler that Danish Resistance activists had become intolerable. SS-*Staf* Dr Rudolf Mildner, BdS Denmark, was unable to cope with the situation because the Danish police not only failed to assist him but co-operated with the resistance movement. Hitler ordered terror to be fought with terror, believing that the Danish people would then force the police to take strict counter-measures against all acts of terrorism. SS-*Staf* Mildner could not carry out those orders. He was short of personnel, and his men were not trained in the handling of demolitions. Moreover, they were so well known in Denmark that they would be recognized immediately, which would defeat Hitler's purpose. The HSSPF confessed that the situation was out of the control and that he was unable to offer any help or advice.

Himmler therefore ordered members of the *Sonder Lehrgang* Oranienburg, who were thugs experienced in the use of explosives, to be transferred to SS-*Staf* Milder's staff. Radl emphasized that it should be possible to verify the fact that the persons sent from VI S were member of the *Sonder Lehrgang* Oranienburg because the *Sonder Lehrgang* was in existence before Skorzeny took over RSHA *Gruppe* VI S. Radl, however, failed to mention one known member of the operation, who is not a member of *Sonder Lehrgang* Oranienburg. He claims to have sent only an interpreter, 60 years of age, to Operation 'Peter', in February 1944. This man had no connections with the SD but was from the *Luftwaffe* and had relatives in Denmark whom he wanted to see.

Radl states that RSHA *Amt* IV was able to provide only the leader for the expedition, SS-*Stubaf* Naujocks (now POW), who had been investigating black market activities for BdS Belgium. Naujocks for some reason did not take part in the actual operation.

SS-*Hstuf* von Foelkersam selected the men from VI S and sent them to Copenhagen. Radl remembers the following names:

SS-*Hstuf* Peter
SS-*Ostuf* Fritz Himmel
SS-*Ustuf* Ludwig Huf
SS-*Uschaf* Walter Glässner
SS-*Uschaf* Hans Holzer
SS-*Uschaf* Renner

The necessary materials were supplied by RSHA *Gruppe* VI F, while papers were issued by the BdS Denmark. All members had aliases in Denmark but these were not known to *Gruppe* VI S. From February to August 1944, reports on the operations were submitted every two months. One copy was sent to RSHA *Amt* IV and one to RSHA *Amt* VI which was read by Schellenberg, Skorzeny, Radl and von Foelkersam. The reports were not signed by Peter. Why the operation was called 'Peter' was not known to Radl and the fact that SS-*Ustuf* Peter was involved appears to him to be a coincidence.

In July 1944, RSHA *Amt* IV compiled a report on the Danish situation for Hitler. This report stated that the number of 'Danish acts of terrorism' was six to eight times as large as Peter's acts. On the other hand, figures given by Radl show that attempted or actual assassinations by the Danish Resistance numbered 30 to 35, while Peter's number eight to ten; Danish attacks on industry 90 to 95, Peter's 15 to 18; attacks on public gatherings by the Danish Resistance 20 to 25, and by Peter

30 to 35. Radl prepared a memorandum for RSHA *Amt* IV, signed by Skorzeny, to the effect that VI S should be kept out of these matters, and that the responsibility should be borne by *Amt* IV.

In August 1944, RSHA *Amt* IV sent an expedition for similar purposes to Denmark, consisting of about ten men commanded by SS-*Stubaf* Philipp. One of the members was SS-*Ustuf* Horst Issel, who may have come from RSHA *Amt* I.

In September 1944 the RSHA VI S men returned. Two reports of their activities in Denmark were sent to VI S4. Radl did not read the reports, which went directly to Schellenberg.

The activities of the Danish Resistance, aided by the British, were so intense that by the end of 1944 the counter-terror had become ineffective. Radl states that the Danish Schalburg Korps, composed of Danish *Waffen*-SS, also committed acts of terrorism in Denmark. They were said not to have had any official connection with the BdS or the HSSPF.

Projected Petain Kidnapping.

In addition to the account of the operation in interrogation report IIR-Radl 12 AG dated 4 June 1945, Skorzeny mentions the following members of the operation:

SS-*Ostuf* Adrian von Foelkersam	I-a, Commanding Officer of 1.Company
SS-*Ustuf* Gerhard Ostafel	Skorzeny's adjutant
SS-*Ustuf* Gert Schiffer	Platoon Leader
SS-*Ustuf* Claus von Bremen	Platoon Leader
SS-*Hstuf* Erwin Schmiel	Administrative Officer
SS-*Ostuf* Herbert Bramfeldt	Aide

The troops taking part in the operation were quartered on the Vichy airfield and patrolled the roads eight to ten kilometers from the center of the town of Vichy.

Operation 'Charlie'.

This operation was carried out in September December 1944 on orders of SS-*Brif* Schellenberg and planned by SS-*Ostuf* Charles Hagedorn and SS-*Hstuf* Arno Besekow. The agent involved was SS-*Ostuf* Neumann alias Nebel.

His mission was to establish contact with and to organize the 'Lit' group in Paris, to locate a drop area for supplies, and to establish a new *Anlaufstelle* (contact address). Nebel was to cross the front lines near Belfort. There was to be no W/T communication and upon completion of the mission he was to return.

After an absence of about eight weeks Neumann returned by way of the front lines. According to his report, the efficiency of Allied counter-intelligence precluded any large scale activities in France. Little was left of the 'Lit' group and no old contact address remained. A new contact address was established in a southern suburb of Paris and a drop area for supplies was found nearby.

Operation 'Charlemagne'.

This operation was carried out by *Leitstelle* II *West* in November and December 1944. Four or five groups were sent out, one to the Langres plateau, one into the Rhone valley, and one into the vicinity of Vichy.

The purpose was to establish contact with the White Maquis. Agents were recruited by Ltn. Frank through the French government at Sigmaringen. *Leitstelle* II *West* operated a W/T station with which contact could be made when necessary.

Neither names of agents nor the contact address are known. It is believed that followers of Darnand and Doriot were used. Results of the operations are unknown.

Operation 'Jeanne' ('Henriette').

This operation was carried out by RSHA *Gruppe* VI S4 and SS-*Jagdverband Süd-West*, supplemented by personnel from SS-*Jagdverband Nord-West*. It took place from November 1944 until January 1945 and was directed by Besekow with Hagedorn handling administrative details.

The mission was to establish contact with the I-net in Belgium. Two groups were sent out, one consisting of two Flemmings, one of these a W/T operator; and the other of two Flemmings and one Flemish woman W/T operator. The Flemmings were furnished by the Flemish Company of SS-*Jagdverband Nord-West* and remained in Belgium near Liege and Antwerp. None of their names are known. Communications were maintained with them by the W/T station of RSHA *Gruppe* VI F/H.

Both groups reported that nothing remained of the I-net and that they were waiting for supplies and personnel to be furnished by the Flemish Company of SS-*Jagdverband Nord-West*.

Operation 'Toto'.

This operation was carried out by RSHA *Gruppe* VI S4 and SS-*Jagdverband Süd-West* in December 1944 by order of the *Wehrmachts Führungsstab* under the direction of SS-*Ostuf* Hagedorn.

The mission was to attack the pipeline running north from Marseille by means of explosives and incendiaries and to attack fuel dumps near the front lines. Operations were to take place behind the front lines in the Alsace area and in the Rhone valley. Four groups of five to seven men each were sent out. Upon completion of the mission they were to join the White Maquis of the I-net in France; names of the participants are not known. It was known, however, that one fuel dump in the front area was blown up.

No W/T equipment was provided.

Operation 'Schlange'.

This operation was carried out in December 1944 by VI S and SS-*Jagdverband Süd-West* on orders of the *Wehrmachts Führungsstab* and in cooperation with the I-c of 5.Army. SS-*Ostuf* Hagedorn was in charge of the four or five groups, comprising five to seven men each.

The mission was the destruction of the pipeline running east from Le Havre by means of explosives and incendiaries, and attacks on fuel and ammunition dumps in the area facing the 5.Army sector. Personnel was to return if possible or to join the White Maquis.

Neither names nor results of this operation are known.

Panzer Brigade 150.

At the end of October 1944, Skorzeny was informed of the plans for the Ardennes Offensive by Hitler and *Generaloberst* Jodl at the *Führer Hauptquartier*. He was ordered to activate Panzer Brigade 150 with SS-*Ostubaf* Willi Hardieck as Commanding Officer.

The mission of this unit was to seize the bridges across the Meuse, to operate as shock troops, and take advantage of the element of surprise. It was activated at the *Truppenübungsplatz* (manouver area) at Grafenwohr in November 1944 and was composed of the following elements:

(1) Approx. 1,000 volunteers from the army, Navy, *Luftwaffe* and *Waffen*-SS of whom 120 officers and 600 men formed a *Kommando*-Company and the rest were divided among other units of the Brigade.
(2) Two Companys of SS-*Jagdverband Mitte*—360 men.
(3) Two Companys of *Fallschirm Jäger* Battalion 600—380 men.
(4) Two Battalions of KG 200—600–800 men, *Luftwaffe* parachutists.
(5) Two Panther Panzer Companys—240 men.
(6) Three Panzer Grenadier Companys—520 men.
(7) Two Anti-Tank Companys—200 men.
(8) One Heavy Mortar Company—100 men.

All figures given above are approximate. The total strength of the Brigade was 3,000 men, of whom 300 to 400 were dressed in American uniforms. When the unit was committed, all non-combat elements remained at *Truppenübungsplatz* Wahn, south of Cologne [Köln], reducing the Brigade to a combat strength of 2,400 men. Before the offensive, in early December 1944 Skorzeny made a tour of the various Army Headquarters on the Western Front, in order to familiarize himself with the plan of action.

At the start of the operation, three or four reconnaissance teams of three men each were sent out, dressed in American uniforms and equipped with jeeps. Two sabotage teams of five men each in American uniforms, driving ¾-ton trucks, were sent against enemy-held bridges. One reconnaissance and one sabotage team came back. It had been planned to commit 300 to 400 men as similar missions but this proved impossible when the offensive did not sustain itself.

The losses of the Panzer Brigade, equally distributed among its component units, were 20% dead and wounded. When SS-*Ostubaf* Hardieck was killed during operations, Skorzeny assumed personal command of the unit.

Operation 'Silberfuchs'.

After the German retreat from Finland, it was decided to organize a resistance movement in Norway. SS-*Jagdverband Nord-West* sent an SS-*Untersturmführer* whose name is unknown to Norway for this purpose. He was unsuccessful and *Gruppe* VI S requested RSHA *Amt* I to supply someone familiar with Norway to take charge of the operation. BdS Oslo sent SS-*Hstuf* Helmuth Romeick to Friedenthal for training. He then returned to Norway to recruit agents, and is believed to have sent 20 to 30 men to *Kampfschule* Neustrelitz. Romeick's recruiting activity in Norway was called *Unternehmen* 'Silberfuchs'.

At the time of the German surrender, the resistance movement had not been organized.

Operation 'Honfeld'.

This operation was carried out by SS-*Jagdverband Süd-West* in January 1945 on the Alsatian front. SS-*Ostuf* Honfeld, two NCOs, and one enlisted man, all of 2.Company SS-*Jagdverband Süd-West*, participated in the mission of destroying a transformer approx. ten kilometers behind the front lines. After two and a half days during which they placed the explosive charge and observed enemy activity, the group returned. Through the use of a time delay the transfomer was blown up during the third night.

2. Operations in the East.

Operation 'Panzerfaust'.

It was known to the Germans that Admiral Horthy [in Hungary] had established contact with Tito [in Yugoslavia] in an attempt to negotiate a separate peace with Russia. In September 1944 Skorzeny got orders from Hitler and Himmler to plan Horthy's abduction. For this purpose a force was placed at his disposal, consisting of:

(1) One reinforced Company of SS-*Jagdverband Mitte* (250 men). Acting Commanding Officer was SS-*Ostuf* Heinz Manns.
(2) One reinforced Company of *Fallschirm Jäger* Battalion 600 (250 men). Acting Commanding Officer was SS-*Ostuf* Joachim Marcus.
(3) Two parachute Companys of KG 200 (*Luftwaffe*). Commanding Officer was Major Schluckebier.
(4) Four Companys of officer-candidates from the Wiener Neustadt Officer Training School (approx. 700 men).

This force was to operate in Budapest under the command of *General der Panzertruppe* Ulrich Kleemann, former defender of Rhodes, to whom Skorzeny was subordinated.

Organization took place in Vienna. The following *Führungsstab* officers took part:

SS-*Hstuf* von Foelkersam (Chief of Staff)
SS-*Hstuf* Radl (deputy Chief of Staff)
SS-*Ostuf* Gallent (deputy)
SS-*Ustuf* Lochner (Administrative Officer)
SS-*Hstuf* Nuke (C.O., SS-*Jagdverband Mitte*)
SS-*Hstuf* Milius (C.O. Company of *Fallschirm Jäger* Batl. 600)

In addition, Skorzeny could dispose of elements of the 22.Hungarian SS Division, the 106th and 108th Panzer Brigades and picked numbers of the *Luftwaffe* stationed in Hungary.

Skorzeny took up residence in Budapest in the beginning of October 1944, and had his office in General Kleemann's Headquarters, while the troops were quartered in the suburbs.

In Budapest he met SS-*Gruf* Pfeffer-Wildenbruch, Commander of the *Waffen*-SS for Hungary; SS-*Ogruf* Winkelmann, the HSSPF Hungary; SS-*Ogruf* von dem Bach-Zelewski, who was sent by *Führer Hauptquartier*; SS-*Staf* Geschke, BdS Hungary; and the Ambassador to Italy, Dr Rahn.

On 16 October 1944 orders came from Ambassador Veesenmayer to General Kleemann to start the action. Skorzeny with a small force arrested Horthy's son, a friend and the two Tito representatives.

Several high German officials such as Pfeffer-Wildenbruch, Veesenmayer and the German military *attache* were on the Burg Berg. Horthy ordered the Hungarian troops to be concentrated around the Burg Berg and made a radio speech asking for a separate peace. Skorzeny then threw a cordon around the Hungarians. Horthy received an ultimatum, expiring at 0600 hours the following morning, stipulating that the peace offer was to be officially revoked and the troops withdrawn.

After its expiration, Skorzeny broke through with a Tiger Tank Company and a Company of *Fallschirm Jäger* Battalion 600 and took the Burg Berg. Horthy, however, had already surrendered to Pfeffer-Wildenbruch. The next day Horthy was taken by special train to Munich.

Operation 'Freischütz I–IV'.

These operations were undertaken in order to contact the isolated *Kampfgruppe* Scherhorn, composed of 2,500 men, in the Minsk area of Russia. Four groups of 10–15 men were organized by SS-*Jagdverband Ost* and the SS-*Jagdverbände Führungsstab* on direct orders from Himmler. Each group was under the command of a German officer, but had also two Russian members. They were equipped with W/T sets.

The groups set out in October/November 1944 from East Prussia and were dropped near Minsk. Group I and II were to march eastwards in search of *Oberstleutant* Scherhorn and his men, while *Gruppe* II and IV searched westwards. One group under SS-*Ustuf* Schiffer found Scherhorn after three weeks. Originally they planned to return by land, but this was impossible because the men were too exhausted. Instead arrangements were made to supply the party by air and actually rations, medicine and ammunition were dropped 8 or 10 times. The evacuation of the force by air from former partisan airstrips had to be abandoned in view of the Russian offensive against East Prussia. It retired according to orders towards Germany in two advance parties and two main bodies (*Nord* and *Süd*). Last radio contact occurred late in January or early February 1945.[2]

Of the other groups, two were never heard of and one returned to Germany.

Operation 'Sonnenblume'.

The purpose of this operation was to establish contact with the Ukrainian Nationalist Movement, UPA, in order to determine how many Germans were fighting with UPA bands and to report on the guerilla situation in the Ukraine.

The operation was started by *Mil Amt* in September/October 1944, under the command of *Hauptmann* Kirn, a competent young officer who had been personally authorized by Himmler to deal with UPA. Kirn was Commanding Officer of a FAK Trupp, 202 or 203, which belonged to *Leitstelle* II *Ost für* FAK. He had some 15 men including two officers, eight NCOs and three Ukrainians.

UPA had strong groups operating against the Russians throughout the Ukraine. Some of them comprised as many as 3,000 men, tying up whole Russian divisions. UPA distrusted the Germans who had not kept their promise, given in 1941, to form an independent Ukrainian state. Instead, their leader in Berlin, Bandera, had been arrested with his followers.

After the German retreat from the Ukraine, many German soldiers stayed behind in pockets. Some of them were captured and turned over to UPA, others voluntarily joined UPA ranks. UPA had clandestine W/T and personal contact with members of the Ukrainian movement working in labor camps in Germany. Apart from this, UPA established connections with Germany through Kirn's organization in the Ukraine.

UPA's condition for cooperating with the Germans in resisting Soviet troops was the liberation of Bandera and his followers. Radl presumes that this condition was presented to the Germans through the clandestine W/T service. At first RSHA *Amt* IV refused, for fear that this might result in uprisings of Ukrainians in German labor camps, but in October 1944 it consented to release Bandera at a pre-arranged place.

In October 1944 Kirn and his men went through the front lines to the western Ukraine. Here he made his survey of Germans fighting with UPA and conferred with the leaders of the movement. Large numbers of German officers and enlisted men were accounted for. In November 1944 he was picked up by a Junkers Ju 52 aircraft and returned to Germany. This terminated Operation 'Sonnenblume'. From then on Kirn maintained contact with UPA both by W/T and by courier.

UPA's efforts were not motivated by sympathy for Germany, but by hate of their common enemy. Any illusions raised by German's repeated assurances of help to create an independent Ukrainian state, were shattered when Vlassov issued the Prague Manifesto. Germany apparently backed Vlassov's ideas of a greater Russia, which were incompatible with Ukrainian independence. Radl points out that Vlassov was in a difficult position. If he had promised Ukrainian independence, he would have lost whatever backing he still had for a greater Russia.

Kirn's efforts to support UPA was interrupted in January 1945 when the Russians advanced and he had to retreat with his *Kommando* to Silesia, where he attempted to build up resistance against the Russians with a group of nationalistic Poles.

Operation 'Landfried'.
When Roumania was lost in September 1944, Himmler ordered this operation, which is also known under the name '*Sonder Unternehmen* Girg'. A member of SS-*Jagdverband Mitte*, SS-*Hstuf* Walter Girg and 30 men supplied the Germans in Transylvania with weapons, assisted them to retreat to Germany with their families, blew up bridges and obstructed passes in the Carpathians, and made a reconnaissance mission. They operated behind the Russian lines, in Russian, Roumanian and Bulgarian uniforms, according to the territory.

Operationally the undertaking was under command of SS-*Ogruf* Phleps. In January/February 1945, fiften men were committed, who operated 700 kms behind the lines. They were divided into an eastern group, a western group and a central group. The first obstructed three passes and located approx. 2,000 men from the Ploesti anti-aircraft batteries in the vicinity of Kronstadt, of whom 250 were brought back. The western group brought back German residents and collected intelligence.

The central group was under the command of Girg. It placed demolitions in the Rotenturm Pass, south of Hermannstadt and observed Russian preparations in that vicinity. On one occasion they marched for about 15 kms in a Russian column. They were discovered and condemned to death. Girg however managed to escape from the firing squad and to reach German lines. He submitted a report containing valuable information on Russian order of battle and was awarded the Ritterkreuz.

In January 1945 Girg came back from another operation in the Danzig area. He was arrested by the commandant of the city of Kolberg on suspicion of being a 'Seydlitz sympathiser' and was sentenced to death. When he offered to defend the city at the most vulnerable spot, the commandant became convinced to Girg's political reliability and released him. He returned to Friedenthal in early March 1945 and joined Skorzeny.

Operations 'Gemsbock I–VI'
Between October and November 1944 six operations took place in north-west Roumania where many Germans were settled. The purpose was to establish contact

with the invasion net and the groups were equipped with W/T sets. Each group consisted of between three and five men mostly Germans from Roumania, drawn from SS-*Jagdverband Süd-Ost*, within which there was an SS-*Jagd Einsatz* Rumänien under SS-*Ostuf* Müller.

All but two members of one group were captured by the Russians shortly after landing.

Operations 'Steinbock I–III'.

These took place between October and December 1944 to strengthen the Iron Guard in Rumania. They were carried out in the territory north of Bucharest. There were three to five men with W/T equipment in each group.

Operations 'Regulus I–VI'.

Leitstelle II *Süd-Ost* undertook six operations between October and December 1944. The groups were dropped by parachute to establish contact with the Roumanian Army and the resistance movements. Small groups were used, consisting partly of German enlisted men, partly of Roumanian volunteers.

The undertakings were successful.

Operations 'Forelle I–II'.

In October 1944 *Jagd Einsatz* Donau of SS-*Jagdverband Süd-Ost* made attempts to make traffic on the river Danube unsafe by blowing up bridges and shipping. The operation, including swimming saboteurs, was under the command of SS-*Ostuf* Stanzig and SS-*Ustuf* Ludwig Wouters, who had a ship called the 'Walter', equipped with radio, arms and ammunition. It was found impossible to attack the bridges because they were seized too quickly by the Russians. A limited success was attained by blowing up a pontoon bridge with the aid of floating mines, and by sinking approx. 10,000 tons of shipping with magnetic charges.

'Forelle II' was an operation by the same unit to breakthrough to Budapest and deliver 600 tons of food and ammunition. It took place on the night of 31 December 1944 and although the 'Walter' ran aground on a sandbank 20 kms from Budapest, SS-*Ostuf* Stanzig succeeded in loading the goods onto a small cargo ship and transporting them to Budapest. W/T communications was maintained with the 'Walter' for five days, after which there was complete silence. A special patrol sent out by SS-*Jagdverband Ost* to find out what had happened reported that the ship had been abandoned.

Operations 'Schlange'.

These operations SS-*Jagdverband Süd Ost* in Serbia all had names of snakes, such as 'Sandviper', 'Blind-Schleicher', 'Kreuzotter', 'Hornviper', and 'Rindelnatter'. According to Radl there were some ten groups of 20 men each, who were to allow themselves to be overrun by the Russians and then attempt to establish W/T contact with the staff of SS-*Jagdverband Süd-Ost*. He thinks that some of them were connected with Mihailovich.

The groups were to maintain radio silence for some four weeks and until April 1945 no W/T contact had been established.

Operations 'Abendstern', 'Fixstern' and 'Polarstern'.
All these operations were organized by SS-*Jagdverband Süd-Ost* in Hungary. There were several more of these undertakings, all bearing names of stars. The largest was 'Abendstern' which was carried out in November 1944. It comprised approx. 100 Hungarians and 10 German instructors who were left behind in the lines in the vicinity of Szeged to perform sabotage activities against enemy supply lines. No reports were received.

Skorzeny mentions the following 'Stern' undertakings:

In October 1944 ten men were left behind the enemy lines in the Banat [the border areas of western Roumania and eastern Yugoslavia]. No reports were received, as the group did not have W/T.

In November–December 1944, three or four patrol operations took place on Lake Balaton (Plattensee) in Hungary. It is known that an ammunition and a fuel dump were blown up.

In January 1945, two reconnaissance missions were carried out south of Lake Balaton.

In March 1945, approx. 80 Hungarians stayed behind in the Bakony forest, they maintained W/T contact with the Honved Ministry.

In March 1945, two groups of 10–12 men each were left behind the lines south of Lake Balaton. No reports were received.

Operation 'Stieglitz'.
This operation was originated by SS-*Jagdverband Süd-Ost* in the fall of and winter of 1944 and early 1945, involving a resistance movement in Hungary. No details are known.

Operation 'Wildkatze'
SS-*Jagdverband Ost* made plans with the *Wehrmacht Führungsstab Ost* and *Fremde Heere Ost* for eight to ten operations in the Baltic States and Poland. However, only the first one materialized. Its purpose was to harrass communications lines and to round up German stragglers. In February 1945 SS-*Stubaf* Dr Pechau and some ten to fifteen men were dropped by parachute south-west of Lodz. The results are not known, as none of them returned and they had no W/T equipment.

Operations by *Dienststellen* 2000 and 3000.
No actual operations are known, except that attempts were made to work in Syria and Palestine with the aid of Greek merchants.

Projected Attack on Russian Industry.

In November 1943 plans were made to impair the Russian war production in the Urals. Skorzeny believes that Speer was the originator of the idea. The Speer Ministry put special emphasis on the destruction of the blast furnaces at Magnitogorsk. Skorzeny was of the opinion that an attack on the power system which supplied a vast net of very large plants would be more effective. He objected to the original plan to *Jäger* Battalion 502.

When Army Group *Mitte* collapsed in June 1944 near Minsk, the bases for the planned operations were lost. New detailed plans were worked out for an attack against the Moscow industrial regions, but were never used.

Annex V

Technical Sabotage Information

The development and manufacture of sabotage equipment and special weapons were carried out by RSHA *Gruppe* VI F and *Mil Amt* D/T. The individual components of sabotage material were often purchased from private firms.

Gruppe VI F occupied two houses in Douglas Strasse, Berlin-Schmargendorf, with workshops and laboratories, and in the spring of 1944 took over a part of Friedenthal, which was closed off from *Gruppe* VI S and to which access could be obtained by special permission only. VI F also had several camps in the neighbourhood of Berlin.

Mil Amt D/T had workshops and a camp at an abandoned factory at Quenz and in barracks on the factory grounds.

In February and March 1945 standard packages (*Einheit Paketen*) weighing approx 2 kilograms were made up and distributed as follows:

To WERWOLF	500 packages
SS-*Jagdverband Süd-West* and SS-*Jagdverband Nord-West* (especial *Einsatz* Flandern)	100 packages
SS-*Jagdverband Süd-Ost*	200 packages
SS-*Jagdverband Ost* (for *Unternehmen* Wildkatze)	200 packages

In each package were:

4 All-purpose Nipolit Charges
2 Nipolit hand grenades
1 Nipolit pressure-release bomb
1 Nipolit incendiary bomb (hexagonal)
1 ZZ 42 push-pull igniter
Safety fuse
Detonating fuse
Blasting caps
GAC delays

Skorzeny's knowledge of German sabotage material is rather limited, he has, however, mentioned certain items that were hitherto unknown.

1. Hexagonal incendiary bomb made of Nipolit, about one foot [30 cm] long and an inch to a inch-and-a-half [2.5–4 cm] in diameter.
2. Mark IV clockwork delays with 6 and 28 day maximum delay time.
3. *Hell- und Dunkel Zünder*, or *Verdunkelungszünder*. A delay containing a selenium cell and a Leclanche battery. It can be made to function when light falls on the cell or when light ceases to fall on the cell. When the battery runs down, the delay functions automatically. It seems possible that about twenty of these were manufactured by KTI for RSHA *Gruppe* VI S.
4. A delay set off by a high frequency radio signal. Maximum signal distance 300 meters [910 feet]. These were in the experimental stage only.
5. *Schienendruckzünder*. A railway pressure igniter for attachment to a rail. The igniter remains inactive as long as there is no traffic on the line but is armed by the pressure of the first passing train. It can be adjusted for a maximum time delay after arming of 14 days. Possibly it is bobby-trapped so that replacement of the metal safety pin in the safety pin-hole causes it to function.
6. Nipolit hand grenade with Allways fuse.
7. All-purpose Nipolit charge (*Einheitsprangkörper*) made jointly by *Mil Amt* D/T and WASAG. This charge weighs approx 300 grams and is rectangular in shape with grooves cut in each face, presumably to give a hollow charge effect.
8. *Abscherzünder*. A delay operating on a shearing principle. A striker is held under spring-tension by a metal schaft which under the tension of the spring gradually breaks down. The body of the delay is telescopic in the sense that the tension of the spring can be adjusted by elongating the barrel.

RSHA *Gruppe* VI F was experimenting with this delay but it had not been put into production.

Annex VI

Poison Bullets

Skorzeny has made the following admissions regarding the manufacture and issue of poison bullets under his direction:

Live Bullets

At Skorzeny's request the *Kriminal Technisches Institut der Sipo* (KTI), Berlin, manufactured special 7.65 caliber bullets containing poison. The poison was an aconite compound and escaped through slits in the sides of the bullets.

The bullets were supplied to Skorzeny at Friedenthal. He issued approx. six each to *Hauptmann* Hellmers, Commanding Officer of *Leitstelle* II *West für Frontaufklärung* in October 1944 and to SS-*Ostubaf* Hardieck of 150 Panzer Brigade in November 1944.

Skorzeny at first tried to persuade the interrogators that these bullets were manufactured and issued solely for suicide purposes. He readily agreed, however, that Hellmers was most unlikely to have wanted them for such a reason. He finally admitted that they were intended for assassinations. He claims that they were not to be used without special orders.

Simulated Bullets

Skorzeny admitted that special equipment was provided for suicide purposes in the form of poison ampoules hidden in fountain pens, automatic pencils, cigarette lighters, and bullets. This bullet is not to be confused with those mentioned above. It is simple a receptacle for the poison ampoule and cannot be fired from a weapon.

Annex VII

Plan of Friedenthal (as of March 1945)

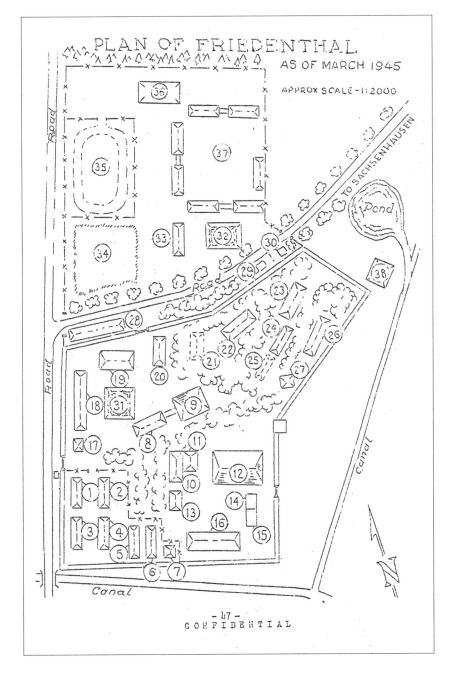

Plan of Friedenthal (as of March 1945)

RSHA *Gruppe* VI F Area.
Admission by special pass only.

1–4.	Wooden barracks
2.	Offices
3.	Workshop
4.	Parachute store room
5–6.	Stone Warehouses. Contains chemical laboratory, photographic dark room, ammunition and weapons storage.
7.	Blacksmith workshop

SS-*Jagdverbände Führungsstab* Area.

8.	Ground floor: Quarters for officers of the *Führungsstab*
	2nd floor: Quarters of Chief of Staff and I-a; offices of the *Führungsstab*
	3rd floor: NCOs quarters.
9.	Ground floor: Offices of Skorzeny and Radl; waiting room, officers' club; library; mess
	2nd floor: Offices of Besekow, Bramfeldt, Schmiel
	3rd floor: Quarter for Skorzeny, Dr Wetz, Radl, Schmiel, Besekow
10.	Garage and stables
11.	Weapons store room of I-b; small repair workshop
12.	Shed
13.	Garage and saddle shop
14.	Kennels
15.	Small stables
16.	Garage and repair shop
17.	Sentry box
18.	HQ Company barracks and orderly room
19.	Cinema (unfinished), used for storage
	Ground floor: Dispensary
	2nd floor: *Führungsstab*, Chief of Staff, I-a, I-b
20.	*Führungsstab*, I-b, I-c, map room
21.	Lecture hall (unfinished)
22.	Officer's quarters
23.	W/T operators' quarters
24.	Telephone, teletype, amd W/T exchange
25.	Hospital (unfinished)
26.	Women's quarters
27.	Ammunition dump; several smaller dumps in woods

28.   Barracks; administrative personnel and guards
29.   Private home
30.   Quarters of secretaries, Kopfheise and Krüger sisters
31–32.   Reservoirs

SS-*Jagdverband Mitte* Area (until 31 January 1945)

33.   HQ Company
34.   Athletic field
35.   Riding ring
36.   Stables
37.   1. 2. and 3. Company area
38.   Boat shed

Annex VIII

Personalities

SS-*Ostubaf* Karl Appel, RSHA VI S3, C.O. Heinrichsburg Sabotage School. Last seen in Berlin, Oct 1944; April–Sept 1944, at Heinrichsburg; engineer by profession; Bavarian (?).

SS-*Stubaf* Alexanders Auch, SS-*Jagdverband Ost*. Born Leningrad; went with SS-*Jagdverband Ost* to Eastern front at Troppau.

SS-*Hstuf* Alfred Backhaus, RSHA VI C (Russia). Last seen in Berlin, March 1945.

SS-*Stubaf* Josef Bäurle, instructor at SS-*Junkerschule* Bad Tölz. Has one leg amputated.

Kapitän z. See Theodor Freiherr von Bechtolsheim, RSHA VI, *Mil Amt*, I-a. Last seen in Berlin, March 1945.

Fräulein Hildegard (?) Beirich, RSHA VI S1 (receipt and despatch section). Evacuated to Hof, dismissed, March 1945.

SS-*Ostubaf* Rudolf Benesch, Commanding Officer SS-*Jagdverband Süd-Ost*. Earlier Major in Brandenburg Division, until Sept. 1944 with *Streifkorps* Croatia; finally joined SKA at Ennstal, Austria; Reserve Police officer.

SS-*Ogruf* Gottlob Berger, Chief SSFHA. Last seen in Berlin, January 1945.

SS-*Ostubaf* Heinrich Bernhard, RSHA VI B, *Referent* for France. Last seen at Waldburg during January 1945.

SS-*Staf* Hermann Bickler, RSHA VI B *Beauftragter* in Paris, December 1943. Last seen in Berlin durinng the summer 1944.

SS-*Hschaf* Gottfried Bitterwolf, RSHA VI S1 (Receipts and Despatch Section).

Oberltn. Walter Bittner, RSHA *Mil Amt* D; came from *Abwehr*.

SS-*Stubaf* Ottomar Blumenthal, SS-*Jagdverbände Führungsstab* from March 1945. End April 1945, volunteered for 6.SS-Pz.Army, possibly went to Army Group Schörner. Last seen at Radstatt, May 1945; left arm missing.

Fräulein Gisela Bölling, work of office of RSHA VI S4. Discharged at Puch, 1945.

SS-*Ostuf* Bolz, SS-*Jagdverbände Führungsstab* (with Gerhardt). Last seen at Hof, May 1945.

Oberltn. Bolzin, RSHA *Mil Amt* A, and adjutant to Sandberger. Last seen in Berlin, April 1945.

SS-*Ustuf* Bouwens, SS-*Jagd Einsatz* Donau. Last seen in Vienna, October 1944; German or Belgian; missing since 31 December 1944 on Unternehmen Forelle II.

SS-*Hstuf* Herbert Bramfeldt, head of RSHA VI S4. Last seen at Radstatt early March 1945, later joined SKA in Carinthia.

Major Friedrich Brandt, *Abwehr* II then *Leitstelle* II *West* in charge of a FAK.

SS-*Ostuf* Ulrich Breitenfeld, RSHA VI S1. Discharged at Hof, March 1945.

Oberst i.G. Georg Buntrock, chief of RSHA *Mil Amt* F. Last seen in Berlin, March 1945.

SS-*Stubaf* Gottlieb Bussinger, RSHA VI D, operations in Finland. Last seen in Berlin, April 1945.

SS-*Stubaf* Fritz Carstens, RSHA VI Kult (liaison officer with *Reichkulturkammer* in Berlin). Last seen in Berlin, April 1945.

Fräulein Rosita Cassier, mistress of Besekow, RSHA VI S4. Born 1918, speaks French, English, Spanish, Italian. Looked after some five families of VI S4 agents in Badenweiler. Suspected to have worked for Allied Intelligence Service.

SS-*Hstuf* Holger-Winding Christensen, RSHA VI F/H (Radio section). Last seen in Berlin, January 1945.

Oberltn Günther Cornand, RSHA VI Z/B. Last seen in Berlin, early April 1945.

SS-*Ostuf* Rudolf Danziger, RSHA VI Wi. Last seen in Berlin, January 1945.

SS-*Hstuf* Heinrich Deharde, SS-*Jagdverband Süd-West*. Killed in action on the river Werra, 1945.

SS-*Hschaf* Ernst Deppert, RSHA VI A, Berlin, mail room. Last seen in Berlin, April 1945.

SS-*Hstuf* Willi Dethier, SS-*Jagdverband Nord-West*. Killed in action on Eastern front, 1 February 1945.

Oberstltn. Eckhardt von Dewitz, RSHA *Mil Amt*; came from Luftwaffe. Last seen in Berlin, March 1945.

SS-*Ostuf* Gaston Dobrovich, RSHA VI S4 (possibly worked with Kienast).

SS-*Hstuf* Erhard Döhring, RSHA VI, *Referent* for Sweden. Last seen in Berlin, beinning 1945; arrested May 1945 in Norway.

SS-*Hstuf* Karl Döring, RSHA VI B, *Referent* for North Africa and Southen France). Last seen at Waldburg, March 1945.

SS-*Hstuf* Dreibholz (*sic*), Commander of HQ Company, SS-*Jagdverbände*, from November 1944. Last seen at Teisendorf at the end April 1945.

SS-*Stubaf* Hans Duffner, RSHA VI S4; 1945, in charge of operations from the Alsace across the lines. Last seen at Friedenthal in January 1945.

SS-*Ustuf* Karl-Otto Ebeling, SS-*Jagdverband Ost*. March–April 1945 in action on Eastern front at Troppau.

SS-*Stubaf* Hans-Wilhelm Eggen, RSHA VI, Schellenberg's man in Switzerland. Last seen in Berlin during March 1945.

SS-*Ustuf* Karl Egner, SS-*Jagdverband Untersuchungsführer*; RSHA III and VI. Last Seen in Friedenthal at end March 1945.

Major Dr Kuno Ehrmann, Chief of RSHA *Mil Amt* D/T from January 1945.

Hauptmann Dr Werner Eisenberg, deputy head *Zentralbüro*, RSHA *Mil Amt* D. Last seen in northern Bavaria at end April 1945.

SS-*Ostuf* Walter Eisenmenger, SS-*Jagdverband Süd-West*. End April 1945 went to 6.SS-Pz.Army on Eastern front.

SS-*Hstuf* Josef Faulhaber, RSHA VI F, occasional instructor at Seehof and Heinrichsburg training schools. April 1945 released by RSHA VI F, and fought on Eastern front as Regimental Commander where wounded.

Oberstltn. Kurt Fechner, commander of *Leitstelle* II *Süd-Ost*.

Oberltn. Murad Ferid, RSHA VI *Mil Amt* D (*Gruppe Süd-Ost*); commander FAK 201 in Belgrade. Arrested by US forces, May 1945.

Ltn Frank, *Leitstelle* II *West*; liaison officer with Doriot and Darnand.

SS-*Hstuf* Werner Franz, RSHA VI Wi, Berlin. Dismissed beginning 1945.

Korv.Kapitän Fritz Frauenheim, Chief of Staff of KdK (Navy). Last in Berlin during January 1945.

Angestellter Erwin Frinke, RSHA VI F, Photographic Laboratory.

SS-*Hstuf* Karl Fucker, with Division *Nord* in Finlad, 1943; *Fallschirm Jäger* Battalion 502, 1943–1944; commander, SS-*Jagdverband Mitte*; finally joined SKA in Hochkönig. Last seen in Salzburg, end April 1945.

SS-*Ostuf* Wilhelm Gallent, SS-*Jagdverbände Führungsstab*; April 1945, went to 6.SS-Pz.Army on Eastern front.

Oberltn. Gotthard Gambke, from *Abwehr* to RSHA *Mil Amt* D (*Gruppe Süd-Ost*). Last seen in Berlin-Birkenswerder, February 1945.

Major Karl-Edmund Gartenfeld, commander *Kampfgeschwader* (KG) 200. Last seen in Berlin during March 1944.

SS-*Hstuf* Hans Gerlach, commander SS-*Jagdverband Süd-West*. Reported missing in action before his arrest by US forces.

Hauptmann Giel, with SS-*Jagdverband Ost* in Bohemia, 1945. Last seen in Friedenthal during November 1944.

SS-*Hstuf* Hermann Giese, RSHA VI D, Berlin. Dismissed from *Amt* VI at the beginning of 1945.

SS-*Hstuf* Walter Girg, SS-*Junkerschule* Klagenfurt and *Fallschirm Jäger* Batl. 502 before appointment as Commander, SS-*Jagdverband Mitte*. Finally joined SKA in Lofer. Last seen in Salzburg during March 1945.

528   RSHA: Reich Security Main Office—Organisation, Activities, Personnel

SS-*Hstuf* Otto Gödtel, RSHA VI S3 and head of administration at Heinrichsburg training school. Dismissed probably end 1944 or early 1945.

SS-*Hstuf* Dr Emil Görns, Medical Officer of SS-*Jagdverband Nord-West*. 1945, went with SS-*Ostuf* Fucker from the Oder front to the SKA in Hochkönig, Austria.

SS-*Ostuf* Hans Graalfs, RSHA VI S, SS-*Jagdverbände Führungsstab* I-c. Early May 1945 was SKA (Annaberg). Went in direction of Salzburg to find Skorzeny and not heard from since.

SS-*Ustuf* Walter Gramzow, worked on Skorzeny's personal staff before sent to join *Sonder Einsatz Abteilung* zbV. Last seen in Hof during March 1945.

SS-*Ustuf* Gunar Grapmanis, came to SS-*Jagd Einsatz* Baltikum as a specialist for Latvia until March 1945. Last seen in Friendenthal during March 1945.

SS-*Ostuf* Charles Hagedorn, RSHA VI S4, on staff of SS-*Jagdverband Süd-West*. Last seen in Friedenthal in November 1944.

Oberst Haigel, Commanding Officer of *Kampfgeschwader* 200 (*Luftwaffe*), April–November 1944. Last seen in Berlin during November 1944.

SS-*Stubaf* Dr Walter Hammer, *Gruppenleiter* RSHA VI E, May 1943–March 1944, when succeeded by Waneck.

SS-*Hstuf* Hans Hartmann, RSHA VI A (*Hausverwaltung*), Berlin. Last seen in Berlin in April 1945.

SS-*Ustuf* Johannes Hein, RSHA VI S, SS-*Jagdverbände Führungsstab* in charge of W/T operations. Probably remained in Hof, March 1945.

SS-*Stubaf* Wolfram Heinze-Rogee, SS-*Jagdverband Ost*. His brother SS-*Stubaf* Eberhard Heinze, killed in action at Hohensalza with SS-*Jagdverbänd Süd-Ost* on 22 January 1945. Last seen in Friedenthal in March 1945

SS-*Ustuf* Rudolf Henn, SS-*Jagdverbände Führungsstab*.

Major der Schutzpolizei Hensel. Last seen in Friedenthal during March 1945.

SS-*Ogruf* Maximilian von Herff, chief of SSPHA (SS-*Personalhauptamt*). Last seen in Berlin during March 1945.

Vize Admiral Hellmuth Heye. Admiral of the Naval KdK units. Last seen in Kiel during Janaury 1945.

SS-*Hstuf* Otto Heyer, RSHA VI C, *Referent* for Near East. Last seen in Salzburg in April 1945.

SS-*Stubaf* RR Dr Klaus Huegel, *Beauftragter* RSHA VI B with BdS Italien. Last seen in Verona, Italy, in June 1944.

SS-*Hstuf* Werner Hunke, SS-*Jagdverbände Führungsstab*, I-a in Divion Schwedt; later joined SKA. Last seen in Annaberg near Salzburg, May 1945.

Major d.Luftwaffe Hurlin, RSHA *Mil Amt*, liaison officer officer with KG 200. Last seen in Berlin during April 1945.

SS-*Hstuf* Erich Jäckert, SS-*Jagdverbände Führungsstab*. End 1944, transferred to army; has one foot amputated.

Dr Janbeck, RSHA VI F, chemist. Last seen in Berlin during January 1945.

SS-*Hstuf* Arvid Janevics, *Waffen-Führer* with SS-*Jagdverband Ost*. Beginning

January 1945 went on mission to the Baltics States and did not return.

SS-*Staf* Juuling (*sic*), Estonian or Latvian, Political Adviser at SS-*Hauptamt*. From February 1945 with SS-*Jagd Einsatz* Baltikum as specialist for Estonia (?). Last seen at Friedenthal during March 1945.

SS-*Ostuf* Rudolf Käfer, construction engineer with SS-*Jagdverbände*, Headquarters Company, at Friedenthal. Probably dismissed at Teisendorf, April 1945; might have joined 6.SS-Pz.Army.

SS-*Hstuf* Alfred Kallweit, SS-*Jagdverbände Führungsstab*, in charge of the technical department of the Signals Section. Dismissed at Hof in March 1945 as a war casualty.

Frau Grete Kaulbach (or Kaulpach), secretary in RSHA VI S3. Dismissed in Hof, March 1945.

SS-*Ostuf* Helmut Kienast, RSHA VI S4, agent operations into France. Dismissed in April 1945, possibly at Hof.

SS-*Ostuf* Dr Wolfram Kirchner, from Brandenburg Divison to Referent in RSHA VI F; 1945, with SS-*Jagdverband Süd-Ost* in Hungary. Arrested by US forces in Austria, May 1945.

Hauptmann Kirn—see Dietrich Witzel, below.

SS-Hstuf Werner Kleber, RSHA VI E, Croatia and Vienna. Last seen in Vienna during October 1944.

SS-*Stubaf* Hans Kleinert, RSHA VI C/Z (Zeppelin) and latterly, RSHA VI A3. Last seen in Berlin during April 1945.

SS-*Ostuf* Konstantin Klinkert, SS-*Jagdverband Mitte*; war invalid. Dismissed at Hof, 1945.

SS-*Ustuf* Anton Knorr, SS-*Jagdverbände Führungsstab*, I-b office. Had only a few weeks with the *Führungsstab*, in April 1945 to the Eastern front with Gerhardt.

Major Dr Hans Koch, *Abwehr Leitstelle* II *Süd-Ost* and FAK. Released in September 1944 due to ill health.

SS-*Ustuf* Köster, RSHA VI S, SS-*Jagdverbände Führungsstab*. Surrendered or taken prisoner at Teisendorf, April 1945.

Frau Grete Kopfheise, secretary of Skorzeny, RSHA VI S. Dismissed at Puch, 1945.

Fräulein Amalien Kottschlag, secretary of Winter, RSHA VI S3. During winter 1944–1945 at *Kampfschule* Neustrelitz; dismissed at Friedenthal, beginning April 1945.

SS-*Ustuf* Konrad Kutschke, RSHA VI S, *Betreuungsoffizier* in *Sondereinheit Abteilung* zbV. 1945, went to the Oder front with Division Schwedt.

SS-*Ostuf* Gerhard Lackner, SS-*Jagdverbände Führungsstab*. Last seen on Skorzeny's train at Pongau or Klammstein, April 1945.

SS-*Ostuf* Lang, SS-*Jagdverband Süd-Ost*.

Oberltn. Lange, with *Kampfgeschwader* (KG) 200; volunteered for suicide missions. Last seen in Berlin during March 1945.

SS-*Stubaf* Dr Heinz Lange, RSHA VI D (USA dept), Berlin. Last seen in Berlin during March 1945.

SS-*Stubaf* Werner Lassig, *Gruppenleiter* RSHA VI F from May 1943. Last seen in Berlin during March 1945.

SS-*Ustuf* Karl Liebe, RSHA VI F location at the Friedenthal site.

SS-*Ustuf* Mathias Liebhart, from SS-*Hauptamt*; liaison officer between SS-*Jagd Einsatz* Rumänien and RSHA VI E in Vienna. Last seen in Vienna during January 1945.

SS-*Ustuf* Kurt Loba, came from RSHA VI B where participated in line crossers in France, to RSHA VI S4. After a few months returned to VI B.

SS-*Ustuf* Ronald Lochner, came from SSFHA in November 1944 to SS-*Jagdverbände Führungsstab*. Released after the the death of his brother.

Major Dr Roland Loos, RSHA *Mil Amt* D.

Hauptmann Hans Lormis, RSHA *Mil Amt* D (*Gruppe Süd-West*). Last seen in Berlin-Birkenwerder during February 1945.

SS-*Stubaf* Hermann Lumm, RSHA VI C/Z (Zeppelin operations against Russia). Last seen in Berlin during March 1945.

Fräulein Alice Mackert, temporary interpreter with RSHA VI S4. Also concerned with the welfare of the foreign agents. Last seen in Berlin during January 1945.

SS-*Hstuf* Joachim Mahlow, RSHA VI S, SS-*Jagdverbände Führungsstab*. Remained at Teisendorf, April 1945.

Oberstltn. Johannes Mauritius, chief of RSHA *Mil Amt* D/T until January 1945.

SS-*Staf* Otto Meyer (*sic*), SS-*Jagdverbände Führungsstab*. End April 1945, joined 6.SS-Pz.Army on the Eastern front.

SS-*Ostuf* Werner Meyer, RSHA VI S4 as assistant to Besekow; then with SS-*Jagdverbände Führungsstab* before finally joining the SKA in Austria. Last seen in Austria, April 1945.

Major Mengler, RSHA *Mil Amt* D, administration.

SS-*Hstuf* Ulrich Menzel, SS-*Jagdverbämde Führungsstab*. Towards end of 1944 traferred to the Wehrmacht.

SS-*Stubaf* Siegfried Milius, Commanding Officer *Fallschirm Jäger* Batl. 600. March 1945, regimental commander with the *Germanisches* SS-Pz.Korps on the Eastern front at Schwedt.

SS-*Hstuf* Erich Müller, came from SS-*Hauptamt* to SS-*Jagd Einsatz* Roumania as platoon leader. Last seen in Vienna during November 1944.

SS-*Stubaf* Herbert Müller, *Gruppenleiter* RSHA VI A, May 1943–February 1944 when succeeded by Sandberger. Last seen in Waldburg during November 1944.

SS-*Ostuf* Franz Nebenführ, came from SD work in Greece to RSHA VI S4 agent operations. Last seen in Linz (Austria), during April 1945 with SKA (Kärnten group).

SS-*Ostuf* Werner Neisser, carried out *Abt.* VI work with BdS Paris, 1943–1944; then VI S work in Italy with Operation Zypresse until the collapse. Arrested in French Zone, 1945.

SS-*Stubaf* Walter Otten, RSHA VI counter-espionage, Berlin. Last seen in Berlin during April 1945.

SS-*Hschaf* Pahlow, RSHA VI S3, assistant to Bramfeldt and schools programs. Last seen in April 1945 on Skorzeny's train at Pongau, Austria. Joined SKA.

SS-*Ustuf* Herbert Pahnke, RSHA VI A (*Hausverwaltung und Verpflegung*). Last seen in Berlin during April 1945.

SS-*Ustuf* Franz Paul, RSHA VI G, Berlin, then RSHA VI E in Vienna. Last seen in Berlin during December 1944.

Ltn. Paulus, RSHA *Mil Amt* D, parachute specialist and *Luftwaffe* liaison officer.

SS-*Stubaf* Dr Manfred Pechau, Director of the Seehof Training School in The Hague, 1944, and finally with SS-*Jagdverband Ost* with the remainder of *Jagd Einsatz* Baltikum on the Oder front at Troppau. Last seen in Friedenthal during March 1945.

SS-*Ustuf* Hans Peter, first with *Sonder Lehrgang* Oranienburg them *Jäger* Battalion 502. In 1945 transferred from the *Führungsstab* to SS-*Jagdverband Ost*. 1945, reported missing in action at Hohensalza.

SS-*Hstuf* Pfriemer (*sic*), SS-*Jagd Einsatz* Donau in Austria, 1945. Last seen in Linz during April 1945; has left hand amputated.

SS-*Stubaf* Philipp (*sic*), posted from RSHA IV to BdS Denmark; he returned two months later having been found unsuitable.

SS-*Stubaf* Dr Wolfgang Pinder, SS-*Jagdverbände Führungsstab, Untersuchungsführer* in charge of disciplinary matters from November 1944. Arrested by British forces.

SS-*Hstuf* Hugo Podlech, RSHA VI S1 *Verwaltungsführer*; latterly with SS-*Jagsverbände Führungsstab*. Last seen at Hof in early April 1945.

SS-*Ustuf* Juhan Prikask, *Sonder Einsatz Abteilung* zbV with KdK at Laspezia (Italy). Operated an improved model of the 'Neger II' (human torpedo). Missing in action after an operation in the Mediterranean off the French coast at Nice, October 1944.

Oberltn. Ramke, RSHA *Mil Amt* D, chief of *Referat Ost*.

SS-*Hstuf* Heinrich Reinel, with RSHA VI F in 1943, and BdS BdS Budapest in 1944 mounting Hungarian resistance movements. Was to join RSHA VI S at Heinrichsburg training school but refused.

SS-*Ostuf* Helmut Riedl, SS-*Jagdverbände Führungsstab*, assistant I-c officer in the Kartenstelle. Last seen at Hof during late March 1945.

SS-*Ustuf* Rinne, SS-*Jagdverband Ost*, assistant I-c officer. Last heard of in action on the Eastern front at Troppau, 1945.

SS-*Hstuf* Hellmuth Romeick, SS-*Jagdverband Nord-West* with BdS Oslo. Remained in Norway until the collapse.

SS-*Ustuf* (or SS-*Ostuf*) Rowohl (*sic*), officer in Brandenburg Division when came to SS-*Jagdverband Süd-Ost* and *Jagd Einsatz* Ungarn. Missing, believed killed in action near Neusiedlersee, south of Vienna, during April 1945.

SS-*Hstuf* Kurt Rybka, *Fallschirm Jäger* Batl. 500. Wounded in the attack on Tito's headquarters in Yugoslavia, June 1944.

SS-*Ostuf* Dr Hans Schäffner, RSHA VI F/H radio and technical services. Last seen in Berlin during March 1945.

SS-*Ustuf* Ernst Schenkel, came from RSHA VI A to RSHA VI S in December 1944. Assistant *Verwaltungsführer* with SS-*Jagsvrbände Führungsstab*. Last seen at Friedenthal in March 1945 and later at Teisendorf where dismissed as a war casualty (one foot amputated).

SS-*Hstuf* Erwin Schmiel, head of RSHA VI S1. Last seen in Radstatt, beginning March 1945; joined SKA (Kärnten group).

SS-*Ustuf* Karl Schmitt, RSHA VI S4 assigned to SS-*Jagdverband Süd-Ost* (*Jagd Einsatz* Ungarn) as political adviser and interpreter. Last seen in Linz (Austria) during April 1945.

Hauptmann Dr Hans Schöneich, RSHA *Mil Amt* D (*Gruppe West*), Berlin. Last seen during January 1945 at Berlin-Birkenwerder.

SS-*Ustuf* Walter Schreiber, in charge of *Jagd Einsatz* Donau and from September 1944 with swimming saboteurs (*Flusskämpfer*). Last seen in Vienna during Janaury 1945; believed missing in action since the Remagen bridge operation.

SS-*Ostuf* Kurt Schröter, SS-*Jagdverbände Führungsstab*, assistant I-z officer from December 1944. Last seen at Teisendorf at the end of April 1945.

SS-*Ostuf* Hubert Schürmann, *Fallschirm Jäger* Battalion 600; later joined the SKA.

Jean Schutt, Belgian (Wallonian or Flemish) agent of RSHA VI S4. Last seen in Berlin during March 1945.

SS-*Hstuf* Gerhard Schwager, from December 1944 in charge of Friedenthal defence, subordinate to Camp Commandant Oranienburg. Latterly, SS-*Jagdverbände Führungsstab*, I-c section responsible for radio and leaflet propaganda. Last seen at Friedenthal, end March 1945.

SS-*Ostuf* Otto Schwerdt, SS-*Jagdverband Mitte*, later with SKA. Last seen on Skorzeny's train at Annaberg and Radstatt, April–May 1945.

SS-*Hschaf* Hans Schwinn, SS-*Jagdverband Süd-West*, I-C. Last seen at Friedenthal during December 1944.

Oberstltn i.G. Kurt Semper (Rendel-Semper), RSHA *Mil Amt*, I-a and Liaison Officer with KG 200 and operations. Last seen in Berlin during mid April 1945.

SS-*Ostuf* Wilhelm Senger, SS-*Jagdverbände Führungsstab*. Transferred to the Army in November 1944.

SS-*Stubaf* Peter Siepen, Chief of Havel Institute, RSHA VI F/H, March 1943–November 1944. Last seen in Berlin during November 1944.

SS-*Hstuf* Dr Helmut Slama, RSHA VI S, SS-*Jagdverbände Führungsstab*. Joined the SKA but was released at the beginning of May 1945 owing to ill health, Oberdonau area.

SS-*Ostuf* Albert Söldner, came from Brandenburg Division (*Streifkorps* Italien) to SS-*Jagdverbänd Süd-West* as Transport Officer. Last with *Jagd Einsatz* Italien. Last seen in Val Martello, southern Tyrol, 1945.

Fräulein Lina Sommer, RSHA VI S, mail section. Dismissed due to ill-health in October 1943.

SS-*Hstuf* Jan Jacobus Sprey, worked for Knolle at Seehof Training School at The Hague. Committed suicide 15 March 1944 (Haaren, Holland).

SS-*Hstuf* Emil Steiner, SS-*Jagdverband Süd-Ost*, I-a officer, from December 1944. Joined the SKA (Ennstal), April 1945.

SS-*Ostuf* Arnold Steinlein, SS-*Jagdverbände Führungsstab*, II-b officer. Last seen at Hof, March 1945, probably dismissed as a war casualty (walks with crutches).

SS-*Ostuf* Gustav Steinmetz, came from RSHA VI CZ (Zeppelin operations) to RSHA VI S3 in the summer 1944; instructor in demolitions at training schools. 1945, probably remained at Neustrelitz school or went with SS-*Jagdverband Nord-West*.

SS-*Stuschaf* Heinz Stöck, RSHA VI S4. Dismissed at Hof in March 1945.

SS-*Hschaf* Stolzenburg, SS-*Jagdverbände Führungsstab*, ammunition specialist with I-b section, November 1944–April 1945. Last seen at Friedenthal at the end of March 1945; possibly went with Gerhardt to the Eastern front.

SS-*Ustuf* Eberhardt Straub, Adjutant with SS-*Jagdverband Nord-West*. Wounded on the Oder front, beginning February 1945, and hospitalized.

SS-*Hstuf* "Strukfuss or Streckfuss", Chief of the Signals Company, SS-*Jagdverbände Führungsstab*, with Division Schwedt on the Oder front. Last seen in Salzburg at the end of April 1945.

SS-*Hstuf* Karl Stüwe, *Gestapo* officer from Hamburg, later attached to RSHA VI S for work in Croatia. Reported killed or taken prisoner in Croatia, 1945.

SS-*Ustuf* Tietjen, SS-*Jagdverband Ost*, I-c section. April 1945 with unit fighting on the Eastern front at Troppau.

Major (Rumanian army) Toba Hathanul, originally with Roumanian SS-*Jagdverband* combatting partisans. December 1944 at Friedenthal when assigned to SS-*Jagdverband Süd-Ost*.

Standartenführer (*Waffen Führer*) Tuling, an elderly man from Estonia or Latvia assigned to SS-*Jagd Einsatz* Baltikum. Last seen in Friedenthal and then Hof, March 1945.

SS-*Hstuf* Wolfgang Überschaar, SS-*Jagdverbände Führungsstab*, specialist in I-b section, and from January 1945 Liaison Officer to *Heeres Waffenamt*. April 1945, possibly with Army Group Rendulic in Austria.

SS-*Hstuf* Herbert Urbanneck, in December 1944 came from RSHA IV A to SS-*Jagdverbände Führungsstab* as *Verwaltungsführer*. End April 1945 transferred to 6.SS-Pz.Army on the Eastern front, and in May 1945 seen at Radstatt.

Hauptmann Hans Urmann, *Leitstelle* II *West*.

SS-*Hstuf* Pieter van Vessum, *Sonder Lehrgang* Oranienburg and *Fallschirm Jäger* Battalion 502. Transferred to the *Wehrmacht* in summer 1944.

SS-*Ostubaf* Karl Walter, until February 1945 with Brandenburg Division as *Oberst* and wounded; came to SS-*Jagdverbände Führungsstab* as Chief of Staff to replace von Foelkersam. April 1945 with SKA in Austria.

Feldwebel or *Unteroffizier* Warthmann (or Worthmann) with SS-*Jagdverbände*

Führungsstab, August–October 1944. Anxious to go on missions to Spain or Portugal. Transferred to SS-*Jagdverband Süd-West* but left (deserted?) after a few days.

SS-*Ostuf* Alois Weber, SS-*Jagdverbände Führungsstab* as Transport Officer (Section V-K). Was to be transferred, but wanted to remain with Skorzeny and work for Besekow (RSHA VI S4). Last seen on the Eastern front at Schwedt, February 1945.

SS-*Ustuf* Alfred Wehr, SS-*Jagdverbänd Führungsstab*, assistant to Weber in the Transport Section. Last seen in Friedenthal at the end of March 1945.

Hauptmann Weiss, SS-*Jagdverbände Führungsstab*, II-b officer. In March 1945 transferred to SS-*Jagdverband Ost* or *Süd-Ost*.

Korv.Kapitän Alfred von Weiss, *Leitstelle* II *Süd-Ost für* FAK. Released at the beginning of 1945.

SS-*Ustuf* Dr Karl Welle, SS-*Jagdverband Süd-West*; after his mission to Holland may have transferred to SS-*Jagdverband Nord-West*.

SS-*Stuschaf* Josef Westphal, RSHA VI F, in charge of the ammunition dump.

SS-*Hstuf* Dr Wilhelm Wetz, Medical Officer with RSHA VI S; SS-*Jagdverbände Führungsstab*. Last seen at Annaberg in May 1945 waiting to surrender.

SS-*Ustuf* Wichmann, SS-*Jagdverbände Führungsstab*, administration, and in February 1945 to Schwedt Division on Eastern front. April 1945 possibly in north Germany.

SS-*Stubaf* Dr Albert Widmann, specialist in KTI (RSHA V). Last seen in Friedenthal during February 1945.

SS-*Ustuf* Max Windhövel, *Verwaltungsführer* with RSHA VI S, and then with SS-*Jagdverbände Führungsstab*. Last seen in Hof, March–April 1945.

SS-*Hstuf* Heinrich Winter, sabotage instructor at Neustrelitz, then SS-*Jagdverband Nord West*. Commander of the *Jagdkommando* at Mauterndorf, Austria, waiting to surrender with Skorzeny, May 1945.

Hauptmann Dietrich Witzel used the alias "Kirn" and with *Leitstelle* II *Ost* and FAK 202, working on operations into Ukraine.

SS-*Hstuf* Erwin Zeidler, from February 1945, I-c officer SS-*Jagdverband Ost*. Last seen in Friedenthal during March 1945.

Hauptmann Zierjaks, RSHA *Mil Amt* D, Officer Records.

Oberleutnant Ziukas, came from SS-*Hauptamt* to SS-*Jagd Einsatz* Baltikum as Lithuanian specialist and political adviser in February 1945. Last seen in Friedenthal during March 1945.

Notes:

* The National Archives, Kew, KV 2/403: USFET, 12th US Army, MFIU No. 4, Interrogation Report 4/6 dated 31 May 1945 by Otto Skorzeny, "The Werwolf Organization"; this report is available at US NARA, RG 498 Box 80.

* The National Archives, Kew, KV 2/1327: USFET, 12th US Army Interrogation Center, Intermediate Interrogation Report dated 4 June 1945, by Karl Radl, "RSHA VI S".

* The National Archives, Kew, KV 3/180: USFET, 12th US Army, Consolidated Interrogation Report (CIR) No. 4 dated 22 July 1945, by Otto Skorzeny and Kar Radl, "The German Sabotage Service".

1 US Holocaust Memorial Museum, Washington DC, RG-18.002M reel 10: details from February and March 1945 of activities by SS-*Jagdeinsatz* Baltikum and *Unternehmen* Wildkatze L.

2 Pavel and Anatoli Sudaplatov, *Special Tasks. The Memoirs of an Unwanted Witness – A Soviet Spymaster* (1994), pp 168-169, reveals Schernhorn group was nothing less than a massive Soviet deception operation. The Scherhorn group had been overrun in August 1944 and the deception began with Scherhorn itself and his own radio operator.

13

Situation Report No. 21: *Amt* VI of the RSHA—*Gruppe* VI Wi (Wirtschaft)

(Note: This Situation Report should be read in conjunction with War Room Publication Reference S.F.52-8-11 dealing with the penetration of German Industry by the Intelligence Service for espionage purposes. This paper is largely confined to the origins, development and personalities of *Gruppe* VI Wi.)

1. RSHA *Amt* VI at the end of 1941.
When Schellenberg took over the direction of RSHA *Amt* VI in the latter half of 1941, its record during the first two years of its existence had been such that its continued existence was threatened by the opposition of the other RSHA *Ämter* and of the Foreign Office. Energetic measures were necessary on the part of Schellenberg to justify a new lease of life for the *Amt*, and the various reforms he introduced are dealt with in the Liquidation Reports on the *Löndergruppen*, where immediate action was required in order to improve the work of the *Amt* as a whole. Together with these immediate changes, however, Schellenberg pursued a long term policy envisaging a complete reform in the working methods of the *Amt*, and it is into this larger frame work that *Gruppe* VI Wi fits, both in its origins and development.

2. The geographical character of RSHA *Amt* VI.
Quite apart from the general inefficiency of its personnel and its direction, RSHA *Amt* VI to Schellenberg suffered from major defects in organisation, which defects, if not remedied, would have made any substantial improvement impossible. The work of the *Amt* had been conceived on purely geographical lines, and apart from the very small *Gruppe* VI F dealing with W/T communications, the *Amt* was composed only of *Ländergruppen*, each responsible for different territories, without any attempt at co-ordination in their work and without any centralised evaluating sections. The territorial division itself was arbitrary and necessarily lent

itself to over-lapping and friction, and meant in addition that *Ländergruppe* had to be self-contained in any special or technical aspect of its work. This is readily appreciated by comparison with the organisation of the *Abwehr*, which contrived to have both a territorial and functional division of work. In RSHA *Amt* VI the function division was completely lacking.

3. Defects of the system.
The inherent defects in such an organisation can be readily appreciated; it meant in effect that one *Gruppe* worked in complete ignorance of the work of the other *Gruppen*; it meant also that liaison with other agencies (if it had existed) could not be effected through any central body, but that each *Gruppe* would require to maintain its own liaison; and while the information received by the *Gruppen* did in fact originate in different territories this did not imply that the same type of information was not received by various *Gruppen*—a point of special importance in dealing with the economic rather than the political side. In the *Abwehr* on the other hand information on more specialised lines was channeled through functional representatives to a central department in Berlin. Schellenberg appreciated these defects, and the existence of such departments as the *Zentral-Büro*, VI *Kult*, VI *Wi*, and VI G, before the end bear evidence of his efforts to remedy them. This was however a slow process, and even at the end the system was still in a state of evolution. Schellenberg's broad policy and long term planning were therefore aimed at the creation of a centralised evaluation section, and at the establishing of functional as opposed to regional sections. RSHA *Gruppe* VI Wi had its roots in this broad policy.

4. The creation of *Sonderreferat* VI Wi in 1941.
On the economic side the first attempt was in the creation of the *Sonderreferat* VI Wi at the end of 1941. This was a small section under SS-*Stubaf* Sebastian, who had as his assistants SS-*Stubaf* Ulenberg, SS-*Hstuf* Zeischka and SS-*Hstuf* Westergaard. The functions of this *Sonderreferat* were comparatively restricted, the section being required to assist the *Ländergruppen* in matters relating to foreign exchange, questions of commercial interest such as imports and exports, and in the more important aspect of the employment in commercial firms both at home and abroad of agents recruited by the *Ländergruppen*. It is to be noted therefore that the *Referat* was not an *Erfassungsreferat*, and neither attempted to recruit agents for its own purposes, not acted as an evalutaory section for economic information obtained by the *Ländergruppen* through its agents. Its function was purely advisory. Nor was its creation particularly welcomed by the *Ländergruppenleiter*, ever jealous of their own rights and authority, for on such authority was the importance of the *Gruppenleiter* himself based. This early period was therefore merely a tentative start; it was not until the early summer of 1942 that any effort was made to extend the scope and authority of the *Referat*.

5. Extensions in June 1942.

In June 1942 SS-*Hstuf* Zeidler was appointed to takeover the *Referat*, which now came under the control of RSHA *Gruppe* VI A. With his appointment the *Referat* was given a much wider assignment, as Schellenberg now proposed that it should run its own information network both at home and abroad, supplementing the already existing networks controlled by the *Ländergruppen*, concentrating its efforts on the facilities afforded by industrial firms.

This more ambitious programme was however doomed to failure, not only because of the inevitable conflict with the *Ländergruppen* themselves, but because the monthly budget granted to the *Referat* was not enough to allow the *Referat* to recruit and pay agents of the type such a scheme required. The *Referat* functioned on lines similar to VI *Kult*, exploring on behalf of the *Ländergruppen* the possibilities that the industrial field provided.

6. Functions of *Referat* VI Wi in 1942–1944.

VI Wi continued therefore primarily as an advisory *Referat*; it arranged on behalf of the *Ländergruppen* suitable commercial cover for agents chosen to work abroad, and gave advice on all matters concerning foreign trade and exchange, necessary to the *Ländergruppen* in their work abroad. But its extended functions now included close liaison with the home Ministries interested in economic matters, while it also acted as an *Auswärtungsreferat*, as it received from the *Ländergruppen* information on economic matters, which it evaluated and passed to the various Reich Ministries interested; and just as VI *Kult* exploited the cultural field, VI Wi sought out prospective agents for the *Ländergruppen* among businessmen whose duties necessitated journeys abroad. To a certain degree therefore Schellenberg had succeeded in creating a centralised functional *Referat* on the economic aspect of RSHA *Amt* VI work, but had not succeeded in extending its representations outside of Germany itself, on the lines of *Abwehr* I Wi. The gap was closed only with the absorption in the summer of 1944 of I Wi into VI Wi.

7. Organisation of *Referat* VI Wi.

The organisation of the *Referat* (subordinated to RSHA *Gruppe* VI A) during this period was a simple one, and was on the following lines:

Referent	SS-*Stubaf* Zeidler
Foreign Exchange Section	SS-*Ostuf* Danzinger
Travel Questions Section	SS-*Ostuf* Franz
	SS-*Stubaf* Rehwagen
Food Section	SS-*Ostuf* Baumer
Industrial Section	SS-*Ostuf* Schönpflug
	SS-*Ostuf* Wachter

SS-*Ostuf* Warger
SS-*Ostuf* Göring
SS-*Ostuf* Warsinki
SS-*Hstuf* Lindt
Angestellter Lindenberg
Angestellter Hoose

8. The absorption of *Abwehr* I Wi in July 1944.

The original plan evolved in the discussions relating to the absorption of the *Abwehr* into RSHA *Amt* VI in the early part of 1944 envisaged that only the *Abwehr* I Wi *Referate* of the *Abwehrstellen* would come under the control of VI Wi, the technical sections, IT/LW, I/WT, and I/MT remaining in the new RSHA *Mil Amt* as *Gruppe* T. After the July 1944 plot, however, the *Abwehr* lost further ground, and the whole of I Wi, including the technical sections, was absorbed, the new *Gruppe* of *Amt* VI being formed with the designation VI Wi/T. with SS-*Staf* Schmied as *Gruppenleiter*. At lower levels the I Wi *Referate* became subordinated to the corresponding SD-*Abschnitte*, but it is to be noted that in order to conceal the connection between the two, it was laid down that the RSHA VI Wi officers within Germany were not to be housed within the offices of the SD. This order was symptomatic of a conscious effort on the part of Schellenberg to develop economic espionage to the best advantage.

9. Results of the absorption.

The immediate consequence of the absorption of *Abwehr* I Wi was that RSHA VI Wi/T now had for the first time its own network of agents and was not dependent on the *Ländergruppen* as its sole source or supply of information. The effect, the I Wi organisation remained comparatively unaffected, the only major change being that its reports were now passed to RSHA VI Wi/T, and the broad division of work in the new *Gruppe*, a division dictated by circumstances, was that the former *Abwehr* I Wi network continued to function as an *Erfassungsreferat*, while the former RSHA VI Wi acted as the *Auswärtungsreferat* [i.e. a collection agency and an evaluation agency].

At the same time however the new-found strength of *Gruppe* VI Wi encouraged two further lines of development—a much closer liaison with interested agencies, such as the *Reichswirtschaftministerium* [Economics Ministry], and the *Feldwirtschaftamts*, for which liaison officers were appointed, together with a direct approach to leading industrial firms, for their assistance in extending the field of economic espionage. The results of this approach are dealt with in the War Room Publication on German Economic Espionage. In addition *Gruppe* VI G was given the task of setting up a special institute dealing with the requirements of VI Wi/T, absorbing at the same time the functions of the already existing Hamburg *Weltwirtschaftsarchiv* von Hausleiter.

10. The organisation of RSHA *Gruppe* VI Wi/T.

The organisational structure of the new *Gruppe* is shown at Appendix I. It will be seen that the former *Referat* VI Wi was largely transferred to the new *Referat* VI Wi/T/2 and VI Wi/T/3, the *Auswärtung* and Liaison *Referate*, while *Abwehr* I Wi became the *Erfassungsreferat* VI Wi/T/1. In the same way the technicaql section of *Abwehr* I Wi became the special *Referat* VI Wi/T/T, composed of former *Abwehr* personnel, except that the *Referat* was placed under the command of SS-*Staf* Ogilvie.

11. Special points.

No attempt is made in this paper to evaluate the results achieved by the former *Abwehr* I Wi. The only SD development resulting from the creation of *Gruppe* VI Wi/T was that VI Wi could now runs its own agents. There is little to indicate that this was developed, though SS-*Staf* Ogilvie is reported to have sent agents to Switzerland and Spain with specific assignments for VI Wi/T/T. The more important aspect of RSHA *Gruppe* VI Wi, the penetration of German industry by the German Intelligence Services, is dealt with in the War Room Publication mentioned in paragraph 9 above.

12. Main sources:

SS-*Staf* Ogilvie	*Referent*, VI Wi/T/T
SS-*Staf* Sandberger	*Gruppenleiter* VI A
SS-*Brif* Schellenberg	*Amtschef* VI
SS-*Stubaf* Zeidler	*Referent*, VI Wi (1942–1944)
Oberst Dettinger	*Referent*, VI Wi/T/T/1

This report was issued by W.R.C.3a. on 4 December 1945

Appendix I

Organisation of RSHA VI Wi/T

Gruppenleiter	SS-*Staf* Schmied
Adjutant	SS-*Ostuf* Pint
Personal Assistant	SS-*Ostuf* Danziger
Personal Assistant	SS-*Ustuf* Dietl

Referat	*Sachgebiet*	*Referent*
VI Wi/T/1	Economic Erfassung	*Oberstltn* Dähne
	SS-*Stubaf* Rehwagen	
	SS-*Hstuf* Lindt	

VI Wi/T/2	Economic *Auswertung*	SS-*Stubaf* Abendroth
	SS-*Ostuf* Warger	
	SS-*Hstuf* Zeischka	
	SS-*Ostuf* Lüttgendorf	
VI Wi/T/3	Liaison with Industry	SS-*Hstuf* Wachter
	SS-*Hstuf* Franz	
	SS-*Ostuf* Warger	
	SS-*Ostuf* Baumer	
	SS-*Ostuf* Göring	
VI Wi/T/4	Administration	SS-*Stubaf* Zeidler
	SS-*Ostuf* Pint	
VI Wi/T/T	SS-*Stubaf* Ogilvie	
	SS-*Hstuf* Nordheim	
VI Wi/T/T/1	Organisation	*Oberstabing.* Dettinger
VI Wi/T/T/2	Basic Research	*Oberstabing.* Fischer
VI Wi/T/T/3	High Frequency	*Oberstabing.* Sonnet
VI Wi/T/T/4	Aircraft Engines	*Haupting.* Lohmann
VI Wi/T/T/5	Armaments	SS-*Hstuf* Augsburg
	SS-*Ustuf* Börstling	
Liaison Officer to Economics Ministry		SS-*Stubaf* Syrup
	SS-*Ustuf* Boes	
Liaison Officer to Ministry of Food		SS-*Stubaf* von Swindern
Liaison Officer to Ministry of Armaments Production		SS-*Stubaf* Eggen
Liaison Officer to the Reichsbank		*Hauptmann* Hübbe
Liaison Officer to Reichsgruppe Insurance		*Hauptmann* Ruperti
Liaison Officer to Transport Ministry		*Oberbahnrat* Keller

Note: Of the above Liaison Officers, SS-*Stubaf* Syrup, SS-*Ustuf* Boes, SS-*Stubaf* von Swindern, and *Oberbahnrat* Keller were detached from their respective Ministries to RSHA VI in an honorary capacity only.

Appendix II

Alphabetical Index of RSHA *Gruppe* VI Wi personnel, 1941–45

Note: This list contains only SD personnel, and does not include those *Abwehr* characters who joined VI Wi/T after the absorption of the *Abwehr* in summer 1944. Personnel known to be arrested are underlined.

Rank & Name	Referat	Remarks
SS-*Stubaf* Hermann <u>Abendroth</u>	VI Wi/T/2	arrested British Zone
SS-*Hstuf* Arthur Augsburg	VI WI/T/T/5	
SS-*Ustuf* Josef Baumer	VI Wi/T/3	
SS-*Ostuf* Erich Becker	VI Wi/T/T/2	
Kriminalsekretär August Beer	VI Wi	VI Wi, 1943
SS-*Ustuf* Friedrich Börstling	VI Wi/T/T/5	
SS-*Ustuf* Erich Boes	VI Wi	Liaison Officer to Ministry of Economics
SS-*Ustuf* Wilhelm Boldt	VI Wi	VI Wi, 1943
Angestellter Johannes Charles	VI Wi	VI Wi, 1943
SS-*Ostuf* Rudolf <u>Danziger</u>	VI Wi/T	Personal Asst to *Gruppenleiter*; arrested British Zone
SS-*Ustuf* Hans Dietl	VI Wi/T	Personal Asst to *Gruppenleiter*
SS-*Stubaf* Hans-Wilhelm <u>Eggen</u>	VI Wi/T	Liaison Officer to Armaments Ministry; arrested in Italy
Angestellter Reinhold Fabritus	VI Wi/T/2	
SS-*Stubaf* Dr Ludwig Fritscher	VI Wi/T	Liaison Officer to the Press
SS-*Ostuf* Franz Göring	VI Wi/T/3	
Angestellter Werner Hoose	VI Wi	left VI WI, March 1943; joined firm Jauch Hühner, Bucharest
Hauptmann Hübbe	VI Wi/T	Liaison Officer to *Reichsbank*
Oberbahnrat Keller	VI Wi/T	Liaison Officer to Ministry of Transport
SS-*Hstuf* Hans Lichtenegger	VI Wi/T	Liaison Officer to RSHA VI E
Angestellter Lindenberg	VI Wi/T/3	
SS-*Hstuf* Dr Lindt	VI Wi/T/1	
SS-*Hstuf* Erich Lüttgendorf	VI Wi/T/2	
SS-*Sturmmann* August Niederauer	VI Wi	VI Wi, 1943
SS-*Hstuf* Karl-Heinz von Nordheim	VI Wi/T/T	
SS-*Staf* Dr Hans <u>Ogilvie</u>	VI Wi/T/T	*Referent* VI Wi/T/T; arrested in US Zone
SS-*Ostuf* Dr Otto Pint	VI Wi	Adjutant to Gruppenleiter
Ranft	VI Wi/T/3	
SS-*Stubaf* Herbert Rehwagen	VI Wi/T/1	
Hauptmann Ruperti	VI Wi/T	Liaison Officer to *Reichsgruppe* Insurance
Angestellter Rudolf Schlatter	VI Wi	VI Wi, 1943
SS-*Ostuf* Egon <u>Schönpflug</u>	VI Wi	transferred to BdS Italy, 1943; arrested in Italy
SS-*Staf* Prof. Dr Robert Schmied	VI Wi/T	*Gruppenleiter* from summer 1944
Angestellter Dr Halvor Sudeck	VI Wi	VI Wi, 1943

SS-*Stubaf* Dr Günter Syrup	VI Wi/T	Liaison Officer to the Ministry of Economics
SS-*Stubaf* von Swindern	VI Wi/T	Liaison Officer to the Ministry of Food
SS-*Hstuf* Alfred Ulenberg	VI Wi	VI Wi, 1943; later RSHA VI A
SS-*Hstuf* Erich Wachter	VI Wi/T/3	
SS-*Ostuf* Robert Warger	VI Wi/T/3	
Angestellter Hans-Dieter Warsinski	VI Wi	
SS-*Hstuf* Julius Westergaard	VI Wi	*Referent*, RSHA VI A in 1940; VI Wi, 1941-42; RSHA VI E
SS-*Stubaf* Dr Hans-Martin <u>Zeidler</u>	VI Wi/T/4	*Referent*, VI Wi 1942–44; arrested British Zone
SS-*Hstuf* Viktor Zeischka	VI Wi/T/2	

Note:

* The National Archives, Kew, KV 3/182: Situation Report No. 21, RSHA VI Wi (Wirtschaft).

14

RSHA VI Z

Counter Intelligence War Room created a very short Situation Report for RSHA VI Z. It was numbered No. 22 and issued by W.R.C.1/A on 7 March 1946. They held off creating a Liquidation Report until receiving more information. In particular they awaited an interrogation report from French Intelligence who had detained *Oberstleutnant* Dr Hans Freund, RSHA VI Gruppenleiter Z.

When the interrogation report of Freund arrived, over 300 pages in French, it was decided to take the much simpler measure of accepting what they had already. This included another French interrogation report, that of *Hauptmann* Hans Geilich of the *Abwehr* whose "report covers the entire organisation of VI Z, with details of personalities and with particular reference to the activities of Referat VI ZD of which Geilich was in charge, and which dealt with Sweden, Finland, U.S.A. and England."

CIWR also had interrogation reports of *Abwehr* officers carried out by US Intelligence. These included reports of Major Albert Gleichauf dealing with VI Z West, and *Oberstleutnant* Robert von Tarbuk dealing with VI Z Ost. In Italy, CSDIC had issued interrogation reports of *Rittmeister* Hans von Pescatore dealing with VI Z Switzerland and Major Benno von Braitenberg dealing with VI Z Italien.

The interrogation of von Pescatore was unsatisfactory and he failed to completely describe his VI Z activities. On the other hand, von Braitenberg was much more forthcoming about his VI Z activities in Italy:

Interrogation report CSDIC/CMF/SD 75 issued on 8 October 1945 includes this assessment of Braitenberg:

There is no doubt that Braitenberg was one of the most efficient members of the German Intelligence Service in Italy, with an original turn of mind, considerable industry and a well-developed security sense. He complains that the end came too soon, as he was on the point of achieving a great deal in the field of penetration. This attitude is perhaps typical of the man, as despite his avowed patriotism he appears to have been more interested in achieving results for his own glory rather than for the good of his country. At first he was determined to refuse all answers which might implicate his agents, remarking that even if ordered to talk by his superiors he would still refuse, but as this determination diminished he began to talk freely, with obvious pride in his capabilities, and it is now thought that he has given an almost if not entirely complete picture of his work. Braitenberg keeps no secret of his continued admiration for Hitler, and attacks any of his compatriots who deface his memory. He believed in a Germany victory up to the end and though he sees that for the moment Germany is helpless there is no doubt that, given the chance, he would do all in his power to resuscitate his own dream.

Reliability: Good.

Gruppe **VI Z, RSHA.**

(a) Formation and Functions:
When Braitenberg was in Sofia about the end of July 1944 forming three FATs, 387, 388 and 389 from *Kriegsorganisation* [KO—*Abwehr* office] Bulgarien, he was told by *Oberst* Wagner, alias 'Delius', then still *Leiter* KO Bulgarien, that the latest result of the merger of the *Abwehr* with the RSHA was the creation of two departments to deal with counter-espionage to take the place of the former III F of the *Abwehr*. RSHA *Gruppe* VI Z, under *Oberstleutnant* Freund, who had been *Sachbearbeiter* III F for the South-East at the *Amt Ausland Abwehr*, was to deal with counter-espionage abroad, and *Referat* IV/III/F, under *Oberst* Rohleder at Eiche near Potsdam, was to control counter-espionage in German territory (Inland). Both VI Z and IV/III/F were to come administratively under the RSHA *Mil Amt*, operationally under RSHA *Amt* VI and *Amt* IV respectively. Wagner also said that as KO Bulgarien was being disbanded, and he was going to take over the newly formed KdM Ungarn, he would like Braitenberg to be VI Z *Leiter* attached administratively to him in Budapest. Braitenberg agreed, and in the first week in August 1944 flew to Berlin to see Freund, who told him that when he returned to Sofia he would find orders waiting for him confirming the Budapest appointment.

These orders were not there when Braitenberg returned, and he spent the rest of August and part of September in Budapest while the relative functions of VI Z and IV/III/F were thrashed out in Berlin. RSHA *Amt* VI maintained that the term 'abroad' meant that VI Z should control all [stress in original] counter-espionage work for the RSHA outside Germany proper, and RSHA *Amt* IV held that territories abroad which were occupied by the Germans should count as German territory (Inland). In the end the dispute was settled, and it was ruled that wherever there was a BdS the counter-espionage inside the respective territory should be carried out by a *Referat* IV/III/F, and where necessary a VI Z representative in the same territory should conduct counter-espionage in enemy or enemy-occupied countries. In neutral countries, because there was no BdS, a VI Z *Dienststelle* was to be attached to the KO, to carry out counter-espionage both inside the country, and in contiguous non-German countries.

This arrangement inevitably meant overlapping of the work of the two departments. To take an example, the VI Z *Dienststelle* in Switzerland under *Rittmeister* von Pescatore, did not immediately hand over to IV/III/F in Italy a counter-espionage case it was handling just because an agent crossed the Swiss border into what was technically IV/III/F territory. Similarly, Braitenberg, if an agent of his had succeeded in being given a mission by the Allied Intelligence Services, in Allied occupied territory, and had obtained contact addresses and the names of other agents already despatched to North Italy, would not have given the case immediately to IV/III/F but would followed it up himself. There was nothing laid down on this point, however, by the RSHA. Another example of overlapping, which cannot be called inevitable, is that Braitenberg also worked against Switzerland from North Italy; he was sent documents by RSHA VI Z dealing with the Allied Intelligence Services in Switzerland, and presumed that this was an indication that he should also concern himself with that country, though his orders were to conduct counter-espionage against Allied occupied territory. Freund never ordered him to cease these activities.

Braitenberg also planned to work against France from North Italy, and in fact despatched one agent on a mission there, to which Freund also raised no objections. In fact Braitenberg is certain that he found an agent who could profitably be despatched to the Middle East or even to China that would have been within his sphere of operations, though of course his chief concern was with Allied occupied territory since no other VI Z *Dienststelle* was responsible for that area.

Another example of overlapping of VI Z and IV/III/F (and IV/2, department of the regional *Gestapo* office organisation responsible for counter-espionage) work in North Italy, which may have been similar to the arrangements made elsewhere, is that Braitenberg came to an agreement with BdS Italian, *Abteilung* IV, whereby he would follow up counter-espionage cases in North Italy if he had first discovered them himself; this would not normally have arisen if he had not attempted to get agents into Allied occupied territory or Switzerland by contact with Allied Intelligence Services circles already in North Italy. Once such contacts had been made with SS-*Sturmbannführer* Dr Kranebitter, *Leiter Abteilung* IV of BdS Italien, agreed that they were better followed up by Braitenberg rather than by *Abteilung* IV, until such time as both he and Braitenberg agreed it was necessary to strike.

(b) Organisation.

Braitenberg knows very little about VI Z personalities or *Dienststellen* apart from VI Z Italien. VI Z Italien was formed in September 1944, and von Braitenberg believes that about the same time *Dienststellen* were formed in Sweden, Spain,

Portugal, Switzerland, Hunagry and the Czech Protectorate. He does not know about other territories; what arrangements were made for work against France, for instance, or Great Britain, from the Reich.

All VI Z *Dienststellen* were given cover names of flowers. Braitenberg saw a list sent him by Freund, but can only remember the cover name of VI Z Schweiz (Switzerland) which was 'Agate'. VI Z Italien was known as 'Astrid'.

Apart from Freund, Braitenberg knows of only two officers at VI Z Berlin, *Hauptmann* Kraigher and *Hauptmann* Geibel, who signed some communications he received. He believes that *Hauptmann* Klausnitzer was VI Z *Leiter* in Prague, and *Sonderführer* 'K' Kleinhampl for a time was VI Z *Leiter* Ungarn in Budapest till he was killed in early 1945 or the end of 1944. *Rittmeister* von Pescatore was VI Z Schweiz (von Pescatore mentioned when interrogated that he was *Leiter* III F, KO Schweiz, from 1 January 1944 until his surrender on 25 May 1945, and made no mention of a VI Z appointment. Braitenberg is certain that von Pescatore was actually the VI Z *Leiter*, as he saw his name on Freund's list, and it is logical to suppose that counter-espionage in Switzerland formerly performed by III F should have passed to VI Z in view of the arrangement in other neutral countries). *Oberstleutnant* Dr Wagner, according to Braitenberg, was *Leiter* VI Z Sweden.

(c) Activities.
Braitenberg can give almost no information on the work of VI Z *Dienststellen* other than his own, as he had no liaison with them. He received from Freund lists of names of persons in Switzerland and North Italy who had been established as connected with the Allied Intelligence Services by VI Z Schweiz, but knows nothing of the means by which they were obtained. He knows one VI Z agent in Sweden, Senise, the nephew of the former Italian Police Chief (secret number GV 175, the 'G' indicating an agent in contact with the enemy), who came to VI Z Italien in March 1945. Senise was in touch with British Intelligence Service circles in Stockholm, who believed him, according to Freund, to be a double agent working for them. Senise specialised on information on the results of V weapons in Great Britain.

3. VI Z Italien.

(a) Formation.
In the first weeks of September 1944 Braitenberg received in Budapest orders from RSHA *Mil Amt* telling him to report to KdM Salzburg and then set up an organisation for long-range contacts in Allied-occupied Italy. The orders were so vague that when he arrived at KdM Salzburg, *Oberstleutnant* Wünsche, the *Kommandeur*, thought that *Abwehr* I work was indicated, and intended keeping Braitenberg in Salzburg to operate from there against Italy. von Braitenberg thought it certain that VI Z work was meant, and the matter was settled by a

phone call to Freund, who told von Braitenberg to go to Italy and look around for a suitable location for his *Dienststelle*, to be known as VI Z Italien. He said that operationally Braitenberg would be directly responsible to RSHA VI Z, and administratively would come under *Oberst* Engelmann, who was then in Italy as the senior representative of the RSHA *Mil Amt*.

Braitenberg went straight to Verona and called on SS-*Brigadeführer* Dr Wilhelm Harster, the BdS Italien, to ask for advice on a suitable location for his work. Harster suggested that he could best operate from Verona where he would be in a central position and would have the signals facilities of the BdS. Braitenberg asked whether he might draw money through the BdS and also have the use of other purely administrative facilities as it would be very convenient for him if he was going to be in Verona himself; Harster was agreeable, and Freund also raised no objections, though technically Braitenberg should have been administered by a RSHA *Mil Amt* representative. Most of his routine signals were in fact sent through the *Mil Amt* net from *Funkleitstelle* Italien, Verona.

After a further short visit to Salzburg, Braitenberg came to Verona in the latter part of September 1944 to begin work. He did not take any staff with him, though Freund had offered him some assistants, as he preferred to begin the initial work on his own. He had arranged with Harster to draw all office equipment from the BdS pool. Harster also gave him the use of an office-cum-bedroom in the *Abteilung* I/II block on the first floor, Room No. 127. He requisitioned villas at Via Nino Bixio 21 and later Via dei Mille 5, and was given the use of two cars by Harster, which he drove himself. He was later given the use of a third car, belonging to the *Abteilung* V agent Count Senni.

(b) Liaison and relations with other Counter-Espionage agencies.

Braitenberg had come to Verona with no information whatsoever from Freund on the Allied Intelligence Services in Allied occupied territory, and the first thing he did, even before getting his staff together, was to try to acquire some from *Abteilung* IV under SS-*Stubaf.* Kranebitter and *Referat* IV/III/F both of BdS Italien under Major Schneweis, and from FAK 309 under *Oberst* Steinberg. Schneweis was extremely impolite to him, and told him that he did not see the necessity for yet another counter-espionage unit in the area, and that everything was already known about the Allied Intelligence Services in Allied occupied territory. At this surprising news Braitenberg asked him to let him see some IV/III/F and III F reports so that he could get in the picture, but after hunting through his documents Schneweis produced only one old report giving vague facts about espionage, W/T and sabotage schools at Bari and Brindisi; Braitenberg had heard of the existence of these schools during his time in the Balkans. He received no more information from IV/III/F during the time he was in Italy, even after Schneweis' departure about December 1944; though he asked his successor *Rittmeister* Lang to let him see reports containing information on Allied occupied territory and later on Switzerland, this in fact was never done. Braitenberg thinks this was due to forgetfulness and inefficiency, not unwillingness to co-operate. Steinberg was also asked to supply reports of interest to Braitenberg, but never did so. Kranebitter was more co-operative, but even from *Abteilung* IV he received little of value. He read a long summary of old IV reports in Kranebitter's office, giving several locations of Allied Intelligence Services schools in Bari, Brindisi, Naples and elsewhere, with names of officers and agents in training and despatched; he made extracts from this and sent them to Freund, but this was the only report of the kind which Braitenberg read.

Subsequent relations were as follows. The arrangement between Braitenberg and Kranebitter by which he could follow up counter-espionage cases in North Italy which he had discovered himself has been discussed in Para. 2.a. Braitenberg did not give Kranebitter details of such cases if he thought that they required more working on by VI Z *Italien*, though he usually gave him the broad outlines, again, if he obtained the names of persons believed to be pro-Allied though not connected with the Intelligence Services through whom he hoped in the future to be able to get his agents to Allied occupied territory or Switzerland he listed them in the VI Z files but did not report them to *Abteilung* IV. This was because he did not trust *Abteilung* IV not to arrest them before he had had a chance to use them, and in fact on two occasions, much to Braitenberg's annoyance, *Abteilung* IV arrested men without his knowledge or approval.

Braitenberg made a tentative suggestion to Kranebitter on one occasion that he should be allowed to interrogate some of the agents arrested by *Abteilung* IV, and IV/III/F. He found once or twice that agents whose names he had discovered through his own people had already been arrested by *Abteilung* IV without his knowing about it, and when he asked Kranebitter for information on the results of their interrogations he was told that the report had been sent to Gossensass for filing. Moreover, as he was not getting reports, he hoped to be able to obtain some information on the Allied Intelligence Services in Allied occupied territory from agents who had been despatched to North Italy. Nothing, however, came of this suggestion, as *Abteilung* IV was far too jealous of its own sphere, though Kranebitter himself might have been willing to arrange it.

Because of a desire to be independent, Braitenberg did not ask *Abteilung* IV for names of possible contacts through whom he could get his own agents to Allied occupied territory or Switzerland, and preferred to let his agents discover such contacts for themselves. Similarly, though *Grenzbefehlstelle West* could have been useful to Braitenberg in putting him on to smugglers, etc., who might get his agents into Switzerland, he preferred to find such means for himself, as he did not want to reveal his plans to the *Leiter*, SS-*Hauptsturmführer* Vötterl, for security reasons, and and also wanted to show Freund that he was capable of running his own business without depending on the SS.

Soon after coming to Italy Braitenberg asked Freund what his position was in regard to W/T Playbacks, as he thought that these should be logically belong to VI Z Italien, because they were concerned with long-distance contacts with Allied occupied territory—the actual term of reference for his work. Freund replied that he should take over the whole of this sphere except that *Abteilung* IV were authorised to run play-backs of a political nature. Braitenberg did not follow up this point, as he was far too understaffed to undertake further commitments.

Kranebitter, who appeared anxious to eliminate the muddle of conflicting departments, himself suggested to Braitenberg not long after his arrival in Italy that he should take over the whole of IV/III/F work in North Italy as well as running VI Z Italien; it was evident that he was not satisfied with the work of Schneweis and Lang. Braitenberg replied that he would do so on condition that he was not operationally subordinate to *Abteilung* IV, but as in the nature of the organisation this was impossible Kranebitter dropped the suggestion.

Summing up, Braitenberg remarked that the efficiency of counter-espionage was greatly hampered by the lack of a central co-ordination agency which could pass relevant reports to the respective departments, as the departments themselves would not co-operate. Braitenberg was himself unwilling to co-operate, both for security reasons and from a desire to be independent.

(c) Liaison and relations with *Abteilung* VI of BdS Italien and *Unternehmen* 'Cypresse'.

On arrival in Verona, Braitenberg found that his old friend Dr Otto Begus was running *Unternehmen* 'Cypresse', and he maintained a close liaison with him until the time when he left Verona in early 1945. Dr Begus told Braitenberg what little he knew on conditions in the Allied occupied territory from the agent's point of view, check-posts, fondness of negro drivers for vino, etc. and also helped him considerably in his early attempts to work in Allied territory. From *Abteiling* VI Braitenberg tried to obtain information on conditions on the other side, but found that almost nothing was known as no VI agent had been despatched let alone returned. He gathered a few hints which had been collected from *Abwehr* agents who had performed missions, on the lines of what Dr Begus had told him. He saw one good report about March 1945 from a VI agent who had returned from a mission giving considerable detail of his experiences in interrogation centres, but cannot now remember the details or the name of the agent. (Comment: this was probably the Luzzatto report).

In December 1944 Braitenberg obtained permission from *Abteilung* VI to borrow SS-*Unterscharführer* Lechner to brief an Allied agent whom he wanted to be given an apparently genuine mission from the Germans and then despatched to Allied occupied territory. This was the only one of its kind, and Braitenberg avoided contact with *Abteilung* VI as far as he could, as he did not get on well with Huegel and mistrusted their security. He often gave his agents cover missions purporting to come from *Abteilung* VI, with the false name of an officer but a description of an actual member of the *Abteilung*; he did not always mention these arrangements to *Abteilung* VI.

(d) Staff.

This remained extremely small throughout Braitenberg's period in Italy, as he preferred to handle everything on his own. Personnel were:

Fräulein Thiel	Typist-secretary (Oct. 1944–April 1945).
Uffz Rudolf Müller	Interpreter and general admin duties (Nov. 1944–April 1945).
Zeno Botta	Recruiter and general admin duties (end Sept. 1944–April 1945).
Signora Ada Botta	Cook and housekeeper at von Braitenberg's villa (end Sept. 1944–April 1945).
Fräulein von Möllhausen	Typist-secretary and interpreter (Dec. 1944–early April 1945).
Silvestri	Chauffeur (end March 1944–April 1945).
Biva	Butling duties in von Braitenberg's villa (Oct. 1944–April 1945).

Fräulein Thiel was presented to Braitenberg by Harster. She was one of the most reliable members of his staff, but had almost nothing to do with agents. Müller had worked for Braitenberg when he was *Leiter* Konst. Skoplje of KO Bulgarien, and was sent to him by Freund at von Braitenberg's request, but though he had briefed agents in Jugoslavia he did not do so in Italy, and was concerned with driving and repairs, buying various requirements and arranging billets, keeping accounts, etc. Both the Bottas had worked for Braitenberg as agents in Jugoslavia, where Botta had formerly been Commanding Officer of a Fascist Albanian Battalion, and had collected information for the Frauenschaft organisation. She claims to be a medium, as did her husband. Braitenberg found them to be agents of IV/III/F with BdS Italien, and asked Schneweis to release them to him, which he did. However, Braitenberg did not use them as agents as Botta was too well-known and his wife he considered too hysterical. Botta found him a few agents, but was chiefly employed on supplying such things as cigarettes for agents and looking after Braitenberg's household. *Fräulein* von Möllhausen was more or less forced on Braitenberg by Harster. She was the sister of *Generalkonsul* Möllhausen; Braitenberg describes her as stupid but well-meaning woman who was of little use to him; he never let her into the picture of what he was doing. Silvestri was formerly the chauffeur of the *Abteilung* VI agent Count Senni, who was arrested in March 1945 for fraud, and Braitenberg took over Silvestri and the car; Silvestri had previously run errands for him.

…

(e) Recruiting and training of Agents.

Having discovered what he could about the Allied Intelligence Services in Allied occupied territory, which was not much, and of that little Braitenberg can now remember no details and turned to the problem of finding agents. He had hoped to be able to borrow some from IV/III/F, but finding no response there, except in the release of the Bottas, he turned to Dr Begus for assistance. Dr Begus in fact provided nearly half of Braitenberg's agents, 13 out of a total of 30. The rest came from unwanted applicants for *Abteilung* VI, Botta, *Ten.Colonel* Bassi, who had heard of Braitenberg through Dr Begus, Freund in Berlin, his chief agent 'Osiris' or '*Frau* Hoffmann' [real name, Madame France Erkner, a French woman], and FAK 211, through *Meldekopf* 'Heinrich'.

Braitenberg's agents received no training in the normal sense of the word, as they required no technical knowledge for their missions. The first agents he despatched to Allied occupied territory had a comparatively short briefing, but later he took more time over his instruction in mission and cover story, and in some cases rehearsed the agent day after day for a period of weeks, putting trick questions as if he were an Allied interrogating officer picking holes in the stories.

(f) Operational Aims, Methods amd Results.

Aims.

Braitenberg's conception of his duties was based on his experience of *Abwehr* III F work in the Balkans. As he saw it, his job was primarily to cause the capture of enemy agents in North Italy through contacts achieved in Allied occupied territory, rather than to collect all possible details on the Allied Intelligence Services organisation; in other words he was to work for exactly the same ends as IV/III/F, only he was to exploit long-distance contacts and IV/III/F would work exclusively on contacts in North Italy. As already stated in Para. 2.a., above, this work would have overlapped if a VI Z agent had succeeded in discovering the Intelligence Service circles in Allied occupied territory the names of agents in North Italy, as Braitenberg would then have followed up the case himself. This did in fact happen in the case of an agent sent to Switzerland, Morelli, when Braitenberg followed up contacts in North Italy obtained as a result of the mission.

Though he told his agents to find out what they could of the personalities, training methods and above all locations of Allied Intelligence Service organisations he was not so much interested in this as in obtaining the names of agents and contacts in North Italy, as he thought the important thing was to catch agents, not to collect a mass of facts which would to a large extent be of no operational interest. It does not appear to have occurred to him that a detailed knowledge of the Allied Intelligence Service organisation would have been of value in the interrogation of captured agents, and he is of the opinion that all captured agents would reveal all they knew without difficulty. He also remarked that if the Germans had been able to reckon with an advance then there might have been some point in collecting everything possible about enemy Intelligence Service organisation from the point of view of future raids on the headquarters, but as this was not the case the matter was comparatively unimportant. No directives were ever received from Freund on the subject, and Braitenberg followed his own ideas in the policy he adopted.

Line-crossers to Allied Occupied Territory.

Braitenberg's first idea was to sent agents across the lines direct to Allied occupied territory. Two agents of *Unternehmen* 'Cypresse', Pesce and Terraciano, were given additional VI Z missions to fulfil if they completed their missions for Dr Begus, and were despatched in October and November 1944 respectively. Three other line-crossers were given independent VI Z missions; two, Dionisio and Simotti, were despatched in November 1944 and January 1945 respectively, and the third, *Signorina* Gollin, was despatched in December 1944, but turned back from no-man's-land. Braitenberg had originally intended Simotti to be overrun in Bologna, to spare him the danger of crossing the lines, but this plan was changed when the fall of Bologna was delayed. Another agent, 'Castagno', was despatched in early March 1945, but turned back after changing his mind in no-man's-land.

The methods of operation of these line-crossers in Allied occupied territory were different, Pesce and Terraciano, after fulfilling their missions for Dr Begus were to try to get to know Italians connected with the Allied Intelligence Services, possibly those engaged in tracking down Fascists, and then gradually work their way into the branch which despatched agents to North Italy, relying on the acceptance of the cover stories supplied by Dr Begus; Dionisio, Simotti and Gollin were to give themselves up immediately they crossed the lines and say they had been forced to accept military or political missions for the German Intelligence Services, which they did not wish to fulfil. Each was given what Braitenberg considered to be a strong motive for wanting to return to North Italy, and he hoped that this, coupled with their 'voluntary' surrender and hints that they were willing to work for the Allied Intelligence Services, would induce the Allies to offer them missions as Allied agents. Cover missions, cover stories to explain their acceptance of these missions, and 'cover stories within cover stories', i.e. motives which the German Intelligence Services had allegedly told them to give for accepting the missions, were provided in each case. 'Castagno', who was a Jugoslav and could not be given a convincing cover mission to tell Allied Intelligence Services, was to contact Italian friends of his in Allied occupied territory, get enlisted in the Italian Army and try to be transferred to the Intelligence Section.

The reason behind the plan that Simotti, Dionisio and Gollen should give themselves up immediately was as follows. Braitenberg argued that if they confessed to having had missions from the Germans, then the Allied Intelligence Services would be bound to interrogate them and show interest, so that they would be brought into close and speedy contact with the circles they were to penetrate. He did not think that this would cause the Allied Intelligence Services to be suspicious.

If on the other hand they reported to the Allied authorities with some personal excuse for crossing the lines, without 'admitting' a mission from the Germans, Braitenberg thought that they would not automatically be brought into contact with the Allied Intelligence Services; if again they offered their services to the Allies, either at once or later it would have been difficult for them to produce a satisfactory story which would have reconciled this offer with their alleged purely personal reason for crossing the lines. They had to have a reason for returning soon to North Italy, and those who crossed the lines for voluntary personal reasons were unlikely to have a reason strong enough for them to return. And Braitenberg did not have such a low opinion of the Allied Intelligence Services as to believe that they would swallow a story that anyone had crossed the lines specifically to offer to work as an agent for them, when he could have found ample scope for such activities in North Italy. He decided, then, that the ostensible reason for his agents' crossing would have to be a mission forced on them by the Germans.

Braitenberg did not believe at the the time that the elaborate cover stories he prepared for these agents would be broken by the Allied Intelligence Services. He thought that the very fact of an agent's confession to a mission would dispose belief in his genuineness from the Allied point of view. If their services as Allied agents were not accepted he expected that they would be allowed to go free, after perhaps a short period in a refugee camp, and that they would then be able to return to him on their own. He based this belief on what he was told of German counter-espionage interrogations, which were said to be fairly casual unless there were good reason to suspect the subject.

Attempts at despatch through Allied Intelligence Services.
In October 1944 Braitenberg decided that a far better method of getting his agents to Allied occupied territory to play them onto an Allied Intelligence Service net in North Italy and get them despatched through enemy channels as supposedly genuine Allied agents to contact the Allied Intelligence Service in Allied territory and carry messages for the respective network. What made him renounce almost entirely the idea of sending agents across the lines on his own account was an announcement in the Italian newspapers or on the wireless. It was reported that several German agents had been executed for espionage in Allied occupied territory, common talk at the BdS that no agents had returned from missions, and the refusal of Gollin, in December 1944, to go forward into Allied territory after she had twice been in no-man's-land. He thought that agents would feel more confident and also have a far better chance of being accepted in Allied territory if they were accepted as genuine Allied agents before they crossed the lines, as he hoped that Allied intelligence net that accepted them would first announce their eventual arrival in Allied territory.

A number of agents made contact with Italian groups or individuals working for Allied intelligence according to the new plan, and in their attempts to be sent to Allied territory on missions for these groups succeeded in discovering in three cases very considerable detail about their membership and activities. These cases were the penetration of the *Partito d'Anzione* in Milan and Verona, the Arbizzani W/T group in Milan and Treviso and a SIM group in Venice. '*Frau* Hoffmann' was the only agent who was actually given a mission—by the *Partito d'Anzione*—but was not despatched before Braitenberg left Verona at the end of April 1945.

Some of the agents whom Braitenberg set to contacting Allied Intelligence Service circles were told to say that they were agents working for the German Intelligence Services, either from compulsion or because they were planning to harm the Germans by giving the Allies what information they picked up, or both. Braitenberg hoped that this method of 'frank confession' would make suspicion of a double agent unlikely, and would also attract the Intelligence Service circles concerned with the possibility of using these agents in a double game themselves. However, this meant that these agents could not be despatched through Allied Intelligence Service channels, which was Braitenberg's original plan when he adopted the system of contact with the Allied Intelligence Services in North Italy, as in that case they could have had no convincing reason to give their German Intelligence Service employers for their prolonged absence; accordingly Braitenberg had to plan to despatch them on his own, and to invent bogus missions which they could tell the Allied Intelligence circles with which they were in contact.

A special case, and the only one of its kind, was that of Morelli, a relative of Field Marshal Messe, whom Braitenberg had 'recruited' in December 1944 through '*Frau* Hoffmann'. Morelli believed her to be genuinely pro-Allied and on her suggestion was taken on as a BdS agent—this was the case in which Braitenberg borrowed the services of Lechner, see Para. 2.c, above—with the idea of going to Allied occupied territory and joining the Allied Intelligence Service with the help of Messe. Braitenberg's idea was that when he retuned with a mission for the Allies he would given full details of what he had learnt, including names of agents and contacts in North Italy, to '*Frau* Hoffmann'.

Work against Allied Intelligence Services in Switzerland.
In October 1944 Braitenberg began to turn his attention to Switzerland. Freund, as already mentioned in Para. 2.a, above, had sent him names of persons suspected of being connected with the Allied Intelligence Services in Switzerland and Braitenberg took this to mean that he was to go ahead with work against Allied Intelligence and its collaborators in that country. In February and March 1945 three agents succeeded in getting into Switzerland; one saw the British Consul in Lugano, with no result, one was thrown out by the Swiss after a short period of detention, one, Morelli who was actually trying to get from Switzerland to Allied occupied territory by an Allied air route via Madrid, was let out from a refugee camp by a pro-Allied Swiss police official who gave him valuable Intelligence Service contacts in North Italy. As a result of this information Braitenberg was able to carry out his successful penetration of the SIM group in Venice referred to above.

Braitenberg soon realised that there was no hope of obtaining visas for agents he proposed sending to Switzerland, except in the case of one with business contacts for whom he tried to obtain one, without success, from the Swiss Consulate in Milan. He therefore told them to try to get in touch with persons in touch with Allied Intelligence Service circles or with frontier smugglers and thus find a way of crossing on foot. Some were to tell the Swiss, if stopped, that they had important news to give to an Allied Consulate, and Braitenberg thought that the pro-Allied attitude of the Swiss would ensure that they were taken there; some were to establish contact with partisans in North Italy and discovered through courier routes to Switzerland, if possible acting as the couriers themselves, what help the partisans were received from Allied circles in Switzerland and from whom they were receiving it. The story that agents were to tell at the Allied Consulates was on the same lines as the cover stories given to his line-crossers to Allied occupied territory, that they had been forced to accept a mission from the Germans which they did not want to fulfil, though they had to return for personal reason to North Italy. Braitenberg hoped that they would then be given missions for the Allies. After he began thinking of work on Switzerland Braitenberg planned more missions of this nature that for Allied occupied territory in southern Italy, as agents accepted them more readily, knowing that they would not be executed whatever happened, and if their request to be taken to an Allied Consulate was not accepted all that would probably happen was expulsion back to Italy; and if they were acting as couriers for partisans and were caught by the Swiss they would be able to invent some excuse for their presence in Switzerland without mentioning espionage. The agent for whom Braitenberg tried to obtain a Swiss visa was to get in touch with Allied Intelligence circles through his business contacts.

Work against Allied Intelligence Services in France.

In November 1944 Braitenberg obtained from Dr Begus a woman agent with relatives in France, and despatched her at the beginning of April 1945 with the task of getting a mission from Allied Intelligence Services in that country. She was to go via Switzerland and try to enlist the help of an Allied Consulate to get her to France.

Espionage on Codes and Ciphers.

Freund sent Braitenberg a request in March 1945 which led him to undertake a new field of work. The request was for information on the old and new British Naval cipher and on the French 'Empire' code. Braitenberg gave 'Frau Hoffmann' the task of discovering what she could of the British ciphers, in Naples, in addition to her penetration mission, and the woman agent despatched to France was to do the same for the French 'Empire' code. An agent for whom he was planning a penetration mission in Allied occupied territory in April 1945 was also given the straight espionage mssion of discovering what he could of the British ciphers (he was not despatched), and another agent who had been given the mission in January 1945 of discovering routes and landing points of Allied submarines engaged in espionage operations on the Adriatic coast was told that if possible he was to find out how one of these submarines might be captured; Braitenberg hoped then to discover cipher documents on board. He imagines that this purely espionage mission was given to VI Z because the Germans considered the information of such importance that all likely intelligence channels were being tapped.

Special tasks from RSHA VI Z.

In additon to the request for information on Allied ciphers, Freund asked Braitenberg on two occasions to find out the whereabouts of individuals in North Italy who were believed to be connected with Allied Intelligence Services in Switzerland, one of them being Baron Parilli. On another occasion he asked Braitenberg to find out the whereabouts of a Hungarian Consul and of a Yugoslav, Ingenieur 'Ivo', in whom he said the Allies were interested, and whom he thought might be used as a double agent. Nothing came of these requests. On another occasion, in March 1945, Freund asked Braitenberg to locate and visit a *Contessa* Bassenge whom SS-*Brigadeführer* Schellenberg wanted to employ as an agent. She was a relative of Baron Parilli. Braitenberg visited her, and her reply was negative.

Proposed Post-Occupational network.

Freund suggested to Braitenberg in October or November 1944 that he should think about the setting up of a post-occupational network of agents who were to find work with the Allied Intelligence Services and also transmit military intelligence, presumably while in training or waiting for missions. Braitenberg opposed this idea, as in his view it would have been far too risky for an agent deliberately to cultivate Allied Intelligence circles and at the same time transmit to the Germans. Besides, he did not consider an espionage task proper for a counter-espionage unit. Freund did not press the matter, and Braitenberg heard no more about it. He did temporarily earmark one agent for such a role in case Freund insisted.

Despatching Methods.

The early line-crossers were all despatched through SS-*Obersturmführer* Müller of *Abteilung* VI at *Sipo* and SD *Aussenkommando* Bologna. Agents for Switzerland were to cross the frontier on foot by means discovered by themselves. Braitenberg heard from Freund that there was an American air service from an airfield near Lausanne to Madrid, and a British line from there to Rome, and hoped to make use of this to get agents to Allied occupied territory via Switzerland, but he did not succeed. The agent who was given the espionage task on the British Naval ciphers was launched into no-man's-land by Einheit IDA in March 1945, but refused to continue, and a passage was then booked for him through *Dienststelle* Carmen; his [parachute] drop was postponed however, and Braitenberg then arranged with

Kapitän-Ltn. Sessler, I(M) San Remo and with *Kapitän-Ltn.* Ullrich, commanding officer 611 Flotilla KdK, for him to be despatched by sea from La Spezia at the beginning of April 1945. This too fell through. Braitenberg had previously booked this passage for '*Frau* Hoffmann', whose departure had to be delayed.

Bogus missions and Briefers.

All bogus missions which Braitenberg made up for his agents were of a very simple nature, so that he did not have to invent a period of training in Allied armies, etc., when it would have been difficult to make up details of an espionage school that did not exist and also difficult not to give away useful information if he chose one that did exist. In some cases agents were given bogus missions by *Abteilung* VI, with a briefing officer with a false name but the real description of an actual member of the *Abteilung*, so as to give weight to the cover story, if the Allied Intelligence Service knew of the officer by description, without revealing any real names. Braitenberg also told his agents to say that the names of officers were almost certainly false for security reasons. In two cases, Braitenberg gave the same particulars about briefing officers to two different agents, as he did not want the Allies to become suspicious at an apparent glut of fresh officers to the *Abteilung*. In other cases he told the agents to say that they been given missions by members of unidentified unit they had met casually, and that they had never been taken to an office. Braitenberg did not think that this fact would appear suspicious, as in the Balkans almost all briefing was done away from German Intelligence Service premises.

On one occasion he gave a bogus military espionage mission to an agent purporting to have been employed by *Abteilung* VI. He did not think this would be suspicious either, as he had been told that *Abteilung* VI also collected military information as a sideline to its political activities.

Agents' documents.

All agents except one were despatched or intended to be despatched under their own names. The exception was the case of '*Frau* Hoffmann' who was always known in North Italy under this false name, and in addition was provided with a false identity card produced by the G *Staffel* OBSW (*Oberbefehlshaber Süd-West*—military commander) issued in Florence as part of the elaborate cover story made up for her mission. As Braitenberg's agents were to contact openly Allied Intelligence Service circles or their collaborators there was no reason for them to have false documents.

False counter-espionage material.

Braitenberg gave a good deal of counter-espionage material to some of his agents, chiefly to double agents in contact with Allied Intelligence circles in North Italy, to impress the intelligence services with their worth and reliability. He applied for permission to use certain short-term and local items, facts on air-raid damage, troop movements etc., either to Harster or to the Ic OBSW. Long-term material on new weapons etc., he submitted to Freund for his approval, or requested him for the material in the first place.

Summary of results.
Despite his immense activity Braitenberg had achieved relatively little by the time of the collapse, though he had several missions planned and in course which promised well. His knowledge of the actual organisation of the Allied Intelligence Services in Allied occupied territory was little more than when he first came to Verona, though, as he has himself said, this was not his main interest. What little more he did learn did not come through his own agents, but from the two reports of *Abteilung* IV and *Referat* IV/III/F at BdS Italien, and he has now forgotten details of these. The same is true of Switzerland; all his knowledge came from lists sent him by Freund of Allied Consuls and suspected intelligence collaborators. He can now remember only the names of Air Commodore West in Geneva and Major de Garston in Lugano.

The only success scored by Braitenberg in his real function, obtaining names of Allied Intelligence Service circles in North Italy through long-distance contacts, was when Morelli obtained the name of a contact in Venice from a Swiss police official, which resulted in successful penetration of the Venice SIM group. Apart from that he penetrated very successfully the Allied Intelligence circle of *Partito d'Anzione* in Milan, discovering some 35 names and/or descriptions of important members, and the Arbizzani W/T group in Milan and later Treviso, which had been transmitting valuable information to Allied occupied territory. His work here resulted in the group's liquidation. He also discovered other isolated names of people known or believed to be connected with Allied Intelligence Services, but either they were known already to *Abteilung* IV or *Referat* IV/III/F (BdS Italien) or appeared to be of little importance or Braitenberg had no time to follow them up.

The above is the sum total of Braitenberg's achievements. The rest was in the planning stage.

What little Major Benno von Braitenberg achieved in North Italy for RSHA VI Z was matched by *Oberstleutant* Robert von Tarbuk in Prague for VI Z *Ost*. Agents recruited as line-crossers who did not want to cross the lines, and plans made that never came to fruition due to the German collapse.

USFET CI Final Interrogation Report (CI-FIR) No. 63 dated 19 January 1946 of *Oberstleutnant* Robert von Tarbuk, head of VI Z *Ost*:

The re-organization of the *Abwehr* was announced at a conference in Salzburg, 16 and 17 May 1944. Kaltenbrunner presided and the conference was attended by RSHA *Amtsgruppenleiter* IV and VI, *Amtsgruppenleiter* of OKW/*Abwehr Ausland*, all heads of *Amts*, and heads of Walli I, II and III. Tarbuk attended as the representative of of *Abwehr Ast* Bucharest.

The assembly was informed of the incorporation of the *Abwehr* into the RSHA. *Oberst* i.G. Georg Hansen was scheduled to speak but he did not appear. Instead, Müller and Schellenberg [RSHA *Amtschef* IV and VI, respectively] reviewed the origin, historical development, and significance of the *Abwehr*. In an optimistic address *Reichsführer*-SS Himmler announced that Hitler had personally assured him that setbacks on all fronts would be overcome by the development of new weapons.

Disposition of *Abwehr* agencies.
The *Truppen-Abwehr, Referate* III-H, III-L, III-M and III-Kgf remained under the *Wehrmacht*. *Abwehr* III-C (Administrative Supervision) and III-Wi were incorporated into RSHA *Amt* IV (*Gestapo*). The *Erkundungs- und Abwehr-Dienst*, with the exception of III-F, was attached to RSHA VI as *Mil Amt*. *Abwehr* I became *Kommando* Meldegebiet and was incorporated into *Mil Amt* C, while *Abwehr* II was renamed *Mil Amt* D. The disposition of III-F ("passive" and "active" espionage, counter-espionage, and enemy information service) remained an unsettled question. Müller, RSHA *Amtschef* IV, insisted that all the functions of *Abwehr* III-F should be absorbed by *Amt* IV, while Schellenberg claimed that "active" espionage fell within his sphere and should be incorporated into his political *Auslandsdienst*.

Disposition of *Abwehr* III-F.
Oberst Joachim Rohleder, head of III-F, and his subordinate, *Oberstleutnant* Dr Hans Freund, constantly disagreed. Freund now sought to become chief of a *Referat* himself. He induced Schellenberg to persuade Kaltenbrunner to split III-F into separate spheres in October 1944.

   Oberst Rohleder was put in charge of "passive" and domestic espionage, which was incorporated into RSHA *Amt* IV as IV 3/a2, while Freund was named head of "active" espionage and counter-espionage abroad, which was incorporated into RSHA VI as VI Z.

The Vermehren Case.
One of the decisive factors inducing Himmler to incorporate the *Abwehr* into the RSHA was the Vermehren case.

   Gefreiter Dr Erich Vermehren was chief agent of *Abwehr* I in Istanbul, Turkey. His subordinate, Dr Kolachevsky, and Vermehren's wife Elisabeth had also been assigned to Istanbul to spy on Allied forces in the eastern Mediterranean area, including Egypt. Himmler learned in 1944 that all three of them had sold out to the Allies [they went over on 27 January 1944]. Himmler uttered the words *Der ganzen Haufen, von Canaris angefangen, ist ein Verräternest* ("The whole lot of them, from Canaris on down, are a bunch of traitors"), and went to see Hitler to propose the *Abwehr* reorganization.

   Freund was despatched to Istanbul, July 1944 (sic) to investigate the Vermehren case and the part played by his agent, Dr Leverkühn, in the affair. Leverkühn, a member of the German Consulate General in Istanbul, had formerly been Vermehren's law partner in Berlin and his Commanding Officer in the Army. Leverkühn was cleared of suspicion.

Freund later boasted that he had been able to effect Kolachevsky's arrest by convincing British Intelligence that the latter was still a German agent.

RSHA *Amt* VI Z:

Division of VI Z.

Oberstleutnant Freund divided VI Z into four departments:

> VI Z *West*, under *Oberst* Ehinger,
>
> VI Z *Nord*, under *Hauptmann* Salzinger (?),
>
> VI Z *Süd*, under *Rittmeister* Pictorius (von Pescatore) in Switzerland,
>
> VI Z *Ost*, under *Oberstleutnant* Tarbuk in Prague.

He also created *Referat* VI Z/E (*Erfassung und Erkundung*) headed by Freund's deputy, *Hauptmann* Kraigher. Freund activated separate departments for Turkey, Spain, and Portugal. *Hauptmann* Geilich, who was a member of Freund's headquarters in Berlin, Tirpitzufer, was in charge of the department for Turkey.

Function and Organization on VI Z *Ost.*

Freund ordered Tarbuk to assume charge of VI Z *Ost* in November 1944 and gave him the choice of headquarters in Vienna or Prague. Tarbuk chose to establish his HQ in Prague, at 5 Platz der Wehrmacht, together with the *Kommando* Meldegebiet. VI Z *Ost* was attached to *Kommando* Meldegebiet Prague but Tarbuk received his orders directly from Freund.

The territory of VI Z *Ost* included all of Z Europe. The chief function of VI Z agents was to spy on the enemy communications net. Tarbuk placed his main agents in Meldeköpfe which were successively located in Budapest, Vienna (December 1944), Graz and Stein am Anger [now Szombathely, Hungary]. The main agents were free to choose their own subordinates.

VI Z *Ost* could only submit its reports to BdS Prague, SS-*Oberführer* Dr Erwin Weinmann, at two-weekly intervals because the German communications system was disrupted by Allied operations.

Personnel of RSHA *Amt* VI Z *Ost.*

Chief:	*Oberstltn.* Robert Tarbuk.
Deputy:	*Hauptmann* Klausnitzer, formerly *Ast* Prague, III-F.
Evaluation & Editing:	*Sonderführer* Strauss, formerly *Ast* Sofia.
Abwehr aide:	*Obergefreiter* Wegener, formerly *Ast* Sofia.
Messenger:	*Gefreiter* Tobisch, formerly *Ast* Sofia.
Driver:	*Feldwebel* Esch, formerly *Ast* Salonika.
Office Chief:	Eschner (civilian employee)

Liaison:	*Hauptmann* Lang, formerly *Stapo* Prage, IV 3c2, who joined VI Z *Ost* in February 1945.
Secretaries:	*Fräulein* Rosemann, *Fräulein* Noack, *Frau* Cebser.
Meldekopf Vienna:	*Oberltn.* Schlandt; von Pahlen (civilian employee)
Meldekopf Stein am Anger:	*Ltn.* Ballon.
Meldekopf Graz:	*Hauptmann* Göbel, formerly Ast Sofia.

Hauptmann Fiedler, formerly *Asts* Vienna, Belgrade.

Gefreiter Richter, formerly *Asts* Breslau, Sofia.

Driver: *Unteroffizier* Trainkner.

Secretary: *Frau* Orendi, formerly *Ast* Athens.

Funkspiele: *Oberltn.* Bernard.

<u>Selection and commitment of Agents.</u>

The dissolution of the Balkan *Aussenstellen* (except *Ast* Bucharest), which started August 1943, released many agents for duty elsewhere. Because of the Russian advance more agents retreated slowly toward the Protectorate. The Meldeköpfe were therefore well provided with men who were willing to work, but who were none too eager to venture behind the enemy lines. Since many of these agents had come from Sofia and were accustomed to the easy method of obtaining information via Turkey, it was imperative that better agents be recruited.

For this purpose Tarbuk obtained the aid of a Russian citizen, Dr Wolochoff (also 'Parsifal'), a very able man who recruited a number of Polish agents. These were known as the 'Polish Group'. Among them was a couple named Koslowsky, who were brought to Prague to train as radio operators. Their training was never completed. The Polish Group was extremely anxious to work against the USSR inasmuch as almost all of them were members of 'AK', the Polish anti-Soviet resistance movement.

There was also a 'Ukrainian Group' under Major von Korab (aliases Dr Majewski, Dr Novotny), which came to Prague after the dissolution of *Ast* Krakow.

Plans were under way to activate a 'Hungarian Group', but it never actually operated.

A 'Spanish Group' was transferred to VI Z *West* and Tarbuk knows nothing of its activities.

Most of the agents of these groups were reluctant to cross the front lines into enemy territory. Consequently much information had to be obtained from refugees and deserters.

<u>Agents attached to VI Z *Ost* and the 'Spanish Group'.</u>

(a) Group I (Ukrainian Group)

      Leader: Major von Korab; office at Jungmannstrasse 30, Prague.

      Agents: Hladky

               Korzan

Fritz

Messer

Laniecki

Kruck

Ilona

(b) Group II (Polish Group)

Leader: Dr Wolochoff; office at Tischlergasse 29, Prague.

Agents: Koslowski and his wife Dorota

Piarecki

Janaszek

Erich Schulz

Scheinhorst

(c) Group III (Hungarian Group)

Leader: Consul and Hungarian Lt.Col. Liszay; received orders from Meldekopf
          Vienna

Agents   Liszay (son), radio operator

Puszta-Szeredi

Kovaczi

P…….. (?)

(d) Group IV (Spanish Group), not personally known to Tarbuk.

Agents: Faerber and his wife, radio operators, who were to operate in Madrid.

Kovacz II, was to operate in Lisbon.

Kamaras, was to reside in Lisbon.

(e) Group V.

Leader: Oriensky, received his orders from Berlin via
          Meldekopf Stein am Anger.

Agents: Kovacz III (alias Tibor)

Vhrovac, received orders directly from Meldekopf Stein a.A.

Wiesinger, editor of the German newspaper in Hungary.

(f) Group VI (Russian Group).

Leader: Hurnuraki, received orders from Meldekopf Graz

Agents: Grabentschikoff

Ing. Ite.

(g) Unattached agents:

Kratschmer, Anton (alias Tony)

Worm (alias Richard)

Reinprechter (alias Franzl)

Ruszysz (Rust?) (alias Franz)

Tartaglia (alias E 4 P)

Krizek (aliases Dicker, E 3 P)

Bitzer (alias Hinrich)

Deteindre

Gregora

Dr Feroroff

VI Z *Ost* in Prague also ran a radio *Funkspiel* in 1944 under the name "Mandoline".

In order to mislead Allied Intelligence, two German agents, Willi Rau and a Serbian with the alias of 'Yokl' became informants. Rau had contacted the British and 'Yokl' worked with the Americans. These men were recruited by *Abwehr* officers Dr Leverkühn and Major Lechner (alias 'Aladin') in Istanbul. Their ruse was so successful that they even managed to obtain radio sets from the Allies.

When Major Fabian returned from *Ast* Sofia, Rau and 'Yokl' provided him with unimportant intelligence information for Allied consumption.

Rau proposed to British Intelligence agents that they use Weigl, a telegraph employee in Prague. The British replied that they were not fond of Weigl but that they would accept any news that was transmitted to them.

Weigl never actually operated the radio, but Postal Inspector Pommert (Erich or Kurt) operated a radio station from Priesterseminar, Schubert Platz, under the alias of 'Mandoline'. Every Sunday at 1000 hours he contacted London and provided the British with false information supplied by *Oberstleutnant* Freund. The British were primarily interested in naval affairs and were seldom interested in political problems. Freund sometimes answered their questions truthfully on the assumption that the Allies had managed to obtain prior access to the information.

Rau was able to maintain contact with the British until 22 April 1945. They had even promised to open an account for him in Switzerland, but Tarbuk does not know whether this plan was actually executed.

Notes:

* The National Archives, Kew, KV 3/110: interrogation report CSDIC/CMF SD 75 dated 8 October 1945, of Benno von Braitenburg.
* The National Archives, Kew, KV 3/111, USFET CI Final Interrogation Report (CI-FIR) No. 63 dated 19 January 1946, of Robert von Tarbuk.

15

Liquidation Report No. 23:
Amt VII of the RSHA

This report contains an account of the historical development of *Amt* VII, together with a list of personalities.

INDEX

Part I: The origins of *Amt* VII
Part II: The Period after the Formation of the RSHA
Part III: The Creation of *Amt* VII in 1941
Part IV: The Function of *Amt* VII
Part V: Miscellaneous

Appendix I: The Organisation of *Amt* II in 1939–1940
Appendix II: The Organisation of *Amt* VII in 1941
Appendix III: The Organisation of *Amt* VII in 1944–1945
Appendix IV: Alphabetical Index of Personalities, 1939–1945
Amt VII of the RSHA

Part I

The Period before the Creation of the RSHA

(a) Dr Six and the *Schriftumstelle*

The origins and development of *Amt* VII of the RSHA is in fact the personal history of its first *Amtschef*, SS-*Staf* Dr Franz Alfred Six. Dr Six has a long history in the

SD. In 1935 after graduating as a doctor of philosophy at Heidelberg University, where he had studied journalism and political science, he joined the SD-*Hauptamt* where his scholarship, mediocre though it was, was likely to give him a position of some importance.

Later in the same year he took over the *Schriftumstelle* of the SD-*Hauptamt* in Leipzig. The *Schriftumstelle* was a section of the *Kulturamt* of the SD, and its functions were to provide the *Kulturamt* with an analysis of the ideological and political content of current publications. These reports were passed by the *Kulturamt* to the SD-*Hauptamt* in Berlin, which was responsible for further distribution to other departments, such as the Propaganda Ministry and the *Gestapoamt*.

(b) The Re-organisation of the SD-*Hauptamt*

The SD-*Hauptamt* was re-organised into *Zentralabteilungen* of which the following are relevant to the history of RSHA *Amt* VII:

Abteilung I/3	Press and Schriftum
I/3/1	Press and Literary Investigations and Press Archives
I/3/2	Library relating to Freemasonry, Sorcery and Witchcraft
Abteilung II/1	SD-Inland (*Nachrichtendient über politische- und weltanschauliche Gegner*)

In this re-organisation SS-*Staf* Dr Six was given command of *Abteilung* I/3 which represented in fact a continuation of his duties as head of the *Schriftumstelle* and the *Presse Abteilungen* of the SD-*Hauptamt*. Thereafter the rise of Six to a position of authority in the SD-*Hauptamt* is quite remarkable. By early 1937 he was appointed *Leiter* of *Abteilung* II/1, and shortly afterwards *Leiter* of *Zentralabteilung* II/2, where he profited as a result of a quarrel between Heydrich and Professor Höhn, who had been *Abteilungsleiter* until then.

(c) The position of Dr Six before the creation of the RSHA

Immediately prior to the foundation of the RSHA in 1939, Six held a position of great authority in the SD-*Hauptamt*. It should be noted for example that *Zentralabteilung* II/2, of which he was *Leiter*, was in fact a forerunner of the later *Amt* III of the RSHA, and Six had as his *Referent* at this time SS-*Gruf* Ohlendorf, who was later to become RSHA *Amtschef* III.

Six was a man of ambition to whom his career meant everything, and the subsequent decline of *Amt* VII of the RSHA is due in no small measure to the difference between the authority which Six enjoyed before the foundation of the RSHA and his comparative eclipse after the RSHA had finally been established.

Part II

The period after the formation of the RSHA

(a) The Absorption of the SD-*Hauptamt*:

When Heydrich set up the RSHA in the latter half of 1939 the various *Abteilungen* of the SD-*Hauptamt* were absorbed into the new *Ämter* of the RSHA. Of the *Abteilungen* of the SD-*Hauptamt* mentioned in Part I (b), *Abteilungen* II/2 became the new *Amt* III under SS-*Gruf* Ohlendorf, while *Abteilung* II/1 was incorporated into the *Gestapoamt*, which became the new *Amt* IV. Six for his part became *Amtschef* of the new *Amt* II, which on broad lines carried on the functions of the former *Abteilung* I/3, but it should be noted that the investigation department of *Abteilung* I/3/1 passed over to the new *Amt* III. The original organisation of the new *Amt* II is shown at Appendix I.

(b) The Position of Six as *Amtschef* II:

Though Six had in fact relinquished his authority over *Abteilung* II/2, as that *Abteilung* had now become *Amt* III under Ohlendorf, together with his control of the old *Abteilung* II/1, an analysis of the breakdown of *Amt* II at Appendix I shows that Dr Six still remained a comparatively powerful *Amtschef* in the RSHA. The title of the new *Amt* II—*Gegnerforschung*—was still sufficiently wide to give the *Amt* a considerable amount of scope. Although the *Amt* was now defined as a research department, its activities were not confined merely to providing a reference library, and at the same time went far beyond the study of the sects which had been the province of the former *Abteilung* I/3 and the SD-*Hauptamt*. Broadly speaking, *Gruppe* A and *Gruppe* B of the new RSHA *Amt* II represented the old *Abteilung* I/3, giving the *Amt* the subjects on which research should be conducted, while *Gruppe* C and *Gruppe* gave it a territorial sphere of interest of the widest possible scope in so far as they covered both Germany itself and the Ausland.

(c) *Amt* II and its relations with *Amt* III:

It is not difficult to appreciate that in the scramble for power between the new *Amtschef* in the setting up of the RSHA, Dr Six should have his work cut out to preserve for *Amt* II the scope given to *Gruppe* C and *Gruppe* D. SS-*Uschaf* Spengler, who had been in the old *Kulturamt* when Ohlendorf joined that section in 1935, had now become SS-*Stubaf* Spengler in the new *Amt* III as *Gruppenleiter*

III A on cultural matters, and shared with Ohlendorf, the *Amtschef*, the latter's resentment at the encroachment of *Gruppe* C of *Amt* II on the wide subject of *Deutsche Lebensgebiete*, the special duty of *Amt* III. Ohlendorf's resentment was based not only on his desire for *Amt* III to be given the widest possible scope, but also because he had been Six's subordinate in the SD-*Hauptamt*, while Spengler, in his capacity as *Gruppenleiter* of the Cultural Section of *Amt* III, was anxious that the records which *Amt* II had inherited from *Abteilung* I/3 and to which he had largely contributed, should be with him in his new capacity.

(d) *Amt* II and its relations with *Amt* VI:

Nor was it likely that Schellenberg, when he became acting RSHA *Amtschef* VI in the latter part of 1941, was likely to look with any favour on *Gruppe* D of *Amt* II and its interest in the Ausland. Indeed much depended on Schellenberg's reaction to *Amt* II in 1941. Schellenberg did indeed discuss the future of *Amt* II with Six, and again in 1942, by which time *Amt* II had become *Amt* VII, with a view to making use of it for the purpose of *Amt* VI. Schellenberg was throughout his career as RSHA *Amtschef* VI most anxious to organise a proper evaluation research section for the *Amt*, and *Amt* VII would have appeared the proper foundation for such a section. Schellenberg however finally decided on the creation of *Gruppe* VI G, and *Amt* VII then ceased to interest him. One of the chief contributing factors in this decision of Schellenberg's was the inefficiency of the personnel in *Amt* VII. Six himself was ambitious rather than capable and his successor Dittel was not the type to appeal to Schellenberg.

(e) The decline of *Amt* II in 1941:

The breakdown of the new RSHA *Amt* VII shown in Appendix II tells its own story. It will be seen from this chart that the former *Gruppe* II C has now become a mere sub-section in the new *Gruppe* VII B, while a similar fate has befallen the old *Gruppe* II D, which now becomes *Gruppe* VII B6. Already therefore by 1941 Dr Six has lost his fight, and the subsequent history of RSHA *Amt* VII is one of whittling away of functions and personnel. This state of affairs could not of course appeal to Dr Six. RSHA *Amt* VII was for him a vehicle for his own ambition. He himself was not an erudite type to whom research would appeal for its own sake. Indeed he did not appreciate either the value of research or the methods by which it should be conducted. When therefore by early 1942 it was apparent that *Amt* VII was no longer destined to be an influential *Amt* of the RSHA, and was likely to disappear into insignificance, Dr Six had to seek elsewhere for some other star to which to hitch his wagon. His interest in *Amt* VII continued to decline, and by early 1943 he did in fact transfer to the Foreign Office at the request of Ribbentrop, and characteristically enough, his interest in *Amt* VII came to an abrupt end.

(b) The development of *Amt* VII after the departure of Dr Six:

By 1943 therefore RSHA *Amt* VII was in an unenviable position. The driving force of the ambitious Dr Six had been replaced by the scholarly and meek personality of SS-*Hstuf* Paul Dittel. *Amt* III had a covetous eye on the VII library. Schellenberg had already decided on the creation of a new *Gruppe* VI G to perform the functions which *Amt* VII might have performed, and the dissolution itself of the *Amt* was urged from time to time by the other RSHA *Amtschefs*. By this time too Heydrich had been replaced by Kaltenbrunner, whose mentality naturally led him to despise 'the intellectual old men', though it must be said that Kaltenbrunner's judgment was a relative one, as the staff of *Amt* VII were intellectual only in comparison with the normal run of SS officers. The staff of *Amt* VII was not in fact suited to research work, and in addition was steadily depleted by the transfer of the physically fit members to operational units. If therefore RSHA *Amt* VII continued to exist, it did so on sufferance. Indeed by December 1943 a complete re-organisation of the *Amt* took place whereby *Gruppe* VII B and *Referat* VII C1 were virtually dissolved, the *Amt* working to all intents and purposes as a single *Gruppe*. As however VII B and VII C had records which were considered worth preserving, they continued to exist on paper. Had the material been available at the time, the liquidation report on *Amt* VII might well have been written in 1943.

…

Part IV

The Function of RSHA *Amt* VII

(a) *Referat* VII A1—Library:

Each *Amt* of the RSHA maintained its own reference library for the subjects of particular interest to the *Amt*. The library of *Amt* VII was therefore not a reference library but a research library on the general subjects covered by *Amt* VII. It contained some 200,000 to 300,000 volumes, mainly on masonic, church, Marxist and Jewish subjects, which were never properly classified and catalogued. The library was little used apart from other *Gruppen* of *Amt* VII itself. The library was evacuated in early 1943 to various parts of Bohemia and Thuringia [due to Allied air-raids].

(b) *Referat* VII A2—Press Archives:

The Press Section was originally intended to provide the other *Ämter* of the RSHA with a daily review of the world press. This scheme was dropped by 1942 after which date the section merely collected various press cuttings of interest for circulation to the other *Ämter* but even this practice fell into disuse. The Press Archives were evacuated to Plaue in Thuringia in March 1943.

(c) *Referat* VII B1—Freemasonry Evaluation:

As stated above, the *Gruppe* VII B was virtually dissolved in December 1943. *Referat* VII B1 evaluated all reports of Freemasonry obtained from other sources, such as *Amt* III, from one of the few VII representatives abroad—SS-*Ostuf* Stüber with the BdS Frankreich, and from other ministries such as the Propaganda Ministry. *Referat* VII B1 was usually disregarded in its evaluations of such material.

(d) *Referat* VII B2—Evaluation of material on Jewry:

This *Referat* issued a review every three weeks summarising Press information on the Jewish Question. These reports tended to be too objective to be welcomed by other departments. The *Referat* obtained most of its material from *Referat* VII A1.

(e) *Referat* VII B3—Evaluation of material on Church questions:

This section was probably the most ineffective section of an ineffective *Amt*. The interests of both *Amt* III and *Amt* IV in Church matters was far too strong for VII B3 to be allowed to function in any way. A certain amount of work was done on ecclesiastical history.

(f) *Referat* VII B4—Evaluation of Marxist material:

This section did research work on standard Marxist literature and filed press articles on Marxism, mainly obtained from the Swiss Press. Its activity served no useful purpose whatever. Again the influence of *Amt* IV was far too strong for *Amt* VII.

(g) *Referat* VII B5—Evaluation of material on Liberalism:

VII B5 was an ambitious venture by Six to carry out research into political and philosophical thought in German history with the object of proving that the Nazi state and Liberalism were quite irreconcilable. Close liaison with *Gruppe* VII C had been envisaged but again the objectivity of *Amt* VII was distasteful to *Amt* III and the venture came to nought.

(h) Referat VII B6—Political opponents:

VII B6 was another *Referat* to have a short life; it had been set up in 1941 as a special research section investigating the ideological and political tendencies of

German *émigré* circles abroad: it had to depend on VII A1 and on the foreign press for its material. VII B6 ceased to function early in 1943.

(i) *Referat* VII C1—Masonic Archives:

This section dealt with research into Masonic records in Germany and maintained archives which were rarely consulted by outside agencies.

(j) *Referat* VII C2—The Masonic Museum:

As previously mentioned VII C2 disappeared in 1943. Its previous existence had been a tenuous one. The section collected exhibits of Masonic regalia.

(k) Referat VII C3—Witchcraft:

This section has also been referred to as the H-*Referat* (the *Hexen Referat*). Its original function had been to trace the influence of the Catholic Church on mediaeval witchcraft. Both Himmler and Heydrich had shown interest in the subject but once again when objective research conflicted with their preconceived views, interest waned. VII C3 ceased to function independently by late 1944.

Part V

Misceallaneous

(a) The Failure of *Amt* VII:

It will be seen from this account of the history of *Amt* VII that it failed completely in the tasks which were assigned to it. The reasons for this failure are very easy to appreciate: the functions of the *Amt* were vague and undefined from its inception, and in any case the research fields which the original *Amt* II was meant to embrace would have entailed a far higher standard of academic ability in the personnel of the *Amt* than was ever available to it. The very scope accorded to *Amt* II was to prove its undoing as its spheres of interest were fated to clash with those of the other *Ämter*, the heads of which were not disposed to accord to another *Amt* subjects of research which they felt could best be done within their own *Ämter*, not because the *Amtschefs* thought in terms of maximum efficiency and co-ordination, but in terms of their own authority and power. The *coup de grâce* was administered by the *Amtschef* himself, when Six abandoned the *Amt* to seek fresh fields for his ambition. A further difficulty was that the *Amt* could not at one and the same time conduct research objectively and find favour with official policy, a factor which was to influence *Amt* III and to a lesser extent, RSHA *Amt* VI in the conduct of their affairs.

It had often been thought that with the appointment of Six to the Foreign Office, RSHA VII represented a penetration of that ministry on behalf of *Amt* VI. It is now quite clear that such was not the case and that from 1942 onwards the work of *Amt* VII had no real purpose and never at any time had any sinister espionage motives. It is known that Six did in fact keep on fairly good terms with Schellenberg after he left *Amt* VII. But the connection was a purely personal one and neither represented any effective penetration of the Foreign Office nor any extension of *Amt* VII interests.

It is also quite clear that RSHA *Amt* VII had no interests and no representatives outside the *Reich*: the one exception was the very minor representation in the BdS Frankreich but this activity had no hidden significance.

(b) Arrests:

Ther number of arrests of personnel is small but in view of the above paragraph, this is of little importance. The acting *Amtschef*, SS-*Ostubaf* Dittel has told all that need be known about the *Amt* and its activities and further interrogation could be of academic interest only. Other arrests are shown in Appendix IV.

(c) Main Sources:

The C.S.D.I.C. (U.K.) report on Dittel (PF.602,120) SIR 1723 on 13th September [1945] contains a full account of the development and functions of the *Amt*. The only other report which need be mentioned is that of SS-*Ostubaf* Patin (PF.602,096) of RSHA VII C3.

W.R.C. 3.a.
17 October 1945.

Appendix I

The Organisation of RSHA *Amt* VII in 1939–40

Amt II – *Gegnerforschung*

Amtschef – SS-*Staf* Dr Franz Alfred Six

Gruppe	Referat	Sachgebiet	Referent
Gruppenleiter II A (position vacant)			
II A		<u>*Grundlagenforschung*</u>	
	II A1	*Presse*	SS-*Ostuf* Helmut Mehringer
	II A2	*Bibliothek*	SS-*Ostuf* Dr Justus Beyer
	II A3	*Archiv*	SS-*Ostuf* Dr Paul Dittel
	II A4	*Aufkunftei*	SS-*Ostuf* Karl Burmester
	II A5	*Verbindungsstelle Deutsche Bücherei*	SS-*Ostuf* Ernst Nitsche
Gruppenleiter II B (position vacant)			
II B		<u>*Weltanschauliche Gegner*</u>	
	II B1	*Freimaurerei*	SS-*Hstuf* Hans Richter
	II B2	*Judentum*	SS-*Hstuf* Hans Richter
	II B3	*Politische Kirchen*	SS-*Stubaf* Albert Hartl
	II B4	*Marxismus*	SS-*Ostuf* Rolf Mühler
	II B5	*Liberalismus*	SS-*Ostuf* Rolf Mühler
Gruppenleiter II C (position vacant)			
II C		<u>*Inlandprobleme*</u>	
	II C1	*Kulturforschung*	SS-*Ostuf* Dr Andreas Schick
	II C2	*Rechts- und Staatsforschung*	vacant
	II C3	*Wirtschaftsforschung*	vacant
	II C4	*Staatsicherung*	vacant
	II C5	*Volkssicherung*	vacant
Gruppenleiter II D (position vacant)			
II D		<u>*Auslandsprobleme*</u>	
	II D1	*Ost*	SS-*Ostuf* Erich Hengelhaupt
	II D2	*Südost*	SS-*Schaf* Dr Emil Steudle
	II D3	*Süd*	SS-*Ostuf* Karl Hass
	II D4	*Frankreich*	SS-*Ostuf* Dr Andreas Biederbick
	II D5	*Eng.Imperium*	SS-*Ustuf* Johannes Neumann
	II D6	*Kolonien und Pazifisch Raum*	SS-*Ostuf* Friedrich Hanke

Appendix II

The Organisation of RSHA *Amt* VII in 1941

Amt VII – Ideological Investigation
Amtschef – SS-*Staf* Dr Franz Alfred Six
Adjutant - SS-*Stubaf* Karl Radke
Administration - SS-*Hstuf* Walter Braune

Gruppe	*Referat*	*Sachgebiet*	*Referent*
Gruppenleiter VII A – SS-*Ostubaf* Paul Mylius			
VII A	Compilation		
	VII A1	Library	SS-*Hstuf* Dr Justus Beyer
	VII A2	Press	SS-*Hstuf* Helmut Mehringer
	VII A3	Information	SS-*Hstuf* Karl Burmester
Gruppenleiter VII B (position vacant)			
VII B	Evaluation		
	VII B1	Freemasonry and Jews	vacant
	VII B2	Political Churches	SS-*Hstuf* Dr Friedrich Murawski
	VII B3	Marxismus	SS-*Ustuf* Horst Mahnke
	VII B4	Opposition Groups	SS-*Ostuf* Rolf Mühler
	VII B5	Domestic Problems	SS-*Hstuf* Dr Andreas Schick
	VII B6	Foreign Problems	vacant
Gruppenleiter VII C (position vacant)			
VII C	Archives		
	VII C1	Archives	SS-*Hstuf* Dr Paul Dittel
	VII C2	Museum	vacant
	VII C3	Special Tasks	SS-*Ostuf* Dr Rudolf Levin

Appendix III

The Organisation of RSHA *Amt* VII in 1944–45

Amt VII – Ideological Research
Acting *Amtschef* – SS-*Ostubaf* Dr Paul Dittel

Gruppe	*Referat*	*Sachgebiet*	*Referent*
Gruppenleiter VII A (position vacant)			
VII A	Compilation		
	VII A1	Library	SS-*Hstuf* Karl Burmester
	VII A2	Press	SS-*Hstuf* Karl-August Focke
Gruppenleiter VII B (position vacant)			
VII B	Evaluation		
	VII B1	Freemasonry	SS-*Stubaf* Erich Ehlers
	VII B2	Jewry	SS-*Hstuf* Dr Heinz Ballensiepen
	VII B3	Churches	vacant
	VII B4	Marxismus	SS-*Ostuf* Georg Heuchert
	VII B5	Liberalismus	SS-*Stubaf* Dr Andreas Schick
Gruppenleiter VII C (position vacant)			
VII C	Special Research		
	VII C1	Masonic Archiv	SS-*Ostubaf* Dr Paul Dittel
	VII C2	Masonic Museum	SS-*Stubaf* Hans Richter
	VII C3	Witchcraft	vacant

Appendix IV

Alphabetical Index of RSHA *Amt* VII Personalities 1939–1945

(Arrested personalities are underlined)

Name	*Referat*	Remarks
SS-*Hstuf* Dr Hans Ballensiepen	VII B2	Evacuated to Leipa (Bohemia) in 1944
SS-*Hstuf* Dr Justus Beyer	VII A1	Transferred to *Wehrmacht* in 1940
SS-*Ostuf* Dr Andreas Biederbick	II D4	*Referent* II D4 in 1940; then transferred to RSHA *Amt* III
SS-*Ostuf* Martin Biermann	VII C3	End 1943 transferred to Belgrade for general SD duties; returned sick
SS-*Stubaf* Walter Braune	VII C1	In charge of evacuated archives in Bohemia; previously in VII A3
SS-*Ustuf* Walter Brüderle	VII Gst.	*Leiter Geschäftsstelle Amt* VII; still in Berlin end 1944
SS-*Stubaf* Karl Burmester	VII A1	Left Berlin 22 April 1945 with Dittel for Schwerin
SS-*Ostubaf* Dr <u>Paul Dittel</u>	VII	*Leiter* RSHA VII; arrested
SS-*Ostuf* Dr Otto Eckstein	VII B3	Evacuated to Leipa (Bohemia), 1944
SS-*Stubaf* Erich Ehlers	VII B1	Evacuated to Bohemia, 1944
SS-*Ostuf* Karl Engelmann	VII A1	
SS-*Ustuf* Willi Flemming	VII B4	
SS-*Ustuf* Heinz Fichtner	VII A1	Mid 1943 posted to *Einsatzkommando* on Eastern Front
SS-*Hstuf* Karl-August Focke	VII A2	Evacuated with files to Denkdorf in Bayerischer Wald
SS-*Hstuf* Dr Günther Franz	VII	
SS-*Ustuf* Dr Heinz Gürtler	VII B1	In VII B1, 1939–1941; killed in action on Eastern Front, 1944 [with *Waffen*-SS]
SS-*Ustuf* Hans Hahn	VII C1	
SS-*Ostuf* Friedrich Hanke	II D6	*Referent* II D6 in 1940
SS-*Ostubaf* <u>Albert Hartl</u>	II B3	*Referent* II B3 in 1940; later RSHA VI Kult; arrested in American Zone
SS-*Hstuf* Karl Hass	VII B6	*Referent* II D3 in 1940; transferred to RSHA VI in Italy, 1943
SS-*Ostuf* Richard Heddergott	VII B2	
SS-*Ostuf* Erich Hengelhaupt	II D1	*Referent* II D1 in 1940; transferred to RSHA VI C

SS-*Ostuf* Georg Heuchert	VII B3	Transferred to Bohemia, 1944
Dr Erich-Joachim Heymann	VII B4	
SS-*Ostuf* Helmut Hirt	VII A1	Transferred to RSHA *Amt* III, mid 1943
SS-*Ostuf* Wilhelm Hucks	VII A3	Transferred to RSHA *Amt* VI, mid 1943
SS-*Ostuf* Helmut Jonas	VII A1	
Angestellte Dr Walter Kellner	VII A1	Evacuated to Leipa (Bohemia), 1944
SS-*Ostuf* Horst Kunze	VII B2	
SS-*Schaf* Dr Willi Leuthardt	VII A2	Killed on Eastern Front
SS-*Stubaf* Dr Rudolf Levin	VII C3	Killed in action near Konitz, Feb 1945
SS-*Hstuf* Horst Mahnke	VII B4	Went with Six as his personal secretary in the Foreign Office
SS-*Stubaf* Herbert Mehringer	VII A2	Killed in Munich air-raid, late 1944
SS-*Ostuf* Fritz Möckel	VII A1	
SS-*Stubaf* Rolf Mühler	VII B6	1942–1944, KdS Marseille
SS-*Hstuf* Dr Friedrich Murawski	VII A2	Originally with VII C3; later removed from RSHA
SS-*Ostubaf* Paul Mylius	VII	Vertreter to Six, 1941–1943
SS-*Ostuf* Neumann-Rippert	VII	In RSHA VI C12 when transferred to *Amt* VII in 1944
SS-*Ostuf* Ernst Nitsche	II A5	*Referent* II A5, Jan 1940
SS-*Ostubaf* Dr <u>Wilhelm Patin</u>	VII C3	Arrested
SS-*Ostuf* Willi Pösch	VII B1	1943–1944, with BdS Belgrade; then returned to *Amt* VII B
SS-*Stubaf* Karl Radke	VII	Adjutant to Six in 1941
SS-*Hstuf* Alfred Reissmann	VII C3	Transferred to RSHA VI B1 (Vatican) in late 1944; died Dec 1944
SS-*Stubaf* Hans Richter	VII C2	*Referent* VII C3 when SS-*Hstuf*
Angestellte Hans Riegelmann	VII C1	
SS-*Stubaf* Dr Rolf Oebsger-Röder	VII	Deputy *Amtchef* in 1940
SS-*Hstuf* Dr Heinz Röthke	VII B2	With BdS Hungary, Oct 1944; investigations into Jewry
SS-*Ostuf* Hans-Wilhelm Rudolph	VII B4	Transferred to RSHA VI D, 1942
SS-*Ostuf* Heinz Rust	VII A2	Killed on Eastern Front
RuKR Dr Ernst Schambacher	VII	Begin 1944, transferred from RSHA V
SS-*Stubaf* Dr <u>Andreas Schick</u>	VII B5	Arrested in British Zone
SS-*Hstuf* Gerhard Schmidt	VII A1	
SS-*Brif* Dr Franz Alfred Six	VII	RSHA *Amtchef* VII; March 1943 transferred to Foreign Office
SS-*Stubaf* Dr Günther Stein	VII A1	Evacuated to Leipa (Bohemia), 1944
SS-*Oschaf* Dr Emil Steudle	II D2	*Referent* II D2, 1940; transferred to RSHA VI as SS-*Ostuf*
SS-*Ostuf* Karl Stuber	VII B1	Attached to BdS Paris, late 1941; killed in an air-raid, Aug 1944

SS-*Stubaf* Friedrich Suhr	VII	Deputy *Amtschef* to Six in 1940 after Oebsger-Röder; went East in 1941
SS-*Hschaf* Wilhelm Tieke	VII A2	Transferred to *Waffen*-SS
SS-*Ustuf* Alfred Wenzel	VII C3	With BdS Paris, early 1944
SS-*Ustuf* Philipp Willius	VII B2	

Supplementary information about RSHA VII

Interrogation Report CSDIC/CMF/SD 64 dated 29 Aug 1945 of SS-*Ostubaf* Georg Elling: "*Amt* VII was first formed as a separate entity in late 1939 under SS-*Staf* (later SS-*Brif*) Six. Until then it had been *Gruppe* 1 of *Amt* II concerned with investigation of internal opposition groups; this *Gruppe* had been organised in two *Referats*, political and non-political, as follows:

Referat II 11 : non-political (*Weltanschauliche Gegnerformen*).
   111   Freemasonry
   112   Jewry
   113   Churches and Sects

Referat II 12 : political (*politische Gegnerformen*).
   121   Marxism
   122   Liberalism
   123   Reactionary nationalism

"Of these two *Referate* II 11 was by far the more important.

"In 1939 when the RSHA re-organisation took place it was decided to define the work more clearly and separate the investigations of opposition groups that were of immediate interest from those of a mere historical character, the former passing to their natural home in *Amt* IV [*Gestapo*], the latter being the task of the new *Amt* VII. The two *Referate* were re-named *Gruppen*—with all the emphasis on the non-political as previously—but Source is unable to give the exact numbering.

"This organisation continued until the end, although with the departure of Six in summer 1943, the department lost its chief driving force and would probably in time have disappeared. Source is of the opinion that *Amt* VII was in fact kept going chiefly to satisfy Six's personal ambitions and rivalry with Ohlendorf of RSHA *Amt* III.

"The type of work done by *Amt* VII included such things as research into the bases of Freemasonry, the origins and history of Christianity, the political aims of the Roman Catholic Church, the problems of separation of State and Church, etc. It was in connection with the latter type of research that Source had contact with the *Amt*.

"The offices were located in Berlin-Schöneberg, Emserstrasse (*sic*) and included a large library which was enriched during the course of the war by large numbers of books from the occupied countries.

"Source estimates the total staff at about twenty-five which included SS-*Brif.* Six the *Amtschef*, SS-*Ostubaf* Dittel his 2 i/c, SS-*Stubaf* Burmester the administration officer, SS-*Ostubaf* Dr Patin responsible for investigating the political tendancies of the Roman Church, SS-*Stubaf* Dr Schick for history of the Church and the origin and development of Freemasonry, Dr Murawski for Christian origins, Father Duchene a former member of the Pallottine Order and latterly a fanatical Nazi, and Dr Kellner the librarian. Source's chief contacts were with Schick, Murawski and Duchene.

"The *Amt* had as a rule no representatives outside Germany, although it sometimes sent one of its staff to conduct investigations in an occupied area, or search for books that would be of use to the library."

Notes:

* The National Archives, Kew, KV 3/249: Liquidation Report No 23, RSHA VII.
* US National Archives, College Park, RG 498, Box 20: interrogation report CSDIC/CMF/ SD 64 dated 29 August 1945 of SS-*Ostubaf* Georg Elling.

16

RSHA *Amt* N

Amt für Nachrichtenverbindung

On 1 September 1944 *Chef der Sipo und des* SD, SS-*Obergruppenführer* Dr Ernst Kaltenbrunner, created within RSHA the *Amt für Nachrichtenverbindung*. SS-*Standartenführer* Richard Sansoni was appointed its RSHA *Amtschef*.

The new *Amt* N bore responsibility for the following specialised areas with a staff of over 700 men and women:

1. Telephone and teleprinter services (*Drahtnachrichtenwesen*). Training personnel telephone and teleprinter operators.
2. Radio (W/T) operators and their training; there was a radio training course held in Fürstenberg.
3. Procurement and administration of all communications equipment and provision of codes and cyphers for the RSHA through the *Chef des Fernmeldewesens* RFSS.
4. Distribution and servicing of all communications equipment at the locations of the Security Police (*Gestapo* and *Kripo* offices) and the Security Service (SD offices) across the *Reich*.

The personnel for this new *Amt* came from the absorption of RSHA II C 1 and II C 2.

Although RSHA *Amt* N was officially charged with procurement, Schellenberg insisted on getting his own equipment, operators and codes from the Havel Institute. This cleavage was so great that on one occasion a W/T operator from the Havel Institute refused to transmit messages even for Kaltenbrunner.

Amt N was never completely organised. The usual red tape and rival jealousies helped to stunt its growth and efficiency. A telephone line at RSHA, for instance, could not be repaired by *Amt* N. *Amt* N had to be informed, but the actual repair work had to be done by the *Oberpostdirektion*. Or if a W/T set failed, *Amt* N would repair it unless the set belonged to RSHA *Mil Amt* or RSHA *Amt* VI, in which event *Amt* N was not allowed to touch it.

Counter Intelligence War Room (CIWR) did not provide a Liquidation or Situation Report on the activities of RSHA *Amt* N, despite Sansoni being in British custody until 1948. No interrogation report of Sansoni has so far been declassified by British intelligence agencies.

However, CIWR did receive information from a USFET interrogation of SS-*Stubaf* Wilhelm Höttl and a British interrogation from Italy of SS-*Ustuf* Heinz Müller.

Höttl stated *Amt* N was a very recent creation. It had been formed during 1944, while previously its tasks had been assigned to a *Gruppe* in *Amt* II (II D). With the extension of the communications network of the RSHA, the creation of a special staff section meeting these requirements had become necessary. *Amt* N had under its control all communications nets used by the RSHA or any of its agencies. The main means used were radio, teleprinter, and telephone.

During the time of its greatest expansion, the teleprinter net alone had several hundred extensions. This does not include the numerous Geheimschreiber automatic encoding and decoding teleprinter machines. The radio net reached its greatest extent with the greatest advance of the German troops. *Sipo* units were attached to various military echelons and frequently their only means of contact with the central office [RSHA Berlin] was by radio communication. The telephone net was also well developed.

An interesting innovation was the so-called *Konferenzapparat*. Kaltenbrunner and all his *Amtschefs* had one of these telephones, as had several ministers and other high functionaries. The number of extensions was very small (maybe about 50). There was only one central, automatic switchboard, and by dialling a two-figure number any of the other subscribers could be contacted, without having to go over the various office switchboards. This ensured both speed and secrecy of the conversations on this net.

The personnel in this section consisted of technical experts. The *Amtsleiter* (*sic*), SS-*Staf* Sansoni, was a communications specialist, while two *Referenten*, Walther and Marks, were experts on teleprinter and radio, respectively."

[Note: this interrogation report uses 'teletype' and this has been changed to 'teleprinter'—'teletype' is a US communications company.]

In Italy, SS-*Ustuf* Heinz Müller was in charge of W/T communications at the BdS Italien, stationed in Verona, from December 1943 until the collapse. He was captured by British forces at Vipiteno (Sterzing) on 3 May 1945 attempting to escape to Austria through the Brenner Pass. Müller was brought down to the Allied interrogation centre near Rome (CSDIC/CMF) and his interrogation report was issued on 24 July 1945:

2. Internal W/T Communications of Bds Italien.

(a) W/T network.
The W/T network consisted of one Control Station and 17 outstations. They are listed below in ascending order of call-signs (the collective call-sign being SDN, that of Milan SDN 1, of Trieste SDN 2, and so forth).

1. Milan	10. Merano
2. Trieste	11. Mira (Venice)
3. Parma	12. Fasano (Höchster SSuPF)
4. Genoa	13. Pola
5. Terlano (BdS Garage)	14. Novara
6. Turin	15. Innsbruck
7. Verona (after Sept 1944)	16. Sondrio (*Grenzstelle* Como)
8. Bologna	17. Forst (*Grenzstelle*)
9. Bolzano	

Müller stated that *Aussenkommando* Parma did not have a W/T station because he had very few sets to allot, and it was not considered an important enough post. *Grenzstelle* Sondrio of *Grenzbefehlstelle* West, Como, implored Müller to let him have W/T equipment, as the partisans in his area were continually cutting his [telephone] lines to Como. The *Leiter* agreed to provide his own operator, and Müller gave him a set. The station at Fasano, for communication with the *Höchster* SSuPF [Wolff], was maintained by by the BdS, and was separate from he stations of the *Höchster* SSuPF staff itself.

Until September 1944 the control station was at Verona, but it then moved to Colle d'Isarco (Gossensass) leaving an outstation. The control station was also in touch with RSHA central W/T station in the *Reich* (since early 1944 at Fürstenberg near Berlin).

(b) Organisation and Personnel.
For purposes of administration and discipline, supplies of apparatus and traffic supervision, the above W/T network came under RSHA *Amt* N, the successor to RSHA *Referat* II C1.

Male personnel were drawn from three SS-Signals Training Depots at Unna (Westphalia), Nuremberg and Vipiteno (Sterzing) in South Tyrol. Female signal auxiliaries came from the SS-*Reichsschule* in Schloss Oberehnheim, near Strasbourg.

The control station consisted of two male W/T operators, one of them the station superintendent, two male cipher clerks and seven or eight female signal auxiliaries who were trained for both duties.

(c) Equipment.

I. Control Station.

The control station had one KST receiver manufactured by Körting Radio, Berlin. It had between six and eight valves and was worked off the mains electricity at 220 volts AC.

It had three transmitters:

(a) A 1.2 KW transmitter, probably with 8–10 valves. This was damaged and put out of action end October 1944.
(b) A 260 watt Italian Safar AC transmitter. It was capable of working at the following voltages: 110, 145, 160, 165, 180, 210, 220 and 260. It had about 12 or 15 valves and was worked off the mains electricity.
(c) A 1000 watt Italian Safar transmitter. It had four large valves and was worked off the mains electricity at 200 volts AC. An unsatisfactory model.

II. Outstations.

These had 70 watt Lorenz transmitters. The receivers were either KST or Radione. KST sets could only work on 220 volts, Radione sets either 125 or 220 volts.

(d) Traffic.

I. Volume.

Total turnover at the control station was about 1000 to 1500 signals per month while it was at Verona; after the move to Colle d'Isarco the volume dropped off slightly and a greater proportion of the traffic consisted of signals for re-transmission.

The outstations had a monthly average varying between about 45 and 80 signals according to the station.

The outstation with the largest volume of traffic in recent months was Verona, with Trieste second and Bolzano third. Fasano, the W/T station with the Höchster SSuPF, was comparatively quiet.

II. Nature of Traffic.

The bulk of all important communications was sent by teleprinter, except when the cables were cut by bombing. Most of the messages passed over the air [i.e. by radio (W/T) messaging] concerned signal control, indents, personnel and administrative matters in general.

Some of the W/T traffic consisted of messages of other services (Army, Police) transmitted by the BdS signal network out of courtesy.

(e) W/T Procedure.

I. Call-Signs and Frequencies.

The call-sign for the control station was SND, the outstations having call-signs SND 1 to SND 17, as given in Para 2a, above. The call-sign of the RSHA Central

W/T Station was SNA, the collective call-sign was SNÄ 1. These call-signs were never altered.

The frequency for communication between control and the outstations was 5015 kcs. Outstations could communicate with each other on the same frequency if not engaged by control; other wise they used either 4055 or 4505 kcs (Müller is not sure which).

II. Times of Communication.

Fixed times of communication between control and the outstations were: 0800 hrs (sometimes changed to 0700 hrs), 0930 hrs (sometimes changed to 1000 hrs), 1215 hrs, 1615 hrs, 1800 hrs and 2100 hrs.

Times of communication between control and the RSHA Central Station at Fürstenberg were 0900, 1400, 1700 and 1900 hrs.

III. Procedure in general.

The forms of procedure were precisely laid down and wireless discipline was strictly observed. Communication between outstations required the permission of the central station. The use of redundant or unofficial signals was forbidden.

IV. Contact procedure (Outstations).

At the fixed time the control station would give a collective call:

"SNÄ 1 SNÄ 1 SNÄ 1 DE SND QRU QRU? AR K"

to which the outstations would reply in order, 1–17. Thus Milan (SND 1) would respond with:

"V DE SND 1" repeating this until control interrupted with a series of dots, indicating that it had heard Milan. The latter would then send "QRU" (if it had no communication to make), "QZS" (if it had a message for control) or "QES SND" with the number of another outstation (if it had a message for that outstation) or finally, a combination of call-signs following QZS (if it had messages for more than one station). Control would then reply:

"R EB SND 2 K"

to which Trieste (SND 2) would respond in the same way as Milan. The next station to be called would be Parma (SND 5), and so on to 17

Control then broadcast to the group, first mentioning by QSA O any station from which it had not heard a response, secondly dismissing those outstations which it had not heard a response, secondly dismissing those outstations which had not made, or been made, an offer of a message. This might be done by either naming the latter or, if they were in a majority, by dismissing all except those which had offered messages, or been named as addressee…

<u>V. Priorities.</u>
"KR" indicated urgency, "KRKR" still greater urgency. Provision had also been made at end 1944 for the highest priority, "KRF" meaning '*Dringender Führerfunkspruch*' (Urgent Officer Message). Müller, however, states that the latter was never used in his experience.

If during the preliminary call and answer as described above, a station included "KR" or "KRKR" in its offer of a message, it would be given precedence as soon as the preliminary call and answer procedure for the whole network had been completed, but the procedure of the collective call would not be interrupted.

"QUA" indicated that a message required an immediate answer.

(f) Ciphers.
All W/T traffic was enciphered by the Enigma machine.

3. Internal Signals Communications of the RSHA.

When the SD-*Hauptamt* was merged in the RSHA in 1939, the central W/T station of the SD-*Hauptamt* became, with the addition of other personnel, the RSHA central W/T station, and came under RSHA *Referat* II C1, also informally referred to as the *Technisches Referat*, which handled all W/T signals matters. *Referat* II C2 dealt with line signals, telephone and teleprinter. In summer 1944 the above *Referate* were reformed into RSHA *Amt* N, which then controlled all internal communications for *Sipo und* SD-*Dienststellen* of the RSHA. For instance, it controlled matters of pay and promotion of signals personnel, provided signals stores, traffic instructions and ciphers. Signals personnel attached to various *Dienststellen* were directly responsible to RSHA *Amt* N. The *Amt* had a small W/T station of its own.

For some time after the RSHA was set up, most signals personnel continued to be SD, but later an increasing number of wounded members of the *Waffen*-SS and *Sipo* personnel were taken on as signallers. Müller made frequent reference to the 'SD W/T network', instead of the *Sipo und* SD network.

RSHA *Amt* N itself, according to Müller, came under an organisation known as *Chef Fernmeldewesen*, though he is not certain of its exact authority. He believes that it was responsible for the technical supervision and co-ordination of <u>all</u> SS signals communications both within and outside the *Reich*, including those of the *Waffen*-SS. It was first located at Wilhelmstrasse 100, Berlin, but towards the end of 1944 moved into the building opposite because of air-raid damage to No. 100 (Amt N then moved into No. 100). The *Chef Fernmeldewesen* was responsible for the SS Signals Depots at Unna (Westphalia), Nuremberg and Vipiteno (Sterzing) in South Tyrol, and the Signals School for female auxiliaries at Schloss Oberehnheim near Strasbourg. During the last year Müller believes that male personnel were trained only for the *Waffen*-SS, and were seconded to the *Allgemeine* SS, and the RSHA networks as required. Müller understands that it was intended to bring the W/T networks of the *Orpo* (*Ordnungspolizei*) also under the control of the *Chef Fernmeldewesen*, but does not know whether this was done.

4. Personalities.

(a) BdS Italien W/T networks.

Frau Anneliese Arnold	SS-*Nachrichtenhelferin*; W/T operator at W/T Control Station, Sept. 1944–April 1945; war widow; German.
SS-*Oschaf* Ludwig Bachmann	W/T operator at Novara W/T station, January–April 1945; previously at Rovereto; Austria.
SS-*Oschaf* Hans Bichler	W/T operator at Terlano W/T station; latterly at Calle d'Isarco; Austrian.
SS-*Sturmmann* Braun	W/T operator at W/T Control Station April 1945; now a POW.
Fräulein Hildegard Britze	SS-*Nachrichtenhelferin*; W/T operator at W/T Control Station, Feb. 1944–April 1945; Berliner.
Fräulein Liesel Burckhardt	SS-*Nachrichtenhelferin*; W/T operator at Mira W/T Station, Dec. 1944–April 1945; German.
SS-*Ustuf* Georg Eigenbrod	Signals master of Verona outstation, Sept. 1944–Jan. 1945, then posted to Bratislava; German.
Fräulein Herta Englisch	SS-*Nachrichtenhelferin*; W/T operator at Verona outstation, and April 1944–April 1945 on detached duty at W/T Milan outstation, then hospitalized.
Fräulein Gertrud Fabich	SS-*Nachrichtenhelferin*; W/T operator at Verona W/T Control Station, Nov. 1944–April 1945; German.
SS-*Oschaf* Otto Fritz	W/T operator at Turin W/t outstation, Feb.–April 1945; previously at Bologna and Verona W/T stations; Berliner.
Fräulein Amalie Gössl	SS-*Nachrichtenhelferin*; W/T operator at Verona W/T Control Station; from the Sudetenland.
SS-*Oschaf* Otto Heit	Cipher clerk at Verona W/T Control Station, Aug. 1944–April 1945; now POW.
Fräulein Gertrud Herget	SS-*Nachrichtenhelferin*; cipher clerk at Verona W/T Control Station, Oct. 1944–April 1945; German.
Fräulein Irmgard Herzog	SS-*Nachrichtenhelferin*; cipher clerk at Fasano W/T Station, Aug.1944–April 1945; German.
SS-*Schaf* Hans Hohensee	W/T operator at Verona W/T Control Station, Aug. 1944–April 1945; now POW.

SS-*Oschaf* Hans Holzer	W/T operator at Merano W/T Outstation Oct.1944–April 1945; Austria.
SS-*Oschaf* Horst Kubica	W/T operator Trieste W/T Outstation, Jan.–April 1945; German.
SS-*Oschaf* Hans Kuckuck	W/T operator Verona W/T Control Station, March–April 1945.
Fräulein Erika Labusch	SS-*Nachrichtenhelferin*; W/T operator at W/T Control Station Verona, Nov. 1944–April 1945; German.
Fräulein Erna Legle	SS-*Nachrichtenhelferin*; W/T operator at Fasano W/T Station, Aug. 1944–April 1945.
SS-*Schaf* Willi Mohr	Cipher clerk at Verona W/T Station; at Colle d'Isarco, May 1945.
Fräulein Johanna Müller	SS-*Nachrichtenhelferin*; cipher clerk at Bolzano W/T station, May 1944–April 1945; *Volksdeutscher* from Lodz.
Zollsekretär May	W/T operator at Forst W/T Station to April 1945.
SS-*Oschaf* Karl Neumann	W/T operator at Innsbruck W/T Station, Jan.–April 1945; previously at RSHA *Amt* N W/T Station in Berlin; Austrian.
Fräulein Inge Petzold	SS-*Nachrichtenhelferin*; cipher clerk at Merano W/T Station, Jan.–April 1945; German.
Fräulein Elly Pörschke	SS-*Nachrichtenhelferin*; W/T operator at Verona W/T Control Station, later in Colle d'Isarco, April 1944–April 1945; East Prussian.
SS-*Oschaf* Werner Rabiger	W/T operator at Pola W/T Station, Oct. 1944–April 1945; previously at Trieste W/T Station; Berliner.
SS-*Hschaf* Fritz Reissenweber	W/T operator at Verona W/T Control Station, March–April 1945; previously on the Russian front; Berliner.
SS-*Hschaf* Karl Rupprecht	Instrument mechanic from RSHA *Amt* N, on detached duty to BdS Italien W/T network, 1944–April 1945; used to test W/T sets; Berliner.
SS-*Uschaf* Josef Schauer	W/T operator at Ceno W/T Station, Dec. 1944–April 1945; Austrian; now POW.
SS-*Oschaf* Franz Scheler	In charge of Verona W/T Control Station, Oct. 1943–April 1944; German; now POW.
Fräulein Liselotte Schellenberg	SS-*Nachrichtenhelferin*; cipher clerk at Verona W/T Control Station, April 1944–April 1945; on occasional detached duty at other W/T Stations.
SS-*Uschaf* Josef Steiner	Instrument mechanic at Verona W/T Control Station, July 1944–April 1945; now POW.
SS-*Oschaf* Richard Timm	W/T operator at Milan W/T Station, Oct. 1944–April 1945; German.

Fräulein Helga Wauer	SS-*Nachrichtenhelferin*; W/T operator at Verona W/T outstation, Sept. 1944–April 1945.
SS-*Oschaf* Ludwig Wieser	W/T operator at Bologna W/T Station to April 1945, then at Colle d'Isarco; Austrian.
Fräulein Friedel Worbs	SS-*Nachrichtenhelferin*; W/T operator at Bolzano W/T Station, May 1944–April 1945; German.

(b) RSHA *Amt* N and *Chef Fernmeldewesen*.

SS-*Ustuf* Werner Georgi	In charge of ciphers at RSHA *Amt* N; in Vipiteno (Sterzing) in May 1945.
SS-*Brif.* Wilhelm Keilhaus	*Chef Fernmeldewesen* who succeeded Sachs in summer 1944.
SS-*Hstuf* Wilhelm Marks	*Referent* W/T at RSHA *Amt* N; formerly *Leiter*, RSHA *Zentralfunkleitstelle* in Berlin until spring 1944.
SS-*Ustuf* Adolf Potter	Adjutant to *Chef* RSHA *Amt* N, to April 1945.
SS-*Ogruf* Ernst Sachs	*Chef Fernmeldewesen* to summer 1944.
SS-*Staf* Richard Sansoni	*Amtschef*, RSHA *Amt* N, 1944–1945.
SS-*Oschaf* Hans Schlüter	W/T operator at RSHA Central W/T Station, 1940–1945, initially in Berlin then in Fürstenberg.
SS-*Ustuf* Hans Stein	*Leiter*, RSHA *Zentralfunkstelle*, Berlin, spring 1944–May 1945; earlier, W/T operator at BdS Oslo and BdS Italien.
SS-*Oschaf* Karl Wallach	W/T operator at RSHA *Zentralfunkstelle* in Berlin and Fürstenberg, 1943–May 1945.
SS-*Stubaf* Kurt Walter	RSHA *Amt* N, *Referent* Telephones and Teleprinters

(c) BdS Norwegen W/T Network.

SS-*Anwärter* Barthel	W/T operator at Bergen W/T Station, April 1941.
SS-*Hschaf* Lothar Bechmann	In charge of W/T Control Station in Oslo, April 1940– early 1942 when transferred to a *Waffen*-SS signals unit, Nuremberg
SS-*Anwärter* Bollerey	W/T operator at W/T Control Station in Oslo, March 1941.
SS-*Hstuf* Wilhelm Cubasch	In charge of the BdS Norwegen W/T Network, April 1940–1942 when transferred to Vienna.
SS-*Hschaf* Hans Höpping	W/T operator and mechanic at W/T Control Station in Oslo, April 1940–mid 1942 when transferred to Berlin.
SS-*Schaf* Othmar Langgoth	W/T operator at W/T Control Station in Oslo, April 1940–April 1945.
SS-*Anwärter* Lehmann	W/T operator at W/T Control Station in Oslo, April 1941.
SS-*Oschaf* Sepp Rademacher	W/T operator W/T Station Stavanger, April 1940–mid 1941 when transferred to BdS Riga; later SS-*Ustuf* and in charge of W/T Station Budapest; believed killed.

SS-*Oschaf* Heinz Rathai	W/T operator at W/T Control Station in Oslo, 1940–Dec. 1944; did detached duty in Stavanager and other W/T Stations; RSHA *Amt* N W/T Station Fürstenberg, Jan.–May 1945.
SS-*Schaf* Karl Rössel	W/T operator at W/T Central Station in Oslo, April 1940–mid 1941, then at W/T Station Tromsö.
SS-*Oschaf* Max Sebastian	W/T operator at W/T Station Trondheim, April 1940–mid April 1941, then transferred to Russian front.

Notes

* The National Archives Kew, KV 3/189.

17

Training Schools of the *Sicherheitspolizei* and the *Sicherheitsdienst*

Counter Intelligence War Room did not create a liquidation or situation report on this aspect of the German intelligence services. They did, however, create a questionnaire to be asked of SS-*Stubaf* Horst Kopkow, SS-*Stubaf* Harro Thomsen and SS-*Ostubaf* Gustav Adolf Nosske who were held at CSDIC/WEA Interrogation Centre at Bad Nenndorf, Germany. Their Sixth Combined Interim Report, IR 62, dated 8 May 1946, has the result of their interrogation.

I. Principal *Sicherheitspolizei* Schools

1. The following details have been supplied by Kopkow; Thomsen and Nosske have no additional information to give on this subject.

A. *Reichsschule der Sipo und des* SD, Prague

2. This was a centre for applicants for the Senior Executive Grade and Medium Executive Grade of service in the *Sipo*, where members of the *Sipo* and SD who wished to become SS-*Führer* reported to be examined on their general educational attainments.

Kopkow believes the school was situated in the country residence of the Czech industrialist Petschek near Prague. Candidates stayed for about a week and the whole proceedings were most informal; there was no 'barracks' discipline and candidates were examined by means of casual questions which were interspersed in general conversations with their examiners.

B. *Führerschule der Sipo und* SD, Berlin-Chalottenburg

3. This school, which was situated at Schloss Strasse 1, Berlin-Charlottenburg, was the actual specialised training centre for candidates for the senior grades of

service in the *Sipo*. Auxiliary short-term courses were also held here at this school for candidates for the medium grades of service.

4. The Kriminal Museum, which was attached to it, consisted of a comprehensive collection of material, supplied by all the regional stations in the *Reich*, used for instructional purposes. This material was kept and annotated from a criminal police viewpoint and not from a political police angle.

5. This school, which had existed prior to 1933 on a small scale as a *Kriminal Institut*, became *Führerschule der Sipo und des* SD in 1936. The head of the *Kriminal Institut*, until 1936, was ORR Linnemann, later SS-*Ostubaf*; Kopkow believes that he was finally *Leiter* of the *Kripo* Regional Station Hanover; he was certainly one of the most capable and best-known German criminologists. SS-*Ostubaf* ORR Hellwig was Commandant from 1936 to 1941–1942 and was succeeded by SS-*Ostubaf* Hotzel, who is not known to Kopkow.

6. The teaching staff of the school consisted of officials such as *Kriminalkommissäre*, and *Kriminalräte*, and *Regierungsräte*, most of whom came from the *Kripo*. All teaching had to be abandoned at end 1943 or very early 1944 owing to the extensive bomb damage to the school buildings [during air-raids]. All the instructional material in the *Kriminal* Museum was completely destroyed and thereafter the courses for the senior grades of the *Sipo* were transferred to the *Sipo Schule*, Rabka, near Zakopane.

C. *Sicherheitspolizeischule*, Rabka

7. This school was established as a war emergency measure; originally it was an examination centre for SS-*Untersturmführers* of the BdS Cracow; it became the school for the senior grades in the *Sipo* early in 1944. This school, however, always lacked almost all the necessary training material, lecturers and instructional facilities, such as had been made available to its forerunner in Charlottenburg by such institutions as Berlin University.

D. *Sicherheitspolizeischule*, Fürstenberg/Mecklenburg

8. This establishment trained the medium grades of the service in the *Sipo*. It was the most modern of all the *Sipo* schools and was constructed only at the beginning of the war. It possessed, besides all the usual material for teaching, a collection of instructional material gathered from regional stations throughout Germany, and a collection of instructional films. One department dealt with the training of W/T operators for work in the *Sipo*. The staff was similar to that at the *Führerschule der Sipo und des* SD in Charlottenburg, the majority of the instructors being *Kripo* officials.

9. At this establishment *Grenzpolizei* (*Grepo*) personnel were trained after the special *Grenzpolizeischule* at Pretzsch/Elbe was closed. In general much more importance was attached to physical training at this school than at Charlottenburg. The Commandant, until October 1944, was SS-*Oberführer Oberst der Polizei*

Trümmler; he afterwards took over either an Inspekteurstelle of the *Sipo und* SD [IdS] or *Befehlshaberstelle* [BdS] in western Germany. His successor until the final collapse was SS-*Ostubaf* ORR Dr Kaussmann.

E. *Grenzpolizeischule*, Pretzsch

10. SS-*Oberführer Oberst der Polizei* Trümmler was Commandant of this establishment before he was transferred to Fürstenberg. Here *Grepo* officials were trained in their frontier police duties prior to being posted to the frontier regional stations. When the school at Fürstenberg was opened, this school at Pretzsch was closed. *Grepo* officials were thereafter trained alongside other *Sipo* officials at Fürstenberg.

F. *Kriminal Technisches Institut* (KTI)

11. In a broad sense this establishment was connected with *Stapo* training in so far as *Stapo* specialists, in any of the branches it dealt with, either provided information for the institute or were themselves instructed in any new developments in such technical fields as sabotage.

12. The main task of the KTI, was, of course, to the technical training of all *Kripo* staff of the *Kripo* regional stations. Such officials when trained were posted to the technical investigation departments of the *Kripo* regional stations. The KTI dealt with research into explosives, fire-arms, ammunition, etc., and had at its disposal the best laboratories and frequently referred to RSHA *Amt* IV's *Referat* IV A2a [Kopkow's own department] for advice and assistance.

II. Recruiting and Training of *Sipo* Personnel

13. The *Sipo* offered four grades of career:

a)   Lower Grade (*Unterer Dienst*)
b)   Medium General Grade (*Mittlerer Einfacher Dienst*)
c)   Medium Executive Grade (*Mittlerer Gehobener Dienst*)
d)   Senior Executive Grade (*Leitender Dienst*)

G. Lower Grade

14. Prison warders, messengers, telephone operators, drivers, caretakers, etc., were all in this category and were employees at the *Sipo* as distinct from being officials. They were in many cases in receipt of better pay than the junior officials of the Medium General Grade.

H. Medium General Grade

15. Junior departmental officials, prison administrators, chief messengers of the large regional stations, telephone and W/T supervisors, etc., were in this grade.

Some of these graduated from the Lower Grade, but such promotions were not frequent and from a financial point of view they were not advantageous, because, unless the individual concerned had hopes of progressing and becoming at least a somewhat higher grade official, it was preferable for him to remain an employee rather than become an ill-paid official. Most of the candidates for this grade of service came from the *Orpo* and were men who had completed twelve years' service therein (in some exceptional cases they entered after eight years' service). The *Wehrmacht*, the *Waffen*-SS and civil life also provided smaller numbers of candidates for this grade of service. All candidates were trained at the *Stapo* and *Kripo* regional stations [*Leitstellen*] and attended a two to three months' course at a *Sipo* school. If they passed the examination at the end of this course, they were promoted *Kriminal* or *Polizei Sekretär*. Further promotion to *Kriminal* or *Polizei Obersekretär* involved further practical training at regional stations and another two to three months' course at a *Sipo* school. Still further promotion to *Kriminal Inspektor* was possible without further examination, but occurred only when vacancies were available in establishments.

16. The underlying principle applicable to all junior officials in this grade was that there should be no promotion without practical training at the regional station [i.e. *Stapoleitstellen* and *Stapostellen*]; the courses at the *Sipo* schools were only intended to co-ordinate the various aspects of this practical training preparatory to an examination of the candidates. No exceptions were made to this procedure; even particularly capable young officials, earmarked by their superiors for eventual promotion to higher positions, had to pass the preliminary examinations and have their full periods of training at the regional stations.

I. Medium Executive Grade

17. The Medium Executive Grade of the *Sipo* was parallel to the Medium Grade of the *Orpo*; it consisted of *Kriminalkommissäre*, *Kriminalräte* and Kriminal Direktoren, equivalent to *Polizei Inspekteure*, *Polizei Oberinspekteure* and *Polizei Räte*. Before 1939 more than half of the officials in this grade of the service came direct from civil life, but during the war there were simply no young men left among the the civil population with suitable qualifications and candidates had to be drawn from the Medium General Grade. This was a temporary measure which was generally recognised as being unsatisfactory, as it meant a continual weakening of the General Grade to fill the vacancies in the Executive Grade.

18. Candidates for this grade of the service, coming from civil life, had to attend at the *Sipo* School in Berlin-Charlottenburg, where they were subjected to examination for about a week. No specialised knowledge was expected at this juncture, but they were subjected to general knowledge tests, and above all, their general behaviour and political outlook were studied. The examination often included severe physical tests. Up to 1939 not more than 30% of the candidates passed the examinations; those who failed were not allowed to make any further attempts to enter either the

Sipo or the *Orpo*. Successful candidates were then sent to *Stapo*, *Kripo*, SD and, very often, to *Orpo* regional stations in turn for practical training in all branches of police work.

19. After completion of this training candidates were returned to the *Sipo* School at Charlottenburg for an eight to twelve months' course, which culminated in a final examination. This examination was often attended by foreign police officials; Kopkow recalls that Bulgars and Chinese certainly attended the school for a period. Successful candidates were then posted to regional stations as *Kriminalkommissäre* for a probationary period of six months, after which they were as a rule confirmed in that rank.

20. As regards the candidates for the Medium Executive Grade who were selected from the ranks of the Medium General Grade, it was found that, when they attended the special examinations at the *Sipo* School in Charlottenburg, which they had to do in the same manner as the civilian candidates, a greater proportion failed to come up to the required standards and had to be eliminated. Those who were successful were promoted in the same way as the civilian candidates to *Kriminalkommissar*.

21. Although further promotion in this grade of the service was very largely dependent on length of service, the following factors were also taken into consideration:

a) whether the official was a National Socialist and member of the Party,
b) whether he had at least endeavoured to become a member of the SS,
c) whether he was married,
d) and if he was married, whether his family had a number of children commensurate with the length of time he had been married.

J. Senior Executive Grade

22. In the *Kripo* the position in this grade were for the most part filled by senior officials who had advanced through their ability and seniority in years of service from the Medium Executive Grade, but in the *Stapo* the situation was somewhat different and the Senior Executive Grade was filled very largely by persons with academic qualifications.

23. As early as 1935/1936, Dr Best had ordered that, as they became vacant, the senior posts should be filled by qualified lawyers, as he considered that such persons would be best suited to carry out the more important duties of the *Gestapo* (as part of the German internal administration) in their dealings with *Landräten*, *Regierungspräsidenten* and other Party officials. Kopkow maintains that this policy was only partly successful in that, although the status of the *Gestapo* was probably enhanced by the incorporation of such persons, the work was not done so thoroughly as it might have been in those branches which required above all a purely specialised knowledge on the part of their executives (e.g. such branches as the counter-intelligence and anti-sabotage departments).

24. Kopkow believes that it was for this reason that during the war a system was inaugurated whereby young *Kriminalkommissäre* and SD-*Führer* were selected by special examination and given the opportunity of an extensive education at the expense of the State, and, after taking the *Referendar* and State examinations were employed in the *Innere Verwaltung* (*Innenministerium, Oberregierungspräsidium* and *Landratsämtern*); after practical experience they were placed in leading positions of the branch for which they were considered best suited, *Kripo, Stapo* or SD. At the end of the war the first group of about thirty candidates had been dealt with in this manner and further groups were in process of being trained, among them being many who had been wounded on active service.

K. General conditions throughout the Service

25. Although the *Sipo* was made up mainly of officials, it was deliberately organised on a military basis. Officials wore SS uniform and held SS rank, and during the war they were provided Soldbücher and paid Wehrsold.

26. Being officials, the personnel came under the '*Deutsche Beamtengesetz*'; disciplinary matters, questions of tenure of office, pensions etc. were all regulated by this law. Officials of the *Sipo* were relieved of all other Party service; if they held any Party position they had to relinquish it on joining the Sipo.

27. Physical training was looked upon as important. One of the conditions of promotion was participation in the sporting events for the *Reich- und Wehrsportabzeichen*. Tests in physical prowess with different standards for the varying age groups were carried out every year until the outbreak of the war.

L. Transfers of officials from *Kripo* to *Stapo* and *vice versa*

28. The majority of the officials appointed when the *Stapo* was founded in 1933 were men drawn from the *Kripo*; Kopkow is of the opinion that from 1933 to 1939 there were only very few and special isolated instances of further transfers from *Kripo* to *Stapo*.

29. On the outbreak of war, however, and purely as a wartime emergency measure, quite a large number of the younger *Kripo* officials were lent, some to the *Geheime Feldpolizei* and a rather smaller number to the *Stapo*. This was not a voluntary transfer and the officials concerned did not welcome the change at all. Kopkow states that he does not think that after this there were any further large transfers of personnel from *Kripo* to *Stapo*; he believes, however, that some of the *Kripo* personnel who had been transferred managed to arrange to be returned to the *Kripo*, but if this happened, the *Kripo* had to find a substitute for the official returned to them. Kopkow states that there were of course cases of special officials being transferred from one service to the other for reasons concerning the work carried out by the individual concerned; for example, there was at one period a *Stapo* official, who had previously been at the *Stapo* regional station in Allenstein, in charge of the *Kripo* regional station in Berlin, but Kopkow is unable to specify the reasons for such special appointments and transfers.

Additional information relating to the background of what Kopkow calls the "Senior Executive Grade" or "*Leitender Dienst*" can be found in the interrogation of SS-*Ostubaf* Georg Elling. In 1941 and again in 1942–1943, SD officer Georg Elling lectured on religion at the *Führerschule der Sipo und des* SD, Berlin-Charlottenburg. In 1943 Elling was posted to Italy where he became an adviser on Vatican affairs for the RSHA VI. When the Allies began occupying southern Italy, Elling moved into Vatican City where he remained throughout the occupation. He surrendered to the British occupiers of Rome in July 1945 and interned. Elling was interrogated by CSDIC/CMF in Rome and his resultant interrogation report dated 29 August 1945, makes mention of the "*Leitender Dienst*" scheme.

5. School for *Sipo und* SD Leaders.

In early 1941 plans were made on the initiative of Heydrich to start special courses for young members of the *Sipo und* SD, who showed promise in their work, to enable them to study law under the auspices of the SD with a view to giving them responsible positions (a school for lower grades of *Sipo* and SD already existed). The course was to last four years and was intended for those who had reached at least Matriculation standard [Abitur] and the rank of SS *Untersturmführer*. Those selected were first to complete two years law study at a University situated in a town where there was an IdS; this was to give them a chance while studying to gain an insight into the actual work of the *Sipo* and SD and enable them to decide in which branch (III, IV, V) they particularly wished to interest themselves. The final two years were to be at the University of Berlin and during this time they were to be housed at the *Sipo* and SD School in Charlottenburg and hear lectures there by experts. During this four years' course pay and promotion were to be regular with all fees paid. At the conclusion of the course an examination was to be set which if successfully passed would entitle the student to the rank of SS *Sturmbannführer* and a responsible position.

The lectures at the school were intended to cover the theory and practice of law, religious life and practice, history of the Churches, Socialism, Freemasonry and other political movements, economics, literature and art: they were to be thoroughly objective. The regular lecturers included SS *Sturmbannführer* Dr Zirpins (theory and practice of law), SS *Sturmbannführer* Dr Hubig (literature and art), SS *Sturmbannführer* Dr Pechau (political movements in particular Marxism), source [Elling] and two others whose names are forgotten. In addition lectures were given by guest lecturers from the RSHA, usually *Amtschefs* or *Gruppenleiter*. Source was to lecture on philosophy (*Weltanschauung*) which was to include the history of the Churches, Congregations and religious Orders, Freemasonry, Jewry and canonical law.

In actual fact the School never functioned in the way it was intended and remained a plan. It was open for the Spring and Summer terms 1941 (Feb–June) and then broke up owing to the outbreak of war with Russia. During this period source gave two series of lectures to groups of twenty-five students each: all were young officers of the *Sipo* and SD (chiefly the former) who had already completed their legal training in the ordinary way. The subjects lectured on were: The history of the Roman Catholic Church, Canonical Law, the religious Orders, their significance in Germany and their efforts in colonisation. Great interest was shown in these subjects especially in the educational ideas of the religious orders. Source did not touch on Freemasonry or Jewry partly from lack of time, but also because he was unaware that his views did not coincide with those of the RSHA. The ground covered by the other lecturers is unknown to Source.

The School came under [RSHA] Amt I and was originally *Gruppe* I F (Leadership and Training of recruits); this was later in June 1941 changed to I B. The *Gruppe* was run at first by SS *Standartenführer* Erwin Schulz and later by SS *Obersturmbannführer* Hotzel who had as far as source knows a staff of only two, apart from the lecturers mentioned above. Hotzel continued in charge of the training of recruits at least until Sept. 1943 and it was under his auspices that Source conducted the lectures given at the school in 1942/43.

The courses were carried on at the Police School in Charlottenburg, Schloßstrasse/Spandauerstrasse, while the library (under SS *Hauptsturmführer* Dr Seeger) and students quarters were housed in a nearby block of flats. It was intended to build a proper school for *Sipo* and SD Leaders outside Berlin later, a scheme which as far as Source knows was never even started.

SS-*Stubaf* Horst Kopkow who provided most of the information above on training schools, could have been more informative about his own training course for *Kriminalkommissar*. He had attended the KK-course at *Führerschule der Sipo des* SD, Berlin-Charlottenburg, between October 1937 and 2 July 1938. Perhaps Kopkow did not want to mention that after successfully completing the course he was quickly fast-tracked from *Stapostelle* Allenstein in far-off East Prussia to *Gestapoamt* Berlin, and never returned to Allenstein. However, Kurt Bethke of *Gestapo* Köslin had gone through the *Kriminalkommissar* selection process and began the nine months course for *Kommissars* at *Führerschule der Sipo und des* SD, Berlin-Charlottenburg, from August 1940 until April 1941. Bethke was captured by US forces in May 1945 and quickly interrogated. In his wide ranging interrogation he gave a reasonably full description of the syllabus at his *Kriminalkommissar* course in Berlin:

'*Führerschule der Sipo*, Charlottenburg.

'From Aug 1940 until Apr 1941 Bethke attended courses at the *Führerschule der Sicherheitspolizei*, in Berlin-Charlottenburg. Upon graduation he was made *Kriminal Kommissar* "*auf Probe*" (on probation).

Admission. Police officials of medium rank (*mittlere Beamtenlaufbahn*), such as Bethke, are suggested as candidates by their respective agencies (*Dienststelle*). Others, particularly men without police experience, are suggested by the SS. The final decision on admission to the *Sipo* school is made by the RSHA.

Organization.

a. Administration

Kommandeur	SS-*Stubaf* Hellwig. After March 1941.
Deputy	SS-*Staf* Schulz
Stabsführer	Name unknown.
Adjutant	Name unknown.
Administrative Department	*Pol O/Insp Nau* (similar to the *Abt* I of a *Stapostelle*).

b. Number and Duration of Courses
Course for:

Kriminal Assistenten Anwärter	2 months
Kriminal Inspektoren Anwärter	4 months
Kriminal Kommisar Anwärter	9 months

c. Organization of the Course for *Kriminal Kommissar Anwärter*
The total number of students in Bethke's class was 60, ten of whom were career policemen. The balance were SS men, who were substantially younger and without previous police experience. Nevertheless, the latter received preferential treatment throughout the course according to Bethke. The class was divided into two sections of 30 men each. Classes were held from 0800 to 1200 or 1300 every day. The afternoon was reserved for individual work, weapons training and sports. The students had to live in barracks on the post.

d. Schedule and Staff
The following subjects were taught generally with one instructor for each subject:

Penal Law	KR Langen
	KR Halswig
Political Police	KR Stindt
National Political Instruction	name forgotten
Police Law	name forgotten
Criminology	name forgotten
Criminal Police Tactics	KK Lingen
Counter Espionage	KR Kluthe
Sport and Drill	SS-*Ustuf* Linke

Teaching Methods.
The instruction was given for the most part in lecture form by the staff, though occasionally students had to give lectures. Oral quizzes were frequent. Once in a while a practical exercise was conducted; e.g. a murder case would be dealt with in detail. Throughout the nine months' course two written tests were taken.

<u>Assignment of Graduates.</u>
After graduation the students returned to their respective agencies, pending decision by the RSHA on individual assignments.

<u>Notes on Instruction.</u>
The course of Political Police dealt mainly with the historical development of this form of police and presented the following topics:
a. Origins in Greece and Egypt.
b. Russian 'Ochrana'.
c. French Fouche system.
d. Origins in Germany.
e. Absorption of political police by the *Gestapo*.
f. Organization of the RSHA.
g. Communism, Marxism, Internationalism, Jews, Freemasons, the Political Church, the Black Front, Bündische Jugend, Catholic Church, and others.
h. Examination of practical cases with description of the means of action the *Gestapo* might take, such as:
   1. Police warning. (*Staatspolizei Warnung*)
   2. Initiation of prosecution by the courts. (*Einleitung eines gerichtlichen Strafverfahrens*)
   3. Financial Fine. (*Verhängung eines Sicherungs Geldes*)
   4. Short term arrest up to 21 days. (*Verhängung Kurzfristiger Haft bis zu 21 Tagen*)
   5. Transfer to a concentration camp. (*Überführung in ein KL*)'.

Notes

* The National Archives, Kew, KV 2/1501: CSDIC/WEA, 6th Combined Interrogation Report, IR 62, dated 8 May 1946, "Training Schools of the *Sicherheitspolizei* and the *Sicherheitsdienst*", by Horst Kopkow, Harro Thomsen and Gustav Adolf Nosske.
* US National Archives, College Park, RG 498 Box 20: interrogation report CSDIC/CMF/SD 64 dated 29 August 1945 of SS-*Ostubaf* Georg Elling.
* US National Archives, College Park, RG 498 Box 80: USFET, 12th Army, interrogation report CIR 4/2 dated 23 May 1945, of SS-*Ostuf* KK Kurt Bethke.

18

Liquidation Report No. 26: RSHA *Militärisches Amt*

A. Preface.

There is set forth first below a brief summary of the fall and dissolution of the old *Amt Auslandsnachrichten und Abwehr* and the place allotted to its remains in the RSHA. This is followed by a general picture of the *Mil Amt* headquarters organisation. In conclusion, there appears a general appreciation of the *Mil Amt's* place in the German Intelligence Services. Other and more detailed papers in the Liquidation/Situation series dealing with the *Mil Amt*, e.g. *Abteilung*, A, B. C, etc., KdMs, FAKs, etc., should therefore, be read with reference to this paper. For a fuller and more comprehensive account of the fall of the *Abwehr* and related matter see War Room publication "The German Intelligence Service and the War", S.F.52/20, 1 December 1945.

B. Events Leading up to RSHA Absorption of the *Abwehr*.

Until the turn of the tide of the war in 1942, the *Abwehr*, the Intelligence Service of the OKW, lived on the success of the German armies, which was naturally but erroneously taken to imply good operational intelligence, and on the success of its own counter-espionage which was considerable. However, from November 1942 when the Allies landed in North Africa, until June 1944 when they landed in France, occurred a period of crisis which led to the fall of the *Abwehr*, the direct connection with this period being the *Abwehr's* regular and conspicuous failure in respect of Allied strategic intentions. Important underlying causes of such failure most certainly were Canaris' own anti-Nazi attitude; his management of the *Abwehr* as a personal organisation, resulting in some suspicion on the part of the OKW itself; his poisoning of the entire establishment by his weakness for intrigue; his incapacity for organisation; and the absence of a centralised intelligence evaluation facility.

These factors, coupled with the growing and inescapable financial corruption and political disaffection of influential officers of the OKW and *Abwehr* and the competition of Himmler's S.S. Intelligence Service, rendered the ultimate collapse inevitable. As the Nazi Party's control over matters purely military was accelerated by German military reverses, Himmler, as Intelligence Chief of the Party, rose with it at the expense of the General Staff and the *Abwehr* so that, by 1943, RSHA *Amt* VI under Schellenberg, although not necessarily more competent, had become a serious rival of the *Abwehr*, ever ready to exploit *Abwehr* failures and no longer confining itself to political intelligence.

The immediate causes, which, however, were only cumulative, of the fall of Canaris and the *Abwehr* occurred at the beginning of 1944 and were (1) the Vermehren incident in Istanbul where three members of the *Abwehr*, who had official status in the German Embassy, deserted to the Allies; and (2) the expulsion by the Spanish Government, yielding to Allied pressure and ignoring Canaris' counter pleas, of *Abwehr* members considered responsible for the successful sabotaging of Allied shipping. Following this latter event, Canaris, in February 1944, was sacked and *Oberst* Georg Hansen became *Abwehr* chief, *Amtsgruppe Ausland*, which had also been under Canaris, and became responsible directly to the OKW/ WFst. A series of negotiations and conferences between high representatives of the RSHA and the *Abwehr* were concluded by a final session at Salzburg in May 1944 which resulted in the abolition of the *Abwehr* as from June 1944 and the creation of a new organisation, the RSHA *Militärisches Amt*.

C. Subordination of the *Mil Amt* and RSHA *Amt* VI.

The Salzburg decision, which preserved much of the original form and personnel of the *Abwehr* under the authority and as a branch of the RSHA, is unimportant as regards detail, for within two months the Generals' Putsch of 20 July 1944 had taken place and failed, thus enabling the Party to substitute for the Salzburg formula a far more radical solution. The period of executions, suicides, dismissals from service, etc., following on the failure of the plot against Hitler, is well known. Deprived of virtually all of its leaders and even of many of its lesser figures, the fragmentary remains of the *Abwehr* as RSHA *Militärisches Amt* were now, in the more important spheres, placed under the direct rule of Schellenberg's RSHA *Amt* VI. The fusion of the *Militärisches Amt* with *Amt* VI, however, brought little in the way of noticeable increases in the direction of efficiency. There was neither the time nor the personnel to bring about a complete overhaul and the new organisation, even up to the time of the German collapse, was in many respects confused and experimental and subject to the inconsistencies and improvisations inevitable when one organisation takes over another that is at least as fully developed as itself. In fact, the reorganisation, by and large, made little difference to the ordinary *Abwehr* officer, either in his methods of reporting or in his immediate subordination. Thus, while the result was a complete triumph for the S.S. on a high level, it represented compromise in the lower strata. Aside from the question of control, it is probably safe to say that the main effect of this change on the intelligence side at least, was to reorganise on a geographical basis as opposed to the old Service branches of the *Abwehr*.

D. Disposition of Old *Abwehr* Functions.

1. *Abwehr Abt.* I and *Abt.* Z.

Viewing the situation more particularly, all the remains of *Abwehr* I (positive intelligence), including I.G. and I.i, were incorporated into the *Mil Amt*, notably *Abteilungen* B. C. E and G. An important exception involved the old *Abwehr* I Wi, IT/LW, IH/T, IL/T and IM/T which were taken over to form *Gruppe* VI Wi/T, and its *Referate* VI Wi/TT of RSHA *Amt* VI. The functions of old *Abwehr Abt.* Z were distributed, for the most part, between RSHA *Amt* I, *Amt* II *Gruppe* A and B, and *Mil Amt Abt.* A.

Sonderkommando 'DORA'.

Originally a part of old *Abwehr* I, *Sonderkommando* 'Dora' was taken over into the *Mil Amt*, but was made responsible directly to Schellenberg, continuing its previous task of producing situation and survey maps based on scientific and geological research. The Commanding Officer was Major Gericke.

Grenadier Regiment 1001.

This was set up originally as a holding unit for non-German I, II and III FAK and FAT personnel in the East and South-East, and met a similar fate. Commanding Officer was *Oberst* Naumann.

2. *Abwehr* II.

Abwehr II was responsible for sabotage and subversion and passed to *Mil Amt*, *Abt.* D whose head, SS-*Ostubaf* Otto Skorzeny, was also head of RSHA *Gruppe* VI S and who, although technically under Schellenberg, was responsible only to Kaltenbrunner and Hitler.

The Brandenburg Division.

The Brandenburg Division was always closely associated with *Abwehr* II, passed to the control of the *Wehrmachtführungsstab* of the OKW, but later was reconstituted in the Balkans as the fifth *Lehrregiment* of the Division which finally came under the *Mil Amt* as a holding and training unit for I as well as II work and was renamed *Lehrregiment Kurfürst*. The Commanding Officer was Major Partl.

3. *Abwehr* III.

Abwehr III was responsible for counter-espionage and the security of the *Wehrmacht*. Briefly, this section was broken up between RSHA *Amt* IV (*Gestapo*) and RSHA *Gruppe* VI Z, the latter formation comprising a small section taken over from *Abwehr* III F for counter-espionage and penetration in satellite and neutral countries not easily accessible to the *Gestapo*. In addition, old *Abwehr* III Kgf (security of POW camps) and *Abwehr* III W/H, L and M (security of the Armed Forces) were transferred to the OKW/WFst/*Truppenabwehr*, but later went into the *Mil Amt*, finally to *Mil Amt* I in about March 1945.

4. *Abwehrleitstellen*, *Kommandos* and *Trupps*.

Following the dissolution of the *Abwehr* and until December 1944, the *Abwehrleitstellen*, *Abwehrkommandos* and *Trupps* first of all experienced changes in terminology, the prefix '*Abwehr*' being replaced by '*Frontaufklärung*'. Their personnel were transferred to the *Mil Amt*, but they were subordinated to the OKW *Wehrmachtführungsstab*/Ic *Wehrmacht*. This illogical division, most certainly designed to save the face of the OKW, was only temporary, for in about December 1944, *Abt*. F of the *Mil Amt* was established to control this old *Abwehr* mobile structure. This change was, however, essentially unimportant, as alike in the *Abwehr* and the *Mil Amt*, the *Leitstellen*, FAKs and FATs were, to all intents and purposes, dependent on *Wehrmacht* command through the agency of a *Mil Amt* officer (attached as liaison officer responsible to the Ic of an *Oberbefehlshaber*, Army Group or Army) who continued to be known by his old *Abwehr* title as Ic/ AO (= *Abwehroffizier*).

5. *Abwehrstellen* and *Kriegsorganisationen* (KOs).

The old *Abwehr*'s regional organisation, both within and without Germany, while being taken over bodily into the RSHA *Mil Amt*, did undergo certain changes at the hands of RSHA. Its stations were renamed '*Kommando der Meldegebiete*' but generally not restaffed, and were responsible to RSHA *Mil Amt* for the restricted functions allocated to that body.

Inside Germany and Austria, the work of the KdMs (formerly Asts) were subjected to a much closer control than previously; they were not to work on their own, independently of one another and of their headquarters; incompetent or unimportant KdMs were dissolved and merged with the more active and important stations adjacent to them, as indicated below. In addition, there was a virtual if not total suppression of old *Abwehr* II work, the KdMs losing this in favour of Skorzeny enterprises, another indication of RSHA policy of centralisation. Briefly, the loss of old *Abwehr* III work also resulted in the station head (now known as *Kommandeur*) no longer doubling as Ic/AO of the AK of the area as had previously been the case. Thus, under the *Mil Amt*, the KdMs inside Germany were to become purely executive arms of the operational sections of *Mil Amt* B (for the West) and *Mil Amt* C (for the East). The final alignment of KdMs inside Germany and Austria (and Czechoslovakia) were as follows for *Mil Amt* B:

KdM Hamburg	absorbed *Asts* Hanover, Kiel and Wilhelmshaven
KdM Köln	absorbed *Ast* Münster/W.
KdM Munich	absorbed *Ast* Nuremberg
KdM Stuttgart	
KdM Wiesbaden	absorbed Ast Kassel
KdM Salzburg	

and for *Mil Amt* C:

KdM Berlin	absorbed *Ast* Dresden
KdM Stettin	absorbed *Asts* Königsberg and Danzig
KdM Breslau	absorbed *Asts* Poznan and Krakau
KdM Vienna	
KdM Prague (Protectorate)	

Outside Greater Germany the regional organisation of the old *Abwehr* was alone subjected to greater central control; and, to counter the previous weakness, the tendency under the RSHA *Mil Amt* was to bring together all of its activities in a neutral country, for example, under the local KdM (formerly KO) and to encourage close liaison between heads of all such KdMs and heads of the local RSHA *Amt* VI stations. Largely as a security measure, staffs of KdMs in neutral countries were severely reduced in order that only the essential specialists needed diplomatic cover. In addition, the old *Abwehr Gruppe* III, I Wi, and IT/LW work was removed from the KdMs abroad and incorporated into the local RSHA *Amt* VI stations. Here again, the KdMs were answerable to *Mil* B or *Mil* C, depending on their locations, whether East or West. Under *Mil* B were:

KdM Switzerland
KdM Spain
KdM Portugal
Führungsstelle Italy

while under *Mil* C were:

KdM China
KdM Sweden
KdM Turkey
KdM Finland (from October 1944, *Sonderkommando Nord*).

6. RSHA *Mil Amt* headquarters organisation.

While RSHA *Mil Amt*, more closely than anything else, corresponded to a successor of the old *Abwehr*, it had no personality or policy apart from that of RSHA. For example, the surviving distinction between RSHA *Amt* VI proper and the *Mil Amt*, such as it was, was in the nature of their work, not in the chain of their responsibility or in their directing personalities.

Schellenberg's personal 'Cabinet': The head and most of the important personalities of *Mil Amt* were also—and first—the head and directors of RSHA *Amt* VI. Thus, at the top was SS-*Brigadeführer* Schellenberg, *Amtschef Amt* VI/*Mil Amt* and his so-called personal 'Cabinet'. *Oberleutnant* Cornand was Schellenberg's Adjutant while SS-*Ostubaf* Dr Wilhelm Schmitz was his Personal *Referent*.

Liaison with *Amtsgruppe Ausland* and the *Ausw.Amt* was maintained through SS-*Ostubaf* Dr Rudolf Oebsger-Röder, while liaison with KG 200 was maintained through Major Hurlin. In this regard and of special *Mil Amt* significance, were the three Service liaison officers who were accredited to the *Mil Amt* as I.a. Marine, *Heer* and *Luft*. These positions, also held directly under Schellenberg, will be covered more fully below.

Abteilungschefs: The directing head of the different *Amt Amt Abteilungen* (and of *Amt* VI *Gruppen*, where dual capacities existed) and the deputies were as follows:

Abt A	Internal Administration	
	Abteilungschef:	SS-*Staf* Martin Sandberger, RSHA VI A
	Deputy *Abteilungschef*:	*Oberstltn.* Lienhardt
Abt B	Intelligence in the West	
	Abteilungschef:	SS-*Staf* Eugen Steimle, RSHA VI B
	Deputy *Abteilungschef*:	Major i.G. Taysen
Abt C	Intelligence in the East	
	Abteilungschef:	*Oberst* Ohletz
	Deputy *Abteilungschef*:	Major Elting
Abt D	Sabotage and Subversion	
	Abteilungschef:	SS-*Ostubaf* Otto Skorzeny, RSHA VI S
	Deputy *Abteilungschef*:	Major Loos
Abt E	Secret Communications	
	Abteilungschef:	*Oberstltn.* Boening, RSHA VI F
	Deputy *Abteilungschef*:	Major Foretschkin
Abt F	*Frontaufklärung*	
	Abteilungschef:	*Oberst* i.G. Buntrock
	Deputy *Abteilungschef*:	*Oberstltn.* i.G. von dem Knesebeck
Abt G	Forged documents, secret writing etc.	
	Abteilungschef:	*Oberstltn.* Boening, RSHA VI F
	Deputy *Abteilungschef*:	*Oberstltn.* Müller
Abt i	Deception	

Abteilungschef:	*Kapt.z.See* von Bechtolsheim
Deputy *Abteilungschef:*	*Obltn.* Naber

As may be noted above, *Abt* C was an exception to the general rule of control of *Mil Amt Abteilungen* by *Gruppenleiters* of RSHA *Amt* VI. In this regard, it is interesting to observe that Ohletz was brought into the old *Abwehr* in the spring of 1944 as a result of pressure from the *Luftwaffe* for improved service in the realm of air intelligence, while his deputy, Major Elting, was a former *Abwehr* officer of long-standing and the only one to hold such an important position in the *Mil Amt*.

Abt F can hardly be considered an exception to the general rule since its function was peculiarly limited to the realm of military intelligence. However, neither its head, *Oberst* Buntrock, nor his deputy, *Oberstltn.* von dem Knesebeck, were in the old *Abwehr*, and it would appear that they were handpicked for the post by the RSHA.

In theory, at least, what has just been said regarding *Abt* F may be extended to *Abt* i, since it was conceived that its function, deception, was specially involved in the sphere of military operations. While von Bechtolsheim, who negotiated its establishment, is given above as *Abteilungchef* of i, doubt exists as to whether, during its very short existence, anyone was ever formally appointed or installed as *Abteilungschef*.

I.a Marine, *Heer* and *Luft*: According to Schellenberg, I.a. Marine, I.a. *Heer*, and I.a. *Luft* were staff officers who had primarily the task of maintaining permanent and good liaison with the intelligence sections, personnel offices and the staffs of their respective Services. They were to put before their supreme commanders all problems of the RSHA concerning material and personnel, and were to occupy themselves intensively with the matters of reinforcements and training for *Mil Amt*, and operational intelligence and deception requirements of the three Services. Schellenberg's view was that these matters had not been understood by the three Services in the days of Canaris and Hansen and that consequently, inadequate support and cooperation had been forthcoming from the *Wehrmachtführungsstab*.

These positions were occupied as follows:

I.a. Marine	*Kapt.z.See* von Bechtolsheim
I.a. *Heer*	*Oberstltn* von dem Knesebeck
I.a. *Luft*	*Oberstltn* Ohletz; succeeded in 1945 by Major i.G. Randell and/or *Oberst* i.G. Semper.

The best account of the work of these I.a.'s comes from von Bechtolsheim who, it may be noted, was not previously a member of the old *Abwehr*, but was brought in from active service with the Germany Navy when the RSHA *Mil Amt* was formed. Generally, the work of von Bechtolsheim as I.a. reflects also, it would seem, the nature of the work carried out by his two counterparts.

While von Bechtolsheim points out that he gave certain training lectures at courses run by *Lehrregiment Kurfürst* and made certain inspection trips to various KdMs, his normal function was to receive all intelligence questionnaires and requests from the OKM (III SKL) and distribute these to the relevant branches of the *Mil Amt* for answer. Much of the detail connected with this work was carried out by telephone directly between the officer in the *Mil Amt* to whom the request had been handed and III SKL, so that once a question or enquiry had been placed or a scheme set in motion, von Bechtolsheim might or might not have heard of subsequent developments or details.

As previously point out, von Bechtolsheim was instrumental in establishing *Abt*.i. He carried the burden of this work since his two counterparts, von dem Knesebeck and Ohletz were, as indicated above, occupying other positions as well, the former being Deputy *Abteilungschef* of *Abt*.F. and the latter *Abteilungschef* of *Abt*.C.

Basically, Schellenberg's idea concerning the need for these I.a.'s was quite sound, but it is reasonably clear that their accomplishments were limited and by the end of the war had not fulfilled, or in fact had time to fulfil, all the tasks for them as conceived by Schellenberg.

F. General Appreciation and Conclusion.

RSHA *Amt* VI itself, like the *Abwehr* which it absorbed, had a tradition of failure and incompetence in spite of a few isolated, but well advertised, successes. In fact, it has been recognised that in some respects the old *Abwehr* was even superior to *Amt* VI, especially in the field of personnel. However, it was against a background of general failure, un-coordinated efforts and fights for political favouritism in all phases of intelligence activities that Schellenberg conceived the idea of a united intelligence service (*Einheitlicher Deutscher Geheim Meldedienst*) operating under one direction and with (as had not been true in the past) the benefit of centrally pooled information, centrally controlled cryptography and co-ordinated deception policy and facilities. The personality of Schellenberg was the determining factor in the later history and last days of the German Intelligence Services as was the personality of Canaris in its earlier phases but, generally, no more effective. He had no support from Kaltenbrunner either in his attempts to improve the efficiency of the SD Intelligence Services or in his attempts to convert Himmler to defeatism. Schellenberg began too late (summer of 1944); his grandiose plans were not and could not have been realised. Thus, the advent of the *Mil Amt* did not, in general, alter the destiny of the German intelligence services.

The remains of the old *Abwehr* had only three sources of intelligence which were considered of any value—one in Lisbon (Fidronne alias 'OSTRO'), one in Stockholm (Kraemer), one in Vienna (Klatt)—and the genuineness of all three was rightly doubted. Like the *Abwehr*, the *Mil Amt* possessed no first rate source of intelligence which was not known to or penetrated by the Allies. In fact, it has been concluded that nowhere in the entire RSHA, *Mil Amt* included, were there developed any new sources of genuine secret intelligence.

The *Mil Amt*'s plan for the future, both inside and outside Germany, were only envisaged in relation to continued central direction and military resistance or, at the very least, something less then unconditional surrender. At the time of the German military collapse, *Mil Amt* headquarters and regional stations were wholly or partly in dissolution. During the last weeks of military resistance, the *Mil Amt* was drastically reduced in size and split in two sections—*Mil* B and C being placed under SS-*Ostubaf* Waneck, RSHA *Gruppenleiter* VI E; *Mil* E and G were joined with *Mil* D under Skorzeny; while *Mil* A and probably F and i were dissolved—and it appears that the only important officers retained in an active capacity following this last minute reorganisation were Major Foretschkin of *Mil* E and Major Meissner of *Mil* C.

The *Mil Amt* no longer exists and, as such, is not a threat to Allied security.

The main sources of information for this report:

> Walter Schellenberg, RSHA *Amtschef* VI/Mil.
> Martin Sandberger, RSHA VI A and *Abteilungschef Mil* A.
> Theodor Freiherr von Bechtolsheim, RSHA *Mil* i, I.a. Marine.
> Otto Skorzeny, RSHA VI S and *Abteilungschef Mil* D.
> Werner Ohletz, RSHA VI, *Abteilungschef Mil* C.

This report was issued by W.R.C.1./A. on 11 January 1946.

Note

* The National Archives, Kew, KV 2/192: Liquidation Report No.26, RSHA *Militärisches Amt*.

19

Situation Report No. 27:
RSHA *Mil Amt* A

A. Origin and History.

When the RSHA absorbed the *Abwehr* in the summer of 1944, *Abteilung* A of the *Militärisches Amt* was formed to cover matters of administration and organisation for the *Mil Amt*. *Oberstleutnant* Engelhorn, Hansen's deputy, was probably first *Abteilungschef Mil* A; but owing to his participation in the 20 July 1944 plot againt Hitler and his subsequent demise, he was succeeded by SS-*Staf* Martin Sandberger on 22 July 1944 who, on 1 January 1944 had become *Gruppenleiter*, RSHA VI A. In this dual capacity Sandberger was immediately responsible to Schellenberg. Thus, *Mil Amt* A and RSHA *Gruppe* VI A, after the events of 20 July 1944, were linked not only at the top by a common head, but more extensively fused, although a conscious or formal division was maintained by *Mil Amt* A1 through A4, described below) corresponded to the first four *Referate* of RSHA *Gruppe* VI A. The continuation of *Abt.* A, as such, was due partly to a RSHA agreement with the OKW, and partly to the fact that certain matters of finance and, above all, questions of personnel, could be facilitated by the *Wehrmacht*.

Mil Amt A was the first of the eight *Abteilungen* of the *Mil Amt*. Theoretically, *Abt* A was a kind of successor to *Abteilung* Z of the old *Abwehr*, with the following known exceptions: (a) ZR (legal) went into RSHA VI A/R; (b) certain sub-sections of ZF (finance) went to RSHA II A1 and II B1; (c) ZF/7 (pensions) was abolished; (d) part of ZA (administration of personnel) went to RSHA I/*Mil. Pers* (general appointments and postings).

To begin with, a large part of *Mil Amt* A was situated mainly at Zossen (cover name 'Zeppelin'), the headquarters of the old *Abwehr* II; then, in July 1944, or possibly later that year, there was removal to Belinde II Camp north of Baruth. In January 1945, the various sections of *Mil Amt* A were spread between Belinde II, Belinde I and Waldburg, a camp situated between Koppin and Fürstenwalde. By mid March 1945, *Mil Amt* A with *Mil Amt* B has been reported to have moved to Seedorf Camp near Lauenburg in Thuringia. In April 1945, *Mil Amt* A was near Innsbruck, and apparently being dissolved.

B. Organisation of RSHA *Mil Amt* A.

As already indicated, RSHA *Mil Amt* A dealt mainly with the administrative and organisation for the *Mil Amt*. Following the abortive 20 July 1944 plot and the absorption of *Mil Amt* by RSHA *Amt* VI, *Abteilung* A was composed as follows (for additional personnel, see para. G):

Abteilungschef:	SS-*Staf* Martin Sandberger, (also *Gruppenleiter* VI A)
Deputy *Abteilungschef:*	*Oberstltn*. Lienhardt
Mil A:	Organisation of the *Mil Amt* (the secretariat of the HQ). This section absorbed part of *Abwehr* ZA (local and internal administration).
Referent:	*Oberstltn*. Gressler (formerly *Abwehr* ZO) until December 1944; the *Oberstltn* Lienhardt who also acted as deputy to Sandberger
Mil A 1/N:	Telecommunications of the *Mil Amt*.
Referent:	Major Woithe
Mil A 1/ZK:	Central Registry of the *Mil Amt*. This section was the old *Abwehr* ZK (*Zentralkartei*).
Referent:	*Oberltn*. Hübner
Mil A 1/KFZ:	Internal transport system of the *Mil Amt*.
Referent:	Major Rahn
Mil A 2:	Financial matters of the *Mil Amt*. *Mil* A 2 comprised part of the old *Abwehr* ZF (finance), namely *Abwehr* ZF/2 (personnel in neutral countries) and ZF/8 (foreign exchange dealings).
Referent:	SS-*Hstuf* Schuler (also *Referent*, RSHA VI A2)
Mil A 3:	Personnel and recruiting of the *Mil Amt*.
Referent:	SS-*Stubaf* Olbrück
Mil A 4:	Training of the *Mil Amt*; (a) General, political and language training; and (b) Training schedules.
Referent:	unknown

Mil A 5:	Headquarters administrative staff of the *Mil Amt*.
Referent:	Major Kunckel
Mil ZB:	*Mil Zentralbüro* existed in name only, and its staff was simultaneously that of RSHA VI A/*Zentralbüro*.

From December 1944, the old *Abwehr* III D (Deception) card index under *Ltn.* Naber, then with the '*Truppenabwehr*', came under the care of *Kapt. zur See* von Bechtolsheim (Ia Marine, *Mil Amt*) and was transferred to *Mil Amt* A.

This was a part of Schellenberg's program for the further development and co-ordination of deception work. As part of *Mil Amt* A, and with no other intelligence-active counterpart in RSHA *Gruppe* I A, this arrangement obviously left much to be desired. Thus, in March 1945, deception was established as a separate *Abteilung*, *Mil Amt* i.

C. *Mil* A 1/ZK (Central Registry).

Oberltn. Hübner was head of this section which comprised the Central Registry of the old *Abwehr*. Hübner by dint of long, industrious and energetic service, had virtually 'risen from the ranks'. Of the card indices and records which he maintained in *Mil* A 1/ZK, a mjor portion was destroyed in February 1945 at the Waldburg Camp; after moving to Probstzelle (Thuringia), the remainder was destroyed in April 1945.

D. *Mil* A 2 (Finance).

While the information thus far available concerning the finance and financial procedures of the old *Abwehr* and the RSHA *Mil Amt*, as such, are sketchy and incomplete, the following may be of some interest:

Previous to the absorption of the *Abwehr* into the RSHA, the *Dienststellen* of the *Abwehr* drew their funds from *Abwehr Abteilung* ZF (Finance). These funds consisted of:

(a) German currency.
(b) Foreign currency.
(c) Gold.
(d) Raw materials and army merchandise.

Abwehr ZF itself had no funds, but drew the necessary currencies, gold and merchandise from the following main sources:

(a) The *Reichswirtschaftsministerium* (foreign currencies).
(b) The Four Year Plan (foreign currencies).

(c) The secret fund of the OKW (German currency).

(d) The *Heeresnachschublager* (Army Stores).

Foreign currencies furnished by the old *Abwehr* by the *Reichswirtschaftsministerium* had averaged a monthly total of 1,000,000 RM. The *Aussenstellen* (*Asts*) had monthly allotments of foreign currencies while the *Kriegsorganisations* (KO's) drew funds not only directly through ZF but also indirectly through the home *Asts*, such as Hamburg, Munich etc. *Abwehrdienststellen* in South America are known to have drawn some funds from the frozen assets of local German business firms. In at least some cases, both at home and abroad, other and less formal sources of funds were not left unexploited. The *Abwehr* had avoided operating through normal banking channels abroad but, according to Düsterberg (RSHA *Amt* II, formerly *Leiter Abwehr* ZF), the RSHA latterly used foreign banks abroad to finance some agents.

After the establishment of the RSHA *Mil Amt*, the various *Mil Referents*, apart from their regular monthly requirements, made application directly to *Mil Amt* A2 for all additional needs. The KdMs had both open and secret funds drawn from the *Mil Amt* through regular established channels. However, the former were accounted for by the local BdS Finance Section while the latter were not.

Schellenberg's view was that the financial needs and requirements of the *Mil Amt* should be brought into line procedurally and otherwise with those of RSHA *Amt* VI. Thus, in October 1944, a system of monthly conferences with representatives of the *Reichswirtschaftsministerium* was introduced. At these conferences the various currency budgets of RSHA *Amt* VI and the *Mil Amt* were discussed and detailed financial arrangements of the *Mil Amt* were submitted. One of the principal objectives of this procedure was a reduction of expenditure to a reasonable ceiling. The function of *Mil Amt* A2 was simply that of submitting requests for funds to RSHA *Amt* II which, generally, was responsible for allocation of funds for needs throughout the RSHA.

Sandberger estimated that the *Mil Amt*'s monthly requirements ran to about 500,000 to 600,000 RM. This, however, does not represent the *Mil Amt*'s total financial dealings, as some funds were obtained from the pay office of the *Wehrkreis* or Army funds. According to Schellenberg, the *Mil Amt*'s annual allocation through RSHA *Amt* II was 8,000,000 RM.

E. *Mil Amt* A3 (Personnel.)

Although *Mil Amt* personnel were considered sufficient in quantity, the percentage of well-qualified officers was very small. This deficiency was due largely to the fact that Canaris had not given proper attention to the question of personnel recruitment and replacement in the old *Abwehr*. Promotion in the *Abwehr* was another major flaw, since officers attached to the *Abwehr* were placed lower in seniority on the promotion lists of their respective Services. Many senior officers who normally would have pressed for a proper personnel policy were General Staff officers attached to the *Abwehr* for given periods; therefore, they had neither a long-term interest in the *Abwehr* nor a willingness to stir up muddy waters.

Great efforts were made by Schellenberg and Sandberger to improve this personnel situation in the course of 1944. They had conferences with the personnel heads of the *Wehrmacht*, explaining to them the needs of the *Geheime Meldedienst* and the necessity of making personnel continually available to RSHA *Amt* VI and the *Mil Amt*. Improvement in this regard was one of the tasks of the Ia *Heer* office, Ia Marine office and Ia *Luft* office. Eventually, a system was evolved whereby the *Abteilung* heads gave their requirements to RSHA *Mil Amt* A3, *Leiter* SS-*Stubaf* Olbrück, who then passed them on to the RSHA *Amt* I/*Mil.Pers. Gruppenleiter Oberstltn.* Hübner. *Amt* I/*Mil.Pers.* forwarded exact requirements to the Personnel *Amts* of the *Wehrmacht* which arranged, through *Amt* I/*Mil.Pers.*, postings to the *Mil Amt*. By the autumn of 1944, the *Mil Amt* was permitted more selection from among available officers. In spite of these efforts, however, no material improvement in the personnel situation occurred, as it was too late in the war for any system to have had the desired effect.

F. Conclusion.

As previously indicated, information thus far available on RSHA *Mil Amt* A is nothing like complete. Any attempt to estimate success or failure would probably be misleading. However, as indicated sketchily above, some changes, considered to be improvements, were undertaken; and, in this regard, it is only too obvious that *Mil Amt* A, as such, had no individuality apart from the RSHA.

G. Known Personnel of *Mil Amt* A.

(personnel now under arrest are underlined.)

Blume, *Ober Reg.Inspektor, Mil* A Legal expert (formerly *Abwehr* ZR).
Eckardt, SS-*Stubaf., Mil Amt* A4.
Engelhorn, *Oberstltn.*, probably first *Abteilungschef Mil Amt* A; also Hansen's deputy; executed in the autumn 1944.
Gressler, *Oberstltn., Referent Mil Amt* A1 until Dec. 1944 (formerly *Abwehr* ZO).
Hübner, Oberltn., *Leiter Mil Amt* A1/ZK (formerly *Abwehr* ZK). Not identical with *Oberstltn.* Hübner, RSHA *Amt* I.
Janssen, SS-*Hstuf., Mil Amt* A4.
Jess, *Hauptmann, Mil Amt* A5.
Dr Jörges, Harald, *Mil Amt* A2 (formerlt *Abwehr* ZF).
<u>Dr Jürgen, Herbert</u>, *Hauptmann, Mil Amt* A1 (lawyer, formerly *Abwehr* ZO).

Krantz, *Oberstabsintendent, Mil Amt* A2 (formerly *Abwehr* ZF).

Kunckel, Major, *Referent Mil Amt* A5.

Lienhardt, *Oberstltn., Referent Mil Amt* A1 from Dec. 1944, and also deputy to Sandberger.

Naber, *Ltn.,* from Dec. 1944 transferred from *Truppenabwehr* to *Mil Amt* A; in March 1945 went to *Mil Amt* i.

Olbrück, SS-*Stubaf., Referent Mil Amt* A3.

Paulick, *Stabszahlmeister, Mil Amt* A2.

Person, Major, *Mil Amt* A3 (formerly *Abwehr* I/*Chefgruppe*).

Pfennig, *Hauptmann, Mil Amt* A5 (formerly *Abwehr* I/*Chefgruppe*).

Rahn, Major, *Mil Amt* A1/KFZ.

Sandberger, Martin, SS-*Staf., Abteilungschef Mil Amt* A and *Gruppenleiter* RSHA VI A.

Dr Schön, *Oberfeldrichter, Mil Amt* A4.

Schollmayer, *Oberltn.,* may have been *Mil Amt* A.

Schuler, SS-*Hstuf., Referent Mil Amt* A2 and RSHA *Amt* II A2.

Wacks, *Hauptmann, Mil Amt* A3.

Woithe, *Hauptmann, Referent Mil Amt* A1/N.

Wolf, *Feldwebel, Mil Amt* A1/N.

Wiesinger, *Polizeirat,* RSHA VI representative for *Mil Amt* A2.

Zirkel, *Oberzahlmeister, Mil Amt* A2 (formerly *Abwehr* ZF).

H. Main Sources of Information.

Walter Schellenberg, RSHA *Amtschef* VI/*Mil.*

Martin Sandberger, *Abteilungschef, Mil Amt* A, *Gruppenleiter* RSHA VI A.

Düsterberg, former *Leiter Abwehr* ZF, then RSHA *Amt* II.

Dr Herbert Jürgen, formerly *Abwehr* III C6, the RSHA *Mil Amt* A1.

This report was issued by W.R.C.2. on 5 March 1946.

Supplementary information.

On 30 January 1946, MI 5 received an USFET interrogation report, CI-CIR 11 dated 10 January 1946. It was a 'report on KdM Prague compiled from information obtained from *Oberst* Dehmel, *Fräulein* Reichert and *Hauptmann* Berthelsen'. Annex II of this report, entitled 'Cache Construction Projects' sheds light on an activity by RSHA *Mil Amt* A that is not reflected in the CIWR Situation Report No. 27 above.

1. Mole Operation (*Maulwurf Aktion*).

When *Oberltn*. Ritter, formerly with a *Front Auklärung* [FAK] unit in Bulgaria, was attached to KdM Prague in December 1944, he brought with him the concept of mole (*Maulwurf*) operations, which he had learned from the Red Army. This was caching of money and valuables in enemy countries, or in areas about to be occupied by the enemy. The hidden funds were to be used for the payment of agents.

As the war began to draw nearer to home, the *Mil Amt* ordered KdM Prague to construct such caches behind a line which at first ran roughly from Moravska Ostrava to Vienna, and later from Glatz (Upper Silesia) to Linz. As usual, there was little cooperation between the various intelligence headquarters, and in Slovakia, which was KdM Vienna territory, Prague was only permitted to do the actual construction work, but not to utilize any of Vienna's agents for the Mole Operation.

Since it could not be foreseen what kind of currency the USSR would authorize for this area, the caches were to be filled with valuables which were to be furnished by RSHA *Mil Amt* A.

Dehmel requested Berthelsen's advice on the Mole Operation in order to prepare directives for the burial places to be selected and the type of packing to be used. Berthelsen and Dr Schindler provided waterproof paper, and in January 1945 Seefeld drew 50,000 RM worth of jewels, which were packed into 45 containers and forwarded to various *Meldeköpfe* for burial. There the paper packages were put into sealed boxes and provided with a number. 145,000 RM worth of jewels were drawn during March 1945 and were packed into approx. 150 packages. Receipts were given, but Dehmel refused to countersign them. According to Dehmel, none of the valuables promised by *Mil Amt* A ever arrived; all funds and valuables buried in the course of the Mole Operation had been drawn from confiscated Jewish property.

Note

* The National Archives, Kew, KV 3/194: Situation Report No. 27, RSHA *Mil Amt* A; also USFET, interrogation report CI-CIR 11 dated 10 January 1946 by Dehmel, Reichert and Bertholsen.

Situation Report No. 28: RSHA *Mil Amt* B

I. History & Organization.

1. Introduction.
The story of the re-organization of the German Intelligence Services in 1944 has been covered in other War Room publications, in particular in Liquidation Report No. 26 on *Mil Amt* Headquarters, where the role of *Mil Amt Abteilung* B in the general secret intelligence field is explained…

2. Operational Area.
Mil Amt B's function was the collecting of secret military intelligence from the West, and was thus a parallel organization to *Mil Amt* C, which had the duty of collecting similar information from the East (see Situation Report No. 29). Geographically, *Mil Amt* B's area of operations included, roughly, all countries west of a line drawn from the Skagerrack to the Gulf of Venice, thus including Norway, Denmark, the Low Countries, France Italy, the Iberian Peninsula, the United Kingdom and the Americas. The primary aim of *Mil Amt* B, therefore, was to obtain military information on the Western Allies, using the other countries as intelligence bases. The work of *Mil Amt* B was thus identical with that of *Abteilung* I *West* of the old *Abwehr*.

3. *Mil Amt* B and RSHA *Amt* VI.
As in the case of *Mil Amt* C, the fact that from July/August 1944 onwards the *Abwehr* at least in part, was integrated into RSHA *Amt* VI, did not entail much change for the *Abwehr* I officers working in the various *Aussenstellen* (*Asts*) and *Kriegsorganisationen* (KOs—KdMs) under *Mil Amt* B; the change was for them, in the main, one of name only. Centrally, however, there was an almost complete change of personnel, important officers having been implicated in the Generals'

Putsch of 20 July 1944. SS-*Staf.* Eugen Steimle, *Gruppenleiter* RSHA VI E, became, in addition, *Abteilungschef Mil Amt* B in August 1944, succeeding as head of *Mil Amt* B, *Oberstltn.* Kübart, previous *Leiter* I H *Amt Abwehr* and close associate of *Oberst* Hansen. Steimle's deputy on the *Mil Amt* side was Major Adalbert von Taysen who, in August 1944, was appointed Deputy *Abteilungschef*, RSHA *Mil Amt* B. Immediately before joining *Mil Amt*, von Taysen, a professional soldier, had served as Ia and Ib officer in infantry and armoured units. von Taysen was admirably unqualified for intelligence work, and Steimle used him merely as an office superintendent. Thus, in contrast to *Mil Amt* C, *Mil Amt* B came under the complete domination of RSHA VI.

4. Organization.
The internal organization of RSHA *Mil Amt* B was similar to that of *Mil Amt* C, being divided into two main sections (*Unterabteilungen*):

> *Sichtung*, or evaluation, and
> *Beschaffung*, or gathering of intelligence.

There was also a small administrative section, the *Zentralgruppe*.

(a) *Unterabteilung Sichtung (Mil B/S)*, which concentrated on the evaluation of intelligence reports, was further subdivided functionally into service departments, namely:

Mil B/S *Heer*	-	exploitation of military intelligence,
Mil B/S *Luft*	-	exploitation of air intelligence,
Mil B/S Marine	-	exploitation of naval intelligence.

The head of each subdivision maintained liaison either directly with the corresponding service Ic officer or with the service Ic office through the intermediary of the special liaison officers created by Schellenberg (the Ia's *Heer*, *Luft* and Marine) to stimulate the interest and cooperation of the service chiefs in RSHA *Mil Amt* matters. The latter was the official channel but, in practise, the former was more usual. The *Sichtung* officers passed on to *Unterabteilung Beschaffung* (see below) requests for information from the services; they had no connection with the KdMs or with agents. The head of *Mil* B/S was *Oberstltn.* J.L. von Dewitz, described by Steimle as an expert on British and American Air Forces, and an officer particularly suited for intelligence work. von Dewitz was also head of *Mil* B/S *Luft*.

(b) *Unterabteilung Beschaffung (Mil B/B)*, was responsible for all aspects of the collection of intelligence, including the development of new sources of information and the exploitation of existing ones; it dealt with demands for information forwarded by the *Sichtung* section, passing them downwards to the appropriate

KdM or outstation for action. This department worked mainly through the KdMs (the successors of the I *Referenten* of the old KOs and *Asts*), though it did employ certain agents or groups directly. Intelligence collected was passed to the *Sichtung* section for evaluation and forwarding to OKH/*Fremde Heer West*, OKL/*Fremde Luftwaffe West* or *Seekriegsleitung* as the case happened to be.

Unterabteilung Beschaffung was subdivided geographically into four *Gruppen*, namely:

Gruppe B/I	-	covering Denmark, Norway and Holland,
Gruppe B/II	-	covering France and Belgium,
Gruppe B/III	-	covering Spain and Portugal,
Gruppe B/IV	-	covering Switzerland and Italy.

(Note: the above geographical divisions are taken from information supplied by Steimle, and are believed to indicate the final alignment. Both von Taysen and Sandberger give alightly different pictures.)

The four *Gruppen*, in turn, directed the work of the KdMs, maintaining closer contact with, and control over, such outstations that had existed under the old *Abwehr*. However, the KdMs still retained considerable latitude in the execution of their tasks. Each *Gruppe* was responsible for direction, according to Steimle, as follows:

Gruppe B/I	-	KdM Hamburg,
Gruppe B/II	-	KdM Köln and KdM Wiesbaden and, by March 1945, KdM Stuttgart,
Gruppe B/III	-	KdM (or KO) Spain, KdM (or KO) Portugal and, until March 1945, KdM Stuttgart,
Gruppe B/IV	-	KdM Munich, KdM Salzburg, KdM (or KO) Switzerland and *Führungsstelle* Italien.

(Note: von Taysen indicates that *Gruppe* B/I was responsible for the United Kingdom and that *Gruppe* B/III was responsible for South America, while Sandberger indicates that both North and South America came under *Gruppe* B/III. On the basis of information available, the Americas and the U.K. were probably not included specifically under one of the *Mil* B/*Beschaffung Gruppen*, but were targets for the combined efforts of RSHA *Mil Amt* B and its KdMs, particularly KdM Hamburg and KdMs Spain and Portugal.)

RSHA *Mil Amt* B/*Beschaffung* was probably headed by *Oberstltn.* J.L. von Bohlen, who was also head of *Gruppe* B/III. von Bohlen was highly regarded by Steimle, who successfully pleaded for his retention in the *Mil Amt*, following his (von Bohlen's) departure for Chile, where he had been *Luftwaffe Attaché*, and his rumoured political unreliability.

5. Important RSHA *Mil Amt* B officers.

The more important officers of RSHA *Mil Amt* B were as follows:

Abteilungschef	-	SS-*Staf* Eugen Steimle
Deputy *Abteilungschef*	-	Major von Taysen
Mil B/Z (*Zentralgruppe*, administration)	-	Major Amsink
Mil B/S (*Sichtung*)	-	*Oberstltn* von Dewitz (Leiter)
Mil B/S *Heer*	-	Major Graf Schwerin
Mil B/S *Luft*	-	*Oberstltn* von Dewitz
Mil B/S Marine	-	*Korv.Kapt.* R(i)ed(e)l
Mil B/B (*Beschaffung*)	-	*Oberstltn* von Bohlen (Leiter)
Mil B/B I	-	*Hauptmann* von Vleuten; succeeded in April 1945 by Major Kempf
Mil B/B II	-	*Korv.Kapt.* Humpert
Mil B/B III	-	*Oberstltn* von Bohlen
Mil B/B IV	-	*Oberltn* Ho(h)mann

6. Locations and final disintegration.

In August 1944, RSHA *Mil Amt* B was located at Camp Belinde at Baruth, south of Berlin. In September 1944, the *Abteilung* evacuated to Camp Waldburg near Berlin, but in March 1945, another move took the *Abteilung* to Castle [Schloss] Lauenstein in Thüringen. By April 1945, *Mil Amt* B was at Tegernsee, Bavaria. While parts of *Mil Amt* B may have been located during the last hectic days at other places, the above are believed to indicate the principal movements of the greater portion of the *Abteilung*.

In April 1945, Steimle states that he dismissed von Taysen, who, as previously indicated, was inexperienced, but who, in addition, was apparently not happy with his subordination to the SD. By this time, information reveals that *Mil Amt* B was in a thorough process of disintegration. Little work was done as the entire German Intelligence Service was in such a state of disorganization; disputes among officers were frequent, and all, apparently, were more concerned regarding personal future plans than with the future of this crumbling organization.

II. Sources of Information.

1. General.

The major part of RSHA *Mil Amt* B's secret intelligence came from its subordinate formations, the KdMs inside German territory and the KdMs (formerly KOs) in neutral or friendly countries. These stations were, for the most part, still staffed by officers of the old *Abwehr*; but, in general, staffs had been reduced for the sake of both efficiency and security. Apart from the KdMs, one direct source of information inherited from the old *Abwehr* that is worth mentioning, is the agent Paul Fidrmuc (alias 'Ostro'), who was controlled by *Mil Amt* B and located in the Iberian Peninsula.

2. The KdMs.

a) KdM Hamburg, controlled by *Mil Amt* B/B1, worked on greater scale than any of the other principal targets being the U.K. and the Americas. The procurement of naval intelligence maintained a high priority, with military and economic intelligence assuming less importance. Hamburg, in mid 1944, absorbed *Aussenstelle* Hannover, Kiel and Wilhelmshaven. Brazil, Turkey and the Iberian Peninsula were areas which KdM Hamburg devoted considerable effort.

b) KdM Munich, controlled by *Mil Amt* B, *Gruppe* B IV, KdM (formerly *Aussenstelle*) Munich engaged almost exclusively, until the collapse of the Fascist Government in Italy, in economic intelligence in the Balkans and Northern Italy. The KdM also acted as a training depot for German Intelligence Service personnel destined for other stations. When the KdM was established in the summer of 1944, it absorbed *Aussenstelle* Nürnberg. Apart from a few initial successes by *Abt* I in the Balkans, the work of *Aussenstelle*/KdM can, with reasonable certainty, be considered ineffective.

c) KdM Salzburg, the old *Aussenstelle* Salzburg was principally an old *Abwehr* III station, but in the overall German intelligence service picture it was never considered more than a third-rate institution. After its conversion to a KdM, the station was definitely ineffective and was so considered by *Mil Amt* B, *Gruppe* B IV which controlled KdM Salzburg.

d) KdM Stuttgart, this station was controlled by *Mil Amt* B, *Gruppe* B II from March 1945 onwards. Prior to conversion of the station from an *Aussenstelle*, it had been fairly active and its personnel were men of considerable ability. However, activity became substantially frustrated because the *Aussenstelle* was frequently used as a staff tank for other stations and was confronted with considerable jurisdictional conflicts with other stations. By the time the *Aussenstelle* became a KdM in mid 1944, it had depreciated substantially and, as a KdM, accomplished little or nothing of significance.

e) KdM Wiesbaden, during its early history this station, as an *Aussenstelle*, experienced considerable activity and was primarily concerned with work against France and was especially interested in intelligence necessary to the German invasion of France in 1940. Following the collapse of France, the *Aussenstelle* had its headquarters with the German Armistice Commission which afforded cover for at least some of its activity. In early 1944, Wiesbaden was selected as the *Abwehr* headquarters responsible for the co-ordination of the first post-occupational netwrok in northern France and the Low Countries. When *Aussenstelle* Wiesbaden became a KdM in mid 1944, it absorbed *Aussenstelle* Kassel. KdM Wiesbaden was controlled by *Mil Amt* B, *Gruppe* B II.

f) KdM Köln, this outstation was originally Nest Köln under *Aussenstelle* Münster/W. and was concerned almost exclusively in economic espionage. The Nest met with some success in the Argentine, and was active in French North Africa, Spain, Portugal, Sweden, Switzerland and Turkey; certain of its activities were also against the U.K. and the U.S.A. In mid 1944, Nest Köln became KdM Köln and absorbed its former controlling station, *Aussenstelle* Münster/W., which had never enjoyed any prominence in the German intelligence service. Under the *Mil Amt*, KdM Köln was controlled by *Mil Amt B, Gruppe* B II.

3. RSHA *Mil Amt* B stations in neutral and friendly areas.

The situation, briefly, regarding *Mil Amt* B stations outside Germany as as follows:

a) *Führungsstelle* Italien: This station was set up in Merano in March 1945 and was under the direction of Hans Wolfram von Engelmann to control espionage in Italy under the direction of *Mil Amt* B, *Gruppe* B IV. *Führungsstelle* Italien was not a large station but did control the following units:

Jacob: W/T School in Merano under *Hauptmann* Hofmayer which was the coordinating station for all German W/T agents in Italy, links being maintained with mobile German Intelligence Service formations.

Aussenstelle Milan: Primarily responsible for the recruitment of agents.

Meldekopf Como: A contact station for formations in Switzerland and also active in the recruitment of agents.

Meldekopf San Remo: Active in connection with coastal missions.

Meldekopf Venice: Training School.

Aussenstelle Verona.

Frontaufklärung work in Italy was controlled separately and was a continuous source of conflict for *Führungsstelle* Italien in the execution of its work. Principal personnel of *Führungsstelle* Italien included the following: *Oberst* von Engelmann, Commanding Officer; *Hauptmann* Matl, Deputy C.O.; *Kapt.Ltn.* Rhotert; Major Peters; *Oberltn.* Oettl and *Hauptmann* Koch.

b) KdM Spain: Due to German participation in the Spanish Civil War and the personal friendship between Admiral Canaris and General Franco, the *Abwehr* until early 1944 enjoyed a particularly favourable position in Spain. By 1941 German intelligence service activities in Spain became more or less centralised under the old K.O. Spain located at Madrid. This Station, in any event, was the controlling office for Nest Barcelona, Nest San Sebastien, Nest Algeciras, Nest Tetuan and other smaller stations, mostly shipping observation posts on the coast. For obvious geographical reasons as well as its neutrality, Spain was a favourable location for espionage activities of other German intelligence service formations whose activities in Spain were not controlled by K.O. Spain. On numerous occasions this fact was a source of conflict and confusion. Probably, the most important work of the organisation under K.O. Spain was its observations on Allied shipping in and about Gibraltar. Another activity which met with some success was the sabotage of Allied shipping in Spanish waters which, however, was the immediate cause of the ejection from Spain under Allied pressure, of many characters. This action of the Spanish Government was also one of the spring-boards for RSHA pressure against the *Abwehr* just prior to the re-organisation in 1944. About this time, *Freg.Kapt.* Leissner (alias 'Lens'), *Leiter* K.O. Spain was replaced by *Oberstltn.* Kleyenstuber who became head of KdM Spain which was controlled by RSHA *Mil Amt* B, *Gruppe* B III. Leissner however, continued to pose as *Leiter* of the KdM as this was thought to give Kleyenstuber an opportunity to re-organise the KdM unobstrusively. There are indications they Kleyenstuber's mission was to organise an espionage organisation for Spain which would in fact have been separate and apart from the KdM. According to Steimle, Kleyenstuber was to complete a general house-cleaning for the German intelligence services in Spain and co-ordinate the efforts of KdM Spain with those of other KdMs whose activities extended into Spain. Speculation on these points will, however, be resolved when the Interrogation Report on Kleyenstuber, who is now in Allied hands, becomes available. On the basis of information available it is relatively certain that so far as secret military intelligence operations are concerned, KdM Spain was most certainly less valuable to the *Mil Amt* that the old K.O. Spain had been to the *Abwehr*.

c) <u>KdM Portugal</u>: KdM Portugal was under the command of *Oberstltn.* Fredirici. Whatever success the KdM may have had while yet a K.O. under the old *Abwehr*, it seems relatively certain that its success under the *Mil Amt* was quite questionable. Like the *Abwehr* in Spain, one of the activities in Portugal was the observation of Allied shipping in and about Portuguese harbours and along the Portuguese coast. There was some *Abwehr* III F activity, as well as the forwarding of agents to neutral territory abroad. Among the principal characters associated with KdM Portugal are the following: Hans Bendixed, in charge of naval espionage; Alois Schreiber, successor to Otto Kurrer (alias 'Kamler'), in charge of military espionage; Major Wenzlau, air intelligence; and Dr Rudolf Baumann, sabotage and subversion. On of the more important personalities in Portugal on the counter-espionage side was Fritz Cramer. Under the *Mil Amt*, KdM Portugal was controlled by *Mil Amt* B, *Gruppe* B III.

d) <u>KdM Switzerland:</u> In 1942 *Kapt.z.See* Johannes Meissner (alias 'Peters') assumed command of K.O. Switzerland from *Oberstltn.* Knabbe. Important officers in Berne, were as follows: I (H) Major von Mühlen and *Sonderführer* Dr Albert; I (Wi) Major Gerl and *Sonderführer* (Z) Wetzel; III F, *Rittmeister* von Pescatore and *Obergefreiter* Willi Diert. Main sub-stations of the K.O. were at Geneva, Zürich and Lugano. The work carried out by the Swiss station was predominately III F. However, von Pescatore had a poor opinion of this work and ascribes its ineffectiveness to 1) the efficiency of the Swiss police, 2) general dislike of the Swiss for the Germans, and 3) general *Abwehr* inefficiency.

Some success of III F work in Switzerland was attained, however, in the penetration of Allied Intelligence Services, particularly the Polish and Russian.

After the arrest of some 100 agents by the Swiss in mid 1943, Canaris issued a general order restricting the activities in Switzerland to these against the Allies. This, no doubt, was prompted by a general desire to make the Swiss less apprehensive and therefore less diligent regarding counter measures. After mid 1944, KdM Switzerland was controlled by *Mil Amt* B, *Gruppe* B IV; but, on the basis of available information, the station as a KdM was certainly no more, and probably less, important than it had been prior to the absorption of the *Abwehr* into the RSHA *Mil Amt.*

4. The Spanish Intelligence Service.
Regardless of what co-operation there may have been between the *Abwehr* under Canaris and the Spanish intelligence service, Steimle states that neither official nor semi-official co-operation between Spanish Intelligence agencies and the *Abwehr* existed. Steimle does indicate, however, that some intelligence was obtained through 'subordinate Spanish military units', but this was found to be of poor quality and not useful. Although the precise accuracy of Steimle's statements in this regard, may be open to some question, it would seem safe to conclude that following the downfall of Canaris and the advent of the RSHA *Mil Amt*, nothing useful was gained by the latter from Spanish official intelligence sources.

5. Agents of RSHA *Mil Amt* B.
The few agents employed directly by *Mil Amt* B were inherited from the old *Abwehr*. Of these, the most important, as previously indicated, was Paul Fidrmuc (alias 'Ostro') who was controlled directly by RSHA *Mil Amt* B, *Gruppe* B III. The network under Fidrmuc was considered by Steimle to have been especially successful in England, although this source was occasionally under the suspicion of being Allied controlled. However, the genuineness of this source, which quite rightly should have been doubted, was highly thought of—according to Steimle—by the armed forces. Fidrmuc is now in Allied hands and, presumably, his interrogation report when published will clarify any remaining doubts as to the 'Ostro' net.

III. Conclusion.

RSHA *Mil Amt* B was no more successful in its secret intelligence work in the West than the old *Abwehr*. No new known sources of any significance were developed. The most obvious cause for this failure was, no doubt, the general chaotic situation which began overtaking the Germans at about the same time that the 'revitalised German Intelligence Service' came into being. Steimle rather obviously was more interested in *Gruppe* VI B and, therefore, stands in considerable contrast to Ohletz, *Abteilungschef* RSHA *Mil Amt* C, who, in varying degrees, not only succeeded in combatting SS encroachment but served as a stabilising force for the *Abwehr* remnants concerned with the East. From his interrogation report, it is rather clear that Steimle had only a very general picture of RSHA *Mil Amt* B and would have required much more time and knowledge before much of significance could have been accomplished under his leadership.

IV. Known Personnel of RSHA *Mil Amt* B.

(Those now under arrest are underlined.)

<u>Steimle</u>, SS-*Staf* Eugen	*Abteilungschef*
von Taysen, Major i.G.	Deputy *Abteilungschef*
Amsink, Major	
Apitsch, *Hauptmann*	*Gruppe* B II
Bohlen, Major	*Gruppe* B II
von Bohlen, *Oberstltn.*	*Gruppe* B III
Bohny, *Korv.Kapt.*	
von Borstel, Jäga	assistant to Amsink
Carnap, *Oberltn.*	*Gruppe* B III
von Dewitz, *Oberstltn.*	
Diemke, *Oberltn.*	*Gruppe* B IV
Flenten, *Hauptmann*	*Gruppe* B I
Hohmann, *Oberltn.*	*Gruppe* B IV
Humpert, *Korv.Kapt.*	*Gruppe* B II
von Keller, *Korv.Kapt.*	*Gruppe* B III
Kempf, *Hauptmann*	*Gruppe* B I
Köcher, *Ltn*	
von Kriess, *Hauptmann Freiherr*	
<u>Kuhnke,</u> *Oberltn.*	
<u>Kurrer</u>, *Hauptmann*	
von Lossow, *Hauptmann*	Gruppe B I
Meyer-Burkhard,	
Plötz, *Oberltn.*	*Gruppe* B III
Pohlmann, *Ltn*	*Gruppe* B III
<u>von Redl</u>, *Korv.Kapt.*	*Gruppe* B III
Richter,	*Gruppe* B III
Rotmann,	*Gruppe* B III
Schlovin, *Lt.z.See*	
Schmidt, *Oberltn.*	
von Schwerin, Major Graf	
Truxa, *Hauptmann*	*Gruppe* B II
von Vleuten,	*Gruppe* B I
Wagandt, *Hauptmann*	
Werner, *Kapt.Ltn.*	

Wiedemann, *Sonderführer*
Weiss, *Sonderführer*
Wimmer-Lamquet, *Ltn.* Franz
Winkler, *Ltn.*   *Gruppe* B IV
Zibis, Major

V. Main Sources of Information.

SS-*Staf* Eugen Steimle
Major von Taysen
Oberltn. Kuhnke
Hauptmann Kurrer

This report was issued by W.R.C.1./A. on 26 March 1946.

Note: The National Archives, Kew, KV 3/193, Situation Report No. 26, RSHA *Mil Amt* B.

21

Situation Report No. 29: RSHA *Mil Amt* C

I. History & Organization.

1. Introduction.

The story of the re-organisation of the German Intelligence Services in 1944 has been covered in other War Room publications, in particular in Liquidation Report No. 26 on the RSHA *Mil Amt* headquarters, where the role of *Mil Amt Abteilung* C in the general secret intelligence field is explained...

2. Operational Area.

RSHA *Mil Amt* C was formed in August 1944 with the main function of collecting secret military intelligence from the East, and was thus a parallel organisation to *Mil Amt* B which had the duty of collecting similar information from the West. Geographically, *Mil Amt* C's area of operations included theoretically all countries East of a line drawn from the Skagerrak to the Gulf of Venice, that is Norway, Sweden, Finland, Russia, the Balkans, the Near and Middle East and the Far East; but its primary aim was to obtain military information on Russia, using the other countries as intelligence bases. The collection of information on Allied intentions and strengths in the Eastern Mediterranean was a secondary, although important task. The work of *Mil Amt* C was thus identical with that of *Abt* I *Ost* of the *Abwehr*.

3. RSHA *Mil Amt* C and RSHA *Amt* VI.

The fact that from July/August 1944 onwards the *Abwehr*, at least in part, was integrated into RSHA *Amt* VI, did not entail much change for the *Abwehr* I officers working in the various *Aussenstellen* and *Kriegsorganistions* (KdMs) under *Mil Amt* C; the change was for them, in the main, one of name only. Centrally, however, there was an almost complete change of personnel, the more important *Abwehr* officers having been implicated in the Generals' *Putsch* of 20 July 1944. *Oberstltn.*

Ohletz was appointed *Abteilungschef* of *Mil Amt* C in August 1944, and held that post until the end. He was a regular *Luftwaffe* officer who had been connected with the *Abwehr* only since the beginning of 1944, and had been imprisoned for a short while on the charge of implication in the July 1944 plot. His second-in-command, Major Elting, on the other hand, was an experienced *Abwehr* officer. Thus *Mil Amt* C in contrast to *Mil Amt* B, managed to escape from complete domination at the hands of RSHA *Amt* VI.

4. Organisation.

The internal organisation of RSHA *Mil Amt* C was similar to that of *Mil Amt* B, being divided into two main sections (*Unterabteilungen*):

> *Sichtung*, or evaluation, and
> *Beschaffung*, or gathering of intelligence.

There was also a small administrative section, the *Zentralgruppe*.

a) *Unterabteilung Sichtung*, which concentrated on the evaluation of reports, was further subdivided functionally into service departments, namely –

Mil C/Si	(*Heer*)
Mil C/Si	(*Luft*)
Mil C/Si	(Marine)

The head of each subdivision maintained liaison either direct with the corresponding service Ic officer or with the service Ic office through the intermediary of the special liaison officers created by Schellenberg (the Ia officers *Heer*, *Luft* and Marine) to stimulate the interest and co-operation of the service chiefs in RSHA *Mil Amt* matters. The latter was the official channel but, in practice, the former was more usual. The *Sichtung* officers passed on to *Unterabteilung Beschaffung* (see below) requests for information from the services; they had no connection with the KdMs or with agents.

b) *Unterabteilung Beschaffung*, was responsible for all aspects of the collection of intelligence, including the development of new sources of information and the exploitation forwarded by the *Sichtung* section, passing them downwards to the appropriate KdM or outstation for action. This department worked mainly through the KdMs (the successors of the I *Referaten* of the old KOs and *Aussenstellen*), though it did employ certain agents or groups of agents directly.

Unterabteilug Beschaffung was subdivided geographically into four *Gruppen* –

> *Gruppe* Fernost (FO), covering China, Japan and Manchukuo.
> *Gruppe* Ostsüd (OS), also referred to as *Südost* (SO), covering the Balkans and Middle East.

Gruppe Russland (R), covering Russia.
Gruppe Skandinavien (SK), covering Sweden and Finland.

(Note: These geographic divisions appear to have been altered from time to time. Ohletz, for example, refers to *Südost* for the Balkans, Nahost for Turkey and the Middle East, Fernost for the Far East, and *Ost* covering Scandinavia and all countries bordering Russia. It is believed, however, that the four sections as described above constituted the final grouping.)

These four *Gruppen* in turn directed the work of the KdMs. There was here a much closer contact between *Mil Amt* C and the KdMs than had existed in the *Abwehr* between *Abteilung* I and the *Aussenstellen* and KOs, although the KdMs still retained much latitude in the execution of their tasks. Each *Gruppe* was responsible for direction as follows:

FO (Far East)	:	KdM (or KO) China.
SO or OS (South East)	:	KdM Vienna and KdM Turkey, i.e. KONO (KO Nahost).
R (Russia)	:	KdMs Breslau, Berlin and Prague.
SK (Scandinavia)	:	KdM Stettin, KdM (or KO) Sweden, KO Finland (later *Sonderkommando Nord*).

5. Important RSHA *Mil Amt* C officers.

The more important officers of RSHA *Mil Amt* C were as follows:

Abteilungschef	:	*Oberstltn.* Ohletz
Deputy *Abteilungschef*	:	Major Elting
Mil C/Z (*Zentralgruppe*)	:	*Hauptmann* Clemens
		Ltn. Becker

Unterabteilung Sichtung (Mil Amt C/Si)

Leiter	:	*Korv.Kapt.* von Crassmann (1944)
		Major Bechtle (1945)
Mil C/Si (*Heer*)	:	*Hauptmann* Bliedung
Mil C/Si (Marine)	:	*Korv.Kapt.* von Grassmann (1944)
		Oberltn.z.See Seeburg (1944–1945)
Mil C/Si (*Luft*)	:	*Regierungsrat* Dr Ungeheuer

Unterabteilung Beschaffung (Mil Amt C/Be)

Leiter	:	*Korv.Kapt.* Paulus
Deputy *Leiter*	:	Major Bechtle (1944)
Mil C/SK (Scandinavia)	:	Major Paulus

		Oberltn. Bürklin
		Oberltn. Johann Walter Berg
Mil C/SO (Balkans, ME)	:	*Korv.Kapt.* von Herz
		Major Bechtle (1944)
		Ltn. Ulshofer (Middle East)
		Hauptmann Merkel
		Ltn.z.See Schäfer (Iran)
Mil C/R (Russia)	:	*Hauptmann* von Lossow
		Hauptmann Walther
Mil C/FO (Far East)	:	*Hauptmann* Flage

6. Locations and final disintegration.

From August 1944 until January 1945, RSHA *Mil Amt* C was at Waldburg camp, 40 miles/64 kms east of Berlin. In January 1945 part of *Mil Amt* C, including the W/T section, moved to Belzig, near Berlin, using the cover-name of 'Husar'. The large part, originally intended for Thuringia, moved eventually south to quarters in a villa in the Chiemsee, southern Bavaria. In April 1945 the section near Berlin moved to Seebruck. By then, however, Ohletz had, on his own initiative, disbanded what remained of RSHA *Mil Amt* C, as he was afraid that RSHA *Amt* IV [*Gestapo*] had designs on his department.

In fact, Ohletz resisted the approaches of RSHA *Amt* VI officers, who were suggesting that the German Intelligence Services should, after military collapse, carry on 'illegal' activities. Ohletz' view on this matter is expressed in his observation in March 1945 to Sandberger, namely, 'that he (Ohletz) was not cut out to run around in the mountains wearing a false beard'. Ohletz did, however, agree in April 1945 to hand over *Mil Amt* C to Major Meissner, friendly with RSHA *Amt* IV, knowing full well that *Mil Amt* C as such, was already non-existent. Ohletz' only plans had been dependent upon the continued existence and functioning of the German Armies either alone or in conjunction with the Allies against Russia.

II. Sources of Information.

1. In general.

The major part of RSHA *Mil Amt* C's secret intelligence came from the subordinate formations, the KdMs inside German territory and the KdMs (formerly the KOs) in neutral or friendly countries. These stations were, for the most part, still staffed by *Abwehr* officers, although many of the *Leiters* were newly appointed; in general, the staffs had been reduced for the sake both of efficiency and security. Apart from the KdMs, there was in the Balkans a somewhat exceptional intelligence team, inherited from the *Abwehr*, whose principals were Richard Klauder (alias 'Klatt') and Ira Land (alias 'Longin'); known respectively as *Luftmeldekopf Südost* and *Gruppe* Lang, these agents were controlled directly by RSHA *Mil Amt* C with the help of KdM Vienna. See also para 3(d) below, concerning the agent *Ltn. Dr. Kraemer*. A further rather doubtful source of information was the Japanese intelligence service in Europe, and collaboration with the Hungarian intelligence service was of some value.

2. The KdMs.
The situation regarding the KdMs inside Germany and Austria are as follows:

a) <u>KdM Berlin</u>, under *Oberst* Stolze was controlled nominally by RSHA *Mil Amt* C/R. The KdM's chief function was the cultivation of high-level contacts in Berlin, but as most foreign diplomats had left the much-bombed capital, nothing of value to *Mil Amt* C came from this quarters.

b) <u>KdM Breslau</u>, under *Oberst* Wieser and later *Oberstltn.* Horaczek, worked under RSHA *Mil Amt* C/R, but produced no information of significance and had to withdraw in haste before schemes for a post-occupational network in its area had passed the planning stage.

c) <u>KdM Prague</u>, controlled by RSHA *Mil Amt* C/R, was exceptional in that it was commanded not by a *Wehrmacht* officer but by the BdS Protectorate, SS-*Staf* Dr Erwin Weinmann. This station was rather more active than KdM Berlin or Breslau, having one interesting agent, Wollmann (alias 'Herold'), who, using a source in Sweden, produced much information on Russia; but as he was suspected of being controlled, he was dismissed in autumn 1944. KdM Prague also attempted, on *Mil Amt* C's instructions, to establish a stay-behind network which was known as the Beachcomber Net, and had the ingenious intention of recruiting Czech agents in such a way that they were to believe that they were working against the Russians for the benefit of the English. The Beachcomber Net was not ready in time.

d) <u>KdM Stettin</u>, was less affected by the creation of the *Mil Amt* than any other KdM in the eastern half of Germany, continuing unaltered its former I.M. work. An *Aussenstelle* in Copenhagen had, as its principal task, the maintaining of liaison with KdM Sweden, but this broke down when it was most needed. KdM Stettin was controlled by RSHA *Mil Amt* C/SK.

e) <u>KdM Vienna</u>, was the most important of the KdMs, supplying *Amt Mil* C/SO with the bulk of its information. *Korv.Kapt.* von Herz, head of *Mil Amt* C/Beschaffung, spent three months in Vienna correlating or liquidating the mass of intelligence units that had concentrated there, following the German withdrawal from the Balkans (remnants of *Aussenstelle* Bucharest, KdM Hungary, KO Bulgaria, etc.). Vienna was the control station for W/T agents long established by the *Abwehr* in the Middle East, and also helped in the management of Kauder (alias 'Klatt'). But, conditions were too chaotic for such a top-heavy intelligence machine to function smoothly. Results were on the whole poor. The post-occupational schemes were all failures.

3. The KdMs in neutral or friendly areas (formerly KOs—*Kriegsorganisationen*)
The situation regarding the KdMs outside Germany and Austria was as follows:

a) <u>KdM (or KO) China.</u> In June 1940, *Korv.Kapt.* Werner Schuler went to China on behalf of *Amt.Ausland/Abwehr* I.M. to investigate the possibility of establishing a shipping intelligence service there. After Schuler's arrival in Shanghai, he was joined in September 1940 by one Siefken (alias 'Smith') and one Remicke (alias 'Richter'), and a *Dienststelle* was established in the German Consulate. During the early phases of their work Schuler, according to Berlin instructions, was not to work against Russia or Japan. Thus, most of the work of the *Dienststelle* was limited to reporting on shipping, as previously planned. Initially, communication with Berlin was via the W/T facilities of an Italian depot ship '*Lepanto*' and Rome; but later Remicke established communications with Berlin via the German Embassy in Peiping [Beijing].

Early in 1941 Siefken was replaced by Major Eisentrager, an *Abt* I Wi officer previously at KO Bulgaria, under whose command the *Dienststelle* became known as KO China. The reporting of economic intelligence particularly against Russia, became at that time a principal function although, according to Schuler KO China was subordinate to *Referat* IM/FC. Subordination to *Referat* IM/FO, *Kapt.z.See* Gartmann, Berlin, reputedly continued until mid 1944.

Reports indicate that KO China, at least by 1943, had outstations in Canton, Peiping and Harbin (Manchukuo), and that in 1944 permission was granted for the establishment of a W/T intercept station in Shanghai. There may have been a station in Nanking, also, as Ohletz indicates that Eisentrager was succeeded, at least since August 1944 by Major Schmalschlager who, in fact, may have moved the Shanghai office to Nanking.

The principal source of KdM China (which was taken over en bloc from the old *Abwehr* and controlled by *Mil Amt* C/FO) was Wolfgang Schenke (alias 'Borodin' and 'Boris'), ex-correspondent of the *Völkischer Beobachter*, who produced little of interest on China or Japan but some useful information on Russia.

German intelligence work in China and environs was complicated by the dissimilarity of German/Japanese interests. Until the very end, Russia and Japan were not at war, and, for example, the Japanese vigorously opposed KdM work in Harbin and, in fact, arrested in early 1943 one Ivor Lissner in Hainking (Manchuria) who was reporting against Russia, allegedly with success. At least much of the information reported by the KdM was obtained from the Japanese.

Last-minute plans for a revised *Mil Amt* organisation in China, namely a new KdM at Nanking headed by *Oberst* Schubert, fell through for lack of time.

b) <u>KO Finland and *Sonderkommando Nord.*</u> Finland had always been a useful base for information on Russia. The so-called KO Finland was in reality little more than the development of *Freg.Kapt.* Cellarius' excellent personal relations with Finnish military and political circles; he made use, too, of Esthonian contacts. There was no agent network in Finland; instead, information was liberally exchanged between the Finnish General Staff and Cellarius. When KO Finland was disbanded on 2 September 1944 on the German evacuation of Finland, Cellarius was much criticised for having not organised an agent network. However, in spite of this criticism and of Cellarius' long friendship with Canaris, on his return to Germany. Cellarius was in late September 1944 given the task by *Oberstltn.* Ohletz of re-establishing contact with his Finnish informers. The new organisation under RSHA *Mil Amt* C/SK was small, consisting of Ltn. Rolf Horn and some non-commissioned officers, and was given the name of *Sonderkommando Nord.*

A number of Finnish seamen from internment camps were trained in W/T work and the use of secret inks, but could not be established in time. Contact with Finnish circles was re-established as the result of a visit by *Ltn.* Horn to Sweden, when it was arranged that the Japanese Military *Attache*, Makate Onadera, should forward information from certain Finnish officers to Berlin. In February 1945, Cellarius and Alarich Brohs of RSHA *Gruppe* VI D, pooled their resources and went by submarine to the Finnish coast to re-establish Finnish contact. The Finnish Colonel Fabritius (alias 'Dr Jonas') was brought back to Germany, and later returned by parachute to Finland. Given more time the efforts of Cellarius would probably have ended successfully.

c) KO Nahosten (KONO). (Also referred to as KO or KdM Turkey.) The appointment of *Kapt.z.See* Erich Pfeiffer, one of the more experienced and successful *Abwehr* officers, as Leiter of KONO was made by *Oberst* Hansen in the last days of the *Abwehr.* With the creation of the RSHA *Mil Amt*, KONO was controlled by RSHA *Mil Amt* C/SO, and had as its task the collection of military intelligence from Syria, Iraq, Palestine, Egypt and Iran. The internment of German nationals in September 1944, together with the defection of one of the organisers of the post-occupational network in Turkey, prevented any useful work in this area under the *Mil Amt.*

d) KdM (or KO) Sweden, under *Oberst* Dr Hans Wagner until his expulsion from Sweden early in 1945, is important mainly because of the agent in Stockholm, *Ltn* Dr Karl Heinz Kraemer, who reported principally on statistics concerning the air forces in England. Kraemer, an agent inherited by *Mil Amt* C from the old *Abwehr*, towards the end was supervised, theoretically, by Major Wenzlau, a *Mil Amt* C representative in Stockholm who worked independently of the KdM except for purposes of pay, etc. Since, however, most of Kraemer's information concerned the Western Front, it was passed by *Mil Amt* C to *Mil Amt* B. Some information, probably from Japanese and Finnish sources, was also reported by Kraemer. Both Wenzlau and later Major Paulus, head of *Mil Amt* C/SK, attempted to increase the intellience out-put from Sweden, but neither met with any material success.

Opinions on Kraemer's reports, according to Ohletz, were very divergent, varying from 'invaluable' to 'obvious controlled material'. Major Friedrich Busch, who had been succeeded by Wenzlau, openly doubted Kraemer's *bona-fides*; for this reason, in fact Buch was recalled, as his attitude was considered to be only 'playing into the hand of the SD, who were on the look-out for sticks with which to beat the *Mil Amt*.' Significant is the fact that, according to Ohletz, Wenzlau too, failed to control Kraemer. Significant also is the fact that Ohletz' hatred of the SD was greater than his desire for an honest agent.

4. The Japanese Intelligence Service.

Co-operation with the Japanese Intelligence Service in Europe had been very loose under Canaris and remained unsatisfactory during the time of RSHA *Mil Amt C*'s existence. In spite of a dinner in December 1944, where Kaltenbrunner, Schellenberg and Ohletz were present, together with leading Japanese, closer collaboration did not result. There was a meagre exchange of intelligence, but it is claimed that the Japanese never fulfilled their side of the bargain. On the other hand, it has been claimed that a report by Kraemer from Sweden forwarned the Japanese about the Leyte battle. General Onadera in Stockholm was the head of the Japanese Intelligence Services in Europe, while a Japanese journalist, Enometo, was an important agent. In the early months of 1945, the Japanese offered the Germans facilities at their Embassies for installing W/T stations and for arranging meeting points for agents; but this offer was refused by Schellenberg, RSHA *Amtschef* VI/ *Mil Amt*.

While information to hand is, as yet, vague and unsatisfactory, the German intelligence efforts in the Far East, such as they were, seem to have been at Japanese sufferance. In the field of air intelligence at least, *General Ltn.* von Gronau, Air *Attache* to Tokyo admittedly failed. In the fact the Ic LW [*Luftwaffe*] Tuburungstat observed that subsequent to the entry of Japan into the war, the shortage of information from the Far East was even more acute. *Oberstltn.* Kleyenstüber of *Abwehr* I LW had suggested in 1943 that he be sent to Japan as *Abwehr* representative to open a KO Japan. This plan was speedily rejected, as the difficulty of such an undertaking was rightly recognized. The Japanese had requested the replacement of von Gronau. Thus, in 1944, plans were made for an intelligence mission to Japan headed by General Kessler; but, as departure from Germany was delayed until April 1945, the plan was never executed.

5. Hungarian Intelligence Service.

Ohletz maintained direct contact with certain officers of the Hungarian General Staff. *Oberst* von Kohoutek was *Mil Amt* C's liaison officer with Hungarian intelligence agencies; and arrangements were made for certain *Mil Amt* C agents who had been threatened with arrest by the *Gestapo* to be taken over by the Hungarians. While further details are sketchy and uncertain, exchanges of information between German intelligence services and the Hungarians are not believed to have been of more than local value.

6. Agents of RSHA *Mil Amt* D.

The few agents employed directly by RSHA *Mil Amt* C were inherited from the old *Abwehr*. Of these the most important were Ira Lang (alias 'Longin') and Richard Kauder (alias 'Klatt'); the reports of both these agents on Russian military activities were considered very valuable by the OKW. Lang was a former Czarist Guards officer with his own W/T at Bratislava and was believed to have a source in the Russian General Staff. Four or five reports were received from him daily.

Richard Kauder (alias 'Klatt') was a Jew who had reported from Sofia and had been forced to move to Budapest in the summer of 1944. He furnished reports on the Russian Army and Air Force, the former of which were considered excellent. However, RSHA *Gruppe* VI Z discovered that almost his sole source was Ira Lang; but this case still remains somewhat of a mystery, pending further investigation.

III. Conclusion.

RSHA *Mil Amt* C was no more successful in its secret intelligence work in the eastern half of Europe than the old *Abwehr*. The causes of this failure were many. The most obvious perhaps was the constant rivalry of the SD, which Ohletz succeeded in combatting, in so far as he was able to resist the infiltration of SS officers into the more important posts of *Mil Amt* C; he was fortunate in remaining on good terms with Schellenberg. Another reason for failure was doubtless the retention of too many officers at the KdMs, whose outlook was still that of the old *Abwehr* days. Shortage of W/T equipment, shortage of time to organise post-occupational networks were contributory factors. But perhaps more serious was the tendency of nearly all German Intelligence Service officers to believe implicitly in the genuineness of the few agents who had been long established, their lack of critical analysis of reports received and their unwillingness to entertain the notion that their agents might be under Allied control. Even when, as in the case of Kauder (alias 'Klatt') and Kraemer, there were, and rightly so, serious doubts as to their reliability, and it was found difficult to cut a loss on the spot.[1]

IV. Known Personnel of RSHA *Mil* Amt C.

(Note: personnel known to be under post-war arrest are underlined.)

Bechtle, Major:	Deputy *Leiter, Mil Amt* C/*Unterabteilung Beschaffung*, and of *Mil Amt* C/SO, 1944. *Leiter, Mil Amt* C/*Unterabt. Sichtung*, 1945
Becker, *Ltn.d.Luft.*:	*Mil Amt* C/Z, *Zentralgruppe* (Admin.)
Berg, *Oberltn.* Johann Walter:	*Mil Amt* C/SK.
Bliedung, *Hauptmann*:	*Mil Amt* C/*Sichtung* (Heer)
Brennscheidt, *Feldwebel*:	*Mil Amt* C/FO.

Bürklin, *Oberltn.*:	*Mil Amt* C/SK.
Clemens, *Hauptmann*:	*Mil Amt* C/Z, *Zentrale Gruppe* (Admin.)
Elting, Major:	Deputy *Abteilungschef*
von Grassmann, *Korv.Kapt.*:	*Mil Amt* C/*Sichtung*, 1944. *Unterabteilungs-chef* and Si/Marine
von Herz, *Korv.Kapt.* Alfred:	*Leiter, Mil Amt* C/*Beschaffung* and of *Mil Amt* C/SO, with temporary posting to KdM Vienna, Oct 1944–Jan 1945; also *Leiter*, KdM Stettin, April 1945.
Höstermann, *Hauptmann*:	*Mil Amt* C/Z.
Hossbach, *Oberltn.*:	*Mil Amt* C/*Sichtung* (*Heer*).
Herr, *Oberkriegsverwaltungsrat*:	*Mil Amt* C/SO.
Kühne, *Oberltn.*:	*Mil Amt* C/R or C/FO.
von Lossow, *Hauptmann*:	*Mil Amt* C/R.
Lüdtke, *Hauptmann*:	*Mil Amt* C/*Sichtung* (*Luft*).
Meissner, Major:	April 1945, appointed to succeed *Oberstltn.* Ohletz as *Abteilungschef*, but *Mil Amt* C had by then been dissolved.
Merkel, *Hauptmann*:	*Mil Amt* C/*Sichtung*, perhaps earlier C/SO.
Ohletz, *Oberstltn.* Werner:	*Abteilungschef*, RSHA *Mil Amt* C.
Paulus, Major:	*Mil Amt* C/SK.
Plage, *Hauptmann*:	*Mil Amt* C/FO.
von Redl, Korv.Kapt.:	*Mil Amt* C/*Sichtung* (Marine).
Rieckhoff, *Freg.Kapt.*:	*Mil Amt* C/*Aussenstelle* Danzig until Jan 1945; then liaison officer to Vlassov.
Schäfer, *Ltn.z.See*:	*Mil Amt* C/SO.
Seeberg, *Oberltn.z.See*:	*Mil Amt* C/*Sichtung* (Marine).
von Stahl, *Ltn*:	*Mil Amt* C/*Sichtung* (Marine), 1944.
Stark, Major:	*Mil Amt* C, *Leiter der Kurierstelle*.
Tiemann, *Ltn* Dr:	*Mil Amt* C/Z.
Ulshofer, *Ltn.*:	*Mil Amt* C/SO (or OS).
Ungeheuer, *Regierungsrat*:	*Mil Amt* C/*Sichtung* (*Luft*); met. specialist.
Vossköhler, *Lorv.Kapt.*:	*Mil Amt* C. (?)
Walther, *Hauptmann*:	*Mil Amt* C/R.
Wehner, *Kapt.*:	*Mil Amt* C/*Sichtung* (Marine).
Wenzlau, Major Heinrich:	*Mil Amt* C/(?), Aug–Sept 1944; sent to Sweden, Sept 1944.

V. Main Sources.

Oberstltn. Werner Ohletz	*Abteilungschef, Mil Amt* C
Korv.Kapt. Alfred von Herz	*Leiter, Mil Amt* C, *Beschaffung*

Korv.Kapt. Werner Schuler   *Abwehr*, I M.
Oberst Schubert   *Luftwaffe* Diplomatic *Korps*.

This report was issued by W.R.C.1/A on 12 March 1946.

Notes

* The National Archives, Kew, KV 3/195: Situation Report No. 29, RSHA *Mil Amt* C.
1 The intelligence sources of Kraemer and Klauder/Klatt were investigated by Britain's security service, MI 5, after the war. Kraemer provided plausible intelligence being 'recycled information or simply fabricated' (see his MI 5 name files at The National Archives, Kew, KV 2/144 to 157). Kauder/Klatt intelligence information was similarly investigated by MI 5 and believed to be mostly Russian deception material. See The National Archives, Kew, KV 2/1495 to 1499. More recently, a huge volume has appeared examining the Klatt intelligence from newly declassified British, American, Swiss and former Soviet sources; Dr Winfried Meyer, *Klatt. Hitlers jüdischer Meisteragent gegen Stalin: Überlebenskunst in Holocaust und Geheimdienstkrieg*, Metropol Verlag, Berlin, 2015 (1287 pages).

22

Liquidation Report No. 30: RSHA *Mil Amt* D

A. Commanding Officers.

Major Naumann (alias Neubert), until July 1944.
SS-*Ostubaf* Otto Skorzeny, from July 1944.

B. History.

Formation: *Mil Amt* D of the RSHA was formed out of *Abwehr Abteilung* II when the RSHA took over control of the *Abwehr* in mid 1944.

Location: *Mil Amt* D originally had its headquarters in the Tirpitzufer, Berlin. Part of it later moved to Lager Zossen but by July 1944 the whole organisation, using cover name 'Belinde', was located at Baruth.

Duties: *Mil Amt* D was responsible for the direction and control of all operations in sabotage and subversion carried out by various *Leitstellen*, FAKs and FATs under its control. At the end of 1944 these last units were also subordinated to the newly formed RSHA *Mil Amt* F and as a result of this dual control, *Mil Amt* D received very little information on the activities of the FAKs and FATs and for the most part concentrated on the organisation of larger scale operations than those carried out by *Mil Amt* F, which was chiefly engaged in the supervision of operations to be carried out directly behind the front lines. Usually general directives only were issued by *Mil Amt* D to FAKs and FATs via the *Leitstellen*, local commanders being permitted to carry out instructions as they thought best, but in cases of large-scale operations involving greater difficulties, large sums of money or with possible political implications, more detailed plans were drawn up by *Mil Amt* D and forwarded to *Leitstellen*. In addition to these duties, *Mil Amt* D held records of all sabotage dumps laid by FATs.

Changes in control after the plot against Hitler (20 July 1944): In July 1944, after the unsuccessful plot against Hitler in which a number of *Abwehr* II officials were involved, *Mil Amt D* was taken over by SS-*Ostubaf* Otto Skorzeny, RSHA *Gruppenleiter* VI S, with Major Naumann, the previous *Leiter*, as his deputy. Officers of the SS were gradually appointed to posts formerly filled by members of *Abwehr Abt* II and to some extent the activities of the organisation were reduced, work that would normally have been carried out by *Mil Amt* D being taken over by Skorzeny's newly created SS-*Jagdverbände*. In particular the SS-*Jagdverbände* became responsible for the entire control of European Resistance Movements and carried out all operations behind the Russian lines, the activities of the FAKs in the East being confined to territory nearer Germany.

Movements after October 1944: In October 1944 *Mil Amt D* moved to Birkenwerder so that Skorzeny, from his headquarters at Friedenthal, could maintain better control of the organisation. In February 1945 the unit, then using *Feldpostnummer* 59994 and cover name 'Dorett', moved once again, this time to Bad Elster-Adorf, where it remained until April 1945 when it was located for a short time before its dissolution at Reith im Winkel in Upper Bavaria.

Sub-divisions of *Mil Amt* D: To carry out the duties referred to above, *Mil Amt* D was sub-divided as follows:

(1) *Gruppe Verwaltung* (Administration): Under Major Eisenberg and divided into the following sections:

IIa	-	under *Hauptmann* Zierlake, in charge of officer personnel.
IIb	-	under *Hauptmann* Bittner, in charge of NCOs and OR personnel
IIc	-	under *Oberltn.* Boldt, in charge of social decorations.
IIe	-	under *Oberltn.* Neumann, in charge of Administration.
IVa	-	under *Stabsintendent* Thodt, in charge of finances, expenses.
IVb	-	under *Oberzahlmeister* Scherfling, in charge of pay, salaries.

In addition, a Camp Commandant under Major Menger and a Registry under Zander were maintained.

(2) *Gruppe Technik (Mil D/T):* Under Major Ehrmann, formerly under *Oberstltn.* Mauritius. Situated near Brandenburg/Havel, this *Gruppe* was responsible for the preparation and collection of sabotage equipment and its supply to FAKs and FATs. For research in explosives etc. the *Gruppe* established the Tegel Laboratories under Dr Günther. *Gruppe Technik*'s main divisions were:

Referat Verwaltung. Administration.

Referat Fertigung. In charge of development and manufacture of explosives, etc.

Referat Waffen und Geräte. In charge of weapons, sabotage material.

The *Gruppe* took over from *Abt* II/T the Quenz sabotage school.

(3) *Referat AP (Auswertung und Planung):* Under Hauptmann Kniesche. In charge of sifting of information and planning of operations.

(4) *Referat Luft:* Under *Ltn.* Paulus. Liaison with the *Luftwaffe* and carrying out of missions when aircraft were used.

(5) *Verbindungsorganisation (VO) Berlin:* Under Major Erfling. Liaison with other sections of the *Mil Amt* in Berlin. Liaison was also maintained with the SS-*Jagdverbände* and an offshoot of this *Gruppe*, known as VO T Berlin, maintained liaison between *Gruppe Technik* and Berlin.

(6) *Referat Ost:* Under *Oberltn.* Gotthard Gambke, formerly under *Oberstltn.* Ernst zur Eikern. On the formation of *Mil Amt* D, *Referat Ost* took over the duties of the former *Gruppe Ost* of *Abteilung* II, which had had been responsible for the organisation of sabotage activities in Russia, Finland and the Baltic States. It was also in administrative control of *Leitstelle* II *Ost* and its subordinate FAKs and FATs. Its main divisions were:

Ost Verwaltung	-	Internal administration.
Ost K	-	Custody of all reports from FAKs and FATs; collecting and editing of information on the morale of the population in Russia territories, rate of Russian production, etc., sifting of information received from FAKs and FATs for forwarding to interested sections of the *Mil Amt*.
Ost F	-	Matters concerning missions, if volunteers of non-German nationality were employed.
Ost J	-	Matters concerning the insurrection of nations against enemy-occupying forces; study of political problems; organisation of partisan movements.

Referat Ost maintained the training establishments *Sonderlager Luckenwalde*, *Forstschutzkommando Bergwacht* and *Arbeitsvermittlung Kirchhain*.

(7) *Referat Süd-Ost:* Cover name 'Coran'. Under *Oberltn.* Dr Murad Ferid (alias 'Ferst'), formerly under *Ltn.* Niklasch. Responsible for the organisation of sabotage activities in the Balkans and Near Eastern countries and in administrative control of *Leitstelle* II *Süd-Ost* and its subordinate FAKs and FATs. Its principal duties were the collection of information received from FAKs and FATs via the *Leitstelle* and the supply to the *Leitstelle* in Vienna of necessary supplies from Berlin. Its main divisions were:

Süd-Ost Verwaltung. Administration.
Süd-Ost/Süd.
Süd-Ost/Nord.
*Süd-Ost/*MO (Middle East)
*Süd-Ost/*OR (Orient).

(8) <u>*Referat West*</u>: Under *Hauptmann* Schöneich, formerly under Major Astor. Responsible for the organisation of sabotage activities in Scandinavia, England, France and North America. In administrative control of *Leitstelle* II *West* and its subordinate FAKs and FATs. Its main divisions were:

> *West/Verwaltung.* Administration.
> *West/Nord.*
> *West/Nordwest.*
> *West/Süd.*
> *West/Südwest.*

(9) <u>*Referat Süd-West*</u>: Under *Hauptmann* Lormis. Responsible for the organisation of sabotage activities in South America, Africa, Italy and the Iberian Peninsula.

W/T Links: *Mil Amt* D maintained its own W/T station, cover name 'Tundra', through which contact was established with those parts of *Mil Amt* D which were not all in the same place. It was also in touch with its *Leitstellen* through the main *Mil Amt* radio station in Berlin.

C. Subordinate Formations.

> *Leitstelle* II *Ost.*
> *Leitstelle* II *Süd-Ost.*
> *Leitstelle West.*
> *Leitstelle Süd.* Dissolved in 1945, when FAK 211 took over its duties.

D. Special Establishments.

Sonderlager Luckenwalde: Founded in 1941 about 32 miles (50 kms) south of Berlin by *Gruppe Ost* of *Abwehr Abteilung* II to train Russian POWs to operate as sabotage agents behind the Russian lines. During the winter of 1943/44 a printing shop was set up at the Lager for the production of propaganda leaflets in Russian and short courses were given in the handling of small printing presses. The camp, under *Hauptmann* Küper, was later taken over by *Referat Ost* of *Mil Amt* D as a training centre for Russian, Baltic and Eastern German personnel who were subsequently to join *Abt* II Trupps on the Eastern Front. The Lager is known to have given detailed training to selected groups of agents who were later sent on '*Unternehmen*' organised by *Mil Amt* D. It was also used as a centre for the preparation of sabotage equipment used in '*Unternehmen* H' of FAK 212. Early in 1945 the unit, with the exception of the administrative personnel, moved to Bad Liebenstein (Thuringia). A short time later the administrative personnel were evacuated to Bad Elster (south, towards the Bavarian/Czech border).

Forstschutzkommando Bergwacht (or Camp Sol): Founded in the spring of 1944 *Gruppe Ost*, the camp, under *Ltn*. Otto Breuer (alias Bremer), was located at Sol (or Sohl) in the district of Saybusch, Upper Silesia. Its students were principally of Caucasian and Turkestan origin and were trained for long-range sabotage missions. It was taken over by *Referat Ost* of *Mil Amt* D in 1944 and was administered by KdM Breslau. In January 1945 it was evacuated to Luckenwalde. It was last reported in the Ohrdruf area.

Arbeitsvermittlung Kirchhain: Organised by *Referat Ost* in 1944 when *Mil Amt* D moved to Baruth where no foreign nationals or agents were allowed. Located at Kirchhain it acted as a recruiting centre and transit point for agents who were to carry out special missions. Refugees from the Eastern Front were also housed there with a view to being used later on *Abt.* II work. *Sonderführer Niebuhr* (alias Naufeld) was in charge of the camp which was later evacuated to Leinsfelde in Südharz.

Quenz Sabotage School: Cover names 'Quatsch' and 'Quelle'; *Feldpostnummer* 155553. Situated on the shores of Lake Quenz (Brandenburg), the school was founded in September 1939 as a training camp for *Lehrregiment* Brandenburg z.B.V. 600. Under *Oberstltn*. Mauritius and later Major Poser, it was taken over by *Abt.* II/T and used as a sabotage instruction centre for *Abt* II agents. When *Mil Amt* D was formed from *Abt* II, the Quenz school became subordinate to *Gruppe Technik*.

Lehrregiment Kurfürst: This unit of the Brandenburg Division was originally based in Kamenz and acted as a training and replacement unit for all German Intelligence Services. In 1944, the Regiment under Major Michael Partl, was taken over by *Abt.* II. On the dissolution of *Abt.* II, *Mil Amt* D assumed responsibility for the Regiment, which acted as a general training centre for *Mil Amt* personnel and instructors for some of *Mil Amt* D's special '*Unternehmen*'. Early in 1945 the *Lehrregiment* moved to Ziegenrück in Thuringia and in April 1945 moved again, this time to Fritzens near Innsbruck, Austria, where it disbanded.

Grenadier Regiment 1001, the Märchen Regiment: This Regiment was formed in November 1943 as an administrative, holding and training unit for volunteers of non-German origin, in the service of *Abt.* II. It was originally under *Oberstltn*. Putz and located at Kamenz with the *Lehrregiment Kurfürst*. Early in 1944, it was transferred from *Abt.* II to the *Wehrmacht Führungsstab*, *Abteilungchef* Ic and in the summer of the same year was taken over by *Mil Amt*, probably in close association with *Mil* D. At the same time the Regiment moved to Jicin (Jitschin, Czechoslovakia), and *Oberstltn*. Marwede became its Commanding Officer. Late in 1944 Major Naumann, formerly second in command of *Mil Amt* D, succeeded Marwede as *Leiter* of the Regiment. In February 1945 the Regiment was stationed at Marienbad. Two training camps were maintained by the Regiment, at Baden near Vienna, and in the neighbourhood of Graz, Austria. Trainees chiefly comprised nationals of Eastern European countries who were to operate on the Eastern and South-Eastern fronts. Plans were made for members of the Regiment to operate on the other fronts, but these never materialised.

E. Main Enterprise.

A large number of special '*Unternehmen*' (enterprises, operations) were carried out by *Mil Amt* D and its *Leitstellen*, FAKs and FATs. Operations summarized below are, as far as is known, the most important of those which were organised by *Mil Amt* D. Untertakings carried out by the subordinate formations of *Mil Amt* D are dealt with in Liquidation Reports on the respective units.

Unternehmen Ginster: Organised by *Referat Ost*, the personnel for this operation were recruited from the Azerbaijan tribe, were about ten in number and led by a certain Lermatov. Training, which was completed by August 1944, was carried out at Luckenwalde Camp and the agents were to be dropped by parachute near Baku in the Caucasus. The operation was not carried out owing to the unfavourable military situation.

Unternehmen Kolibri: This operation, carried out in October 1944, was under the direction of *Referat Ost* and *Referat Luft* and consisted of a raiding expedition in the Strya/Stanislau area with the object of contacting Ukrainian partisans and leaders of the Ukrainian revolutionary army and ascertaining from them the possibility of further German soldiers remaining behind the lines. A group of approximately ten Germans were slipped through the lines into Russian territory, where they remained for about a month. This was considered a very successful operation.

Unternehmen Mohr: This operation was controlled by *Referat Ost* in co-operation with FAK 202. A party of Caucasians were trained at Luckenwalde Camp and transferred to *Forstschutzkommando* Bergwacht. Their mission and the result are not known.

Unternehmen Brennessel: This operation, under *Referat Ost*, was formed from part of the unsuccessful undertaking 'Linde', controlled by FAK 202, in which members of a Caucasian tribe were to have parachuted into their own country to foment armed resistance to the Russians. In April 1944, approx. thirteen Caucasians of *Unternehmen* Brennessel were dropped by parachute at Emba on the Caspian Sea with the mission of making contact with rebel bands, fomenting insurrection and committing acts of sabotage. The group was equipped with four W/T sets, but no contact was ever established and the fate of the group is unknown. A second Brennessel II was planned to find out what had happened to the previous undertaking, but this was never put into operation.

Unternehmen Transit: Under *Oberltn.* Ferid of *Referat Süd-Ost*, this operation was planned in 1944 to equip Roumanian National Resistance Group with weapons, etc., and to hide arms and explosives in suitable districts for use in the event of a Soviet occupation of Roumania. The operation was not carried out because of Roumania's sudden secession from the German Alliance.

F. Important Agents.

None reported.

G. Appreciation of Success or Failure.

RSHA *Mil Amt* D's success was hampered to some extent by rival organisations such as *Mil Amt* F and the SS-*Jagdverbände*, both of which took over work which had formerly been carried out by *Mil Amt* D. Priority for supplies of men and material was given to the SS-*Jagdverbände*, this hindering still further *Mil Amt* D's arrangements for carrying out its '*Unternehmen*'. These undertakings were for the most part not very successful, as plans frequently had to be abandoned owing to unfavourable military situations. The Brennessel undertaking, which succeeded in reaching its destination in the Caspian Sea area, failed to establish any W/T contact with *Mil Amt* D and nothing more was heard of its personnel. *Mil Amt* D's schools were very active in carrying out their training duties.

Sources of information:

SS-*Ostubaf* Otto Skorzeny, Commanding Officer, *Mil Amt* D.
Major Dr Werner Eisenberg, Head of *Gruppe Verwaltung*.
Oberltn. Dr Murad Ferid, Head of *Referat Süd-Ost*.
Oberltn. Gotthard Gambke, Head of *Referat Ost*.
Ltn. Dr Hans Raupach, Deputy Head of *Referat Ost*.
Gefreiter Sergius Peters, member of *Referat Ost*.

This report was issued by W.R.C.1/G, 19 January 1946.

Note:

*   The National Archives, Kew, KV 3/118, Liquidation Report No. 30, RSHA *Mil Amt* D.

23

Liquidation Report No. 31: RSHA *Mil Amt* E

A. Introduction.

This paper, as its title indicates, deals primarily with RSHA *Militärisches Amt Abteilung* E. However, and as in other such papers in the *Mil Amt* series, *Amt Mil* E's function as it was previously carried out in the old *Amt Ausland/Abwehr* will be covered herein only to the extent of supplying necessary, available background...

B. Old *Abwehr* Ii.

The old *Abwehr Abteilung* Ii, which may be considered the predecessor of *Mil Amt* E, was the branch of *Amt Ausland/Abwehr* responsible for supplying the other branches of the *Abwehr* with, for the most part, wireless personnel and communications. *Oberstltn.* Rasehorn (alias 'Rasom') was head of *Abwehr* Ii in Berlin.

The two main central W/T stations of the old *Abwehr* Ii were at Stahnsdorf, cover name 'Speer', and at Belzig, cover name 'Burg'. The former, built in about 1938, grew inadeqate with increased radio traffic and was largely displaced by the latter in about 1940. Apart from ordinary routine business traffic, agents' reports also passed through the network controlled by these centres, which were linked with such important *Abwehr* W/T stations as those at Vienna, Sigmaringen, Köln and Hamburg. Belzig was known as OKW *Aussendienststelle* Belzig and its *Feldpostnummer* was 10176. *Hauptmann* Niese was the Commanding Officer.

Abwehr Ii departments at the various *Aussenstellen* supervised the radio activities of these intelligence posts which, in the west at least, drew their equipment, replacement parts, codes and personnel from *Abwehrleitstelle* Frankreich (France); the latter in turn drew its equipment, personnel, etc. from *Abteilung* Ii in Berlin. Only on rare occasions was equipment obtained locally. Some training of W/T personnel was also carried on in the Ii departments of the various *Aussenstellen*.

At the beginning of 1944, when the *Aussenstellen* beyond the German frontier in the west became mobile, their W/T personnel were either assigned to *Leitstellen*, *Abwehrkommandos* or—*trupps*, or transferred to *Abwehr* stations inside Germany. As *Frontaufklärung* units existed on the Eastern Front at an earlier date, Ii responsibilities for the communications of these mobile intelligence units arose at the same period in this area.

A plan had existed even before the war to incorporate all *Abwehr* W/T personnel into a single military unit, but not until 1944 was agreement reached between *Amt Ausland/Abwehr* and the OKW Signal Liaison Department (WNV—*Wehrmachtnachrichtenverbindung*) for the formation of a new signals regiment of this kind. *Nachrichten* Regiment z.b.V. was organised, at least on paper, about April–June 1944 and became 506 *Nachrichten* Regiment in July 1944, though the organisation plan did not receive final approcal until the autumn of 1944. Roughly coinciding, at least in point of time, with this re-organisation of W/T personnel was the general re-organisation of the *Abwehr* into the RSHA *Mil Amt*.

C. Formation of *Mil Amt* E, & Absorption by RSHA VI F.

When the old *Abwehr* was re-organised in about June 1944, *Mil Amt* E was created from the old *Abteilung* Ii. However, after the events of 20 July 1944 and the subordination of the *Mil Amt* to Schellenberg's RSHA *Amt* VI, *Oberstltn*. Boening, *Gruppenleiter* RSHA VI F, became also *Abteilungschef Mil Amt* E and C, the work of these *Abteilungen* corresponding roughly to that of RSHA *Gruppe* VI F. In the meantime, *Oberstltn*. Rasehorn had been replaced by Major Poretschkin (alias 'Potemsky') who, under Boening, became Deputy *Abteilungschef Mil Amt* E.

Briefly, RSHA *Mil Amt* E had the task of maintaining secret communications of the *Mil Amt* by W/T, land line and carrier pigeon. By far the most important function was the organisation of the W/T network of the *Mil Amt*, which involved responsibility for all radio communications of the *Mil Amt* both at home and abroad, including communications of the *Leitstellen*, FAKs and FATs, and for all related technical matters. In this capacity *Mil Amt* E's heaviest task was the supply of men (W/T operators) and materials (W/T sets), both of which became in increasingly short supply. Only after the advent of *Mil Amt* E were any of the *Mil Amt* stations linked by teleprinter, a move which dispensed with unnecessary W/T traffic.

No major changes are believed to have been resulted in the work of *Mil Amt* E until the early spring of 1945 when a new section, RSHA VI F (BFN) was set up with the responsibility of providing W/T intelligence apparatus for *Mil Amt* E and RSHA VI F (H). Towards the end of the war, however, Schellenberg resolved to unite even more closely *Mil Amt* E and C and RSHA *Gruppe* VI F, his principal reason being the attainment of closer organisational unification of all technical means. A contributing reason also was the increased supply difficulties resulting from bombing [air-raids]. Numerous deficiencies had emerged in connection with the communications of RSHA *Gruppe* VI F (*Havelinstitut*), and Schellenberg had agreed with the *Waffen*-SS, that all W/T personnel should be embodied in the *Waffen*-SS, and that a SS-*Funknachrichten* Regiment *der Waffen*-SS, should be created for this purpose. While the mobilisation instructions in this regard appear to have been prepared, there is no evidence that the plan, which would probably have covered all RSHA W/T personnel, was ever actually executed.

Under Kaltenbrunner's order of 26 April 1945, SS-*Ostubaf* Skorzeny, *Gruppenleiter* RSHA VI S and *Abteilungschef Mil Amt* D, was placed in charge also of *Mil Amt* E and C, as well as RSHA *Gruppe* VI F.

D. RSHA *Mil Amt* E Headquarter Organisation, Jan 1945.

1. *Abteilungschef.* Oberstltn. Boening was *Mil Amt* E *Abteilungschef,* in addition to being *Abteilungschef Mil Amt* C and *Gruppenleiter* RSHA VI F.
2. Deputy *Abteilungschef* and Commanding Officer 506 *Nachrichten* Regiment: Major Poretschkin, in addition to being Deputy *Abteilungschef Mil Amt* E, was also C.O. of 506 *Nachrichten* Regiment; and it appears that all *Mil Amt* E officers were technically on the strength of this Regiment whose headquarters, as well as those of *Mil Amt* E, were at Stahnsdorf, south-west Berlin suburbs.
3. Important Staff Officers: Poretschkin's adjutant was *Hauptmann* Hardtke, later succeeded by *Oberltn.* Mohns. *Hauptmann* Schulz reported to have been adjutant, in fact may have been the Belzig administrative officer. *Oberltn.* Oesterle, generally known as Poretschkin's assistant, was also chief of the 506 *Nachrichten* Regiment radio section. The technical staff at Stahnsdorf included also *Oberstltn.* Gehrts, *Sonderführer* Grunberg and *Oberltn.* Karwan.
4. *Zentralegruppe.* According to Schellenberg, there was, directly under the *Abteilungschef Mil Amt* E and his Deputy, a central group (*Zentralegruppe*) which dealt with codes and other specialist matters, in addition to matters of personnel and administration. Either as subdivisions of the *Zentralegruppe* or subordinate units responsible to the *Zentralegruppe* were, according to Schellenberg, the following:

   a) *Gruppe Betriebsfunk* (general radio matters)
   b) *Gruppe Agentenfunk* and *Ausbildung* (W/T sets for agents, and training)
   c) *Gruppe Fabrikation* (manufacturing; a large part of the W/T sets were manufactured at Pischwitz & Würzen).

5. Regimental HQ, 506 *Nachrichten* Regiment: This HQ was the official channel for dealing with the three *Wehrmacht* services on such questions as personnel. At *Mil Amt* E/506 *Nachrichten* Regiment HQ were the 9th, 10th,

11th and 12th Companys of the Regiment. The companys were disposed as follows:

a) 9th Company: At Belzig, cover name 'Burg', which was known as '*Funkzentrale*' (Radio Centre). There was an operations company handling the communications of Regimental Headquarters. All messages which arrived at 'Burg' were re-transmitted to the various sections of the *Mil Amt*. Commanding Officer was *Hauptmann* Soujon.

b) 10th Company: At Nischwitz, west of Leipzig, was a technical company (workshop unit) dealing with the maintenance of all equipment. Commanding Officer Major Stein, also in charge of stores.

c) 11th Company: At Belzig, was a replacement and training unit. Commanding Officer *Hauptmann* Soujon. *Ltn* Langguth was in charge of training. (There are conflicting reports regarding the disposition of the 10th and 11th Companys and it is possible that the Company at Nischwitz was the 11th Company, and the Company at Belzig the 10th Company.)

d) 12th Company: Existed for the purpose of carrying on the books all personnel of the Regiment stationed outside Germany (only three instances known to Poretschkin were Spain, Portugal and, for a while, Turkey.)

6. <u>Movements.</u> Regimental HQ and most probably RSHA *Mil Amt* E, also, evacuated to Obing or vicinity, cover name 'Wiese', in Bavaria in April 1945 where they carried on until the end of the war. The *Ausweichstelle* for Belzig was Seedorf in Thuringia, cover name 'Lago', to which the 9th and 10th or 11th Companys probably retreated before finally joining the Regimental HQ at Obing. To complete the organisation of the evacuated departments of RSHA *Amt* VI and *Mil Amt* in the '*Alpenfestung*', two mobile W/T stations were set up, one operated by *Mil Amt* E/506 *Nachrichten* Regiment at Fritzens and the other run by RSHA *Amt* VI F (H) at Eichert.

E. Codes and Ciphers—OKW/CHI.

As may be expected, RSHA *Mil Amt* E had the immediate responsibility for supplying ciphers and checking their security, but this was done in conjunction with OKW/CHI. The latter's principal function was the deciphering of intercepted messages and, conversely, the development of hand and machine ciphers for German use and the supervision of secret telephone and teleprinter sets. *Oberst* Höpfner was chief of OKW/CHi, while *Oberinspektor* Menzer was the OKW/CHi officer responsible for the supply of codes and ciphers to, among others, RSHA *Mil Amt* E/506 *Nachrichten* Regiment.

F. Carrier Pigeons.

Little information, indeed, has come to light from interrogation reports concerning the use of carrier pigeons, and such as has become available is sketchy. Thus, *Hauptmann* Koegl, W/T officer at KdM Prague, for example, was order by *Mil Amt* E to investigate the possibility of using carrier pigeons in February 1945. This venture was proposed as a possible improvement in communications which had become bad owing to lack of equipment. There is little evidence, however, that this program ever materialised even to a small extent. It must be assumed that similar plans prevailed elsewhere, but it is doubtful whether any more success ensued.

G. 506 *Nachrichten* Regiment.

As indicated in Paragraph A above, this Regiment was formed in the autumn of 1944 for the purpose principally of centralising W/T personnel administratively and creating a replacement pool. The Regiment consisted of four battalions of three or four companys each. As previously indicated, the 9th, 10th, 11th and 12th Companys are reported to have been at Regimental Headquarters at Stahnsdorf. The remaining units of the Regiment were set up on a geographical basis dependent on the RSHA *Mil Amt* organisations in the Field to which they were attached. Generally, of course, the Regiment had the task of providing all required W/T personnel for the maintenance of communications of the *Mil Amt* at all levels, including *Frontaufklärung* and *Lehrregiment Kurfürst*. Personnel of the Regiment never had any more contact with agents than was absolutely necessary for the execution of their communications mission.

Battalion Commanders and Company Commanders, in most cases, worked on the location of the KdM of the area, but were only technically subordinate to the KdM. Commanding Officers were also called *Funkstellenleiters*.

The W/T personnel were drawn from all three sections of the *Wehrmacht*, and were accommodated in military units (i.e. *Funktrupps* or Zugs or Companys). For technical and disciplinary purposes they remained under the command of the Regiment, though they continued to belong to their old formation and wore their original uniforms. The activation of the Regiment was never formally announced to many of its members, who often work were completely unaware of their membership.

The complement of the Companys probably varied according to the amount of work designated to them. Thus, the 2nd Company/1st Battalion had a strength of 130, including W/T operators and administrative staff, made up of 75 W/T operators working at stations other than Company Headquarters, about 45 operators at Company Headquarters and 10 administrative staff. The Companys of the 2nd Battalion had a strength of approx. 130 mean each, but in practise the 4th Company had about 90 men and the 5th and 6th Companies approx. 60 men each.

The activities of the Battalions and their Companys (other than the Headquarters Companys) were as follows:

1. 1st Battalion Headquarters, at Vienna, cover name 'Koni', controlled by FULEI S.S.O. (Balkans and Italy), handled all communications to and from Italy and the Balkans. Commanding Officer, *Oberstltn. Oberregierungsrat* Hotzel, succeeded by Major Mangelsdorff (alias 'Mucius') on 1 December 1944. *Oberltn* Trabandt was adjutant. *Oberltn* Matz was in charge of W/T traffic, also chief instructor of agents at Belgrade and Vienna, and dealt with R-*Netz* from Vienna. In March 1945, Battalion Headquarters with the 1st and 3rd Companys, moved to Obing, and possibly at the beginning of May 1945 in the direction of Berchtesgaden.

   1st Company/1st Battalion, at Vienna with Battalion Headquarters, cover name 'Wera'. Commanding Officer, Major Mangelsdorff, succeeded by *Oberltn* Hantschel, who was also Commanding Officer of the 3rd Company. This Company dealt with the communications to and from Vienna, also manned listening posts in Austria. In January 1945, *Hauptmann* Koegl set up a W/T station at KdM Prague which was to be controlled from Vienna; but owing to lack of equipment, this line of communications does not appear to have been very effective. 1st Company moved with Battalion Headquarters to Obing in March 1945.

   2nd Company/1st Battalion, at Merano, cover name 'Jakob'. Commanding Officer, *Hauptmann* Matthias Hofmaier (alias 'Dohna'). *Ltn* Sieber was on the staff. This Company dealt with the W/T communications and serviced W/T stations in Italy, including the FAKS and FATs in that area, and was also responsible for the BALDO net whose function was the collection and dissemination of information on Partisans and the establishment of a PO organisation; the Company supplied W/T operators, sets and procedure. 'Jakob' also controlled Munich, cover name 'Monika'. An emergency station was at Sand, cover name 'Bergbahn', to which a retreat was attempted. On 3 May 1945 the Company with the equipment withdrew from Merano and moved to Schlanders-Reschenpass (mountain pass between Italy and Austria), then to Grauen, command post of Battle Group Kotz. W/T sections were never committed with the Battle Group.

   3rd Company/1st Battalion, at Vienna, cover name 'Wald' (?). Commanding Officer, *Oberltn* Hantschel. Deputy C.O., *Oberltn* Hellwig. This Company was also attached to Battalion Headquarters and was run in conjunction with the 1st Company owing to the large volume of communications to and from Vienna. Evacuation was the same as the 1st Company.

   13th Company/1st Battalion, at Belgrade, later Agram (Zagreb), cover name 'Bernhard'. *Hauptmann* G.E. Weber was probably the first Commanding Officer, succeeded by *Hauptmann* Flade, his adjutant. Deputy C.O., *Oberltn* Hundt. This Company served the FAKs of Army Group F and the personnel of Station 'Biene' (a relay station located at Liebach in Graz, Austria) which maintained liaison between several FATs of Army Group F. (According to Poretschkin, this unit was known as the 16th Company, motorised.)

2. <u>2nd Battalion Headquarters</u>, at Wiesbaden, cover-name probably 'Palme', controlled by FULEI WEST. Commanding Officer, *Oberstltn* Johann Gottlieb Rauh (alias 'Rapp'), succeeded by *Hauptmann* Prodehl (alias 'Peter') on 1 December 1944. *Hauptmann* Böttcher (alias 'Fahne') was adjutant. Staff included *Ltn* Cierkes for a short time, and *Oberltn* Dobbart, wire communications expert. This Battalion handled all communications to and from the West, excluding England and the western hemisphere. Battalion staff supervised military, technical and coperational matters, and the Companys maintained actual contact between KdM Sigmaringen (Stuttgart), KdM Wiesbaden and KdM Köln and Regimental Headquarters. Headquarters was destroyed in an air attack on 2 February 1945. Towards the end of the war the Battalion moved to Sesslach in Coburg.

    4th Company/2nd Battalion, at Sigmaringen, cover name 'Sonja'. Commanding Officer, *Oberltn* Kart Hientzsch (alias 'Heros'), who succeeded *Hauptmann* Fränznick (alias 'Fechner') in August 1944. The Company worked mainly on the communications of KdM Stuttgart, cover name 'Tubus'. From a strictly technical point of view, the Company also commanded the MK W/T stations at Singen, Lörrach and Strasbourg. From the end of February 1945, the Company gradually moved towards Arlburg. Latest station was in the vicinity of Oberlech, somewhere between Langen and the Bavarian frontier.

    5th Company/2nd Battalion, at Wiesbaden, cover name 'Wilja', with Battalion Headquarters. The station was also known as 'Eiserne Hand'. Commanding Officer, *Hauptmann* Fränznick (alias 'Fechner'). The W/T station was expanded on the activation of the FAKs and FATs, and the Company probably maintained some of their communications, as well as dealing with those of KdM Wiesbaden.

    6th Company/2nd Battalion, at Köln-Bensburg until January 1945, then at Bad Wildungen, cover name 'Konrad'. *Feldpostnummer* 19864. Commanding Officer, *Hauptmann* Dr Schwarzenberg (alias 'Sander'). Staff included *Ltn* Snaders (alias 'Schrammel'). The Company consisted of four W/T platoons and one encoding and decoding section called '*Kommando*'. Each platoon consisted of 6–12 operators and gave 24-hour coverage in 6-hour shifts.

    17th Company/2nd Battalion: According to Poretschkin, this Company carried personnel detached to the FAKs in the western theatre and was under the command of the 2nd Battalion. This information is questionable, as Schlottmann, Commanding Officer of the 3rd Battalion was supposed to have operated the Nordnetz with the 1st and 2nd Zug of this Company (see below).

3. <u>3rd Battalion Headquarters</u> at Hamburg. Commanding Officer, *Oberstltn Oberregierungsrat* Werner Trautmann (alias 'Dr Hans Thiele'), succeeded

by *Oberstltn* Hans Albert Wilhelm Schlottmann (alias 'Schrader') on 1 December 1944. *Ltn* Wein dealt with supply and telephone and teleprinter communications. Battalion handled all communications to and from the North, as well as agents' communications to and from England and the western hemisphere. The Commanding Officer was known as *Funkleiter Übersee* for the *Mil Amt*. The Battalion also controlled the W/T network in Norway.

7th Company/3rd Battalion, at Wohltorf outside Hamburg, cover name 'Domaene', W/T station for Battalion Headquarters. Commanding Officer, *Oberstltn* Schlottmann (alias 'Schrader'). The Company was responsible for receiving and transmitting all W/T traffic to and from agents. Instructors and technicians were supplied for the network in Denmark—FAK 140. The Company was individed into three sections: i) I—administration, ii) II—TS Technical—responsible for W/T sets and stores, iii) III-FU—Operational. 'Domaene' was intended as control for stay-behind net for Denmark.

8th Company/3rd Battalion, at Krugsdorf near Pasewalk. Commanding Officer, *Kapt.Ltn.* Griese. The Company dealt with the communications of KdM Stettin which had a number of W/T posts in the areas east of Danzig, and for which the Company probably supplied operators and technicians. W/T personnel were trained with the Company for a stay-behind net of KdM Stettin on the German Baltic coast. Originally, Krugsdorf had been planned as an alternative to Wohltorf (7th Company) in the event of withdrawal. However, owing to the Russian advance, the station was evacuated to Wohltorf in March 1945.

18th Company/3rd Battalion. According to Poretschkin, this Company carried personnel detached to the FAKS in Denmark and Norway. It seems possible that Poretschkin has confused the numbers of this unit, and that in fact the Company with the 17th (rather than the 18th) under the command on the 3rd Battalion, and the 18th Company was under the command of the 2nd Battalion (see above).

4. <u>4th Battalion Headquarters</u>, probably at Warsaw, controlled by FULEI OST. Commanding Officer, *Hauptmann* Bödigheimer. Battalion staff included *Oberltn* Kahlau. There are many conflicting reports as to the exact set-up of the Battalion and its Company. Poretschkin states that the Battalion handled all personnel detached to the *Frontaufklärung* on the Eastern Front. Under the Battalion were the 13th, 14th and 15th Companys. However, according to Baun, Commanding Officer of *Leitstelle* I *Ost*, the 4th Battalion consisted of the 15th, 16th and 17th Companys, and worked with *Leitstelle* I *Ost für Frontaufklärung* for maintaining communications. The normal complement for *Frontaufklärung* units in the East was two Companys, plus one other Company which dealt with all other W/T traffic of the *Geheime Meldedienst* in the East. Finally, Hientzsch, Commanding Officer of the 4th Company/2nd Battalion gives the information that the 4th Battalion consisted of the 12th, 14th, 15th and 16th Companys, and served the FAKs and FATs operating on the whole of the Eastern Front.

From this it will be seen that there is no conflict in evidence as to the 14th, 15th and 16th Company; but as the other Companys reported on the Eastern Front, that is, the 12th, 13th and 17th, there is conflicting evidence.

H. Known Personnel of *Mil Amt* E & 506 *Nachrichten* Regiment.

(Note: personnel known to be under postwar arrest are underlined.)

Bödigheimer, *Hauptmann*—Commanding Officer, 4th Battalion.

Boening, *Oberstltn*—Commanding Officer of RSHA *Mil Amt* E and C, and RSHA *Gruppe* VI F; transferred to *Amt* Vi, 1943.

Böttcher, *Hauptmann*—adjutant, 2nd Battalion.

Dobbart, *Oberltn*—wire communications expert, 2nd Battalion.

Fenner, *Ministerialrat*—RSHA *Amt* VI.

Flade, *Hauptmann* Hermann—Commanding Officer, 13th Company/1st Batl.

Fränznick, *Hauptmann* Fritz—Commanding Officer, 5th Company/2nd Batl.

Freese, *Ltn*—Chief of *Funkstelle Westerwald* (*Leitstelle* I *West*) from Nov 1944, successor to Prodehl.

Gaber, *Korv.Kapt.*—supervised W/T traffic between Sigmaringen and Spain; cover name for his station, 'Nevo'.

Gehrts, *Oberstltn*—*Referent* for technical matters at Stahnsdorf.

Gierkes, *Ltn*—with 2nd Battalion for a short time.

<u>Griese</u>, *Kapt.Ltn.*—Commanding Officer, 8th Company/3rd Batl.

Grunberg, *Sonderführer*—radio engineer, Chief of technical section of Regt. at Stahnsdorf; and chief engineer of *Mil Amt* E.

Hantschel, *Oberltn*—Commanding Officer, 1st and 3rd Company/1st Batl.

Hardtke, *Hauptmann*—adjutant to Poretschkin.

Hellwig, *Oberltn*—Deputy C.O., 3rd Company/1st Batl.

<u>Hientzsch,</u> *Oberltn* Karl—Commanding Officer, 3th Company/2nd Batl.

Höpfner, *Oberst*—Chef OKW/WNV/CHI.

<u>Hofmaier,</u> *Hauptmann* Matthias—Commanding Officer, 2nd Company/1st Batl.

Holey, *Hauptmann* Hugo—technical supervisor to 1st Batl.

Hotzel, *Oberstltn* ORR Hans—Commanding Officer, 1st Battalion, until 1 December 1944.

Hundt, *Oberltn*—Deputy C.O., 13th Company/1st Batl.

Kähler, *Oberstltn*.

Kahlau, *Oberltn*—with 4th Batl.

Karwan, *Oberltn*—W/T engineer, technical section at Stahnsdorf.

Koegl, *Hauptmann*—at KdM Prague.

Kretschmar, *Hauptmann* Siegfried—chief of W/T Company of *Lehrregiment Kurfürst*.

Langguth, *Ltn*—10th Company, in charge of training.

Laue, *Oberltn* Werner (?)—*Funkleiter* of FAK *Abwehr* II *West*, station cover name 'Menuet'; possibly with RSHA VI S in 1945.

Mangeldorff, Major—Commanding Officer, 1st Company/1st Batl; then C.O. 1st Battalion from1 December 1944.

Matz, *Oberltn*—in charge of W/T traffic of 1st Battalion; also dealt with R-*Netz* from Vienna.

Mettig, *Major*—OKW/CHI, also *Mil Amt* E.

Mohns, *Oberltn*—succeeded Hardtke as adjutant to Poretschkin.

Mundhenke, *Ltn.*

Niese, *Hauptmann*—*Leiter* of Belzig W/T station prior to formation of 506 *Nachrichten* Regiment.

Nünke, *Ltn*—Ii Oslo, probably member of 3rd Battalion.

Oesterle, *Oberltn* Alphons—Chief of W/T station of Regiment; assistant to Poretschkin.

Poretschkin, Major—Commanding Officer, 506 *Nachrichten* Regiment, and Deputy C.O. of RSHA *Mil Amt* E.

Prodehl, *Hauptmann*—Commanding Officer, 2nd Battlion from 1 December 1944; previously W/T officer of *Leitstelle* I *West*.

Rasehorn, Major—*Referent* of *Abwehr* Ii at Stahnsdorf prior to formation of 506 *Nachrichten* Regiment, probably the first C.O. of the Regiment.

Rauh, *Oberstltn* Johann—Commanding Officer, 2nd Battlion until 1 Dec. 1944.

Scherer, *Oberregierungsrat*—RSHA *Mil Amt* E.

Schlottmann, *Oberstltn* Hans—Commanding Officer, 3rd Battalion from 1 Dec. 1944; also Commanding Officer of 7th Company/3rd Battalion and possibly also of the 17th Company.

Schmidt, *Hauptmann*—possibly sttaioned in Bulgaria employed for installation of new W/T sets.

Schulz, *Hauptmann*—reported as adjutant to 506 *Nachrichten* Regiment; may have been in charge of administration at Belzig.

Schulze, SS-*Oberscharführer*—*Mil Amt* E.

Schwarzenberg, *Hauptmann* Dr Johannes—Commanding Officer, 6th Company/ 2nd Battalion.

Sieber, *Ltn*—on staff of 2nd Company/1st Battalion.

Snaders, *Ltn*—on staff of 6th Company/2nd Battalion.

Soujon, *Hauptmann*—Commanding Officer, 9th Company and either 10th or 11th Company at Belzig.

Stein, Major—*Dienststellenleiter Nischwitz* (10th or 11th Company) and in charge of Stores.

Trautmann, *Oberstltn* ORR Werner—Commanding Officer, 3rd Battalion until 1 December 1944.

Weber, *Hauptmann*—probably first Commanding Officer, 13th Company/1st Battlion; then chief of school at Striegau.

Wein, *Ltn*—3rd Battalion, in charge of supply and telephone and teleprinter communications.

I. Main Sources of Information.

Oberstltn Rauh
Oberstltn Schlottmann
Oberstltn Trautmann
Major Poretschkin
Hauptmann Hofmaier
Oberltn Hientzsch
Hauptmann G.E. Weber
SS-*Gruf.* Walter Schellenberg
SS-*Staf* Martin Sandberger
Oberst Baun
Obergefreiter Kleeberg

This report was issued by W.R.C.1./A on 6 February 1946.

Note:

*   The National Archives, Kew, KV 3/117: Liquidation Report No. 31, RSHA Mil Amt E.

24

Liquidation Report No. 32: RSHA *Mil Amt* F

A. Status of Mobile *Abwehr* Prior to Establishment of *Mil Amt* F.

In February 1944 *Amt Abwehr* ordered the stationary *Aussenstellen* in the West to fall into line with the mobile organisation which existed on the Russian front. There, *Frontaufklärung* (front reconnaissance) had been systematically organised in the form of mobile *Abwehr Kommandos* (FAKs) and *Abwehr Trupps* (FATs) since 1941 for the purpose of conducting the work of the *Abwehr* in the field with the armies. Though the *Amt Abwehr* in Berlin was responsible for establishing general policy, FA units, with military status, were immediately subordinate to the OKW and were under the tactical command of the Ic officers of army groups and armies. These FAKs and FATs on all fronts, together with their controlling *Leitstellen*, were of three types, corresponding to the three kinds of *Abwehr* work –

1. The active gathering of intelligence;
2. Sabotage and subversion;
3. Counter-espionage.

Eventually the term *Abwehr* was dropped and these units became known as *Frontaufklärung Leitstellen*, FA Kdos (FAKs) and FA *Trupps* (FATs)…

During the course of the mid 1944 re-organisation of the *Abwehr* into RSHA *Mil Amt*, *Frontaufklärung* remained immediately subordinate to the OKW and suffered little change. However, as a result of discussions in March and April 1944, an office entitled '*Chef* Ic *Wehrmacht*' was instituted in the WFSt (Army General Staff). This comprised (a) the *Abteilung* FA under *Oberst* Naumann and (b) the *Abteilung Truppenabwehr* (deception work) under *Oberst* Martini. *Oberst* i.G. von Süsskind-Schwendi was *Chef* of this office. Later in the summer of 1944, this WFSt office was renamed '*Chef* F.T. *Wehrmacht*' (*Chef der* FA *und*

Truppenabwehr), Süsskind-Schwendi remained as *Chef*. In addition, the *Mil Amt* was authorised to exercise a so-called right of operational jurisdiction (*fachliches Weisungsrecht*) over *Frontaufklärung*. RSHA *Mil Amt* B and C dealt with FA I matters, *Mil Amt* D with FA II, and FA III was dealt with by RSHA *Amt* IV. In fact, practical experience called for close co-operation between the *Mil Amt* and *Frontaufklärung*, for the former had at its disposal trained replacements, signal apparatus and other facilities for intelligence work, while the OKW, in general, was unfamiliar with many of these matters.

B. Establishment of RSHA *Mil Amt* F.

From an efficiency point of view, the office '*Chef* F.T. *Wehrmacht*' was an unsatisfactory solution for *Frontaufklärung*, as considerable difficulty was experienced in handling information from FA, much of it being of value to the *Mil Amt* as well as the Army commands. This was obviously due to the lack of co-operation between the RSHA and the OKW; the latter attempted to resist any interference on the part of the RSHA. Even in the old *Abwehr* days, FA had been the subject of much controversy.

Authority between the *Abwehr* and the OKW was never clearly defined, with the result that orders were continually countermanded, and petty jealousies became major issues, often to the detriment of a military operation. In addition, the RSHA had incessantly attempted to control *Frontaufklärung*; and after formation of the *Mil Amt*, the RSHA intensified their aggressiveness in the fight for supremacy. By November 1944, it was apparent that Süsskind-Schwendi was fighting a losing battle against RSHA; also, the military situation was deteriorating and producing the unenviable position whereby the FAKs and FATs were overlapping functionally, and were sometimes physically to the rear of the KdMs.

Finally in mid November 1944, Keitel and Himmler ordered that the *Frontaufklärung* establishment should be absorbed by the RSHA *Mil Amt* to form *Mil Amt* F, effective from 1 December 1944. *Oberst* i.G. Buntrock, formerly Ic officer with Army Group A, was chosen by Keitel as *Chef*, *Mil Amt* F. Buntrock was thought by Keitel to be agreeable to the [Nazi] Party, while at the same time sufficiently sympathetic with the OKW to give some opposition to the RSHA. He was known as *Chef* of *Mil Amt* F and *Chef* FA (*Frontaufklärung*). The *Truppenabwehr* remained with the AFSt.

The FA Leitstellen with their FAKs and FATs were subordinated to *Mil Amt* F, but they continued to accept directions and missions from the Ic officers of the military formations to which they were attached and responsible. At the same time they continued to report intelligence, etc., to the competent specialist branch of the *Mil Amt* (B, D and C) and RSHA *Amt* IV.

Buntrock, on his appointment, immediately had to contend with much jurisdictional controversy and the intensified efforts of the RSHA to assume

Wehrmacht power over *Frontaufklärung*. Orders were being countermanded and Schellenberg refused to interfere. RSHA *Gruppe* VI B and VI C showed definite interest in *Frontaufklärung* I, Skorzeny of RSHA *Gruppe* VI S and *Mil Amt* D insisted on taking over *Frontaufklärung* II; in the *Frontaufklärung* III field, Müller, RSHA *Amtschef* IV, wanted control, as did Freund of RSHA *Gruppe* VI Z, who attempted to annex the remaining long-distance connections (neutral countries). All W/T personnel of the *Frontaufklärung* were incorporated in *Mil Amt* E as members of 506 *Nachrichten* Regiment and *Mil Amt* G absorbed the G-*Staffels* (counterfeit documents, etc.).

By the end of December 1944, it was obvious that *Frontaufklärung* would soon completely collapse if the position were not clarified. Therefore, Buntrock brought the matter to the notice of Keitel, Jodl, Kaltenbrunner and Schellenberg. The outcome of this was that Buntrock drafted an order establishing the function and jurisdiction of RSHA *Mil Amt* F—*Chef* Front *Aufklärung*, which was accepted and approved in February 1945. This order, briefly, was as follows:

1) The Departmental *Chef Frontaufklärung* with its subordinate units (FAKs and FATs) formed part of the RSHA.
2) *Chef* FA (*Frontaufklärung*), who headed RSHA *Mil Amt* F, was subordinated –
   (a) in matters pertaining to military command (*Truppendienstlich*) to the *Chef* OKW [Keitel], but in all other respects to the RSHA;
   (b) in operational jurisdiction, for FA I and FA II to the head of RSHA VI *Mil Amt* (Schellenberg), for FA III to the head of RSHA IV (Müller).
   All *Frontaufklärung* units to take their orders from *Chef* FA; i.e. matters pertaining to operational jurisdiction, military command, discipline and tectical employment in the field. However, FA units attached to army commands were subordinate to local Ic officers for the three last named functions.
3) The subordinate unit of FA *Leitstellen*, FAKs and FATs, were specialised organisations which could only operate effectively under the control of *Chef* FA.
4) Missions of *Frontaufklärung* –
   (a) The sole purpose of *Frontaufklärung* was to act as a military intelligence service of the fighting front.
   (b) The three types of *Frontaufklärung* and the work designated to them, remained as before (para A).

In March 1945, an addendum to this order, defining the jurisdiction of FA III, was drawn up by Major Gänzer, FA III *Referent* in RSHA *Mil Amt* F and signed by Kaltenbrunner. This limited the activities of FA III to the immediate area of operations only, and should this in any way affect the security of the *Reich*, the *Sipo* had the power to step in and assume control.

According to Buntrock, the imminence of Germany's collapse prevented the full execution of the plans reflected by these orders.

C. Organisation of RSHA *Mil Amt* F.

1. Headquarters.

Buntrock, although formerly an Ic officer, had no specialised experience in gathering tactical and strategic information of the FA I, II and III categories. Therefore, on his appointment to RSHA *Mil Amt* F, he immediately surrounded himself with specialists in FA I, II and III. The set-up at the headquarters of *Mil Amt* F was as follows:

Chef Amt F and *Chef* FA	:	*Oberst* i.G. Buntrock
Deputy *Chef* F	:	*Oberstltn* i.G. von der Knesebeck (also *Mil Amt* Ia, *Heer*)
I *Referent*	:	*Oberltn* Schattnow
II *Referent*	:	*Hauptmann* Gildermeister
III *Referent*	:	Major Gänzer
Quartermaster (Supply)	:	*Oberstltn* Links
Referent, I Personnel	:	Major Rosenfeld
Referent, III Personnel	:	*Hauptmann* Lenz
Adjutant to Buntrock	:	*Oberltn* Heinen

In January 1945, Headquarters of RSHA *Mil Amt* F was situated at Belinde II, moving to Ludwigstadt in March, and finally in April 1945 at Seeon/Chiemsee, where it was soon dissolved.

2. *Leitstellen* controlled by RSHA *Mil Amt* F.

FA-*Leitstellen* I, II and II *Ost*—in the field subordinate to WFSt, Fremde *Heere Ost*.

FA-*Leitstellen* I, II and III *West*—in the field subordinate to *Ob.Befehlsh. West*, *Abt* Ic office.

FA-*Leitstellen* I, II and II *Süd-Ost*—in the field subordinate to *Ob.Befehslh. Süd-Ost*, *Abt* Ic office.

These *Leitstellen* controlled their respective FAKs, which in turn controlled the FATs subordinate to them.

3. Personnel and Training.

RSHA *Mil Amt* F dealt with the supply of *Frontaufklärung* personnel which was considered far below standard in December 1944. Consequently, Buntrock immediately stated his claim for a percentage of the graduates from the *Lehrregiment Kurfürst*, where all *Mil Amt* personnel received their practical and final training. He also asked that he should be consulted regarding the curriculum, since it was essential that these graduates should be adequately trained in *Frontaufklärung* matters so as to expedite field appointments.

Grenadier-Regiment 1001 came under the jurisdiction of *Chef Frontaufklärung*, and in December 1944 consisted of a staff located near Prague and two camps near Graz (Austria). Originally this Regiment had dealt with –

(a)   Personnel records of V-*Leute* [informants]
(b)   Placement of V-*Leute* who were no longer needed by the intelligence agencies for further missions, and
(c)   The recruiting and schooling of new V-*Leute*.

In January 1945, jurisdiction of this Regiment was transferred to Schellenberg, because investigations showed that *Leitstellen* preferred to recruit, train and assign their own V-*Leute*, and were unwilling to furnish the Regiment with particulars of V-*Leute*.

Since *Frontaufklärung* had no replacement unit of its own, it appears that one Company of *Ersatz* Bataillon 600 was designated as a FA replacement company. (Buntrock believed that this Battalion was a replacement unit for the *Geheime Feldpolizei*.) When *Frontaufklärung* became part of RSHA *Mil Amt* F this FA replacement company was separated from the Battalion and placed under the *Mil Amt*. Efforts were made to incorporate it into the *Lehrregiment Kurfürst*, thereby making the latter the central replacement pool for the whole of *Frontaufklärung*. However, this was prevented by the end of the war.

4. Situation regarding *Mil Amt* D.
Even prior to the formation of RSHA *Mil Amt* F, *Mil Amt* D had considered *Frontaufklarung* II within its exclusive sphere; and in August 1944, Skorzeny without consulting the OKH authorities, had gone the length of ordering *Frontaufklärung* II FAKs and FATs to ignore *Wehrmacht* orders. Consequently, the OKH lost the use of *Frontaufklärung* units at a time when its need was most urgent. Buntrock, on his appointment as *Chef* of *Mil Amt* F, was fully aware of Skorzeny's motives for incorporating *Frontaufklärung* II in his SS-*Jagdverbände*, and at the same time realised that the army authorities did not have adequate knowledge of the uses to which FA II could be put. In spite of the fact that *Mil Amt* D had slowly become *de facto* in charge of FA II, Buntrock continued to oppose Skorzeny until the end of the war. One of Buntrick's reasons was his disapproval of Skorzeny's methods, which he believed detrimental to the German people and a danger to the *Wehrmacht* personnel recruited for FA II work; another reason was the feeling that once FA II had been completely ceded to *Mil Amt* D, then the other sections of RSHA would lay claim to the remaining *Frontaufklärung* units. This difficulty with *Mil Amt* D would appear to explain the absence of of a *Referent* for FA II personnel within the organisation of RSHA *Mil Amt* F.

D. Last Days of *Mil Amt* F.

During April 1945, the RSHA apparently dissolved *Frontaufklärung* as a service, and certain FA I units were ordered to operate with Skorzeny's SS-*Jagdverbände*. Buntrock opposed this order, and even after a stormy conference with Kaltenbrunner on 1 May 1945, declared that only the OKW had the right to order such an action. The German capitulation put an end to this controversy.

Buntrock apparently had plans for maintaining a skeleton staff of RSHA *Mil Amt* F personnel in the area of Chiemsee (Bavaria), since he was of the opinion that, eventually, there would be war between the Eastern and Western Allies; had this been the case, he considered that his *Frontaufklärung* units, with their intelligence knowledge of the Eastern enemy, would be of immediate use to the Western powers. This scheme did not materialise however, for by the end of April 1945, *Mil Amt* F appears to have had little or no contact with the subordinate Leitstellen and most of the *Frontaufklärung* records had been destroyed. Finally, on 1 May 1945, after a discussion with General Winter, Jodl's assistant on the WFSt, Buntrock ordered the disbanding of *Frontaufklärung*, and all his staff officers were notified that they were free to go.

E. Appreciation of Success or Failure.

The formation of RSHA *Mil Amt* F so near the end of the war, prevents an appreciation of its success or failure. Had this department, as a central administrative office for *Frontaufklärung*, been conceived during the early formation of the *Mil Amt*, a certain measure of success might have been achieved. Buntrock states, however, that the operations of *Frontaufklärung* I in the East were more succdessful than in the West.

F. Known Personnel of RSHA *Mil Amt* F.

(Note: those officials reported under postwar arrest are underlined.)

<u>Buntrock</u>, *Oberst* i.G. Georg	*Chef, Mil Amt* F and *Chef* FA.
Classen, *Oberltn*	*Mil Amt* F, Personnel
<u>Gänzer</u>, *Hauptmann* Johannes	*Mil Amt* F; formerly III F, Warsaw
Gildermeister, *Oberltn*	*Mil Amt* F; formerly *Abwehr* II
Heinen, *Oberltn*	Adjutant to Buntrock
Hörmann, *Hauptmann* Dr	*Mil Amt* F I; formerly FAK 190
<u>von dem Knesebeck</u>, *Oberstltn* i.G.	Deputy *Chef Mil Amt* F
Lenz, *Hauptmann*	*Referent* for III personnel
Links, *Oberstltn*	*Mil Amt* F, Quartermaster
Raupuch, Dr Hans	*Mil Amt* F

Rosenfeld, Major	*Referent* for I personnel
Schattnow, *Oberltn*	*Mil Amt* F, *Referent* I
Stark, *Hauptmann*	*Mil Amt* F, I
<u>Strohecker</u>, *Hauptmann* Dr	*Mil Amt* F, I; formerly FAK 120

G. Main Sources of Information.

Oberst i.G. Georg Buntrock
SS-*Staf* Martin Sandberger

This report was issued by W.R.C.1/A on 27 March 1946.

Note

*   The National Archives, Kew, KV 3/196: Liquidation Report No. 32, RSHA *Mil Amt* F.

25

Liquidation Report No. 34:
RSHA *Mil Amt* i

Introduction.

Mil Amt i (usually written with the small letter presumably to differentiate it from a Roman I) was a grandiose conception which in fact never materialised. Thus, what was intended to have been a powerful department co-ordinating all German deception activities, emerged merely as an abortive successor to the old *Abt.* III D of *Amt Ausland/Abwehr.*

Abt. III D, Amt Ausland/Abwehr.

Briefly, III D served as a registry of deception sources and as a channel by which chicken-feed was passed from the OKW to III F *en route* for the *Aussenstelle* concerned. It had never been of major importance as a department, and its peak period had occurred before the war, since when it played a progressively less important role. On the dissolution of the *Abwehr*, in the summer of 1944, III D had been transferred to the OKW/WFSt/*Truppenabwehr*.

Deception Possibilities.

Schellenberg seems to have been the first to realise the lack of co-ordination in the field of deception, and to see the need for a single powerful organisation to deal with this important side of the German Intelligence Services' war effort, a side possessing considerable potentialities. With this purpose in mind, Schellenberg proceeded to form a new branch, which came into being in the following manner.

Formation.

In July 1944, Schellenberg ordered von Bechtolsheim, *Mil Amt* Ia Marine, to exploit the possibilities of the *Truppenabwehr*, into which III D, with its card-index under a certain *Ltn* Naber, had been incorporated. Schellenberg knew that the first step in his scheme was to acquire this index, as it constituted a complete record of persons who had been, or were being, used to feed deception material to Allied Intelligence Services. In about December 1944 *Ltn* Naber, with his cards, was transferred to the control of *Mil Amt* A. von Bechtolsheim, however, felt that, as a part of *Mil Amt* A, deception work would inevitably become side-tracked and, in March 1945, he persuaded Schellenberg to create an entirely new department in the charge of a staff officer of Major's rank, with the result that *Mil Amt* i was formed. When, shortly afterwards, the *Mil Amt* disintegrated, a senior officer had not yet been appointed, unless Major Kiesewetter, former *Truppführer* FAT 365, known to have been transferred either to *Mil Amt* F or *Mil Amt* i, but to have taken ill and therefore unable to commence work, was to have filled the post.

Scope and Activities.

It is almost certain that *Mil Amt* i never in fact had the opportunity to function, although Schellenberg, as will be seen, suggests somewhat vaguely that it participated in various deception schemes. von Bechtolsheim, probably a more reliable source on the subject, states categorically that it was never able to commence work. At all events, it is more than questionable whether *Mil Amt* i would in any circumstances have been the final word on deception, as it seems obvious that deception policy would have been decided by the Military High Command. This view is supported by an interesting captured policy directive signed by Jodl, head of the *Wehrmachtführungsstab*, showing the importance the High Command attached to deception, and mentioning the existence of a central approval committee with the WFSt for all matters of operational deception, to which *Wehrmacht* sections were to submit their proposals. *Mil Amt* i's initial task, according to the same circular, was to register all technical military material released for W/T playing-back purposes.

Schellenberg, on the other hand, states that *Mil Amt* i, in liaison with SS-*Stubaf* Horst Kopkow of RSHA *Amt* IV [IV A2], received after lengthy negotiations, the right to participate in using existing W/T contacts for performing deceptive operations, and may have actually engaged in one such scheme.

Conclusion.

Although it is clear that *Mil Amt* i failed to achieve anything during its brief existence, it is quite probable that is Schellenberg's idea for the centralisation of deception activity had originated earlier in the war, some measure of improvement over former deception methods would have been effected.

This report was issued by W.R.C.1.d on 8 January 1946.

Notes:

* The National Archives Kew, KV 3/119: Liquidation Report No. 34, RSHA *Mil Amt* i.

Suggested Reading about RSHA

Banach, J., *Heydrichs Elite. Das Führerkorps der Sicherheitspolizei und des SD 1936–1945* (Verlag Ferdinand Schöningh, Paderborn, 1998)

Black, P., *Ernst Kaltenbrunner: Ideological Soldier of the Third Reich* (Princeton: University Press, 1984)

Browder, G. C., *Foundations of the Nazi Police State. The Formation of Sipo and SD* (Lexington: The University Press of Kentucky, 1990)

Browder, G. C., *Hitler's Enforcers. The Gestapo and SS Security Service in the Nazi Revolution* (Oxford: University Press, 1996)

Dams, C., and Stolle, M., *The Gestapo: Power and Terror in the Third Reich* (Oxford: University Press, 2014)

Paehler, K., *The Third Reich's Intelligence Services. The Career of Walter Schellenberg* (Cambridge: University Press, 2017)

Paul, G./M., Klaus-Michael (eds.), *Die Gestapo—Mythos und Realität* (Darmstadt: Primus Verlag, 1996)

Paul, G./M., Klaus-Michael (eds.), *Die Gestapo im Zweiten Weltkrieg. 'Heimatfront' und besetztes Europe* (Darmstadt; Primus Verlag, 2000)

Tyas, S., *SS-Major Horst Kopkow: From the Gestapo to British Intelligence* (Stroud: Fonthill Media, 2017)

Wildt, M., *Generation des Unbedingten. Das Führerkorps des Reichssicherheitshauptamtes* (Hamburg: Hamburger Edition GIS Verlagsges, 2002)